Handbook of Research Methods in Developmental Science

Blackwell Handbooks of Research Methods in Psychology

Created for advanced students and researchers looking for an authoritative definition of the research methods used in their chosen field, the *Blackwell Handbooks of Research Methods in Psychology* provide an invaluable and cutting-edge overview of classic, current, and future trends in the research methods of psychology.

- Each handbook draws together 20–25 newly commissioned chapters to provide comprehensive coverage of the research methodology used in a specific psychological discipline.
- Each handbook is introduced and contextualized by leading figures in the field, lending coherence and authority to each volume.
- The international team of contributors to each handbook has been specially chosen for its expertise and knowledge of each field.
- Each volume provides the perfect complement to non-research based handbooks in psychology

Handbook of Research Methods in Industrial and Organizational Psychology
Edited by Steven G. Rogelberg

Handbook of Research Methods in Clinical Psychology
Edited by Michael C. Roberts and Stephen S. Ilardi

Handbook of Research Methods in Experimental Psychology
Edited by Stephen F. Davis

Handbook of Research Methods in Developmental Science
Edited by Douglas M. Teti

Handbook of Research Methods in Developmental Science

Edited by

Douglas M. Teti

Blackwell
Publishing

BLACKWELL PUBLISHING

350 Main Street, Malden, MA 02148-5020, USA

9600 Garsington Road, Oxford OX4 2DQ, UK

550 Swanston Street, Carlton, Victoria 3053, Australia

The right of Douglas M. Teti to be identified as the Author of the Editorial Material in this Work has been asserted in accordance with the UK Copyright, Designs, and Patents Act 1988.

First published 2005 by Blackwell Publishing Ltd

First published in paperback 2006 by Blackwell Publishing Ltd

1   2006

Library of Congress Cataloging-in-Publication Data

Handbook of research methods in developmental science / edited by Douglas M. Teti.—1st ed.
    p. cm. — (Blackwell handbooks of research methods in psychology ; 4)
    Includes bibliographical references and index.
    ISBN 0-631-22261-8 (hardcover : alk. paper)
1. Developmental psychology—Research—Methodology.   I. Teti, Douglas M., 1951–   II. Series.

    BF713.5.H36 2005
    155'.072—dc21

2004007787

ISBN-13: 978-0-631-22261-3 (hardcover : alk. paper)
ISBN-13: 978-1-4051-5395-9 (paperback : alk. paper)
ISBN-10: 1-4051-5395-4 (paperback : alk. paper)

A catalogue record for this title is available from the British Library.

Set in 10.5/12.5pt Adobe Garamond
by Graphicraft Ltd, Hong Kong
Printed and bound in the United Kingdom
by TJ International Ltd, Padstow, Cornwall

The publisher's policy is to use permanent paper from mills that operate a sustainable forestry policy, and which has been manufactured from pulp processed using acid-free and elementary chlorine-free practices. Furthermore, the publisher ensures that the text paper and cover board used have met acceptable environmental accreditation standards.

For further information on
Blackwell Publishing, visit our website:
www.blackwellpublishing.com

Contents

Contributors

Roger Bakeman, Department of Psychology, Georgia State University, Atlanta, Georgia

Marian J. Bakermans-Kranenburg, Faculty of Social Science, Leiden University, Leiden, The Netherlands

John E. Bates, Department of Psychology, Indiana University, Bloomington, Indiana

Patricia J. Bauer, Institute of Child Development, University of Minnesota, Minneapolis, Minnesota

Jennifer G. Boldry, Department of Psychology, Montana State University, Bozeman, Montana

Laurel Bornholt, School of Development and Learning, University of Sydney, Sydney, Australia

Marc H. Bornstein, National Institute of Child Health and Human Development, Bethesda, Maryland

Grace I. L. Caskie, Gerontology Center, University Park, Pennsylvania State University, Pennsylvania

Jana Chaudhuri, Eliot Pearson Department of Child Development, Tufts University, Medford, Massachusetts

Raymond Debus, School of Development and Learning, University of Sydney, Sydney, Australia

Deborah F. Deckner, Georgia State University, Atlanta, Georgia

Elizabeth Dowling, Eliot Pearson Department of Child Development, Tufts University, Medford, Massachusetts

Nancy Eisenberg, Department of Psychology, Arizona State University, Tempe, Arizona

Alan Fogel, Department of Psychology, University of Utah, Salt Lake City, Utah

Chun-Shin Hahn, National Institute of Child Health and Human Development, Bethesda, Maryland

Donald P. Hartmann, Department of Psychology, University of Utah, Salt Lake City, Utah

O. Maurice Haynes, National Institute of Child Health and Human Development, Bethesda, Maryland

Christine Reiner Hess, Department of Psychology, University of Maryland, Baltimore County, Baltimore, Maryland

Allison Holmes, Human Development, University of Maryland, College Park, Maryland

Hui-Chin Hsu, Department of Child and Family Studies, University of Georgia, Athens, Georgia

Keng-Yen Huang, Department of Psychology, University of Maryland, Baltimore County, Baltimore, Maryland

Femmie Juffer, Faculty of Social Science, Leiden University, Leiden, The Netherlands

Deborah A. Kashy, Michigan State University, East Lansing, Michigan

Michael E. Lamb, Faculty of Social and Political Sciences, Cambridge University, Cambridge, United Kingdom

Manuela Lavelli, Department of Psychology and Cultural Anthropology, University of Verona, Verona, Italy

Richard M. Lerner, Eliot Pearson Department of Child Development, Tufts University, Medford, Massachusetts

Nanmathi Manian, National Institute of Child Health and Human Development, Bethesda, Maryland

Herbert Marsh, SELF Research Centre, University of Western Sydney, Australia

John J. McArdle, Department of Psychology, University of Virginia, Charlottesville, Virginia

Daniel Messinger, Department of Psychology, University of Miami, Coral Gables, Florida

Amanda Sheffield Morris, Department of Psychology, Arizona State University, Tempe, Arizona

Claire Novosad, Indiana University, Bloomington, Indiana

Andréa P.F. Pantoja, Department of Psychology, California State University, Chico, California

Steven C. Pitts, Department of Psychology, University of Maryland, Baltimore County, Baltimore, Maryland

Justin H. Prost, Department of Psychology, Arizona State University, Tempe, Arizona

Vicenç Quera, University of Barcelona, Barcelona, Spain

Craig T. Ramey, School of Nursing and Health Studies, Georgetown University, Washington, DC

Sharon L. Ramey, School of Nursing and Health Studies, Georgetown University, Washington, DC

K. Warner Schaie, Department of Human Development and Family Studies, University Park, Pennsylvania State University, Pennsylvania

Kelly Robinson Todd Schmidt, Department of Psychology, University of Maryland, Baltimore County, Baltimore, Maryland

Ronald Seifer, Department of Psychiatry and Human Behavior, Brown University School of Medicine, Providence, Rhode Island

Tracy L. Spinrad, Department of Psychology, Arizona State University, Tempe, Arizona

Elizabeth A. Stormshak, College of Education, University of Oregon, Eugene, Oregon

Catherine S. Tamis-LeMonda, National Institute of Child Health and Human Development, Bethesda, Maryland

Douglas M. Teti, Department of Human Development and Family Studies, University Park, Pennsylvania State University, Pennsylvania

Karen L. Thierry, National Institute of Child Health and Human Development, Bethesda, Maryland

Marinus H. van IJzendoorn, Faculty of Social Science, Leiden University, Leiden, The Netherlands

Theodore D. Wachs, Department of Psychological Sciences, Purdue University, West Lafayette, Indiana

Dale Walker, Schiefelbusch Institute for Life Span Studies, University of Kansas, Kansas City, Kansas

Steven F. Warren, Schiefelbusch Institute for Life Span Studies, University of Kansas, Kansas City, Kansas

Janet A. Welsh, Center for Child/Adult Development, University Park, Pennsylvania State University, Pennsylvania

Jamie J. Winters, Department of Psychology, University of Maryland, Baltimore County, Baltimore, Maryland

Philip W. Wirtz, Department of Psychology, George Washington University, Washington, DC

Preface

The impetus for this *Handbook* stems in part from my cumulative experience in offering graduate-level courses in research methods in developmental science. It became clear that successful, comprehensive, meaningful instruction in developmental research methods needed to include information in five different, yet interrelated, domains: (1) developmental designs, (2) issues in measurement, (3) data analysis, with a particular emphasis on "change," (4) intervention methods designed to promote development, and (5) emergent developments in the field, and the methods used in forging them.

The present volume, to a great extent, reflects this experience. Its five sections pull from some of the foremost intellects in the field to write about methodological issues pertaining to the domains indicated above. Part I "Developmental Designs," for example, provides chapters that present on "staple" (Schmidt and Teti), complex (Schaie and Caskie), microgenetic (Lavelli et al.), experimental (Holmes and Teti), and quasi-experimental designs (Pitts et al.) in developmental research. In "General Issues in Developmental Measurement" (Part II), a variety of measurement issues particular to developmental science are discussed, including measurement of constructs that develop over time (Bates and Novosad), using parents vs. observers to collect data (Seifer), the validity of child reports (Marsh et al.), emic vs. etic perspectives in developmental measurement (Teti & Huang), and conceptualizing and measuring "context" (Lerner et al). Part III, "Developmental Intervention: Traditional and Emergent Approaches in Enhancing Development," has chapters devoted to a review of empirical findings and methods used in promoting development across a wide spectrum of developmental domains, including socioemotional (Juffer et al.), intellectual (Ramey & Ramey), language (Warren & Walker), and social competence (Stormshak & Welsh), and Hess has contributed a fifth chapter on enhancing development in high-risk infants. In Part IV, "Analytic Issues and Methods in Developmental Psychology," three chapters are devoted to the conceptualization and analysis of change (Hartmann, McArdle, and Wirtz), a fourth addresses analytic strategies for dealing with dyadic interaction (Kashy & Boldry), and a fifth presents methods and procedures for analyzing behavioral streams (Bakeman et al.). Finally, Part V, "New Directions in Developmental Research," targets a variety of developing lines of research in the field, and the methods used in studying them. These include emotion regulation (Eisenberg et al.), person-environment "fit" (Wachs), memory development in infancy (Bauer), validity of children's eyewitness accounts of child abuse (Lamb & Thierry), and new approaches to the study of fetal development, language development, and the development of play (Bornstein et al.).

The contents of the chapters in this volume are designed to be accessible and readable. Graduate students, and upper-level undergraduate students, should find this volume to provide useful coverage of topics that are basic to the field and topics that may be of particular relevance to their own interests. The same should be true for more experienced developmental scientists, who wish to use this *Handbook* as a means of learning about new areas of interest, or getting a fresh perspective on areas for which they already have some pre-existing knowledge.

This *Handbook* is the culmination of many years of thought about the nature of research in developmental science. It does not presume to cover all topics of interest. However, I hope it will be of use, as both a reference and a text, to a broad array of professionals with interests in developmental science.

Douglas M. Teti, PhD
Professor of Human Development
The Pennsylvania State University

PART I

Developmental Designs

CHAPTER ONE

Issues in the Use of Longitudinal and Cross-Sectional Designs

Kelly Robinson Todd Schmidt and Douglas M. Teti

Baltes, Reese, and Nesselroade (1977) defined the task of developmental science as *"the description, explanation, and modification (optimization) of intraindividual change in behavior and interindividual differences in such change across the life span"* (p. 84, italics in original). This task was embraced by many over the last 100 years, and indeed the discipline has yielded a wealth of knowledge about the physical, cognitive, emotional, and social development of individuals across the life span.

Developmental research has traditionally been conducted using one of two methodologies. One involves the repeated measurement of a sample of individuals, usually at the same age at the start of the study, over a period of time, termed a *longitudinal* study. The "task" in longitudinal studies is to find meaningful associations between age changes and changes in specific outcome behaviors or abilities of interest. The second involves the measurement of several samples of differing ages simultaneously, termed a *cross-sectional* study, in which the task is to discover age group differences in particular behaviors or abilities.

This chapter reviews these two approaches from the vantage point of the general developmental model, discusses the advantages and pitfalls of each, and highlights exemplars of each from the developmental literature.

The Developmental Function and the General Developmental Model

Wohlwill (1970a) defines a variable as "developmental" when it changes with age in a generally uniform and consistent way across individuals and environments. He asserts that our interest should not be in looking for significant age-related differences but in discovering the nature of the age function – its shape and form. The developmental function is defined as "the form or mode of the relationship between the chronological age of the individual and the changes observed to occur in his responses on some specified dimension of behavior over the course of his development to maturity" (Wohlwill, 1973, p. 32). Wohlwill (1973) asserted that extending the concept of the developmental function to the whole life span was not useful because of the challenge of studying the life span longitudinally, the lack of measurable change in some aspects of behavior at maturity, and the difficulties in ascertaining the onset of aging. There are many life-span developmental researchers, however, who take issue with this premise and have conducted interesting, valuable research on "mature" individuals (e.g., Schaie, 1996; Schaie & Caskie, this volume; Siegler & Botwinick, 1979).

The parameters that make up the developmental function were explicated in a seminal paper by Schaie (1965), who is widely credited with laying out the paradigm of developmental research that has shaped research for over three decades and continues to do so. The three parameters that define developmental change according to Schaie's (1965) general developmental model are *age*, *cohort*, and *time of measurement* (also called *period*). *Age* is commonly defined as chronological age; this definition is not without some controversy, as will be discussed later. *Cohort* is defined as a group of individuals experiencing an event or set of events associated particularly with that cohort (a cohort-defining event) (Mayer & Huinink, 1990). The most frequently used cohort-defining event is the birth of an individual. Time of measurement is most typically defined according to calendar time, although this definition too has been questioned by some (e.g., Schaie, 1986).

According to the model, different developmental research designs can be seen as combinations of the three variables. Simple longitudinal and cross-sectional designs are defined by the ages of interest to the researcher, the cohort(s) from which the sample is drawn, and the time or times of measurement. More complex developmental designs are proposed under the model, but these are discussed by Schaie and Caskie in Chapter 2. When used in cross-sectional research, the age variable really taps *interindividual differences*. When used in longitudinal research, it taps *intraindividual change* (Schaie, 1983, 1984, 1986). The cohort variable is an *individual differences* variable, while time of measurement or period is an *intraindividual change* variable.

These three variables by definition are not independent; that is, once two of these three parameters are determined, the third is automatically defined (Baltes, 1968; Schaie, 1965, 1986). This means that age – the variable most often of interest to developmental researchers – is always inevitably confounded with either cohort or time of measurement. Schaie (1986) pointed out that this is because we tend to define each variable in terms of calendar time, and proposed designs for unlinking calendar time from the variables in order to get at the independent effects of them (e.g., defining cohort more broadly than time of birth) (see Chapter 2, this volume). These designs, such as cross-sequential and cohort-sequential designs, appear infrequently in the developmental literature.

Schaie's general developmental model has been subjected to much criticism over the years (e.g., Baltes, 1968; Baltes, Reese, & Nesselroade, 1977). Strict adherence to it requires the researcher to make some perhaps untenable assumptions, such as assuming that one variable in the model has no effect on the dependent variable (Schaie, 1986). Another limitation of the model is that it assumes that change occurs incrementally over time with age in a linear fashion (Kosloski, 1986). This in fact may not be true for many developmental functions such as personality traits. Finally, some have argued that the model is really only useful for describing change, not for explaining it (Baltes, Reese, & Nesselroade, 1977).

In spite of these criticisms, the general developmental model has spurred much thought about how development should be studied. Because age, cohort, and time of measurement serve as proxies for other causal variables (Hartmann & George, 1999), the model has forced researchers to think more creatively and complexly about developmental processes. The goal for many developmental researchers is to understand the contribution of age to the developmental function, but it should be clear that researchers need to investigate the contributions of age, cohort, and time of measurement to the developmental function because they are inextricably linked.

Simple Cross-Sectional Designs

The simple cross-sectional study consists of at least two samples of different ages drawn from different cohorts and measured simultaneously. For example, a researcher might want to examine the social strategies used to enter a group of children by 6-, 8-, and 10-year-olds. This research approach stems from the assumption that when an older age group is drawn from the same population as a younger age group, the eventual behavior of the younger group can be predicted from the behavior of the older group (Achenbach, 1978). Thus, a researcher can examine the relationship between earlier and later behavior without actually waiting for development to occur (Achenbach, 1978). Longitudinal conclusions are typically drawn from cross-sectional data, but the validity of this is questionable (Achenbach, 1978; Kraemer et al., 2000).

Cross-sectional studies are relatively inexpensive, quick and easy to do, are useful for generating and clarifying hypotheses, piloting new measures or technology, and can lay the groundwork for decisions about future follow-up studies (Kraemer, 1994). They provide information about *age group differences* or *interindividual differences* (Miller, 1998). They do not, however, provide information about *age changes* or *interindividual differences in intraindividual change* (Miller, 1998; Wohlwill, 1973). That is, the results of the above-mentioned study on socialization might reveal differences among 6-year-olds, 8-year-olds, and 10-year-olds, but they would not inform us of how and when these differences emerge and how the behaviors evolve over time.

Cross-sectional studies are subject to many methodological concerns and limitations. They cannot answer questions about the stability of a characteristic or process over time (Miller, 1998), and information is lost because of the use of averages to create group means (Wohlwill, 1973). A researcher planning to conduct a cross-sectional study needs to ensure at the outset that the measurement instruments (e.g., personality tests, intellectual assessments, etc.) he/she plans to use measure similar things at each age and are valid for each age under investigation (Miller, 1998). Another criticism of cross-sectional studies is that their external validity (i.e., generalizability) is possibly affected by historical/ cultural differences between cohorts (Achenbach, 1978). For example, if one were studying the development of some reading behaviors, the comparability of a first grade class and a third grade class within the same school would be compromised if the first graders were exposed to a new reading curriculum that the third graders never experienced. This would represent a historical event that renders the cohorts non-equivalent. This problem, termed the age by cohort confound, is perhaps the most serious limitation of the cross-sectional design; that is, one cannot easily separate the effects of age from the effects of belonging to a particular cohort, especially if that cohort is defined by birth. Miller (1998) argues that the seriousness of this problem relates to the dependent variable: the more "basic" or "biological" the variable (e.g., heart rate, visual acuity), the less likely it is that the cohort effect will be present. It also depends on the age span of the sample: the wider the spread, the more likely a cohort effect could be operating. This is particularly problematic in aging or life span research.

Another major risk of the cross-sectional method is that the researcher will unwittingly create bias in the samples through flawed selection procedures, especially if random assignment to age groups is not possible (Baltes, Reese, & Nesselroade, 1977; Flick, 1988; Hertzog, 1996; Kosloski, 1986; Miller, 1998; Wohlwill, 1973). Traditional experimental research methods (e.g., Cook & Campbell, 1979) mandate the formation of groups that are identical except for the variable of interest, which in this case is age. Matching on variables other than age could result in a non-representative sample; for example, if one were comparing 25-year-olds and 75-year-olds, matching on educational level (e.g., college graduate) would yield a positively biased sample of 75-year-olds. That is, 75-year-old college graduates would be less representative of their age cohort in terms of education, than would the 25-year-olds of their age cohort. Furthermore, if the entrances and exits of individuals from the sampling population are not random, then the researcher is at risk for making incorrect inferences about the developmental process under investigation (Kraemer et al., 2000). For example, if one is interested in the relation between age and the move toward assisted living, one must account for the fact that entering or exiting an assisted living facility is not a random occurrence but is most likely related to factors associated with age. Adopting a cross-sectional approach to studying this developmental process would not permit the identification of predictors associated with moving into assisted living, whereas adopting a longitudinal approach would allow such analyses.

The basic premise for using the cross-sectional approach is that we can draw conclusions about intraindividual age-related changes from observing interindividual differences. This requires the strong assumption that participants in all comparison groups are equivalent in all respects save chronological age. Indeed, it is commonly held that the longitudinal inferences drawn from cross-sectional research are not seriously misleading, when in fact this might not be valid (Hertzog, 1996; Kraemer et al., 2000). One's ability to draw inferences from cross-sectional research is affected by factors such as how time is measured, the type of developmental trajectory of the developmental process (i.e., fixed trait, parallel trajectories, or nonparallel trajectories), the reliability of measurement, and the time of measurement (i.e., fixed or random for all subjects) (Kraemer et al., 2000). Furthermore, Kraemer and colleagues (2000) suggest that cross-sectional research done as pilot studies for subsequent longitudinal studies in fact might actually serve to discourage longitudinal research because they intimate that the answers are already known.

Examples of cross-sectional studies

Flavell, Beach, and Chinsky (1966) employed the cross-sectional design in a study which examined the use of verbal rehearsal strategies for a memorization task among children at three ages: kindergarten, second grade, and fifth grade. Ten boys and girls of each age were matched on grade and sex, and were instructed to remember the order of pictures presented. The children wore a "space helmet" with a visor that allowed the experimenters to watch the children's mouths. The study revealed that most kindergartners did not use verbal rehearsal strategies, while most fifth graders did. This study therefore generated intriguing hypotheses about the development of memory strategies during middle childhood.

Gopnik and Astington (1988) examined the apparent developmental changes in representational thought in 3-, 4-, and 5-year-old children. In one experiment they used deceptive objects such as a candy box containing pencils and asked the children to guess the contents of the box before opening it. Once the surprising contents were revealed, the children were asked what they thought was in the box before it was opened. The youngest children tended to maintain that they knew pencils were in the box, even though they guessed "candy" earlier, while the older children demonstrated some awareness of the appearance/reality distinction. The experimenters also had the children complete a false belief task in which they asked the children, "X has not seen this box, what will s/he think is in the box?". Again, the younger children incorrectly stated that X would think pencils were in the box, while older children tended to correctly recognize that the appearance of the box would lead one to think candy was in the box.

Thus, cross-sectional research designs can be quite useful in their ability to demonstrate age group differences in developmental processes such as cognition and memory, but it is essential that one remember that inferences about *how* and *when* these changes emerge and evolve over time are impossible to make. Furthermore, the age by cohort confound makes untangling the independent effects of each variable difficult.

Simple Longitudinal Designs

An obvious solution to the shortcomings of the cross-sectional research strategy would appear to be a strategy in which a sample of participants of a given age and from a given cohort were observed over a period of time – that is, employing the longitudinal research design. As Campbell (1988, p. 43) noted, "There are few issues that evoke greater agreement among social scientists than the need for longitudinal as opposed to cross-sectional studies."

Miller (1998) defined longitudinal designs as "repeated tests that span an appreciable length of time" (p. 27). The notion of "repeated tests" is not well defined, and frequently seems to be conceived of as two occasions, which has been found questionable by some (e.g., Rogosa, 1995). The concept of "appreciable length of time" appears to vary with the developmental level of the sample. For example, one week between testing does not likely constitute a longitudinal study for a 5-year-old, but might for a newborn.

Longitudinal designs are useful and necessary in that they allow us to focus on intraindividual change, developmental sequences, and co-occurring social and environmental change that enable one to develop theoretical/explanatory accounts of whatever change occurs (McCall, 1977). They are perhaps most valued due to the fact that they permit a direct measure of age changes – intraindividual development over time (Farrington, 1991; Miller, 1998). Also, the researcher can examine interindividual differences in intraindividual change (Baltes & Nesselroade, 1979). Longitudinal designs permit the investigation of individual consistency or change and let the researcher look at early–later relationships (Farrington, 1991; Miller, 1998; Wohlwill, 1973). Longitudinal studies allow construction of the shape of the developmental function and let the researcher examine differences between individuals in terms of the entire developmental function, not just at a particular age (Wohlwill, 1970b, 1973).

The researcher conducting a longitudinal study can explore the causes of intraindividual change because this methodology meets one necessary, but not sufficient, criterion for making causal inferences: time ordering (Baltes & Nesselroade, 1979; Campbell, 1988; Farrington, 1991; Pellegrini, 1996; Wohlwill, 1973). That is, one can examine antecedents and consequences and make some reasonable speculations about causality. However, Schaie (1988) noted that, although observations in a longitudinal study are by definition time ordered unidirectionally, this does not mean that time-ordered change is unidirectional. Although many developmental processes may be unidirectional over certain time periods of the life span, others are likely to be cyclical or recursive.

Threats to Validity in Longitudinal Research

In spite of the apparent benefits of the longitudinal research strategy, it is expensive, time consuming, and labor-intensive. Furthermore, longitudinal research designs are quite vulnerable to many of the threats to validity commonly associated with quasi-experimental research, namely selection, attrition, instrumentation, and regression to the mean (Shadish, Cook, & Campbell, 2002). The process of assembling an appropriate sample for a longitudinal study is no easy task. Sampling depends upon whether the researcher is doing a prospective or a retrospective study. In a prospective study, the sample is constructed based on the independent variable (e.g., if one were interested in studying the long-term effects of prenatal exposure to alcohol, one would recruit newborns exposed to alcohol in utero), while in a retrospective study it is assembled based on the dependent variable (e.g., if one were interested in assessing the long-term effects of an early intervention program, one could recruit graduates of a Head Start program) (Jordan, 1994). Also the researcher must decide upon which type of population from which to sample: a normal representative population (e.g., birth cohort, school and adult cohorts, community cohorts) or nonrepresentative population (e.g., specialized cohorts such as twin, adoptees, identified patients, etc.) (Mednick, Griffith, & Mednick, 1981). The advantages of using a representative sample are the increased generalizability of the findings, the ability to study a variety of phenomena (e.g., social and medical variables), and the ability to obtain incidence and prevalence data on diseases and illnesses (Baltes, Reese, & Nesselroade, 1977; Goldstein, 1979; Mednick, Griffith, & Mednick, 1981; Schaie, 1977; van der Kamp & Bijleveld, 1998). However, a representative sample can become less representative over time; that is, a population may change over time so that a sample studied at Time 2 may no longer be representative of the population as it was at Time 1 (Baltes, Reese, & Nesselroade, 1977; Goldstein, 1979; Mednick, Griffith, & Mednick, 1981; Schaie, 1977; van der Kamp & Bijleveld, 1998).

It is desirable to obtain a sample that is readily available and cooperative over the length of the study, but this is quite challenging for most researchers, and doing so may in fact create sampling bias (Achenbach, 1978; Miller, 1998). One can do screenings at the outset of a study to maximize the possibility of obtaining a sample that is high in cooperation and stability, but the sample might become biased in the process (Jordan, 1994). However, noncooperative and mobile families/individuals are likely to be quite different from cooperative stationary ones, so including them in a sample might bias the sample anyway (Jordan, 1994).

Thus, the researcher must take into account the problems associated with constructing and maintaining a sample over the course of a longitudinal study. The researcher planning to do a longitudinal study must decide between selecting a large sample for which less detailed information can be collected and to which less time and effort can be devoted to reducing attrition, or a smaller sample where external validity may be compromised but in which one can devote greater effort and time to obtaining more detailed, process-oriented data (Bergman & Magnusson, 1990).

Sample attrition is probably one of the most common and frustrating problems faced by longitudinal researchers. Attrition is problematic in that non-responders usually differ from responders in ways that might be related to the variables being studied (Bergman & Magnusson, 1990; Goldstein, 1979). It can also be problematic for the researcher studying several groups over the same period of time, such as in a treatment study, when participants in one group drop out at a higher rate than those in other groups (Miller, 1998). Goldstein (1979) advises researchers to plan for attrition and thus plan to trace subjects. Jordan (1994) recommends obtaining the name, address, and phone number of a relative most likely to know the participant's address in the future as a way to prevent attrition. Another suggestion for situations in which a participant has moved away is to enlist the help of a colleague in that area to conduct any testing or interviewing (Jordan, 1994). Thus the researcher can potentially control some types of attrition, such as that caused by lack of interest, relocation, or active refusal, but cannot control factors related to age such as physical decline which may impede participation (Schaie, 1977).

The missing data that is a result of attrition is problematic for the longitudinal researcher. One can use data collected on earlier occasions to make inferences about nonresponders (Goldstein, 1979), and Flick (1988) reviews a number of statistical solutions to the problem of missing data. Jordan (1994) asserts that it is not necessarily true that a missing subject is missing forever, since he or she may be recovered at a later point in time, if the researcher plans ahead to allow for such situations. It might be well worth the effort to try to recover subjects lost at one point in time, as can be seen in the results of a longitudinal study of adult intellectual development conducted by Siegler and Botwinick (1979). Adults between 60 and 94 years of age participated in 11 test sessions over 20 years, beginning in 1955 and ending in 1976. Significant attrition occurred over the course of the study as expected due to illness and death, but study procedural requirements also contributed to attrition because subjects who did not complete the entire test battery at a session were eliminated, and furthermore a subject's score at any one point in time could only be counted if he or she had been tested at each previous time. Siegler and Botwinick (1979) graphed IQ scores at time 1 by test session and found that IQ scores were dramatically higher for those who completed more sessions than for those who completed less, so that those who completed the 11 sessions appeared to have higher intellectual ability than those who dropped out. Thus the intellectually superior participants made it through the procedural requirements of test completion and attendance at all sessions. The researchers concluded that inferences about adult intellectual development made on results such as these could be quite misleading.

Another potential threat to the validity of a longitudinal study is *testing*, where performance by participants is enhanced due to practice or familiarity with the measurement tools and/or procedures. It has been noted that participating in a longitudinal study may actually change the course of growth and development because of a heightened awareness of the phenomena under investigation (Goldstein, 1979). The presence of a testing effect means that a sample has become less representative of the underlying population (Schaie, 1977). When examining the data for practice effects, one must first take into account attrition (Schaie, 1996). Practice effects can be lessened by the use of alternate forms and nonreactive measures (Wohlwill, 1973), and may be less of a problem for developmentally less mature participants. Miller (1998), for example, points out that testing is not likely to be a significant problem in infant research.

Instrumentation represents yet another validity threat. Often it is the case that researchers need to use different instruments at different ages, and one cannot assume that the same phenomena is being measured at each time (Baltes, Reese, & Nesselroade, 1977; Goldstein, 1979; Schaie, 1977). Even if the same instrument is used, interpretations of the results at each time of measurement could be different (Goldstein, 1979). Alternatively, an assessment tool might be appropriate across the age range under investigation but be cohort-specific, which limits generalizability (Schaie, 1977). Schaie (1988) suggests that the problem of measurement equivalence over time could be due to developmental discontinuities of the behavior in question (see Hartmann, this volume). Even if a variable can be measured identically at two points in time, however, it is still likely that the distribution of scores will change over time, which means that the *meaning* of a score may change (Achenbach, 1978).

Other instrumentation-related problems include the fact that tests and instruments are susceptible to "aging" and might even become obsolete, or at least undergo changes in validity and/or reliability (Baltes, Reese, & Nesselroade, 1977; Jordan, 1994; Mednick, Griffith, & Mednick, 1981; Miller, 1998; Schaie, 1977). Study personnel might also change significantly over the course of a longitudinal study, affecting the overall procedures of the study and the administration of the assessment tools (Jordan, 1994). The researcher should keep in mind that personnel will likely grow in psychometric skills over the course of a study (Jordan, 1994). In addition, definitions and measurement of the independent and dependent variables will likely change over time (Achenbach, 1978; van der Kamp & Bijleveld, 1998). Moreover, theories and hypotheses might become outdated as a study progresses and thus requires reformulation in light of findings along the way or other data from outside sources (Farrington, 1991; Jordan, 1994; Mednick, Griffith, & Mednick, 1981).

Regression to the mean is yet another potential problem in longitudinal research. Buss (1979) points out that repeated measures on the same variable introduce the possibility of regression toward the mean, especially when sampling extreme scores in a population, and researchers should seek to separate out true score changes from measurement error. Regression to the mean is also observed when error variance decreases over time (i.e., as reliability increases), so that researchers should also examine variance over time (Buss, 1979). According to Baltes and colleagues (1977), regression to the mean is mostly a problem when a sample is observed on only two occasions and when the sample is divided into subgroups along a continuum. One way to minimize regression to the mean as well as testing and instrumentation threats to validity is to draw independent samples at each time of testing (Kosloski, 1986).

The simple longitudinal research design is also susceptible to a *cohort effect*, which might impact both the internal and external validity of a study (Achenbach, 1978; Baltes, Reese, & Nesselroade, 1977; Bergman & Magnusson, 1990). That is, a particular cohort under investigation may have some unique characteristics or experience some unusual event that makes it unlike another cohort of the same age. This problem can be partially mitigated by obtaining some cross-sectional data on relevant variables (Bergman & Magnusson, 1990).

Finally, the validity of a simple longitudinal research study can be threatened by the age by time of measurement confound. In fact, Schaie (1977, 1983) suggests that this threat is most likely to impact such a study because it consists of only one cohort and thus makes separating out the independent effects of age and time of measurement impossible. For example, a researcher studying anxiety during adolescence would have to take into account time of measurement issues if he/she was collecting data both before and after the terrorist incidences of September 11, 2001; age alone could probably not explain any developmental changes seen among this cohort of adolescents. Following Miller (1998), the age by time of measurement confound is likely to be less serious when more "basic" or "biological" variables are under consideration, but perhaps more serious with outcome variables that are likely to be influenced by historical events that co-occur with age (e.g., attitudes about risk-taking).

Conceptual and Planning Considerations in Longitudinal Research

Friedman and colleagues (1994) argue that longitudinal research, especially follow-up research in which some sample is studied after completing a treatment or intervention, has tended to be atheoretical and driven largely by the availability of assessment tools such as IQ tests, rather than by theory or methodological considerations. They point out that IQ tests historically were intended to be predictor rather than criterion variables, which is not how they are frequently used. In addition, they assert that the choices made about sources of data seem to be determined by factors other than methodological considerations.

Indeed, the conceptualization, methodology, and data analyses of longitudinal studies need to be tightly linked, but this frequently does not happen in large-scale studies (Campbell, 1988). Several writers advise the researcher to be broad-minded and eclectic when developing theories and choosing measures and to plan for studies to be multi-purpose and multidisciplinary (Bergman & Magnusson, 1990; Mednick, Griffith, & Mednick, 1981; Mednick, Mednick, & Griffith, 1981). Adopting such an approach will likely minimize the problem of fading relevancy (Bergman & Magnusson, 1990). The researcher must anticipate the possibility, however, that the methods of measurement, scales of measurement, and the meaning of scores will change over time during the course of the study when looking for patterns of stability and change (Achenbach, 1978).

Many researchers offer practical suggestions with regard to planning and implementing a longitudinal study. It behooves the researcher planning a study to be flexible, especially in light of the possibility of sleeper effects (i.e., effects that emerge a considerable time later) or simply the length of time it takes for some phenomena to manifest themselves. This is particularly applicable to longitudinal research involving infants (Mednick, Mednick, & Griffith, 1981). Longitudinal studies require more careful planning than cross-sectional research studies as well as consistent funding over time and a major time commitment from the head researcher and other personnel, which makes such undertakings demanding. Many note that the expense and time investment required of a well-done longitudinal study is commonly a deterrent to such an endeavor (Bergman, Eklund, & Magnusson, 1991; Miller, 1998; Wohlwill, 1973). With regard to expense, Mednick, Griffith, and Mednick (1981) point out that a longitudinal study may especially be expensive initially as staff training and the purchase of new equipment and materials are required. The researcher committed to conducting a longitudinal study must be willing to cope with a slow rate of return on the amount of work invested (Wohlwill, 1973) and also realize that no researcher can study across the life span (Baltes, Reese, & Nesselroade, 1977).

Planning involves theory, organization, and administration of the study (Bergman, Eklund, & Magnusson, 1991). Jordan (1994) notes that planning is essential, because an enormous amount of data will be collected that need to be processed. It is important for the researcher to pay very close attention to data collection and storage, and to take advantage of opportunities to collect additional data on subjects (Mednick, Griffith, & Mednick, 1981). Goldstein (1979) recommends that the researcher try to anticipate future data needs and try to be redundant in the early stages of the research project. Others suggest collecting data in a way that would allow them to be used in different ways and from different theoretical perspectives, as well as keeping them in their most basic form (i.e., raw data rather than composites or summary measures) to allow for other uses (Bergman & Magnusson, 1990).

With respect to personnel issues, it is suggested that the researcher train staff well in advance of the designated time for collecting data (Jordan, 1994). Jordan (1994) further advises against blind testing because of the need to build rapport and a relationship over time, although this view is contrary to that most commonly held by experimental researchers and will likely depend on the nature of the study being conducted. Study personnel who are not blind might introduce expectancy bias into the data, which can affect things like how a construct is operationalized and how raters operate (Bergman & Magnusson, 1990). To prevent staff turnover, it has been suggested that researchers can maintain investment in a longitudinal study by publishing as much as possible (Mednick, Griffith, & Mednick, 1981), although it has been pointed out that the publication of earlier waves of research could potentially impact subsequent behaviors (van der Kamp & Bijleveld, 1998).

In planning a longitudinal study the researcher would be wise to review Rogosa's (1995) "myths" about longitudinal research, particularly in regards to determining the number of times of measurement. One such myth is that two times of measurement constitutes a longitudinal study. Although one can plot the amount of change observed between two points in time, one cannot determine the shape of the growth curve from only two data points. Moreover, if the change function is not a straight-line function then time of measurement can be quite influential. Rogosa (1995) recommends the use of multiple measurement points and growth curve data for the best statistical analysis and examination of individual growth trajectories over time.

Planning is also essential with respect to time of measurement. Goldstein (1979) states that it is almost inevitable that there will be some variation around the targeted sampling age, and this should not be problematic if it is small and random, but if the variation in time of measurement is large it could pose a problem. For example, the findings of a study could be impacted by time of measurement effects if developmental change on some attribute is rapid, if there is skew in the sampling, or if there is some relationship between the time of measurement and the average value of the measurement (e.g., seasonal variations in phenomena such as physical growth). Goldstein recommends sampling throughout the year to avoid this.

An Example of a Simple Longitudinal Study: The Dunedin Study

Silva and colleagues (Silva, 1996; Silva & McCann, 1996) conducted a noteworthy longitudinal study of over 1,000 infants born at one hospital in Dunedin, New Zealand. Infants born between April 1, 1972 and March 31, 1973 were enrolled and assessed at birth, 3, 5, 7, 9, 11, 13, 15, 18, and 21 years of age. The objectives of the study were to examine the health, development, and wellbeing of the participants at each age. This study led to 555 publications by April 1995 (Silva & McCann, 1996). What makes the Dunedin study particularly remarkable is the very low attrition rate: 97 percent of participants were followed at ages 18 and 21. Over the course of the study the participation rate dropped as low as 82 percent at age 13, but the researchers were able to implement aggressive retention measures such as flying participants who had moved away back to New Zealand and using interviewers in other locations such as Australia. Attrition analyses were conducted and revealed no significant differences between dropouts and those who remained in the study between ages 3 and 11 except on socioeconomic status and single motherhood.

Silva (1996) writes that the costs of the study were minimal in the beginning because the services of many volunteers were used, but over the years the costs increased. These were covered in part by government agency funding or grants, but in addition academics and professionals as part of their jobs did work. He notes that costs increased at the age 9 testing period because testing sessions increased from one half-day to a full day. The costs for the age 21 testing sessions were considerable because of the expenses involved in flying participants back to New Zealand and paying incentives. If the entire study had been funded as a yearly contract, it is estimated that it would have cost $1 million a year, which really is not such an unreasonable amount of money considering the wealth of health and developmental data that has been generated by this study.

Thus the simple longitudinal research design can be a powerful method for gaining knowledge of developmental processes, but it is fraught with methodological and practical problems that make it challenging to complete. Clearly one does not embark upon such a study without careful planning and a great deal of patience since the rate of progress will be inevitably slow, especially in the early years of the study. During the planning phase, it is essential that the researcher spend considerable time developing theories and conceptualizing relationships between variables, especially in light of the fact that many developmental researchers have tended to regard time and cohort as confounds while seeking only pure age effects. According to Schaie (1984) this is a "static and ahistorical" (p. 2) approach. A review of the variables laid out by the general developmental model – age, cohort, and time of measurement – and the meaning of each variable within the developmental function might be helpful to the researcher.

Special Considerations Regarding Age, Cohort, and Time of Measurement

Age as a variable

Age is commonly used as an independent variable in developmental research and as "the central marker of development in biological and psychological research on developmental phenomena" (Bergman & Magnusson, 1990, p. 26). Hertzog (1996) warns, however, that chronological age only imperfectly maps onto maturational, psychological, and social aging processes. It is not necessarily a correlate of time of onset or duration of a particular behavior, and is not the same thing as biological age (Bergman & Magnusson, 1990; Schaie, 1988). Indeed, development needs to be understood as a function of both chronological and biological age, as well as birth cohort and time of measurement. Age thus should not be conceptualized as a causal variable, but rather as a proxy variable for a host of co-occurring, co-varying processes and events that can be more meaningfully used to account for age-related change. Variables such as biological maturation, years of schooling, and specific experiences are some prime examples (Miller, 1998).

It is clear, therefore, that age is not a singular variable but is multiply defined by a number of variables. Wohlwill (1970a) makes this case strongly in stating that age is:

at best a shorthand for the set of variables acting over time, most typically identified with experiential events or conditions, which are in a direct functional relationship with observed developmental changes in behavior; at worst it is merely a cloak for our ignorance in this regard (p. 30).

Cohort as a variable

Similarly, Baltes, Cornelius, and Nesselroade (1979) state that developmental researchers should not automatically begin a study by assuming that age is the most important explanatory variable for a phenomenon under investigation. This is true especially for samples of adolescents and adults, when cohort effects could potentially be much more explanatory than age. However, for the most part, the role of cohort effects in developmental processes has been presented descriptively rather than empirically (Baltes, Cornelius, & Nesselroade, 1979).

Baltes, Cornelius, and Nesselroade (1979) also note that the researcher's approach to dealing with the cohort variable depends on the nature of the research question. It could be seen as error, which is most probably true of child researchers who examine basic processes such as learning and cognition. It also could be seen as a dimension of external validity/generalization. Only a sequential strategy will separate out cohort-specific or between-cohort differences from "true" ontogenetic development (see Schaie & Caskie, this volume). The cohort variable also could be treated as a theoretical and process variable, but this is difficult to do because it requires explication of the "form and nature of cohort change that is judged to be developmental, the need for such concepts as stages or transitions in representing cohort change, and the types of explanatory mechanisms involved in producing cohort change" (Baltes, Cornelius, & Nesselroade, 1979, p. 80).

Kosloski (1986) makes a persuasive argument that defining a birth cohort simply by a shared discrete period of time does not automatically mean that members of that cohort shared experiences, so that the "cohort effect" might be meaningless in some instances. At other times, however, it makes sense to expect that historical events will impact individuals of varying ages differentially. Defining cohort by birth says little about what specific events "define" that cohort, and is likely to be of little real use (Kosloski, 1986).

Cohort can be related theoretically to development through the use of a model explicated by Baltes and Nesselroade (1979). They assert that there are three influences on behavioral development: normative age-graded, normative history-graded, and nonnormative. Normative age-graded influences are those most highly correlated with chronological age, and include processes such as biological maturation and socialization processes that are widely experienced across time and cohorts. Normative history-graded influences are those biological and social processes that are more culturally based and that are presumed to affect most members of a cohort, such as entering school. Nonnormative influences are those biological and social processes that do not impact most members of a cohort, such as illness, disability, divorce, and unemployment. These all operate simultaneously over time, which leads to between-cohort differences in developmental change as well as within-cohort differences (Baltes, Cornelius, & Nesselroade, 1979). Schaie (1986) adapts this framework when he proposes a method of composing cohorts that result in cohorts free from chronological age, thus allowing the researcher to more fully examine the parameters of development as set forth by the general developmental model without the constraint of calendar time.

Nesselroade and Baltes (1974) conducted a study that demonstrated a cohort effect. Longitudinal sequences of cohorts born in 1954, 1955, 1956, and 1957 and tested every year from 1970 to 1972 were used. Over 1,800 subjects were drawn from public schools in West Virginia and given personality and ability tests. Data analyses showed significant main effects of time of measurement on 7 of 10 personality variables and significant main effects of cohort on 2 of 10 personality variables. The main effects of cohort on the personality variables Independence and Achievement can be seen in Figure 1.1. The 14-year-olds tested in 1972 scored much higher in Independence than 14-year-olds tested in 1970 or 1971, while the 14-year-olds tested in 1970 scored higher in Achievement than 14-year-olds tested in 1971 and 1972. The researchers interpreted these findings as suggesting that the social-cultural context is more influential than maturation in adolescent personality development. This study is also important in that it demonstrated retest effects for the mental abilities testing, and attrition influenced the findings, such that those who remained in the study performed better than those who dropped out.

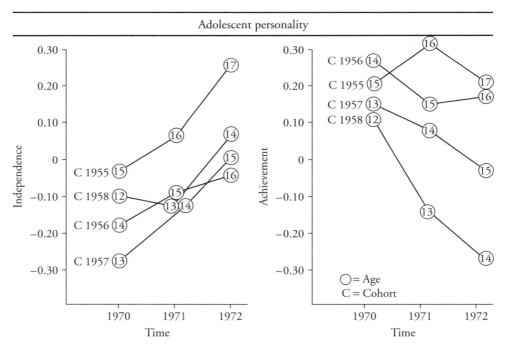

Figure 1.1   Differences in adolescent personality development as a function of the cohort effect. (From Baltes, Cornelius, & Nesselroade (1979). Copyright 1979 by Academic Press. Reprinted by permission.)

Time as a variable

The contribution of time to the developmental function has perhaps been the least understood, and, like the cohort variable, it has tended to be treated as a confound rather than an integral part of development (Schaie, 1984, 1986). Simply acknowledging the influence of time, which can be defined as a marker for historical events (Kosloski, 1986), does not give it explanatory power; it begs the question of what is the underlying psychological process (Caspi & Bem, 1990). Historical time is an essential parameter of developmental research, according to Schaie (1986), because it provides an important context for development.

Schaie (1986) suggests redefining time of measurement in terms of the impact of events on life-span development, which would separate the variable from calendar time. When attempting to determine what influences and processes might be important in terms of historical time, Schaie (1984) suggests looking for "societal changes in technology, customs, and cultural stereotypes that might constrain behavior" (p. 8). The researcher needs to make some conceptualization of historical causation as being distal or proximal as this affects the spacing of observations in longitudinal research (Baltes & Nesselroade, 1979). Finally, it is probably most important for the researcher studying adult/life-span development to hypothesize about the contribution of historical time to the developmental process since it is most likely influential in adulthood (Schaie, 1984, 1986). Indeed, the adult development researcher studying individual differences is really studying cohort and period effects according to Schaie (1986).

Conclusions

Donaldson and Horn (1992, p. 213) noted that "age, cohort, and time constitute a muddle. They are redundant quantities that cannot be independently varied to produce unique contributions to a dependent variable." Psychologists, they argue, tend to ignore cohort and time variables because they are the domains of other disciplines and assert that psychologists alone will not be able to construct a general model of development which takes into account the effects of age, cohort, and period. This is a strong call for interdisciplinary scholarship in developmental research. Indeed, the complexities seen in separating out the influences of age, cohort, and time of measurement on human development mandate the creation of complex models of development which will require the expertise of many disciplines (Baltes, Cornelius, & Nesselroade, 1979; Donaldson & Horn, 1992). At the very least, one undertaking a cross-sectional or simple longitudinal study should recognize that the best solution to the problem of separating age, period, and cohort effects is to measure directly those things that the variables index (Kosloski, 1986).

As indicated above, simple cross-sectional and longitudinal designs have been criticized severely over the years. At the same time, we would argue that, despite the flaws inherent in simple developmental designs, they remain high on the list of design choices when one is interested either in testing or generating hypotheses about developmental phenomena. Indeed, there is no better design than the longitudinal design for identifying age-related developmental change, and competent use of this and the cross-sectional design requires that one understand, in a proactive way, the issues and pitfalls associated with each, and plan data collection strategies and choose dependent variables so as to minimize concerns about threats to validity. We endorse Miller's (1998) point that nearly everything we know about developmental processes is the result of cross-sectional or longitudinal designs. Despite their limitations, we expect these methods will continue to be used by students of human development for many years to come.

References

Achenbach, T. M. (1978). *Research in developmental psychology: Concepts, strategies, and methods.* New York: Free Press.

Baltes, P. B. (1968). Longitudinal and cross-sectional sequences in the study of age and generational effects. *Human Development, 11*, 145–71.

Baltes, P. B. & Nesselroade, J. R. (1979). History and rationale of longitudinal research. In J. R. Nesselroade & P. B. Baltes (eds.), *Longitudinal research in the study of behavior and development* (pp. 1–39). New York: Academic Press.

Baltes, P. B., Cornelius, S. W., & Nesselroade, J. R. (1979). Cohort effects in developmental psychology. In J. R. Nesselroade & P. B. Baltes (eds.), *Longitudinal research in the study of behavior and development* (pp. 61–87). New York: Academic Press.

Baltes, P. B., Reese, H. W., & Nesselroade, J. R. (1977). *Life-span developmental psychology: Introduction to research methods.* Monterey, CA: Brooks/Cole.

Bergman, L. R. & Magnusson, D. (1990). General issues about data quality in longitudinal research. In D. Magnusson & L. R. Bergman (eds.), *Data quality in longitudinal research* (pp. 1–27). New York: Cambridge University Press.

Bergman, L. R., Eklund, G., & Magnusson, D. (1991). Studying individual development: Problems and methods. In D. Magnusson, L. R. Bergman, G. Rudinger, & B. Torestad (eds.), *Problems and methods in longitudinal research: Stability and change* (pp. 1–31). New York: Cambridge University Press.

Buss, A. R. (1979). Toward a unified framework for psychometric concepts in the multivariate developmental situation: Intraindividual change and inter- and intraindividual differences. In J. R. Nesselroade & P. B. Baltes (eds.), *Longitudinal research in the study of behavior and development* (pp. 41–59). New York: Academic Press.

Campbell, R. T. (1988). Integrating conceptualization, design, and analysis in panel studies of the life course. In K. W. Schaie, R. T. Campbell, W. Meredith, & S. C. Rawlings (eds.), *Methodological issues in aging research* (pp. 43–69). New York: Springer-Verlag.

Caspi, A. & Bem, D. J. (1990). Personality continuity and change across the life course. In L. Pervin (ed.), *Handbook of personality theory and research* (pp. 549–75). New York: Guilford.

Cook, T. D. & Campbell, D. T. (1979). *Quasi-experimental design and analysis issues for field settings.* Chicago, IL: Rand McNally.

Donaldson, G. & Horn, J. L. (1992). Age, cohort, and time developmental muddles: Easy in practice, hard in theory. *Experimental Aging Research, 18*, 213–22.

Farrington, D. P. (1991). Longitudinal research strategies: Advantages, problems, and prospects. *Journal of the American Academy of Child and Adolescent Psychiatry, 30*, 369–74.

Flavell, J. H., Beach, D. R., & Chinsky, J. M. (1966). Spontaneous verbal rehearsal in a memory task as a function of age. *Child Development*, *37*, 283–99.

Flick, S. N. (1988). Managing attrition in clinical research. *Clinical Psychology Review*, *8*, 499–515.

Friedman, S. L., Haywood, H. C., & Livesy, K. (1994). From the past to the future of developmental follow-up research. In S. L. Friedman & H. C. Haywood (eds.), *Developmental follow-up: Concepts, domains, and methods* (pp. 3–26). San Diego, CA: Academic Press.

Goldstein, H. (1979). *The design and analysis of longitudinal studies: Their role in the measurement of change*. New York: Academic Press.

Gopnik, A. & Astington, J. W. (1988). Children's understanding of representational change and its relation to the understanding of false belief and the appearance-reality distinction. *Child Development*, *59*, 26–37.

Hartmann, D. P. & George, T. P. (1999). Design, measurement, and analysis in developmental research. In M. H. Bornstein & M. E. Lamb (eds.), *Developmental psychology: An advanced textbook* (4th edn., pp. 125–95). Mahwah, NJ: Lawrence Erlbaum Associates.

Hertzog, C. (1996). Research design in studies of aging and cognition. In J. E. Birren & K. W. Schaie (eds.), *Handbook of the psychology of aging* (4th edn., pp. 24–37). San Diego, CA: Academic Press.

Jordan, T. E. (1994). The arrow of time: Longitudinal study and its applications. *Genetic, Social, and General Psychology Monographs*, *120*, 469–531.

Kosloski, K. (1986). Isolating age, period, and cohort effects in developmental research: A critical review. *Research on Aging*, *8(4)*, 460–79.

Kraemer, H. C. (1994). Special methodological problems of childhood developmental follow-up studies: Focus on planning. In S. L. Friedman & H. C. Haywood (eds.), *Developmental follow-up: Concepts, domains, and methods* (pp. 259–76). San Diego, CA: Academic Press.

Kraemer, H. C., Yesavage, J. A., Taylor, J. L., & Kupfer, D. (2000). How can we learn about developmental processes from cross-sectional studies, or can we? *American Journal of Psychiatry*, *157*, 163–71.

Mayer, K. U. & Huinink, J. (1990). Age, period, and cohort in the study of the life course: A comparison of classical A-P-C analysis with event history analysis or Farewell to Lexis? In D. Magnusson & L. R. Bergman (eds.), *Data quality in longitudinal research* (pp. 211–32). New York: Cambridge University Press.

McCall, R. B. (1977). Challenges to a science of developmental psychology. *Child Development*, *48*, 333–44.

Mednick, B. R., Mednick, S. A., & Griffith, J. J. (1981). Some recommendations for the design and conduct of longitudinal investigations. In F. Schulsinger, S. A. Mednick, & J. Knop (eds.), *Longitudinal research: Methods and uses in behavioral science* (pp. 285–95). Boston, MA: Martinus Nijhoff.

Mednick, S. A., Griffith, J. J., & Mednick, B. R. (1981). Problems with traditional strategies in mental health research. In F. Schulsinger, S. A. Mednick, & J. Knop (eds.), *Longitudinal research: Methods and uses in behavioral science* (pp. 3–15). Boston, MA: Martinus Nijhoff.

Miller, S. A. (1998). *Developmental research methods* (2nd edn.). Upper Saddle River, NJ: Prentice-Hall.

Nesselroade, J. R. & Baltes, P. B. (1974). Adolescent personality development and historical change: 1970–1972. *Monographs of the Society for Research in Child Development*, *39* (1, serial no. 154).

Pellegrini, A. D. (1996). *Observing children in their natural worlds: A methodological primer*. Mahwah, NJ: Lawrence Erlbaum Associates.

Rogosa, D. (1995). Myths and methods: "Myths about longitudinal research" plus supplemental questions. In J. M. Gottman (ed.), *The analysis of change* (pp. 3–66). Mahwah, NJ: Lawrence Erlbaum Associates.

Schaie, K. W. (1965). A general model for the study of developmental problems. *Psychological Bulletin, 64*, 92–107.

Schaie, K. W. (1977). Quasi-experimental designs in the psychology of aging. In J. E. Birren & K. W. Schaie (eds.), *Handbook of the psychology of aging*. New York: Van Nostrand.

Schaie, K. W. (1983). What can we learn from the longitudinal study of adult psychological development? In K. W. Schaie (ed.), *Longitudinal studies of adult psychological development* (pp. 1–19). New York: Guilford.

Schaie, K. W. (1984). Historical time and cohort effects. In K. A. McCluskey & H. W. Reese (eds.), *Life-span developmental psychology: Historical and generational effects* (pp. 107–21). New York: Academic Press.

Schaie, K. W. (1986). Beyond calendar definitions of age, time, and cohort: The general developmental model revisited. *Developmental Review, 6*, 252–77.

Schaie, K. W. (1988). Methodological issues in aging research: An introduction. In K. W. Schaie, R. T. Campbell, W. Meredith, & S. C. Rawlings (eds.), *Methodological issues in aging research* (pp. 1–11). New York: Springer-Verlag.

Schaie, K. W. (1996). *Intellectual development in adulthood: The Seattle Longitudinal Study*. New York: Cambridge University Press.

Shadish, W. R., Cook, T. D., & Campbell, D. T. (2002). *Experimental and quasi-experimental designs for generalized causal inference*. Boston, MA: Houghton Mifflin.

Siegler, I. C. & Botwinick, J. (1979). A long-term longitudinal study of intellectual ability of older adults: The matter of selective subject attrition. *Journal of Gerontology, 34*, 242–45.

Silva, P. A. (1996). The future of the Dunedin Study. In P. A. Silva & W. R. Stanton (eds.), *From child to adult: The Dunedin Multidisciplinary Health and Development Study* (pp. 259–66). Auckland, New Zealand: Oxford University Press.

Silva, P. A. & McCann, M. (1996). An introduction to the Dunedin Study. In P. A. Silva & W. R. Stanton (eds.), *From child to adult: The Dunedin Multidisciplinary Health and Development Study* (pp. 1–23). Auckland, New Zealand: Oxford University Press.

van der Kamp, L. J. T. & Bijleveld, C. C. J. H. (1998). Methodological issues in longitudinal research. In C. C. J. H. Bijleveld & L. J. T. van der Kamp (eds.), *Longitudinal data analysis: Designs, models, and methods* (pp. 1–45). London: Sage.

Wohlwill, J. F. (1970a). The age variable in psychological research. *Psychological Review, 77*, 49–64.

Wohlwill, J. F. (1970b). Methodology and research strategy in the study of developmental change. In L. R. Goulet & P. B. Baltes (eds.), *Life-span developmental psychology: Research and theory* (pp. 149–91). New York: Academic Press.

Wohlwill, J. F. (1973). *The study of behavioral development*. New York: Academic Press.

CHAPTER TWO

Methodological Issues in Aging Research

K. Warner Schaie and Grace I. L. Caskie

Introduction

The purpose of this chapter is to examine some of the central issues in research on aging. Most of the content of the chapter, although oriented towards the special issues facing researchers interested in the life stages of adulthood and old age, is equally relevant to the study of earlier life stages. These earlier stages are characterized by the rapid growth and differentiation of behaviors. By contrast, growth slows in young adulthood, and middle adulthood is characterized by long-lasting stability, while early old age shows decline occurring in some but not all individuals. In advanced old age, rapidly declining performance is then the norm. A perhaps even more important distinction is provided by the fact that studies of early development are typically conducted over short temporal periods and limited age ranges while studies of adulthood cover large age ranges and may extend across different historical eras.

We begin this chapter by delineating the differences in conclusions that can be drawn from cross-sectional (or age-comparative designs) as contrasted to longitudinal (or within-group follow-up) research designs. Sequential research designs and related analytic strategies are then considered as possible ways to ameliorate the deficiencies of single time point cross-sectional and single-cohort longitudinal studies. Finally, we turn to an analysis of the threats to the internal validity of studies of adulthood and aging.

Cross-Sectional versus Longitudinal Designs

In developmental research, it is important to be clear about whether a study addresses age differences or age changes. Cross-sectional (or age-comparative) designs provide information about *age differences* by comparing groups of different people who vary in age but are assessed at the same point in time. In contrast, longitudinal (or within-group follow-up) designs involve the observation of the same individuals at two or more different times; thus, such data represent *age changes*.

Perhaps the best way to understand the differences between cross-sectional and longitudinal designs is to consider how the designs vary along the dimensions of age, cohort, and time (or period). Schaie (1965) presented a general developmental model that proposed that any developmental change could potentially be decomposed as being influenced by one or more of these three independent dimensions. These issues were also addressed in the sociological literature by Mason et al. (1973) and Ryder (1965). Schaie's general developmental model is reviewed below.

The general developmental model characterized the developmental status of a given behavior B to be the function of three components (i.e., age, cohort, and time), such that $B = f(A, C, T)$. In this context, age (A) refers to the number of years from birth to the chronological point at which the individual is observed or measured. Cohort (C) denotes a group of individuals who enter an environment at the same point in time (usually but not necessarily at birth), and time of measurement (T) indicates the temporal occasion on which a given individual or group of individuals is observed or measured. We note that the three components are confounded in the sense that once two are specified, then the third is known, similar to the confounding of temperature, pressure, and volume in the physical sciences. For example, if an individual from a cohort born in 1950 (C) is to be assessed in the year 2010 (T), then it is known that the age (A) of that individual will be 60 years at the assessment. Nevertheless, despite their confounded nature, each of the three components is of primary interest for some questions of interest in the developmental sciences, and it would be useful to estimate the specific contribution attributable to each component.

Both the traditional longitudinal design, following one group of individuals over several occasions, and the traditional cross-sectional design, measuring several age groups at one time point, are simply special cases of Schaie's general developmental model, in which one of the three dimensions does not vary, while the other two are confounded. Specifically, in cross-sectional studies, no differential time (i.e., period) effects can be observed because the data are all collected at one point in time. In addition, age and cohort are confounded in the cross-sectional design because the age groups being studied must, by definition, be drawn from different birth cohorts. Because age and cohort are confounded in a cross-sectional design, it cannot be known if any differences between age groups that may be found are actually due to age or whether such differences could be attributed to cohort differences.

In contrast, single-cohort longitudinal studies, by definition, cannot reflect any cohort differences, but confound the effects of age changes in the dependent variable with time (period) effects occurring over the calendar time during which change is assessed. Because the single-cohort longitudinal study confounds changes in age with changes due to the passage of time, we cannot be assured with this type of design that any observed behavioral change is due to a maturational change as opposed to an environmental change. For example, suppose that in 1997 we had asked a group of 20-year-olds their opinions about the level of security they would find acceptable for air travel. If we reassessed this group in 2002 (at age 25) and found that they would accept a greater amount of security measures for air travel, we could not be certain whether this increase was due to a change in age from 20 to 25 or to events that had occurred during the five years between assessments.

Investigators have sometimes compared samples of individuals at different ages (i.e., the cross-sectional method) and concluded that differences found on the dependent variable could be attributed to chronological age. However, research on the adult development of mental abilities has shown wide discrepancies between cross-sectional and longitudinal data collected on the same subject population over a wide age range. For some dependent variables, substantial age differences obtained in cross-sectional data were not replicated in longitudinal data, while for other dependent variables, longitudinal age changes reflected more profound decrement than was shown in the comparable cross-sectional age difference patterns (Schaie, 2004; Schaie & Strother, 1968).

Given the confounds involved in both the traditional cross-sectional and single-cohort longitudinal designs, it is unlikely that a single cross-sectional data set or even a single longitudinal data set would be able to answer many theory-based questions (Schaie, 1992, 2000; Schaie & Hofer, 2001). Further, although the necessity of longitudinal data for the study of age changes and intraindividual development is clear, such studies are plagued by their impracticable time line if one is interested in a large age range, such as the entire adult age span. However, data acquisitions that are structured as cross-sectional or longitudinal sequences (Schaie & Baltes, 1975; Baltes, 1968) can allow an initial data collection to be suitably extended so that theory-based questions about development can be answered (Schaie, 1992; Schaie & Willis, 2002). Sequential strategies, described in the next section, have been proposed to address these concerns.

Sequential Studies and Analysis Strategies

Sequential studies can be either cross-sectional or longitudinal. A *cross-sectional sequence* consists of two or more cross-sectional studies, covering the same age range, conducted at two or more times. For example, we might compare age groups ranging in age from 25 to 75 in 2005 and then repeat the study in 2015 by obtaining a new sample of individuals in each of the age groups, covering the same age range of 25 to 75 years. In contrast, a *longitudinal sequence* consists of two or more longitudinal studies, using two or more cohorts. For example, we might begin by studying a group of 25-year-olds in 2005, planning to assess these individuals every ten years until they reach age 75 in 2055. This is a simple, single-cohort longitudinal study. In 2015, if we also begin studying a new cohort of 25-year-olds, also planning to assess these individuals every ten years until they reach age 75, the data from these two single-cohort longitudinal studies comprise the simplest case of a longitudinal sequence.

To summarize, longitudinal sequences use the same sample of individuals from two (or more) cohorts repeatedly, while cross-sectional sequences use independent random samples of individuals (each observed only once) from cohorts covering the same age groups at two (or more) different points in time. The critical difference between the two approaches is that the longitudinal sequence permits the evaluation of intraindividual age change and interindividual differences in rate of change, about which information cannot be obtained from cross-sectional sequences.

Schaie's "most efficient design" (Schaie, 1965, 1977, 1994; Schaie & Willis, 2002) combines cross-sectional and longitudinal sequences in a systematic way. The "most efficient design" first requires the identification of a population frame that provides a reasonable representation of the full range of the dependent variables to be studied. Optimally, the population frame should be a natural one, such as a school system, health plan, broadly based membership organization, or the like. Also, the population should be fairly large, so that it is possible to assume that members leaving the population will on average be replaced by other members with similar characteristics, maintaining the consistency of the population (i.e., sampling with replacement). In the most efficient design, an age range of interest is defined at Time 1 and is sampled randomly at intervals that are optimally identical with the time chosen to pass between successive measurements. For example, if 10 years will elapse between the first and second measurements, then the samples should be drawn in 10-year age intervals. At Time 2, previous participants from the Time 1 data collection are retrieved and restudied, providing short-term longitudinal studies of as many cohorts as there were age intervals at Time 1. The whole process can be repeated multiple times with retesting of previous subjects (adding to the longitudinal data) and initial testing of new samples (adding to the cross-sectional data). A hypothetical data collection with three time points using Schaie's most efficient design is shown in Figure 2.1.

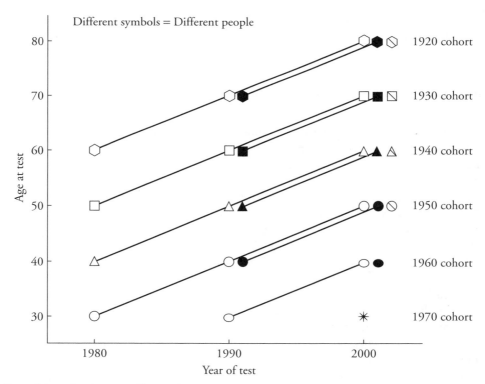

Figure 2.1   Schaie's most efficient design. (From Schaie & Willis (2002). Copyright 2002 by Prentice-Hall. Reprinted by permission.)

Table 2.1 Summary of the key features of the cohort-sequential, cross-sequential, and time-sequential analysis strategies

	Minimum requirements				
Strategy	*Ages*	*Cohorts/samples*	*Times*	*Contrasts*	*No effect*
Cohort-sequential	2	2	3	Age × Cohort	Time
Cross-sequential	3	2	2	Cohort × Time	Age
Time-sequential	2	4	2	Age × Time	Cohort

Data from the "most efficient design" or comparable designs can be analyzed in several ways to answer different research questions. Based on his 1965 general developmental model, Schaie described three sequential analysis strategies: the cohort-sequential strategy, the cross-sequential strategy, and the time-sequential strategy. It is important to note that the strategies proposed by Schaie should be viewed primarily as data analysis strategies rather than as data collection designs (Schaie & Baltes, 1975; Baltes, Cornelius, & Nesselroade, 1979; Schaie, 1994). Table 2.1 summarizes the key points of these three strategies and can be used as a reference as we explain the details of each strategy in the rest of this section.

Cohort-sequential (CS) analysis strategy

Developmental scientists often find the cohort-sequential strategy of greatest interest because it explicitly differentiates intraindividual age changes that occur within a cohort from interindividual differences between cohorts. This strategy also permits a check of the consistency of age functions over successive cohorts, thereby offering greater external validity than would be provided by a single-cohort longitudinal design. Cohort-sequential designs are often required to test hypotheses about phenomena assumed to follow the irreversible decrement model of aging, in which a maximal level of functioning is reached at some point in adulthood and thereafter involves linear (or linearly accelerating) and irreversible decrement (Schaie, 1977). The irreversible decrement model of aging is most appropriate for variables on which performance may be dominated by the level of efficiency of the peripheral sensory functions and by psychomotor speed, variables that typically decline with age.

The cohort-sequential strategy requires that at least two cohorts each be assessed for at least two age levels. Thus, as the example in Table 2.2 shows, this strategy requires at least three times of measurement. In other words, to compare the 1920 and 1930 birth cohorts in the example at ages 60 and 70, we would need data that were collected in 1980 (on only the 1920 cohort), in 1990 (on both cohorts), and in 2000 (on only the 1930 cohort).

When using the cohort-sequential analysis strategy, a critical assumption is the absence of time-of-measurement (T) effects on the behavior or variable being studied. This

Table 2.2   Cohort-sequential strategy

| | Age at data collection | |
Cohort	60	70
1920 cohort	1980	1990
1930 cohort	1990	2000

assumption may be parsimonious for many psychological variables, but others may still be affected by "true" period effects or by other internal validity threats such as differences in instrumentation or experimenter behavior across test occasions. For example, the terrorist attacks on September 11, 2001 were experienced by most American citizens alive at the time of the event. Variables such as level of anxiety or perceptions of security may vary greatly depending on whether they were measured before or after the event. Yet, other variables, particularly those that depend on physiological development (e.g., grip strength), will be virtually unaffected by period effects. The question arises, then, how violations of the assumption of no time-of-measurement effects would be reflected in the results of the cohort-sequential analysis. Logical analysis suggests that all estimated effects will be perturbed, although the most direct evidence of the violation would be shown in a significant C (cohort) by A (age) interaction (cf. Schaie, 1973). However, the lack of such an interaction does not necessarily guarantee the absence of T effects.

Accelerated longitudinal designs   A design proposed by Bell (1953) called the accelerated longitudinal design is also referred to as a cohort-sequential design by some researchers (see, e.g., Duncan et al., 1999; Anderson, 1993, 1995; Duncan, T. E., Duncan, & Hops, 1994; Duncan, S. C., Duncan, & Hops, 1996). However, it should be pointed out that the data generated by the accelerated longitudinal design differ from the data used in Schaie's cohort-sequential strategy. As shown in Table 2.1, the most basic case of Schaie's cohort-sequential strategy requires a minimum of three time points and uses complete information on two ages for two cohorts. In contrast, the accelerated longitudinal design collects data on each cohort at each time point, but not at every age, and thus incorporates missing data into the data matrix by design, as shown in Table 2.3. Under the assumption of no cohort differences, the information from the cohorts in an accelerated longitudinal study is then "linked" to examine an extended developmental trajectory. The convergence of the cohorts' developmental trajectories can be tested, and such tests will be stronger for cohorts with more overlapping time points (Anderson, 1993, 1995; McArdle & Anderson, 1990). Although the data necessary for the cohort-sequential strategy in Table 2.2 can be obtained from Table 2.3 (i.e., the columns for ages 60 and 70), the data generated by the accelerated longitudinal design actually corresponds more closely to the data used by the cross-sequential analysis strategy described next.

Table 2.3 Accelerated longitudinal design

	Age at data collection			
Cohort	50	60	70	80
1920 cohort		1980	1990	2000
1930 cohort	1980	1990	2000	

Table 2.4 Cross-sequential strategy

	Year of data collection	
Cohort	1970	2000
1920 cohort	Age 50	Age 80
1950 cohort	Age 20	Age 50

Cross-sequential (XS) analysis strategy

The basic cross-sequential strategy uses data collected from at least two cohorts at two times of measurement. For example, in Table 2.4, we compare a cohort born in 1920 to a cohort born in 1950 at two time points – 1970 and 2000. This analysis strategy is most appropriate when the variable of interest is expected to be independent of age but not independent of time-of-measurement. For example, we may be interested in how much the sexual attitudes of these cohorts differ in 1970 versus how much these cohorts' attitudes differ in 2000. The assumption that changes in the variable under study are not due to age or change with age at a uniform rate makes it possible to differentiate between cohort (C) trends and time-of-measurement (T) trends. However, if time-of-measurement effects are slight or nonexistent, the assumption that the variable is independent of age could be examined by estimating age changes (e.g., 20 to 50 and 50 to 80) because the individuals are obviously older at the second time of measurement. In fact, although the focus of the cross-sequential strategy is to contrast cohort differences with changes due to the passage of time, if the data in Table 2.4 were reorganized by age rather than by time, they would be identical to the data collected in the accelerated longitudinal design described in the previous section (Tonry, Ohlin, & Farrington, 1991).

The cross-sequential strategy's assumption that age (A) has no effect on the variable of interest may be hard for most developmental researchers to accept. However, this approach may be useful when longitudinal data are available only for a limited number of measurement occasions but extend over a wide range of cohort groupings. For example, suppose that a study was begun in 1970, examining individuals born in the 1910, 1920, 1930, 1940, and 1950 birth cohorts, and a repeated measurement was taken on all individuals in 1980. Despite having conducting her study for 10 years, the researcher cannot yet implement a cohort-sequential analysis strategy to examine age by cohort differences because three measurement occasions are required for that strategy. However, a cross-sequential analysis strategy, requiring only two measurement occasions, could be used in this case. Given a strong developmental theory about the nature of the confounded *A* effects, this strategy can also be used to obtain information about potential *A* effects represented in the *C* and *T* components. For example, if our hypothetical researcher analyzed her data after the second data collection with a 4 cohort × 2 times analysis of variance (ANOVA) and found significant interactions between cohort and time, she could conclude that there were positive age changes for some cohorts and negative age changes for other cohorts. This information could then be examined to obtain an idea of age changes from age 20 to age 80 (also see Schaie, 1996; Schaie & Strother, 1968). Although it is always preferable to estimate parameter effects from the most appropriate design – one that makes the correct limiting assumptions – one must often settle for something less than the optimal, whether this be a temporary expedient or whether dictated by the phenomenon being studied.

Time-sequential (TS) analysis strategy

The time-sequential strategy compares at least two age levels at a minimum of two times of measurement. An example of this strategy is shown in Table 2.5. In this example, a sample of 20-year-olds and a sample of 50-year-olds were drawn in 1970 and new, independent samples of 20-year-olds and 50-year-olds were drawn in 2000. Unlike the prior two analysis strategies that used repeated measures data, this strategy uses all independent samples. In other words, although the 1950 cohort is assessed in both 1970 and 2000, the data are drawn from two different samples from that cohort.

The time-sequential strategy examines whether the difference between the two age groups is the same or different at the two times of measurement. In other words, does the difference between the two age groups remain stable or does it change over time? The difference between 20-year-olds and 50-year-olds may be the same in 2000 as it was in 1970, or it may have narrowed or widened, depending on the variable that is assessed. For example, the difference between 20-year-olds and 50-year-olds in the amount of computer usage is likely to be much greater in 2000 than it was in 1970, while the

Table 2.5   Time-sequential strategy

	Year of data collection	
Age	*1970*	*2000*
20	1950 cohort – S_1	1980 cohort
50	1920 cohort	1950 cohort – S_2

S = Sample.

difference between 20-year-olds and 50-year-olds in how many words can be recalled from a list may be the same in 2000 as it was in 1970.

The time-sequential strategy is most appropriate when one assumes that the behavior being studied follows a decrement with compensation model of aging. In this model, one expects age decrement past maturity, but also allows that significant environmental remediation may compensate for the maturationally programmed deficit. This type of model may be most appropriate for variables such as fluid intelligence and other psychological variables where speed of response is involved. The time-sequential strategy permits the separation of age differences from time-of-measurement differences, assuming only trivial cohort effects.

Assessing Attrition and Practice Effects in Developmental Studies

Campbell and Stanley (1967) described eight different threats to the internal validity of quasi-experiments. One of these, maturation, represents no threat to the validity of developmental studies whose purpose is to test hypotheses about the effects of aging. The remaining seven threats represent rival hypotheses to the effect of aging; these include the effects of history (time), selection (cohort), experimental mortality (attrition), testing (reactivity or practice effects), instrumentation, statistical regression, and certain interactions of these effects. The effects of time and cohort were discussed in the sections above. In the next section, we will review how the three sequential analysis strategies described in the previous section can be extended to combine controls for the effects of time and/or cohort with the assessment of attrition and/or practice effects (see also Schaie, 1988). It must be noted, however, that the most controlled design is not necessarily the best. Implementing such controls can be costly in terms of experimenter efforts and resources and should be done only when absolutely necessary to ensure the integrity of a study.

Attrition effects

In a simple pre-test/post-test design, a cross-sectional attrition analysis can be performed by comparing participants who returned for T_2 to those present at T_1. However, this analysis only addresses how the baseline characteristics of the sample have changed due to attrition and cannot address whether those participants who dropped out would have changed more or less on the dependent variable than the remaining sample, had they remained in the sample. Three or more time points would be necessary to obtain an estimate of the effects of attrition on the measurement of age changes. Also, a simple attrition analysis at T_2 does not account for the possible confounding of attrition with practice or the interaction of attrition with maturation or selection (cohort).

Controlling for time and attrition   One way to assess the effects of both time and attrition is to consider two longitudinal samples carried over the same age range: that is, one sample is followed from T_1 to T_2 and a second sample is followed from T_2 to T_3. The members of each sample are then classified according to whether they returned for their second assessment or dropped out (i.e., were only assessed once). The cohort-sequential example that was presented in Table 2.2 can provide a context for this analysis. In the example presented in Table 2.2, the age range of 60 to 70 years was examined for a sample born in 1920 and a sample born in 1930. The 1920 cohort sample was assessed in 1980 (T_1) and 1990 (T_2), while the 1930 cohort sample was assessed in 1990 (T_2) and 2000 (T_3). To examine the effects of time and attrition, a 2 (time of measurement: 1980 or 1990) $\times$ 2 (attrition status: returned at age 70 or dropped out) ANOVA could then be performed on the data collected at age 60 for both samples. Because only the first measurement points are considered for either sample in this type of analysis, practice effects are controlled but cohort effects are not controlled.

A more general and interesting format for this analysis uses an extension of the time-sequential strategy and allows the component of variance associated with age to be assessed in addition to the components for time and attrition. This analysis requires obtaining at least one additional data point for each of the independent samples included in the time-sequential analysis. This additional data is only used to classify each individual's attrition status; in other words, this additional assessment point for each sample does not enter into the analysis.

To give an example of this analysis, let us begin with a basic time-sequential strategy comparing 50-year-olds and 60-year-olds at two times in history (1980 and 1990). The four cells marked "$R + D$" in Table 2.6 represent the four samples used in a basic time-sequential strategy assessing time and age. To extend this example to also assess attrition, as many individuals as possible are retrieved from the two samples first assessed in 1980 and are reassessed in 1990 (i.e., at age 60 for Sample 1 from the 1930 cohort and at age 70 for the sample from the 1920 cohort sample), and as many individuals as possible from the two samples first assessed in 1990 would be reassessed in 2000 (i.e., at age 60 for the sample from the 1940 cohort and at age 70 for Sample 2 from the 1930 cohort). This additional data is used only to classify the individuals in the original four samples as having returned (R) or having dropped out of the study after the first assessment (D).

Table 2.6 Extension of the time-sequential strategy to assess time $\times$ attrition

Time of test	Age		
	50	60	70
1980	1930 cohort $-$ S_1 ($R + D$)	1920 cohort ($R + D$)	
1990	1940 cohort ($R + D$)	1930 cohort $-$ S_2 ($R + D$)	
		1930 cohort $-$ S_1 (R^*)	1920 cohort (R^*)
2000		1940 cohort (R^*)	1930 cohort $-$ S_2 (R^*)

S = Sample; R = returned for second assessment; D = dropped out after first assessment.
*This data is used only to classify individuals as those who returned or dropped out and does not enter into the analysis.

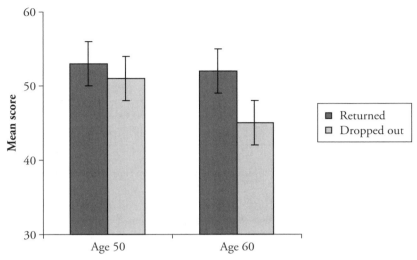

Figure 2.2   Example of an age × attrition interaction.

The ANOVA framework would again be used for this analysis, now using a 2 (age: 50 or 60) × 2 (time of test: 1980 or 1990) × 2 (attrition status: returned or dropped out) design. The attrition status main effect and its interactions with age and time provide information about the differential patterns of attrition by age and by time. For example, if a significant main effect were found for attrition, one possible conclusion is that the sample that returned had higher scores on average than those who dropped out. On the other hand, if a significant interaction for age by attrition such as that shown in Figure 2.2 were found, one could conclude that, of the sample measured at age 60, those who returned were likely to have higher scores than those who dropped out while no such difference was found for the sample measured at age 50.

Controlling for cohort and attrition   Extending the standard cohort-sequential design allows attrition effects to be crossed with cohort and age. Table 2.7 extends the cohort-sequential example in Table 2.2. An additional assessment of each of the two cohort samples at a third age (i.e., age 80) would be added to the original cohort-sequential design. Specifically, the 1920 cohort sample would again be assessed in 2000 at age 80, and the 1930 cohort sample would be assessed in 2010 at age 80. This final assessment of both samples at age 80 would be for the purpose of identifying dropouts only and would not enter into the analysis. The analysis of age, cohort, and attrition is performed for all individuals who were measured twice ($R + D_2$) as a repeated measures ANOVA (i.e., 2 age (repeated) × 2 cohort × 2 attrition status [R versus D_2]). A significant age × attrition interaction would provide evidence of differential age changes on the dependent variable for the group that returned versus the group that dropped out.

An alternative analysis method for examining age, cohort, and attrition involves extending the independent samples variant of the cohort-sequential analysis strategy. In the independent samples variant, an independent sample is drawn from each cohort

Table 2.7   Repeated measures extension of the cohort-sequential strategy to assess cohort ×
attrition

Cohort	Age at data collection		
	60	70	80
1920 cohort	1980 $(R + D_1^* + D_2)$	1990 $(R + D_2)$	2000 (R^*)
1930 cohort	1990 $(R + D_1^* + D_2)$	2000 $(R + D_2)$	2010 (R^*)

R = Returned for second and third assessment; D = dropped out after first assessment.
*This data is used only to classify individuals' attrition status and does not enter into the analysis.

Table 2.8   Independent samples extension of the cohort-sequential design to assess cohort ×
attrition

Cohort	Age at data collection		
	60	70	80
1920 cohort	C_1S_1 $(R + D)$	C_1S_2 $(R + D)$ C_1S_1 (R^*)	C_1S_2 (R^*)
1930 cohort	C_2S_1 $(R + D)$	C_2S_2 $(R + D)$ C_2S_1 (R^*)	C_2S_2 (R^*)

C = Cohort; S = sample; R = returned for second assessment; D = dropped out after first assessment.
*This data is used only to classify individuals as those who returned or dropped out and does not enter into the
analysis.

at each age studied, rather than repeatedly assessing the one sample drawn from each
cohort. In Table 2.8, the four samples that would be included in the independent
samples variant of the basic cohort-sequential strategy are marked "$R + D$." To include
an assessment of attrition effects, a repeated measurement would be added for each
of these four samples at the next time point. This additional data (marked R^*) is only
used to assign the attrition status and does not enter into the analysis. The analysis is
performed as a 2 (age: 60 or 70) × 2 (cohort: 1920 or 1930) × 2 (attrition status:
returned or dropped out) ANOVA. In this analysis, a significant interaction of age
and attrition indicates that the difference between the group that returned and the
group that dropped out varied based on whether the group was measured at age 60
or age 70.

Controlling for time, cohort, and attrition It is also possible to specify analysis designs that
allow the crossing of attrition effects with both time and cohort. These designs involve
extensions of the cross-sequential strategy. Table 2.9 demonstrates that an additional
measurement point would be necessary to determine dropouts following the second

Table 2.9 Repeated measures extension of the cross-sequential strategy to assess cohort × time × attrition

Time of test	Cohort birth year	
	1920	*1930*
1980	Age 60 $(R + D_1^* + D_2)$	Age 50 $(R + D_1^* + D_2)$
1990	Age 70 $(R + D_2)$	Age 60 $(R + D_2)$
2000	Age 80 (R^*)	Age 70 (R^*)

R = Returned for the second and third assessments; D_1 = dropped out after the first assessment; D_2 = dropped out after the second assessment.
*This data is used only to classify individuals as those who returned or dropped out and does not enter into the analysis.

Table 2.10 Independent samples extension of the cross-sequential strategy to assess cohort × time × attrition

Time of test	Cohort birth year	
	1920	*1930*
1980	$C_1S_1 \ (R + D)$	$C_2S_1 \ (R + D)$
1990	$C_1S_2 \ (R + D)$	$C_2S_2 \ (R + D)$
	$C_1S_1 \ (R^*)$	$C_2S_1 \ (R^*)$
2000	$C_1S_2 \ (R^*)$	$C_2S_2 \ (R^*)$

C = Cohort; S = sample; R = returned for second assessment; D = dropped out after first assessment.
*This data is used only to classify individuals as those who returned or dropped out and does not enter into the analysis.

assessment. The repeated measures design requires classification into dropouts and survivors after the first and second assessments. Attrition at the second time point consequently is confounded with practice effects. The analysis of time, cohort, and attrition is performed for individuals who were measured twice $(R + D_2)$ as a 2 (time, repeated) × 2 cohort × 2 attrition status repeated measures ANOVA.

If independent samples from each cohort are used instead of repeated measurements on the same cohort samples, practice effects are now controlled for, but each independent sample must be assessed twice for each level of the design. In Table 2.10, the four samples that would comprise the basic cross-sequential strategy with independent samples are marked "$R + D$." The data from the reassessment of each of these four samples at the next time point is used only to determine attrition status. The analysis can be performed as a 2 (time: 1980 or 1990) × 2 (cohort: 1920 or 1930) × 2 (attrition status: returned or dropped out) ANOVA.

Practice effects

The possible inflation of longitudinal change estimates because of practice effects can be studied by comparing individuals at the same age who are retest returnees with the performance of individuals assessed for the first time at T_2. However, such a comparison involves the comparison of an attrited sample with a random sample. The mean values for the longitudinal group should therefore be adjusted for attrition to permit a valid comparison. The appropriate adjustment is the difference between returnees and the entire sample at baseline (rather than the difference between returnees and dropouts). Similar analyses can be conducted to assess the continuing effect of practice at additional assessment points in the study.

Controlling for time and practice The effects of time and practice for a particular age level can be examined with a minimum of four independent samples and three measurement occasions. Data collected at T_2 or T_3 are compared for samples of equivalent age that were either assessed at the previous time point or that are assessed at T_2 or T_3 for the first time. Returning to the cohort-sequential example in Table 2.2 where a sample from each of two cohorts was assessed at ages 60 and 70, suppose that another sample from each of the two cohorts had been drawn and only measured at the second age studied (i.e., age 70). Then, the two original samples (measured twice) are the "practiced" groups at age 70, and the two new samples are the "unpracticed" groups. An analysis of the data collected at age 70 contrasts time of measurement with practice. Cohort is confounded with time of measurement in this analysis in that all of the data collected in 1990 (i.e., T_2) was from the 1920 cohort and all of the data collected in 2000 (T_3) was from the 1930 cohort.

A more general formulation of this analysis that balances ages at pre-test is an extension of the time-sequential strategy that also crosses age with time, and practice. An example of this analysis strategy is shown in Table 2.11. The four starred samples represent the basic data required in a time-sequential design. These four samples are retested at the next time point, creating the practiced groups. At the retest time points,

Table 2.11 Extension of the time-sequential strategy to assess age × time × practice

Time of test	Age at data collection		
	50	60	70
1980	1930 cohort − S_1^*	1920 cohort − S_1^*	
1990	1940 cohort − S_1^*	1930 cohort − S_2^*	
		1930 cohort − S_1 (P)	1920 cohort − S_1 (P)
		1930 cohort − S_3 (U)	1920 cohort − S_2 (U)
2000		1940 cohort − S_1 (P)	1930 cohort − S_2 (P)
		1940 cohort − S_2 (U)	1930 cohort − S_4 (U)

S = Sample; P = practiced; U = unpracticed.
*This data does not enter into the analysis but is required to establish differential levels of practice.

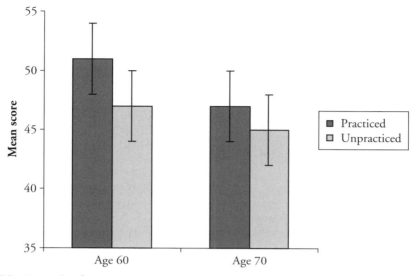

Figure 2.3   Example of an age × practice interaction.

four new (unpracticed) samples are drawn and tested. Thus, the data used for this analysis comes from at least eight samples (four at each of two age levels), half of which are pre-tested at an earlier occasion before generating the data that enter into this analysis.

The analysis can then be performed as a 2 (time: 1990 or 2000) × 2 (age: 60 or 70) × 2 (practice level: practiced or unpracticed) ANOVA. A significant main effect for practice might demonstrate that those who had been pre-tested showed significantly higher levels of performance at retest than those who were first tested, regardless of age or time of measurement. A significant age × practice effect would reflect age-specific practice effects. Figure 2.3 shows an example of such an interaction where practice has greatly increased the performance of the 60-year-olds but only had minimal benefit for the 70-year-olds. It should be noted that this analysis confounds practice with attrition. The implication of this confound is that the practiced sample is also an attrited sample.

Controlling for cohort and practice   The cohort-sequential design with independent measurements can be expanded to permit crossing of age, cohort, and practice. A minimum of two samples is required at each age level for each cohort, half of whom have received practice at a previous data point that does not enter the analysis. Consequently, a minimum of four assessment points will be required for this design, which also confounds practice with attrition.

The four starred assessments in Table 2.12 represent the four original sets of data used in the basic independent samples variant of the cohort-sequential strategy. Each of these four samples is retested at the next time point; at each retest point, a new independent sample is also drawn from each cohort and tested for the first time. The analysis of cohort, practice, and age can be performed as a 2 (age: 70 or 80) × 2 (cohort: 1920 or 1930) × 2 (practice status: practiced or unpracticed) ANOVA. A significant cohort

Table 2.12   Independent samples extension of the cohort-sequential design to assess cohort ×
practice

Cohort	Age at data collection		
	60	*70*	*80*
1920 cohort	$C_1S_1^*$	$C_1S_2^*$ $C_1S_1 \ (P)$ $C_1S_3 \ (U)$	$C_1S_2 \ (P)$ $C_1S_4 \ (U)$
1930 cohort	$C_2S_1^*$	$C_2S_2^*$ $C_2S_1 \ (P)$ $C_2S_3 \ (U)$	$C_2S_2 \ (P)$ $C_2S_4 \ (U)$

C = Cohort; S = sample; T = time; P = practiced; U = unpracticed.
*This data does not enter into the analysis but is required to establish differential levels of practice.

× practice interaction indicates that the effect of practice on the dependent variable differed by cohort.

Controlling for time, cohort, and practice   Once again, for those adult age levels when age effects can be assumed to be trivial, it would be possible to cross time, cohort, and practice by extending the cross-sequential design with independent measurements. The minimum design here would require three assessment points. That is, each of the four possible cohort/time-of-measurement combinations (at T_2 and T_3) would require two samples, one of which received practice at T_1 or T_2. Table 2.13 provides an example of the data necessary to perform the 2 (time: 1990 or 2000) × 2 (cohort: 1920 or 1930) × 2 (practice status: practiced or unpracticed) ANOVA to examine the components of time, cohort, and practice.

Table 2.13   Independent samples extension of the cross-sequential design to assess time ×
cohort × practice

Time of test	Cohort birth year	
	1920	*1930*
1980	Age 60 – $C_1S_1^*$	Age 50 – $C_2S_1^*$
1990	Age 70 – $C_1S_2^*$ Age 70 – $C_1S_1 \ (P)$ Age 70 – $C_1S_3 \ (U)$	Age 60 – $C_2S_2^*$ Age 60 – $C_2S_1 \ (P)$ Age 60 – $C_2S_3 \ (U)$
2000	Age 80 – $C_1S_2 \ (P)$ Age 80 – $C_1S_4 \ (U)$	Age 70 – $C_2S_2 \ (P)$ Age 70 – $C_2S_4 \ (U)$

C = Cohort; S = sample; T = time; P = practiced; U = unpracticed.
*This data does not enter into the analysis but is required to establish differential levels of practice.

Designs crossing practice and attrition

Using the independent measurement designs allowed the effects of attrition to be assessed while controlling for practice. The converse approach (assessing the effects of practice while controlling for attrition) is not feasible because study participants returning for a second assessment represent, by definition, only the group of retest survivors. It is possible, however, to cross attrition and practice if, rather than comparing only those who returned and those who dropped out after T_1, we also consider dropout after T_2. In this case, a prior occasion of data not entering the analysis would be required for half of our groups, and all individuals must be followed to the occasion beyond the last analysis point, to determine dropouts and survivors for each subset. All the designs described can be treated in this manner, but an additional assessment occasion is required. Thus, designs crossing practice and attrition with either cohort or time will require four assessment occasions. The design that crosses attrition and practice with both cohort and time will require a minimum of five occasions.

Summary

The study of adult development has benefited markedly from shifts in methodological paradigms as well as from the application of innovative methods particularly suited to the study of behaviors occurring across age and time. In this chapter, we first focused on the need to determine whether the investigator is interested in age differences or age changes. We then discussed multiple observation analysis strategies suitable for distinguishing the effects of age, cohort, and time of measurement. To review, the cohort-sequential strategy contrasts cohort with age; the cross-sequential strategy contrasts age with time; and the time-sequential strategy contrasts time with age. Finally, we discussed controlling threats to the internal validity of studies. We showed how the basic analysis strategies can be extended to provide assessments of practice and attrition in addition to the effects of age, cohort, and time.

References

Anderson, E. R. (1993). Analyzing change in short-term longitudinal research using cohort-sequential designs. *Journal of Consulting and Clinical Psychology, 61,* 929–40.

Anderson, E. R. (1995). Accelerating and maximizing information from short-term longitudinal research. In J. M. Gottman (ed.), *The analysis of change* (pp. 139–63). Mahwah, NJ: Lawrence Erlbaum Associates.

Baltes, P. B. (1968). Longitudinal and cross-sectional sequences in the study of age and generation effects. *Human Development, 11,* 145–71.

Baltes, P. B., Cornelius, S. W., & Nesselroade, J. R. (1979). Cohort effects in developmental psychology. In J. R. Nesselroade & P. B. Baltes (eds.), *Longitudinal research in the study of behavior and development* (pp. 61–87). New York: Academic Press.

Bell, R. Q. (1953). Convergence: An accelerated longitudinal approach. *Child Development, 24,* 145–52.

Campbell, D. T. & Stanley, J. C. (1967). *Experimental and quasi-experimental designs for research.* Chicago, IL: Rand McNally.

Duncan, S. C., Duncan, T. E., & Hops, H. (1996). Analysis of longitudinal data within accelerated longitudinal designs. *Psychological Methods, 1,* 236–48.

Duncan, T. E., Duncan, S. C., & Hops, H. (1994). The effects of family cohesiveness and peer encouragement on the development of adolescent alcohol use: A cohort-sequential approach to the analysis of longitudinal data. *Journal of Studies on Alcohol, 44,* 588–99.

Duncan, T. E., Duncan, S. C., Strycker, L. A., Li, F., & Alpert, A. (1999). *An introduction to latent variable growth curve modeling: Concepts, issues, and applications.* Mahwah, NJ: Lawrence Erlbaum Associates.

Mason, K. G., Mason, W. H., Winsborough, H. H., & Poole, W. K. (1973). Some methodological problems in cohort analyses of archival data. *American Sociological Review, 38,* 242–58.

McArdle, J. J. & Anderson, E. R. (1990). Latent variable growth models for research on aging. In J. E. Birren & K. W. Schaie (eds.), *Handbook of the psychology of aging* (3rd edn., pp. 21–44). San Diego, CA: Academic Press.

Ryder, N. B. (1965). The cohort as a concept in the study of social changes. *American Sociological Review, 30,* 843–61.

Schaie, K. W. (1965). A general model for the study of developmental problems. *Psychological Bulletin, 64,* 92–107.

Schaie, K. W. (1973). Methodological problems in descriptive developmental research on adulthood and aging. In J. R. Nesselroade & H. W. Reese (eds.), *Life-span developmental psychology: Methodological issues* (pp. 253–80). New York: Academic Press.

Schaie, K. W. (1977). Quasi-experimental designs in the psychology of aging. In J. E. Birren & K. W. Schaie (eds.), *Handbook of the psychology of aging* (pp. 39–58). New York: Van Nostrand Reinhold.

Schaie, K. W. (1988). Internal validity threats in studies of adult cognitive development. In M. L. Howe & C. J. Brainerd (eds.), *Cognitive development in adulthood: Progress in cognitive development research* (pp. 241–72). New York: Springer-Verlag.

Schaie, K. W. (1992). The impact of methodological changes in gerontology. *International Journal of Aging and Human Development, 35,* 19–29.

Schaie, K. W. (1994). Developmental designs revisited. In S. H. Cohen & H. W. Reese (eds.), *Life-span developmental psychology: Theoretical issues revisited* (pp. 45–64). Hillsdale, NJ: Lawrence Erlbaum Associates.

Schaie, K. W. (1996). *Intellectual development in adulthood: The Seattle Longitudinal Study.* New York: Cambridge University Press.

Schaie, K. W. (2000). The impact of longitudinal studies on understanding development from young adulthood to old age. *International Journal of Behavioral Development, 24,* 267–75.

Schaie, K. W. (2004). *Developmental influences on adult intelligence: The Seattle Longitudinal Study.* New York: Oxford University Press.

Schaie, K. W. & Baltes, P. B. (1975). On sequential strategies in developmental research: Description or explanation? *Human Development, 18,* 384–90.

Schaie, K. W. & Hofer, S. M. (2001). Longitudinal studies in research on aging. In J. E. Birren & K. W. Schaie (eds.), *Handbook of the psychology of aging* (5th edn., pp. 55–77). San Diego, CA: Academic Press.

Schaie, K. W. & Strother, C. R. (1968). A cross-sequential study of age changes in cognitive behavior. *Psychological Bulletin, 70*, 671–80.

Schaie, K. W. & Willis, S. L. (2002). *Adult development and aging* (5th edn.). New York: Prentice-Hall.

Tonry, M. H., Ohlin, L. E., & Farrington, D. P. (1991). *Human development and criminal behavior: New ways of advancing knowledge.* New York: Springer-Verlag.

CHAPTER THREE

Using Microgenetic Designs to Study Change Processes

Manuela Lavelli, Andréa P. F. Pantoja, Hui-Chin Hsu, Daniel Messinger, and Alan Fogel

The process of change represents a main, central issue for the study of development. Basic and applied researchers in developmental science have aimed their research work at answering several key questions related to the problem of change. How does change occur? What mechanisms produce change? What conditions are likely to promote the emergence of change in development? Another related question concerns the stability versus instability of new behavioral patterns that emerge as a consequence of an intervention. What are the relationships between variability and stability in developmental processes? Does the emergence of new behavioral patterns tend to suppress the old patterns or to coexist with them? Nevertheless, observing and understanding how change occurs has been recognized to be a quite difficult and challenging task (Miller & Coyle, 1999; Siegler & Crowley, 1991). This is despite recent advances in both theoretical perspectives and methods focused on change processes that have brought considerable progress in the research field (see "Microgenetic designs as promising tools," below). Part of the challenge is due to the complexity of conceptualizing change processes. It is our contention, however, that the main problem appears to come from the difficulty of devising and implementing appropriate methods for studying change *while* it is occurring (Fogel, 1990; Kuhn, 1995; Siegler, 1995), instead of comparing pre- and post-change behavioral patterns.

In this chapter, we aim to illustrate a research design, referred to as microgenetic designs, specifically devised for documenting change processes in development. First, we discuss the limitations of traditional research designs to capture ongoing processes of change. We then present microgenetic designs through an illustration of their key characteristics. This is followed by a review of the theoretical foundations of microgenetic designs as well as some of the historical and current observational and experimental studies based on microgenetic designs, illustrating their possibilities. In particular, we give a detailed presentation of the relational-historical approach as a particular form of microgenetic design devised to study developmental change processes in interpersonal relationships. Examples from our studies are given to illustrate the steps of a research program informed by the relational-historical approach. In the following sections of the chapter, we describe different quantitative and qualitative strategies that can be used to analyze data collected through microgenetic designs. Finally, we discuss the advantages of using microgenetic designs, suggesting new directions for microgenetic research.

Traditional Designs versus Microgenetic Designs

The main methodological difficulty in studying developmental change processes is that traditional research designs do not involve a direct observation of change *while* it is occurring (Kuhn, 1995). In both cross-sectional and longitudinal designs the researcher can see the *products* of change, not the *process*. Essentially, what these kinds of designs do is to compare the infants' or children's target behavior (e.g., the interactive behavior, or the behavior shown during a task) at different ages: cross-sectional studies compare the behavior of different children, whereas longitudinal studies compare the behavior of the same children at different ages. On the one hand, cross-sectional designs provide information on the characteristics of the target behavior in large groups at different ages. On the other hand, longitudinal designs yield important information on changes within cases, allowing one to compare those changes across different cases. Consequently, longitudinal designs afford more opportunities for the researcher to obtain insight on patterns of stability/instability of multiple individuals over time. Nevertheless, due to their time-consuming nature, longitudinal designs are often based on a small number of observations collected at widely spaced intervals. This strategy, however, has the potential to mask the intra-individual variability that is so important for those interested in how change occurs.

Another related limitation in most longitudinal designs is that the time interval between observations is usually too long to capture the ongoing process of change. Thus, the kind of information gained by such longitudinal designs is more like that in a series of a few snapshots taken across a wide span of time than the continuous flow of information in a movie (Siegler, 1995). As a result, transitional behavioral patterns, such as pre-reaching movements (Thelen et al., 1993) and strategies for adding numbers (Siegler & Jenkins, 1989), developed in brief periods of rapid change that could help clarify how infants/children make a transition in a specific domain may be completely missed using a "snapshot" approach.

Microgenetic Designs as Promising Tools

One promising approach to studying change processes and individual differences in development is offered by microgenetic designs as these are specifically aimed to allow the researcher to closely observe *processes of change*, instead of *products*. As the name implies, microgenetic designs are focused on the *microgenesis* of development, that is, on the moment-by-moment change observed within a short period of time for an elevated number of sessions. Usually, the observational time includes relatively short (weeks, months) but rapidly changing developmental periods.

Two main premises underlie the use of microgenetic designs. The first is that only by focusing on the *microgenetic details* of children's (and their partners') behavior in particular contexts (e.g., interactive and/or task-oriented contexts) is it possible to gain the type of fine-grained information that is necessary to understand change processes. The second premise is that observing and understanding changes at the micro-level of real time is fundamental to understanding changes at the macro-level of developmental time. This premise is rooted in Werner's (1948) hypothesis on the commonalities underlying changes that occur on different time scales, and strengthened by recent advances in the dynamic systems perspective within developmental science (see "Theoretical foundations and current studies," below).

Although the term "microgenetic method" has been predominantly associated with research within a more cognitive orientation, researchers of different theoretical perspectives have also advocated and adopted microgenetic designs. Only in the last decade, however, has the use of microgenetic designs been increasing and widening to investigate a range of different domains. Some of these domains include early emotional development (e.g., de Weerth, van Geert, & Hoijtink, 1999; Messinger, Fogel, & Dickson, 1999), mother–infant communication (e.g., Hsu & Fogel, 2003; Lavelli & Fogel, 2002), motor development (e.g., Thelen et al., 1993), early language development (e.g., Ruhland & van Geert, 1998), social writing (Jones, 1998), attention (Miller & Aloise-Young, 1996), memory (Coyle & Bjorklund, 1997), young children's problem-solving strategies (Chen & Siegler, 2000), and the effects of instructional procedures (Siegler, 2002). Such "explosion," we believe, is probably due to advances in both theoretical perspectives and data analysis strategies for the study of change processes. But what characterizes microgenetic designs?

Key characteristics of microgenetic designs

Regardless of the researchers' theoretical perspectives and the developmental domains under investigation, microgenetic designs are defined by the following key characteristics:

1   Individuals are observed through a period of developmental change. That is, the *changing individual* is the fundamental unit of analysis.
2   Observations are conducted *before*, *during*, and *after* a period during which rapid change in a particular domain occurs. That is, observation is not simply conducted before and after the change takes place.
3   There is an *elevated density* of observations within the transition period. That is, observations are conducted at time intervals that are considerably shorter than the time intervals required for the developmental change to occur. For instance, if a

developmental change takes place over several months, then observations should be conducted weekly or even more frequently (Fogel, 1990, 1997).

4 Observed behaviors are *intensively analyzed*, both qualitatively and quantitatively, with the goal of identifying the processes that give rise to the developmental change (Siegler & Crowley, 1991).

In the existing developmental literature, the change in behavioral patterns examined in observational studies is most likely to occur spontaneously, whereas in experimental studies, the change is most likely to be elicited. Either way, the goal of microgenetic designs is to accelerate the change process, or carefully observe the change process, by providing participants with a high concentration of experiences and opportunities, over a relatively short period of time (weeks, months) (Kuhn & Phelps, 1982). Of particular note, this strategy has been claimed as extremely useful to test potential control parameters, that is, those factors that according to a dynamic systems perspective shift the observed system into new behavioral configurations (see Thelen, 1990). In the case of changes that are hypothesized to occur across years, microgenetic designs also appear to be a useful alternative provided that a sampling of behaviors over a long period of time would be very expensive and time-consuming. But what are the theoretical roots of microgenetic designs? Microgenetic designs, especially microgenetic experimental designs, are deeply rooted in the history of developmental science. Their foundations are found within different theoretical perspectives.

Theoretical Foundations and Current Studies

Around the mid-1920s, the term "microgenesis" was coined by Werner as an extension of the German word *Aktualgenese* used by Sander (Leipzig group of Gestalt psychologists) to describe an experimental technique devised to evoke the genesis and development of percepts in the laboratory setting, thus yielding development as an object of observation for the researcher (Catan, 1986).

Werner shared the same interest in experimentally evoking developmental phenomena to closely observe them. Hypothesizing similarities between change processes at different developmental levels, Werner (1948) devised a set of techniques to scale down developmental phenomena of different extensions in time and at different developmental levels to experimentally reconstruct what he called "microgenesis," i.e., the activation and the developmental process of a particular competence in a miniaturized, accelerated form. Werner's work was cited and supported by Vygotskij (1978).

According to Vygotskij, macrodevelopmental changes (changes that occur over months and years) arise from the process of microdevelopmental changes (changes that occur over real time) observed in the context of social interactions. The interactions between a child and a supportive adult lead to questions, examples, and demonstrations that gradually change a child's performance, thereby allowing the child to perform activities that s/he could not accomplish alone. Thus, within this sociocultural perspective, a microgenetic analysis of the moment-to-moment changes observed during social interaction is used as a dynamic assessment of a child's "zone of proximal development." The microgenetic method also operates as a means to explore the mechanisms through which cultural factors structure the organization and development of the individual's communicative and cognitive strategies.

Current microgenetic approaches guided by sociocultural theory

The sociocultural theory discussed above represents a conceptual framework guiding some of the current studies using microgenetic analyses to investigate the development of problem-solving strategies in social-collaborative contexts. Compared to those studies that investigate the effects of collaboration on cognition using pre- and post-test designs, studies using microgenetic analysis present the advantage of gaining a wide range of information about the *process of change* in both the ensemble and the individuals. In these microgenetic studies, the natural course of the partners' behavior is videotaped over the time of one or more problem-solving sessions, and later analyzed in detail. Provided that such cognitive processes are expressed verbally and non-verbally through the joint activities observed during interaction, microgenetic analysis allows the researcher to track and correlate specific moment-to-moment changes to the changes observed in the participants' cognitive performance (Miller & Coyle, 1999).

For example, in preschoolers, microgenetic analysis has been used to document the transition from other-regulated to self-regulated problem-solving strategies (Wertsch & Hickmann, 1987; Wertsch & Stone, 1978). With regard to graduate students in a problem-solving interaction, microgenetic analysis showed that the microdevelopmental sequence (i.e., the moment-to-moment progression in understanding an unfamiliar device; Granott, 1993) followed the same progression predicted at skill levels by dynamic-skill theory, demonstrating a parallelism between microdevelopments and macrodevelopments (Fischer & Granott, 1995).

In the late 1970s, the spread of Vygotskij's theory associated with the shift in developmentalists' attention to microdevelopment within adult–child interaction constituted a turning point in the explosion of microgenetic designs to investigate change processes in social contexts. Examples include a study by Bruner (1983), where the ontogenesis of speech was examined through careful observation of two mother–infant dyads during spontaneous play every other week from 3–5 to 18–24 months. Studies conducted by Fogel (1977; 1985), Trevarthen (1977), and Papousek and Papousek (1984) also provided detailed documentation of the development of mother–infant face-to-face interaction through weekly or even more frequent observations of parent–infant dyads between the second and the sixth months of life.

Post-Piagetian microgenetic approaches to cognitive development

The emergence of microgenetic designs within the context of post-Piagetian studies was primarily affected by the work of Barbel Inhelder and Annette Karmiloff-Smith, who turned their attention from Piaget's general and atemporal analyses of cognitive structures to real-time analyses of the procedures and strategies that children generate in specific task situations (Inhelder et al., 1976; Karmiloff-Smith, 1984). These scholars highlighted the importance of examining the intimate relationship between changes at the micro-level (e.g., the processes through which a child reaches the solution of a particular problem during an experimental session) and changes at the macro-level (e.g., the participant's general cognitive systems for encoding reality), advocating an in-depth microgenetic approach. Such an approach, as Karmiloff-Smith observed (1993), has had important repercussions for Anglo-Saxon researchers, who turned their interest from the analysis of *products* to the analysis of *processes*. This shift is reflected on the developmental analyses focused on the microgenetic details of how children solve tasks, rather than whether their answers are right or wrong.

Such analyses allowed investigators to uncover that some of the children who gave a wrong answer during simple numerical and conservation tasks also showed a discrepancy between their verbal output and their non-verbal gestures during problem-solving (Alibali & Goldin-Meadow, 1993). The simultaneous expression of conflicting beliefs through verbal and non-verbal outputs was thus hypothesized and demonstrated to be an index of a transitional state of cognitive change (Goldin-Meadow, Alibali, & Church, 1993).

The use of microgenetic designs within the area of cognitive development has also revealed other interesting phenomena related to change processes and the conditions that precede a developmental change, such as the coexistence of multiple strategies, switching strategies within a single trial, and utilization deficiencies (see Miller & Coyle, 1999, for a review), recently observed also in toddlers' behavior during a tool-use task (Chen & Siegler, 2000).

Dynamic systems perspective within developmental psychology

The most recent theoretical foundation for microgenetic research is represented by the application of the dynamic systems perspective – i.e., an interdisciplinary approach that provides a model for the study of change processes – within developmental psychology (Fogel & Thelen, 1987; Thelen & Smith, 1994; van Geert, 1994). Substantially, the dynamic systems perspective aims to address the problem of describing, and thus explaining, the ways in which complex systems (including biological systems such as individuals) change over time. The focus is on how changes at the micro-level of relationships between a system's constituents give rise to new patterns of behavior at macro-levels. Accordingly, new patterns of activity emerge from the mutual relationship between constituents coming from the individual and environment, and not from a maturational or teleological plan within the individual. Due to the property of self-organization characteristic of complex systems, the constituents of a system act together to constrain the multiple actions of other constituents so that the complex system coheres into stable patterns of behavior called "attractors" (Prigogine & Stengers, 1984). Action schemes, emotions, and cognition as well as communication patterns in social systems can be conceptualized as attractors (Fogel, 1993; Lewis, 1995; Thelen, Kelso, & Fogel, 1987). Most attractors are dynamically stable; that is, although attractors constitute processes of change that occur in time, they preserve their integrity across a wide variety of conditions. This dynamic stability implies processes of both stability and change between attractors. Therefore, from a dynamic systems perspective, development is conceptualized as the reorganization of prior attractors and the emergence of new attractors through self-organization processes observed at the micro-level (Fogel & Thelen, 1987; Thelen & Smith, 1994).

Two different models have arisen within the dynamic systems perspective: a model based on quantifying the physical parameters of a given system, and a qualitative model focused on the information that is present in systems (Pattee, 1987). According to the physical-quantitative model, stability is observed when changes at the micro-level are maintained within the boundaries of existing attractors. A transition to a new attractor occurs when a change in the relationships among the constituents of a system reaches a critical value that takes that system beyond the boundaries of their existing attractors (Lewis, 1995; Prigogine & Stengers, 1984). For example, the rapid deposition of subcutaneous fat in the first postnatal months, and then the overtaking of a critical fat/muscle mass or strength ratio in the infant's legs was found to be a crucial control parameter for the "disappearance" of newborn stepping reflex (Thelen, Fisher, & Ridley-Johnson, 1984).

According to the information-qualitative model, changes in the constituents of a system at the micro-level create the conditions for the emergence of new attractors. Thus, the transition to a new attractor occurs when new information is generated; that is, when the difference generated within microchanges is perceived as meaningful or "a difference that makes a difference" (Oyama, 1985). For example, if the infant turns his/her gaze away from the mother, looking at a toy, and the mother perceives this change as a momentary disengagement of attention, she can then try to regain her infant's attention by using other familiar actions that have been previously successful. If, however, the mother perceives the change in the infant's gaze as a new interest (i.e., meaningful difference), she may follow her infant's gaze, picking up a toy, and showing its properties to the infant. Through these meaningful microchanges, a new pattern of communication emerges based on play with objects (Fogel & Lyra, 1997). This example illustrates that the process of transition between attractors in real time is thought to be a source for developmental change.

Whether within a physical-quantitative model or informational-qualitative model, microgenetic designs are advocated as imperative to understand how, in certain conditions, changes at the micro-level maintain a system's relative stability, while, in other conditions, microscopic changes give rise to developmental innovations. Accordingly, the process of developmental change is best revealed when researchers focus on key developmental transition periods, and intensive observations are conducted before, during, and after a key developmental transition (Fogel, 1990; Thelen & Ulrich, 1991). This is because the often fortuitous contingent series of events that give rise to a developmental change are most likely to be observed through frequent observations during periods of increased variability, or transition periods (Fogel, 1995, 2000).

Microgenetic research informed by the dynamic systems perspective has been leading important advances in understanding change processes in early infant development. Physical-quantitative models have often examined main motor developmental transitions observed during the first year of life. For example, to investigate the onset of reaching, Thelen and collaborators observed four infants in a standard reaching task and in a play session with their parents weekly, from 3 to 30 weeks of age; that is, before, during, and after the transition to reaching (Spencer et al., 2000; Thelen et al., 1993). Microgenetic analysis afforded opportunities for the discovery of dramatic individual differences not only in the age of reach onset – ranging from 12 to 22 weeks – but also in the strategies used by the infants to get the toy.

Due to the limited success of quantitative models in capturing the element of meaning/information inherent in interpersonal communication, a particular approach to microgenetic research has been recently devised by Fogel and collaborators (Fogel, 1995, 2000; Fogel & Lyra, 1997) to document change processes in interpersonal relationships. This methodological approach will be presented in detail in the next section.

Microgenetic Designs to Study Interpersonal Relationships: A Relational-Historical Approach

Based on the dynamic systems perspective and recent advances in life history qualitative research as well as quantitative methods to study change, a new methodological approach, referred to as the relational-historical approach (Fogel, 2000; Fogel & Lyra, 1997), uses microgenetic designs to study developmental change processes in interpersonal relationships. The approach rests on the assumption that interpersonal relationships have regularly recurrent patterns that regulate the communication and emotional closeness of the participants. Within a dynamic systems perspective, these patterns of communication between interactive partners are attractors in a relational landscape. Further, part of the developmental process of relationships includes historical process constituted by patterns of communication as they are formed, maintained, transformed, and dissolved over time. It follows, then, that an important assumption of this methodological approach is that relationship patterns repeatedly observed over a period of rapid change constitute the minimum unit of analysis. Another important assumption is that real-time changes may represent significant innovations for the participants, and thus have the potential to launch developmental changes.

Compared to other current microgenetic approaches, the contributions of the relational-historical approach include a focus on relationship patterns (rather than single components of relationships), and a historical perspective of change processes (provided that change is viewed as arising out of earlier system processes, although not entirely constrained by those processes). Thus far, this approach has been applied to study change in early mother–infant relationship within normally developing dyads across major developmental transitions reported in the literature. It is our contention that the relational-historical approach can be fruitfully extended to clinical populations. It is also suggested that it can be applied to analyzing change processes in relationships in periods of crucial transitions across the life span such as the transition to parenthood, first experiences of a child in a day-care center, family dissolution, or the child–therapist relationship in a process of physical rehabilitation.

The relational-historical approach includes the following main characteristics:

1   use of multiple case study method;
2   intensive observations across a key developmental transition;
3   identification of patterns of communication (referred to herein as "frames");
4   use of quantitative analyses of real-time sequences and developmental trajectories of patterns of communication combined with qualitative descriptions of the historical emergence of change and stability within dyadic communication.

Multiple case study method

The relational-historical approach is guided by the assumption that as the researcher invests time in multiple intensive observations of a small number of cases, there are considerable opportunities to observe in great detail the dynamics of change (Fogel, 1990; Thelen, 1990; van Geert, 1994). On the contrary, when time and resources are divided across many cases, as in more traditional research designs, it is inevitable that fewer observations can be made on each case.

The use of case studies in research inquiry refers back to the work of early baby biographers, who believed that only by collecting a substantial number of detailed case histories could general laws of development be constructed (Wallace, Franklin, & Keegan, 1994). Case studies have also been systematically used in the clinical literature, in Piaget's studies, in single-case behavioral analysis research, and in studies of language development (Thorngate, 1987; Wallace, Franklin, & Keegan, 1994). In all these kinds of case studies, the validity, meaningfulness, and insights generated from qualitative inquiry have more to do with the information richness of the cases selected and the observational/analytical capabilities of the researcher than with the sample size (Patton, 1990).

Furthermore, from a dynamic systems perspective, interpersonal relationships are thought to evolve through historical transitions between attractors, and it thus becomes essential to trace developmental trajectories of communication within each single relationship across developmental shifts. These individual developmental trajectories become the primary data source. Accordingly, once individual developmental trajectories are identified, it may be possible to compare and group subjects on the basis of developmental path, and not on the basis of developmental outcome (Thelen, 1990).

In one of our studies (Lavelli & Fogel, 2002), we documented the process of emergence of inter-dyad differences in early mother–infant face-to-face communication. Sixteen primiparous mother–infant dyads were videotaped weekly during spontaneous face-to-face communication at home, from age 1 to 14 weeks (i.e., before, during, and after the 2 months developmental transition). Developmental trajectories were traced for the duration of face-to-face communication as well as for other communication patterns observed in the data, using a multilevel modeling technique (see "Data analysis strategies applied to microgenetic designs," below). Results showed that the trajectories of mother–infant face-to-face communication were similar and increasing during the early weeks of life, but diverged around 2 months. After the second month of life, two different groups of dyads were identified on the basis of their developmental trajectories: one group with trajectories that continue to increase in the duration of face-to-face communication, the other group with trajectories that peak and then begin to decrease. A first investigation of system factors that may have contributed to the trajectories' divergence uncovered significant differences between the two groups related to the duration of the infants' wakefulness, gaze at the mother, and emotional expression during the period immediately prior to the divergence of trajectories. These findings illustrate how individual differences can be profitably studied comparing the overall patterns of the individual developmental trajectories, and not only the individual outcomes. As a result, these findings point toward the benefits of using the multiple case study method.

Finally, the quality of data collected using the multiple case study method depends to a great extent on the relationship that investigators build up with the research participants. This is because multiple intensive observations require considerable commitment on the part of the families involved in the study. For example, in an intensive longitudinal data collection conducted by Fogel and collaborators, 13 mothers brought their infants to a laboratory setting weekly for the entire first year of the infant's life, biweekly for the second year, and in some other cases until the end of the third year. During that period, the research staff formed close ties with each mother–infant dyad, and during particular periods such as holidays or family crises, staff also helped mothers to arrange their activities to find time to go to the laboratory each week. The mothers thus became active collaborators, taking their role in the research very seriously.

Intensive observations across key developmental transitions

Another advantage of the multiple case study method is that the researcher can isolate a particularly interesting developmental transition in order to study how individuals, dyads, or groups navigate across that transition. The fundamental principle of microgenetic designs informed by the relational-historical approach is to isolate a key developmental transition – that is, a well-documented change in infant/child development – and then to study the corresponding change processes in relationship patterns (e.g., mother–infant relationship) before, during, and after the transition. Similarly, in applied research, a particular period of developmental intervention can be isolated to document change and stability in the relationship between child and educator, or child and therapist, before, during, and after the intervention.

In one of our research programs (Fogel, 1998), we aim to document the process by which individual differences in patterns of attention and emotion arise developmentally in infants' social relationships with mothers, by making intensive observations across key developmental transitions. Four key developmental transitions in the first two years of life are closely examined: the transition to exogenous control, coinciding with the onset of social smiling and an increase in the infant's gazing at mother, around 2 months; the transition to visually directed reaching and the onset of systematic interest in objects, around 4 months; the transition to conventional communication and the onset of shared attention and emotion between mother and infant, around 12 months; and the transition to mirror self-recognition and the onset of self-related attention and emotions such as mastery, pride, and internal state language, around 18 months.

For example, the dataset focused on the first transition was collected using weekly observations of face-to-face play from birth to $3^1/_2$ months of age in 16 mother–infant dyads. Preliminary analysis indicated that the emergence of smiling is coupled with the emergence of active attention to the mother's face during the second month, confirming the well-documented 2-month developmental transition (Lavelli & Fogel, 2000). Multilevel modeling further revealed that inter-dyad differences in the duration of face-to-face play emerged toward the end of the second month, supporting the hypothesis that individual differences emerge during periods of increased variability as developmental transition periods. These findings illustrate the importance of conducting intensive observations across transition periods. A third important component of the relational-historical approach is its use of frames as the minimum unit of analysis.

Frame analysis: identifying stability and change in patterns of communication

According to the relational-historical approach, interpersonal relationships are historically developing systems of communication characterized by a relatively small number of attractors that tend to be stable under the dynamics of the system self-organization. These patterns are called "frames" (Fogel, 1993; Goffman, 1974; Kendon, 1985) and constitute the minimum unit of developmental analysis. Frames are "segments of co-action that have a coherent theme, that take place in a specific location, and that involve particular forms of mutual orientation between participants" (Fogel et al., 1997, p. 11). For example, in the context of the mother–infant relationship, commonly observable frames are feeding, comfort, attention getting, protoconversation, greeting, attachment behavior, and various kinds of play. Different frames are historically coupled with each other through real-time transitional processes – that is, processes of change engaged by the participants when their relationship changes from one communication frame to another (Fogel & Lyra, 1997).

The variability of action within the same frame on repeated occasions indicates that frames, conceived of as attractors, have a dynamic stability. Each time a frame is reconstituted in a relationship, small variations in the participants' attention, location, co-orientation, or topic of communication create a sense of ongoing novelty within sameness (Fogel, 1993; Stern, 1985). At the same time, however, this intrinsic variability also represents the potential for another level of change, that is, microchanges that begin transforming the existing frame, thereby opening opportunities for the emergence of a new frame. Microgenetic designs are therefore used to capture developmental change processes in interpersonal relationships through the analysis of microscopic variability observed within and between communication frames. A particular procedure, called frame analysis (Fogel, 1998), was developed to accomplish this aim. Frame analysis consists of three phases:

1 the identification of the most frequently occurring frames in the data;
2 the coding of real-time onsets and offsets of frames from the videotaped records;
3 the observation of changes within and between frames through microanalytic coding of real-time sequences of actions within frames and transitional actions between frames.

With respect to frame identification, once the specific communicative situation and the level of analysis are set according to the aim of the study, frames can be identified and distinguished on the basis of four criteria:

1 the direction of the participants' attention;
2 the participants' location;
3 the participants' postural co-orientation;
4 the topic of their communication.

Taken together, these microscopic criteria aim to capture the relational quality of segments of interpersonal communication that cohere into relationship patterns.

Once frames are identified, the coding of real-time onsets and offsets of frames for all the observation sessions is essential. This second phase of the frame analysis provides important grounding for examining stability and change across the key developmental transition and for observing changes within and between frames in real time. It is during this second phase that inter-coder reliability is measured. The last phase of the frame analysis consists of the microanalytic coding of both the participants' actions within and between frames. This is necessary to examine the sequences and co-occurrences of actions within frames, as well as the types of actions that form the transitions between frames. Standard sequential analysis methods (see "Data analysis strategies applied to microgenetic designs," below) are thus used in combination with narrative descriptions of those real-time changes (see "Qualitative analysis applied to microgenetic designs," below). The goal is to shed some light on the microgenesis of change in interpersonal communication – that is, to examine those real-time change processes that open possibilities for a developmental change.

Combining quantitative and qualitative analyses

Once frames, actions within frames, and transitions between frames have been coded, they are amenable to quantitative analysis. The relatively small number of cases does not preclude the use of parametric statistical analysis because an elevated number of observations within cases is gathered. Although the results from studies guided by the relational-historical approach are not intended to be generalized to the larger population, statistical analysis can be used as a means to identify regularities across cases. These regularities can then serve as hypotheses to be tested on larger samples. Further, the relational-historical approach rests on the premise that general principles of relational developmental change can be ascertained by studying each dyad separately. This allows the researcher to learn about both commonalities and differences between dyads in their developmental *process*.

In our studies guided by the relational-historical approach, we apply recently developed techniques to examine complex sequential processes in both real time and developmental time. These include, but are not limited to, the study of developmental trajectories for the real-time durations of frames and actions within frames using multilevel modeling (for more details, see "Data analysis strategies applied to microgenetic designs," below). When examining communication processes quantitatively, however, part of the methodology requires the breakdown of events into discrete sequences of codes for "individual" action. Therefore, since within the relational-historical approach codes are initially defined as relational actions, and analysis of sequences and co-occurrences arises from the theoretical recognition of action as relational-historical, the burden is on the investigators to guide the reader from the details of technique back to a relational-historical interpretation. One way to accomplish this is to combine quantitative approaches with qualitative analysis. One of the goals of the qualitative-narrative analysis is to place the quantitative findings into a historically coherent relational whole. The focus is then on the examination of frames as globally stable dynamic patterns. The quantitative analyses can provide a picture of systematic changes in frequencies and durations of frames, actions within frames, and frame transitions. The qualitative-narrative analysis thus complements the understanding of change processes as it can reveal whether the newly emerging frames arise from innovation introduced into the historical background frames (for more details, see "Qualitative analysis applied to microgenetic designs," below).

As mentioned earlier, the primary goal of applying a microgenetic design is to investigate change processes and individual differences in development. Due to the requirements of a microgenetic design, such as coverage of a developmental transition in its entirety, high density in time interval of data collection, and the intense nature in data extraction (e.g., microanalytic behavioral coding), the resultant quantitative data are characterized by smaller sample sizes and a larger number of observations. These features are different from data collected by applying a traditional longitudinal design, which are typically characterized by large sample sizes from just a few data time points. Therefore, a variety of unique data analysis techniques are called for. The next section provides an overview of data analysis strategies for detecting both developmental and real-time changes utilizing microgenetic designs.

Data Analysis Strategies Applied to Microgenetic Designs

Detecting within- and between-individual differences in developmental changes

Four different data analysis strategies have been applied to analyze data collected based on a microgenetic design:

1 normative-oriented approach, in which developmental changes are determined by group averages;
2 idiographic individual-oriented approach, in which replication of findings by multiple cases is the focus of investigation;
3 individual growth-modeling approach, in which detecting the shape of the developmental trajectory is the primary interest;
4 multivariate individual-oriented approach, in which the pattern of change is investigated on the basis of an array of indexes with a single individual and replication with multiple cases over time.

Of particular note, all four strategies are applicable not only to observational data but also to any quantitative data extracted from diaries, interviews, case reports, and questionnaires.

Normative-oriented approach This approach refers to using the individual as the unit of analysis and summarizing across individual analyses to make generalizations about groups or subgroups of individuals over time based on the central tendency. Repeated-measures analysis of variance, with the time variable as the within-subjects factor, is a typical strategy. Trend analysis can then be performed to fit the orthogonal polynomials to specific developmental curves in detecting the developmental trajectory of the group of individuals in the follow-up analysis.

Due to the intensive nature of a microgenetic design, individuals are observed at many more time points than in a traditional longitudinal study. In order to apply repeated-measures strategies, data need to be collapsed to reduce the number of levels of the time variable. A repeated-measures ANOVA method is the dominant approach in psychological research for the examination of developmental change (Hertzog & Rovine, 1985). This strategy is simple and straightforward, and can be easily performed with many off-the-shelf statistical packages. Nevertheless, despite the fact that the unit of analysis is the individual, the result of analysis is only pertinent to individuals as a group. As a result, information pertinent to each of the individuals is missing. Only the norm-ative pattern of developmental trend based on central tendencies is revealed at a group level, which may not reflect the developmental change of any individual in the group (Bates & Appelbaum, 1994).

Idiographic individual-oriented approach Focusing on within-individual differences, this approach refers to empirical investigation of individuals and their correlates over time in psychological research (Jaccard & Dittus, 1990). Like the normative-oriented approach, the unit of analysis in an idiographic approach is the individual. However, instead of performing statistical analysis with individuals at a group level, the analysis is performed separately for each individual case by case. Results from each individual are then later summarized or aggregated to show the overall pattern of within- and between-individual differences in development. In essence, a multiple case study method is applied in this approach.

Graphical display and visual inspection of individual data against time (e.g., daily or weekly) have been suggested as the first step for analysis (Bakeman & Robinson, 1997). However, visual analysis is notorious for its subjectivity, unreliability, and insensitivity in detecting less pronounced changes. Statistical evaluations are often desirable tools to detect whether a significant change has occurred or whether a developmental pattern has emerged (Busk & Marascuilo, 1992; Franklin et al., 1996). Two alternative statistical techniques are available for this case-by-case approach: ordinary least-squares regression and polynomial regression.

Ordinary least-squares regression analysis can be applied to detect linear patterns of developmental changes. Linear regression analysis may be performed separately for each mother–infant dyad to reveal the developmental trajectory of different behavioral patterns (see Messinger, Fogel, & Dickson, 1999). Polynomial regression analysis can also be utilized to approximate the nonlinear developmental trend within each individual (see de Weerth, van Geert, & Hoijtink, 1999). This case-by-case method not only preserves the individual as the unit of analysis, but also serves as replications within the same study. The replicating findings with multiple individual cases would reduce the likelihood of obtaining spurious results (Bates & Appelbaum, 1994). However, the drawback of this approach is that multiple tests of significance with several individuals may inflate the Type I error. To obtain an estimate of the significance at population level, a meta-analytic technique has been suggested (Glass, McGaw, & Smith, 1981, cited in de Weerth, van Geert, & Hoijtink, 1999).

An idiographic individual-oriented approach to data analysis can provide a wealth of information based on a case-by-case analysis of each individual. Unfortunately, the results from each of the individual cases under investigation do not necessarily yield a coherent single picture of the development. Systematic empirical examination of the similarities and/or differences among individuals is necessary. Deriving a valid and reliable coefficient of similarity is needed in future studies.

Individual growth-modeling approach This approach refers to the investigation of individual development within the context of a group of individuals, focusing on the shape of growth trajectories at both the individual and the group levels. This approach not only permits one to answer the "within-individual" level (level-1) research questions, but also allows one to unravel the "between-individual" level (level-2) research questions (Willett, 1997). At the within-individual level, the focus is on the developmental change within the individual. The questions are about the rate (e.g., dramatic or gradual increase) and shape (e.g., linear or curvilinear) of the development for each individual. At the between-individual level, the primary question is about whether the trajectory of developmental change is different from one individual to another, and about the individual and/or contextual characteristics that contribute to the between-individual differences in developmental trajectories. Furthermore, it may also be possible to address the question of whether individuals' developmental trajectories are predictive of different patterns of developmental outcome (see Nagin & Tremblay, 1999, for examples).

The growth-curve modeling method has been applied to examine early language (Huttenlocher et al., 1991), infant vocal development (Hsu & Fogel, 2001), and infant–mother interaction (e.g., van den Boom & Hoeksma, 1994). The sample sizes of these studies are relatively small ($N \leq 30$) and data were collected from more than 6 time points (the most intensive one has 20 time points). Several computer programs are devoted to performing the modeling of growth curves. MLn (Multi-Level analysis; Woodhouse, 1996) and HLM (Hierarchical Linear Modeling; Bryk & Raudenbush, 1992; see Chapter 18 for details) are the two commercially available programs. Results of a comparative study suggest that the available programs derive the same solutions for the estimated parameters (Kreft, de Leeuw, & Kim, 1990, cited in Willett, 1997).

Multivariate individual-oriented approach The approaches discussed above are primarily univariate methods – only one variable (measured repeatedly over time) is under consideration in the analysis. One might ask what if several variables are measured and collected repeatedly from the same individual over time. In this case, a multivariate approach would be necessary. P-technique factor analysis is a useful statistical strategy to examine within- and between-individual differences when a large number of variables are collected from a single individual intensively across time (Hooker et al., 1987; Jones & Nesselroade, 1990). This technique is different from a typical R-technique factor analysis, in which the patterns of variables (or factors) are formed on the basis of a group of variables collected from a large sample of individuals. The goal of P-technique factor analysis is to identify how groups of variables change together across time within the same individual. A minimum of 100 observations has been suggested for this technique (Jones & Nesselroade, 1990). The factor scores derived from the factors can be further examined for trends over time with linear or curvilinear orthogonal polynomials by follow-up analyses. Developmental changes in the underlying structure of the individual behaviors or characteristics can then be revealed. To replicate the findings from separate individuals, the degree of congruence of factor patterns between individuals can be performed by a congruence assessment (Harman, 1967). This evaluation of congruence reveals the between-individual differences or similarities. However, like univariate analysis strategies, autocorrelation within each variable from repeated observation with the same individual may distort the pattern of factor loadings in the P-technique (Gorman & Allison, 1997). Recently, dynamic factor models, which allow for autocorrelation, have been developed. Such models may be an alternative to the P-technique method (see Wood & Brown, 1994). In the next subsection, we provide data analysis strategies specifically used for measuring real-time changes.

Quantitative measures of real-time change

A precept of microgenetic methods is that real-time change occurring during an actual interaction or cognitive task sheds light on development. The quantitative methods reviewed here rest on the premise that by analyzing a behavioral stream into its constituents and examining how the constituents are organized, we can shed new light on the processes being observed. In this subsection, we review quantitative methods for understanding how behaviors are related in real time and summarize statistical methods for assessing developmental change and stability in these patterns. Our focus is on interactions between an infant and caregiver. But the methods reviewed can be generalized to other participants (such as a therapist and client) or generalized to the analysis of different behaviors of a single individual (such as a toddler in a non-interactive learning paradigm).

In all behavioral and interactive processes, we distinguish between at least two different streams or modalities of action. These might be the speaking turns of two adolescents or the facial expressions and vocalizations of a single infant. Codes are chosen to distinguish behaviors within each of these modalities (e.g., speaking and not speaking). Having coded one's data, there are different approaches to documenting associations between behaviors in time. We focus on:

1   measures of the overlap between two behaviors;
2   measures of the frequency with which one behavior occurs during another;
3   measures of the sequencing of two behaviors.

These measures of temporal association produce different but complementary views of behavior and interaction.

The overlap or co-occurrence of two behaviors may be the simplest and most common case of a temporal association in the developmental literature (e.g., Weinberg & Tronick, 1994). To illustrate, mother smiling and infant gazing at mother's face tend to occur simultaneously (Kaye & Fogel, 1980). This association can be documented by comparing the percentage of time in which mothers are smiling and infants are gazing at their mothers' faces with the percentage of time in which mothers are not smiling and infants are gazing at their mothers' faces (Messinger, Fogel, & Dickson, 1998). Alternate measures of temporal overlap are log odds and Yule's Q (Bakeman, McArthur, & Quera, 1996). All produce robust measures of the degree of co-occurrence between two behaviors.

Co-occurrences indicate that a pattern exists, but do not shed light on how it forms. To understand how co-occurrences form, it is useful to examine how frequently one behavior begins (or ends) during a different behavior. Continuing with the same example, mothers smile more frequently when their infants are gazing at them than when their infants are gazing elsewhere. Infants, however, do not gaze at their mother more frequently when she is smiling. In fact, infants gaze *away* from their mothers more frequently when their mothers are smiling than when they are not smiling. It appears to be mothers, not infants, who are most directly responsible for creating the co-occurrences between mother smiling and infant gazing at mother (Messinger, Fogel, & Dickson, 1998). This case illustrates how a frequency analysis can pinpoint the proximal source of a pattern documented by a co-occurrence analysis and, more generally, how different types of analyses can provide complementary perspectives on real-time interactions.

The stability of co-occurrence analyses can also be directly combined with the focus of frequency analyses (Messinger, Fogel, & Dickson, 2001). The idea is to document the overlap of two behaviors, but only when the overlap begins with the onset of the behavior of particular interest. In an illustrative example, we tabulated the proportion of time infants engaged in different types of smiling while their mothers were already smiling or not smiling. Only those co-occurrences that began with the infant engaging in a particular type of smiling were examined; co-occurrence that began with the mother smiling or ceasing to smile were not examined. Conceptually, this allowed us to focus on how infants smiled in response to their mother smiling, rather than the reverse (Messinger, Fogel, & Dickson, 2001). More generally, this case illustrates how different types of analyses of real-time behavior can be combined to focus on specific research questions.

One difficulty with both co-occurrence and frequency techniques is that they do not efficiently document complicated sequences involving two different behaviors. Yale and her colleagues (Yale et al., 1999) suggest an efficient schema for classifying the temporal overlap of two behaviors. One behavior can be embedded in the other. An infant, for example, can gaze at the mother's face, smile, then stop smiling, and, finally, gaze away from the mother. Alternatively, one behavior can begin during another but then outlast it. A smile, for example, can begin during a gaze at the mother's face but then continues, ending only after the infant has looked away from the mother. Different sequences of behavior can be tallied by hand or by using the display function of specialized software. The difficulty lies in determining whether specific sequences occur more often than expected by chance.

Newly developed simulation software surmounts this problem (Yale et al., 1999). The temporal progression or stream of actions is simulated independently within each behavioral modality. So, for example, actual periods of gazing at and away from the mother's face are combined in random order (with the proviso that the two actions always alternate) to create a simulated session. The simulated gaze session is combined with a simulated session of facial expressions created in the same fashion. The number of different patterns of gaze–smile sequences expected by chance in a given interactive session is determined by running the simulation repeatedly (e.g., 2,000 times). A summary z score is then created that indicates the degree to which a given infant at a given age sequences actions into a specific pattern at greater than chance levels. Simulation analyses are of great interest because they have the potential to document complex patterns of real-time behavior and (see next section) how they change with time.

The co-occurrence, frequency, and sequential techniques outlined above create summary measures of real-time behavior. Developmental researchers in general and microgenetically oriented researchers in particular are typically interested in how development occurs for an individual or within an interactive dyad. For this reason, it is optimal to calculate measures of relationship between two variables – measures of co-occurrence, frequency, and of sequential organization – for the individuals or dyads that comprise a sample. The same set of statistical tests can then be performed on all these measures of association. The binomial test indicates whether a higher proportion of participants show associations between behaviors than the proportion expected by chance (Hays, 1988). Parametric tests (e.g., t-tests and Fs from repeated-measure ANOVAs) indicate whether the mean level of association between behaviors is greater or less than that expected by chance. When measures of association are calculated repeatedly (as in a microgenetic design) they can be subjected to the longitudinal analyses discussed in the previous sessions. Qualitative techniques for exploring and documenting developmental change in these real-time patterns are the subject of the next section.

Qualitative Analysis Applied to Microgenetic Designs

Another crucial component of our microgenetic investigations includes the qualitative description of the historical emergence of change and stability within dyadic communication, using frames as the unit of analysis. The term qualitative analysis, however, refers to a broad range of techniques utilized by social scientists, including developmental scientists, who aim to explicitly include the interpretative nature of research inquiry into their investigations. Among the various forms of qualitative methods, we focus on Polkinghorne's (1995) discussion of narrative analysis because it has been helpful in providing tools for our developmental investigations of early mother–infant relationships.

Polkinghorne (1995, p. 15) defines narrative analysis as ". . . the procedure through which the researcher organizes the data elements into a coherent developmental account." Narrative analysis allows the real-time changes that constitute the developmental process of early mother–infant relationships to be captured as part of a historical and coherent whole. In order to adapt Polkinghorne's narrative analysis to our microgenetic investigations of early development, we have created a series of analytic steps that we utilize with our longitudinal videotaped data of mother–infant transactions (e.g., Pantoja, 1999; Pantoja, Nelson-Goens, & Fogel, 2001).

Narrative analysis steps

The first step of the narrative analysis consists of watching and re-watching each of the videotaped records of the mother–infant interaction. The goal is to develop initial impressions and interpretations of the unfolding of the dyad's communication development in the changing context of their relationships. This is important as it provides the investigator with a preliminary view of both stable and changing components of the mother–infant relationship.

As our second step, we create chronological narratives for each dyad – that is, the description of the observed phenomena in terms of sequences of events. As qualitative researchers, we recognize that as the investigator transforms the observational data into text, s/he may not describe every dyadic action occurring at the level of real time. The process of writing sequence narratives implies an interpretation. Similar to the decisions made during the identification of frames, the interpretation implied in the sequence narratives is guided and refined by the research problem in question.

In our third step, the sequence narratives become the main data. When the study includes multiple cases, the investigators inductively derive the frames by session for each dyad, and the frames that emerge from each dyad inform the other frames – this is an iterative process also known as the constant comparative method (Denzin & Lincoln, 1994; Strauss & Corbin, 1990).

The fourth step includes the rereading of the sequence narratives, bearing in mind the frames that originated from the previous step. The purpose is to create short stories that synthesize the meaningful elements of each session. With these short stories, we begin to configure the dyadic actions involved in early communication development by means of a preliminary plot that emerges from the data. We then move to our fifth step. The objective is to emplot these short stories into a narrative that synthesizes the *history* of communication development for individual dyads.

When the study includes more than one case, the goal of the final step is to capture the regularities, if any, across dyads in the way they develop and transform their relationship history over time (for an example, see Fogel, 1995). At this level, the investigator aims to create a story strongly "characterized by the integration" (Ricoeur, 1991, p. 22) of the multiple historical narratives. This is another level of narrative analysis in which the observer moves towards a synthesis of the multiplicity of events into a complete and meaningful story.

Concluding Remarks

This chapter presented microgenetic designs as a promising approach advocated by researchers of different theoretical perspectives to studying change processes in development.

At the beginning of the chapter, we introduced central issues related to the problem of change that traditional designs fail to address. Now, we synthesize the benefits of using microgenetic designs, considering how some of these issues can be tackled by such designs. We then discuss objections addressed to the use of microgenetic designs, as well as costs and limitations. Finally, we indicate new directions for microgenetic research.

Advantages of microgenetic designs

The studies described in the different sections of the chapter illustrate the kinds of issues that microgenetic designs can address that more traditional designs cannot. To synthesize, the focus on microgenetic details of the sequence of children's (and their partners') behavior during close observational or experimental sessions over a period of rapid change allows researchers a direct observation of the change processes. This includes the observation of short-lived transitional behaviors that would not be detected within more aggregated analyses. Microgenetic designs thus can address the issue of how change occurs, at least at the level of detailed descriptions of change processes, and convey both quantitative and qualitative aspects of change, shedding some light on the nature of transitional states.

Because of the density of observations, microgenetic designs allow researchers to trace individual developmental trajectories for a particular behavior across the age range investigated, thus highlighting stable and changing components of behavioral patterns. This allows for the identification of transition points from the prevalence of a behavioral pattern to the prevalence of another pattern that could not be detected through more typical longitudinal designs. Therefore, microgenetic designs allow researchers to investigate intraindividual variability; that is, to address the issue of stability and instability of individual behaviors across time and different conditions. As discussed earlier, such designs can also address the question of individual differences in the acquisition of new patterns of behavior both in terms of transitional strategies as well as rate and time of developmental changes.

Finally, microgenetic designs allow for the identification of the conditions under which changes are most likely to occur. As a means to closely examine the mechanisms underlying the change investigated, microgenetic designs allow researchers to formulate hypotheses about the potential parameters responsible for the change, and test their hypotheses through microgenetic experimental studies. Thus, microgenetic designs increase our understanding of change processes, fostering the possibility of explaining, in addition to describing, such processes.

New directions for microgenetic research

The elevated costs involved in microgenetic research make it essential that the period of intense sampling substantially coincides with a period during which the rate of change is particularly rapid. A research field within which the use of microgenetic designs is becoming particularly fruitful, because of the omnipresence and rapidity of change, is that concerning developmental processes during the very first years of life. Recent microgenetic studies on early emotional and communicative development, as well as motor development, are stimulating the widespread use of such designs by illustrating that they are leading to great advances in understanding early developmental change processes.

In addition, recent advances in dynamic systems perspective have been contributing to the theoretical support to use microgenetic designs as a means to document change and stability in development. Microgenetic approaches have been fruitfully extended to studying change processes in different domains of development, thereby highlighting new directions for enriching microgenetic research. We think that these directions are essentially represented by:

1   a research focus on naturally occurring behaviors in social contexts;
2   a focus on the communication and relationship between elements in a dynamic system, rather than a focus on a "disconnected" individual;
3   a historical perspective on change processes in which change arises out of the earlier systems processes.

We believe that, with recent advances in quantitative and qualitative techniques for analyzing the emergence of variability in developmental change processes, microgenetic designs can fruitfully be extended to studying multiple cases in different populations.

Finally, after outlining the costs and benefits of microgenetic designs in the context of developmental research, we would like to encourage clinicians as well as those interested in education and public policy to explore the possibilities of applying the microgenetic principles discussed in this chapter in their respective areas of interest. Some of the principles presented throughout this chapter may be particularly suitable to early intervention programs. How could we promote change and growth through simple manipulations in the everyday details that constitute the lives of children and families? This is a new direction for microgenetic research that is yet to be developed.

Note

Correspondence concerning this chapter should be addressed to the first author, Manuela Lavelli, Dipartimento di Psicologia e Antropologia Culturale, Università degli Studi di Verona, via S. Francesco 22, 37129 Verona, Italy. Electronic mail may be sent to manuela.lavelli@univr.it.

References

Alibali, M. W., & Goldin-Meadow, S. (1993). Gesture-speech mismatch and mechanisms of learning: What the hands reveal about a child's state of mind. *Cognitive Psychology, 25,* 468–573.

Bakeman, R. & Robinson, B. F. (1997). When Ns do not justify means. In L. B. Adamson & M. A. Romski (eds.), *Communication and language acquisition: Discoveries from atypical development* (pp. 49–72). Baltimore, MD: Paul H. Brookes.

Bakeman, R., McArthur, D., & Quera, V. (1996). Detecting group differences in sequential association using sampled permutations: Log odds, kappa, and phi compared. *Behavior Research Methods, Instruments and Computers, 28*(3), 446–57.

Bates, E. & Appelbaum, M. (1994). Methods of studying small samples: Issues and examples. In S. H. Broman & J. Grafman (eds.), *Atypical cognitive deficits in developmental disorders: Implications for brain function* (pp. 245–80). Hillsdale, NJ: Lawrence Erlbaum Associates.

Boom, D. C. van den & Hoeksma, J. B. (1994). The effect of infant irritability on mother–infant interaction: A growth-curve analysis. *Developmental Psychology, 30*, 581–90.

Bruner, J. (1983). *Child's talk. Learning to use language.* New York: Norton.

Bryk, A. S. & Raudenbush, S. W. (1992). *Hierarchical linear models: Applications and data analysis methods.* Newbury Park, CA: Sage.

Busk, P. L. & Marascuilo, L. A. (1992). Statistical analysis in single-case research: Issues, procedures, and recommendations, with applications to multiple behaviors. In T. R. Kratochwill & J. R. Levin (eds.), *Single-case research design and analysis: New directions for psychology and education* (pp. 159–85). Hillsdale, NJ: Lawrence Erlbaum Associates.

Catan, L. (1986). The dynamic display of process: Historical development and contemporary uses of the microgenetic method. *Human Development, 29*, 252–63.

Chen, Z. & Siegler, R. S. (eds.) (2000). *Across the great divide: Bridging the gap between understanding of toddlers' and older children's thinking.* Monographs of the Society for Research in Child Development, serial no. 261, vol. 65, no. 2. Oxford: Blackwell.

Coyle, T. R. & Bjorklund, D. F. (1997). Age differences in, and consequences of, multiple- and variable-strategy use on a multitrial sort-recall task. *Developmental Psychology, 33*, 372–80.

Denzin, N. K. & Lincoln, Y. S. (1994). Introduction: Entering the field of qualitative research. In N. K. Denzin & Y. S. Lincoln (eds.), *Handbook of qualitative research* (pp. 1–17). Newbury Park, CA: Sage.

de Weerth, C., van Geert, P., & Hoijtink, H. (1999). Intraindividual variability in infant behavior. *Developmental Psychology, 35*, 1102–12.

Fischer, K. W. & Granott, N. (1995). Beyond one-dimensional change: Parallel, concurrent, socially distributed processes in learning and development. *Human Development, 38*, 302–14.

Fogel, A. (1977). Temporal organization in mother–infant face-to-face interaction. In H. R. Schaffer (ed.), *Studies in mother–infant interaction* (pp. 119–52). New York: Academic Press.

Fogel, A. (1985). Coordinative structures in the development of expressive behavior in early infancy. In G. Zivin (ed.), *The development of expressive behavior: Biology–environment interactions* (pp. 249–67). Orlando, FL: Academic Press.

Fogel, A. (1990). The process of developmental change in infant communicative action: Using dynamic systems theory to study individual ontogenies. In J. Colombo & J. Fagen (eds.), *Individual differences in infancy: Reliability, stability, prediction* (pp. 341–58). Hillsdale, NJ: Lawrence Erlbaum Associates.

Fogel, A. (1993). *Developing through relationships.* Chicago, IL: University of Chicago Press.

Fogel, A. (1995). Development and relationships: A dynamic model of communication. *Advances in the Study of Behavior, 24*, 259–90.

Fogel, A. (1997). Information, creativity, and culture. In C. Dent-Read & P. Zukow-Goldring (eds.), *Evolving explanations of development. Ecological approaches to organism–environment systems* (pp. 413–43). Washington, DC: American Psychological Association.

Fogel, A. (1998). Development of emotion and attention. Grant proposal MH57669 supported by the National Institute of Mental Health.

Fogel, A. (2000). Systems, attachment, and relationships. *Human Development, 43*, 314–20.

Fogel, A. & Lyra, M. (1997). Dynamics of development in relationships. In F. Masterpasqua & P. Perna (eds.), *The psychological meaning of chaos* (pp. 75–94). Washington, DC: American Psychological Association.

Fogel, A. & Thelen, E. (1987). Development of early expressive and communicative action: Reinterpreting the evidence from a dynamic systems perspective. *Developmental Psychology, 23,* 747–61.

Fogel, A., Dickson, L. K., Hsu, H., Messinger, D., Nelson-Goens, C., & Nwokah, E. (1997). Communication of smiling and laughter in mother–infant play: Research on emotion from a dynamic systems perspective. In K. Caplovitz Barrett (ed.), *The communication of emotion: Current research from diverse perspectives* (pp. 5–24). San Francisco, CA: Jossey-Bass.

Franklin, R. D., Gorman, B. S., Beasley, T. M., & Allison, D. B. (1996). Graphical display and visual analysis. In R. D. Franklin, D. B. Allison, & B. S. Gorman (eds.), *Design and analysis of single-case research* (pp. 119–58). Mahwah, NJ: Lawrence Erlbaum Associates.

Geert, P. van (1994). *Dynamic systems of development: Change between complexity and chaos.* Hemel Hempstead: Harvester Wheatsheaf.

Goffman, E. (1974). *Frame analysis: An essay on the organization of experience.* Cambridge, MA: Harvard University Press.

Goldin-Meadow, S., Alibali, M. W., & Church, R. B. (1993). Transitions in concept acquisition: Using the hand to read the mind. *Psychological Review, 100,* 279–97.

Gorman, B. S. & Allison, D. B. (1997). Statistical alternatives for single-case designs. In R. D. Franklin, D. B. Allison, & B. S. Gorman (eds.), *Design and analysis of single-case research* (pp. 159–214). Mahwah, NJ: Lawrence Erlbaum Associates.

Granott, N. (1993). Patterns of interaction in the co-construction of knowledge: Separate minds, joint efforts, and weird creatures. In R. H. Wozniak & K. W. Fischer (eds.), *Development in context: Acting and thinking in specific environments* (pp. 183–207). Hillsdale, NY: Lawrence Erlbaum Associates.

Harman, H. H. (1967). *Modern factor analysis.* Chicago, IL: University of Chicago Press.

Hays, W. L. (1988). *Statistics* (4th edn.). New York: Holt.

Hertzog, C. & Rovine, M. (1985). Repeated-measures analysis of variance in developmental research: Selected issues. *Child Development, 56,* 787–809.

Hooker, K., Nesselroade, D. W., Nesselroade, J. R., & Lerner, R. M. (1987). The structure of intraindividual temperament in the context of mother–child dyads: P-technique factor analyses of short-term change. *Developmental Psychology, 23,* 332–46.

Hsu, H. & Fogel, A. (2001). Infant vocal development in a changing mother–infant communication system. *Infancy, 2,* 87–109.

Hsu, H. & Fogel, A. (2003). Stability and transitions in mother–infant face-to-face communication during the first 6 months: a microhistorical approach. *Developmental Psychology, 39,* 1061–82.

Huttenlocher, J., Haight, W., Bryk, A., Seltzer, M., & Lyons, T. (1991). Early vocabulary growth: Relation to language input and gender. *Developmental Psychology, 27,* 236–48.

Inhelder, B., Ackerman, E., Blanchet, A., Karmiloff-Smith, A., Kilcher, H., Montangero, J., & Robert, M. (1976). Des structures cognitives aux procédures de découvertes. Esquisse de recherches en cours. *Archives de Psychologie, 44,* 57–72.

Jaccard, J. & Dittus, P. (1990). Idiographic and nomothetic perspectives on research methods and data analysis. In C. Hendrick & M. S. Clark (eds.), *Research methods in personality and social psychology* (pp. 312–51). Newbury Park, CA: Sage.

Jones, C. J. & Nesselroade, J. R. (1990). Multivariate, replicated, single-subject, repeated measures designs and P-technique factor analysis: A review of intraindividual change studies. *Experimental Aging Research, 16,* 171–83.

Jones, I. (1998). Peer relationships and writing development: A microgenetic analysis. *British Journal of Developmental Psychology*, *68*, 229–41.

Karmiloff-Smith, A. (1984). Children's problem solving. In M. E. Lamb, A. L. Brown, & B. Rogoff (eds.), *Advances in developmental psychology* (vol. 3, pp. 39–90). Hillsdale, NJ: Lawrence Erlbaum Associates.

Karmiloff-Smith, A. (1993). Beyond Piaget's "epistemic subject": Inhelder's microgenetic study of the "psychological subject". *Archives de Psychologie*, *61*, 247–52.

Kaye, K. & Fogel, A. (1980). The temporal structure of face-to-face communication between mothers and infants. *Developmental Psychology*, *16*, 454–64.

Kendon, A. (1985). Behavioral foundations for the process of frame attunement in face-to-face interaction. In G. P. Ginsburg, M. Brenner, & M. von Cranach (eds.), *Discovery strategies in the psychology of action*. Orlando, FL: Academic Press.

Kuhn, D. (1995). Microgenetic study of change: What has it told us? *Psychological Science*, *6*, 133–9.

Kuhn, D. & Phelps, E. (1982). The development of problem-solving strategies. In H. Reese (ed.), *Advances in child development and behavior* (vol. 17, pp. 1–44). New York: Academic Press.

Lavelli, M. & Fogel, A. (2000). Attention-related expressions during early mother-infant face-to-face communication. Paper presented at the International Conference on Infant Studies, July, Brighton, UK.

Lavelli, M. & Fogel, A. (2002). Developmental changes in mother–infant face-to-face communication: Birth to 3 months. *Developmental Psychology*, *38*, 288–305.

Lewis, M. (1995). Cognition–emotion feedback and the self-organization of developmental paths. *Human Development*, *38*, 71–102.

Messinger, D. S., Fogel, A., & Dickson, K. L. (1998). When infants gaze and mothers smile: Competing agenda? Paper presented at the International Conference on Infant Studies, April, Atlanta, GA.

Messinger, D. S., Fogel, A., & Dickson, K. L. (1999). What's in a smile? *Developmental Psychology*, *35*, 701–8.

Messinger, D. S., Fogel, A., & Dickson, K. L. (2001). All smiles are positive, but some smiles are more positive than others. *Developmental Psychology*, *37*, 642–53.

Miller, P. H. & Aloise-Young, P. (1996). Preschoolers' strategic behaviors and performance on a same-different task. *Journal of Experimental Child Psychology*, *60*, 284–303.

Miller, P. H. & Coyle, T. R. (1999). Developmental change: Lesson from microgenesis. In E. K. Scholnick, K. Nelson, S. A. Gelman, & P. H. Miller (eds.), *Conceptual development: Piaget's legacy* (pp. 209–39). Mahwah, NJ: Lawrence Erlbaum Associates.

Nagin, D. & Tremblay, R. E. (1999). Trajectories of boys' physical aggression, opposition, and hyperactivity on the path to physically violent and nonviolent juvenile delinquency. *Child Development*, *70*, 1181–96.

Oyama, S. (1985). *The ontogeny of information: Developmental systems and evolution*. Cambridge, MA: Cambridge University Press.

Pantoja, A. P. F. (1999). Emotional development from a relational-historical approach: The story of one mother–infant dyad. Doctoral dissertation, University of Utah, Salt Lake City, Utah.

Pantoja, A. P. F., Nelson-Goens, G. C., & Fogel, A. (2001). A dynamical systems approach to the study of early emotional development in the context of mother–infant communication. In A. F. Kalverboer & A. Gramsbergen (eds.), *Brain and behavior in human development*. Dordrecht: Kluwer.

Papousek, H. & Papousek, M. (1984). Qualitative transitions in integrative processes during the first trimester of human postpartum life. In H. F. R. Prechtl (ed.), *Continuity of neural functions from prenatal to postnatal life* (pp. 220–41). Oxford: SIMP, Blackwell Scientific.

Pattee, H. H. (1987). Instabilities and information in biological self-organization. In F. E. Yates (ed.), *Self-organizing systems: The emergence of order.* New York: Plenum.

Patton, M. Q. (1990). *Qualitative evaluation and research methods* (2nd edn.). Thousand Oaks, CA: Sage.

Polkinghorne, D. E. (1995). Narrative configuration in qualitative analysis. *Qualitative Studies in Education, 8(1),* 5–23.

Prigogine, I. & Stengers, I. (1984). *Order out of chaos: Man's new dialogue with nature.* New York: Bantam Books.

Ricoeur, P. (1991). Life in quest of narrative. In D. Wood (ed.), *On Paul Ricoeur: Narrative and interpretation.* London: Routledge.

Ruhland, R. & van Geert, P. (1998). Jumping into syntax: Transitions in the development of closed class words. *British Journal of Developmental Psychology, 16,* 65–95.

Siegler, R. S. (1995). How does change occur: A microgenetic study of number conservation. *Cognitive Psychology, 25,* 225–73.

Siegler, R. S. (2002). Microgenetic studies of self-explanation. In N. Granott & J. Parziale (eds.), *Microdevelopment. Transition processes in development and learning* (pp. 31–58). Cambridge, MA: Cambridge University Press.

Siegler, R. S. & Crowley, K. (1991). The microgenetic method: A direct means for studying cognitive development. *American Psychologist, 46,* 606–20.

Siegler, R. S. & Jenkins, E. (1989). *How children discover new strategies.* Hillsdale, NJ: Lawrence Erlbaum Associates.

Spencer, J. P., Vereijken, B., Diedrich, F., & Thelen, E. (2000). Posture and the emergence of manual skills. *Developmental Science, 3,* 216–33.

Stern, D. (1985). *The interpersonal world of the infant.* New York: Basic Books.

Strauss, A. & Corbin, J. (1990). *Basics of qualitative research: Grounded theory procedures and techniques.* Thousand Oaks, CA: Sage.

Thelen, E. (1990). Dynamical systems and the generation of individual differences. In J. Colombo & J. Fagen (eds.), *Individual differences in infancy: Reliability, stability, prediction* (pp. 19–43). Hillsdale, NJ: Lawrence Erlbaum Associates.

Thelen, E. & Smith, L. B. (1994). *A dynamic systems approach to the development of cognition and action.* Cambridge, MA: MIT Press.

Thelen, E. & Ulrich, B. D. (1991). *Hidden skills: A dynamic systems analysis of treadmill stepping during the first year.* Monographs of the Society for Research in Child Development, serial no. 223, vol. 56, no. 1. Chicago, IL: Society for Research in Child Development.

Thelen, E., Fisher, D. M., & Ridley-Johnson, R. (1984). The relationship between physical growth and a newborn reflex. *Infant Behavior and Development, 7,* 479–93.

Thelen, E., Kelso, J. A. S., & Fogel, A. (1987). Self-organizing systems and infant motor development. *Developmental Review, 7,* 39–65.

Thelen, E., Corbetta, D., Kamm, K., Spencer, J. P., Schneider, K., & Zernicke, R. F. (1993). The transition to reaching: Mapping intention and intrinsic dynamic. *Child Development, 64,* 1058–98.

Thorngate, W. (1987). The production, detection, and explanation of behavior patterns. In J. Valsiner (ed.), *The individual subject and scientific psychology* (pp. 71–93). New York: Plenum Press.

Trevarthen, C. (1977). Descriptive analysis of infant communicative behavior. In H. R. Schaffer (ed.), *Studies in mother–infant interaction* (pp. 227–70). New York: Academic Press.

Vygotskij, L. S. (1978). *Mind in society: The development of higher psychological processes.* Cambridge, MA: Harvard University Press.

Wallace, D. B., Franklin, M. B., & Keegan, R. T. (1994). The observing eye: A century of baby diaries. *Human Development, 37,* 1–29.

Weinberg, M. K. & Tronick, E. Z. (1994). Beyond the face: An empirical study of infant affective configurations of facial, vocal, gestural, and regulatory behaviors. *Child Development*, 65, 1503–15.

Werner, H. (1948). *Comparative psychology of mental development*. New York: International Universities Press.

Wertsch, J. V. & Hickmann, M. (1987). Problem solving in social interaction: A microgenetic analysis. In M. Hickmann (ed.), *Social and functional approaches to language and thought* (pp. 251–66). Orlando, FL: Academic Press.

Wertsch, J. V. & Stone, C. A. (1978). Microgenesis as a tool for developmental analysis. *Laboratory of Comparative Human Cognition*, 1, 8–10.

Willett, J. B. (1997). Measuring change: What individual growth modeling buys you. In E. Amsel & K. A. Renninger (eds.), *Change and development: Issues of theory, method, and application* (pp. 213–41). Mahwah, NJ: Lawrence Erlbaum Associates.

Wood, P. W. & Brown D. (1994). The study of intraindividual differences by means of dynamic factor models: Rationale, implementation, and interpretation. *Psychological Bulletin*, 116, 166–86.

Woodhouse, G. (1996). *Multilevel modelling applications: A guide for users of MLn*. London: Institute of Education, University of London.

Yale, M., Messinger, D. S., Cobo-Lewis, A. B., Oller, D. K., & Eilers, R. E. (1999). An event-based analysis of the coordination of early infant vocalizations and facial actions. *Developmental Psychology*, 35(2), 505–13.

CHAPTER FOUR

Developmental Science and the Experimental Method

Allison Holmes and Douglas M. Teti

The primary focus of developmental science has been and continues to be on the manner in which particular phenomena evolve and change with age, and identifying lawful antecedents of change. This volume is testimony to the importance of that enterprise. However, because describing how and why change occurs is developmental science's primary calling, it sometimes creates the impression (especially among non-developmentalists) that the discipline is non-experimental, that developmental scientists are ill-equipped to understand and apply the basic principles of the experimental method, and that laboratory experimental methods have no place in a developmental scientist's methodological arsenal. Indeed, developmental science may in part be responsible for these impressions. McCall (1977), for example, decried attempts by developmental scientists to align with more experimental approaches, emphasizing instead that describing and understanding growth and change in developmental phenomena in naturalistic contexts was much more important to the discipline, and to a broader understanding of human development.

We certainly have no quarrel with this perspective. As we shall see, however, experimentation in service of illustrating developmental processes very much has a place in developmental science. The kind of experimental work we refer to here does not include the well-documented, broad-based, randomized clinical trials that characterize early intervention efficacy research. Rather, we refer to some very basic, yet very elegant, laboratory-based experimental work that has done much to advance the field's understanding of some fundamentally important developmental processes. Indeed, we would argue that developmental science is home to some of the most clever and ingenious experimental work ever devised. This has been especially true of research with infants, whose verbal limitations preclude the use of self-reports as a means for understanding development. For example, it is difficult to determine, from parent report or from naturalistic observation alone, whether an infant prefers music to noise, or whether s/he even perceives a particular sound at all. This chapter discusses how developmental scientists have made use of experimental methods to identify and document perceptual and intellectual capacities in infants and young children, and to test theories of development.

Limitations in Experimental Work with Infants

Like all study designs, experimentation with infants has advantages and shortcomings. For example, experimental manipulations are dependent on and limited by characteristics of the participants. If an experiment involves a motor response, infants' motor capacities and limitations must be taken into account. Four-week-old infants cannot manually engage a small object for a substantial amount of time. Thus, one challenge faced by the developmental experimenter is to choose a behavior to study that is within the infant's developmental repertoire. Head turning, for example, has proved to be a useful dependent variable in studies whose aim is to demonstrate learning capabilities in infants as young as 8 weeks of age (Watson, 1972; Weisberg & Rovee-Collier, 1998).

Developmental considerations also pertain to the nature of stimulus used in infant experimentation, and infant capacities for prehending that stimulus. If you set out to test infants' preference of novel over familiar stimuli, for example, infants must have the capacity to distinguish among the stimuli chosen. Infants in the first few months of life have limited visual acuity (Kellman & Banks, 1998). A very young infant may not be able tell the difference between shades of green, but could more readily differentiate between green and red.

A third factor to consider, which may contribute directly to error variance, is the infant's state of arousal. Optimal infant performance in perceptual, cognitive, and motor domains is most likely to occur in the quiet alert state (Lamb, Bornstein, & Teti, 2002), which in very young, fatigued, ill, or hungry infants may be relatively fleeting and quite brief in duration in comparison to older, well-rested, healthy, or recently fed infants. Indeed, the difficulties frequently encountered in attempts to demonstrate operant conditioning capabilities in neonates has been attributed to developmental limitations in their ability to remain alert long enough to attend to and perceive contingent relations between their behavior and stimulus consequences thereof (Weisberg & Rovee-Collier, 1998).

Despite these limitations, very young infants have proved to be a very viable population for experimental study when careful consideration is given to design and measurement. Utilizing a natural ability of infants, sucking, DeCasper and Fifer (1980) were able to manipulate the rate of sucking with 3-day old infants. In this experiment, a baseline measure of the infant's rate of sucking was first obtained. When the interval between the infant's sucking bursts reached levels specified by the researchers, a recording of the mother's voice was played for the infant. When the interval did not reach this pre-specified level, another woman's voice was played. Infants altered sucking intervals to produce their own mother's voice, thus demonstrating that infants only 72 hours old were capable of perceiving contingencies between their behavior and an environmental event and could be operantly conditioned. The success of this experiment was due in part to the choice of a behavior (sucking) for the dependent variable that took advantage of the fact that infants are predisposed to attend selectively to human voices (Glenn & Cunningham, 1983) and thus the contingent stimuli used in this experiment could be readily discerned by the infants. DeCasper and Fifer demonstrated that newborns can learn from the consequences of their actions, can discriminate between human voices, and prefer the sound of their own mother's voice to another woman's voice. This example illustrates nicely the effectiveness of developmentally tailored experimental approaches in documenting infant capabilities.

Common Paradigms

There are four common experimental paradigms used with infants and young children: habituation/novelty preference, operant conditioning, search techniques, and deferred imitation. Each paradigm will be described and examples of how it has been used will be given. Of course, more than just these four paradigms have been used in the literature, but this chapter will focus on these in particular to highlight the power of the experimental method in documenting developmental processes and testing developmental theories.

Habituation/novelty preference

The habituation/novelty preference paradigm is used to determine an infant's ability to discriminate between two or more stimuli. The basic paradigm has two steps. In step one, the experimenter repeatedly exposes the participant to a stimulus and records the responses to the stimulus. Exposure to the stimulus ceases once the participant no longer orients toward or responds to the stimulus (i.e., the participant habituates to the stimulus). In step two, a new or novel stimulus is introduced and the participant's response to the new stimulus is observed. Evidence of discriminating between the two stimuli is provided if the infant shows conspicuously increased attention and orientation to the novel stimulus. If the infant evinces similar responses to both the old and new stimuli, that is taken as evidence that s/he is not capable of discriminating between the two stimuli.

This paradigm has been used to test infant perceptual skills and memory. For example, Ghim (1990) tested whether 3- and 4-month-old infants could perceive whole forms through subjective contours. Are these young infants capable of seeing in the mind's eye a figure that is not actually drawn on a page? As seen in Figure 4.1a, the contour of a square can be perceived even though the picture is only of four incomplete circles with the angles aligned. In one study, infants were habituated to subjective contours of a square (Figure 4.1a) and then were presented during novelty preference trials with either Figure 4.1b, c, or d, each of which does not contain the subject

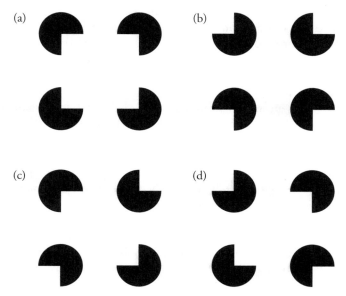

Figure 4.1   Four stimulus patterns used in Ghim's (1990) experiments. (a) This pattern produces subjective contours forming a square. Patterns (b)–(d) do not produce subjective contours of a whole figure. Reprinted from *Infant Behavior and Development*, 13, H.R. Ghim, Evidence for perceptual organization in infants: Perception of subjective contours by young infants, pp. 271-91. Copyright 1990, with permission from Elsevier.

contours of a square. Infants oriented to and fixated longer on the new nonsubjective contour stimuli in Figures 4.1b, c, and d than they did on the subjective contours of a square provided in Figure 4.1a. This indicated that the infants discriminated the subjective contour of a square (in Figure 4.1a) from the nonsubjective contour stimuli (Figures 4.1b, c, and d). Moreover, infants who were habituated to one nonsubjective contour stimulus were later unable to discriminate between other nonsubjective contour stimuli during the novelty preference trials. That is, infants were unable to discriminate among Figures 4.1b, c, and d, whereas they reliably discriminated between Figure 4.1a and Figures 4.1b–d. The habituation/novelty preference paradigm, in this case, enabled researchers to determine that preverbal infants as young as 3 to 4 months of age could perceive whole forms through subjective contours.

Categorization, or the ability to group a series of items according to a perceptual or conceptual feature, is another aptitude that can be researched using a habituation/novelty preference experimental design with young participants. Similar to procedures used in visual perception, infants are presented with exemplars from the same category until they are habituated. Then they are presented with a novel exemplar from the habituation category and an exemplar from a different category. If the infant orients and selectively attends to the different category exemplar, then formation of the habituated category is inferred. In one study with 10- and 13-month-olds, categorizations of land animal and sea animal were tested (Oakes, Coppage, & Dingel, 1997). During the familiarization/habituation phase, infants were presented with exemplars from the land animals group (tiger, horse, dog, and zebra) or the sea animals group (killer whale, harp seal, humpback whale, and dolphin) one at a time, with each exemplar presented three times. Then all infants, regardless of whether they were familiarized with land animals or with sea animals, were presented with a novel exemplar from land animals (rhinoceros), a novel exemplar from sea animals (manatee), and an exemplar from a novel category (vehicle, e.g., car). That is, each infant was presented with a new animal from a category s/he was familiar with, an animal from a new category, and a non-animal item. The older infants attended longer to the novel, out-of-category animal (i.e., if familiarized with land animals, the infant attended longer to the sea animal) and to the novel category exemplar (i.e., the car). Thus, if an infant had habituated to land animals, the infant regarded a sea animal and a car as different from the familiar land animals. The younger infants, though, dishabituated to the novel category exemplar only. So if an infant had habituated to land animals, the infant regarded a sea animal as the same as a land animal and a car as different from the familiar land animals. Thus, only 13-month-old infants demonstrated categorization of land animals, sea animals, and non-animals; 10-month-olds demonstrated understanding of a global animal category.

Using habituation/novelty preference, categorization skills have even been demonstrated with infants 6 months of age and younger (Arterberry & Bornstein, 2001; Hayne, 1996). Typically, infants are habituated to one or a few exemplars (e.g., toy cat, dog, fish) from a common category, animals. During the novel testing trial, the infants are presented with an exemplar (e.g. car) from a different category (vehicle). The ability of the infant to have formed the category of animals is inferred if infants attend more to the novel, out-of-category stimulus (car) than they attend to the last presented in-category stimulus (fish). Thus, the habituation-novel responsiveness paradigm has enabled researchers to discover infants' propensities to organize their worlds and to test the extent of those mental processes.

Operant conditioning

With language-limited participants, operant conditioning paradigms have proved to be quite useful in documenting infant perceptual capabilities and preferences. Researchers who use operant conditioning paradigms with infants must take into account young infants' limitations in perceiving a contingency between their behavior and a stimulus consequence. Very young infants do indeed have this capacity, provided that the interval between the target behavior and the ensuing stimulus event is brief, and that other distracting stimuli are eliminated (Watson, 1966, 1972). The basic procedure is to take a baseline measure of the infant's behavior (whatever it may be), then follow that behavior contingently with a stimulus known to have reinforcement value for that behavior. The assumption is that if the infant learns the contingency between her/his behavior and the reinforcer, the experimenter can expect the infant to increase the frequency of the target. An assumption inherent in this conditioning paradigm is that the infant will be able to perceive the contingency between behavior and the contingent stimulus.

Butterfield and Siperstein (1972) used an operant conditioning paradigm to explore newborns' preference of music over noise. The type of auditory stimulus, "music" or noise, was made contingent on specific sucking patterns infants displayed. Certain patterns triggered the playing of music while another pattern resulted in noise. When the infants altered their sucking patterns to hear music over noise, it was inferred that, given the choice between the two, infants prefer music. This experiment was particularly important because it demonstrated, via an operant conditioning paradigm, that newborns are "pre-wired" to prefer auditory stimulus that is rhythmic and melodic over random, "white" noise.

One particular operant conditioning derivative that has been used to study the categorization abilities of infants is the mobile conjugate reinforcement paradigm. This method makes use of 2- to 6-month-old infants' ability to learn, while lying face up in a crib, to make an overhead mobile move by kicking their feet (Rovee-Collier & Shyi, 1992). By connecting the infant's leg to the mobile with a ribbon, the infant can learn the contingency of moving her/his leg and moving the mobile. Moreover, the intensity of the reinforcement is proportional to the intensity of the infant's response (conjugate reinforcement) and thus, the harder the infant kicks, the greater the amount of movement is produced in the mobile. Typically, a baseline measure of infant foot kicks is taken for 3 minutes prior to the attachment of the ribbon around the infant's ankle. The baseline phase is followed by a 9-minute reinforcement period during which the ribbon is connected from the infant to the mobile hanging above the infant's crib. Thus, when the infant moves her/his leg, the mobile moves with the same intensity and vigor as the kick. After the reinforcement phase is a 3-minute post-training session. The infant's foot is disconnected from the mobile and the rate of foot-kicking is measured as a test of the infant's immediate retention of the event.

The mobile conjugate reinforcement paradigm is used to test categorization using a simple forgetting procedure and a reactivation procedure. In the simple forgetting procedure, the infant is trained on a variety of different mobile exemplars on different days. Training is then followed by a delay of a day or more, followed in turn by a 3-minute post-training, non-reinforcement retention phase, during which the infant is presented with a novel mobile that is not moving and not connected to the infant's foot. If the infant's rate of foot-kicking is similar to the rate observed during the actual training (when the foot and mobile were connected), it suggests that the infant views the novel mobile as belonging to the same category as the exemplars used during training. If the infant's foot-kicking rate does not differ from the baseline rate, categorization is not assumed.

Greco, Hayne, and Rovee-Collier (1990) used this simple forgetting procedure with 3-month-old infants who were trained with mobiles that suspended five same-sized colored blocks with either the number 2 or the letter A showing, with the color of the character (either the 2 or the A) varying during the three training days (e.g., Day 1: blue A; day 2: green A; day 3: red A). Then the infants experienced a 24-hour delay. The test phase consisted of the infants viewing one of four novel mobiles (not connected to their foot) while their foot-kicking rate was measured. Infants' foot-kicking rates were highest in response to the nursery mobile (mobile elements consisting of five objects such as a bird, horse, baby doll, boot, and doll) and next highest in response to the stars mobile (mobile elements consisting of two large stars with streamers underneath), indicating some degree of categorization; the nursery and stars mobile were perceived as being in the same category as the training mobiles. The rainbow (mobile consisted of a large rainbow with streamers along the entire bottom) and butterfly (mobile consisted of a single butterfly sitting in a ring with two rods suspended underneath) mobiles had levels of foot-kicking similar to the pretraining baseline levels. Thus, it was inferred that the infants did not place the rainbow and butterfly mobiles in the same category as the training mobiles.

The reactivation procedure is a variation of the simple forgetting paradigm and can also test infant categorization in the mobile reinforcement paradigm. During the reactivation procedure, the infant is given a "reminder" session designed to reactivate the infant's memory of the training event prior to the retention test. The reminder session involves a 3-minute, noncontingent exposure to a mobile that was used in the training phase. In this session, movement of the mobile is produced by the experimenter at a rate similar to that produced by the infant during training, but the infant's foot and the mobile are not connected, so the infant cannot control the mobile's movement during the reminder. Evidence for categorization, involving a novel mobile, is assessed hours or days later using the procedure described earlier.

Search technique

A third common paradigm used in the experimentation with infants and young children is the search technique. The search technique specifically tests infants' recall. Typically, the procedure involves the experimenter hiding a toy while allowing the infant to see where the toy is being hidden. Then the experimenter allows the infant the opportunity to seek out the toy. Evidence of the infant's memory is determined by whether an exhibited search is appropriate and successful. The search technique procedure is comparable to verbal or pictural recall tests. Instead of studying a list of words or pictures and then recalling (writing or telling) items, the infant watches a sequence of events, and is expected to remember the last step in the process, and then actively look for the object.

Reznick, Fueser, and Bosquet (1998) used the search technique to demonstrate age differences in infants' memory skills. With 7- and 9-month-olds, an experimenter hid a toy in one of three wells in front of the infant and allowed her/him to search after a short delay. Indicating little memory of the toy-hiding sequence, 7-month-olds equally searched all three wells for the toy. The 9-month-olds were more successful in their searching, however, finding the toy more often than expected by chance.

Seeking to further refine our understanding of infant memory with 8- to 12-month olds, Ahmed and Ruffman (2000) used Piaget's "A not B" task with a twist. The Piagetian "A not B" task involves the experimenter continually hiding the toy in location A and then allowing the infant to retrieve the toy. Typically, the infants are successful. Then, in full view of the infant, the experimenter hides the toy in location B and again allows the infant to retrieve the toy. Frequently, infants in this age range erroneously look in location A, despite having watched the experimenter hide the toy in location B. As expected for infants of that age, Ahmed and Ruffman (2000) found that the infants made the "A not B" error when searching for the toy.

Capitalizing on other skills common to 8- to 12-month-olds, Ahmed and Ruffman (2000) gave this classic Piagetian task a twist with a non-search element. Essentially, the twist was a violation of expectations. First, the experimenter hid the toy in location A and retrieved the toy from location A, a perfectly possible and logical sequence of events. Then the experimenter hid the toy in location B, but (impossibly) retrieved it from location A. Infants stared longer when the toy was retrieved from location A (the impossible consequence) than from location B (possible consequence). Thus, even though the infants could not themselves retrieve the toy when it was hidden at location B, the fact that they fixated longer on location A in the impossible sequence suggested that they were still able to remember the correct location of the toy. Ahmed and Ruffman were able to define more accurately when infants have the ability to recall simple event sequences by taking creative license with a classic technique and simplifying the demands on the infant.

Deferred imitation

Deferred imitation is another common experimental paradigm that tests infant memory recall. This procedure tests the infant's ability to imitate a modeled sequence of events after a nontrivial time delay. Deferred recall does not emerge until about 18 months of age, according to Piagetian theory (Piaget, 1952), but Barr, Dowden, and Hayne (1996) demonstrated that 6-month-old infants could defer imitation. The experimenters modeled a three-step sequence of (1) removing a mitten from a puppet's hand, (2) shaking the mitten (which rang a bell inside the mitten), and (3) putting the mitten back on the puppet's hand. After a 24-hour delay, infants were given the puppet and mitten. Most of the infants showed memory of the content of events: 75 percent of the infants would repeat one out of the three events. But only the remaining 25 percent of the infants showed memory of the sequence of events. That is, only 25 percent of the infants would repeat at least two of the events in the order shown. Thus, 6-month-old infants had memory for the content of individual events but not yet for the temporal order of events. Deferred imitation has provided some important insight about the emerging memory skills of first-year infants, who at one time were believed to be incapable of extensive recall.

Representation and Memory in the First Year

The four common approaches mentioned above (habituation/novelty preference, operant conditioning, search techniques, and deferred imitation) give a brief glimpse into some experimental/developmental research with infants and young children. Both the habituation/novelty preference and operant conditioning procedures can be easily used to tap into infant sensory skills, preferences, and categorization skills. Further, innovative approaches such as the search technique and deferred imitation have been invaluable in documenting the existence of infants' recall much earlier in development than expected only two decades ago. As exemplified above, infants as young as 6 months of age can remember the content of a series of events, and at 8 months of age appear to understand and accurately remember where a toy is hidden.

Collectively, these experiments demonstrate that infants' capacities for learning, perception, and memory are much greater than was imagined prior to 1980. For example, infants are capable of rudimentary categorization as early as 3 months of age and are capable of forming detailed categories by 10 months. Infants are also capable of learning even within a few days of birth. To further illustrate the power of the experimental method in illustrating developmental process, we turn now to a series of experiments, most of which have been conducted in the past decade, focusing on infants' capacities for mental representation that directly challenge Piaget's formulations regarding the emergence of representation during the first two years of life.

Piaget's Theory

From observations of his own children, Jean Piaget (1952) provided a stage theory of cognitive development from birth to adolescence in *Origins of Intelligence in Children*. The innovative basis for Piaget's theory was that infants learn and come to understand the world by their direct interactions with it. Thus, Piaget is credited with viewing infants as active agents as opposed to passive recipients of information in their own learning.

The first of Piaget's developmental stages, and the focus of this section, is the sensorimotor stage occurring from birth to two years of age. As the name implies, Piaget postulated that infants explored and learned about their world with their senses and actions rather than mentally thinking and internally processing the information. In fact, the ability to mentally represent the external world is the key end product at the conclusion of the sensorimotor stage, around 18 to 24 months of age.

The sensorimotor stage is further divided into six substages. The first substage spans birth to 1 month of life and is characterized by the newborn reflexes and the infant having minimal understanding of her/his place in the environment. The second substage spans 1 month to 4 months after birth, wherein the infant shows increases in the ability to coordinate movements and impact the surrounding world. Primary circular reactions, the tendency of infants to repeat simple actions that resulted in satisfying outcomes by chance, are evidence of infants' newfound control and understanding. The third substage, from 4 months to 7 months of age, is characterized by a growth in more complex motor skills and infants' ability to focus their attention on the outside world. In this substage, infants now repeat actions that produce interesting effects in their environment, which Piaget called secondary circular reactions. The fourth substage is estimated to occur from 7 to 10 months. Here infants appear to engage in intentional or goal-directed behavior as seen by the infants' capacity to uncover a hidden object. Finding hidden objects further implies that infants have some notion of the object's continued existence despite the lack of sensory information to support that conclusion. However, this understanding of the permanence of objects is rudimentary, as evidenced by infants' common commission at this age of the "A not B" error, discussed earlier. The fifth substage spans about 10 to 18 months of age. Cognitive advancement is demonstrated by tertiary circular reactions, where the infant repeats behaviors with variation to provoke new and varied effects in the external environment. Object permanence is matured such that infants no longer commit the "A not B" error, but infants do not have full grasp of permanence to anticipate and search for objects without some trial and error. The last substage of the sensorimotor stage takes place from 18 to 24 months. Mental representation is the noteworthy milestone in this substage, as exemplified by the toddler's ability to imagine and internally visualize the location of an invisible object.

Challenges to Piaget's Theory

Piaget's theory of cognitive development is unrivaled in elegance and scope, and there is empirical corroboration for many of his proposed developmental achievements and for the sequences in which they occur. The theory has clearly served as the foundation for the study of infant cognition, but recent experimental research has challenged Piaget's formulations and basic assumptions.

Perhaps the greatest empirical challenges to Piaget's theory of sensorimotor development come from findings indicating that the capacity for mental representation of the physical world, and the emergence of object permanence, appear much earlier in development than Piaget supposed. Two lines of experimentation contribute to this conclusion. The first is represented by the work of Baillargeon (1994, 1995, 1998; Baillargeon, Kotovsky, & Needham, 1995) and Spelke (1994; Spelke & Hermer, 1996), who demonstrated that infants' capacity for perceiving and representing the physical world is much better developed than Piaget ever thought. The second line of research is represented by the work of Meltzoff and Moore (1997, 1998, 1999), who demonstrated that infants can imitate selected facial expressions of others within minutes after birth, indicating that a rudimentary capacity to represent the external world may be present at birth. We discuss each of these lines of research in turn.

Demonstrating that infants appear to possess knowledge about the permanence of objects much sooner than Piaget would have predicted, Spelke et al., (1992) used habituation and violation-of-expectation procedures with $2^{1}/_{2}$-month-old infants. With a platform, two thin boxes (one taller than the other), a ball, and a screen, Spelke et al. tested object permanence by having infants watch the trajectories of the ball as it rolled across the platform. Infants were first presented with a view of the entire platform with the ball on its extreme left and the smaller of the two boxes sitting on its edge on the extreme right. Infants were then habituated to a sequence in which the screen was lowered in front of the right half of the platform, completely occluding the right half of the platform and the small box. Next, the ball was rolled from left to right across the platform and disappeared behind the screen, after which the screen was elevated to show the ball against the box.

Following the habituation phase, infants were shown two events, a "possible" event and an "impossible" event (a violation of expectations). For each of these events, the infants were placed in front of the platform, on the right edge of which the smaller box had been placed, with the taller box placed on the platform a few inches to the left of the smaller box. The screen was again lowered in front of the platform and the smaller box, but only partially occluding the taller box. The ball was then rolled from left to right across the platform until it disappeared behind the screen, and then the screen was raised. In the possible event, the ball rested against the taller box, which is what would be expected. In the impossible event, the ball rested against the smaller box. Duration of infant looking was significantly longer to the impossible event than to the possible event. Such findings suggest that infants at $2^{1}/_{2}$ months followed the ball's trajectory even after it disappeared behind the screen, understood that it was impossible for the ball to roll through the solid taller box, and expected the ball to be stopped by the taller box. When it did not, infants showed surprise and looked longer.

According to Spelke et al. (1992), these findings give evidence of representational abilities in infants as young as 2 months of age. By this age, infants appear to understand that objects move cohesively (i.e., object parts remain connected as they move) and continuously through space.

Building on this work in a series of experiments on infants' developing knowledge of everyday events, Baillargeon (1994, 1995, 1998; Baillargeon, Kotovsky, & Needham, 1995) proposed that infants are innately endowed with specific learning mechanisms that enable rapid acquisition of knowledge about event categories (e.g., events in which an object collides with another object, becomes occluded by another object, or supports another object) and object categories (e.g., animate objects, inanimate objects that move, and inanimate objects that do not move). Infants first learn about the event or object concept as a generalized whole, and with experience gradually accumulate knowledge about variables that are relevant to the concepts of physical causality. For example, at $2^{1}/_{2}$ months of age, infants' understanding of collision is relatively simple. They expect any moving object to displace any stationary object on impact and show surprise when this does not occur. By about 6 months of age, infants can understand that a large moving object will, on impact, displace a stationary object further than will a small moving object. By 8 months, infants begin to take the stationary object's shape into account in determining whether it will be displaced by a moving object. Thus, Baillargeon and Spelke argue that the ability to mentally represent events and objects is either innate or achieved by 2 to 3 months of age. This is at least 15 months before Piaget predicted that this ability would emerge and challenges the Piagetian notion that infants learn solely by their direct interaction with their environment.

Meltzoff and Moore's (1998, 1999) work on infants' imitation of facial expressions within the first month of life also leads to the conclusion that a capacity for representation is present from birth. However, they hold that representational capacity continues to develop after birth, and that object permanence is not complete until about 9 months of age, resulting from innumerable interactions between the infant and the physical and social worlds. This view is embodied in what Meltzoff has termed representational-development theory.

In brief, representational-development theory posits that infants have the capacity for representation, allowing them to acquire and retain information about the world through observation and perception long before they act on objects. The ability to imitate various facial expressions has been demonstrated in infants less than 1 month old. These observations indicate that, from birth, infants form mental representations of events from observation alone and can reproduce these events immediately. Note that these data contrast with Piaget's contention that infants do not imitate until 10 to 12 months of age and do not develop representational abilities until 18 to 24 months. Perhaps even more compelling are observations that infants can engage in deferred imitation of a model's novel actions on an object as early as 6 months of age (almost a full year before Piaget said it occurred) and of a model's facial expressions within the first 2 months of life. For example, Meltzoff (1988) had 6- to 9-month-old infants observe an adult model lean forward and press a panel with his forehead (a highly unusual, novel behavior). One week later, the infants who had viewed this behavior, and a control group of infants who had not, returned to the laboratory and were presented with the panel. No control infants exhibited the forehead-to-panel response, whereas 66 percent of the infants who had previously witnessed this behavior did. Furthermore, Meltzoff and Moore (1999) demonstrated that 6-week-old infants who saw an adult model's facial gestures could reproduce these expressions 24 hours later when they saw the same adult displaying a neutral face.

Other work documents that very young infants have the ability to represent external actions that persist across time and contexts (Meltzoff & Moore, 1997). Meltzoff and Moore (1999) termed this capacity representational persistence and argued that it was not equivalent to the representational capacity of infants in the second year of life. Rather, representational persistence is viewed as the beginning state of infant cognition, which continues to develop with maturation and the infant's ongoing experience with the world. Most importantly, Meltzoff's representational persistence does not imply awareness of object permanence, which requires the understanding that objects exist continuously in the world. Indeed, Meltzoff and Moore (1999) argue that the experimental work of Spelke and Baillargeon provides evidence that young infants recognize an object's *identity*, which serves as a prerequisite for, but is not the same as, object permanence. Understanding object identity then could be conceptualized as the recognition of an object's physical characteristics such that objects can be compared, differentiated, or accepted as the same.

Distinguishing between infants who understand object permanence (and, therefore, object identity as well) and infants who understand object identity, but not yet object permanence, required another creative experimental design. Moore, Borton, and Darby (1978) provided such information using a visual tracking experiment with 5- and 9-month-olds. The infants watched a ball pass in continuous movement from left to right behind two nontransparent split screens. The ball passed behind the first screen and then emerged from behind the second screen without passing through the open gap between the two screens. The ball that emerged from the second screen looked exactly like the ball that disappeared behind the first screen. Moore, Borton, and Darby (1978) hypothesized that infants with an understanding of object permanence would perceive this state of affairs as a violation of expectations. If only one ball was involved, it should have been occluded by the first screen, become visible between the two screens, been occluded again by the second screen, and become visible again when it reemerged from behind the second screen. Infants with object permanence would regard the ball that emerged from the second screen as a new ball and scan the edges of the first screen for the original, thus showing that they perceived the first ball as continuing to exist even though it disappeared. In contrast, infants who understand object identity but not yet object permanence should not perceive the event as a violation of expectations because the ball that emerged from the second screen was identical to the ball that disappeared behind the first screen. Moore and colleagues also expected that infants who understand object identity, whether or not they had also achieved object permanence, would be sensitive to changes in the features and trajectory of an object as it moved from left to right behind a nontransparent screen.

Moore, Borton, and Darby (1978) used three tasks in this experiment. In the permanence task, as described above, a ball moving from left to right passed behind a first screen and then emerged from behind a second screen, which was displaced to the right of the first screen, without passing through the open gap between the two screens. The ball that emerged from the second screen looked exactly like the ball that disappeared behind the first screen. In the feature task, a ball moved behind a screen but a box emerged from the other side of the screen along the same trajectory (i.e., the object changed in appearance when it emerged from the other side of the screen). In the trajectory task, a ball moved behind a screen but emerged from the other side sooner than expected based on its initial speed.

As predicted, both 5- and 9-month-old infants were sensitive to identity violations. They looked away from the object that emerged from the right side of the screen, which differed from the original in terms of features or trajectory, and scanned the edges of the screen in apparent search for the original. However, only the 9-month-old infants showed such behavior in the permanence task. The 5-month-old infants did not search for the original ball, presumably because they perceived the ball that emerged from the second screen to be the same ball that disappeared behind the first screen. These findings collectively showed that object permanence emerges some time between 5 and 9 months of age and that what appeared as evidence for object permanence in younger infants (e.g., Spelke et al., 1992) was actually evidence for object identity. So infants as young as 2 months of age have knowledge of object identity, but do not achieve object permanence until 9 months of age.

Thus, although Meltzoff, Spelke, and Baillargeon agree that representational capacity exists from birth, Meltzoff and Moore (1998, 1999) argue that the ability to represent events and objects across time and space, which they term representational persistence, does not imply the understanding that objects exist in the world as permanent entities. Rather, early representational persistence predisposes infants to maintain the identity of objects, which serves as a developmental precursor to object permanence. Again, Meltzoff, Spelke, and Baillargeon's arguments posit higher cognitive abilities to infants months sooner than Piaget theorized, speaking volumes with regard to the value experimentation in developmental science can offer in identifying and understanding basic developmental processes.

Conclusions

Describing growth and change in developmental phenomena, and identifying the determinants and sequelae of such, will very likely continue to be the primary mission of developmental science. It is clear, however, that the discipline has derived great benefit from experimental methodology when the goal is to triangulate on and uncover basic developmental processes. The experiments described above are ingenious, yet elegant, in their simplicity. They provide illustrations of how developmental researchers can employ basic experimental paradigms to identify and test the limits of infant abilities in order to better understand early development. They show that, even within a few days out of the womb, infants are remarkably capable beings. As the discipline progresses, and with more emphasis than ever before on development and the neurosciences, we expect even greater use of experimentation to understand how the brain reacts to qualitative differences in early experience, and perhaps how differences in such experiences organize brain functioning in particular directions. This is an exciting time in developmental research.

References

Ahmed, A. & Ruffman, T. (2000). Why do infants make A not B errors in a search task, yet show memory for the location of hidden objects in a nonsearch task? In D. Muir & A. Slater (eds.), Infant development: The essential readings. Essential readings in developmental psychology (pp. 216–35). Malden, MA: Blackwell.

Arterberry, M. E. & Bornstein, M. H. (2001). Three-month-old infants' categorization of animals and vehicles based on static and dynamic attributes. *Journal of Experimental Child Psychology*, *80*, 333–46.

Baillargeon, R. (1994). How do infants learn about the physical world? *Current Directions in Psychological Science*, *3*, 133–40.

Baillargeon, R. (1995). A model of physical reasoning in infancy. In C. Rovee-Collier & L. P. Lipsitt (eds.), *Advances in infancy research* (vol. 9, pp. 305–71). Norwood, NJ: Ablex.

Baillargeon, R. (1998). Infants' understanding of the physical world. In M. Sabourin, F. Craik, & M. Robert (eds.), *Advances in psychological science*, vol. 2: *Biological and cognitive aspects* (pp. 503–29). East Sussex: Psychology Press.

Baillargeon, R., Kotovsky, L., & Needham, A. (1995). The acquisition of physical knowledge in infancy. In D. Sperber, D. Premack, & A. J. Premack (eds.), *Causal cognition: A multidisciplinary debate* (pp. 79–116). Oxford: Clarendon Press.

Barr, R., Dowden, A., & Hayne, H. (1996). Developmental changes in deferred imitation by 6- to 24-month-old infants. *Infant Behavior and Development*, *19*, 159–70.

Butterfield, E. C. & Siperstein, G. N. (1972). Influence of contingent auditory stimulation upon non-nutritional suckle. In J. F. Bosoma (ed.), *Third symposium on oral sensation and perception: The mouth of the infant*. Springfield, IL: Thomas.

DeCasper, A. J. & Fifer, W. P. (1980). Of human bonding: Newborns prefer their mothers' voices. *Science*, *208*, 1174–6.

Ghim, H. R. (1990). Evidence for perceptual organization in infants: Perception of subjective contours in young infants. *Infant Behavior and Development*, *13*, 221–48.

Glenn, S. M. & Cunningham, C. C. (1983). What do babies listen to most? A developmental study of auditory preferences in non-handicapped infants and infants with Down's Syndrome. *Developmental Psychology*, *19*, 332–7.

Greco, C., Hayne, H., & Rovee-Collier, C. (1990). Roles of function, reminding, and variability in categorization by 3-month-olds. *Journal of Experimental Psychology: Learning, memory, and cognition*, *16*, 617–33.

Hayne, H. (1996). Categorization in infancy. In C. Rovee-Collier & L. P. Lipsitt (eds.), *Advances in infancy research* (vol. 10, pp. 79–120). Norwood, NJ: Ablex.

Kellman, P. J. & Banks, M. S. (1998). Infant visual perception. In W. Damon (editor-in-chief), D. Kuhn, & R. S. Siegler (vol. eds.), *Handbook of child psychology*, vol. 2: *Cognition, perception, and language* (5th edn., pp. 103–46). New York: Wiley.

Lamb, M. E., Bornstein, M. H., & Teti, D. M. (2002). Development in infancy: An introduction. Mahwah, NJ: Lawrence Erlbaum Associates.

McCall, R. (1977). Challenges to a science of developmental psychology. *Child Development, 48*, 333–44.

Meltzoff, A. N. (1988). Infant imitation after a 1-week delay: Long-term memory for novel acts and multiple stimuli. *Developmental Psychology, 24*, 470–6.

Meltzoff, A. N. & Moore, M. K. (1997). Explaining facial imitation: A theoretical model. *Early Development and Parenting, 6*, 179–92.

Meltzoff, A. N. & Moore, M. K. (1998). Object representation, identity, and the paradox of early permanence: Steps toward a new framework. *Infant Behavior and Development, 21*, 201–35.

Meltzoff, A. N. & Moore, M. K. (1999). A new foundation for cognitive development in infancy: The birth of the representational infant. In E. K. Scholnick, K. Nelson, S. A. Gelman, & P. H. Miller (eds.), *Conceptual development: Piaget's legacy. The Jean Piaget Symposium Series* (pp. 53–78). Mahwah, NJ: Lawrence Erlbaum Associates.

Moore, M. K., Borton, R., & Darby, B. L. (1978). Visual tracking in young infants: Evidence for object identity or object permanence? *Journal of Experimental Child Psychology, 25*, 183–98.

Oakes, L. M., Coppage, D. J., & Dingel, A. (1997). By land or by sea: The role of perceptual similarity in infants' categorization of animals. *Developmental Psychology, 33*, 396–407.

Piaget, J. (1952). *The origins of intelligence in children*. New York: Norton.

Reznick, J. S., Fueser, J. J., & Bosquet, M. (1998). Self-corrected reaching in a three-location delayed-response search task. *Psychological Science, 9*, 66–70.

Rovee-Collier, C. & Shyi, G. C. W. (1992). A functional and cognitive analysis of infant long-term memory. In M. Howe, C. Brainerd, & V. F. Reyna (eds.), *Development of long-term retention* (pp. 3–55). New York: Springer-Verlag.

Spelke, E. S. (1994). Initial knowledge: Six suggestions. *Cognition, 50*, 431–45.

Spelke, E. S. & Hermer, L. (1996). Early cognitive development: Objects and space. In E. Carterette & M. Friedman (series eds.), R. Gelman, & T. K. F. Au (eds.), *Handbook of perception and cognition: Perceptual and cognitive development* (2nd edn., pp. 71–114). San Diego, CA: Academic Press.

Spelke, E. S., Breinlinger, K., Macomber, J., & Jacobson, K. (1992). Origins of knowledge. *Psychological Review, 99*, 605–32.

Watson, J. S. (1966). The development and generalization of "contingency awareness" in early infancy: Some hypotheses. *Merrill-Palmer Quarterly, 12*, 73–94.

Watson, J. S. (1972). Smiling, cooing, and "The Game". *Merrill-Palmer Quarterly, 18*, 323–40.

Weisberg, P. & Rovee-Collier, C. (1998). Behavioral processes of infants and young children. In K. A. Lattal & M. Perone (eds.), *Handbook of research methods in human operant behavior* (pp. 325–70). New York: Plenum Press.

CHAPTER FIVE

Quasi-Experimental Designs in Developmental Research: Design and Analysis Considerations

Steven C. Pitts, Justin H. Prost, and Jamie J. Winters

The goal of this chapter is to introduce researchers in developmental science to the application of quasi-experimental designs. Instances may arise in which a researcher wishes to test the effect of a theoretically defined treatment, yet cannot (or chooses not to) randomly assign individuals to levels of the treatment, thus preventing the researcher from conducting a randomized experiment. The researcher is, of course, still interested in estimating and testing the effect of the treatment program. While it is the case that the randomized experiment offers the most powerful and least ambiguous test of causal hypotheses (Rubin, 1974), quasi-experiments can also be used to test those same hypotheses (Campbell & Stanley, 1966), assuming alternative explanations for observed effects can be ruled out. As will be seen in this chapter, there are a number of considerations and decisions that can be made by the quasi-experimental researcher throughout the research process (i.e., theory, design, and analysis) that vary in their ability to address possible alternative explanations. In this chapter, we introduce the reader to the issues that arise through use of quasi-experimental designs; we explicate several of the "basic" quasi-experimental designs; we discuss the impact of a number of decisions made at the analysis level on resulting estimates of the treatment effect; and we consider a number of design enhancements to the defined quasi-experimental designs that can increase their utility.

We begin with a brief reminder of the distinction between randomized experiments and quasi-experiments. We then consider the consequences of the quasi-experimental design on the validity of the findings resulting from this "type" of study, in general. As the focus of much of developmental science is on change (growth or decline) in the individual(s), we take the opportunity to consider several issues that can arise in the analysis and interpretation of data from longitudinal designs. These are issues that arise at both the design and analysis phase and we attempt to make the reader aware that decisions made at either phase can have differing consequences on the researcher's ability to estimate and interpret treatment effects. The quasi-experimental designs considered in this chapter will be those that are: (a) most likely to be available to researchers in developmental science, (b) most commonly used, and (c) most likely to yield the least biased estimates of the hypothesized treatment effect, provided certain assumptions or design features are met. In consideration of the quasi-experimental designs, we address each design's ability to address alternative explanations for the presence (or absence) of a treatment effect. Throughout the chapter, we attempt to introduce the reader to both traditional and emerging analytical and design techniques, though length constraints prevent consideration of all possible options available to the researcher (see Shadish, 2002, for a good summary of changes in quasi-experimental design and analysis in recent years). Our main messages, however, will be: (1) decisions made at each phase of the research process can affect interpretability of the findings, and (2) quasi-experimental researchers should consider multiple design enhancements to the quasi-experiment, or even multiple quasi-experiments, rather than a single quasi-experiment and/or a single design enhancement.

Quasi-Experiments

Campbell and Stanley (1966) initially introduced the term quasi-experiment to distinguish the randomized experiment (in which participants are randomly assigned to treatment condition) from experiments in which the researcher does not have the benefit of random assignment (quasi-experiments). As with randomized experiments, the goal of quasi-experiments is to draw causal inferences from the study and thus they often have a similar structure to the randomized experiment. As well, quasi-experiments will have some form of a treatment or intervention and will have two or more measurement waves (Cook & Campbell, 1979; West, 2001, personal communication).[1]

Given these specifications, it is clear there is a broad range of possible quasi-experimental designs, each with differing strengths and applications. One might think of two broad categories of quasi-experiments. Designs in which the treatment is administered to some, but not all, participants in the study might be loosely classified as nonequivalent control group designs. These designs typically have a small number of measurement waves and the treatment occurs some time following the first, but prior to the final, measurement. Designs in which participants are measured on a large number of occasions (e.g., 100) and treatment is administered at some point in the "middle" of the measurements can broadly be referred to as interrupted time series designs. Time series designs may or may not have a control group; the instance in which a single group

---

[1]   While Cook and Campbell (1979) discuss a design referred to as "posttest-only design with predicted higher-order interactions" they also acknowledge that this design has a number of potential weaknesses and may not be applicable across a wide variety of settings. We take the position that two or more measurement waves are necessary to provide even a minimum of protection against possible confounding.

is measured over time is referred to as a simple interrupted time series design (Cook & Campbell, 1979). The critical distinction of any time series design is the large number of measurements. Finally, it is noted that for both categories of quasi-experiments the treatment may or may not be literally under the researcher's direct control. Use of data from existing groups exposed to differing levels of a treatment focused on personal responsibility in aged patients of an institutional nursing home (Langer & Rodin, 1976) or use of archival data (e.g., introduction of drunk driving laws, West et al., 1989) are two examples of quasi-experiments in which administration of the treatment was not under the researcher's control.

Implications of nonrandom assignment to group

One benefit of random assignment is the expectation that, on average, the treatment groups will be approximately equal on all extraneous variables (variables other than the treatment condition that are related to the outcome). This increases the researcher's confidence that group differences at post-test are due to the experimental manipulation (see West, Biesanz, & Pitts, 2000 for an accessible discussion of the benefits and rationale of random assignment). When assignment to group is nonrandom, group differences at post-test *may* be due to treatment, but the differences may also be due to underlying differences between the groups on one or more confound variables.[2] In short, one of the issues that arises with respect to quasi-experimental designs of any type is with respect to the internal validity of the study – the actual estimate of the treatment effect is drawn into question and/or may be ambiguous.

Whenever researchers design a study (quasi-experiment, randomized experiment, etc.), they should consider aspects of the design that pertain to the validity of any conclusion(s) drawn from the study. Three types of validity that the researcher should consider are internal validity, external validity, and statistical conclusion validity. Internal validity can be thought of as whether the study provides an unambiguous test of the researchers' hypothesis. External validity concerns how well the findings of the particular study apply to other individuals, treatments, settings, etc. Finally, statistical conclusion validity regards aspects of the statistical test(s) conducted, including statistical power, possible violations of assumptions of the statistical tests, inflated Type I error rate, and reliability of the measures.

When considering differing quasi-experimental designs and possible enhancements to the basic designs, our interest will lie primarily with respect to threats to internal validity and the benefits of the proposed design enhancements to either reduce those threats or assist in their detection. Our focus on internal validity reflects the argument that issues regarding the external validity or the statistical conclusion validity are more difficult to address if the internal validity of the study is not first demonstrated. For example, if it

---

[2] When an extraneous variable is related to both the DV (outcome) and the IV (group) it is traditionally referred to as a confound variable, as the relation between the IV and DV is confounded with the extraneous variable.

is not clear that the results reflect an effect of treatment alone, it is difficult to consider to which populations the treatment effect would generalize or whether statistical power is relevant (i.e., if treatment is confounded with other variables, power does not reflect power for the effect of treatment alone). This is not to say, however, that any one type of validity is more or less important than the other. The type of validity a researcher attends will likely differ as a function of the researcher's goals, and thus other researchers may weight these types of validity differently.

Internal Validity

Establishing the internal validity of a study might be thought of as establishing that the relation between the IV and DV is causal. Alternatively, it might be thought of as the process of ruling out other reasons the IV and DV are related *other than* the IV causes the DV (i.e., ruling out that a third variable causes both the IV and DV). In any given study, a number of possible threats to the internal validity might arise, including selection, history, maturation, statistical regression, mortality, and instrumentation. While these threats can arise in both randomized experiments and quasi-experiments, random assignment to group is designed to mitigate many of these threats. These threats may occur alone, together, or may interact. Following a brief definition of each threat, we turn our attention to the instances more specific to quasi-experiments in which these threats to internal validity interact.

Threats to the internal validity of quasi-experiments

By its very definition, the threat of *selection* is ubiquitous in quasi-experimental research. Selection concerns how participants in the groups were assigned (selected) to the condition. If there is an unknown selection process by which participants are assigned to groups (e.g., self-selection), and thus to treatment condition, the estimate of the treatment effect is brought into question (i.e., are the effects due to treatment or due to selection to group?). *History* effects arise when an event that is not part of the treatment occurs between the pre- and post-test that influences the outcome of interest. *Maturation* regards the individuals' growth (e.g., more awareness, understanding, etc.) between the pre- and post-test that is not related to treatment but *is* related to the outcome of interest. *Statistical regression* can arise when individuals are selected into the study as a function of their extreme standing (high or low) on a variable(s) related to the outcome (e.g., pre-test) that is not perfectly reliable or is temporally unstable. Subsequent measurements (e.g., the post-test) will tend to be less extreme, even in the absence of any effect of treatment. Thus, even if the individual has identical *true* scores at both measurements, his or her *observed* scores will have appeared to change (Pitts & West, under review). *Mortality* is most typically observed in the social sciences as attrition (dropping out of the study) that is related to the outcome of interest (e.g., in a study of adolescent substance use, differential rates of attrition between non-drinkers and heavy drinkers might be expected). Differential mortality results in a specific form of a selection threat and is often discussed in that context. *Instrumentation* threats may arise if the methods of measuring the individual (collecting the data) are different at pre- and post-test. In this instance, the individual may appear as if they have changed, but the change may be due to differing instruments rather than to any effect of treatment.

Selection interactions are particularly problematic threats to the internal validity of a quasi-experiment in which selection interacts with one of the other threats to the internal validity. Many of the design modifications discussed in this chapter allow the researcher to reduce or identify one or more of these selection interactions. As well, sometimes the specific pattern of results of the study can help the researcher rule out the likelihood of one or more of these threats (see West, Biesanz, & Pitts, 2000). Nonetheless, researchers should carefully consider each of the threats to internal validity and selection interactions when conducting quasi-experimental research. While selection can interact with any of the threats to validity, many methodologists consider the following interactions to be the most problematic: selection × history, selection × statistical regression, selection × instrumentation, and selection × maturation.

In selection × history interactions, differing events (not defined as treatment) happen to individuals in each of the groups between the pre- and post-test measurements. In this sense, the history events are confounded with, and masked as, treatment effects. These interactions might arise when the treatment is administered at the group level[3] (e.g., elementary school, inpatient facility, etc.), as individuals in the groups share common administrators, educators, and other staff, as well as components of the treatment.

Selection × statistical regression interactions can arise if the formation of either group was a function of individual standing on correlates of the pre-test (or the pre-test itself) and individuals were selected into the group as a function of high or low scores. This selection may be external (e.g., an agency determines if an individual meets criteria to be in the group) or self-selected, if an individual feels he or she should enroll in a program (join a group) based on their own assessment of a temporally unstable behavior (e.g., they enroll in a program to cut down on drinking based on a recent weekend of "partying"). Selection × statistical regression interactions do not present the same level of threat to internal validity in designs in which membership to group is not a function of extreme scores. For example, selection × statistical regression should not prove a threat in an experiment in which the groups are two elementary schools

---

[3] Additional issues arise with respect to administration of treatment at the group level. This brings into question the "unit of analysis" issue. That is, given that treatment is administered at the group level, analyses of treatment effects should be conducted at the group level – unfortunately, this typically leads to substantial decreases in statistical power. The problem with analyzing data at the individual level is that it is likely that the errors of prediction for individuals within a given group are not independent, thus violating an assumption of most traditional procedures (e.g., regression, ANOVA). Multilevel modeling is a statistical technique that allows estimation of relations at the individual level, while controlling for the dependence among the observations (ICC; intraclass correlation coefficient). Length constraints prohibit consideration of this technique in the current chapter; thus, the traditional assumption of independent errors is made. The interested reader is urged to consult one of several accessible sources regarding multilevel modeling (Bryk & Raudenbush, 1987, 1992; Kreft & de Leeuw, 1998).

that are otherwise approximately equal (similar neighborhoods, enrollment, number of teachers, etc.).

Selection × instrumentation effects may arise when the measure(s) changes between pre- and post-test for one, but not all, of the groups. On the surface, this is one of the easier threats to rule out and/or control. To the extent that the same measuring instrument is used at each wave for each group in the study, this reduces the probability of this threat. Note, however, that a number of scales are designed to be normed for differing age groups (especially for younger children). In some instances, this entails including or deleting scale items for different ages. Though use of these types of scales does not necessarily imply a selection × instrumentation threat, it is something that the researcher should consider when evaluating effects of the treatment.

Selection × maturation effects are particularly relevant to developmental scientists. This threat can arise when the rate of underlying growth (ignoring any effect of treatment) is different in the two (or more) nonequivalent groups. Obviously, differing rates of naturally occurring growth in the groups between pre- and post-test can serve to confound any estimate of an effect of the treatment or intervention in the groups.

Longitudinal Designs

As quasi-experimental designs require multiple measurement occasions (e.g., most nonequivalent control group designs, regression discontinuity design, interrupted time series design), the quasi-experimental researcher should also address predictable issues that can arise in longitudinal designs. Some of these issues (e.g., measurement invariance) directly pertain to specific threats to the internal validity of the study, while others (e.g., attrition) have implications regarding all three types of validity. A thorough discourse of these issues is beyond the scope of this chapter, though our brief attention is not intended to belie their importance.

Measurement invariance

The use of equivalent measures is a necessary requirement to allow estimation and discussion of change over time, as nonequivalent measures can result in positively or negatively biased estimates of change. Differential measurement invariance (in which the measure changes for one, but not all, groups) is, by definition, the selection × instrumentation threat to internal validity discussed above. While cross-group measurement invariance is convenient, it is not as critical as invariance over time. With respect to establishing and testing measurement invariance, multiple indicator constructs are preferred to single item variables, as greater flexibility and tests of assumptions are available (Byrne, Shavelson, & Muthén, 1989; Kenny, 1975; Shadish, 2002). Pitts, West, and Tein (1996) and Widaman and Reise (1997) provide more detailed discussions of the issues of measurement invariance that should prove beneficial to the quasi-experimental researcher.

Attrition

Participant loss is an issue facing all longitudinal researchers, regardless of the design of the study (Little & Rubin, 1987; Tabachnick & Fidell, 2001). While the best solution is to take all possible steps to minimize attrition at the post-test measurement, it is likely that some participant loss will still arise. How the researcher proceeds with respect to estimating the effect of treatment depends on the processes underlying the reason for attrition. Thus, the researcher's goals with respect to missing data are twofold: (1) identify reasons for the missing data (see Jurs & Glass, 1971); and (2) depending on the identified reasons for attrition, adjust the effect of the treatment and/or consider data imputation strategies for those participants with missing data (Little & Rubin, 1987; Little & Schenker, 1995). Two points are noted with respect to identifying the reasons for attrition. First, the approach assumes participants are measured on all relevant pre-test measurements (i.e., the reasons for attrition). Second, as the approach depends on statistical tests to identify reasons for attrition, it is suggested that a more liberal alpha level be used when testing variables believed to influence attrition (e.g., $\alpha = 0.25$; Hansen et al., 1985; Tebes, Snow, & Arthur, 1992).

Developmental referent

Correct identification of the developmental marker (referent) can affect the internal validity and statistical conclusion validity of the study (Nesselroade, 1990). To wit, if measurement wave is used as the referent in a cohort sequential design (see Chapter 1, this volume), this has implications with respect to both the meaning of and variability in the outcome measure, potentially resulting in biased and/or underpowered estimates. It is noted that inclusion of age at initial measurement as a covariate in cohort sequential designs with multiple (3+) waves does not entirely remove the resulting bias in these instances. Thus, as age is often used as the developmental referent, many researchers elect to circumvent the issues related to unequal referents by obtaining samples as homogeneous as possible on age. While this sounds reasonable, the researcher should still consider whether identification of age as the referent is the most appropriate developmental referent (e.g., as opposed to grade level in school).

Nonequivalent Control Group Designs

Cook and Campbell (1979) distinguished eleven differing nonequivalent control group designs, eight of which typically provided interpretable results. The common feature among all these designs is nonrandom assignment to treatment, though not all of the designs have a defined control group. For example, the removed treatment control group and the repeated treatment designs each have only one group. It is also not necessary for all designs to have both pre- and post-test measurement waves. Cook and Campbell

(1979) discuss a design they term the "posttest-only design with predicted higher-order interactions," though they indicate that the applicability of this design is infrequent and interpretability of results is potentially very sensitive to selection artifacts in the sample. Other nonequivalent control group designs discussed were either presented as, or might be thought of as, variants of the untreated control group design (or the no-treatment control group design). In the untreated control group design there are two groups of individuals (not randomly assigned to group). One group serves as the control (no treatment) condition and the other group serves as the treatment condition. Individuals in both groups are measured at pre-test and again at post-test. The untreated control group design, and variants of this design, receives a fair amount of attention in the current chapter not because it is the best design, but because it is likely the most commonly used design. Prior to discussion of the untreated control group design, we briefly take up the regression discontinuity design. While this design is a strong quasi-experimental design, it is not widely used in the social sciences. We summarize the design to the extent that it helps illustrate the issues regarding selection into group that arise in the untreated control group design.

Regression discontinuity design

Of the nonequivalent control group designs defined by Cook and Campbell (1979), the regression discontinuity design is sometimes thought of as distinct from the other designs. In one obvious aspect it is, and this distinction may prove helpful in understanding the threats to internal validity due to selection and selection interactions that arise in the untreated control group design. The regression discontinuity design proves to be a very strong nonequivalent control group design and even approaches randomized experiments with respect to addressing threats to internal validity (Cook & Campbell, 1979; West, Biesanz, & Pitts, 2000). The regression discontinuity design is an alternative when participants are assigned to treatment condition as a function of their standing on some quantitative measure (typically a measure of need or merit). For example, children may be assigned to a "school breakfast and lunch program" based on family income. The outcome may be classroom behavior or some measure of academic performance. In a classic example of the regression discontinuity design, Seaver and Quarton (1976) examined the impact of being placed on the Dean's list (based on Fall quarter GPA) on students' subsequent Winter quarter GPA. The quantitative measure upon which group assignment decisions are made is referred to as the quantitative assignment variable. In the above examples, family income and Fall quarter GPA are the quantitative assignment variables.

In the basic regression discontinuity design, both the pre-test measurement (often the quantitative assignment variable) and the treatment condition are used as predictors of the outcome. In the purest form of results, the regression line describing the relation between the pre-test and the outcome has the same slope in each group. Differences in the *height* of the line (i.e., intercept differences) exist at the point of the treatment, thus introducing a discontinuity in the regression line; this discontinuity reflects the effect of the treatment. West, Biesanz, and Pitts (2000) discuss alternative models that can be used to detect treatment effects that involve more than a simple shift in the intercept, including estimation of the pre-test by treatment group interaction and nonlinear relationships. Of importance to us with respect to the regression discontinuity design is that, "When its assumptions are met, it rules out most of the threats to internal validity and has good external validity for much applied work." (West, Biesanz, & Pitts, 2000, p. 62).

The reason the regression discontinuity design is a strong approach is that, while assignment to treatment condition is not random, it is *known*. In fact, many of the threats to the internal validity of this design that may arise concern instances in which assignment to treatment does not perfectly correspond to values on the quantitative assignment rule (so called "fuzzy assignment" rules). For example, either parents or school officials may underreport a family's income so that the child may partake in the school breakfast program. Thus, the actual mechanism of assignment to treatment is less clear, and threats involving selection begin to surface. This serves to highlight the true difficulty of the untreated control group design – that the mechanism for assignment to treatment condition is not known. It should be noted that though the regression discontinuity design is a strong design, as far as the nonequivalent control group designs are concerned, it still has shortcomings compared to the randomized experiment. Even in the best case scenario (bivariate normality, correctly specified model), the sample sizes needed in the regression discontinuity design are roughly two to three times that needed in the randomized experiment to achieve comparable statistical power estimates.

Untreated control group design

The most typically utilized nonequivalent control group design is the untreated control group design. In this design, individuals are not randomly assigned to condition (treatment and control); however, in virtually all other regards, the design appears structurally similar to a randomized two-group experiment. The selection issues raised by nonrandom assignment to group require the researcher take additional steps to either reduce or allow estimation of any possible threats to the internal validity of the study. To reduce these threats, various design or analytical modifications are often included, with the goal of making the untreated control group design more closely approximate a randomized experiment. As will be seen, the success of these approaches relies heavily on correct identification and measurement of the processes underlying the nonrandom assignment to condition (i.e., the variables underlying potential group differences have been correctly identified and measured).

Analytical strategies to equate groups in untreated control group designs The most commonly employed strategies to equate the groups involve inclusion of covariates in the analysis of group differences at the post-test (i.e., the "ANCOVA" approach). For this discussion, we assume a traditional two-group untreated control group design in which there is a single pre-test and a single post-test measurement and all individuals are measured at the same developmental referent (e.g., measured at the same ages). Conceptually, one may think of two approaches to statistically equate the groups; though, ultimately, the statistical analysis will be the same for both approaches. One approach is to model the selection processes that *led to* the group differences and/or otherwise control for the pre-test group differences. In the second approach, covariates are identified that would predict *post-test differences* between the groups that are *not* associated with the treatment.

For example, a researcher may wish to conduct a study to examine the effects of a novel after-school program on the self-esteem of elementary school children. The new program is administered to all children enrolled in the current after-school program (the treatment group). The control group consists of all children who are not enrolled in the after-school program. Covariates related to selection into the treatment condition may include children with single parents, enrollment in some other afternoon program, and/or the child's interest in the current after-school program. Covariates that might be related to the measure of self-esteem at the post-test would more likely include shared aspects of the two after-school programs, the child's interaction with peers, and/or structured play that occurs in the after-school program. In practice, the researcher may elect to include both "types" of covariates. While the approach of equating groups is theoretically sound and often employed, there are some obvious drawbacks. First and foremost, it is unlikely that the researcher will be able to identify *all* possible sources of selection into group and/or predictors of outcome differences, much less measure them all. Thus, the researcher is more often in a position of choosing the theoretically "best" covariates rather than the full set of covariates. Pragmatically, it is probably reasonable to choose a small set of strong covariates and assume that additional covariates that are not included have relatively small effects. When utilizing this approach, the researcher is advised to test the assumptions that the relation between a given covariate and the outcome is linear in form and does not interact with other predictors and covariates in the model (Aiken & West, 1991; Cohen & Cohen, 1983; Keppel, 1991; Neter et al., 1996).

A second problem that can arise with use of covariates to statistically equate the two groups regards measurement error in the covariates and in the pre-test measurement. In the case of a single covariate (the *measured* pre-test), the presence of measurement error will result in an *underadjustment* of the post-test outcome. A straightforward solution to the presence of measurement error in the case of a single covariate can be found through use of Porter's true score analysis of covariance (see Huitema, 1980, chapter 14). While it is likely that a set of covariates, each measured with error, will also result in an underadjustment of the post-test outcome, Reichardt (1979) notes that it is technically possible for the outcome to be overadjusted in these instances. When multiple covariates are included in the analysis, one response might be to utilize structural equation modeling (SEM) software (e.g., EQS, Bentler, 1995; LISREL, Jöreskog & Sörbom, 1989), which allows estimation of relations between multiple measured variables adjusted for measurement error. As both approaches (i.e., Porter's true score ANCOVA and SEM) are dependent on estimates of reliability, Judd and Kenny (1981) recommend a specificity analysis in which the adjustment for error is made for varying estimates of reliability.

Structural equation models, in which multiple measured variables serve as indicators of underlying latent constructs, provide theoretically error-free measures of each of the constructs and allow direct tests of the assumptions of measurement invariance discussed earlier (Pitts, West, & Tein, 1996). Thus, obtaining multiple indicators provides another approach the researcher may take in response to the presence of measurement error. Moreover, the SEM approach is well suited to examination of change in multi-wave designs as a random effects process through estimation of latent growth curve models (LGC) (Curran, Muthén, & Harford, 1998; Curran & Muthén, 1999; McArdle, 1988; Muthén & Muthén, 2000). Conceptually, the LGC allows individuals to have their own unique estimates of growth, permitting the researcher to test whether the variability in these estimates is systematically related to individual-level variables (e.g., treatment condition). The primary drawbacks of the SEM approach, in general, are the relatively large sample size requirements (which increase as the number of measured variables and hypothesized latent constructs increases), the current inability to estimate an interaction between two continuous latent constructs, and the assumption of multivariate normality in the measured variables. While methodological advances do allow estimation of effects even when the assumption of normality is not met, these procedures require even larger sample sizes (Bentler, 1995).

Matching procedures to equate groups Matching procedures are an attempt to roughly equate the groups through exclusion of noncomparable individuals from the analysis. In its most basic application, individuals in the two groups are matched on the single pre-test measurement of the outcome. This approach has the advantage of producing groups that have approximately the same mean on the pre-test measure. There are, however, a number of potential disadvantages with this approach. Foremost is the fact that participants may need to be dropped from analysis if a match is not available, thus affecting statistical conclusion validity as well as external validity. For disparate groups, matching can also result in rather odd implications regarding the two groups. For example, consider matching groups of students from public versus academically competitive private schools on a standardized scholastic aptitude measure. These two groups likely represent different populations that have different means on the covariates (e.g., the aptitude measure, family income, academic training, etc.). It is easily possible that the resulting matched groups would be comprised of a sample of "lower achieving" private school children (relative to private school peers) and a sample of "higher achieving" public school children (relative to public school peers). Thus, relative achievement is confounded with group membership due to matching the groups, though the goal is to equate the groups. Additional problems with the above strategy of matching include the practical difficulty of finding good matches (especially on a number of covariates) and the problem of regression to the mean (Judd, Smith, & Kidder, 1991).

Matching, however, is not entirely without promise. Rosenbaum and Rubin (1983) proposed the idea of matching on propensity scores. In this approach, the researcher identifies all possible pre-test covariates that might predict membership into the two groups. This set of covariates is then used in a logistic regression to develop a propensity score for each individual that reflects probability of membership in the treatment group. The two groups are then matched on the basis of this propensity score (see Rosenbaum & Rubin, 1984, for an application of this approach). As with the analysis of covariance approach discussed above, this approach depends on the researcher correctly identifying all relevant variables to develop the propensity score.

Design enhancements to the untreated control group design As suggested above, many of the "different" nonequivalent control group designs proposed by Cook and Campbell (1979) might be thought of as modifications of the basic two-group untreated control group design with one pre-test and one post-test measurement. These modifications can prove to be very helpful at identifying or reducing threats to internal validity as well as strengthening the overall untreated control group design. Design modifications that can likely be employed by the majority of developmental scientists utilizing the untreated control group design include measuring additional dependent variables, collecting data from additional control groups (and its correlate, multiple treatment groups), including an additional pre-test measurement, and the short time series design. Researchers are encouraged to use multiple enhancements, as the benefit of these modifications in com-bination can greatly increase the strength of a quasi-experimental design (Higginbotham, West, & Forsyth, 1988; Reynolds & West, 1987).

Nonequivalent dependent variables, as defined by Cook and Campbell (1979), entail the measurement of a single group on two (or more) dependent variables at both pre- and post-test. One DV is hypothesized to be affected by the treatment (reactive DV) and the other DV is hypothesized to *not* be affected by the treatment (nonreactive DV). The two DVs should otherwise be comparable, both in similarity as a construct and (roughly) equally affected by the same threats to internal validity (Cook & Campbell, 1979). Additional benefits of this design may be derived from measurement of a number of nonreactive DVs, each with high reliability (Reynolds & West, 1987). Repeated measures analysis of variance (or multivariate analysis or profile analysis; see Tabachnick & Fidell, 2001; Tatsuoka, 1988) can be conducted to test for a time by treatment interaction. Differences in the amount of pre- to post-test change between the reactive and nonreactive DVs provide support for the unique effect of the treatment (see Reynolds & West, 1987 for an example incorporating this type of design).

By itself, the nonequivalent dependent variables design is probably one of the weakest of the nonequivalent control group designs (Cook & Campbell, 1979; Higginbotham, West, & Forsyth, 1988; Reynolds & West, 1987). In conjunction with other non-equivalent control designs, however, the nonequivalent dependent variables design can provide useful information to the researcher regarding possible threats to internal validity. As proposed by Cook and Campbell (i.e., additional dependent variables meas-ured only in the treatment group; 1979), results can provide information with respect to threats due to selection × history. When nonreactive DVs are measured in both groups, however, this provides additional information regarding effects from the nonequivalent dependent variables design that may be due to selection × instrumentation and/or selection × maturation. Finally, examination of between-groups differences in the nonreactive DVs only may provide the researcher information with respect to possible selection × maturation threats.

Multiple groups have the goal of obtaining an additional control group that did *not* arise through the same selection process(es) as either the treatment or "primary" control groups. In essence, while any one control group differs from the treatment group in unknown ways (other than treatment), additional control groups representative of differ-ent selection processes are not expected to share the same *systematic* reasons for differ-ences from the treatment group other than the treatment itself. While a randomly selected additional control group is ideal (Higginbotham, West, & Forsyth, 1988; Rosenbaum, 1987), the researcher should, at a minimum, search for additional control groups that do not share the same processes that result in selection into either the treatment or other control groups. Careful articulation of the threats to internal validity arising between the treatment group and each of the control groups provides the researcher with greater confidence in the results. In combination with consideration of outcome patterns (see West, Biesanz, & Pitts, 2000), additional control groups can also be helpful in determining which threats to internal validity are, or are not, likely in the study. As the additional control group is not defined by the same selection processes as is the first control group, it would be unlikely to expect the same influences, and hence patterns of change, in the two groups.

Additional *treatment* groups may also be of benefit if: (1) it is possible to obtain an additional treatment group at random from the population, or (2) it can be assumed that the effects of increased treatment dosage are linear and an additional treatment group can be obtained that is similar to the primary treatment group. In the unlikely case that an additional treatment group can be obtained at random, the researcher would again focus on both overall group differences as well as differences between pairs of groups. More likely is the case in which the researcher can obtain an additional treatment group that can be described by similar selection processes as the primary treatment group. If the assumption can be made that increases in treatment dosage are linear, the researcher could assign this second group to receive a larger treatment. Thus, differences between the two treatment groups reflect the effect of the increased dosage of treatment and can be used in conjunction with analyses examining the control group to isolate the effect of treatment and effects due to selection processes (Reichardt, in press). While an additional treatment group may be helpful in estimating effect size of treatment, it is not as strong in identifying threats to internal validity as additional control groups.

Additional pre-test measurement is one of the most straightforward enhancements a researcher can make to address both the selection × maturation and selection × statistical regression threats to internal validity (Cook & Campbell, 1979; West, Biesanz, & Pitts, 2000). The additional pre-test measurement can be used to estimate and test for differences in the rate of growth in the two groups prior to treatment. Moreover, these estimates could then be used to adjust the estimate of the treatment effect (Bryk & Raudenbush, 1987, 1992; Kreft & de Leeuw, 1998). This approach is dependent on the assumptions that the two pre-test measurement waves are sufficient to test for maturation differences in the two groups and that the pattern of pre-test change would remain stable over the full course of the study. Given these two assumptions are met, collection of an additional pre-test measurement can prove invaluable to the researcher, not only for addressing threats to the internal validity of the study, but also for providing estimates of reliability of the measure(s) in each group.

Short time series designs conducted with two groups, or two-group panel studies, provide the strongest approach to evaluating possible selection × maturation and selection × statistical regression threats to the internal validity of the study. In the short time series design, the researcher collects multiple pre-test and multiple post-test measurements in each group. This allows the researcher to estimate and test for group differences in the amount of growth, and form of growth trajectory, both prior to and following administration of treatment. The actual number of measurement waves will vary as a function of the researcher's hypotheses regarding the form of growth in the groups. Ideally, short time series designs include as many post-test as pre-test measurements, thus allowing the researcher to test the equivalence of form of growth both prior to and following treatment (Reynolds & West, 1987). As with the additional pre-test designs, HLM (Bryk & Raudenbush, 1992) and LGC (McArdle & Epstein, 1987; Muthén & Curran, 1997; Pitts, 1999) methodologies prove very beneficial both for tests of within-group differences as well as between-group treatment effects. Moreover, the inclusion of multiple post-test measurements allows the researcher to test additional hypotheses regarding the timing and duration of the treatment effect.

Summary of enhancements to the untreated control group design While the traditional two-group untreated control group design may be one of the weaker of the quasi-experimental designs, there are a number of design enhancements that can be made to this design to reduce or identify threats to internal validity. These enhancements themselves are not necessarily panaceas to the problems that arise through use of the untreated control group design (Cook & Campbell, 1979; West, Biesanz, & Pitts, 2000). The nonequivalent dependent variables design for example, is on its own perhaps the weakest quasi-experimental design (Cook & Campbell, 1979; Reynolds & West, 1987). Results from this design taken in conjunction with results from other untreated control group designs, however, can greatly strengthen the researcher's interpretation, understanding, and confidence in the estimates of a treatment effect. As well, while it may not be possible to find a single ideal control group, collecting additional control groups through differing selection processes can assist in ruling out a number of threats to internal validity. The enhancements that are stronger in ruling out threats to the internal validity of the study may require more effort to put in place and the researcher should weigh the benefits of such a modification relative to possible gains. At a minimum, however, the researcher may wish to strongly consider collecting a second pre-test measurement if possible, since this relatively minor enhancement can be quite successful at identifying selection × maturation and selection × statistical regression threats. In short, the researcher using untreated control group designs should not think of *the best* quasi-experimental design modification, but rather a series of modifications (or series of quasi-experiments) that best serve to address the key hypotheses and rule out likely threats to internal validity.

Interrupted Time Series Designs

The interrupted time series design, as presented earlier, was loosely described as a design in which participants are measured on a large number of occasions both prior to and following a treatment. One advantage of using an interrupted time series design is that the design allows researchers to identify changes in the developmental process after the introduction of a treatment that may extend beyond simple mean or slope changes. Identifying experimentally introduced changes in the developmental process requires that we first understand and estimate the *normative* form of development across time (accomplished with the pre-test measurements).

As well, using time series with large numbers of measurement occasions allows for forms of development to be identified that would not be identifiable with only a few measurements. For example, if development on a specific variable was characterized by a periodic cycle of peaks and valleys with a positive linear trend, analyses would need to include enough measurements to identify this pattern. Now consider adding a treatment to this example of linear and cyclical growth that does not alter the positive linear trend, yet flattens the periodicity (the cycling) in the growth. Were we to consider only the linear trend when evaluating the effects of treatment, we might conclude that treatment had no effect. Whether group differences in the dependencies (e.g., the periodic cycles) reflect an effect of treatment depends on the researcher's theoretical expectations regarding the effect of treatment. At a minimum, these dependencies should be estimated; even if they are not central to the researcher's hypotheses, they can be used to reduce the estimate of error in the observations.

Interrupted time series design considerations

Traditional approaches to the analysis of interrupted time series design strive to remove the variability due to dependencies in the data, thus providing more powerful tests of differences in the underlying trends. West and Hepworth (1991) identified three types of dependence that can occur when considering temporally ordered data. The first form of dependence reflects trends that may exist in the pre-test data. The second form of dependence is due to cyclical components (e.g., the periodicity component described above). The last form of dependency, termed serial dependency, is due to observations being adjacent to each other (autocorrelation). Any of these forms of dependence can lead to potentially misleading results if not appropriately controlled. West and Hepworth (1991) indicate that the appropriate use of many of the available statistical techniques for analysis of time series data require that these forms of dependence be estimated and adjusted for. For an example of this application, see Berman, Meyer, and Coats (1984), who successfully used this approach of controlling for dependencies to evaluate the effects of an inpatient program for alcoholics on multiple dimensions of the MMPI.

Determining the appropriate measurement interval and the length of measurement, primary factors contributing to the efficacy of an interrupted time series design, is critical to correctly estimate and identify underlying cycles. A cycle reflects the systematic variability that is associated with the autocorrelations across measurements (i.e., serial dependency, periodicity). To determine the appropriate measurement interval to capture underlying cycles, the researcher must consider both the pattern of change and frequency of hypothesized cycles across time. For example, if a behavior cycles weekly, then a one-week measurement interval is clearly insufficient to capture this cycle, as each measurement will be made at the same point in the cycle. The appropriate length of measurement (duration of the study) in an interrupted time series is the second major concern when developing a study or when using existing data sources. Identification of a cycle requires a recurring pattern of the cycle; the cycle must be captured at least twice.

Identifying changes due to treatment requires the identification of both pre-test and post-test patterns of change (include cycles, if applicable). Thus, the appropriate study duration will be dependent on the hypothesized cycle length for *both* the pre- and post-test measurements.

The interval between measurements and the duration of the study obviously combine to dictate the total number of measurement occasions. Correctly identifying the number of pre- and post-test measurements is necessary to adequately model the three sources of dependency defined above. Failure to do so could result in unidentified cyclical patterns, biased estimates of pre- and post-test growth patterns, and misleading inferences regarding the effect of treatment. While some authors suggest having 100 or more measurements (Velicer & Harrop, 1983), smaller numbers of waves may be sufficient depending on the goal of the time series analysis and the periodicity in the variable. For example, Berman, Meyer, and Coats (1984) had a total of 20 pre-test and 23 post-test measurements in their evaluation of an inpatient alcoholism treatment program.

Internal validity of the interrupted time series design

Many of the threats to internal validity discussed earlier continue to apply with respect to the interrupted time series design: selection, history, maturation, and instrumentation (Higginbotham, West, & Forsyth, 1988). Threats from selection in the interrupted time series design are somewhat different than previously defined. These are threats that arise if the sample changes in some systematic fashion across measurements. This is most typically a function of attrition, and thus the easiest method of controlling for this threat is an attempt to minimize attrition. Again, as it is likely that some attrition will be present in even the best designs, the researcher should make every effort to examine the correlates of attrition and determine if potential non-random attrition coincided with administration of the treatment. Of importance, to be considered a viable threat to internal validity, the nonrandom attrition would need to arise due to implementation of the treatment (i.e., at some point after the treatment/interruption).

History threats arise when there is an introduction of some other change in the environment that occurs at the same time as the treatment. This threat to internal validity can be very difficult to control for, as it is often unlikely that all possible changes in the environment can be anticipated and/or recognized. Given the absence of a randomly assigned control group, the researcher must attempt to identify any changes in the environment that coincide with the interruption and their possible impact on growth in the variable of interest.

The most obvious benefit of the interrupted time series design is the ability to control for threats to internal validity that might arise due to maturation. In this design, growth in the pre-test measurements serves as an unbiased estimate of normal maturation and can be used to control for post-test maturation, strengthening the researcher's conclusions regarding the effect of treatment. Only in the unlikely instance that the underlying form of normative growth would change at the exact point of treatment administration is this threat considered to be a viable alternative explanation of differences in growth due to treatment.

Instrumentation is likely more problematic when using existing data sets, as the instruments used are not under the control of the researcher. In a designed study, this should be less of a concern as the researcher can maintain the use of the same instrument across the measurements. In an existing data set, this threat to internal consistency should be readily identifiable as a change in measurement that typically occurs at, or shortly after, administration of the treatment.

Time series designs provide a very powerful means to identify developmental processes that are naturally occurring in the absence of treatment (pre-test measurements). The effect of treatment may be evaluated by consideration of the post-test growth relative to the pre-test growth. The treatment may impact the slope or intercept of a regression line, or both. Traditionally, serial and cyclical dependencies are estimated and controlled for, resulting in more powerful tests of changes in the underlying form of growth, though it is also possible that the treatment may affect the cyclical aspects of development, and these patterns themselves can be interpreted. Thus, the interrupted time series design provides a method of evaluating development in the more traditional manner as well as in ways not previously available, allowing evaluation of treatment effects that leads to greater confidence in the validity of the findings of the study.

Conclusion

In this chapter, we sought to introduce the reader to the use of quasi-experimental designs and the issues that arise in the course of designing, analyzing, and interpreting effects from quasi-experimental research. Throughout the chapter, we attempted to emphasize that decisions made at each phase of the research process will affect the researcher's ability to both identify and control for these issues. We elected to focus on just a few of a number of possible quasi-experimental designs. Our decision for this was twofold: (1) we wished to present those designs that we felt were most applicable and/or most commonly used in developmental science, and (2) presentation of a smaller number of designs allowed demonstration of how enhancements to the basic design can address varying threats to the internal validity of the study. As well, we wished to draw the reader's attention to the fact that even basic analytical decisions can greatly impact the findings and interpretations of the results (e.g., mis-specification of covariates in a nonequivalent group design can result in underadjustment of treatment effects).

A final theme throughout this chapter is that the researcher almost always benefits through more information at any phase of research. This may include knowledge of the group assignment process (e.g., the regression discontinuity design), of additional outcomes, of additional control or treatment groups, or of additional measurement waves (e.g., an additional pre-test measurement or an interrupted time series design). This culminates in the suggestion that quasi-experimental researchers should consider designing quasi-experiments that incorporate more than one design modification (or a series of quasi-experiments with complementary design modifications). This approach may be seen as a smaller version of the scientific process in general. While no single study (experiment or quasi-experiment) can be designed such that it rules out or addresses all uncertainty with respect to the effect of a given treatment, a consistent finding of the treatment effect in the literature across a range of studies and designs greatly increases our confidence in the robustness of the effectiveness of treatment (Shadish, Cook, & Campbell, 2002).

Note

Address for correspondence: Steven C. Pitts, Department of Psychology, University of Maryland, Baltimore County, Baltimore, MD 21250. Email: spitts@umbc.edu.

References

Aiken, L. S. & West, S. G. (1991). *Multiple regression: Testing and interpreting interactions.* Thousand Oaks, CA: Sage.

Bentler, P. M. (1995). *EQS: Structural equations program manual.* Encino, CA: Multivariate Software, Inc.

Berman, J., Meyer, J., & Coats, G. (1984). Effects of program characteristics on treatment outcome: An interrupted time-series analysis. *Journal of Studies on Alcohol, 45,* 405–10.

Bryk, A. S. & Raudenbush, S. W. (1987). Application of hierarchical linear models to assessing change. *Psychological Bulletin, 101,* 147–58.

Bryk, A. S. & Raudenbush, S. W. (1992). *Hierarchical linear models: Applications and data analysis methods.* Newbury Park, CA: Sage.

Byrne, B. M., Shavelson, R. J., & Muthén, B. (1989). Testing for the equivalence of factor covariance and mean structure: The issue of partial measurement invariance. *Psychological Bulletin, 105,* 456–66.

Campbell, D. T. & Stanley, J. C. (1966). *Experimental and quasi-experimental designs for research.* Chicago, IL: Rand-McNally.

Cohen, J. & Cohen, P. (1983). *Applied multiple regression/correlation analysis for the behavioral sciences* (2nd edn.). Hillsdale, NJ: Lawrence Erlbaum Associates.

Cook, T. D. & Campbell, D. T. (1979). *Quasi-experimentation: Design and analysis issues for field settings.* Boston, MA: Houghton-Mifflin.

Curran, P. J. & Muthén, B. O. (1999). The application of latent curve analysis to testing developmental theories in intervention research. *American Journal of Community Psychology, 27,* 567–95.

Curran, P. J., Muthén, B. O., & Harford, T. C. (1998). The influence of changes in marital status on developmental trajectories of alcohol use in young adults. *Journal of Studies on Alcohol, 59,* 647–58.

Hansen, W. B., Collins, L. M., Malotte, C. K., Johnson, C. A., & Fielding, J. E. (1985). Attrition in prevention research. *Journal of Behavioral Medicine, 8,* 261–75.

Higginbotham, H. N., West, S. G., & Forsyth, D. R. (1988). *Psychotherapy and behavior change: Social, cultural, and methodological perspectives* (pp. 9–74). Elmsford, NY: Pergamon Press.

Huitema, B. E. (1980). *The analysis of covariance and alternatives.* New York: John Wiley.

Jöreskog, K. G. & Sörbom, D. (1989). *LISREL 7: A guide to the program and applications.* Chicago, IL: SPSS, Inc.

Judd, C. M. & Kenny, D. A. (1981). Process analysis: Estimating mediation in treatment evaluations. *Evaluation Review, 5,* 602–19.

Judd, C. M., Smith, E. R., & Kidder, L. H. (1991). *Research methods in social relations* (6th edn.). Fort Worth, TX: Harcourt-Brace.

Jurs, S. G. & Glass, G. V. (1971). The effect of experimental mortality on the internal and external validity of the randomized comparative experiment. *Journal of Experimental Education, 40*, 62–6.

Kenny, D. A. (1975). A quasi-experimental approach to assessing treatment effects in the nonequivalent control group design. *Psychological Bulletin, 82*, 345–62.

Keppel, G. (1991). *Design and analysis: A researcher's handbook* (3rd edn.). Englewood Cliffs, NJ: Prentice Hall.

Kreft, I. & de Leeuw, J. (1998). *Introducing multilevel modeling.* Thousand Oaks, CA: Sage.

Langer, E. J. & Rodin, J. (1976). The effects of choice and enhanced personal responsibility for the aged: A field experiment in an institutional setting. *Journal of Personality and Social Psychology, 34*, 191–8.

Little, R. J. A. & Rubin, D. B. (1987). *Statistical analysis with missing data.* New York: John Wiley.

Little, R. J. A. & Schenker, N. (1995). Missing data. In G. Arminger, C. C. Clogg, & M. E. Sobel (eds.), *Handbook of statistical modeling for the social and behavioral sciences* (pp. 39–76). New York: Plenum Press.

McArdle, J. J. (1988). Dynamic but structural equation modeling of repeated measures data. In J. R. Nesselroade & R. B. Cattell (eds.), *Handbook of Multivariate Experimental Psychology* (2nd edn.). New York: Plenum Press.

McArdle, J. J. & Epstein, D. (1987). Latent growth curves within developmental structural equation models. *Child Development, 58*, 110–33.

Muthén, B. O. & Curran, P. J. (1997). General longitudinal modeling of individual differences in experimental designs: A latent variable framework for analysis and power estimation. *Psychological Methods, 2*, 371–402.

Muthén, L. K. & Muthén, B. O. (2000). *Mplus: The comprehensive modeling program for applied researchers.* Los Angeles, CA: Muthén & Muthén.

Nesselroade, J. R. (1990). Adult personality development: Issues in assessing constancy and change. In A. I. Rabin, R. A. Zucker, R. A. Emmons, & S. Frank (eds.), *Studying persons and lives.* New York: Springer-Verlag.

Neter, J., Kutner, M. H., Nachtsheim, C. J., & Wasserman, W. (1996) *Applied linear statistical models* (4th edn.). Burr Ridge, IL: Irwin.

Pitts, S. C. (1999). The use of latent growth models to estimate treatment effects in longitudinal experiments. Unpublished doctoral dissertation, Arizona State University.

Pitts, S. C. & West, S. G. (under review). Alternative sampling designs to detect interactions in multiple regression. *Psychological Methods.*

Pitts, S. C., West, S. G., & Tein, J-Y. (1996). Longitudinal measurement models in evaluation research: Examining stability and change. *Evaluation and Program Planning, 19*, 333–50.

Reichardt, C. S. (1979). The statistical analysis of data from nonequivalent group designs. In T. D. Cook & D. T. Campbell, *Quasi-experimentation: Design and analysis issues for field settings* (pp. 147–205). Boston, MA: Houghton-Mifflin.

Reichardt, C. S. (in press). A logic for estimating effects. *Psychological Methods.*

Reynolds, K. D. & West, S. G. (1987). A multiplist strategy for strengthening nonequivalent control group designs. *Evaluation Review, 11*, 691–714.

Rosenbaum, P. R. (1987). The role of a second control group in an observational study (with discussion). *Statistical Science, 2*, 292–316.

Rosenbaum, P. R. & Rubin, D. (1983). The central role of the propensity score in observational studies for causal effects. *Biometrika, 70*, 41–55.

Rosenbaum, P. R. & Rubin, D. (1984). Reducing bias in observational studies using sub-classification on the propensity score. *Journal of the American Statistical Association, 79*, 516–24.

Rubin, D. B. (1974). Estimating causal effects of treatments in randomized and nonrandomized studies. *Journal of Educational Psychology, 66*, 688–701.

Seaver, W. B. & Quarton, R. J. (1976). Regression discontinuity analysis of the dean's list effects. *Journal of Educational Psychology, 68*, 459–65.

Shadish, W. R. (2002). Revisiting field experimentation: Field notes for the future. *Psychological Methods, 7*, 3–18.

Shadish, W. R., Cook, T. D., & Campbell, D. T. (2002). *Experimental and quasi-experimental design for generalized causal inference*. Boston, MA: Houghton-Mifflin.

Tabachnick, B. G. & Fidell, L. S. (2001). *Using multivariate statistics* (4th edn.). Boston, MA: Allyn & Bacon.

Tatsuoka, M. T. (1988). *Multivariate analysis*. New York: Macmillan.

Tebes, J. K., Snow, D. L., & Arthur, M. W. (1992). Panel attrition and external validity in the short-term follow-up study of adolescent substance use. *Evaluation Review, 16*, 151–70.

Velicer, W. F. & Harrop, J. W. (1983). The reliability and accuracy of time series model identification. *Evaluation Review, 7*, 551–60.

West, S. G. & Hepworth, J. T. (1991). Statistical issues in the study of temporal data: Daily experiences. *Journal of Personality, 59*, 609–62.

West, S. G., Biesanz, J., & Pitts, S. C. (2000). Causal inference and generalization in field settings: Experimental and quasi-experimental designs. In H. Reis and C. Judd (eds.), *Handbook of Research Methods in Personality and Social Psychology* (pp. 40–84). New York: Cambridge University Press.

West, S. G., Hepworth, J. T., McCall, M. A., Reich, J. W. (1989). An evaluation of Arizona's July 1982 drunk driving law: Effects on the city of Phoenix. *Journal of Applied Social Psychology, 19*, 1212–37.

Widaman, K. F. & Reise, S. P. (1997). Exploring the measurement invariance of psychological instruments: Applications in the substance use domain. In K. J. Bryant, M. Windle, & S. G. West (eds.), *The science of prevention: Methodological advances from alcohol and substance abuse research* (pp. 281–324). Washington, DC: American Psychological Association.

PART II

General Issues in Developmental Measurement

CHAPTER SIX

Measurement of Individual Difference Constructs in Child Development, or Taking Aim at Moving Targets

John E. Bates and Claire Novosad

Questions about the development of individual differences in social adaptation are of great importance in society and science, but they present researchers with commensurately great methodological challenges. Suppose one wants to determine whether level of activity is a stable characteristic from the newborn to the teenage era. Amount of time spent running might be an appropriate item to assess activity level in a toddler, but this would obviously be an inappropriate item for the newborn; and while teenagers are capable of running, they spend less time doing so than do toddlers. So the researcher has the challenge of creating measures that truly reflect activity tendency, even though the behaviors that express this trait change with development, both qualitatively and quantitatively.

There has been considerable progress in sophistication of measurement in recent decades, but we have not yet reached a point where we can be less than fully mindful of the complexities. We might wish that methodological questions were well resolved, so we could focus entirely on substantive questions. However, methodology has always been an inescapable concern in science, as reflected in the maxim, "what we know depends on how we know it." Sometimes we are blind to methodological blemishes on empirical knowledge, accepting findings that do not mean what we conventionally think they do; and sometimes, because we accept methodological fashions as requirements, we reject findings that might be empirically meaningful. An advantage in focusing on methodology, such as in the present chapter, is that it might augment the ability to critically evaluate research, and ultimately, to develop improved methods and advances in knowledge.

In this chapter, we focus on the measurement of constructs critical for understanding two kinds of social adaptation constructs – temperament and intelligence. These constructs are central in theoretical models of social development. They have been measured at multiple points in development, and have attracted interesting methodological discussion. Current theories of social development are complex and transactional (Collins et al., 2000; Wachs, 2000), so we think of both temperament and intelligence as multiply determined and as participants in a much larger team of influences in development. However, each has been conceived as both an important cause and result of individual differences in social development. The chapter does not focus on the relative merits of specific means of assessment, such as questionnaire versus observation. Each of these has advantages and disadvantages, such as the potential subjective component in the use of questionnaire measures and the difficulty in sampling sufficient numbers of situations in the use of observational measures, as recently detailed by Rothbart & Bates (1998). Instead, this chapter focuses on broader issues in measuring constructs across development, including reliability and validity, and continuity and change.

Temperament is typically defined as biologically based, early-appearing and enduring, basic traits of personality (Bates, 1989b). The concept of temperament encompasses multiple dimensions of individual differences in reactivity and self-regulation (Rothbart & Bates, 1998). Because temperament is a concept we employ to organize the study of psychological phenomena, we regard the definition of temperament as a conceptual tool rather than a fixed standard. At one time, the field tended to assume that things called temperament should appear early in infancy, to avoid the methodological complications of the effects of experience. However, it is now argued that some individual differences fitting the concept of temperament can only appear with development. For example, differences in effortful control of attention, critical in self-regulation, are only apparent with the maturation of the relevant brain systems (Rothbart, Derryberry, & Posner, 1994). Similarly, although many variations in temperament have genetic underpinnings (Goldsmith, Buss & Lemery, 1997), the genes would operate only in transaction with the environment. Nevertheless, constructs of temperament traits presuppose a relatively high level of stability.

Many of these same considerations are also true for the construct of intelligence (McCall, 1986). Intelligence in some form is present early in development, but develops in complex ways. Genetic, biological and environmental factors, and their interactions, all must be considered. While the dictionary defines intelligence as reasoning ability, knowledge, and the ability to learn, researchers are still hotly debating many aspects of the definition of intelligence. Many follow the tradition of Spearman (1904), who identified a "g-factor", an underlying general factor common to the many specific abilities associated with intelligence. At the same time, it is widely recognized that more than "g" is involved in intelligence; for example, each ability has a specific factor associated with it. Cattell was the first to propose that intelligence is composed of two fundamental factors: fluid and crystallized (McGrew & Flanagan, 1998). Fluid intelligence is the capacity to solve novel problems; crystallized intelligence is consolidated knowledge. Others have specified further differentiation in the construct, e.g., speed of decision making and visual and auditory perceptual abilities; however most IQ research is still dominated by the simpler, Spearman tradition (Neisser et al., 1996), despite strong claims for the value of a more detailed view (McGrew & Flanagan, 1998).

Basic Principles

Basic principles of assessment are important in all areas of research on individual differences, including studies of development. We will briefly summarize key principles. We have been influenced by a number of sources in the area of personality or temperament assessment, but especially by the classic text by Wiggins (1973). The most influential source in the area of intellectual assessment has been Sattler (1990). A proper review of the principles themselves could fill volumes, but here we offer merely a brief commentary on issues that come up in developmental studies of temperament and intelligence. All of the issues apply to any form of measurement, whether parental ratings, structured test, or naturalistic observation.

Initial meanings

One begins measurement development with a theoretical concept, such as the trait of fearfulness in novel situations. This individual difference concept probably began as folk observation, but eventually it became specified in more psychological detail, bringing the need for quantification. One then identifies specific behaviors, cognitions, and emotions to describe individuals on this concept in relation to other individuals. In the process of developing measures of a trait, an important early consideration is content validity, or the extent to which the item content meaningfully reflects the concept of interest. This is not usually a problem when the concepts and their situational contexts are clearly delineated. Different traits of temperament, for instance, are differentially related to incentive conditions (Rothbart & Bates, 1998). As an example, the concept of behavioral inhibition to novelty (Kagan, 1998) might be specified by behaviors theoretically indicating anxiety, fear, and distress specifically in response to unfamiliar situations, and not behaviors theoretically indicating anger, nor behaviors in familiar situations. A critical challenge for the developmental researcher is identifying core elements of constructs that might be equivalent despite maturation. Whereas behavioral inhibition tendencies might be activated by the simple approach of a stranger at the age of 18 months, at 36 months the comparable level of activation might require the stranger making a social demand of the child.

Another, related issue at this stage of developing a measure is whether the items mean the same thing to the person who is completing them – the rater, observer or examiner – that they do to the researcher who is building from theoretical concepts. This can be as simple as translating psychological ideas into language that the intended population will understand, or it may involve recognizing more fundamental gaps of experience. For example, when we were developing a measure of temperamental irritability (Bates, Freeland, & Lounsbury, 1979), we tested possible items in preliminary interviews. One item pertained to an infant becoming distressed by crib sheets that had become bunched up or wrinkled. However, this item, contributed by the mother of a difficult infant in a prior generation, drew mostly puzzled looks from mothers in the current, "fitted-sheets" generation. The situations specified in an item must be relevant in the context of the culture under study. This is an especially critical issue in testing intelligence (Neisser et al., 1996). For example, the Comprehension scale of the Wechsler Adult Intelligence Scale–Revised asks why the state requires a license before getting married. This would not likely be meaningful to a person from a country where a license was not a requirement for marriage.

Psychometrics

Assuming adequate conceptual and operational definition of key concepts, the researcher next confronts the issue of reliability of measurement. To the extent that a measure is repeatable, it bolsters confidence that the measure is what it purports to be. Reliability provides a theoretical limit for the validity of the measure, that is, its correlation with other measures of the same construct (e.g., see Meyer et al., 2001). One question is the extent to which the measure is repeatable on different occasions, or the measure's test–retest reliability. The interval between measurements is relevant here, especially if a construct is theoretically subject to rapid development. For example, consider an infant's activity level at the point of transition to walking (Goldsmith et al., 2000). A long test–retest interval might coincide with a developmental reorganization of the phenotypic behavior, and thus yield a misleadingly low estimate of reliability. Too short an interval, on the other hand, might lead to artificially high reliabilities, such as when parents can clearly remember how they rated their child's behavior and are motivated to appear consistent. Fortunately, researchers have typically avoided the periods of rapid developmental reorganization, and it appears that the 1–4-week test–retest intervals that are typically evaluated for measures of psychological constructs in adults are also workable with infants and children in the domains of temperament and intelligence (e.g., see Bates, Freeland, & Lounsbury, 1979; Slabach, Morrow, & Wachs, 1991; Sattler, 1990; Colombo, 1993). It seems likely that shorter test–retest intervals would be needed to fairly test individual constructs in periods of most rapid development, such as in early infancy, than in periods of slower reorganization of behavior patterns and abilities, such as later infancy. However, we are not aware of systematic research on this measurement issue.

Another important kind of measurement reliability is internal consistency. In the questionnaire tradition of measurement, traits are almost always measured by multiple items, inquiring about different but related aspects of a more general trait as well as asking about the same aspects in slightly different ways. This is also appropriate for other forms of measurement, such as naturalistic or structured observation (Rushton, Brainerd, & Pressley, 1983). Aggregation of similar measures of a construct takes advantage of the psychometric principle of independence or randomness of error. According to classical test theory, the statistical variance of each measure, whether a test item or an observation code, is assumed to have a "true" portion and an "error" portion. The psychometric errors are further assumed to be uncorrelated with each other, so when the measured scores are combined, the errors tend to cancel one another, and the composite score is a more accurate reflection of the true variance. Other things being equal, aggregation of a larger number of items into a trait construct will tend to yield a more reliable measure than aggregation of a smaller number of items (Rushton, Brainerd, & Pressley, 1983). However, larger numbers of items and higher internal consistency reliability may not always be advantageous in terms of the validity of a measure, or the degree to which a measure adequately taps its target construct. Little, Lindenberger, and Nesselroade (1999) showed with artificial data that when a construct domain is relatively homogeneous, a smaller number of items may constitute a more efficient (and still valid) measure than a larger number of items; and, in contrast, when the construct domain is complex, lower internal consistency due to a wider sampling of items in the construct domain can result in improved validity. A hypothetical example in the temperament domain might involve measurement of infants' distress. Distress due to feeling ignored by caregivers is conceptually different from distress due to novelty, but individual differences of the two could be correlated with one another, and thus indicate a theoretically interesting, more general negative reactivity dimension. This might mean that a measure focused on one or the other of the subdimensions would have higher internal consistency than a measure combining both kinds of item, but that the more general combination of negative emotionality items would have stronger associations with important criterion measures such as behavior problem outcomes, and thus more validity in this sense. It should also be mentioned that in modern statistics, researchers are not limited to merely assuming random error – they can actually evaluate the accuracy of this assumption by including correlations between the errors of different items in their measurement models (e.g., Bentler, 1980).

A third kind of reliability is between raters. This is not usually considered in instances where two different sources provide ratings on a questionnaire but is especially relevant when multiple observers apply the same coding system to simultaneous observations of the same stream of behavior. Intelligence-relevant behavior is more typically coded in highly structured situations, and examiners are trained to pre-existing criteria, so observer reliability is not generally an issue. In the case of observations of temperament-relevant behavior, however, whether in structured or naturalistic situations, researchers take care to train observers to segment and code the behavior in similar ways, and they present statistical indexes of the degree of similarity, such as correlations and kappa coefficients. However, the point that Little, Lindenberger, & Nesselroade (1999) made about internal consistency reliability might be extended to inter-observer reliability: one can attain excellent rater reliability by defining trivial snippets of behavior, but only achieve measures with weak conceptual meaningfulness. Stated differently, although measurement validity is dependent to some degree on measurement reliability, a highly reliable measure is not necessarily valid. This point is especially relevant when a measurement system taps a construct, such as temperament or intelligence, that evolves both quantitatively and qualitatively with age. Although reliability is an important aspect to consider in assessment, it is possible to have a very reliable tool that does not really hit its conceptual target. As will be described in more detail later, the Bayley scales of infant development are quite reliable at all ages, but assessments under one year of age have little relationship to later IQ (e.g., see Rose & Feldman, 1995), showing that they do not measure the standard construct of intelligence or its developmental antecedents. We now turn to a more formal discussion of validity.

Validity

The notion of validity is a very complex one, but validity is at the core of scientific value of psychological measurement. Research and underlying theory establish a network of meanings and expected relations among measures. Cronbach and Meehl (1955) pointed out that exploration of the network of relations and nonrelations among alternate measures of multiple constructs allows refinement of both theoretical constructs and measures. Especially for constructs of temperament, there are no fixed, "gold standard" measures. Constructs of intelligence may have well-established conventions, but even here, many questions are raised about their meanings (Neisser et al., 1996). So, the process of validating a measure is a meandering, never-ending journey. Sometimes validity is spoken of as a yes–no question, such as when it is argued that parental reports of temperament are not suitable for scientific research (e.g., Kagan, 1998), but others view it more as a multilayered and comparative question (e.g., see Bates, 1994; Mangelsdorf, Schoppe & Buur, 2000; Rothbart & Bates, 1998). A measure may be judged useful or not, depending on the particular objectives of the research; however, this judgment can rarely be a simple one. A number of standard questions are asked about the validity of measures. We will list some of the most relevant of these.

Convergence between related constructs   One question is whether one measure of a construct correlates with another. For example, the temperament construct of difficultness as measured by the Infant Characteristics Questionnaire (ICQ; Bates, Freeland, & Lounsbury, 1979) has shown moderate correlations with other parent-report measures of negative emotionality (e.g., Bates, Freeland, & Lounsbury, 1979; Lemery et al., 1999). In the Lemery et al. (1999) study, the ICQ Fussy-Difficult scale correlated at age 12 months 0.54 with the Infant Behavior Questionnaire (Rothbart, 1981) Distress to Limitations scale and 0.58 with the Toddler Temperament Scale (Fullard, McDevitt, & Carey, 1984) Mood scale. In this example, the correlations all involve convergence between measures using the same method of measurement: all are questionnaires completed by the parent.

A more stringent test of convergent validity would come from comparing measures of a construct using different methods. For example, parental ratings on questionnaires of temperament (or intelligence) constructs would be expected to reflect not simply the theoretical, "true" characteristics of the child, but also characteristics of the parent that might color their perceptions of the child, such as social desirability response set or a generally negative outlook on their experiences (Bates, 1980). Variance in any rating would have subjective, objective, and psychometric error components. To evaluate "method variance," therefore, researchers consider relations between measures from different sources, such as between the ICQ difficultness measure and observational measures, such as frequency of crying (Bates, Freeland, & Lounsbury, 1979; Bates & Bayles, 1984; Goldsmith, Rieser-Danner, & Briggs, 1991) and aversive acoustic qualities of infants' cry sounds (Lounsbury & Bates, 1982). When the convergence between such different measures is greater than would be expected by chance, this provides support for the validity of both kinds of measure. Studies of convergence between questionnaire and observational measures of temperament typically yield validity correlations that are lower than those between a mother and father completing the same questionnaire measure. However, these cross-method correlations are not typically smaller than those between the parent reports and parental characteristics that might be expected to bias the reports, such as social desirability response set (Bates & Bayles, 1984). Thus, the "subjective" component of the parent report of temperament is not larger than the "objective" component. Interestingly, we found that parent ratings of their infants' and toddlers' language development had both a strong objective component, relating to standardized tests of intellectual development and observer ratings of child communication competence, and also a subjective component, relating to mother characteristics such as social desirability in the same way that parent reports of temperament did (Bates & Bayles, 1984).

The validity of most of the widely used intelligent tests has been established by comparisons with each other and with measures one would expect to be related to intelligence. For example, the Stanford-Binet Intelligence Scale and the Wechsler Intelligence Scale for Children–Revised have been shown to correlate highly (Sattler, 1990). These tests have also been found to be related to academic performance. In elementary school IQ correlates about 0.60–0.70 with grades, and also with other indicators related to academic performance, such as dropout rates (Jensen, 1998; Neisser et al., 1996).

Questions about the validity of measures from alternative sources of information are being explored with increasingly sophisticated statistical designs, especially in studies of developmental psychopathology. For example, Fergusson and Horwood (1993) used confirmatory factor analysis to evaluate stability from age 8 to age 12 in constructs of conduct problems, attention problems, and anxiety problems, simultaneously modeling the ratings of teachers, mothers, and the children themselves. The latent factors' stabilities were very high, ranging from 0.82 to 0.98. Keiley et al. (2000) used latent growth curve analysis. This showed that teachers' and mothers' convergence on the trajectory, or rate of change of children's internalizing symptoms across eight years of development, was 0.45 ($p < 0.01$), which was greater than their convergence on the true intercept (the starting value based on the eight-years' data, 0.28, $p < 0.01$). Such designs are applicable to developmentally informative measurement of many other kinds of traits.

Divergence between different constructs   Finding a lower relationship between measures of conceptually different constructs than between measures of the same concept provides support for the discriminant validity of the measures. For example, Goldsmith, Rieser-Danner and Briggs (1991) found that negative emotionality scales from different – mother and daycare teacher – temperament questionnaires for infants, toddlers, and preschoolers tended to correlate more strongly with one another than with distress to novelty temperament scales, and vice versa. This kind of result suggests that the questionnaires are measuring a differentiated set of behavioral qualities, rather than some globally perceived lump, such as "good versus bad" (Bates, 1994). There are similar findings of discriminant validity in intelligence measures. For example, as reviewed by Neisser et al. (1996), speed of comparing line lengths correlates more strongly with performance IQ tests, and speed of comparing words correlates more strongly with verbal IQ (see McGrew & Flanagan, 1998, for similar examples).

Predictive validity From the perspective of developmental science, a critical aspect of the validity of a trait measure is its ability to forecast future characteristics of the child, whether on the same construct or on theoretically related, newly developing constructs. Our temperament research has been strongly focused on questions of prediction of individual differences in children's adjustment. We have noted, for example, tendencies for early fear of novelty to be associated more strongly with the conceptually similar later anxiety problems than with the conceptually different externalizing behavior problems. In contrast, an early tendency to be resistant to control was more strongly associated with later externalizing problems than with the conceptually different anxiety problems (Bates, 1989a). This differential linkage pattern has been confirmed by other researchers more often than not (Caspi, 1998; Goldsmith et al., 2000; Rothbart & Bates, 1998).

One of the first assessments of intelligence in infants was the Bayley Scales of Infant Development, which yields scores of mental and motor development. As previously mentioned, the correlations found between the Bayley mental scores and later measures of IQ are small, and approach zero as the time between tests increases (e.g., McCall, 1986). Infants do vary on time of acquisition of the developmental milestones measured by the Bayley scales, but this variance is probably caused by many factors other than just intelligence, such as qualities of temperament and environment. These findings suggested that "intelligence" as indexed by scales like the Bayley may not be continuous from preverbal infancy to later ages (DiLalla et al., 1990; Laucht, Esser, & Schmidt, 1994; Rose & Feldman, 1990). Interestingly, however, findings using the visual habituation paradigm show more convincing continuity in intellectual performance between infancy and childhood. The visual habituation paradigm measures rates of decline in time looking at the same stimulus and increases in time looking at a novel stimulus. Such measures in infancy have been found to be correlated with later measures of intelligence in numerous studies (Colombo, 1993; Colombo & Mitchell, 1990; DiLalla et al., 1990; Laucht, Esser, & Schmidt, 1994; Rose & Feldman, 1990, 1995). These findings have led many to believe that the duration of fixation may measure some basic component of intelligence, such as speed of processing (Neisser et al., 1996; Rose & Feldman, 1995).

The topic of predictive validity could be addressed at much greater length, but here we use it as an opening to the question that will occupy the rest of this chapter – measurement of continuity and change across development.

Psychological Measurement in a Developmental Context

Continuity and change are the key concepts in developmental science, and, therefore, theoretical and empirical description of these concepts is vital to the field (e.g., Overton, 1998). As Lewis and Starr said in 1979, "At its most basic level, the problem of development is finding order in change, identifying continuities in behavioral systems that are rapidly transforming and reorganizing" (p. 653). We are particularly interested in continuity and change in individual difference constructs.

Describing continuity

In a conceptual typology used by many subsequent authors, Kagan (1971) spoke of two kinds of continuity. Homotypic continuity is stability of individual differences in the same or similar traits across development, e.g., verbal intelligence. This is the emphasis of most of the work relevant to the present chapter. Heterotypic continuity is inferred from correlations between traits that differ on the surface, but have theoretically based, conceptually meaningful links between early and later manifestations of the underlying trait. For example, the correlation between difficult temperament in infancy and aggressive behavior problems (Bates, 1989a) probably reflects, in part, the continuity of a reactive, negative emotionality.

Homotypic continuity Caspi (1998) listed the following specific ways in which homotypic continuity can be seen.

DIFFERENTIAL CONTINUITY

Typically referred to as rank-order continuity or stability, differential continuity is simply a tendency for someone high on a trait at one point in development to remain high relative to others at later points, and vice versa for someone low on the trait. This is the kind of homotypic continuity that is most frequently considered in studies of development. For example, intelligence test scores show relatively high levels of rank-order stability at least when measured past infancy (Sattler, 1990; Colombo, 1993). Temperament and personality measures also show this kind of stability, but not to quite as high a degree as intelligence measures (Caspi, 1998). Temperament is, according to most definitions, present early in life, prior to the influences of experience. Researchers have wished to measure it as early as possible, at least in the earlier years of the study of temperament, in hopes of minimizing the conceptually confounding effects of experience. It is theoretically unlikely, however, that temperament phenotypes, the patterns of behavior that can be observed, are ever fully independent of environmental factors, even in early infancy (Rothbart & Bates, 1998). And, as a general rule, temperament measures in early infancy are found to be less stable than in later infancy and beyond (Caspi, 1998; Goldsmith et al., 2000). For example, Lemery et al. (1999) found that a scale representing fearfulness via multiple scales was correlated 0.42 from age 3 to 12 months, 0.58 from 12 to 24 months, and 0.70 from 24 to 36 months. Interestingly, level of continuity of temperament is itself a trait that has shown genetic heritability (DiLalla & Jones, 2000).

ABSOLUTE CONTINUITY

Absolute continuity is typically measured in terms of group averages, and it is the extent to which individuals (or groups) tend to maintain the same level of a given trait. For example, one could ask if infants' levels of expression of distress decrease over time or stay stable. If one operationally defines "distress" as crying, one would expect distress to be expressed less frequently at 8 months of age than at 6 weeks of age

(St. James-Roberts, 1989; Barr et al., 1989). However, it is unlikely that crying means the same thing across these early months, or that it is by itself a sufficient definition of a temperament trait. A key problem is that development often requires adjustments in the specific contents of the measures of traits, and, as Caspi (1998) noted, "Absolute continuity has no meaning if the 'same' attribute actually refers to different phenotypic expressions of a personality variable" (p. 348). Even when measuring something that is seemingly simple, developmental changes may contribute to differences in performance. For example, reaction time is a measure that has been found to be related to IQ, perhaps due to the underlying trait of speed of processing (Neisser et al., 1996). Anderson and colleagues (1997) assessed reaction time in children aged 7 and 11, and found a developmental progression toward shorter reaction times. However, they concluded that this change was not necessarily due to real changes in speed of processing, but rather due to an unrelated factor, response selection.

STRUCTURAL CONTINUITY

Structural continuity concerns degree of constancy in the operational definition of a trait over time. To the extent that an operational definition remains the same, such as when the same items are used in a scale at different ages, findings of rank-order or absolute stability are more meaningful. If one uses factor analysis of multiple items to create a definition of a particular trait, one may be interested in whether the same items produce similar factors at different points in development. For example, in the Bloomington Longitudinal Study, exploratory factor analyses showed that the difficult temperament factor of the 13-month form of the ICQ (Pettit & Bates, 1984) was similar to, but not exactly the same as, that for the 24-month form (Lee & Bates, 1985). Pedlow et al. (1993) showed that several of their temperament scales were factorially equivalent across infancy to middle childhood.

We attempted to measure temperamental difficultness from about age 6 months to 24 months, a span of time in which there is considerable development of the child's behavioral and emotional repertoire. We wanted to keep the measures as similar as possible for the sake of conceptual comparability, but we also wanted to adjust measures according to the children's age. Lacking precise information about how temperament would be expressed differently at different ages, we made minor alterations in our questionnaire contents based on observations and interviews with parents, adding in items responding to the major change in mobility and self-directedness that occurred with onset of walking around 13 months of age. We then evaluated the interrelations of the items via factor analyses at the different ages, adjusting scale definitions according to the changing factors. This work was done prior to the general availability of confirmatory factor analysis, but our exploratory factor analyses served the purpose. Items that consistently define our construct of difficultness at different ages included daily frequency of irritable/fussy behavior, how much cry/fuss in general, how changeable mood is, and the overall degree of difficulty for a parent. On the other hand, items pertaining to how much attention was required other than for caregiving and how well the infant or toddler played by him- or herself were more strongly associated at the earlier stages of development than at 24 months of age, where this kind of item formed a factor separate from the difficultness factor. It appears that expressions of negative emotionality stemming from a need for parental attention and stimulation become less associated with general negative emotionality as toddlers gain more control over their own levels of stimulation, as a result of their expanded motor and symbolic abilities. Those 13-month-olds who are dependent on their caregivers for stimulation tend to be the same ones who are crying and fussing frequently and perceived as difficult, but those 24-month-olds who are dependent in this way are not necessarily the ones who are negatively emotional in general. We cannot be certain that the 13- and 24-month difficultness factors are structurally equivalent, but even with the content differences, there are still substantial similarities between the factor loadings. In addition, the longitudinal correlation between unweighted composite scores was 0.71 (Lee & Bates, 1985), which provides further support for the assumption of structural continuity.

A historically important example of structural change in measurement in the intelligence domain concerns the span from infancy to early preschool era. As previously mentioned, for a number of years, many thought that intelligence was not continuous from infancy to later childhood, based partially on the lack of significant relationships between such infant assessments as the Bayley or the Gesell and later IQ. However, another reason for the assumption of discontinuity was that the factor structure of the items making up these tests was found to be different at different ages (McCall, Eichorn, & Hogarty, 1977; Reznick, Corley, & Robinson, 1997; Gardner & Clark, 1992). McCall and colleagues (1977), for example, performed a principal components analysis of the items making up the precursor to the Bayley Scales of Infant Development, and found changes in the composition of the principal components at 2, 8, 13, 21, and 30–36 months. They concluded that these changes reflected the development of the cognitive system, from a very subjective understanding of the world to the emergence of ability to form symbolic relationships.

IPSATIVE CONTINUITY

Ipsative continuity concerns stability of a constellation of traits within an individual. For example, does a particular individual stay the same in having a higher level of positive emotionality than negative emotionality? Interest is currently growing in person-centered approaches to describing temperament and personality in development, although it is not a new way of looking at personality. Allport (1937), for example, recommended that personality researchers use idiographic approaches along with the nomothetic ones that dominate the present chapter and most of the research in the field. A study by Caspi et al. (2003) takes an idiographic approach in considering personality predictors, and shows that temperament profiles in early childhood predict a large number of personality and adjustment variables in adolescence and early adulthood. For example, the group with an undercontrolled pattern at age 3 years showed a lower average score on the agreeableness scale at age 26 than the other age three groups, including well-adjusted, confident, reserved, and inhibited (see also Caspi, 2000). However, although this kind of analysis shows that the constructs underlying the early typology are related to later dimensions of personality, it does not establish whether there is continuity of the profile or typology itself. In one relevant study, Asendorpf et al. (2000), showed that a set of three personality prototype patterns – resilient, undercontrolled and overcontrolled – showed stability in classification across a 6-month period in adults. We have found mentions of ipsative or within-individual analysis of intelligence test data in clinical contexts. According to McGrew and Flanagan (1998), there is little empirical support for such analyses using subscale scores from tests such as the Wechsler, but there may be more hope of finding validity for ipsative approaches using a broader spectrum of scales from multiple test batteries.

Heterotypic continuity The basic idea in the notion of heterotypic continuity is that an earlier characteristic predicts a different, but theoretically similar, developmentally appropriate manifestation of the earlier characteristic (Sroufe, 1979). For example, we have found that early unmanageability, measured by the mother-reported ICQ scale of Resistance to Control in early childhood, predicts children's tendency to show externalizing behavior problems as assessed by teacher- or mother-reported Achenbach (1991a,b) scales (Bates et al., 1998). Externalizing behavior problems are not the same thing as temperamental resistance to control, but there is a clear, conceptual coherence between a child's unresponsiveness to parental prohibitions in toddlerhood and oppositional and aggressive tendencies in middle childhood. A second example is the finding of Kochanska, Murray and Harlan (2000) that tendency to focus attention on a set of soft blocks at age 9 months predicted the temperament construct of effortful control (self-regulation) at age 22 months. In the area of intelligence, Sigman and associates (1997) found that infants' visual fixation durations predicted intelligence in 18-year-olds, and that this continuity was moderated by how verbally stimulating their caregivers were. Infants who were "short lookers" ended up with higher IQs, but this depended on having high levels of verbal stimulation available. Again, visual fixation durations in infancy are not the same thing as intelligence, but there is a logical coherence between the two measures in that infants who were quick to process novel stimuli were found to be more intelligent as young adults.

As Caspi (1998) points out, "the investigator who claims to have discovered coherence must have a theory – no matter how rudimentary or implicit – that specifies the 'genotype' or provides the basis on which the diverse behaviors and attributes can be said to belong to the same equivalence class" (p. 350). In the case of the resistance-externalizing link, our preferred theory at the moment is that the core, underlying traits concern motivation and self-regulation, and that these interact with qualities of the discipline environment in producing behavioral adjustment. Bates et al. (1998) showed, for example, that among temperamentally resistant children, those with relatively noncontrolling mothers were more likely to show later behavior problems than were those with controlling mothers. That is, the continuity was evident especially where an environmental counter-force was absent. In addition, although temperamentally non-resistant children with noncontrolling mothers came to show uniformly low levels of externalizing behavior, similarly nonresistant children with highly controlling mothers sometimes came to show higher levels of externalizing behavior than would have been predicted by their nonresistant temperament alone. In short, the adjustment implications of children's temperament depended on the kind of discipline environment they experienced.

Another moderated linkage between temperament and social adjustment is provided by Kochanska (1997): temperamentally fearful children (as assessed in a laboratory task) were more advanced in signs of conscience, or internalized self-control, when their mothers practiced gentle forms of discipline rather than harsh. In contrast, fearless children's conscience development depended on warm, positive forms of relationship with the mother rather than on the absence of harsh control. The examples of temperament–environment interaction in social development illustrate an important principle: continuity of traits is not to be taken for granted.

Continuity is not an automatic process, but rather it requires that things happen in development (Bates et al., 1998; Caspi, 1998). Even if we think of temperament or intelligence as based in genes, the traits would not simply unfold throughout life, but would actively be constructed, in a dynamic, nondeterministic way (Gottlieb, 1995), through myriad transactions between the child and environment. As Caspi (1998) points out, continuity can be due to continuity of environmental characteristics, such as intellectual stimulation, gentle discipline, etc. as well as to genes that incline the individual toward stability, such as temperamental proclivities toward certain emotional and attentional reactions to common situations. Caspi emphasizes that these processes combine in the form of (a) reactive person–environment transaction, such as when a child has acquired a bias toward interpreting ambiguous actions of peers as having hostile intent (Dodge, Bates, & Pettit, 1990), (b) evocative person–environment transactions, such as when a resistant child's tendencies evoke negative reinforcement for coercive behavior (Patterson, Reid, & Dishion, 1992), or (c) proactive person–environment transactions, such as when a verbally adept child goes to the library. Describing continuity process is a challenging task for science. Psychometric measurement and theoretical advances will need to proceed together.

Describing change

Of course, the notion of change was tacitly part of the preceding section on describing continuity. However, increasingly researchers have emphasized that change deserves special attention. We need to think about specific kinds of change, and, just as for continuity, about the processes giving rise to change. Caspi's (1998) discussion of these issues is the most probing and comprehensive we have seen. Following Caspi's analysis, one type of change is essentially due to unsolved methodological problems. If a measure is psychometrically unreliable, a researcher might obtain a misleadingly low cross-age stability correlation on the measure, and mistakenly infer that the low correlation reflects meaningful shifts in individuals' rank orders. A researcher might use the same items at two times separated by a developmental period in which the meaning of the items with respect to the underlying trait has changed. For example, the meaning of crying might change from early infancy to preschool age. In a related way, since the meaning of any behavior depends on its situational context, a researcher might measure behavior in different contexts at different ages, such as measuring the child's negative emotionality in situations that are very challenging for a 1-year-old, but not for a 4-year-old. Finally, a researcher might measure a trait, such as negative emotionality, that shifts at the point of a developmental transition, such as puberty, but measuring this trait at the same age for all children might produce changes in rank orders that would not be observed if the measurements were timed with puberty itself, which, of course, arrives at different ages (Caspi, 1998; Magnusson, 1988).

Modern statistical techniques, such as growth curve models within structural equations, have begun to make it possible to separate change due to methodology from more theoretically meaningful change. For example, Keiley et al. (2000) used a growth curve analysis to chart adjustment trajectories across from kindergarten to 7th grade for both externalizing and internalizing behavior as reported by both teachers and mothers. Among many relevant findings, Keiley et al. showed that, overall, children decreased over time in externalizing behavior problems as rated by their mothers, an effect that was amplified by children's status as being accepted by their peers or not, whereas children very slightly increased in externalizing problems rated by their teachers, an effect that was amplified by children being male as opposed to female. Moffitt et al. (1993) carefully evaluated measurement artifacts in changes they observed in children's IQ from age 7 to 13. It is well known that IQ scores are highly reliable and show stability from one age to another. However, Moffitt et al. pointed out that it was not known how reliable a cross-time *pattern* of IQ scores is – to what extent are individuals' trajectories of IQ reliably measured? Moffitt et al. evaluated the reliability of IQ profiles across ages by comparing two alternate four-scale short-forms of the WISC-R They concluded that, in most cases, changes in IQ represented unreliability of measurement. For 13 percent of their sample, the changes were larger than expected on the basis of chance, which might reflect meaningful changes. However, despite considering a large number of possible predictors of change in these cases, they were unable to specify general factors accounting for the change profiles. Case analysis did allow idiosyncratic explanations, such as one child increasing in IQ in a period of family stability and another decreasing due to trauma.

Assuming that the methodological artifacts can be ruled out, some instances of change, then, can be considered meaningful. Caspi (1998), discussed ways in which changes in trajectories might occur due to relatively discrete transitions or turning points, such as encountering an inspiring teacher or marrying a supportive spouse. The methodological challenge, however, is to empirically account for the effects of such occurrences. It is quite possible that individuals' pre-existing characteristics alter the effects of a given experience. One especially relevant example is the Asendorpf (1994) study of behavioral inhibition from age 4 to age 10 years. Children's initial stranger inhibition scores were largely uncorrelated with their intelligence test scores, but their slopes of stranger inhibition were predicted by their intelligence ($r = -0.29$, $p < 0.05$). Brighter children showed a sharper decrease in fear. Thus, over development, brighter children were more able to modulate their fearfulness.

Statistical modeling of continuity and change

What is called for, then, is not simply ruling out methodological artifacts, but rather describing, both empirically and theoretically, the process by which the continuity or change has occurred. An especially impressive effort to do this in the area of temperament is the study of Lemery et al. (1999). Lemery et al. measured multiple constructs of temperament, with mother reports on several questionnaires at ages 3–48 months. Through a thoughtful and complex process of standardizing the different measures, they created composites measuring positive emotionality, distress-anger, fear, and activity level. Then they evaluated in structural equations several alternative models of how the observed continuities and discontinuities in temperament scores might have occurred. The alternative models were, in essence, the autoregressive simplex model – which posits that stability from time 1 to time 3 is mediated through stability between time 1 and time 2 – and the common factor model – which posits that stability is a reflection of an underlying source affecting all measurement occasions. In other words, the autoregressive simplex model would explain a pattern in which an early level on a trait forecasts later levels more accurately when the time interval is short rather than long, and the common factor model would explain a pattern in which length of interval does not make much difference in strength of prediction. By using structural equations, Lemery et al. were able to control statistically for measurement unreliability. They found that in infancy, a period that is theoretically one of rapid development, the cross-age data (ages 3, 6, 12, and 18 months) for all temperament dimensions could be well explained by the autoregressive simplex model; that is, the model in which all continuity is mediated through intermediate characteristics. However, in addition, for the composites of distress-anger, fear, and activity level, an alternate version of the autoregressive simplex model, in which there was an additional component of continuing influence from the age 3 months measure, also fit the data. For the toddler to preschool data (ages 24, 36, and 48 months), the common factor model fit better for all temperament dimensions than the autoregressive simplex model. The findings of Lemery et al. (1999) suggest that, despite substantial degrees of stability from one time to another, individual differences in temperament are changing, to some degree, throughout infancy. Perhaps this occurs as a result of the many and relatively rapid neurological and psychological developments that occur in this period (Rothbart & Bates, 1998), such as maturation of the anterior attentional system, allowing more flexible, autonomous control of attention, which might affect an infant's ability to regulate emotional distress. The Lemery et al. (1999) findings also suggest that after infancy, stability of temperament dimensions is the main story, rather than change.

The Lemery et al. (1999) study is a model of the kind of work that can now be done in developing measures that work in developmental research. It attends to the basic validity of constructs, evaluating multiple measures simultaneously. It measures constructs longitudinally. And it goes beyond the simple examination of stability correlations to consider in statistical detail multiple, alternative models of possible ways in which the patterns of continuity might have occurred, controlling for key measurement issues of scaling and psychometric error. Such analysis provides an excellent basis for building theory and designing studies to further detail the processes involved in social development. Of course, there is much more to be done, and indeed, that is currently being done. For example, one might wonder about differential or divergent continuity; that is, cross-dimensional relations across time. One might also wonder about possible differences in developmental processes of continuity versus change as revealed by different kinds of measurement, including in addition to the parent report measures, structured laboratory and naturalistic observation measures. Goldsmith and his colleagues are, in fact, engaged in a number of such efforts to advance the measurement of temperament constructs. Goldsmith et al. (2000) provide a valuable review of some of these efforts, including work on the roles of genes in accounting for individual differences in temperament traits as well as in correlations between different temperament traits and in continuity versus change in temperament.

Conclusion

In this brief review we have given some examples of how basic principles of assessment, including reliability and validity, are important in measurement of development. For illustrations, the chapter has focused on the constructs of temperament and intelligence, but the general points about psychometrics would apply to any construct and any form of measurement. Validity is ultimately the most important of the psychometric concepts, and the most complex, especially when considered in a developmental context. The challenge is in finding measures that allow for meaningful description of continuity and change. For both temperament and intelligence concepts, the most interesting scientific questions concern how individuals might maintain a level of continuity on a trait, while at the same time their behavioral, emotional, and cognitive repertoires change radically over the years of development. In the case of temperament, research has moved beyond merely identifying age-appropriate equivalent situations and behaviors to the beginnings of detailed, statistical models of the continuity-change process that take into account traits measured longitudinally and theoretically important, potential factors in development, such as parent–child interactions and genes. In the case of intelligence, we noted major progress in moving beyond the observation that "baby IQ" tests are poor predictors of childhood IQ to discovery of a theoretical component, measurable in infancy, which does predict later IQ – speed of information processing. Although we can sometimes measure continuity of traits in ways that are conceptually straightforward, sometimes our aim needs to be away from the center of the target.

References

Achenbach, T. M. (1991a). *Manual for the Child Behavior Checklist/4-18 and 1991 Profile.* Burlington, VT: University of Vermont, Dept. of Psychiatry.
Achenbach, T. M. (1991b). *Manual for the Teacher's Report Form and 1991 Profile.* Burlington, VT: University of Vermont, Dept. of Psychiatry.
Allport, G. W. (1937). *Personality: A psychological interpretation.* New York: Holt.
Anderson, M., Nettelbeck, T., & Barlow, J. (1997). Reaction time measures of speed of processing: speed of response selection increases with age, but speed of stimulus categorization does not. *British Journal of Developmental Psychology, 15,* 145–57.
Asendorpf, J. B. (1994). The malleability of behavioral inhibition: A study of individual developmental functions. *Developmental Psychology, 30,* 912–19.
Asendorpf, J. B., Borkenau, P., Ostendorf, F., & van Aken, M. A. G. (2000). Carving personality description at its joints: Confirmation of three replicable personality prototypes for both children

and adults. Presented at 1st Expert Workshop on Personality Psychology, Ghent, Belgium, November.

Barr, R., Kramer, M., Pless, I. B., Boisjoly, C., & Leduc, D. (1989). Feeding and temperament as determinants of early infant crying/fussing behavior. *Pediatrics*, *84*(3), 514–21.

Bates, J. E. (1980). The concept of difficult temperament. *Merrill-Palmer Quarterly*, *26*, 299–319.

Bates, J. E. (1989a). Applications of temperament concepts. In G. A. Kohnstamm, J. E. Bates, & M. K. Rothbart (eds.), *Temperament in childhood* (pp. 321–55). Chichester: John Wiley.

Bates, J. E. (1989b). Concepts and measures of temperament. In G. A. Kohnstamm, J. E. Bates, & M. K. Rothbart (eds.), *Temperament in childhood* (pp. 3–26). Chichester: Wiley.

Bates, J. E. (1994). Parents as scientific observers of their children's development. In S. L. Friedman & H. C. Haywood (eds.), *Developmental follow-up: Concepts, genres, domains, and methods* (pp. 197–216). New York: Academic Press.

Bates, J. E. & Bayles, K. (1984). Objective and subjective components in mothers' perceptions of their children from age 6 months to 3 years. *Merrill-Palmer Quarterly*, *30*, 111–30.

Bates, J. E., Freeland, C. B., & Lounsbury, M. L. (1979). Measurement of infant difficultness. *Child Development*, *50*, 794–803.

Bates, J. E., Pettit, G. S., Dodge, K. A., & Ridge, B. (1998). The interaction of temperamental resistance to control and restrictive parenting in the development of externalizing behavior. *Developmental Psychology*, *34*, 982–95.

Bentler, P. M. (1980). Multivariate analysis with latent variables: Causal modeling. *Annual Review of Psychology*, *31*, 419–56.

Caspi, A. (1998). Personality development across the life course. In W. Damon (ed.-in-chief) & N. Eisenberg (vol. ed.), *Handbook of child psychology*, vol. 3: *Social, emotional and personality development* (5th edn., pp. 311–88). New York: John Wiley.

Caspi, A. (2000). The child is father of the man: Personality continuities from childhood to adulthood. *Journal of Personality and Social Psychology*, *78*, 158–72.

Caspi, A., Harrington, H. L., Milne, B., Amell, J. W., Theodore, R. F., & Moffitt, T. E. (2003). Children's behavioral styles at age 3 are linked to their adult personality traits at age 26. *Journal of Personality*, *71*(4), 495–514.

Collins, A., Maccoby, E. E., Steinberg, L., Hetherington, E. M., & Bornnstein, M. H. (2000). Contemporary research on parenting: The case for nature and nurture. *American Psychologist*, *55*, 218–32.

Colombo, J. (1993). *Infant cognition: Predicting later intellectual functioning* (vol. 5). Newbury Park, CA: Sage.

Colombo, J. & Mitchell, D. W. (1990). Individual differences in early visual attention: fixation time and information processing. In J. Colombo & J. Fagen (eds.), *Individual differences in infancy: Reliability, stability and prediction* (pp. 193–227). Hillsdale, NJ: Lawrence Erlbaum Associates.

Cronbach, L. J. & Meehl, P. E. (1955). Construct validity in psychological tests. *Psychological Bulletin*, *52*, 281–302.

DiLalla, L. F. & Jones, S. (2000). Genetic and environmental influences on temperament in preschoolers. In V. J. Molfese & D. L. Molfese (eds.), *Temperament and personality development across the life span* (pp. 33–55). Mahwah, NJ: Lawrence Erlbaum Associates.

DiLalla, L., Plomin, R., Fagan, J. F., Thompson, L. A., Phillips, K., Haith, M., Cyphers, L. H., & Fulker, D. W. (1990). Infant predictors of preschool and adult IQ: A study of infant twins and their parents. *Developmental Psychology*, *26*(5), 759–69.

Dodge, K. A., Bates, J. E., & Pettit, G. S. (1990). Mechanisms in the cycle of violence. *Science*, *250*, 1678–83.

Fergusson, D. M., & Horwood, L. J. (1993). The structure, stability and correlations of the trait components of conduct disorder, attention deficit and anxiety/withdrawal reports. *Journal of Child Psychology and Psychiatry*, *34*, 749–66.

Fullard, W., McDevitt, S. C., & Carey, W. B. (1984). Assessing temperament in one- to three-year-old children. *Journal of Pediatric Psychology*, *9*, 205–17.

Gardner, M. & Clark, E. (1992). The psychometric perspective on intellectual development in childhood and adolescence. In R. Sternberg & C. Berg (eds.), *Intellectual Development* (pp. 16–43). New York: Cambridge University Press.

Goldsmith, H. H., Buss, K. A., & Lemery, K. S. (1997). Toddler and childhood temperament: Expanded content, stronger genetic evidence, new evidence for the importance of environment. *Developmental Psychology*, *33*, 891–905.

Goldsmith, H. H., Rieser-Danner, L. A., & Briggs, S. (1991). Evaluating convergent and discriminant validity of temperament questionnaires for preschoolers, toddlers, and infants. *Developmental Psychology*, *27*, 566–79.

Goldsmith, H. H., Lemery, K. S., Askan, N., & Buss, K. A. (2000). Temperament substrates of personality development. In V. J. Molfese & D. L. Molfese (eds.), *Temperament and personality development across the life span* (pp. 1–32). Mahwah, NJ: Lawrence Erlbaum Associates.

Gottlieb, G. (1995). Some conceptual deficiencies in "developmental" behavior genetics. *Human Development*, *38*, 131–41.

Jensen, A. R. (1998). *The "g" factor: The science of mental ability*. Westport, CT: Praeger.

Kagan, J. (1971). *Change and continuity in infancy*. New York: John Wiley.

Kagan, J. (1998). Biology and the child. In W. Damon (series ed.) & N. Eisenberg (vol. ed.), *Handbook of child psychology*, vol. 3: *Social, emotional, and personality development* (pp. 177–235). New York: John Wiley.

Keiley, M. K., Bates, J. E., Dodge, K. A., & Pettit, G. A. (2000). A cross-domain growth analysis: Externalizing and internalizing behaviors during 8 years of childhood. *Journal of Abnormal Child Psychology*, *28*, 161–79.

Kochanska, G. (1997). Multiple pathways to conscience for children with different temperaments: From toddlerhood to age 5. *Developmental Psychology*, *33*, 228–40.

Kochanska, G., Murray, K. T., & Harlan, E. T. (2000). Effortful control in early childhood: Continuity and change, antecedents and implications for social development. *Developmental Psychology*, *36*, 220–32.

Laucht, M., Esser, G., & Schmidt, M. (1994). Contrasting infant predictors of later cognitive functioning. *Journal of Child Psychology and Psychiatry*, *35(4)*, 649–62.

Lee, C. L., & Bates, J. E. (1985). Mother–child interaction at age two years and perceived difficult temperament. *Child Development*, *56*, 1314–25.

Lemery, K. S., Goldsmith, H. H., Klinnert, M. D., & Mrazek, D. A. (1999). Developmental models of infant and childhood temperament. *Developmental Psychology*, *35*, 189–204.

Lewis, M. & Starr, M. D. (1979). Developmental continuity. In J. D. Osofsky (ed.), *Handbook of infant development* (pp. 653–70). New York: John Wiley.

Little, T. D., Lindenberger, U., & Nesselroade, J. R. (1999). On selecting indicators for multivariate measurement and modeling with latent variables: When "good" indicators are bad and "bad" indicators are good. *Psychological Methods*, *4*, 192–211.

Lounsbury, M. L. & Bates, J. E. (1982). The cries of infants of differing levels of perceived temperamental difficultness: Acoustic properties and effects on listeners. *Child Development*, *53*, 677–86.

Magnusson, D. (1988). *Individual development from an interactional perspective: A longitudinal study*. Hillsdale, NJ: Lawrence Erlbaum Associates.

Mangelsdorf, S. C., Schoppe, S. J., & Buur, H. (2000). The meaning of parental reports: A contextual approach to the study of temperament and behavior problems in childhood. In V. J. Molfese & D. L. Molfese (eds.), *Temperament and personality development across the life span* (pp. 121–40). Mahwah, NJ: Lawrence Erlbaum Associates.

McCall, R. (1986). Issues of stability and continuity in temperament research. In R. Plomin & J. Dunn (eds.), *The study of temperament: Changes, continuities and challenges.* (pp. 13–25). Hillsdale, NJ: Lawrence Erlbaum Associates.

McCall, R. B., Eichorn, D. H., & Hogarty, P. S. (1977). Developmental changes in mental performance. *Monographs of the Society for Research in Child Development, 38* (serial no. 171).

McGrew, K. S. & Flanagan, D. P. (1998). *The intelligence test desk reference (ITDR): Gf-Gc cross-battery assessment.* Boston, MA: Allyn & Bacon.

Meyer, G. J., Finn, S. E., Eyde, L. D., Kay, G. G., Moreland, K. L., Dies, R. R., Eisman, E. J., Kubiszyn, T. W., & Reed, G. M. (2001). Psychological testing and psychological assessment: A review of the evidence and issues. *American Psychologist, 56(2)*, 128–65.

Moffitt, T. E., Caspi, A., Harkness, A. R., & Silva, P. A. (1993). The natural history of change in intellectual performance: Who changes? How much? Is it meaningful? *Journal of Child Psychology and Psychiatry, 34*, 455–506.

Neisser, U., Boodoo, G., Bouchard, T. J. Jr., Boykin, A. W., Brody, N., Ceci, S., Halpern, D. F., Loehlin, J. C., Perloff, R., Sternberg, R. J., Urbina, S. (1996). Intelligence: Knowns and unknowns. *American Psychologist, 51*, 77–101.

Overton, W. F. (1998). Developmental psychology: Philosophy, concepts, and methodology. In W. Damon (series ed.) & R. M. Lerner (vol. ed.), *Handbook of child psychology*, vol. 1: *Theoretical models of human development* (pp. 107–188). New York: John Wiley.

Patterson, G. R., Reid, J. B., & Dishion, T. J. (1992). *Antisocial boys.* Eugene, OR: Castalia.

Pedlow, R., Sanson, A., Prior, M., & Oberklaid, F. (1993). Stability of maternally reported temperament from infancy to 8 years. *Developmental Psychology, 29*, 998–1007.

Pettit, G. S. & Bates, J. E. (1984). Continuity of individual differences in the mother–infant relationship from 6 to 13 months. *Child Development, 55*, 729–39.

Reznick, J. S., Corley, R., & Robinson, J. (1997). A longitudinal twin study of intelligence in the second year. *Monographs of the Society for Research in Child Development, 62*(1).

Rose, S. & Feldman, J. (1990). Infant cognition: individual differences and developmental continuities. In J. Colombo & J. Fagen (eds.), *Individual differences in infancy: Reliability, stability and prediction* (pp. 229–45). Hillsdale, NJ: Lawrence Erlbaum Associates.

Rose, S. A. & Feldman, J. F. (1995). Prediction of IQ and specific cognitive abilities at 11 years from infancy measures. *Developmental Psychology, 31*, 685–96.

Rothbart, M. K. (1981). Measurement of temperament in infancy. *Child Development, 52*, 569–78.

Rothbart, M. K. & Bates, J. E. (1998). Temperament. In W. Damon (series ed.) & N. Eisenberg (vol. ed.), *Handbook of child psychology*, vol. 3: *Social, emotional, and personality development* (pp. 105–76). New York: John Wiley.

Rothbart, M. K., Derryberry, D., & Posner, M. I. (1994). A psychobiological approach to the development of temperament. In J. E. Bates & T. D. Wachs (eds.), *Temperament: Individual differences at the interface of biology and behavior* (pp. 83–116). Washington, DC: American Psychological Association.

Rushton, J. P., Brainerd, C. J., & Pressley, M. (1983). Behavioral development and construct validity: The principle of aggregation. *Psychological Bulletin, 94*, 18–38.

Sattler, J. M. (1990). *Assessment of children* (3rd edn.). San Diego, CA: Jerome M. Sattler.

Sigman, M., Cohen, S. E., & Beckwith, L. (1997). Why does infant attention predict adolescent intelligence? *Infant Behavior and Development, 20*(2), 133–40.

Slabach, E., Morrow, J., & Wachs, T. D. (1991). Questionnaire measurement of infant and child temperament: Current status and future directions. In A. Angleitner & J. Strelau (eds.), *Explorations in temperament* (pp. 205–34). New York: Plenum Press.

Spearman, C. E. (1904). "General intelligence," objectively determined and measured. *American Journal of Psychiatry, 15,* 201–93.

Sroufe, L. A. (1979). The coherence of individual development. *American Psychologist, 34,* 834–41.

St. James Roberts, I. (1989). Persistent crying in infancy. *Journal of Child Psychology and Psychiatry, 30*(2), 189–95.

Wachs, T. D. (2000). *Necessary but not sufficient: The respective roles of single and multiple influences on individual development.* Washington, DC: American Psychological Association.

Wiggins, J. (1973). *Personality and prediction: Principles of personality assessment.* Reading, MA: Addison-Wesley.

CHAPTER SEVEN

Who Should Collect Our Data: Parents or Trained Observers?

Ronald Seifer

Many human development researchers rely on parent report data as a basic foundation for empirical understanding of key phenomena. Although studies employing parent report data are ubiquitous in the literature, some have raised serious questions regarding the utility of research findings using this method. In this chapter I review the reasons researchers employ this approach, some of the downside to parent reports, as well as pros and cons of alternative methods. I also provide an example of a study investigating features of parent reports along with a theoretical framework in which to understand this issue. Finally, I provide a summary and recommendations for appropriate use of parent reports in developmental research. Most of the examples in this chapter will be from research on children's temperament, which has been the source of much debate on the issue of informants used in studies.

Why Query Family Members?

Researchers employ parent reports for many reasons. In general, these reasons all speak to economies in research implementation, with one major exception discussed below. These economies provide opportunities related to the mix of resources, subject availability, researcher time and effort, and alternative technologies.

One of the principal domains where parent reports are used is in the assessment of infant and child temperament. An obvious motivation to use this approach is that *infants and young children cannot provide self-reports* since they neither understand sophisticated language nor produce verbal or written language expressions. Thus, a logical proxy is to query parents about the behavior of their children. This approach has its roots in the

New York Longitudinal Study (NYLS; Thomas et al., 1963), where mothers were interviewed on several occasions during the first years of their child's life about different aspects of behavioral style. About a decade after this study began, the NYLS temperament constructs were incorporated in a parent report questionnaire (Carey, 1970), which became a model on which many other parent report instruments were based.

Questionnaires of this type are an *inexpensive method for collecting information*. Once instruments have been developed, costs associated with their administration are minimal. Researcher time is limited to recruiting study participants, giving the question-naire to parents, and entering and analyzing the resulting data. Parents in turn do the observations as part of their daily activity (more about this below) and it is their time that is used to complete the assessment instrument – these are burdens from which researchers are relieved. Such studies can be done, in fact, without researchers ever laying eyes on the infants and children who are the targets of the investigations. Furthermore, if the study is done via mail, researchers need not ever meet the parents either.

The issue of *parents as natural observers of their children's behavior* is more complex. As alluded to above, in addition to this availability, parents may be optimal informants in other ways. Thus, it is not only for convenience' sake that some have advocated use of parental reports (Rothbart & Bates, 1998). Instead, parents may be viewed as having a uniquely advantageous role in children's lives from the perspective of behavioral devel-opment research. By virtue of their daily sharing of their children's experience, parents amass a corpus of observational data that cannot be duplicated, even by the most diligent and persistent researcher. Furthermore, parents have access to parts of children's days that are typically off-limits to researchers (e.g., awakening in the morning, behavior at large family gatherings). Thus, there is a set of children's behavior that can only be observed and reported upon by parents.

The major advantage of employing parent-report strategies in research is their facilita-tion of research activities that would otherwise not be possible. Access to participants, large sample sizes, inaccessible behavior samples, and extension of limited resources are all mechanisms by which research possibilities are enhanced.

Bad Things Can Happen

The research advantages described in the preceding section come with a price. Of course, every decision made in the conduct of research results from a balancing of advantages and disadvantages. It is the responsibility of scientists to make those decisions that best advance knowledge in the domain under investigation. Concern about parent reports was most evident in the 1980s (Achenbach, McConaughy, & Howell, 1987; Bates, 1980; Hubert et al., 1982; Ivens & Rehm, 1988; Kashani et al., 1985; Kochanska, Kuczynski, & Radke-Yarrow, 1989; Richters, 1992; Richters & Pellegrini, 1989; Sameroff, Seifer, & Elias, 1982; Vaughn, Deinard, & Egeland, 1980). I describe some of the disadvantages of parent-report assessments in this section.

When researchers themselves make judgments about behavior, they apply certain standards regarding the rigor of those judgments. These are the familiar reliability criteria typically seen in research that includes behavior observations. This, of course, is not feasible in studies that employ parent-report questionnaires. As a result, questionnaire studies where respondents are reporting on the behavior of someone else (i.e., functioning as a research observer) may be a collection of *observations from a set of unreliable observers*. A related issue, which may contribute to a lack of reliability among parent-observers, is that parents likely do not have a common normative framework in which to interpret behavior, nor do they necessarily have a large observational base to develop such norms (hopefully in a common way compared with other parent-observers).

Studies employing parent-report instruments are sometimes longitudinal in nature. Parents may be asked to report on similar behaviors across time, on somewhat different aspects of children's behavior, or a combination of the two. In either event, another technical problem in such studies is the potential for rater drift in the parent-observers. Again, when researchers themselves conduct behavior observations, steps are typically taken to guard against drift in the ratings after the establishment of reliability. While this is not yet a standard seen in every published observation study, such procedures have become a characteristic of the highest quality longitudinal observation research projects.

Perhaps the most vexing problem in studies using parent-report is that parents may not simply be contributing random error to the measures, as would be the case for unreliability or some forms of drift, but that they may be adding *systematic error based on biases the parents have about their children*. Such biases can be positive or negative, and they can be conscious or unconscious. Furthermore, these biases may be related to characteristics of the parent, such as race, socioeconomic status (SES) or depression (Sameroff, Seifer, & Elias, 1982; Vaughn, Deinard, & Egeland, 1980). There are many implications for researchers beyond additional error variance in measures. In longitudinal studies, bias can increase the apparent stability of child characteristics beyond that detectable in the actual child behavior. When correlates of child behavior are examined, inflated effect sizes can be produced when the correlate of child behavior examined is in fact a characteristic related to parental bias. In turn, explanatory conclusions may be distorted by the confound between biasing characteristics and the biased reports. For example, depression biases parents to be more negative in attributions about their children (Teti & Gelfand, 1997), then a spurious link between parental symptoms and child behavior may be inferred from data (see Richters, 1992 for a thorough discussion of this issue, including the possibility that depressed mothers' reports may not be negatively biased).

A related problem arises in longitudinal studies where parents report on different domains of child behavior (Campbell et al., 1991; Graham, Rutter, & George, 1973; Earls, 1981; Maziade et al., 1989, 1990; Martin, 1989; Sanson et al., 1991). An example where this occurs in multiple studies is the relation between child temperament and behavior problems. In the large majority of studies on this issue, parents have been the reporters for both domains of child behavior. As a result, the apparent relation between these components of child behavior may be a primary function of using the same reporter rather than of the children (Rothbart & Bates, 1998), a problem sometimes referred to as *shared method variance* or *mono-method bias* (Cook & Campbell, 1979).

What's the Alternative?

The principal alternative to parent-report instruments is direct observation of child behavior. The most obvious question about this approach is – why do so much work? The economies associated with parent reports were clearly documented above, so there must be good reasons to expend the resources to collect this form of data. Before discussing those reasons, I will describe the work involved in some detail.

I noted above that parent-report instruments implicitly use observers (i.e., parents) who have not been trained to reliability criteria. In contrast, one of the basic tasks involved in observational research is *achieving high levels of rater reliability* in order to minimize the amount of error variance (and maximize true score variance) in final measurements. A related activity is to maintain rater reliability when studies are conducted over extended time frames. This involves *identifying standard rating criteria*, *repeated testing of raters* to insure they continue to meet these criteria, and *rejecting data collected during periods where ratings drifted from criteria*. These tasks can be more or less complicated depending on whether ratings are done live or from videotape, and whether simple summary scales or complex time-based ratings are used.

Another factor affecting the amount of error in measurements is the inherent reliability of the phenomenon under study. It is well established that humans (including infants and young children) do not always behave the same way from day to day or from setting to setting (Seifer et al., 1992; O'Brien, Johnson, & Anderson-Goetz, 1989). As a result, studies where individual differences in behavior are of interest need to be attentive to the degree to which stable individual differences can be inferred from the data collected. Test–retest reliabilities of direct observations of children's behavior rarely exceed 0.30 – indicative of a substantial level of instability (Epstein & O'Brien, 1985; Mischel & Peake, 1982). Thus, even if raters are in perfect agreement for single observations, the perfectly observed behavior may still have error in detecting individual differences because the phenomenon is inherently variable. A common solution to this problem is to collect information on multiple occasions and use *aggregates of multiple observations* to reduce the amount of error variance (Epstein & O'Brien, 1985; Martin & Fabes, 2001; Seifer et al., 1994). Such a strategy, of course, multiplies the amount of effort needed to collect reliable information about individual differences in children's behavior. Note that the use of parents as reporters implicitly includes multiple observations in the summary ratings provided by these informants.

Another factor adding to workloads occurs when *video records are collected and analyzed at subsequent points in time*. The obvious convenience factors of this approach underlie its popularity – increased control over the rating process, permanent retention of raw data material, which can be re-analyzed with different rating systems or, in the case of rater drift, with the same rating system, and ability to use ratings that cannot be reasonably accomplished in a live format (e.g., multiple viewings are required, highly precise timing is required). Still, the time to collect the raw data is added to the time needed to rate the behavior, thus increasing the resources necessary to complete the study.

Finally, a higher level of *data processing* is often required when conducting direct observations than when parent-report questionnaires are used. Ratings that employ time-based rating systems require data reduction (sometimes quite complex) that can add substantially to effort in a study. Furthermore, when multiple observations are employed, an additional set of processing to aggregate across measures for each individual is added to the mix.

In sum, there are many substantial increases in workload when direct observations are used in place of parent-report questionnaires. As I noted above, this additional work expends precious resources available for research and limits the scope of what can be studied. So, what is to be gained?

Why Do So Much Work?

One theme I have emphasized throughout is the increase in reliable true score variance, and complementary decrease in error variance, when improved measurement strategies are employed. Such improved measurement has several advantages. The probability of spurious effects is reduced when there is less error in measures – findings that will not replicate because they do not reflect the phenomena under study but instead reflect study-specific measurement artifacts will appear less frequently in the literature. Studies that have stronger measures will have increased power to detect effects actually present in the samples studied. In regression models, for example, when more variance is apportioned to the regression term and less to the error term, the potential for significant findings is increased.

As the theoretical discussion of utility of parental reports advanced over the years, another issue became clear. There is likely value in directly studying the nature of the objective and subjective components of parent reports (Bates, 1980) as one feature of understanding the interplay of child development in the family context. How children actually behave and how parents view that behavior (where is there correspondence? where is there discrepancy? what kinds of discrepancy are apparent?) could provide important insight into the attributions held by parents about their children (Seifer, 2000).

A final issue might be termed truth in lending. When results of parent-report measurements are disseminated, they are almost universally presented as measurements of the children being reported on. Undoubtedly, a portion of the variance in these measures does reflect child behavior. But it is also equally reasonable to assume that a meaningful portion of variance reflects the reporter and not the child. Thus, what is actually being measured is some mixture of the two, and it is incumbent upon researchers to accurately report what their instruments are validly measuring.

A Research Example

We conducted a study to explicitly examine where in the process of rating behavior of children parents may introduce bias into their responses (Seifer et al., in press). As with most of the material I have discussed in this chapter, the study focuses on reports of infant behavioral style. Our basic premise was that some portion of parental report contains systematic variance introduced by the parent, and that manipulating aspects of the reporting process could shed light on the issue. In this study, we focused primarily on the observation portion of the parent-report process by contrasting the agreement with trained observers when reporting on children unfamiliar to the parents (*standard children*) and the parents' *own children*. In particular, we were interested in addressing several questions:

- When observing children in general, do parents understand norms of behavior and rate that behavior in the same way as trained observers?
- Does the introduction of a special relationship with the target child influence the level of correspondence in behavior ratings?

The study took place in our laboratory when children were between 4.5 and 6.5 months of age. The part of the procedure relevant to this discussion occurred following 10 minutes of parent–child interaction that was videotaped. Parents were asked to view ten 2.5-minute segments of videotape: six segments were of standard children, and four were of their own child, which had just been recorded in the laboratory. For each of these ten segments parents rated behavior on a series of temperament rating scales we have used for many years: the Temperament Adjective Triad Assessment (TATA; Seifer et al., 1994). This instrument was designed for repeated assessments occurring over the course of several weeks or within a single day. The TATA yields four summary scales (Mood, Intensity, Activity, Approach).

The six standard-child video segments rated by all parents were also rated by three trained observers from our laboratory. Each trained observer was certified against our reliability standard and had coded several hundred similar behavior segments from a large study of temperament conducted in home settings. The six samples were selected from these home observations such that the sex of the child was not apparent in dress or grooming, and a range of behavior on the four TATA scales was evident in the segments. The scores from these three trained observers were averaged to provide a final rating for the standard children (final reliability coefficients exceeded 0.90). Also, each of the four segments for the study children was rated by one of the trained observers.

The data analysis strategy was a bit out of the ordinary. In the case of the standard children, we collected a profile of 24 ratings by each parent (and we had the same profile from our trained observers). That is, for each 2.5-minutes segment each parent provided four summary scores (activity, intensity, activity, approach), for a total of 24 ratings. For each parent, the profile was compared with the trained observers' aggregate profile using Pearson correlations to yield an index of correspondence.[1] In a similar fashion, profiles of 16 ratings were obtained for the four 2.5-minute segments for each own child, and the data were treated in the same manner.

The results were exceptionally clear. In answer to our first question, parents were indeed able to rate standard children in a manner similar to trained observers. The

---

[1]   We examined these data using more complex methods, such as nested regressions and hierarchical linear models – to account for the random selection of parents as sampling units – and arrived at precisely the same conclusions. I will report only the most straightforward correlation analyses here.

average correlation between profiles of mother ratings and profiles of observer ratings was 0.83 (SD = 0.09). All but one of these correlations was 0.60 or above, and 74 percent were 0.80 or above. In other words, the parents behaved as reliable raters using standard research criteria. In answer to our second question, parents clearly rated their own children differently from the trained observers. The average correlation between profiles of mother ratings and profiles of observer ratings was 0.11 (SD = 0.33). Many of these correlations were negative (32 percent), and only 1 of the 112 correlations exceeded 0.80. Parents were anything but consistent with raters when their own children were the focus.

This finding suggests that parents may be the last people we should choose to provide research information about their own children. When the characteristic of having a special relationship with the target of observations is introduced, the quality of the information obtained declined precipitously. This result should not be surprising – few researchers would allow their trained observers to code behavior of people they know with whom they had a relationship outside of the laboratory.

Another set of findings was that parents rated children as more positive than trained observers. This positive attributional bias was far more pronounced for own children than for standard children. For example, mood ratings (lower scores indicate more positive mood) for *standard children* by trained observers were 2.43 and by mothers were 2.09 (SD = 0.30); for *own children* trained observer ratings were 2.81 and mother ratings were 2.10 – a difference about twice as large. In the next section I provide a theoretical framework in which findings about parental rating of their children's behavior can be understood.

A Theoretical Framework

In articulating a theory of parental behavior when placed in the role of research observer, I draw heavily from Kenny's (1994) Social Relations Model (SRM), which outlined a set of basic principles regarding the general function of person perception (see Chapter 19, this volume). This model is quantitative in nature, describing the components of variation in judgments individuals make of other people. Such an approach matches well with the basic concern – different sources of accuracy and error in parents' ratings of children's behavior.

One fundamental premise of SRM is that relationship partners have perceptions of one another – the judgments made by one of the partners may be conceived in terms of the perceiver (the person making the judgment) and the target (the person the judgment is about).[2] Furthermore, the perceptions made may be conceived as the sum of

---

[2]   Kenny's (1994) formulation cannot be described in full within the constraints of this chapter, and the reader is referred to Chapter 19 of this volume. Two points about material not described are noted here. First, the obvious issue of reciprocity in dyadic relationships is addressed in the model in some detail. Second, the issues peculiar to research design for studying the variance components of person perception within the SRM model are fully discussed in Kenny (1994).

several components: perceiver variance, target variance, relationship variance, and a constant term. *Perceiver* refers to the degree to which an individual perceives targets (in general) as high or low on a trait; *target* refers to the degree to which the target individual is perceived by others (in general) as high or low on a trait; *relationship* refers to the unique view of a particular target by the perceiver, with the general target and perceiver variance controlled; *constant* refers to the average level perceivers (in general) view targets (in general) as high or low on the trait. Of interest in the current context of parent and trained observer rating of child behavior is the relationship component of the judgments.

A general finding from Kenny's review of person perception studies is that perceiver variance accounts for about 20 percent of total judgment variance, target variance accounts for about 15 percent of total judgment variance, and relationship variance accounts for about 20 percent of total judgment variance; the remaining 45 percent of judgment variance is attributed to error. Stated another way, the consensus among raters (which might be viewed as our best estimate of the actual trait level of the target) accounts for only a small portion of variance – less than either the rater characteristics or the relationship factors. Note that these studies examine the judgments that individuals make about one another in laboratory analog social situations.

Several basic explanations are offered for the meaning of relationship variance in person perception (Kenny, 1994). One explanation is that *different information is shared* within a relationship than outside of a relationship. This, in fact, is a point often emphasized in support of parent-report methods. There is special knowledge held by parents that would be very hard to duplicate in trained observers who do not have an ongoing relationship with the target child because of limitations on time and place for interaction with the child.

A second explanation is that *different meaning* may be attached to behavior because of the existent relationship, for which three distinct subcomponents may be identified. Parents may have developed an attributional bias about their child based on expectations and history. These *attributions* can be generally positive or negative, and may have other more specific characteristics. For example, a parent may be biased to view his or her child as highly active because they see that same behavioral style as characteristic of themselves. *Cultural milieu* of the perceiver may also color the judgments made about others. Again, in some cultural groups a parent may value high activity level as an indicator that his or her child is vibrant and competent. Perceivers in a relationship may integrate observations into coherent *narratives*. A growing body of work points to the importance of individually constructed narratives in understanding how families behave with and understand one another (Dickstein et al., 1999; Fiese et al., 1999; Zeanah et al., 1989; Seifer, 2000). In human development research, the term working model has often been used to characterize such narratives.[3] Working models are believed

---

[3]   The narrative method for eliciting information about working models should not be confused with the intended usage of narrative to describe a cognitive script (implicit or explicit) the individuals employ when making sense of events in the world, and in this context, events having to do with the behavior of relationship partners.

to be important for understanding how individuals comprehend the behavior of their relationship partners as well as how they actually behave with those partners (Seifer & Schiller, 1995; Main, Kaplan, & Cassidy, 1985). Furthermore, working models have some degree of endurance over time, and may generalize across relationships to some extent.

Relationships may also promote *idiosyncratic perceptions* by the partners. This aspect of relationship variance may be particularly important in the case of parent reports of young children. This may be viewed as an aspect of perceiver variance, but with specific reference to the relationship with the target. Knowledge of, or affect about, the target gleaned from shared relationship history may influence the judgments made by the perceiver. I also note that there is some conceptual overlap here with the notion of narrative/working models, as some portion of the working models is formed in the context of these pieces of knowledge and feelings about the target.

So, how does all of this systemization of the judgment process help us understand how parent-report measures may provide error-laden information? First, it is important to keep in mind that judgments about others, when made by individuals selected from the general population, do not contain a high degree of consensus, while larger portions may be attributable to the perceiver and the relationship portions of variance. Thus, there is likely to be a large portion of variance in obtained measurements that is not about the actual behavior of the targets. One of the primary functions of training observers to rating criteria is to minimize the perceiver component while maximizing the consensus component of their ratings – this done in a context where raters do not have a relationship with the targets. Second, the SRM provides a set of expectable reasons why individuals having a special relationship with a child will provide systematically biased judgments about their behavior, in line with the conclusion of Achenbach, McConaughy, and Howell (1987) that correspondence among informants varies as a function of the type of relationship the reporters have with the target child. Third, the SRM points to the potential importance of understanding the constructed cognitions parents have about their children when they provide information about the behavior of their children to researchers.

What is important to parents?

The SRM provides a frame for understanding person perception in general, but it is also important to consider special characteristics of parents. When choosing to employ parents as our data collectors, we should keep in mind the basic functions (vis-à-vis their children) that are critical to parents. Most researchers would agree that acting as a dispassionate research assistant is not near the top of the list of these important functions. Instead, we should always keep in mind the primary role of parents of protecting their children. Protection takes the obvious form of shielding children from physical harm, but it can also be manifest as being their child's strongest advocate in a complex social environment. From this perspective, it is reasonable to expect that parents would be motivated to produce overly praiseworthy descriptions of their own children, an expectation consistent with the data I reported above. Furthermore, this protection function may vary systematically with such things as the level of parental distress, which in turn would systematically alter the reported perceptions.

Constructs measured by parent report

Different constructs may be inherently more or less amenable to the use of parent reports. Two examples highlight this point. In the case of infant temperament, the fundamental interest is in the behavior of children. In the case of child behavior problems, the child's behavior is of interest as is the relation with diagnostic classification. In diagnosing childhood disorders, particularly with younger children, information from parents is a critical part of the diagnostic process (American Psychiatric Association, 1994; Zero to Three, 1994). Thus, the applicability of parent reports may be higher where the basic construct incorporates the view of parents.

Metatheoretical issues

Behavioral scientists in the US have been largely guided by an individualist view, a perspective that has generalized to developmental work as well. That is, behavior is often viewed in a decontextualized manner, with a tendency to attribute meaning and causality to individual agents rather than the social and cultural contexts in which the behaviors occur. When addressing issues such as informant reports, this individualist view may lead to theoretical difficulty. The knowledge gained from the parent-report instruments is typically attributed to behavior of the child who is the focus of the report. But, the information emanates from a developmental system organized at the level of a dyadic relationship and likely influenced by other levels of organization, including family, neighborhood, and culture. This failure to recognize the metatheoretical assumptions underlying the empirical investigation can lead to serious problems in the understanding of the phenomena under investigation (Overton, 1998).

An alternative to the individualist perspective is to view the developing child as embodied in the multiple systems that affect development. One manifestation of this embodiment is that an individual must also be understood in terms of the relationships in which that individual participates. Furthermore, it is useful to understand the system as it is organized at the level of these relationships (Bronfenbrenner & Morris, 1998; Magnusson & Stattin, 1998). In the current context, where parent reports are the focus, the relationships of interest will be the parent–child relationships within a family. This shift in the unit of analysis provides an alternative to the individualist perspective when interpreting parent reports. Rather than making the simple attribution that reports are about the child, when interpreted at the relationship level of analysis the reports are seen as reflecting the nature of the relationship. Thus, the information is simultaneously about each of the individuals embodied in the relationship as well as in how the individuals relate to each other. Developmentalists need to struggle with these dialectical oppositions if we are to fully appreciate the meaning of the information we compile (Overton, 1998).

Summary and Integration

The issue of parental reports is vexing for developmental researchers. On the one hand, we have a method that has been used for many years and affords a great degree of economy when used in research. On the other hand, we have a method with some serious shortcomings that render interpretation of data difficult. What's a researcher to do?

One important point to keep in mind when answering this question is that conducting high-quality research requires a series of compromises. Given the lack of precision in our knowledge base in the field of human development, we are necessarily working with a set of research designs and technologies that includes a large degree of uncertainty. Furthermore, the phenomena under study are highly complex and difficult to manipulate, which of course contributes to the difficulty in gaining precise knowledge of the phenomena. Conducting science within such constraints requires that we simplify the scope and expectations of our work in order to accomplish the (sometimes painfully) small steps toward more complete understanding of developmental phenomena.

The nature of these compromises spans the various tasks familiar to researchers. The samples in our studies may be less than optimal (not truly random, smaller than desired, of limited generalizability), measurement scales may violate statistical assumptions, statistical tests may not fully address underlying research questions, protocols may have built in confounds, or measurement tools may include high levels of error. Some of these compromises result from a basic inability to reach beyond the current capabilities of our science, while others result from a balancing of available resources and the quality of resulting answers to research questions.

In the case of parent reports, our decisions are in the domain of errors of measurement in concert with the resources available to conduct the scientific inquiry. When (if ever) is it appropriate to use parent reports instead of direct observation? Are parent reports just as good or superior in any circumstances? How should parent-report or observation data be interpreted? I address each of these questions in turn in the remaining material.

There are many circumstances where parent-report instruments are a reasonable choice in research studies. Most obviously, when correspondence or validation issues between parent reports and observations are the main research question, then the reports become an integral part of the research design. Similarly, when the components of the reports (as outlined in Kenny's SRM model or some other framework) are at issue they again will be a central feature of the research. In circumstances where the behavior of the child is the key element motivating measurement, then I would recommend using a simple rule of thumb. When the child behavior measured (potentially by parent report) is a central construct in the research design, then parent reports may be less desirable. In contrast, where the child behavior is a secondary construct of interest, then the error associated with reports may be more acceptable. The major exception to this rule would be in large-scale survey studies, where two factors are operative. First, the feasibility of observations is very low in such work, making parent reports the only available alternative, other than deciding that the research cannot be conducted. Second, the power afforded by large sample studies may offset some of the negative features associated with the error contained in the reports, although interpretation must be made with caution, as discussed below.

The superiority of parent reports has been suggested (Carey, 1983), based on the fact that parents have a unique observational base that cannot be duplicated by observers. This argument is correct in the limited frame regarding the observational base. As I have attempted to demonstrate in discussion of the research example and the findings from Kenny's SRM, the path from observation to report is not simple and has points where substantial error can enter the process. Thus, I believe the best working conclusion at this time is that direct observation is a clearly superior method when the core question is the actual behavior of the child.

Finally, when interpreting parent-report data, several points must be kept in mind. First, the behavior of the child may be measured with a high degree of error. Second, the error may be systematic and thus less amenable to the usual assumption that measurement errors will simply sum to zero (asymptotically, in large samples) and hence reduce effect size. Instead, the systematic error may result in conclusions based on the biases of the reporter, rather than the behavior of the child. Third, the influence of bias is particularly problematic when the informant is providing multiple data points in the research. This may occur when the same construct is measured on multiple occasions, or when different constructs are assessed. In this situation, the probability is increased of making inappropriate conclusions about children inferred from data where the true underlying relation is between the common biasing factors contained in the multiple parent reports. Fourth, parents can be encouraged to provide more accurate information when reporting about their children, and the utility of the information may ultimately be a function of how well this encouragement has been implemented.

Regarding this last point, Teti and McGourty's (1996) study of the Home Behavior Q-Sort[4] for assessing attachment security (Waters & Deane, 1985) supports the idea that parents can provide more accurate information about their children under the right circumstances. In this study, providing a 2-week period to review the items on the instrument and to observe child behavior with the items in mind, along with completion of the sort under researcher supervision, resulted in substantial informant–observer correspondence. Similarly, when we had parents in our own research complete the same temperament assessment on currently observed behavior on eight occasions, using the same instrument and the same observation period as trained observers, moderate parent–observer correspondence was obtained on aggregated measures of negative emotionality (Seifer et al., 1994). Such findings, while representing exceptions to the rule of how parent reports are obtained, point to the possibility that parents can provide accurate reports in some circumstances. Unfortunately, the extra effort required to accomplish this accuracy negates the greatest appeal of using parents as informants – ease and economy.

---

[4]   This Q-sort method requires the informant to sort 90 items relevant to child secure-base behavior into 10 piles ranging from most like the child to least like the child. The informant's pattern of responses is then correlated to a criterion sort, derived from experts rating a prototypical secure child, to yield a summary index of security.

Overall, the most prudent approach is to use parent reports judiciously in circumstances where they can augment a research agenda with minimal danger of yielding spurious findings. If they are to be used, they are best coupled with reports from other classes of informants and employed with procedures to maximize accuracy; interpretation should be imbued with the cautions outlined above. Whenever possible, researchers' attributions about child behavior should be derived from direct experience with the child. Parents have many crucial roles in our culture. Unfortunately for researchers (and fortunately for children), being a research assistant is not one of those roles.

Acknowledgment

Dr Seifer was supported by grants from the National Institute of Mental Health.

Note

Inquiries may be sent to Dr Seifer at E. P. Bradley Hospital, 1011 Veterans Memorial Parkway, East Providence, RI 02915. Email to ronald_seifer@brown.edu.

References

Achenbach, T. M., McConaughy, S. H., & Howell, C. T. (1987). Child/adolescent behavioral and emotional problems: Implications of cross-informant correlations for situational specificity. *Psychological Bulletin, 101*, 213–32.

American Psychiatric Association (1994). *Diagnostic and statistical manual of mental disorders* (4th edn.). Washington, DC: American Psychiatric Association.

Bates, J. E. (1980). The concept of difficult temperament. *Merrill-Palmer Quarterly, 26*, 299–319.

Bronfenbrenner, U. & Morris, P. A. (1998). The ecology of developmental processes. In R. M. Lerner (ed.), *Handbook of Child Psychology* (5th edn., vol. 1, pp. 993–1028). New York: John Wiley.

Campbell, S. B., March, C. L., Pierce, E. W., Ewing, L. J. & Szumowski, E. K. (1991). Hard-to-manage preschool boys: Family context and the stability of externalizing behavior. *Journal of Abnormal Child Psychology, 19*, 301–18.

Carey, W. B. (1970). A simplified method for measuring infant temperament. *Journal of Pediatrics, 77*(2), 188–94.

Carey, W. B. (1983). Some pitfalls in temperament research. *Infant Behavior and Development, 6*, 247–54.

Cook, T. D. & Campbell, D. T. (1979). *Quasi-experimentation: Design and analysis issues for field settings*. Chicago, IL: Rand McNally College.

Dickstein, S., St-Andre, M., Sameroff, A. J., Seifer, R., & Schiller, M. (1999). Maternal depression, family functioning, and child outcomes: A narrative assessment. In B. Fiese, A. J. Sameroff, H. J. Grotevant, F. S. Wambolt, S. Dickstein, & D. L. Fravel (eds.), *The stories that families tell: Narrative coherence, narrative interaction, and relationship beliefs. Monographs of the Society for Research in Child Development, 64* (serial no. 257, pp. 84–104).

Earls, F. (1981). Temperament characteristics and behavior problems in three-year-old children. *Journal of Nervous and Mental Disease, 169,* 367–73.

Epstein, S. & O'Brien, E. J. (1985). The person-situation debate in historical and current perspective. *Psychological Bulletin, 98(3),* 513–37.

Fiese, B., Sameroff, A. J., Grotevant, H. J., Wambolt, F. S., Dickstein, S., & Fravel, D. L. (eds.) (1999). *The stories that families tell: Narrative coherence, narrative interaction, and relationship beliefs. Monographs of the Society for Research in Child Development, 64* (serial no. 257).

Graham, P., Rutter, M., & George, S. (1973). Temperamental characteristics as predictors of behavior disorders in children. *American Journal of Orthopsychiatry, 43,* 328–39.

Hubert, N. C., Wachs, T. D., Peters-Martin, P., & Gandour, M. J. (1982). The study of early temperament: Measurement and conceptual issues. *Child Development, 53,* 571–600.

Ivens, C. & Rehm, L. C. (1988). Assessment of childhood depression: Correspondence of reports by child, mother, and father. *Journal of the Academy of Child and Adolescent Psychiatry, 27,* 738–41.

Kashani, J. H., Orvaschel, H., Burk, J. P., & Read, J. C. (1985). Informant variance: The issue of parent child disagreement. *Journal of the American Academy of Child and Adolescent Psychiatry, 24,* 437–41.

Kenny, D. A. (1994). *Interpersonal perception: A social relations analysis.* New York: Guilford.

Kochanska, G., Kuczynski, L., & Radke-Yarrow, M. (1989). Correspondence between mothers' self-reported and observed child-rearing practices. *Child Development, 60,* 56–63.

Magnusson, D. & Stattin, H. (1998). Person-context interaction theories. In R. M. Lerner (ed.), *Handbook of child psychology* (5th edn., vol. 1, pp. 685–759). New York: John Wiley.

Main, M., Kaplan, N., & Cassidy, J. (1985). Security in infancy, childhood, and adulthood: A move to the level of representation. In I. Bretherton & E. Waters (eds.), *Growing points of attachment theory and research. Monographs of the Society for Research in Child Development, 50* (serial no. 209, pp. 66–106).

Martin, C. L. & Fabes, R. A. (2001). The stability and consequences of young children's same-sex peer interactions. *Developmental Psychology, 37,* 431–46.

Martin, R. P. (1989). Activity level, distractibility, and persistence: Critical characteristics in early schooling. In G. A. Kohnstamm, J. E. Bates, & M. K. Rothbart (eds.), *Temperament in childhood* (pp. 451–61). New York: John Wiley.

Maziade, M., Cote, R., Bernier, H., Boutin, P., & Thivierge, J. (1989). Significance of extreme temperament in infancy for clinical status in pre-school years I: Value of extreme temperament at 4–8 months for predicting diagnosis at 4.7 years. *British Journal of Psychiatry, 154,* 535–43.

Maziade, M., Caron, C., Cote, R., Boutin, P., & Thivierge, J. (1990). Extreme temperament and diagnosis: A study in a psychiatric sample of consecutive children. *Archives of General Psychiatry, 47,* 477–84.

Mischel, W. & Peake, P. K. (1982). Beyond deja vu in the search for cross-situation consistency. *Psychological Review, 89,* 730–55.

O'Brien, M., Johnson, J. M., & Anderson-Goetz, D. (1989). Evaluating quality in mother–infant interaction: Situational effects. *Infant Behavior and Development, 12,* 451–64.

Overton, W. (1998). Developmental psychology: Philosophy, concepts, and methodology. In R. M. Lerner (ed.), *Handbook of child psychology* (5th edn., vol. 1, pp. 107–88). New York: John Wiley.

Richters, J. (1992). Depressed mothers as informants about their children: A critical review of the evidence for distortion. *Psychological Bulletin, 112,* 485–99.

Richters, J. & Pellegrini, D. (1989). Depressed mothers' judgments about their children: An examination of the depression–distortion hypothesis. *Child Development, 60,* 1068–75.

Rothbart, M. K. & Bates, J. E. (1998). Temperament. In W. Damon & N. Eisenberg (eds.), *Handbook of child psychology: Social, emotional and personality development* (5th edn.,). New York: John Wiley.

Sameroff, A. J., Seifer, R., & Elias, P. K. (1982). Sociocultural variability in infant temperament ratings. *Child Development, 53,* 164–73.

Sanson, A., Oberklaid, F., Pedlow, R., & Prior, M. (1991). Risk indicators: Assessments of infancy predictors of pre-school behavioral maladjustment. *Journal of Child Psychology and Psychiatry, 32,* 609–26.

Seifer, R. (2000). Temperament and goodness of fit: Implications for developmental psychopathology. A. J. Sameroff, M. Lewis, & S. M. Miller (eds.), *Handbook of developmental psychopathology* (2nd edn., pp. 257–76). New York: Plenum Press.

Seifer, R. & Schiller, M. (1995). The role of parenting sensitivity, infant temperament, and dyadic interaction in attachment theory and assessment. In E. Waters, B. E. Vaughn, G. Posada, & K. Kondo-Ikemura (eds.), *Caregiving, cultural, and cognitive perspectives on secure-base behavior and working models: New growing points of attachment theory and research. Monographs of the Society for Research in Child Development, 60* (serial no. 244, pp. 146–74).

Seifer, R., Sameroff, A. J., Anganostopolou, R., & Elias, P. K. (1992). Mother–infant interaction during the first year: Effects of situation, maternal mental illness and demographic factors. *Infant Behavior and Development, 15,* 405–26.

Seifer, R., Sameroff, A. J., Barrett, L. C., & Krafchuk, E. (1994). Infant temperament measured by multiple observations and mother report. *Child Development, 65,* 1478–90.

Seifer, R., Sameroff, A. J., Dickstein, S., Schiller, M., & Hayden, L. (in press). Your own children are special: Clues to the sources of reporting bias in temperament assessments. *Infant Behavior and Development.*

Teti, D. M. & Gelfand, D. M. (1997). Maternal cognitions as mediators of outcome in the context of postpartum depression. In L. Murray & P. J. Cooper (eds.), *Postpartum depression and child development* (pp. 136–64). New York: Guilford.

Teti, D. M. & McGourty, S. (1996). Using mothers versus trained observers in assessing secure base behavior: Theoretical and methodological considerations. *Child Development, 67,* 597–605.

Thomas, A., Chess, S., Birch, H. G., Hertzig, M. E., & Korn, S. (1963). *Behavioral individuality in early childhood.* New York: New York University Press.

Vaughn, B. E., Deinard, A., & Egeland, B. (1980). Measuring temperament in pediatric practice. *Journal of Pediatrics, 96,* 510–14.

Waters, E. & Deane, K. (1985). The Home Behavior Q-set. In I. Bretherton & E. Waters (eds.), *New directions in attachment research. Monographs of the Society for Research in Child Development, 50* (serial no. 209, pp. 41–65).

Zeanah, C. H., Benoit, D., Hirschberg, L., & Barton, M. L. (1989). Working model of the child. Paper presented at the World Association for Infant Psychiatry and Allied Disciplines meeting, Lugano, Switzerland.

Zero To Three/National Center for Clinical Infant Programs (1994). *Diagnostic Classification: 0–3.* Arlington, VA: Zero To Three/National Center for Clinical Infant Programs.

CHAPTER EIGHT

Validating Young Children's Self-Concept Responses: Methodological Ways and Means to Understand their Responses

Herbert Marsh, Raymond Debus, and Laurel Bornholt

The purpose of this chapter is to evaluate methodological approaches to, and empirical support for, assessing the validity of children's responses to self-concept instruments, in particular, for children under the age of eight. In a brief review of the research with older children, we argue that advances in the field are due to new self-concept instruments with sound theoretical and empirical bases, and to improved methodological and statistical approaches to data analysis. Advances in self-concept research with younger children therefore require corresponding improvements in age-appropriate instruments with an emphasis on the validation of responses. The specific aims of this chapter are to evaluate theoretical approaches to, and empirical support for, self-reports by young children that differentiate among multiple dimensions of self-concept; assess the construct validity of children's responses; review self-concept instruments for young children; and outline the special issues in assessment of self-concepts for young children.

One of the main challenges in this field is the prevailing assumption that young children either do not have clearly defined multidimensional self-concepts or that such a multidimensional structure cannot be measured with self-report instruments similar to those used with older children. A thorough evaluation is therefore critical to the advancement of self-concept research for this age group and, more generally, for understanding the role of self-concepts in young children's learning and motivation.

The Context: Historical Perspectives on Self-Concept Research

Theories of self-concept rest on rich philosophical traditions and on the beginnings of psychology; in particular, the work of William James more than a century ago. Although advances in theory, research, and measurement of self-concept were slow during the heyday of behaviorism, there has been a resurgence in the last 25 years. During the 1970s, reviews of self-concept research (e.g., Burns, 1979; Hattie, 1992; Shavelson, Hubner, & Stanton, 1976; Wells & Marwell, 1976; Wylie, 1979) highlighted the need for a good theoretical basis, improved self-concept instruments, and strong methods of analysis.

Construct validity of self-concepts

As with many psychological constructs, self-concept suffers in that "everybody knows what it is." Consequently, few empirical researchers provide theoretical definitions of self-concept, although construct validity is critical to any field of research. Investigations of construct validity of self-concepts can be grouped into within-network or between-network studies. Within-network studies explore the internal structure of self-concept; for instance, distinctions among the content of children's self-concepts about reading, mathematics, sport, and so on. Between-network studies examine relations between self-concepts and other constructs (e.g., performance, personal and social comparisons, feelings and choices) to address substantive theoretical and practical issues. From this construct validity approach, the theory, measurement and empirical self-concept research are intertwined, so that neglect of one will undermine the others.

Shavelson, Hubner, & Stanton (1976) suggested that self-concept research had addressed the substantive between-network issues in self-concept before within-network problems of definition, measurement, and interpretation had been resolved. In reviewing self-concept research, they developed a multidimensional, hierarchical model of self-concept, defined self-concepts in terms of experience and interpretations of the environment that explain and predict actions, and outlined the process of construct validation that they applied to five popular self-concept instruments. The review proposed different ways and means for evaluating construct validity in self-concept research.

Logical analysis examines the consistency of the definition, features of the instrument such as the instructions, item format, and scoring procedures, and the predictions. The purpose is to generate testable hypotheses about the interpretation of test scores. For example, according to Marsh (1993), if self-concept is a multidimensional construct and one of the differentiable dimensions is academic self-concept, then academic accomplishments should be more highly related to academic self-concept responses than non-academic self-concept responses.

Correlational techniques can be used to examine the structure of self-concept and the relations between self-concept and other constructs. Factor analysis, multitrait–multimethod analysis (MTMM), and path analysis are particularly useful in self-concept research.

Experimental techniques are also used to examine sources and consequences, as well as the structure of self-concepts. For instance, experimental evidence that an intervention had substantially more effect on targeted components of self-concept than nontargeted components would contribute to the construct validity of self-concept responses and of the intervention.

Self-concept research with older children and adolescents

Major advances in theoretical models and the development of self-concept instruments during the 1980s and 1990s (see Byrne, 1984, 1996; Harter, 1986; Hattie, 1992; Skaalvik, 1997; Wylie, 1989) emphasized specific self-concept domains rather than one global component (e.g., self-esteem) in studies with older children and adolescents (e.g., Bornholt, 2000b; Marsh & Craven, 1997). Self-concepts of reading, mathematics, social relations, sport, and so on were well differentiated, and sound factor analytic evidence supported the multidimensionality of self-concept responses.

There is a clear need for these advances to be extended for young children (see Bornholt, 1997; Harter, 1983; Marsh, Craven, & Debus, 1991; Penn, Burnett, & Patton, 2001; Stipek & Mac Iver, 1989; Wylie, 1989). Self-concept research with younger children raises important issues (see Harter, 1985) about simplified items or pictorial representations, simplified or new response formats, and individually based interviews instead of standard group administered paper-and-pencil tests. We contend that better multidimensional instruments, based on a rigorous approach to the construct validation, will stimulate progress in theory, research, and practice for young children.

Methodological approaches in self-concept research with older children

Methodological sophistication of self-concept research with older children has increased substantially, from inferential statistics in correlational and experimental designs, to addressing important substantive issues. These advances provide models for future self-concept research with young children. An important feature of recent self-concept research is the use of confirmatory factor analysis (CFA) as a statistical tool to evaluate *a priori* factor structures. Historically, evaluations of the structure of responses to self-concept instruments used exploratory rather than confirmatory factor analyses (see Hattie & Marsh, 1996; Shavelson, Hubner, & Stanton, 1976; Wylie, 1989). Exploratory factor analyses designed to "discover" the underlying factors from a large number of self-referent items (i.e., "throw it in and see what happens") proved largely unproductive. Wylie (1989) compared the instruments reviewed in her 1974 and 1989 monographs on self-concept measures. She noted that more recently developed multidimensional self-concept instruments were more likely to begin with an explicit theoretical basis for the domains rather than relying on atheoretical, empirical approaches to identify the salient factors from a broad collection of items. Even when there were *a priori* factors, exploratory factor analysis was not a fully satisfactory statistical tool. A combination of poorly designed instruments and reliance on exploratory factor analyses meant that observed factors were typically ambiguous and not easily replicated. Although exploratory factor analysis may be used to confirm *a priori* factors, recent advances in CFA provide a more satisfactory hypothesis-testing tool. Self-concept researchers have generally embraced CFA tools to address old questions in exciting new ways as well as to explore new questions. For example, new statistical developments have allowed us to evaluate hypotheses about (a) convergent and discriminant validity for self-concept responses and inferences from reports by teachers, parents, and peers (Marsh & Craven, 1991, 1997), (b) responses to competing multidimensional self-concept instruments, (c) developmental differences in mean profiles and the structure of self-concepts in cross-sectional and longitudinal data (e.g., Bornholt, 1997; Marsh, Craven, & Debus, 1991, 1998; Marsh & Hocevar, 1985), (d) negatively worded items that may confound interpretation of responses, particularly by young children, (e) situations that alter associations between cognitive and affective self-evaluations (e.g., Bornholt & Nelson, 2002; Marsh, Craven, & Debus, 1999), and (f) disentangling self-concept as cause and effect in longitudinal studies (e.g., Marsh, Byrne, & Yeung, 1999; Guay, Marsh, & Boivin, 2003). In brief, CFA and related statistical techniques are becoming a common standard for research with older children. However, Davis-Kean and Sandler (2001) indicated that the application of these procedures is rare in self-concept research with younger children.

Self-Concept Research with Children Younger than Eight

For many developmental, educational, and psychological researchers, self-concepts are a "cornerstone of both social and emotional development" (Kagen, Moore, & Bredekamp, 1995, p. 18; also see Davis-Kean & Sandler, 2001; Marsh, Ellis, & Craven, 2002). It is argued that self-concepts develop early in childhood and that, once established, they are enduring (e.g., Eder & Mangelsdorf, 1997). The development of self-concept is therefore emphasized in many early childhood programs (e.g., Fantuzzo et al., 1996). However, there is surprisingly little systematic research with young children. Davis-Kean and Sandler (2001) emphasized that early childhood programs need a reliable basis for evaluating interventions to enhance children's self-concepts (see Fantuzzo et al., 1996; Penn, Burnett, & Patton, 2001). Currently available inventories for young children use a wide range of techniques, such as pictures, Q-sort, one-to-one interview, questionnaires, and puppets, often with limited success (Byrne, 1996; Wylie, 1989). There is clearly a need to integrate the information from these various techniques.

Developmental issues in the construction of self-concepts

Self-concept indicators for young children There is growing evidence that children as young as four or five years old can make standard self-evaluations (Bornholt, 1997; Penn, Burnett, & Patton, 2001). Other techniques were used by Stipek, Gralinski and Kopp (1990) to ask mothers of 123 toddlers (14 to 40 months) to report on 25 behaviors associated with the development of self-concept. Their results suggested that groups of behaviors develop in a systematic order, such that self-recognition preceded self-description, which preceded emotional and evaluative responses. Harter (1998) emphasizes that the development of language is critical in the development of self. It provides a basis for children to represent themselves, to use personal pronouns, and to construct autobiographical memories of past events that form the basis of a personal "life story." In addition, Howe and Courage (1997) argue that the ability to create an autobiographical memory of self requires self-knowledge. This appreciation of the self is distinct from others in terms of attributes, affects, and thoughts. This cognitive self is a knowledge structure used to organize memories of experiences that happened to "me." This cognitive self emerges in the second year of life, so the lower limit for early autobiographical memories is about two years of age. Subsequent accumulation of memories is linked to improvements in children's ability to maintain information in storage. Howe and Courage's (1997) review argued that infants began to become aware of their separateness from their environment within weeks of birth, recognized their own image in a mirror at 18 months, and correctly labeled their image by 22 months. They concluded that by 18 to 24 months, infants have a self-concept that is sufficiently well developed to provide a basis for the organization of memory about personally experienced events.

In a meta-analysis of the reliability of young children's self-concepts, Davis-Kean and Sandler (2001) argued that young children have both the language and the cognitive ability to discuss the self by the time they are in preschool (see also Bates, 1990; Bornholt, 1997; Damon & Hart, 1988; Lewis & Brooks-Gunn, 1979; Penn, Burnett, & Patton, 2001). In particular, the classic studies by Lewis and Brooks-Gunn showed that children between the ages of 18 and 30 months were able to use self-referent terms, distinguish themselves by feature recognition (the categorical self), correctly identify their size in comparison to other children (e.g., "I am bigger"), and use terms like "I," "mine," and "me" (Lewis & Brooks-Gunn). Davis-Kean and Sandler also emphasized that children can discuss abstract ideas about emotions and inner states. Direct questions need to be explicit (e.g., "Are you a girl or a boy?", "How good are you at drawing?") rather than a vague question such as "Who are you?" (see Damon & Hart, 1988; Eder, 1989).

Eder and Mangelsdorf (1997) outlined theoretical stages in the early development of "personality" with a particular emphasis on dispositional conceptions of the emerging self-concept: (1) organized patterns of behavior reflecting innate temperament and patterns of attachment; (2) nonverbal conception of emotional states; (3) verbal conceptions of emotional states; (4) verbal conceptions of dispositions; and (5) development of a full metatheory of self. They reviewed considerable theoretical and empirical research indicating that self-concept first emerges during infancy (the first two years). Eder and Mangelsdorf emphasized that most personality research with preschool children was based on behavioral observations and reports by others. There was clear evidence of individual differences in broad personality constructs. It was unclear whether there were also corresponding differences in self-concept or phenomenological experience, because these inferences were based on observed behavior. In contrast, self-concept researchers focus on young children's own self-concepts as part of developing social cognition. Early research using open-ended questions suggested that the content of self-concepts became more psychological as children grew older (see Harter, 1983), although Eder and Mangelsdorf's subsequent review suggested that self-concepts developed at a younger age. They argued that because young children can access and retrieve general memories by three years of age and specific memories by four or five, this suggested that the patterns of self-concepts would be similar. In support of this idea, Eder (1990) asked children aged three to eight to respond to pairs of items on personality dimensions presented by puppets. Factor analyses of responses at each age group consistently revealed three logical factors. Eder and Mangelsdorf (1997) concluded "that by 3 years of age, children possess common underlying dispositional constructs for organizing information about themselves" (p. 226).

Hattie (1992; Hattie & Marsh, 1996) reviewed theoretical and empirical support for stages of growth in the development of self-concept, arguing against fixed stages that all persons must pass through. He argued that seven parallel developments are relevant to growing self-concepts: (1) children distinguish self and others, (2) children distinguish self and the environment, (3) changes in major reference groups lead to changes in expectations, (4) attributions are made to salient personal and social or external sources, (5) cognitive processing capacities develop, (6) children develop particular cultural values, and (7) children develop strategies for confirmation and disconfirmation of self-referent information.

Eder and Mangelsdorf (1997) also noted a curious disjuncture in that research with older children, adolescents, and adults focused more on individual differences in the evaluative aspects of self-concept, whereas research with preschool children focused more on categories of self-description. They suggested that the reasons for this disjuncture were that developmentalists placed more emphasis on age differences than individual differences, the instruments used with older children were not suitable for young children, and early preconceptions in the minds of researchers that young children did not demonstrate psychological self-conceptions of themselves. Reliance on open-ended questions was part of the problem in research with preschoolers. It required children to generate language rather than understand ideas and give responses indicative of their conception of self. Such difficulties with features of self-concept inventories may have obscured indications of young children's multidimensional self-concepts. For example, Eder (1990) showed that young children use organizing constructs when evaluating information. Although Eder and Mangelsdorf (1997) argued that children as young as three can use underlying constructs to organize and evaluate information about themselves, they suggested that children cannot articulate metatheories of themselves until the age of seven or eight.

Differentiation among multiple dimensions of self-concept During the 1990s, developmental psychologists addressed progressive differentiation among self-concepts (e.g., Dweck, 1999; Eccles et al., 1993; Eder & Mangelsdorf, 1997; Harter, 1998; Marsh, Craven, & Debus, 1998; Ruble & Dweck, 1995; Wigfield et al., 1997). Harter (1983, 1999) proposed a developmental model in which self-concept becomes increasingly abstract with age. She also emphasized increasing differentiation, from a global perspective of being smart, to more differentiated self-representations in specific school subjects. Harter suggested that during early childhood the young child could construct concrete cognitive representations of observable features of self, but that these were only understood as separate, taxonomic attributes – as "single representations" (see Fischer, 1980). Harter noted that young children have difficulty differentiating actual and desired attributes, and incorporating social comparison information for purposes of self-evaluation, resulting in unrealistically positive self-evaluations. At the next stage of development, Harter (1998) indicated that young children form representational sets of related attributes – what Fischer labeled "representational mappings." However, such self-descriptions were highly reflective of good and bad, resulting in all-or-none or unidimensional thinking. Whereas these self-descriptions sounded like trait labels, Ruble and Dweck (1995) argued that more research was needed to ascertain whether such attributes represented inner qualities to these children. Harter suggested that it was not until middle childhood that children were capable of integrating information from specific features to higher-order generalizations that reflect trait labels – what Fischer referred to as "representational systems." Such self-descriptions represented more balanced representations of underlying competencies that were more closely related to external criteria. Consistent with Harter's framework, there is growing evidence to suggest that the self-concept of children becomes more accurate (in relation to external criteria) with age and increasing cognitive functioning (see also Bouffard et al., 1998; Eccles, 1983; Eccles et al., 1993; Russell, Bornholt, & Ouvrier, 2002; Wigfield et al., 1997; Wigfield & Eccles, 1992).

Research on the domain-specificity of self-concepts for young children (Eccles; 1983; Eccles et al., 1993; Wigfield & Eccles, 1992) draws on an expectancy-value model of educational choice. Here, self-concepts of performance and ability are related to self-perceptions of competence and task value (e.g., interest, usefulness) that contribute to intentions and choice of behaviors (see also Bornholt, 2001). Based on earlier research (e.g., Nicholls, 1979; Stipek & Mac Iver, 1989), Eccles et al. proposed that declining self-concepts for young children reflected an optimistic bias for young children that was tempered by experience as their self-perceptions became more accurate with age. This trend is reinforced by changes in school environments, as educational achievements become more salient and education encourages social comparisons and competition.

Differential distinctiveness hypothesis Shavelson, Hubner, and Stanton (1976) hypothesized that the multidimensionality of self-concept would increase with age, but provided no clear guidelines about how to operationalize and test this hypothesis. Marsh and Hocevar (1985; Marsh & Shavelson, 1985) interpreted this to mean that there should be a systematic decline in the size of correlations among self-concept factors as children grew older. Marsh and Shavelson found support for this hypothesis in that the average correlation among self-concept scales decreased dramatically with age during early preadolescent years. Subsequent research (Marsh, Craven, & Debus, 1991, 1998) with younger children aged 5 to 8 also supported these trends, although Marsh (1989) reported no further declines in the average correlation among scales with age for older adolescents.

Although clearly relevant, this operationalization of the Shavelson, Hubner, and Stanton (1976) hypothesis was too simplistic. Marsh and Ayotte (2003) have proposed the differential distinctiveness hypothesis, whereby there are substantial declines in the sizes of correlations among self-concept factors that are most theoretically distinct, but there is little (or no) decline in the correlations among factors that are most theoretically associated. Making a similar point, Wigfield et al. (1997) suggested that some constructs should become more synchronous – more highly correlated – with age. This rationale is also consistent with the Matthew Effect (see Walberg & Tsai, 1983) where small differences at a young age may lead to larger differences as children grow older. As applied in the differential distinctiveness hypothesis, the extent of differentiation among self-concepts for young children is likely to be magnified with age so that factors that are clearly differentiated for young children become more differentiated with age.

Characteristics of self-concept instruments for young children

Research in developmental psychology by Davis-Kean emphasizes the importance of self-concepts in a variety of early childhood settings, and notes many new self-concept inventories using a variety of methodologies (Davis-Kean & Sandler, 2001; Davis-Kean, 1997). Her meta-analysis of self-concept measurement for preschool children (4 to 7 years of age) provides one of the few studies that integrate information across different methods for measuring self-concept. Indicators of the psychometric quality of the responses included reliability, convergent validity, and discriminant validity. However, there was so little information on convergent and particularly discriminant validity in studies with this age group, that Davis-Kean and Sandler could only consider internal consistency (reliability). Although they considered only the best study for each instrument, only 22 of 57 potential studies met their criteria for inclusion (typically, exclusion was due to lack of reliability information). Design quality was inferred from four characteristics (derived from theory; has *a priori* dimensions; investigated dimensionality; use of confirmatory factor analysis) and was disappointingly low across the instruments. Design quality was not clearly related to reliability estimates for each instrument, but was associated with year of publication.

In the Davis-Kean and Sandler (2001) meta-analysis, reliability was positively associated with age ($r = 0.54$; responses by older children were more reliable), number of items ($r = 0.57$; instruments with more items were more reliable), socioeconomic indicators ($r = 0.47$; responses by middle-class children were more reliable than those by lower-class children), scale type ($r = 0.30$; Likert/rating scale responses were more reliable than dichotomous responses), method ($r = 0.25$; questionnaires were better than instruments based on pictures and other devices), and setting ($r = 0.23$; responses collected in school settings were more reliable than those collected in non-school settings). They also evaluated the extent to which children's age interacted with other predictor variables – particularly the superiority of questionnaires and longer instruments. Age interacted significantly with method of data collection, but the nature of this interaction was somewhat surprising in that the advantage of questionnaires over pictorial formats was stronger for younger (4–5-year-old) children and was negligible for older (6–7-year-old) children. However, these results supported the suggestion of Marsh, Craven, and Debus (1998) that the juxtaposition of the pictures and verbal explanations was more confusing for young children than verbal presentations alone.

The number of items in the inventory is a particularly important issue for the reliability of self-concepts responses by young children. Initially, Davis-Kean (1997) speculated that brief inventories might be better for younger children, even though conventional wisdom suggests that adding more items of parallel content and difficulty increases the internal reliability of a measure. However, on the basis of their meta-analysis, Davis-Kean and Sandler (2001, p. 900) concluded that "regardless of the age of a respondent, if researchers add enough items of parallel content to an instrument, the instrument will be highly reliable." Marsh, Craven, and Debus (1991, 1998) suggested that the number of items in a scale increases reliability, as suggested by measurement theory, but may also give children time to understand and respond more appropriately (i.e., a warm-up effect) so that the quality of responses to items near the end of an instrument is better than that of items near the beginning or in the middle of the instrument.

Self-concept instruments for young children

In the past decade there have been two major reviews of self-concept measures (Wylie, 1989; Byrne, 1996) for different age groups. Both reviewers noted many instruments available for young children, but concluded that only two were sufficiently developed to warrant serious consideration; the Harter and Pike instrument (1984) discussed below and the Joseph instrument (1979), which relies on items from a variety of different domains to infer a global, undifferentiated self-concept. However, for both instruments there was a paucity of psychometric evidence (reliability, stability, factor structure), and the evidence that was available was not particularly encouraging. Given Byrne's review was conducted seven years after Wylie's review, it was disconcerting that there was virtually no further research undertaken that utilized either of these two instruments, so that there was still no adequate information available to evaluate their construct validity. This lack of satisfactory inventories for this age group is surprising, given that theoretical models of self-concept development suggest that young children should be able to differentiate among different components of self-concept. We expect that recent progress in theory, research, and practice that stimulated sound inventories for older children will also stimulate the development of better multidimensional inventories for younger children. In response to this need, researchers (Byrne, 1996; Fantuzzo et al., 1996; Harter, 1983; Harter & Pike, 1984; Marsh & Craven, 1997; Marsh, Craven, & Debus, 1991; Stipek & Mac Iver, 1989; Stipek, Recchia, & McClintic, 1992; Wylie, 1989) recommended the evaluation of potentially more appropriate assessment procedures (e.g., simplified item content, use of direct questions, more appropriate response formats, and individually based interviews instead of group administered paper-and-pencil tests).

An early attempt by Harter and Pike (1984) evaluated support for an *a priori* factor structure for young children aged four to seven. Their instrument included self-concept scales (physical, cognitive, peers, and maternal) using items represented by parallel verbal statements and pictures. They found that below age eight, children either did not understand general self-worth items or did not provide reliable responses, prompting them to exclude this scale from their instrument. Results identified only two factors: Competence (incorporating the physical and cognitive scales) and Social Acceptance (incorporating the peer and maternal scales). The factor structure was less differentiated than the structure typically found for older children, supporting the assumption that the structure becomes more differentiated with age. Marsh, Craven, and Debus (1991) suggested that the failure to separate even the physical and academic components that are so robust in responses by slightly older children was surprising. They suggested that perhaps part of the failure to identify the *a priori* factor structure was due to reliance on exploratory factor analysis rather than stronger confirmatory factor analysis procedures. They noted, for example, that correlations among the physical and academic scales reported by Harter and Pike (rs of 0.43 to 0.56) did not approach 1.0, even after correction for unreliability, and that there was support for their differentiation in relation to other criteria reported by Harter and Pike (e.g., teacher ratings, choice of behavior, being held back a grade). Marsh, Craven, and Debus concluded that Harter and Pike's interpretation was unduly pessimistic about the ability of young children to differentiate among multiple dimensions of self-concept and that it may be premature to conclude that children at this age level can only identify two broad components of self.

Fantuzzo et al. (1996) used the Harter and Pike inventory (1984) in a large study of Head Start participants. However, they were unable to replicate Harter and Pike's two-factor structure, concluding that the instrument "did not yield meaningful or stable constructs" (p. 1078) for their sample and that the administration format was not developmentally appropriate for preschool children. Furthermore, they found no replications of the instrument's factor structure or empirical evaluations of its developmental appropriateness for preschool children in the research literature. Whereas the focus of the Fantuzzo et al. study was on the measurement of self-concept responses, they argued that their study had even broader implications for developmental and early childhood research. More specifically, they emphasized that their results were fundamental to the broader debate about the validity of self-report responses as a research tool for preschool children. On one side of the debate, they cited researchers who argued that preschool self-reports have such questionable validity that only responses by adult respondents should be considered. On the other side of the debate, Fantuzzo et al. cited other researchers who argued for the need to develop self-report methods to assess self-perceptions that were not confounded by biases in responses by parents and teachers. This debate is particularly important in self-concept research where it is broadly assumed (e.g., Marsh, 1990; Marsh & Craven, 1997; Shavelson, Hubner, & Stanton, 1976; Wylie, 1989) that self-concept can only be inferred from self-report responses and that responses by significant others (e.g., parents, peers, teachers) – inferred self-concepts – represent a distinct construct that has theoretically important relations with (self-report) self-concept responses (e.g., Marsh & Byrne, 1993; Marsh & Craven, 1991). Furthermore, Fantuzzo et al.'s failure to find a meaningful factor structure called into question the appropriateness of conclusions based on theoretical research indicating that young children should be able to differentiate among different self-concept factors.

The meaning of children's self-concepts is considered in relation to expectancy-value models of educational choice that focus on how self-concepts and related task values contribute to children's educational plans and behavioral choices (Bornholt, 2001; 2000a; Eccles et al., 1993; Wigfield et al., 1997). Eccles et al. (1993) provided further support for the multidimensionality of self-concept for young children, finding that children in grades 1, 2, and 4 differentiated math, reading, music, and sports self-concepts. In 1997, Wigfield et al. used a multicohort–multioccasion (or cohort-sequential longitudinal) design to assess three age cohorts (children in grades 1, 2, and 4) in each of three successive years. They found that self-concepts declined with age, and that these effects were reasonably consistent over domain and across cohort and longitudinal comparisons. There was also a consistent pattern in test–retest stability coefficients in which stability over time was low for young children and grew steadily with age, although these comparisons were complicated to some extent by age-related differences in reliability (see also Spencer & Bornholt, 2003). Wigfield et al. reported gender effects (favoring boys in math and sport, favoring girls in music and reading) that did not interact with either cohort or time of measurement. Instead, consistent with Marsh (1989; Marsh, Craven, & Debus, 1991), they found that gender differences emerged at an early age and remained reasonably consistent as young children grew older. Finally, teacher and parent ratings of children's competence showed little systematic relation to self-ratings for the youngest children, but were substantially related to self-perceptions for the oldest children. Wigfield et al. also found that in contrast to children's self-perceptions, teacher and parent ratings of the children's competence did not vary as a function of age.

Promising New Self-Concept Instruments for Young Children

Extension of Self Description Questionnaire I with Individual Administration (SDQI-IA)

Marsh, Craven, and Debus (1991, 1998) described a new, adaptive procedure for assessing multiple dimensions of self-concept for children aged 5–8 using the SDQI. They explored the use of pictorial self-concept instruments (e.g., Harter & Pike, 1984) but found that the juxtaposition of the pictures and verbal explanations was more confusing to young children than the verbal presentations alone. In an individual interview format, the 64 positively worded items from the SDQI were administered to large samples of children in kindergarten, 1st grade and 2nd grade. A double binary response strategy was adapted, in part, from Harter and Pike (1984). The interviewer initially asked the child to respond "yes" or "no" to each description. This was always followed by a second probe (i.e., "yes always" or "yes sometimes" or "no always" or "no sometimes"). Children were encouraged to seek clarification of the meaning of any item they did not understand. CFAs (Marsh, Craven, & Debus, 1991; 1998) clearly identified all eight SDQI scales. With increasing age, the differentiation among the eight factors improved, as shown by the decreasing size of correlations among the factors. As part of this research, Marsh, Craven, and Debus (1991) compared this new assessment procedure with the standard group administration procedure in which the same SDQI items were read aloud to groups of children. Kindergarten children were not able to complete this group-administered task. For children in grades 1 and 2, the psychometric properties of group administration responses were substantially poorer than those based on the individual interview responses. Byrne (1996) specifically noted the effectiveness of the Marsh, Craven, and Debus (1991) study in adapting the SDQI for use with very young children. She emphasized that the psychometric properties based on this single study were stronger than those provided by any other instruments specifically designed for very young children, clearly demonstrating the need for further research on this promising adaptation of a well-established instrument.

In a cross-cultural replication, Lee (2002) administered the SDQI-IA to 201 Korean kindergarten children aged 3.4 to 6.4 (mean age = 5 years). Although the children were younger than in the Marsh, Craven, and Debus studies (1991, 1998), they were enrolled in a kindergarten with a systematic curriculum rather than preschool or day-care programs. Replicating administration procedures in the original Marsh, Craven, and Debus

(1991, 1998) research, Lee reported that reliability estimates for the eight SDQ factors varied from 0.69 to 0.81 (median = 0.77) and that the reliability of the total score was 0.93. Factor loadings were consistently high (0.44 to 0.89; mean = 0.71), whereas correlations among the eight factors provided reasonable support for discrimination among the factors. Correlations among the seven specific factors – excluding the global scale – varied from 0.50 to 0.86, whereas the global scale was substantially highly correlated with specific factors (0.67 to 0.93). Lee concluded that the Korean replication provided support for the cross-cultural validity of SDQI-IA responses.

The SDQI-IA was also used successfully with a large group of 211 young children (grades 2–6) with mild intellectual disabilities (IQs between 56 and 75; Tracey, Marsh, & Craven, 2003; also see Russell, Bornholt, & Ouvrier, 2002). The educational placement of children with mild intellectual disabilities remains controversial and debate is often based on the anticipated impact upon self-concept. Labeling theory suggests that special class placement should have a negative effect on self-concepts, whereas social comparison theory predicts the opposite. Tracey, Marsh, and Craven argued that limitations in past research with special education populations included the predominant use of unidimensional measures of self-concept, psychometrically weak instruments, and measures that had not been validated for this population (see also Coleman & Bornholt, 2003; Russell, Bornholt, & Ouvrier, 2002). Children in regular ("mainstream") classes and special support classes completed the SDQI-IA using the individually administered format. CFAs and estimates of reliability revealed that the SDQI-IA was a suitable measure of self-concept for these children. Even for the youngest cohort (grades 2–4), the mean alpha across the eight self-concept scales was 0.86 (range of 0.68 to 0.95). Confirmatory factor analysis clearly identified all eight *a priori* factors; the factor loading for each variable was consistently high on the factor that it was designed to measure (average factor loading = 0.78) and goodness of fit indexes suggested that the *a priori* model provided a good fit to the data. Consistent with theoretical predictions, children in regular classes had significantly lower self-concepts for all three academic scales (Reading, Math, School), for one nonacademic scale (Peers), and for General self-concept, but did not differ from children in special classes for the remaining three nonacademic self-concepts (Parents, Physical Ability, Physical Appearance). Results support the construct validity of the SDQI-IA in this special population, social comparison theory, and the need to consider multiple dimensions of self-concept. The findings suggest that the SDQI-IA is a reliable and valid measure of self-concept for this population of young special education children.

Potential strengths and weaknesses of the measurement procedure A substantial body of research using the SDQI-IA (Marsh, Craven, & Debus, 1991, 1998) provides stronger support for the construct validity of self-concept responses than those based on other instruments reviewed by Byrne (1996) and Wylie (1989). Thus, it is relevant to speculate on the potential strengths and weaknesses in the instrument and in the administration procedure. The individual interview-style administration was an important feature of the strategy used by Marsh, Craven, and Debus (1991) and was more effective than group administration procedures – even when the items were read aloud to children. An important limitation is that individual administration procedures required much more time than the typical group administration procedure, and many statistical procedures require reasonably large sample sizes of at least 200 children and preferably more (e.g., Tanaka, 1987). In the Marsh, Craven, and Debus research the test administration was conducted by a large number of different undergraduate teacher education students with some classroom experience, who were given a two-hour training program consisting of an instructional video and trial administrations. Although these results suggested that relatively inexperienced test administrators easily mastered the testing procedures, even stronger results might have been obtained if the administration had been done by a small number of more highly trained professionals.

Self-concept instruments for young children sometimes combine the use of verbal cues and pictures, but preliminary research reported by Marsh, Craven, and Debus suggested that the pictures were counterproductive – distracting young children from the verbal content of the items. Whereas these results are only suggestive, it would be of interest to pursue these preliminary findings with more fully developed instruments that use a pictorial format.

A significant difference between the Marsh, Craven, and Debus (1991, 1998) studies and most previous research with young children was the length of the questionnaire: 64 items. Whereas the authors were initially concerned about the potential for fatigue, loss of interest, and loss of attention, such that the quality of responses for items near the end of the instrument would deteriorate, they found that these items were psychometrically stronger, not weaker. There was a clear progression of increasing factor loadings for items presented in the first, second, third, and fourth quarters of the instrument. Consistent with the Davis-Kean and Sandler (2001) meta-analysis, these results have important implications for early childhood researchers in that the use of short instruments may be counterproductive and may account for some of the difficulties researchers have in obtaining responses that yield good psychometric properties from young children.

The items used by Marsh, Craven, and Debus (1991, 1998) were from a well-established instrument, designed for older children. A potential limitation of this strategy was that the wording of some of the items (e.g., the term "mathematics") was overly complex for some young children. However, this potential limitation was apparently offset by the flexibility of individual administration in which the meaning of any item could be explained to a child. Instruments specifically designed for young children, such as those reviewed by Byrne (1996) and Wylie (1989) have typically not been used with older children. It is therefore unclear whether apparent problems with many of these instruments are inherent in the instruments or related to their use with young children. If an instrument is not effective with children slightly older than the target population, it is unlikely to be effective with young children.

Self Description Questionnaire Preschool–Individual Administration (SDQP-IA)

Following from the success of Marsh, Craven, and Debus (1991, 1998), a reasonable question is whether the SDQI-IA can be extended to even younger children and still retain reasonable psychometric properties. In pursuing this question, Marsh, Ellis, and

Craven (2002) argued that a growing body of theoretical and empirical research (e.g., Eder & Mangelsdorf, 1997) suggests that children should be able to construct meaningful self-conceptions and differentiate among the components at younger ages than previously assumed. Pilot research indicated that the individual interview style with the double-binary response scale was viable with preschool children aged 4 and 5. However, following suggestions by Chapman and Tunmer (1995), Marsh, Ellis, and Craven found that a question format (e.g., "Can you run fast?") worked better than the declarative format (e.g., "I can run fast") used by Marsh, Craven, and Debus (1991, 1998). Although Marsh, Craven, and Debus (1991) found that the general self-concept scale was well-defined and reliable for young children, extensive piloting suggested that preschool children could not clearly understand these items (also see Harter, 1983; Harter & Pike, 1984). Consequently, this scale was excluded from the SDQP. Marsh, Ellis, and Craven also found that more explicit and specific items enhanced understanding. In particular, the academic self-concept items from the SDQI were not easily understood and were sometimes inappropriate (e.g., preschool children are not given grades in mathematics or English and, typically, have not yet learned to read), so the authors developed new items (e.g., Do you know lots of letters of the alphabet? Do you know lots of different words? Do you know lots of different shapes? Do you like playing number games?). Based on this pilot work, 38 items were developed to represent six self-concept scales (Physical, Appearance, Peers, Parents, Verbal, and Math). Approximately half of the items were new and the rest were slight modifications of original SDQI items.

Using an individual-interview procedure and double-binary response format, young children ($N = 100$, aged 4.0 to 5.6 years) completed the SDQP-IA and a battery of achievement tests. In evaluating responses to the SDQP-IA, Marsh, Ellis, and Craven (2002) focused on traditional psychometric criteria of reliability and factor structure, age and gender differences, and relations with standardized measures of achievement. The psychometric properties were good; the self-concept specific scales were reliable (0.75–0.89; $Md = 0.83$), first and higher-order confirmatory factor models fitted the data well, and correlations among the scales were mostly moderate (−0.03–0.73; $Md = 0.29$). Achievement test scores correlated modestly with academic self-concept factors (rs 0.15 to 0.40), but were nonsignificantly or significantly negatively related to nonacademic self-concept scales. Compared with responses by older children, there were several distinctive features of these results. The correlation between Verbal and Math self-concepts (0.73) was much larger than the near-zero correlations found with children who were more than 10 years old and larger even than those reported for children aged 5–8 (Marsh, Craven, & Debus, 1998). Interestingly, reminiscent of findings by Harter and Pike (1984), the Physical self-concept scale in the Marsh, Ellis and Craven study was somewhat more strongly correlated with the academic self-concept scales than with the other nonacademic self-concept scales. It is plausible that the transition from preschool to kindergarten and early school years, with a greater emphasis on mathematics and reading as formal curriculum areas, reinforced the distinction between Math and Verbal self-concept. Clearly, there is a need for longitudinal research in which the effects of the (gradual) developmental trend of increasing differentiation between Math and Verbal self-concepts and the (abrupt) transitional effects of moving from preschool to regular school are more fully articulated.

Marsh, Ellis, and Craven (2002) also offered advice about the construction of self-report instruments for young children that may also be useful for researchers in other areas. They emphasized that it was important to develop items that were tangible and relevant to children's everyday experience. For example, the Math and Verbal items from the SDQI worked well for young children who had already begun school, but were not appropriate for the preschoolers. As reported by Marsh, Craven, and Debus (1991, 1998; also see Davis-Kean & Sandler, 2001), they concluded that very short instruments were unlikely to result in reliable responses and that pictorial representations seemed to confuse young children. However, they found that introducing a short break with some physical activity in the middle of the test administration was useful. At least for these young children, they also found that phrasing items as questions rather than first-person declarative sentences was more natural. Because they only asked children to make a series of binary choices, the young children were not explicitly asked to make judgments along a continuum (even though the authors combined their binary choices to form a continuum). Most importantly, the individual-interview format allowed the test administrator to establish rapport with the child, ascertain that the child was able to understand the task based on responses to sample items, clarify the meaning of words or expressions that were unfamiliar to the child, and – through the double-binary choice format – provide a double check on the appropriateness of each response.

It is also relevant to point out some limitations in the Marsh, Ellis, and Craven (2002) research and interpretations. There were several technical issues that warrant some concern (small sample size and non-normal response distributions), even though the results were apparently robust in relation to these concerns. Implicit in their interpretations of their CFAs was the suggestion that the preschool children have mental representations of themselves as physically competent (or incompetent), as popular (or unpopular) and so on. In relation to the five categories proposed by Eder and Mangelsdorf (1997), this interpretation corresponds to their fifth category – development of a metatheory of self. Eder and Mangelsdorf claimed, however, that children did not reach this stage until the age of 7 or 8. According to their theoretical model, children in the Marsh, Ellis, and Craven study should only have been at their Stage 4 – possessing underlying dispositional constructs for organizing information about themselves. The Marsh, Ellis, and Craven study, however, was not specifically aimed at distinguishing between these two stages of self-concept development. Children clearly responded to items representing each factor in an internally consistent manner that was distinct from the way they answered items representing other factors. However, the authors did not explicitly test whether the children were able to articulate these underlying constructs fully, but suggested that it would be easier for young children to articulate the underlying constructs that the SDQP was designed to measure (e.g., popularity with peers, physical attractiveness, loved by parents, etc.) than the apparently more abstract personality domains used in the 1990 Eder study (e.g., self-acceptance, self-control, extraversion). Even more problematic, perhaps, was the interpretation of higher-order factors. They were aware, for example, of Harter's often-cited claim (1986, 1998) that higher-order factors were more likely to reside in the heads of factor analytic-oriented researchers than in the minds of children who complete our instruments. They argued that hierarchical CFA was merely a useful tool to explore clusterings of lower-order factors and to evaluate whether relations between the lower-order factors and other relevant variables can be explained in terms of higher-order constructs.

It is also interesting to compare these results based on the new preschool version of the SDQI with Lee's (2002) results based on responses by kindergarten children of a similar age. Both studies provided support for the individual administration procedure and for *a priori*, multidimensional self-concept ratings for children even younger than 5 years of age. The main difference was that Lee reported that the original items from the SDQI-IA were successful, whereas Marsh, Ellis, and Craven modified the items for their younger age group. It is important to note that the Korean children were enrolled in kindergarten with a formal academic curriculum, whereas the Australian children were enrolled in preschools where there was less academic emphasis. Hence, it is interesting to speculate that the appropriateness of the original set of items may have varied according to the structure of the preschool versus kindergarten setting. Indeed, this suggestion is consistent with the Marsh, Ellis, and Craven (2002) suggestion as to why the SDQI-IA worked for kindergarten children but not for preschool children.

Marsh, Ellis, and Craven (2002) concluded that their research with preschool children showed a well-defined multidimensional factor structure with reasonably reliable factors. However, the instrument probably needs more research to ascertain the replicability of the findings and, perhaps, to explore the appropriateness of including multiple dimensions of academic self-concept. Although probably not sufficiently reliable to use as a basis for making judgments about individual children, the instrument should be useful for comparing groups of children and for other research purposes. More generally, the findings provide an important counterperspective to researchers who argue that only responses by adult informants should be used in research with preschool children.

The ASK-KIDS self-concept inventory for children

Self-concepts are cognitive evaluations that integrate knowledge of oneself and corresponding activities (Bornholt, 2000b; Bornholt & Ingram, 2001). A substantial body of theory, and correlational and experimental evidence, supports a self-categorization approach to the sources and consequences of children's self-concepts. In particular, recent studies show the stability and test–retest reliability of young children's self-concepts over time (Spencer & Bornholt, 2003), the personal and social bases of self-concepts that support and constrain choice behaviors, and interventions that enhance particular self-concepts (Bornholt, 2000b; Bornholt & Ingram, 2001; Coleman & Bornholt, 2003). Ongoing research examines context effects on congruence or incongruence of children's self-concepts and feelings about activities (Bornholt & Nelson, 2002).

The Aspects of Self Knowledge (ASK-KIDS) inventory measures self-concepts about activities for 5–12-year-old children (Bornholt, 1997; Russell, Bornholt, & Ouvrier, 2002), with recent advances for preschool children (Penn, Burnett, & Patton, 2001). ASK-KIDS is a brief self-concept inventory that is meaningful to children and useful in clinical and educational settings. There are ten activities: reading, number, drawing, friendship, self-expression, individuality, belonging, movement, body, and appearance activities (see Bornholt, 2000b; Bornholt & Ingram, 2001; Brake & Bornholt, 2002;

Coleman & Bornholt, 2003). ASK-KIDS is readily extended to other activities (e.g., self-concepts about cognitive assessments for young children; Spencer & Bornholt, 2003) and other populations in diverse locations (e.g., children with cognitive impairments and reading difficulties; Coleman & Bornholt, 2003).

ASK-KIDS is administered individually by a trained interviewer, who provides practice items, describes the activity, and reads each item. Direct questions make genuine enquiries (e.g., "How good are you at reading?"), with scripted prompts to clarify terms. There are five items for each self-concept. Children respond using a simple one-to-five dot-point scale (low to high). Their responses create diverse individual profiles, around an optimal point that is just above the mid-point of the scale. There are a few small gender effects, and profiles are unbiased by socioeconomic indicators.

The ASK-KIDS measurement model has ten related yet discrete factors with uncorrelated residuals. Psychometric properties of the measurement models are generally sound (Bornholt, 1997; Bornholt & Nelson, 2002). In particular, responses of young children (under 8 years, $N = 283$) and older children ($N = 379$) create internally consistent self-concepts based on conventional coefficients (alpha 0.6 to 0.8). CFA showed satisfactory goodness-of-fit for younger (ratio ChiSq/df 2.5, RMSEA 0.04) and older children (ratio ChiSq/df 1.5, RMSEA 0.06). For younger children, self-concepts are often uncorrelated (80 percent), with notable exceptions for reading–number ($r = 0.29$), reading–drawing ($r = 0.31$), friends–expression ($r = 0.53$), friends–individuality ($r = 0.45$), individuality–expression ($r = 0.48$), individuality–body ($r = 0.29$), belonging–drawing ($r = 0.48$), body–movement ($r = 0.47$), and body–appearance ($r = 0.36$). For older children, self-concepts were also uncorrelated (82 percent), except for reading–number ($r = 0.59$), reading–drawing ($r = 0.44$), drawing–number ($r = 0.38$), friends–expression ($r = 0.42$), individuality–reading ($r = 0.29$), individuality–drawing ($r = 0.43$), belonging–body ($r = 0.35$), and reading–movement ($r = 0.29$).

In summary, the ASK-KIDS self-concept inventory is brief, meaningful, and useful with younger and older children in educational and clinical settings. The measurement and structural models are confirmed by CFA, and the self-categorization approach to self-concepts is supported by corrrelational and experimental evidence that balances stability and responsiveness of children's self-concepts to experience.

Berkeley Puppet Interviews (BPI; Measelle et al., 1998)

The Berkeley Puppet Interviews (Measelle et al., 1998) are based on earlier research by Eder (1990), and research that shows children can differentiate among multiple dimensions of self-concept at a younger age than typically assumed (Harter & Pike, 1984; Marsh, Craven, & Debus, 1991; Shavelson, Hubner, & Stanton, 1976). The procedure uses an interview format to promote a peer-like communication between the child and two puppets. Children are presented with a pair of bipolar opposite statements that are simple declarative sentences. To engage the interest of the child, each statement is presented by one of the puppets. Children may indicate their choice in a manner most natural to them (e.g., naming the puppet or pointing to the puppet). Materials were administered by undergraduate students following extensive training. The interviews were videotaped and scores assigned by two external observers on a 7-point response scale from (1) low to (7) high. For example, a response "I am dumb too" that matched the original statement would be given a 2, whereas responses "I am really dumb" or "I am kind of dumb" would be given a 1 or 3, respectively. The authors reported high levels of agreement between coders.

The BPI has 60 item-pairs with equal numbers of positive and negative content, used to measure six scales: Academic Competence, Achievement Motivation/Valuing, Social Competence, Peer Acceptance, Depression-Anxiety, and Aggression-Hostility. Results were reported for 97 children in two-parent, largely middle-class families whose oldest child was about to enter kindergarten (T1; mean age = 4.6, SD = 0.47). Follow-up responses were collected from the same children when they had completed kindergarten (T2) and had completed first grade (T3). In addition to the BPI responses, children completed standardized achievement tests and each child's competency and achievement was evaluated independently by each parent and by the teacher.

Responses were internally consistent across age groups (0.59 to 0.75, except for social competence at T1, T2, and T3). Exploratory factor analysis showed that items were closely associated with appropriate factors, with no more than 25 percent of cross-loading over 0.35. The mean correlation among scales decreased from 0.36 (T1), 0.31 (T2), and 0.28 (T3), suggesting more differentiation with age, whereas stability of responses over time increased with age (0.41 for T1/T2; 0.51 for T2/T3; 0.28 for T1/T3). Although there were some stereotypical gender differences (girls higher on Depression-Anxiety, lower on Aggression-Hostility), these were small and consistent over time. Age effects were also small, although self-concepts tended to increase with age. There was also a tendency for parent-inferred self-concepts to increase over time.

Children's BPI scores were associated with teacher ratings on scales (T1, T2, T3), and mother ratings (T2 and T3). Self–other agreement increased systematically with age and was higher for teacher ratings than mother ratings, and for mother ratings than for father ratings. Test scores were significantly related to achievement motivation and depression-anxiety (but not academic competence) at T2 and to achievement motivation, depression-anxiety, and academic competence at T3.

Overall, Measelle et al. (1998) report impressive preliminary support for this new multidimensional measure of self-concept designed for children as young as four years of age – particularly in relation to traditional measures such as those reviewed by Byrne (1996) and Wylie (1989). The main limitation of the puppet method is that it is labor-intensive in terms of training interviewers and coders, administering the BPI, and coding the results based on videotaped responses. There are clear strengths, in that the reliability and stability of children's responses were satisfactory, with clear differentiation among the self-concepts. Relations between BPI scores and informant responses provided support for convergent validity, whereas relations with academic achievement provided support for convergent validity and some support for divergent validity. In summarizing limitations of their research, Measelle et al. (1998) noted the need to replicate their results with larger, more diverse samples – particularly given that the results were apparently based on responses to only 41 of the original set of 60 items selected as being most effective in the same sample. They also indicated that the item pool is not static, as they are attempting to improve items for the six scales and, perhaps, include additional scales.

Summary and Implications

Central to this chapter is the critical debate in developmental and early childhood research about the validity of self-report as a research tool for young children (Fantuzzo et al., 1996). This debate is particularly important in self-concept research because many self-concept researchers argue that self-concept can only be measured by self-report. However, recognizing the importance of perceptions of significant others, these self-concept researchers argue that such inferred self-concept responses must be distinguished from self-concept responses based on self-report responses. The outcome of this debate is also important as a basis for validating claims based on theoretical models of self-concept development, that children as young as four and five years of age should be able to distinguish among multiple dimensions of self-concept. From the perspective of this broad, overarching debate, our most important conclusion was the existence of a clearly defined, multidimensional structure of self-concept based on self-report responses by young children, younger than eight years of age. The apparent failure of previous research with young children apparently reflects problems with the development of appropriate multidimensional instruments and the reliance on weak or inappropriate statistical tools as well as issues that are idiosyncratic to this particular age group. Results with new self-concept inventories demonstrate that young children can distinguish among multiple dimensions of self-concept at a younger age than has been demonstrated in studies based on other self-concept instruments. This provides strong support for like-minded researchers who argue for the importance of self-report as a research tool in developmental and early childhood research. In support of this conclusion, we have summarized preliminary results based on several promising new instruments specifically designed for this age group. We predict that the combination of more appropriate measurement tools, better methodology, and stronger statistical procedures will facilitate a resurgence of good-quality self-concept research with young children.

Acknowledgment

We would like to thank the Australian Research Council, and to acknowledge its financial assistance for this research.

Note

Correspondence in relation to this chapter should be sent to Professor Herbert W. Marsh, SELF Research Centre, University of Western Sydney, Bankstown Campus, Penrith South DC, NSW 1797, Australia. Email: Herb Marsh, H.Marsh@uws.edu.au (also see http://self.uws.edu.au).

References

Bates, E. (1990). Language about me and you: Pronominal reference and the emerging concept of self. In D. Cicchetti & M. Beeghly (eds.), *The self in transition* (pp. 165–82). Chicago, IL: University of Chicago Press.

Bornholt, L. J. (1997). Aspects of self knowledge about activities with young children, *Every Child*, *3*, 15–18.

Bornholt, L. J. (2000a). ASK-KIDS about task choice: Self-concepts and choices of number, reading and drawing activities. In R. G. Craven & H. W. Marsh (eds.), *Self-Concept Theory, Research and Practice: Advances for the New Millennium*, Proceedings of the Inaugural International Conference, Sydney, Oct. 5–6, 2000. Sydney: SELF Research Centre, University of Western Sydney (http://self.uws.edu.au/conferences/2000_Proceedings.pdf).

Bornholt, L. J. (2000b). Social and personal aspects of self knowledge: A balance of individuality and belonging. *Learning and Instruction*, *10*, 415–29.

Bornholt, L. J. (2001). Self-concepts, usefulness and behavioural intentions in the social context of schooling, *Educational Psychology*, *21*, 67–78.

Bornholt, L. J. & Ingram, A. (2001). Personal and social identity in children's self-concepts about drawing, *Educational Psychology*, *21*, 151–67.

Bornholt, L. J. & Nelson, L. (2002). The affective basis of children's self evaluations about cognitive, physical and social activities. In R. G. Craven, H. W. Marsh, & K. B. Simpson (eds.), *Self-Concept Research: Driving International Research Agendas*, Proceedings of the 2nd International Biennial Conference, Sydney, Aug. 6–8, 2002. Sydney: SELF Research Centre, University of Western Sydney (http://self.uws.edu.au/Conferences/2002_Proceedings.htm).

Bouffard, T., Markovits, H., Vezeau, C., Boisvert, M., & Dumas, C. (1998). The relation between accuracy of self-perception and cognitive development. *British Journal of Educational Psychology*, *68*, 321–30.

Brake, N. & Bornholt, L. J. (2002). Optimal physical self concepts for children, *Primary Educator*, *2*, 18–23.

Burns, R. B. (1979). *The self-concept: Theory, measurement, development and behaviour.* London: Longman.

Byrne, B. M. (1984). The general/academic self-concept nomological network: A review of construct validation research. *Review of Educational Research*, *54*, 427–56.

Byrne, B. M. (1996*). Measuring self-concept across the life span: Issues and instrumentation.* Washington, DC: American Psychological Association.

Chapman, J. W. & Tunmer, W. E. (1995). Development of children's reading self-concepts: An examination of emerging subcomponents and their relation with reading achievement. *Journal of Educational Psychology*, *87*, 154–67.

Coleman, C. & Bornholt, L. J. (2003). Reading self concepts and task choices for children with reading difficulties, *Australian Journal of Learning Disabilities*, *8*, 24–31.

Damon, W. & Hart, D. (1988). *Self-understanding in childhood and adolescence.* New York: Cambridge University Press.

Davis-Kean, P. E. (1997). A meta-analysis of preschool self-concept measures: A framework for future measures. *Dissertation Abstracts International Section A: Humanities & Social Sciences*, *57(11-A)*, 4646.

Davis-Kean, P. & Sandler, H. M. (2001). A meta-analysis of measures of self-esteem for young children: A framework for future measures. *Child Development*, *72(3)*, 887–906.

Dweck, C. S. (1999). *Self-theories: Their role in motivation, personality, and development.* Philadelphia, PA: Psychology Press/Taylor & Francis.

Eccles, J. S. (1983). Expectancies, values, and academic choice: Origins and changes. In J. Spence (ed.), *Achievement and achievement motivation* (pp. 75–146). San Francisco. CA: W. H. Freeman.

Eccles, J., Wigfield, Harold, R. D., & Blumenfeld, P. (1993). Age and gender differences in children's self- and task perceptions during elementary school. *Child Development*, *64*, 830–47.

Eder, R. A. (1989). The emergent personologist: The structure and content of $3^1/_2$, $5^1/_2$, and $7^1/_2$-year-olds' concepts of themselves and other persons, *Child Development*, *60*, 1218–28.

Eder, R. A. (1990). Uncovering young children's psychological selves: Individual and developmental differences. *Child Development*, *61*, 849–63.

Eder, R. A. & Mangelsdorf, S. C. (1997). The emotional basis of early personality development: Implications for the emergent self-concept. In R. Hogan, J. Johnson, & S. Briggs (eds.), *Handbook of personality psychology* (pp. 209–40). San Diego, CA: Academic Press.

Fantuzzo, J. W, McDermott, P. A., Manz, P. H., Hampton, V. R., & Burdick, N. A. (1996). The Pictorial scale of perceived competence and social acceptance: Does it work with low-income urban children? *Child Development*, *67*, 1071–84.

Fischer, K. W. (1980). A theory of cognitive development: The control and construction of hierarchies of skills. *Psychological Review*, *87*, 477–531.

Guay, F., Marsh, H. W. & Boivin, M. (2003). Academic self-concept and academic achievement: Development perspectives on their causal ordering. *Journal of Educational Psychology*, *95*, 124–36.

Harter, S. (1983). Developmental perspectives on the self-system. In P. H. Mussen (ed.), *Handbook of child psychology* (vol. IV, 4th edn., pp. 275–385). New York: John Wiley.

Harter, S. (1985). Competence as dimensions of self-evaluation: Toward a comprehensive model of self-worth. In R. L. Leahy (ed.), *The development of self* (pp. 55–122). New York: Academic Press.

Harter, S. (1986). Processes underlying the construction, maintenance and enhancement of self-concept in children. In J. Suls & A. Greenwald (eds.), *Psychological perspective on the self* (vol. 3, pp. 136–82). Hillsdale, NJ: Lawrence Erlbaum Associates.

Harter, S. (1998). The development of self-representations. In W. Damon (ed.), S. Eisenberg (vol. ed.), *Handbook of child psychology* (5th edn., pp. 553–617). New York: John Wiley.

Harter, S. (1999). *The construction of the self: A developmental perspective*. New York: Guilford Press.

Harter, S. & Pike, R. (1984). The pictorial scale of perceived competence and social acceptance for young children. *Child Development*, *55*, 1969–82.

Hattie, J. (1992). *Self-concept*. Hillsdale, NJ: Lawrence Erlbaum Associates.

Hattie, J. & Marsh, H. W. (1996). Future directions in self-concept research. In B. A. Bracken (ed.), *Handbook of self-concept* (pp. 421–62). New York: John Wiley.

Howe, M. L. & Courage, M. L. (1997). The emergence and early development of autobiographical memory. *Psychological Review*, *104*, 499–523.

Joseph, B. W. (1979). *Pre-school and Primary Self-Concept Screening Test: Instruction manual*. Chicago, IL: Stoelting Co.

Kagen, S. L., Moore, E., & Bredekamp, S. (1995). *Considering children's early development and learning: Toward common views and vocabulary* (report no. 95-03). Washington, DC: National Education Goals Pane.

Lee, Kyung-Ok (2002). Measurement structure of SDQ-I and self-concept development of kindergarteners in Korea. In R. G. Craven, H. W. Marsh, & K. B. Simpson (eds.), *Self-Concept Research: Driving International Research Agendas*, Proceedings of the 2nd International Biennial Conference, Sydney, Aug. 6–8, 2002. Sydney: SELF Research Centre, University of Western Sydney (http://self.uws.edu.au/Conferences/2002_Proceedings.htm).

Lewis, M., & Brooks-Gunn, J. (1979). *Social cognition and the acquisition of self*. New York: Plenum Press.

Marsh, H. W. (1989). Age and sex effects in multiple dimensions of self-concept: Preadolescence to early-adulthood. *Journal of Educational Psychology, 81*, 417–30.

Marsh, H. W. (1990). A multidimensional, hierarchical model of self-concept: Theoretical and empirical justification. *Educational Psychology Review, 2*, 77–172.

Marsh, H. W. (1993). Academic self-concept: Theory measurement and research. In J. Suls (ed.), *Psychological perspectives on the self* (vol. 4, pp. 59–98). Hillsdale, NJ: Lawrence Erlbaum Associates.

Marsh, H. W. & Ayotte, V. (2003). Do multiple dimensions of self-concept become more differentiated with age? The differential distinctiveness hypothesis. *Journal of Educational Psychology, 95(4)*, 687–706.

Marsh, H. W. & Byrne, B. M. (1993). Do we see ourselves as others infer? A comparison of self–other agreement on multiple dimensions of self-concept from two continents. *Australian Journal of Psychology, 45*, 49–58.

Marsh, H. W. & Craven, R. G. (1991). Self-other agreement on multiple dimensions of preadolescent self-concept: The accuracy of inferences by teachers, mothers, and fathers. *Journal of Educational Psychology, 83*, 393–404.

Marsh, H. W. & Craven, R. G. (1997). Academic self-concept: Beyond the dustbowl. In G. Phye (ed.), *Handbook of classroom assessment: Learning, achievement and adjustment* (pp. 131–98). San Diego, CA: Academic Press

Marsh, H. W. & Hocevar, D. (1985). The application of confirmatory factor analysis to the study of self-concept: First and higher order factor structures and their invariance across age groups. *Psychological Bulletin, 97*, 562–82.

Marsh, H. W. & Shavelson, R. (1985). Self-concept: Its multifaceted, hierarchical structure. *Educational Psychologist, 20*, 107–25.

Marsh, H. W., Byrne, B. M., & Yeung, A. S. (1999). Causal ordering of academic self-concept and achievement: Reanalysis of a pioneering study and revised recommendations. *Educational Psychologist, 34*, 155–67.

Marsh, H. W., Craven, R. G., & Debus, R. L. (1991). Self-concepts of young children aged 5 to 8: Their measurement and multidimensional structure. *Journal of Educational Psychology, 83*, 377–92.

Marsh, H. W., Craven, R. G., & Debus, R. L. (1998). Structure, stability, and development of young children's self-concepts: A multicohort-multioccasion study. *Child Development, 69*, 1030–53.

Marsh, H. W., Craven, R., & Debus, R. (1999) Separation of competency and affect components of multiple dimensions of academic self-concept: A developmental perspective. *Merrill-Palmer Quarterly, 45*, 567–601.

Marsh, H. W., Ellis, L., & Craven, R. G. (2002). How do preschool children feel about themselves? Unravelling measurement and multidimensional self-concept structure. *Developmental Psychology, 38*, 376–93.

Measelle, J. R., Ablow, J. C., Cowan, P. A. & Cowan, C. P. (1998). Assessing young children's views of their academic, social, and emotional lives: An evaluation of the self-perception scales of the Berkeley Puppet Interview. *Child Development, 69(6)*, 1556–76.

Nicholls, J. (1979). Development of perceptions of own attainment and causal attributions of success and failure in reading. *Journal of Educational Psychology, 71*, 94–9.

Penn, C. S., Burnett, P. C., & Patton, W. (2001). The impact of attributional feedback on the self-concept of children aged four to six years in preschool. *Australian Journal of Guidance and Counselling, 9*, 21–34.

Ruble, D. N. & Dweck, C. (1995). Self-conceptions, person conceptions, and their development. In N. Eisenberg (ed.), *Review of personality and social psychology: Development and social psychology: The interface* (vol. 15, pp. 109–39). Thousand Oaks, CA: Sage.

Russell, L., Bornholt, L., & Ouvrier, R. (2002). Brief cognitive screening and self concepts for children with low intellectual functioning, *British Journal of Clinical Psychology*, *41*, 93–104.

Shavelson, R. J., Hubner, J. J., & Stanton, G. C. (1976). Self-concept: Validation of construct interpretations. *Review of Educational Research*, *46*, 407–41.

Skaalvik, E. M. (1997). Issues in research on self-concept. In M. L. Maehr & P. R. Pintrich (eds.) *Advances in motivation and achievement* (vol. 10, pp. 51–98). Greenwich, CT: JAI Press.

Spencer, F. H. & Bornholt, L. J. (2003). A model of children's cognitive functioning and cognitive self-concepts, *Australian Journal of Learning Disabilities*, *8*, 4–9.

Stipek, D. & Mac Iver, D. (1989). Developmental change in children's assessment of intellectual competence. *Child Development*, *60*, 521–38.

Stipek, D. J., Gralinski, J. H., & Kopp, C. B. (1990). Self-concept development in the toddler years. *Developmental Psychology*, *26*, 972–7.

Stipek, D., Recchia, S., & McClintic, S. (1992). Self-evaluation in young children. *Monographs of the Society for Research in Child Development*, *57*, 100.

Tanaka, J. S. (1987). "How big is big enough?": Sample size and goodness of fit in structural equation models with latent variables. *Child Development*, *58*, 134–46.

Tracey, D. K., Marsh, H. W., & Craven, R. G. (2003). Self-concepts of primary students with mild intellectual disabilities. In H. W. Marsh, R. G. Craven & D. M. McInerney (eds.), *International Advances in self research*. Greenwich, CT: Information Age.

Walberg, H. J. & Tsai, S-L. (1983). Matthew effects in education. *American Educational Research Journal*, *20*, 359–73.

Wells, L. E. & Marwell, G. (1976). *Self-esteem: Its conceptualization and measurement.* Beverly Hills, CA: Sage.

Wigfield, A. & Eccles, J. S. (1992). The development of achievement task values: A theoretical analysis. *Developmental Review*, *12*, 265–310.

Wigfield, A., Eccles, J. S., Yoon, K. S., Harold, R. D., Arbreton, A. J. A., Freedman-Doan, C., & Blumenfeld, P. C. (1997). Change in children's competence beliefs and subjective task values across the elementary school years: A 3-year study. *Journal of Educational Psychology*, *89*, 451–69.

Wylie, R. C. (1979). *The self-concept* (vol. 2). Lincoln, NE: University of Nebraska Press.

Wylie, R. C. (1989). *Measures of self-concept.* Lincoln, NE: University of Nebraska Press.

CHAPTER NINE

Developmental Perspectives on Parenting Competence

Douglas M. Teti and Keng-Yen Huang

Interest in identifying the elements of competent parenting is centuries old (Locke, 1964; Rousseau, 1911). It was not, however, until the early- to mid-twentieth century that genuine theories of parenting emerged (i.e., psychoanalytic and behavioral learning theories), accompanied by systematic efforts at empirical validation. Although these early efforts were, for the most part, unsuccessful, they ushered in a productive era in which competence in parenting became better understood in relation to socially desirable developmental outcomes (see Maccoby, 1992; Teti & Candelaria, 2002, for reviews).

This work is decidedly Western in cultural orientation and cannot escape the inherent circularity that plagues any working definition of parenting competence, namely that parenting competence can only be defined in terms of its propensity to move children toward goals that their culture deems important. In addition, empirical work has varied dramatically in terms of the developmental outcomes under study, and thus in terms of the elements of parenting that appear to promote those outcomes. For example, competent parenting vis-à-vis linguistic and intellectual outcomes is that which is rich in language inputs and responsive to children's communicative bids (Tamis-LeMonda et al., 1996; Warren & Walker, this volume). By contrast, competent parenting with respect to socioemotional outcomes in infancy is that which is "sensitive" to infant distress, needs, and bids for interaction and withdrawal (Ainsworth et al., 1978; Belsky, 1999).

This chapter is concerned with parenting competence in infancy and the preschool years in relation to two broad-based socialization goals: the achievement of a mutual interpersonal parent–child orientation, and the promotion of social competence with adults and peers. Maccoby and Martin (1983) described a mutual interpersonal parent–child orientation as a paramount socialization goal in which both parent and child mutually invest in each other and commit to the relationship, taking into account each other's needs before acting, and expecting their partner to do the same. This kind of mutual investment predisposes the child to attend more closely to parental socialization messages, thus potentiating the parent's effectiveness as a socialization agent, the child's internalization of appropriate standards of conduct, and, in turn, social competence within and outside the family (Kochanska, 1994; Maccoby & Martin, 1983).

In this chapter, we also explore continuity and stability in parenting competence from infancy to the preschool years. In doing so, we are mindful of Baumrind's (1989a) distinction between developmental etic and developmental emic approaches to the study of continuity of developmental constructs over time. Developmental etic approaches address the degree to which a particular construct (e.g., parental responsivity or warmth), and individual performance on it, can be generalized across age. A number of published studies have taken such an approach in examining stability (i.e., the rank ordering of individuals) of parenting competence over time (see Holden & Miller, 1999). Whereas we will examine this work in this chapter, we do not believe an etic approach does justice to the changing complexity of parenting competence from infancy to the pre-school years. Instead, we adopt a developmental emic approach in discussing parenting competence and argue that the construct of parenting competence changes *qualitatively* in the transition from infancy to preschool years, and that parents who may be judged as competent in infancy will remain so in the transition to the preschool years only to the extent that parents can adapt successfully to the qualitatively new and different needs and demands of the preschool-aged child. From this perspective, stability of parenting competence in the infant-to-preschool transition, defined as the degree to which one maintains one's rank order in a sample of individuals across two points in time, can only be assessed against the backdrop of construct discontinuity; that is, what constitutes parenting competence in the infancy period is not isomorphic with the constituents of competent parenting in the preschool years. This chapter is concerned with conceptualizations of parenting competence at both of these age points, with how successful parenting must adapt and change as children grow from infants to preschoolers, and with factors that may influence stability of parenting across these two age points.

Parenting Competence in Infancy

This section draws from attachment theory and research in making the case that competent parenting of infants, especially infants under 18 months of age, can be defined primarily as that which promotes a secure infant–mother attachment and establishes, as a consequence, the beginnings of a mutual interpersonal parent–child orientation. Although John Bowlby (1969) viewed infants' propensity to attach to a caregiver as an outcome of natural selection pressures, he also acknowledged that the quality of this attachment depended upon the overall quality of care. It was Mary Ainsworth, however, who transformed our understanding of the nature of parenting competence in infancy with the identification of three infant attachment patterns (secure, insecure-avoidant, and insecure-ambivalent) and their linkage with quality of maternal care. Her work revealed that the single most important feature of parenting in the formation of a secure infant–parent attachment was parental sensitivity to infant cues and signals. That is, parents who accurately perceived and responded contingently and appropriately to basic infant needs and bids for interaction and withdrawal during feeding, play, and distress were more likely to promote secure infant–parent attachments than were parents who ignored infant needs, rejected or ignored infant interactional bids, and/or who responded to them inconsistently.

The three Ainsworth patterns of attachment, and the developmental significance of secure attachment in infancy for socioemotional competence in the preschool period and beyond, are well known (Berlin & Cassidy, 1999; Cassidy & Shaver, 1999; Teti & Teti, 1996). Detailed coverage of these topics is beyond the scope of this chapter. What is at issue here, however, is evidence that points to secure attachment, and parental sensitivity, in fostering the young child's positive orientation toward and acceptance of the attachment figure as an agent of socialization. Indeed, sensitive parenting and secure attachment during the first year of life appear to promote high levels of infant cooperation with and acceptance of the parent's overtures toward the infant by the second year of life (Ainsworth, Bell, & Stayton, 1974; Londerville & Main, 1981; Stayton, Hogan, & Ainsworth, 1973). In addition, Kochanska and Aksan (1995) later reported on the linkage between parental sensitivity and children's investment in the parent–child relationship. In this study of maternal behavioral correlates of the quality of preschool children's compliance with maternal bids and internalized conduct, maternal warmth, positive affective tone, and responsivity correlated positively with children's levels of "committed" compliance, or compliance that was characterized by a child's willing participation in a mother-guided cleanup task. It thus appears that a positive mutual interpersonal parent–child orientation may be rooted in the quality of parental behavior as early as the first year of life, and that "sensitive" parents have a greater likelihood of fostering such an orientation than do insensitive parents. We turn now to the basic elements of parental sensitivity, and various approaches to its assessment.

Ainsworth's conceptualization and measurement of parenting sensitivity

Parental sensitivity is a construct that is typically associated with the infancy period of life, although it could be argued that being "sensitive" is a quality that should characterize parenting, and indeed all human behavior toward one another, across the life span. It has typically been assessed from observations of parent– (usually mother–) infant interactions, the durations of and contexts for which vary widely, through the use of rating scales. There now exists a plethora of rating scales purporting to measure the sensitivity construct and closely linked derivatives. All such scales, however, are rooted in Ainsworth's (1969; Ainsworth et al., 1978) formulations and measurement approach.

Ainsworth (1969, p. 1) construed maternal sensitivity as "the mother's ability to perceive and to interpret accurately the signals and communications implicit in her infant's behavior, and given this understanding, to respond to them appropriately and promptly." Ainsworth viewed sensitivity as comprised of four components: (1) Awareness of infant signals, requiring parental accessibility and alertness to infant cues; (2) accurate interpretation of infant signals, requiring empathy and freedom from distortion;

(3) prompt, contingent responsivity to these signals; and (4) responding to signals appropriately. Appropriateness of response was judged in terms of how well the response struck a balance between what the infant wanted versus what s/he needed, in the service of maintaining the infant's sense of comfort and security. Frequently, infant wants and needs are one and the same, and a single parental response can satisfy both. For example, picking up a distressed infant and holding the infant upright, against one's chest and shoulder frequently satisfies both what the infant wants (to be picked up and held) as well as what s/he needs (contact comfort, which functions to promote the infant's sense of security). When the infant's wants and needs are not the same, however (as when an infant sees a sharp knife on the table and seeks it out as a play object), an appropriate response is one that acknowledges what the infant wants but redirects the infant toward safer, more "appropriate" playthings. Appropriateness of parental response is also judged in terms of how well it alleviates infant "concerns." An appropriate soothing response, for example, is one that fully satisfies the infant, such that the infant does not wish to be picked up again at the moment s/he is put down.

Ainsworth rated maternal sensitivity on a 9-point scale, with 9 reserved for "highly sensitive" mothers, described as "exquisitely attuned to B's signals" (Ainsworth, 1969, p. 4), showing the ability to take the infant's perspective into consideration, accurately interpreting what the infant wants, and responding contingently and appropriately. A rating of 1, by contrast, was assigned for "highly insensitive" mothers whose focus was only on their own, not their infant's, wishes and needs, and whose response to infant behavior was driven by the mothers' own idiosyncratic tendencies. Intermediate scale points of 7 ("sensitive"), 5 ("inconsistently sensitive"), and 3 ("insensitive") were also behaviorally anchored and defined.

Ainsworth's assessment of parenting sensitivity, especially with regard to the "appropriateness" component, was confounded by how well it "worked" with the infant at the same point in time. Such a confound is inherent in virtually all conceptualizations of sensitivity, fortunately or not, and rating scale systems that have followed in Ainsworth's footsteps have not improved on this problem. Because appropriateness is somewhat bound up by infant response, this suggests that (a) a given parent may look more or less sensitive as a function of individual differences in such temperamentally based (Vaughn & Bost, 1999) dimensions as reactivity and proneness to distress, or (b) a parent faced with the task of parenting two different children who differ substantially in such temperamental dimensions would receive similarly high sensitivity ratings only to the extent that s/he is capable of modifying her/his responses so as to be equally "successful" with both infants. Interestingly, little systematic attention has been given to determining the extent to which individual differences in infant temperament influence ratings of parental sensitivity, and, conversely, the extent to which parental sensitivity ratings would remain consistent across children with widely varying temperaments.

Three additional rating scales were used in Ainsworth's naturalistic observations of mother–infant interactions. These included "Acceptance–Rejection," "Cooperation–Interference," and "Accessibility–Ignoring." Acceptance-Rejection tapped into the mother's ability to resolve any conflicting emotions she had about the baby. High scores were given for a mother who was accepting of the baby regardless of the baby's mood. Low scores were assigned to a mother who was angry and resentful toward the baby.

Cooperation–Interference assessed the degree to which a mother's interactions reflected her belief in her infant as an autonomous being, as indicated by appropriately timing and tailoring her response to the infant's ongoing activity. High scores indicated that the mother rarely interrupted or interfered with her infant's activity, or if she did, it was done by successfully eliciting the infant's willing cooperation. Low scores, by contrast, were used with a mother who characteristically broke into and disrupted infant activity, showing little regard for the infant's autonomy. Finally, Accessibility–Ignoring assessed a mother's physical and psychological accessibility to the infant. High scores were given to a mother who remained accessible and aware of her infant's cues despite the existence of competing environmental distractions. Low scores, on the other hand, were assigned to mothers whose self-absorption was strong enough that it precluded any meaningful attention to infant signals.

These four dimensions were highly intercorrelated ($rs > 0.80$; Ainsworth & Bell, 1969), suggesting that all four scales really assessed the same construct. That these scales were strongly intercorrelated is not surprising, in our view, because each of them can be straightforwardly incorporated, conceptually, into a parenting sensitivity construct. Indeed, it is difficult, if not impossible, to conceive of a sensitive mother who is not accessible to, cooperative with, and accepting of her infant, and we argue that the latter three dimensions are but different manifestations of a sensitivity dimension.

Other Ainsworth-inspired measurement systems

Ainsworth's seminal work on parenting sensitivity led to the development of a host of rating systems that, it is argued, did not stray vary far from Ainsworth's original conceptualizations about what constitutes parenting competence in infancy, at least in relation to promoting a positive, mutual interpersonal parent–infant orientation and early socioemotional development. Some of these systems included parenting dimensions that were also relevant to intellectual and linguistic outcomes, but all of them included either a maternal sensitivity dimension and/or related dimensions that were conceptually linked to a sensitivity construct. There are a number of such systems now available, and although a full review of them is beyond the scope of this chapter, a few deserve mention.

Barnard's (1994) Nursing Child Assessment Satellite Training (NCAST) Parent–Child Feeding and Teaching Scales have achieved much popularity among health professionals who wish to understand the nature and structure of parent–infant interaction in feeding and teaching contexts, especially when infants are compromised medically. The scales have been used for both assessment and intervention purposes and appear to be psychometrically sound and predictive of later development (Bee et al., 1982). Both the feeding and teaching scales have four parenting dimensions, three of which overlap strongly with a parenting sensitivity construct. These include "sensitivity to cues" (ability to detect and respond appropriately to infant cues), "response to distress"(ability to soothe a distressed infant), and "social-emotional growth fostering" (affective quality of the parent response). The fourth scale, "cognitive growth-fostering," measures the kind and quality of caregiver-provided learning experiences (Barnard, 1994; Morriset, 1994).

Other sensitivity-based rating systems that have become popular include the Parent–Child Early Relational Assessment (PCERA; Clark, 1985), whose 29 five-point parental behavioral rating scales include one scale termed "sensitivity," with strong conceptual overlap with Ainsworth's formulations, and a wide variety of individual and families of scales that would be expected to be strongly correlated with, if not differential manifestations of, parental sensitivity. These include contingent responsiveness, expressed affect, structuring and mediation of the environment, expressed attitude, intrusiveness, flexibility/rigidity, and many more. The PCERA also includes an additional 28 scales that assess child behavior, and another eight that assess the parent–child dyad. The sheer number of rating scales in the PCERA make it rather daunting for use in research, and this is complicated further by much conceptual overlap between many of the scales (e.g., there is a parent scale termed "expressed positive affect," another termed "enthusiastic, animated, and cheerful mood," and a third labeled "enjoyment, pleasure expressed toward child." Clark (1999) provided some guidance here with eight factor analytically derived PCERA dimensions (e.g., intrusiveness/sensitivity) that may prove useful to the field. Careful selection of non-overlapping PCERA dimensions have also proved useful. Teti et al. (1991) composited five PCERA parent scales for assessing the quality of mothers' behavior with their preschoolers during free play: anger/hostility (higher scores indicating less anger); enthusiastic, animated, cheerful mood; structuring and mediation of the environment; sensitivity; and flexibility/rigidity. The composited scale, termed "maternal involvement," correlated significantly and positively with the quality of preschool-aged attachment behavior in the home from mothers' sorts of the Attachment Q-Set (Waters & Deane, 1985).

One of the most comprehensive measures of parental sensitivity developed to date is the Maternal Behavior Q-Set (MBQ; Pederson & Moran, 1995a). The MBQ is not a traditional rating scale system but a Q-sorting system, in which the observer is required, after observing the parent with the infant in (typically) a naturalistic setting for a sufficient amount of time (typically two hours or more), to sort a set of 90 descriptors about the parent according to how like or unlike that descriptor was of the parent's behavior during the observation. Cards are sorted into 9 piles of 10 cards each, ranging from "very much like the parent" to "very much unlike the parent." The final set of descriptors were based strongly on Ainsworth's formulations about sensitivity and its components. Typical of q-sort assessments, a "criterion sort" was derived by averaging the sorts of a variety of experts in the field on the topic of parental sensitivity, who were asked to sort the 90 items according to the hypothetically "most sensitive" parent. An MBQ sort for a specific parent is then correlated with the criterion sort, and the stronger the correlation, the more sensitive that parent is taken to be. The MBQ is reliable and correlates strongly with security of infant–parent attachment (Moran et al., 1992; Pederson & Moran, 1995b; Pederson et al., 1990).

MBQ items with high criterion sort scores (i.e., that were viewed by experts as characteristic of a sensitive parent) include "responds accurately to signals of distress," "interactions revolve around B's tempo and current state," "shows delight in interaction with B," "interprets cures correctly as evidenced by B's response," "spontaneously expresses positive feelings to B," and "interventions satisfy B." MBQ items with low criterion sort scores (viewed by experts as uncharacteristic of parental sensitivity) include "provides B with little opportunity to contribute to the interaction," "content and pace of interaction set by M rather than according to B's responses," "consistently unresponsive," "responds only to frequent, prolonged, or intense distress," "actively opposes B's wishes," and "scolds or criticizes B." Note that these items incorporate such dimensions as parental cooperation, intrusiveness, positive affect, negative affect, contingent responsivity to infant cues, appropriateness of response, and flexibility/rigidity. In many rating scale systems, these dimensions are rated separately along with a separate scale for assessing sensitivity. The fact that these dimensions were seen by parenting experts as being either very characteristic of, or very uncharacteristic of, a sensitive parent, supports the premise that these dimensions are not distinct from sensitivity but rather represent different components of sensitive or insensitive parenting.

Finally, a more recently developed set of ratings, the Emotional Availability Scales (EAS), developed by Biringen and her colleagues (Biringen & Robinson, 1991; Biringen, Robinson, & Emde, 1998; Pipp-Siegel, 1998) have risen in popularity over the past decade. Parental emotional availability is captured by four dimensions: sensitivity (responsiveness to the child in terms of timing, appropriateness, flexibility, quality of affect, and ability to resolve conflict), structuring (quality of scaffolding of child behavior, particularly during play, and limit-setting), nonintrusiveness (parent's availability to the infant without being intrusive or overprotective), and nonhostility. The EAS also assess child behavior along dimensions of responsiveness to, and involvement with, the parent. There is an acknowledged strong conceptual overlap between EAS parent dimensions and those developed by Ainsworth (Biringen, 2000). However, Biringen and her colleagues emphasize that the EAS parent scales explicitly take into consideration the behavior of the child in guiding the observer to a particular score. Parental emotional availability is thus construed as a product of mutual parent–child behavioral and affective regulation. The emphasis on this point is important because of prior assumptions, largely implicit, that maternal sensitivity is wholly a characteristic of the mother (Ainsworth et al., 1978; Claussen & Crittenden, 2000). Biringen also emphasizes the need to take into account a child's developmental level, and, unlike other rating scale assessments of parenting quality, has produced different versions of the EAS for infancy/early childhood and for middle childhood (Biringen, Robinson, & Emde, 1998; Pipp-Siegel, 1998). EAS dimensions of sensitivity and structuring/intrusiveness (which combined the structuring and nonintrusive dimensions) were found to be more optimal among mothers of securely attached 12-month-old infants, relative to mothers of insecure infants.

Parenting Competence in the Toddler/Preschool Years

Some rather dramatic developments characterize children as they move from infancy to toddlerhood and the preschool period. These developments, as one might expect, have a significant impact on conceptualizations of parenting competence. The move to the preschool period is characterized by exponential growth in language comprehension and production skills, less dependence on parents and increased connections with the wider world, including extended family and peers, and increased ability, at a rudimentary level, to take another's perspective, especially with regard to feelings and emotions (Crittenden, 1992; Greenberg, Cicchetti, & Cummings, 1990; Teti et al., 1995). Along with such developments, however, comes the need, in Western culture, to learn and internalize standards of conduct with regard to societal norms and in terms of what is "right" versus "wrong" in the treatment of others (i.e., the development of a moral conscience), and the need to control impulses and regulate emotion in accordance with cultural expectations (Cole, Michel, & Teti, 1994; Cusinato, 1994; Edwards & Liu, 2002; Grusec & Goodnow, 1994; Hoffman, 1994; Kochanska, 1993).

The task of parenting thus becomes decidedly more complicated as the child moves out of infancy. Parents now must play an active role in shaping and molding their children so that they learn "proper" behavior toward parents, peers, and other adults, and to do so without active coercion or prompting by the parents, at least in the longer run. Parents of preschoolers become much more concerned than they did when their children were infants about discipline and control, about making maturity demands, while at the same time maintaining positive, harmonious relationships with their children (i.e., a positive, mutual, parent–child orientation).

Integrating discipline with nurturance

Although much of her work focused on school-aged children, Diana Baumrind has nevertheless made an enormous contribution to the understanding of the elements of parenting competence post-infancy (Baumrind, 1966, 1967, 1970, 1980, 1989b, 1991), and her work was a logical extension of previous work of Sears, Maccoby, and Levin (1957) and Baldwin (1948, 1955). Baumrind began by identifying a set of child attributes that she believed represented child outcomes that were highly valued by parents in the United States. These included independence, social responsibility, achievement, peer-friendliness, purposive, and cooperation with parents and other responsible adults. Children high on these attributes were deemed *instrumentally competent*, and competent parenting was taken as that which promoted the development of instrumental competence in children.

Baumrind is most well known for her development of "styles" of parenting that took into consideration how parents fared on four distinct dimensions of parenting: nurturance, control, clarity of communication, and maturity demands. She was primarily interested in the pattern of parental behavior across these four dimensions, rather than in the influence of any single one. *Authoritarian* parents were identified by high levels of control and maturity demands and low levels of nurturance and clarity of communication. These parents placed a premium on absolute obedience in their children and the use of strong punitive measures when such was not obtained. Reciprocal verbal dialogue with children was discouraged. *Permissive* parenting, by contrast, was characterized by high levels of nurturance and clarity of communication, and low levels of control and maturity demands. Permissive parents allowed children much freedom in decision making, were openly accepting and supportive of their children's behavior, and made little effort either to control their children's behavior or set firm, consistent standards of conduct. Finally, *authoritative* parents were high on all dimensions. They were warm and nurturing toward their children, exerted firm, consistent control over their children's behavior, set clear and consistent standards of conduct, and openly acknowledged and incorporated, whenever possible, their children's perspective in disciplinary matters. Discipline thus involved the combined use of reason and power, with reference to set standards of conduct, but not to the point of harsh physical punishment or severe curbs on the child's autonomy.

The cumulative results of Baumrind's work are well known (Baumrind, 1967, 1973, 1989b). The highest levels of instrumental competence were associated with children from authoritative homes. On the basis of observations, standardized tests, ratings, and Q-sorts, children of authoritative parents were found to be more independent and assertive, achievement oriented, friendly with peers, and cooperative with parents. Children in authoritarian homes, by contrast, were found to be more hostile and/or shy with peers, less achievement-oriented, and overly dependent on parents, and children of permissive parents were also found (interestingly) to be overly dependent and to exhibit poor self-control. The similarities between children of authoritarian and children of permissive parents prompted Baumrind's (1973) speculation that neither authoritarian nor permissive parents provided their children with sufficient opportunities to learn to cope effectively with stress and deal adaptively with everyday life challenges. Authoritarian parents characteristically curtail their children's initiatives; permissive parents fail to establish and enforce standards of conduct. The advantages conferred by authoritative parenting for children of all ages with respect to achievement, social competence, and positive relationships with parents have been remarkably consistent both in the United States and abroad, and among minority populations in the US (Aunola, Stattin, & Nurmi, 2000; Deković & Janssens, 1992; Hickman, Bartholomae, and McHendy, 2000; Hill, 1995; Kaufmann et al., 2000; Leung & Kwan, 1998; Querido, Warner, & Eyberg, 2002; Shumow, Vandell, & Posner, 1998; Taylor, Casten, & Flickinger, 1993; Thompson, Hollis, & Richards, 2003).

It thus appears that competent parenting post-infancy, at least in industrialized, primarily Western-oriented cultures, involves considerably greater emphasis on active efforts at control, in terms of curbing children's undesirable impulses, shaping prosocial behavior toward others, and steering children so that they attain developmental milestones at appropriate times in the life cycle. Importantly, however, there remains an equal emphasis on warmth, nurturance, and on responsive dialog with one's children, such that in socializing their children, competent (authoritative) parents take into full account their children's feelings and desires, ongoing activities, and developmental needs. As such, authoritative parenting has much in common, conceptually, with parental sensitivity. Recall that Ainsworth's conceptualization of sensitive parenting included awareness and accurate interpretation of infant cues and responding to them contingently and appropriately. The dimension of appropriateness was evaluated on the basis of the degree to which a parent response struck a balance between what the infant wantedand what s/he needed, in the service of maintaining the infant's sense of comfort and security. When infant needs do not match with infant wants, a sensitive parent strikes this balance by openly acknowledging what the infant wants but skillfully redirecting the infant's attention to a safer or more acceptable pursuit. Authoritative parenting in the preschool years also must strike this balance by, on the one hand, responding to their children contingently and warmly and affirming their emotions (negative as well as positive) and perspectives, but also making use of their children's more developing linguistic and social cognitive skills to communicate appropriate standards of conduct, to do so consistently, and to provide their children with choices that parents can "live with." Thus, at a conceptual level, one can argue that authoritative parenting is but a developmentally more advanced form of parental sensitivity. Like parenting sensitivity in infancy, authoritative parenting incorporates awareness and accurate interpretation of child cues and prompt responding to them. However, it expands qualitatively upon the dimension of appropriateness to include the proper use of control as it applies to establishing standards of conduct toward others, limit-setting, and promoting the attainment of developmental achievements (e.g., using the toilet, learning simple duties such as clean-up after play).

How much control is "too much"?

Defining "proper use of control" in the context of authoritative parenting is informed by socialization literature addressing the linkage between parental disciplinary techniques and children's internalization of standards of conduct. Grusec and Goodnow (1994, p. 4) defined internalization as the "taking over the values and attitudes of society as one's own so that socially acceptable behavior is motivated not by anticipation of external consequences but by intrinsic or internal factors." This process, termed by others as the development of "conscience" (Kochanska, 1993), is arguably the most important goal of parenting efforts. Socialization theorists traditionally have examined the power of three fundamental disciplinary techniques, singly and in combination, in effecting internalization of values: *power assertion*, *love withdrawal*, and *reasoning/explanation* (Grusec & Goodnow, 1994). Power assertion refers to the threat of or actual use of force, physical punishment, or withdrawal pf privileges. Love withdrawal involves ignoring the child or expressing disappointment or disapproval. Reasoning/explanation involves calling attention to the child's misdeed and how it has infringed upon the rights and feelings of others, a process that has been termed *induction*, or *other-oriented induction* (Damon, 1983; Grusec & Goodnow, 1994).

From empirical work, Hoffman & Saltzstein (1967) argued that reasoning/explanation is the single most powerful technique for fostering internalization, with power assertion the least effective and love withdrawal falling in between. Such a finding is certainly consistent with authoritative parenting's high level use of nurturance and clarity of communication in working with their children. However, Hoffman also noted that power assertion and love withdrawal, though by themselves inadequate in promoting internalization, can still serve an important function if used appropriately (i.e., at low levels) and in conjunction with reasoning/explanation. Specifically, for some children, parents may on occasion need to employ low levels of power assertion or love withdrawal to a point necessary for the child to attend to the parent's message. Parents must gauge this accordingly, because an overuse of power assertion will likely direct the child attention away from the parental message and toward the consequences that threaten to follow, or actually follow, the misdeed. Insufficient arousal, on the other hand, could lead the child to pay insufficient attention to the message. Thus, authoritative parenting may involve, on occasion, a combination of reasoning/explanation with just enough coercion, via power assertion or love withdrawal, in the service of communicating standards of conduct clearly and effectively to children.

The success of particular parental socialization strategies also appears to be influenced by child temperament. Kochanska (1993, 1994, 1995, 1998; Kochanska et al., 1998; Kochanska, Murray, & Coy, 1997) has examined the manner in which individual differences in early temperament influence parenting effectiveness, the quality of children's orientation toward and acceptance of parental messages, and children's working understanding of "right" and "wrong," or conscience. In her work, children's susceptibility to anxiety arousal, and thus to the degree of emotional discomfort experienced in response to committing a "transgression," has a bearing on children's predisposition to attend to parental input. Anxiety-prone children should be more sensitive to the emotional content of parents' messages about behavioral expectations, and in turn be more likely to internalize parentally established standards of conduct than should emotionally imperturbable children. Kochanska further argues that individual differences in a second component of temperament, effortful control (which emerges late in the first year of life), also bears on children's internalization to the extent that children with well-developed impulse control are more likely to be able to attend to parental messages than are children with poor impulse control. Thus, gentle socialization approaches, characterized by responsivity, warmth, induction, and low (if any) levels of power assertion and love withdrawal are likely to be most successful with anxiety-prone children, especially those with good impulse control. By contrast, one might anticipate the need to make use of greater levels of power assertion and/or love withdrawal with emotionally imperturbably and/or poorly controlled children. However, excessive use of coercion with such children will likely backfire, as evidenced by the close and unfortunate linkage between attention-deficit hyperactivity disorder and externalizing disorders such as oppositional-defiant and conduct disorders (August et al., 1999). Kochanska (1993) suggests that such children may respond most favorably to simply packaged parental messages that assist children in structuring their behavior and in understanding how it affects others, and by delivering these messages within a context of warmth and nurture. Support for Kochanska's theoretical formulations is accumulating (Kochanska, 1995; Kochanska et al., 1997).

"Authoritative" parental behavior and children's social competence

Unlike parenting sensitivity measurements in infancy, few widely accepted behavioral measurement systems exist for parents of preschoolers that take into consideration an appropriate balance of parental warmth/nurturance, control, and quality of communication. The Emotional Availability Scales (Biringen, Robinson, & Emde, 1998; Pipp-Siegel, 1998), which include versions for parents of children beyond infancy, include limit-setting as one component of an overall "structuring" dimension. However, very little data on the use and validity of these scales with parents of preschoolers are available. Importantly, studies that include assessments of actual parental behavior in the preschool years suggest that children reap socioemotional benefits when parenting in the preschool years achieves a proper blend of nurturance, responsivity, and control. For example, in an investigation of 69 preschoolers at varying degrees of risk for conduct disorder, Denham et al. (2000) found that supportive parenting (positive regard for and emotional support of child), clarity of parental instruction, and clear limit setting during parent–child play at 4.5 years correlated negatively, whereas maternal hostility correlated positively, with children's problem behaviors at 7 and 9.7 years. Further, a measure that composited supportive mothering, quality of instruction, and limit setting at 4.5 years of child age was predictive of decreases in children's externalizing symptom levels over time. These findings were similar to those of Zahn-Waxler et al.(1990), who found that maternal "proactive" parenting of two-year-olds, characterized by an ability to take the child's perspective, structuring the child's peer play, and showing respect for the child's autonomy when using control, was associated with lower levels of behavior problems at five years of age. Importantly, Denham et al. (2000) found that mothers' hostility toward the child in the preschool period was by itself predictive of children's behavior problems at 7 and 9.7 years, and negatively related to decreases in child symptom levels over time. These results provide strong evidence that parental control efforts will likely fail if delivered in the context of negative affect and is consistent with a host of studies emphasizing the debilitating effect of parental anger and negative emotion on children's emotional wellbeing and social adjustment (Crockenberg & Litman, 1990; Cummings, Iannotti, & Zahn-Waxler, 1985; Davies & Cummings, 1995; Dumas & LaFreniere, 1993; Gardner, 1987; Pettit & Bates, 1989; Teti et al., 1995).

Stability of Parenting from Infancy to the Preschool Years

The foregoing illustrates that, whereas competent parenting in infancy has largely been construed in terms of Ainsworth's perspectives on sensitivity and nurturance, competent parenting in the preschool years is characterized by a complex integration of nurturance, control, and quality of communication as parents adapt to the increasingly sophisticated skills and repertoires of the preschool-aged child. The construct of parenting competence undergoes qualitative shifts and is thus discontinuous from infancy to the preschool years. Although parental warmth and responsiveness remain important at both ages, parenting competence in the preschool years is also evidenced by the emergence of reasonable and appropriate parental controls in disciplinary contexts, and clearly conveyed messages to children about appropriate standards of conduct. Parenting so manifested in infancy and preschool would be highly likely to promote a mutual parent–child interpersonal orientation, and children's social competence with peers and familial and non-familial adults. From a developmental emic perspective, then, parenting so manifested would also be considered "stable" across the two age points. Such parents would have manifested successful adaptation to the challenges inherent in the parenting of both infants and preschoolers. Parenting instability, by contrast, could take several forms. One example of instability would be illustrated by parents who are sensitive in infancy, but who then decrease in nurturance and use high levels of inappropriate control in the preschool years, perhaps because they are unable to cope effectively with the increasing challenges brought to bear by a developmentally more sophisticated child. Alternatively, parents who are sensitive in infancy and who maintain warmth and nurturance post-infancy but have difficulty with limit-setting (the quintessential "permissive" parent, from Baumrind's typology) again would be demonstrating instability. Other permutations, of course, exist as well, as for example a parent who may find it difficult to adapt successfully to parenting an infant but whose adaptation improves in the preschool years because of the child's improved communicative and physical abilities.

Interestingly, the literature is surprisingly bereft of studies taking a development emic approach to parenting stability from infancy to the preschool years. A number of studies do exist, however, that examine short-term stability in parenting responsivity and sensitivity in infancy. Interestingly, these studies generally show only low to moderate levels of parenting stability, even within the first year of life. Crockenberg and McCluskey (1986), for example, assessed maternal responsivity to infant distress at 3 months of age using a time-sampling procedure in which 10 seconds bins of observation of the mother–infant dyad were alternated with 10 seconds bins of recording, extended over 3.5 hours of observation. At 12 months, infants participated in the Strange Situation procedure, and maternal sensitivity to infants during the two reunion episodes was rated by a trained coder who was blind to maternal responsivity scores obtained at 3 months. There was no relation between 3-month maternal responsivity and 12-month maternal sensitivity. Further, maternal behavioral change across the infants' first year toward maternal insensitivity was associated with the combination of high infant irritability, as assessed during the first 10 days postpartum using the Brazelton Neonatal Behavioral Assessment Scale, and prenatal maternal attitudes that endorsed the perspective that it was appropriate *not* to respond to a crying baby. Although this study concerns itself only with the first year of life, this finding is important in that it emphasizes the role that child characteristics can play in promoting parental stability or instability over time.

One cannot rule out the possibility that Crockenberg and McCluskey's (1986) inability to document stability over time in parenting competence is related to differences in the manner in which parenting competence was assessed at 3 months versus 12 months of infant age. This lack of stability, however, is actually consistent with a variety of studies examining parenting stability across the first year that find across-time correlations of small to moderate magnitude (Bell & Ainsworth, 1972; Belsky, Rovine, & Taylor, 1984; Heinicke et al., 1983). Further, Pianta, Sroufe, and Egeland (1989) failed to find strong stability from 6-month measures of maternal sensitivity in free play and feeding contexts to 24-month assessments of maternal sensitivity during a problem solving tool-use task and 42-month assessments of maternal sensitivity in a teaching context. Sensitivity in the tool-use task was operationally defined as the sensitivity and skill with which mothers assisted their children in the task, termed Quality of Assistance. Sensitivity in the teaching task was defined as the degree to which mothers recognized and responded sensitively and supportively to their children's cues for assistance, termed Supportive Presence. Intercorrelations among the 6-month, 24-month, and 42-month sensitivity measures did not exceed 0.38, and in one case (between 6-month sensitivity and 24-month Quality of Assistance) was only 0.16, which was not significant.

The foregoing suggests that stability in parenting within infancy, and from infancy to the preschool period, is moderate at best even when conceptually similar assessments of a single construct (i.e., using an "etic" approach to stability) are obtained over time. We refer the reader to Holden and Miller's (1999) comprehensive review of parenting stability examined in a variety of children's age groups. We know very little, however, about the stability of parenting competence from infancy to the preschool years when parenting competence in the preschool years is defined not simply in terms of sensitivity but in terms of the integration, as advocated in this chapter, of warmth/nurturance, control, and quality of communication. Indeed, to date, we have been able to find only one investigation that addresses parental stability from infancy to the toddler/preschool years in this manner. In a study of 308 lower socioeconomic status (SES) parents of preterm infants, Smith, Landry, and Swank (2000) examined the manner in which maternal nurturance/responsiveness and restrictiveness changed from across three age points in development (6, 12, and 24 months), and then assessed the children at 3 years of age on intelligence, language skills, psychiatric symptoms (as reported by mothers), and social responsiveness to mother during a 1-hour home observation. Mothers also reported on the quality of their social supports and their attitudes toward child rearing and child development, specifically in terms of whether children's development was multiply determined and dependent in part on context (a perspectivistic orientation) and in terms of how much parents needed to restrict their children's activities. Smith, Landry, and Swank hypothesized that the most optimal profile would be that in which responsiveness remained high at all points and restrictiveness increased from 6 to 24 months, but not dramatically. Parents showing such a profile, they proposed, would be reflective of the most optimal parental adaptation in their children's move from infancy to toddlerhood, showing high levels of warmth and responsivity at all ages but showing moderate increases in restrictiveness in response to the need to set limits upon their children's behavior. Such parents, from an emic perspective, would evince stability in parenting competence. Home observations of mothers and infants took place during a 60-minute window (separate from that used to assess children's social responsiveness to mothers) in which mothers were asked to feed, bathe, and dress their infants during that time but otherwise to go about their daily routines. Restrictiveness was defined as the proportion of time the mother made any attempt, physical or verbal, to stop the baby's ongoing activity. Warm responsiveness was defined as the composite of ratings of maternal behavior along dimensions of positive affect, concern/acceptance, and responsiveness/flexibility.

Smith, Landry, and Swank used a cluster analytic approach to identify four change profiles. One cluster (*n* = 92), hypothesized to be the most optimal in terms of facilitating child development, was identified by high levels of warm responsiveness at all three age points, and slight to moderate increases, starting from very low levels at 6 months, in restrictiveness across time. From the developmental emic perspective taken in this chapter, such parents exhibited stability in parenting competence from infancy to toddlerhood. A second cluster (*n* = 53) was characterized by very low levels of warm responsiveness across all time points, and increases to high levels of restrictiveness (from moderate levels observed at 6 months) at 12 and 24 months. Such a pattern, Smith, Landry, and Swank hypothesized, was perhaps the most problematic in terms of parental competence, and these parents also exhibited stability, but in parenting *incompetence*. A third cluster (*n* = 70) increased significantly from low restrictiveness at 6 months to a very high level of restrictiveness at 24 months, but also had fairly high levels of warm responsiveness at 6 and 12 months, decreasing to very low levels at 24 months. This cluster, from an emic perspective, displayed competent parenting during the infants' first year but decreased in parenting competence by 24 months, thus displaying instability in parenting competence over time. Finally, a fourth cluster ($n = 93$) showed decreases over time in warm responsiveness from moderate levels at 6 months to low levels at 12 months, followed by an increase to moderate levels by 24 months, and 6- to 12-month increases in restrictiveness to moderate levels by 12 months, followed by a slight decrease from 12 to 24 months. Whereas these mothers may have demonstrated competence in parenting at 6 months, the decrease in responsiveness from 6 to 12 months, followed by only a slight increase from 12 to 24 months, is suggestive of parenting instability across the three age points.

As Smith, Landry, and Swank (2000) hypothesized, the most optimal outcomes for children were associated with the first cluster, in which mothers maintained high levels of warm responsiveness over time and increased only slightly their levels of restrictiveness. Children of these mothers had higher cognitive scores than did children of other mothers, and better social skills than did children of mothers with the hypothetically least adaptive profile (low levels of responsiveness and high restrictiveness at all age points) and children of mothers who evinced some apparent difficulties adapting to their children's changing needs over time (i.e., characterized by reductions in warm responsiveness across the second year of life and strong increases in restrictiveness from 6 to 24 months). Importantly, Smith, Landry, and Swank also reported that mothers in the most optimal cluster were of significantly higher SES, more likely to report higher levels of social supports, and more likely to endorse the most flexible, perspectivistic, and non-restrictive attitudes about child rearing than were mothers in the other clusters.

Smith, Landry, and Swank's (2000) investigation targeted lower SES mothers of preterm infants, and thus it is not clear to what degree these results are generalizable to middle-class parents and parents of full-term infants. What is clear from this investigation, however, is that stability in parenting was observed for only 47 percent of the sample (i.e., stability in parenting competence or stability in parenting incompetence), with the other 53 percent evincing patterns of instability, characterized predominantly by moving from more competent parenting early in the infants' lives to less competent parenting as the children matured. In light of the low levels of stability in parenting in more middle-class samples of full-term infants as reported earlier (e.g., Crockenberg & McCluskey, 1986; Belsky, Rovine, & Taylor, 1984), one cannot hypothesize with any degree of confidence about whether levels of parenting stability, using the developmental emic approach outlined in this chapter, would improve in lower-risk samples. This is clearly an area for future research.

Conclusions

In this chapter we have adopted a developmental emic approach to argue that parenting competence, defined as high levels of warm, contingent, and appropriate behavior in response to child cues and signals in infancy (parental sensitivity), evolves into a qualitatively more complex construct in the preschool years, one that combines warmth and responsiveness with reasonable and appropriate levels of control in disciplinary contexts and clear communication with the child with regard to parental expectations about proper conduct. Parental competence in the preschool years thus maps quite well onto Baumrind's (1967, 1973, 1989b) authoritative parenting construct, and, as reviewed earlier, both parental sensitivity in infancy and authoritative parenting post-infancy are associated with mutually positive, reciprocal parent–child relationships and with children's social competence in the wider world. Establishing "reasonable and appropriate" levels of parental control, of course, rules out the use of excessive coercion and negative parental affect, which, as previous data indicate (e.g., Denham et al., 2000), would not be associated with competent parenting under any circumstance. As discussed earlier, perhaps the most promising and useful formulations regarding the manner in which parental control might be well-tailored to individual children come from Kochanska's work (Kochanska, 1995; Kochanska, Murray, & Coy, 1997), which take into consideration the quality of "fit" between parental socialization behaviors and individual differences in children's temperamental dimensions of fearfulness and effortful control. This work represents an important breakthrough in the field of early socialization research.

Interestingly, there is precious little work that examines stability of parenting from infancy to the preschool years that makes particular use of the developmental emic approach outlined here. The one study that comes closest to doing so (Smith, Landry, & Swank, 2000) suggests that it is reasonable to find both stability and instability in parenting competence represented in samples of parents and children during this transition. In this study, 47 percent of parents demonstrated parenting stability (30 percent showing stability in parenting competence, and 17 percent showing stability in parenting incompetence). Children's capacities for healthy development would, of course, be expected to be maximized under conditions of stability in parenting competence, and minimized under conditions of stability in parenting incompetence. Importantly, however, Smith, Landry, and Swank found 53 percent of mothers who demonstrated instability in parenting competence, and it appeared that these mothers best fit a "competency in infancy" to "incompetency in the preschool years" change pattern. This suggests that instability in parenting may be most likely represented by parents' growing inability to cope with their children's increasingly complex and demanding behavioral repertoire in the move from infancy to the preschool years, although we believe it is important to remain open to the possibility that some parents may evince instability by moving from incompetent to competent parenting in this transition. Such a change pattern may characterize some fathers, for example, perhaps because with development children become less dependent on their mothers and gain motor and communication skills that enable them to become better partners in father–child play routines. Such a pattern is consistent with Clarke-Stewart's (1978) findings of increasing paternal involvement with their young children by the second year of life, although there clearly are many additional sociocultural, socioeconomic, and family-systems factors to consider in assessing for developmental trends in paternal competence. What Smith, Landry, and Swank do suggest, however, is that when parents do not adapt well in the transition from infancy to the preschool years, children's development suffers.

A great deal of work remains to be done in the study of developmentally emic consistencies and shifts in parenting competence in the child's early years. To begin, we need a more comprehensive understanding of how competent-to-incompetent parenting shifts are particularly manifested. One pattern of parental change not identified by Smith, Landry, and Swank (2000), for example, is one in which parents remain warm and responsive to their children both in infancy and the preschool period but show no increases whatsoever in restrictiveness or limit-setting, which would appear to be a move from sensitivity parenting in infancy to permissive parenting in the preschool years. What is not clear from previous research is whether such a change pattern occurs with enough frequency to warrant the study of it in its own right; however, we believe that such a change pattern is theoretically plausible and represents another kind of parental maladaptation, especially among parents of children who lack sufficient impulse control and therefore require adequate and appropriate levels of parental structure and controls. Baumrind (1967, 1973) would argue that such a change would not be adaptive, either for the parent–child relationship or for the child's ability to be competent in the wider world.

Beyond the identification of bona fide parenting change patterns, additional work needs to done to understand how and why consistencies and shifts in parenting competence occur. Parenting, as we know by this point in time, can be predicted on the basis of a parent's developmental history, belief systems, family functioning, social ecology (e.g., stressors and social-marital supports), and psychiatric profile, as well as stable and developing characteristics of the child (Crnic & Low, 2002; George & Solomon, 1999). Quality of adaptation to parenting as the child develops would be expected to be responsive to changes in perhaps any one or more of these domains. It behooves researchers to use these domains to seek theoretically lawful explanations of continuities and discontinuities in parenting competence. For example, is a move from competent parenting in infancy to incompetent parenting in the preschool years a function of a parent's inability or unwillingness to accept and tolerate the child's growing separation and individuation from the parent? Can this be explained by the parent's own developmental history (e.g., overprotective parents, or perhaps a nonautonomous state of mind regarding attachment), the presence of significant psychiatric symptoms, and/or perhaps a belief system that endorses somewhat inflexible, non-perspectivistic, authoritarian attitudes about how to raise children when they get older? Alternatively, do the origins of such instability lie in the parent's social ecology, as when, for example, qualitative shifts occur in the quality of support received from one's partner, in perceived life stress, or some combination of the two? Lastly (but not least), to what extent can qualitative shifts in parenting competence be explained by developing child characteristics, such as high levels of negative mood, proneness to distress, and a growing lack of impulse control, either solely or in interaction with specific parental vulnerabilities?

We believe that questions of this kind are extremely important, not just to the study of parenting, but to a better, more comprehensive, and more dynamic understanding of child development and the factors that influence it. It is our hope that theoretically guided research will be generated with these ends in mind.

References

Ainsworth, M. D. S. (1969). Maternal sensitivity scales. Unpublished manuscript, The Johns Hopkins University. Retrieved August 29, 2003, from http://www.psychology.sunysb.edu/ewaters/552/senscoop.htm.

Ainsworth, M. D. S. & Bell, S. M. (1969). Some contemporary patterns of mother–infant interaction in the feeding situation. In A. Ambrose (ed.), *Stimulation in early infancy* (pp. 133–70). London: Academic Press.

Ainsworth, M. D. S., Bell, S. M., & Stayton, D. J. (1974). Infant–mother attachment and social development: Socialization as a product of reciprocal responsiveness to signals. In M. Richards (ed.), *The integration of the child into the social world* (pp. 99–135). Cambridge: Cambridge University Press.

Ainsworth, M. D. S., Blehar, M. C., Waters, E., & Wall, S. (1978). *Patterns of attachment: A psychological study of the strange situation.* Hillsdale, NJ: Lawrence Erlbaum Associates.

August, G. J., Realmuto, G. M., Joyce, T., & Hektner, J. M. (1999). Persistence and desistance of oppositional defiant disorder in a community sample of children with ADHD. *Journal of the American Academy of Child and Adolescent Psychiatry, 38*, 1262–70.

Aunola, K., Stattin, H., & Nurmi, J.-E. (2000). Parenting styles and adolescents' achievement strategies. *Journal of Adolescence, 23*, 205–22.

Baldwin, A. L. (1948). Socialization and the parent–child relationship. *Child Development, 19*, 127–36.

Baldwin, A. L. (1955). *Behavior and development in childhood.* New York: Dryden.

Barnard, K. E. (1994). What the NCAST feeding scale measures. In G. S. Sumner & A. Spietz (eds.), *NCAST: Caregiver/parent-child interaction manual.* Seattle, WA: University of Washington NCAST Publications.

Baumrind, D. (1966). Effects of authoritative control on child behavior. *Child Development, 37*, 887–907.

Baumrind, D. (1967). Childcare practices anteceding three patterns of preschool behavior. *Genetic Psychology Monographs, 75*, 43–88.

Baumrind, D. (1970). Socialization and instrumental competence in young children. *Young Children, 26*, 104–19.

Baumrind, D. (1973). The development of instrumental competence through socialization. *Minnesota Symposium on Child Psychology* (vol. 7, pp. 3–46). Minneapolis, MN: University of Minnesota Press.

Baumrind, D. (1980). New directions in socialization research. *American Psychologist, 35*, 639–52.

Baumrind, D. (1989a). The permanence of change and the impermanence of stability. *Human Development, 32*, 187–95.

Baumrind, D. (1989b). Rearing competent children. In W. Damon (ed.), *Child development today and tomorrow* (pp. 349–78). San Francisco, CA: Jossey-Bass.

Baumrind, D. (1991). Parenting styles and adolescent development. In J. Brooks-Gunn, R. Lerner, & A. C. Petersen (eds.), *The encyclopedia of adolescence* (pp. 746–58). New York: Garland.

Bee, H. L., Barnard, K. E., Eyres, S. J., Gray, C. A., Hammond, M. A., Spietz, A. L., Snyder, C., & Clark, B. (1982). Prediction of IQ and language skill from perinatal status, child performance, family characteristics, and mother–infant interaction. *Child Development, 53*, 1134–56.

Bell, S. & Ainsworth, M. (1972). Infant crying and maternal responsiveness. *Child Development, 43*, 1171–90.

Belsky, J. (1999). Interactional and contextual determinants of attachment security. In J. Cassidy & P. R. Shaver (eds.), *Handbook of attachment: Theory, research, and clinical applications* (pp. 249–64). New York: Guilford.

Belsky, J., Rovine, M., & Taylor, D. G. (1984). The Pennsylvania Infant and Family Development Project: III. The origins of individual differences in infant–mother attachment: Maternal and infant contributions. *Child Development, 55*, 718–28.

Berlin, L. J. & Cassidy, J. (1999). Relations among relationships: Contributions from attachment theory and research. In J. Cassidy & P. R. Shaver (eds.), *Handbook of attachment: Theory, research, and clinical applications.* (pp. 688–712). New York: Guilford.

Biringen, Z. (2000). Emotional availability: Conceptualization and research findings. *American Journal of Orthopsychiatry, 70*, 104–14.

Biringen, Z. & Robinson, J. (1991). Emotional availability in mother–child interactions: A reconceptualization for research. *American Journal of Orthopsychiatry, 61*, 258–71.

Biringen, Z., Robinson, J. L., & Emde, R. N. (1998). *Manual for scoring the emotional availability scales* (3rd edn.). Unpublished manuscript, Colorado State University, Fort Collins, CO.

Bowlby, J. (1969). *Attachment and loss*, vol. 1: *Attachment*. New York: Basic Books.

Cassidy, J., & Shaver, P. R. (eds.) (1999). *Handbook of attachment: Theory, research, and clinical applications*. New York: Guilford.

Clark, R. (1985). The parent–child early relational assessment. Available from Roseanne Clark, Department of Psychiatry, University of Wisconsin Medical School, 600 Highland Avenue, Madison, WI 53792.

Clark, R. (1999). The Parent–Child Early Relational Assessment: A factorial validity study. *Educational and Psychological Measurement, 59*, 821–46.

Clarke-Stewart, K. A. (1978). And daddy makes three: The father's impact on mother and young child. *Child Development, 49*, 466–78.

Claussen, A. H. & Crittenden, P. M. (2000). Maternal sensitivity. In P. M. Crittenden & A. H. Claussen (eds.), *The organization of attachment relationships: Maturation, culture, and context* (pp. 115–22). Cambridge: Cambridge University Press.

Cole, P. M., Michel, M. K., & Teti, L. O. (1994). The development of emotion regulation and dysregulation: A clinical perspective. In N. A. Fox (ed.), The development of emotion regulation: Biological and behavioral considerations. *Monographs of the Society for Research in Child Development, 59* (nos. 2–3, serial no. 240), 73–100.

Crittenden, P. M. (1992). Quality of attachment in the preschool years. *Development and Psychopathology, 4*, 209–41.

Crnic, K. & Low, C. (2002). Everyday stresses and parenting. In M. H. Bornstein (ed.), *Handbook of parenting*, vol. 5: *Practical issues in parenting* (2nd edn., pp. 243–67). Mahwah, NJ: Lawrence Erlbaum Associates.

Crockenberg, S. & Litman, C. (1990). Autonomy as competence in 2-year-olds: Maternal correlates of child defiance, compliance, and self-assertion. *Developmental Psychology, 26*, 961–71.

Crockenberg, S. & McCluskey, K. (1986). Change in maternal behavior during the baby's first year of life. *Child Development, 57*, 746–53.

Cummings, E. M., Iannotti, R. J., & Zahn-Waxler, C. (1985). Influence of conflict between adults on the emotions and aggression of young children. *Developmental Psychology, 21*, 495–507.

Cusinato, M. (1994). Parenting over the family life cycle. In L. L'Abate (ed.), *Handbook of developmental family psychology and psychopathology* (pp. 83–115). New York: John Wiley.

Damon, W. (1983). *Social and personality development: Infancy through adolescence*. New York: Norton.

Davies, P. T. & Cummings, E. M. (1995). Children's emotions as organizers of their reactions to interadult anger: A functionalist perspective. *Developmental Psychology, 31*, 677–84.

Deković, M. & Janssens, M. A. M. (1992). Parents' child-rearing style and child's sociometric status. *Developmental Psychology, 28*, 925–32.

Denham, S. A., Workman, E., Cole, P. M., Weissbrod, C., Kendziora, K. T., & Zahn-Waxler, C. (2000). Prediction of externalizing behavior problems from early to middle childhood: The role of parental socialization and emotion expression. *Development and Psychopathology, 12*, 23–45.

Dumas, J. & LaFreniere, P. J. (1993). Mother–child relationships as sources of support or stress: A comparison of competent, average, aggressive, and anxious dyads. *Child Development, 64*, 1732–54.

Edwards, C. P. & Liu, W.-L. (2002). Parenting toddlers. In M. H. Bornstein (ed.), *Handbook of parenting*, vol. 1: *Children and parenting* (2nd edn., pp. 45–71). Mahwah, NJ: Lawrence Erlbaum Associates.

Gardner, F. E. M. (1987). Positive interaction between mothers and conduct-problem children: Is there training for harmony as well as fighting? *Journal of Abnormal Child Psychology, 15*, 283–93.

George, C. & Solomon, J. (1999). Attachment and care giving: The care giving behavioral system. In J. Cassidy & P. R. Shaver (eds.), *Handbook of attachment: Theory, Research, and Clinical Applications* (pp. 649–70). New York: Guilford.

Greenberg, M. T., Cicchetti, D., & Cummings, E. M. (1990). *Attachment in the preschool years: Theory, research, and intervention*. Chicago, IL: University of Chicago Press.

Grusec, J. E. & Goodnow, J. J. (1994). Impact of parental discipline methods on the child's internalization of values: A reconceptualization of current points of view. *Developmental Psychology, 30*, 4–19.

Heinicke, C., Diskin, S., Ramsey-Klee, D., & Given, K. (1983). Rebirth characteristics and family development in the first year of life. *Child Development, 54*, 194–208.

Hickman, G. P., Bartholomae, S., & McHendy, P. C. (2000). Influence of parenting style on the adjustment and academic achievement of traditional college freshmen. *Journal of College Student Development, 41*, 41–54.

Hill, N. E. (1995). The relationship between family environment and parenting style: A preliminary study of African American families. *Journal of Black Psychology, 21*, 408–23.

Hoffman, M. L. (1994). Discipline and internalization. *Developmental Psychology, 30*, 26–8.

Hoffman, M. L. & Saltzstein, H. D. (1967). Parental discipline and the child's moral development. *Journal of Personality and Social Psychology, 5*, 45–57.

Holden, G. W. & Miller, P. C. (1999). Enduring and different: A meta-analysis of the similarity in parents' child rearing. *Psychological Bulletin, 125*, 223–54.

Kaufmann, D., Gesten, E., Santa Lucia, R. C., Salcedo, O., Rending-Gobioff, G., & Gadd, R. (2000). The relationship between parenting style and children's adjustment: The parents' perspective. *Journal of Child and Family Studies, 9*, 231–45.

Kochanska, G. (1993). Toward a synthesis of parental socialization and child temperament in early development of conscience. *Child Development, 64*, 325–47.

Kochanska, G. (1994). Beyond cognition: Expanding the search for the early roots of internalization and conscience. *Developmental Psychology, 30*, 20–22.

Kochanska, G. (1995). Children's temperament, mothers' discipline, and security of attachment: Multiple pathways to emerging internalization. *Child Development, 66*, 597–615.

Kochanska, G. (1998). Mother–child relationship, child fearfulness, and emerging attachment: A short-term longitudinal study. *Developmental Psychology, 34*, 480–90.

Kochanska, G. & Aksan, N. (1995). Mother–child mutually positive affect, the quality of child compliance to requests and prohibitions, and maternal control as correlates of early internalization. *Child Development, 66*, 236–54.

Kochanska, G., Murray, K., & Coy, K. C. (1997). Inhibitory control as a contributor to conscience in childhood. From toddler to early school age. *Child Development*, *68*, 263–77.

Kochanska, G., Coy, K. C., Tjebkes, T., & Husarek, S. J. (1998). Individual differences in emotionality in infancy. *Child Development*, *69*, 375–90.

Leung, P. W. L., & Kwan, K. S. F. (1998). Parenting styles, motivational orientations, and self-perceived academic competence: A mediational model. *Merrill-Palmer Quarterly*, *44*, 1–19.

Locke, J. (1964). *Some thoughts concerning education*. New York: Bureau of Publications (original work published 1693).

Londerville, S. & Main, M. (1981). Security of attachment, compliance, and maternal training methods in the second year of life. *Developmental Psychology*, *17*, 289–99.

Maccoby, E. E. (1992). The role of parents in the socialization of children: An historical overview. *Developmental Psychology*, *28*, 1006–17.

Maccoby, E. E. & Martin, J. (1983). Socialization in the context of the family: Parent–child interaction. In E. M. Hetherington (ed.) and P. H. Mussen (series ed.), *Handbook of child psychology*, vol. 4: *Socialization, personality, and social development* (pp. 1–101). New York: John Wiley.

Moran, G., Pederson, D. R., Pettit, P., & Krupka, A. (1992). Maternal sensitivity and infant–mother attachment in a developmentally delayed sample. *Infant Behavior and Development*, *15*, 427–42.

Morriset, C. E. (1994). What the Teaching Scale measures. In G. S. Sumner & A. Spietz (eds.), *NCAST: Caregiver/parent–child interaction manual*. Seattle, WA: University of Washington NCAST Publications.

Pederson, D. R. & Moran, G. (1995a). Appendix B: Maternal Behavior Q-set. In E. Waters, B. E. Vaughn, G. Posada, & K. Kondo-Ikemura (eds.), Care giving, cultural, and cognitive perspectives on secure-base behavior and working models: New growing points of attachment theory and research. *Monographs of the Society for Research in Child Development*, *60* (serial no. 244, nos. 2–3), 247–54.

Pederson, D. R., & Moran, G. (1995b). A categorical description of infant-mother relationships in the home and in relation to Q-sort measures of infant-mother interaction. In E. Waters, B. E. Vaughn, G. Posada, & K. Kondo-Ikemura (eds.), Care giving, cultural, and cognitive perspectives on secure-base behavior and working models: New growing points of attachment theory and research. *Monographs of the Society for Research in Child Development*, *60* (serial no. 244, nos. 2–3), 111–32.

Pederson, D. R., Moran, G., Sitko, C., Campbell, K., Ghesquire, K., & Acton, H. (1990). Maternal sensitivity and the security of infant–mother attachment: A Q-sort study. *Child Development*, *61*, 1974–83.

Pettit, G. S. & Bates, J. E. (1989). Family interaction patterns and children's behavior problems from infancy to four years. *Developmental Psychology*, *25*, 413–20.

Pianta, R. C., Sroufe, L. A., & Egeland, B. (1989). Continuity and discontinuity in maternal sensitivity at 6, 24, and 42 months in a high-risk sample. *Child Development*, *60*, 481–7.

Pipp-Siegel, S. (1998). Assessing the quality of relationships between parents and children: The Emotional Availability Scales. *Volta Review*, *100*, 237–49.

Querido, J. G., Warner, T. D., & Eyberg, S. M. (2002). Parenting styles and child behavior in African American families of preschool children. *Journal of Clinical Child Psychology*, *31*, 272–7.

Rousseau, J. J. (1911). *Émile* (B. Foxley, trans.). London: Dent (original work published 1762).

Sears, R. R., Maccoby, E., & Levin, H. (1957). *Patterns of childrearing*. Evanston, IL: Row, Peterson.

Shumow, L., Vandell, D. L., & Posner, J. K. (1998). Harsh, firm, and permissive parenting in low-income families: Relations to children's academic achievement and behavioral adjustment. *Journal of Family Issues*, *19*, 483–507.

Smith, K. E., Landry, S. H., & Swank, P. R. (2000). The influence of early patterns of positive parenting on children's preschool outcomes. *Early Education and Development*, *11*, 147–69.

Stayton, D., Hogan, R., & Ainsworth, M. D. S. (1973). Infant obedience and maternal behavior: The origins of socialization reconsidered. *Child Development*, *42*, 1057–70.

Tamis-LeMonda, C. S., Bornstein, M. H., Baumwell, L., & Damast, A. M. (1996). Responsive parenting in the second year: Specific influences on children's language and play. *Early Development and Parenting*, *5*, 173–83.

Taylor, R. D., Casten, R., & Flickinger, S. M. (1993). Influence of kinship social support on the parenting experiences and psychosocial adjustment of African-American adolescents. *Developmental Psychology*, *29*, 382–99.

Teti, D. M. & Candelaria, M. A. (2002). Parenting competence. In M. H. Bornstein (ed.), *Handbook of parenting*, vol. 4: *Social conditions and applied parenting* (2nd edn., pp. 149–80). Mahwah, NJ: Lawrence Erlbaum Associates.

Teti, D. M. & Teti, L. O. (1996). Infant–parent relationships. In N. Vanzetti & S. Duck (eds.), *A lifetime of relationships* (pp. 77–104). Pacific Grove, CA: Brooks/Cole.

Teti, D. M., Nakagawa, M., Das, R., & Wirth, O. (1991). Security of attachment between preschoolers and their mothers: Relations among social interaction, parenting stress, and mothers' sorts of the Attachment Q-Set. *Developmental Psychology*, *27*, 440–7.

Teti, D. M., Gelfand, D. M., Messinger, D., & Isabella, R. (1995). Maternal depression and the quality of early attachment: An examination of infants, preschoolers, and their mothers. *Developmental Psychology*, *31*, 364–76.

Thompson, A., Hollis, C., & Richards, D. (2003). Authoritarian parenting attitudes as a risk for conduct problems: Results from a British national cohort study. *European Child and Adolescent Psychiatry*, *12*, 84–91.

Vaughn, B. E. & Bost, K. K. (1999). Attachment and temperament: Redundant, independent, or interacting influences on interpersonal adaptation and personality development? In J. Cassidy & P. R. Shaver (eds.), *Handbook of attachment: Theory, research, and clinical applications* (pp. 198–225). New York: Guilford.

Waters, E. & Deane, K. E. (1985). Defining and assessing individual differences in attachment relationships: Q-methodology and the organization of behavior in infancy and early childhood. In I. Bretherton & E. Waters (eds.), Growing points of attachment theory and research. *Monographs of the Society for Research in Child Development*, *50* (serial no. 209, nos. 1–2), 41–65.

Zahn-Waxler, C., Iannotti, R. J., Cummings, E. M., & Denham, S. A. (1990). Antecedents of problem behaviors in children of depressed mothers. *Development and Psychopathology*, *2*, 271–91.

CHAPTER TEN

Methods of Contextual Assessment and Assessing Contextual Methods: A Developmental Systems Perspective

Richard M. Lerner, Elizabeth Dowling, and Jana Chaudhuri

Since its inception as a field of study within psychology, dating at least to the work of G. Stanley Hall (e.g., 1904; see Cairns, 1998; Dixon & Lerner, 1999), developmental psychology has been interested in understanding the environment, setting, ecology, or context of human development (Bronfenbrenner, 1977, 1979, 2001; Bronfenbrenner & Morris, 1998). This interest has been motivated by both theoretical issues – ranging from one's steeped in biological (e.g., evolutionary) ideas about the source of human development (e.g., Haeckel, 1876; Hall, 1904) to models seeking to identify the environmental stimulus conditions believed to shape human development (e.g., Watson, 1914, 1928; see also Bijou, 1976; Bijou & Baer, 1961, 1965, for later versions of this viewpoint). Interest in the context has been generated also by concerns about how to apply ideas about human development to improve behavior in schools, families, work sites, and other key settings of human life (e.g., see Cairns, 1998; McCandless, 1967, 1970).

More recently, and especially in the last two decades of the twentieth century, the emergence of dynamic, developmental systems perspectives about human development (e.g., Fischer & Bidell, 1998; Ford & Lerner, 1992; Gottlieb, 1992, 1997; Lerner, 1998a, b, 2002; Magnusson, 1999a, b; Magnusson & Stattin, 1998; Thelen & Smith, 1994, 1998; Wapner & Demick, 1998), and the applications of developmental science that it has spawned (e.g., Fisher & Lerner, 1994; Lerner, Fisher, & Weinberg, 1997, 2000a, b; Lerner, Jacobs, Wertlieb, 2003), have provided additional theoretical and societal impetus for understanding the integrative relations that exist between the developing individual and his or her changing, multilevel context.

Given this relatively long and varied history, it is not surprising that developmental psychologists have devised and used a rich and diverse set of methods to appraise the context, or ecology, of human development. The advent in the 1970s of an influential and empirically productive dynamic, life-span view of human development (Baltes, 1987, 1997; Baltes, Lindenberger, & Staudinger, 1998; Baltes, Staudinger, & Lindenberger, 1999; Schaie, 1965; Schaie & Strother, 1968), one which called for an integrative, multidisciplinary approach to the study of people and their contexts, resulted in greater attention being paid by developmental psychologists to the ways that sociologists, anthropologists, historians, economists, political scientists, and other social and behavioral scientists measured the context of human development (e.g., see Elder, 1980, 1998; Hernandez, 1993; Sørensen, Weinert, & Sherrod, 1986; Spanier, 1976a, b). This attention expanded the methodological repertoire that developmental psychologists used to measure the context of individual development, an expansion that involved units of analysis (e.g., birth cohorts, normative and nonnormative historical events) more macro than those usually associated with the individual-level interests and methods of developmental psychologists (e.g., see Elder, Modell, & Parke, 1993).

The life-span view of human development developed by both Baltes (1987, 1997; Baltes et al., 1998, 1999) and by Schaie (1965; Schaie & Strother, 1968) was an instance of the developmental systems idea that, as noted above, emerged towards the end of the last century to predominate the theoretical scene in the study of human development (Lerner, 1998a, b, 2002). The unit of analysis in developmental systems theories is neither the individual nor the context; rather, developmental systems theories are more concerned with the relation between individual and context – more specifically, with a dynamic, or fused, multilevel relation among levels of organization integrated within the developmental system (e.g., Fischer & Bidell, 1998; Lerner, 2002; Thelen & Smith, 1998; Tobach & Greenberg, 1984). Gottlieb (1970, 1983, 1992, 1997) describes the process of integrated change within this fused system as involving *probabilistic epigenesis*. This is:

> the view that the behavioral development of individuals within a species does not follow an invariant or inevitable course, and, more specifically, that the sequence or outcome of individual behavioral development is probable (with respect to norms) rather than certain. (Gottlieb, 1970, p. 123)

Gottlieb explains that this probabilistic character of individual development:

> necessitates a bidirectional structure–function hypothesis. The conventional version of the structure–function hypothesis is unidirectional in the sense that structure is supposed to determine function in an essentially nonreciprocal relationship. The unidirectionality of the structure–function relationship is one of the main assumptions of predetermined epigenesis. The bidirectional version of the structure–function relationship is a logical consequence of the view that the course and outcome of behavioral epigenesis is probabilistic: It entails the assumption of reciprocal effects in the relationship between structure and function whereby function (exposure to stimulation and/or movement of musculoskeletal activity) can significantly modify the development of the peripheral and central structures that are involved in these events. (Gottlieb, 1970, p. 123)

In short, probabilistic epigenesis stands in contrast to the predetermined epigenesis conception, where the key assumption:

> holds that there is a unidirectional relationship between structure and function whereby structural maturation determines function (structural maturation → function) but not the reverse, probabilistic epigenesis assumes a bidirectional or reciprocal relationship between structural maturation and function whereby structural maturation determines function and function alters structural maturation (structural maturation ←→ function). (Gottlieb, 1983, p. 12)

In the contemporary study of human development, scholars involved with testing ideas associated with developmental systems models are concerned with more than using methods that reliably and validly index the context within which development occurs. They are concerned, instead, with developing *relational* measures, or what we may term "developmental contextual methods," that is, methods that usefully appraise the dynamic linkage between an individual and the settings within which he or she reciprocally interacts (Lerner et al., 2003). Such emphases have elevated person-centered analyses (Magnusson, 1999a, b; Magnusson & Stattin, 1998), or perhaps better, person-context relational centered analyses (e.g., Eccles, 2004; Eccles, Wigfield, & Byrnes, 2003; Lerner et al., 2003) to the fore of basic and applied scholarship predicated on developmental systems models.

To reflect the history and current status of the methods involved in integrating the context into the nature of human development, our task in this chapter is twofold. First, we will discuss the theoretical and associated methodological history of the approaches taken to measure the context of human development. This discussion will lead us to the second focus of our presentation: an analysis of the extent to which developmental science has theoretically and empirically appropriate methods available for evaluating the contemporary, developmental systems approach to contextual assessment. In this approach, the dynamic relations between individuals and setting are presumed to propel ontogenetic change across the entire course of life. To begin this discussion we first consider the history, in the scientific study of human ontogeny, of interest in the appraisal of the contexts of development.

The Historical Context of Developmental Psychological Interest in the Context

G. Stanley Hall (1904) fancied himself as the "Darwin of the mind" (Dixon & Lerner, 1999; White, 1968), which meant, to Hall, that he was applying Darwinian evolutionary theory to the description and explanation of human ontogeny. The connection Hall drew between Darwin's ideas and those he proposed to characterize the human life course was mediated by the recapitulationist ideas of the nineteenth- and early twentieth-century embryologist, Ernst Haeckel (1868, 1876, 1905), who – misinterpreting Darwin – claimed that "ontogeny recapitulates phylogeny" (Dixon & Lerner, 1999; Gould, 1977; Lerner, 2002; White, 1968).

Although it is not the purpose of the present chapter to explain either Haeckel's misinterpretation or Hall's resulting misapplication of Darwinian ideas (see Lerner, 2002, for such a discussion), we do note that Hall's use of Darwinian ideas provided an initial, evolutionary context within which to consider the changes that characterized human development across the life span. Hall's recapitulationist ideas framed the study of human development as being embedded within the context of the past settings within which humans lived. To Hall, the outcomes of the evolutionary context are the current features of human ontogeny (Dixon & Lerner, 1999).

One key outcome of Hall's reliance on Darwinian theory was, then, the launching of the field of developmental psychology in a manner that emphasized macro "nature" (e.g., biological heritage, evolution) sources of human development, rather than "nurture" ones (e.g., experiences across ontogeny), as foundational in the shaping of human behavior across the life course. Although few scholars, even contemporaries of Hall (e.g., Thorndike, 1904), accepted Hall's recapitulationism, Hall's prominent students – Arnold Gesell (e.g., 1946) and Louis Terman (e.g., 1916, 1925) – were influential in launching developmental psychology as a field focused on the biological (e.g., maturational, genetic) primacy of the causal factors in human development. This more micro, but equally hereditarian (Rushton, 1999), nature orientation meant that nurture – environmental or, more broadly, contextual – ideas were given secondary status in the study of human development (Dixon & Lerner, 1999; Lerner, 2002).

The contemporary version of these micro, hereditarian, reductionistic, and mechanistic views of the biological context of human development are behavior genetic (e.g., Rowe, 1994; Plomin, 2000) or sociobiological (Rushton, 1999) approaches to human behavior. In some instances of these approaches, any influence of the family or other purportedly key socializing contexts may be reduced to genetic inheritance if, upon computation of heritability coefficients, evidence is found that individual differences in a trait distribution are associated with differences in "gene" distributions in that same population. This approach, which is egregiously and fatally flawed on both conceptual and methodological grounds (e.g., Collins et al., 2000; Gottlieb, Wahlsten, & Lickliter, 1998; Hirsch, 1997; Horowitz, 2000; Lerner, 2002), is, nevertheless, seen by its proponents as constituting a means to bypass the need to study the context of human development. Since all contextual influences can, in principle, be reduced to genetic inheritance, some proponents of this approach believe that there is no reason to be concerned with what they term "socialization science" (Rowe, 1994).

With the advent of the popularity of Behaviorism (Skinner, 1938, 1964; Watson, 1914, 1928) in the early decades of the twentieth century a micro-nurture alternative to understanding the context of human behavior came to counter the macro- and micro-nature ideas of Hall (1904), Gesell (1946), and Terman (1916). The Behavioral, or functionalist (Baer, 1976; Bijou, 1976), perspective embodied in this nurture orientation represented context through the notion of a proximal stimulus environment or reinforcement context (Bijou & Baer, 1961). Within this approach, the figure and ground character of organism and environment was, at times, altered. The organism was seen as the context, locus, or, simply, the host of stimuli that swirled around it (Baer, 1976).

In the main, however, the micro-nurture alternative to the macro- or micro-nature views resulted in a "situationalist" (Bowers, 1973) view of the context of human development. The world outside the organism was said to be independent of it. The organism was regarded as the location for, or host of, the relations between stimuli and responses that comprised ontogenetic behavioral change (Baer, 1976). This organism-independent context – if not reduced to the actual, core constituent elements involved in behavior change – might be termed the "family," "school," "playground," or "community." However, from the point of view of this mechanistic approach, these contexts, when they are reduced to their constituent elements, are the repositories or dispensers of stimuli, understood in "S-R," "S-O-R," or "social learning" frameworks (Lerner, 1986; Overton & Reese, 1973; Reese & Overton, 1970).

Both the nature and the nurture approaches to the conceptualization and indexing of context were based on a premise that there was one core reality in human development, either nature or nurture (Overton, 1998). Believing in this "split" view of human life, both groups pursued research that would enable them to index either the biological or environmental variables that they believed causal in human development. As noted above, the latter decades of the twentieth century saw the emergence of an integrative, life-span approach to human development (e.g., Baltes, Lindenberger, & Staudinger, 1998; Baltes, Staudinger, & Lindenberger, 1999), one that stressed the fusion (Tobach & Greenberg, 1984) and reciprocal, or dynamic (Lerner, 1978; Thelen & Smith, 1998), interrelation of individual and ecological variables.

The intellectual basis of this synthetic view of the bases of human development is found throughout history in seventeenth- through twentieth-century German philosophy and behavioral science (Baltes, 1979, 1983; Brandtstädter, 1998, 1999), in twentieth-century biological ideas pertinent to general systems, dynamic systems, and probabilistic epigenesis (von Bertalanffy, 1933, 1968; Gottlieb, 1992, 1997; Kuo, 1976; Novikoff, 1945a, b; Schneirla, 1956, 1957), and in twentieth-century ideas associated with home economics and human ecology (Bronfenbrenner, 1979, 2001; Bubolz & Sontag, 1993). These influences converged to create interest in the multidisciplinary study of human development and broadened the perspective of developmental psychologists to consider scholarship pertinent to family and life course sociology, the family life cycle, and the U-shaped curve of marital quality (Spanier, 1976a, b; Spanier & Glick, 1980); the demography of children, cohort analysis, and the role of historical and/or life events in differentiating the life paths of cohorts (e.g., Elder, 1974, 1979, 1980, 1998, 1999; Featherman & Hauser, 1978; Hernandez, 1993; Mayer & Huinink, 1990); and the importance of cultural context in providing the developmental niche of individuals and groups (e.g., Shweder et al., 1998).

The contemporary context of the study of context

Coupled with the organismic developmental approaches that elicited sensitivity to the cultural and historical dimensions of the ecology of human development (e.g., Erikson, 1968; Kohlberg, 1978; Vygotsky, 1978), the last 30 years have been marked by appeals to understand how both the macro ecology of human development (Elder, 1998), and, in particular, public policies regarding children, affect individual development (e.g., Bronfenbrenner, 1974; Jacobs, Wertlieb, & Lerner, 2003; Zigler, 1999, 2003). Indeed, in the last two decades of the twentieth century this convergence of interests led to a zeitgeist to "consider the context" (cf. Bloom, 1973). This zeitgeist influenced and was influenced by the growing popularity of dynamic, developmental systems perspectives (e.g., Baltes, Lindenberger, & Staudinger, 1998; Brandtstädter, 1998, 1999; Elder, 1998; Fischer, 1980; Fischer & Bidell, 1998; Ford & Lerner, 1992; Gollin, 1981; Gottlieb, 1983, 1991, 1992; Lerner, 1978, 1998b, 2002; Magnusson, 1995, 1996, 1999a, b; Sameroff, 1983; Thelen & Smith, 1994, 1998; Wapner & Demick, 1998). As noted earlier, developmental systems theory proposes that the context is more than a level of organization central in human development (i.e., a moderator of human development). Rather, it is a constituent component of the very fabric of development (Bronfenbrenner, 2001; Bronfenbrenner & Morris, 1998; Elder, 1998).

The key methodological implication of the developmental systems perspective is that human development must be studied from a relational, integrative point of view. As such, one must make three assessments. These include (a) the person, (b) the context, and (c) the relation between the two. One can have good measures of "a" and "b" but be limited in the measurement of "c." However, a dynamic developmental system is, by definition, a changing system, one wherein any component of the system affects and is affected by all the other components within the system with which it is embedded. Therefore, since understanding developmental systems requires relational units of analysis, the assessment of "c" is critical (Lerner et al., 2003).

To understand the conceptual role that context plays in the contemporary study of human development, methodologies associated with at least two approaches to contextual analysis must be considered. First, we need to review issues and instances of measuring context ("b," above) and, second, we need to assess the degree to which methods exist that allow the context to be related to the individual ("c," above). In both instances, of course, the context may change and, as such, issues in the measurement and analysis of change are central in both approaches.

Change is difficult to assess, even when it is a matter of charting the continuity and/or discontinuity of a single variable over time (Lerner, 2002; Lerner & Tubman, 1989). Systemic change is even more difficult to appraise, given that it involves multivariate and multilevel analysis. While it is important to recognize the importance of the measurement and analysis of change in all approaches to the study of human development, the importance of this issue is arguably elevated in salience when a developmental systems perspective is used to frame scholarship.

The more complicated issues raised in the analysis of change from a developmental systems perspective will be understood best when we compare them to the corresponding issues involved in measuring the contextual level of analysis and the changes it may undergo. We will first discuss methods associated with measuring the context per se. Here, levels of organization ranging from the dyadic through the sociocultural and historical must be considered. In turn, we will discuss the types of methods useful in integrating the individual and the context and, as well, we will consider the "design criteria" involved in developing synthetic person–context developmental methods.

The Context of Human Development: Concepts and Measures

Scholars interested in the measurement of the context of human development have assessed levels of organization ranging from the dyadic through the historical. Numerous models for summarizing these levels and the variables assessed within them may be offered (Lerner, 1998a). However, independent of theoretical differences in terminology and emphasis, these models converge operationally in suggesting the levels that must be appraised in order to adequately depict the context of human development. Accordingly, two examples of such models, both representing instances of developmental systems theory (Lerner, 1998a, 2002), may be used to illustrate this commonality. First, we will discuss Lerner's (1991, 1995, 1996, 1998b) developmental contextual view of human development. Second, we will consider Bronfenbrenner's (2001; Bronfenbrenner & Morris, 1998) bioecological model of human development.

Developmental contextualism

Figure 10.1 presents the developmental contextual view of person–context relations (represented in the figure by child–parent relations) seen from the perspective of this instance of developmental systems theory (Lerner, 1991, 1995, 1996, 1998b, 2002).

As shown in this figure, the inner and outer worlds of a child are fused and dynamically interactive. The same may be said of the parent depicted in the figure and, in fact, of the parent–child relationship. Each of these foci – child, parent, and parent–child relationship – is part of a larger, enmeshed system of fused relations among the multiple levels which compose the ecology of human life (Bronfenbrenner, 1979, 2001). For instance, Figure 10.1 illustrates the idea that both parent and child are embedded in a broader social network and that each person has reciprocal reactions within this network. This set of relationships occurs because both the child and the parent are much more than just people playing only one role in life. The child may also be a sibling, a peer, and a student; the parent may also be a spouse, a worker, and an adult child. All of these networks of relationships are embedded within a particular community, society, and culture. Finally, all of these relationships are continually changing across time and history.

Thus, Figure 10.1 illustrates also that the child–parent relationship and the social networks in which it is located are embedded in still larger community, societal, cultural, and historical levels of organization. Moreover, the arrow of time (history) cuts through all of the systems. This feature of the model underscores the idea that, as with the people populating the social systems, change is always occurring. Diversity within time is created as changes across time (across history) occur. As depicted in Figure 10.1, such diversity introduces variation into all the levels of organization involved in the system. As such, the nature of parent–child relationships, of family life and development, and of societal and cultural influences on the child–parent–family system are influenced by both "normative" and "nonnormative" historical changes (Baltes, 1987; Baltes, Lindenberger, & Staudinger, 1998) or, in other words, by "evolutionary" (i.e., gradual) and "revolutionary" (i.e., abrupt; Werner, 1957) historical changes.

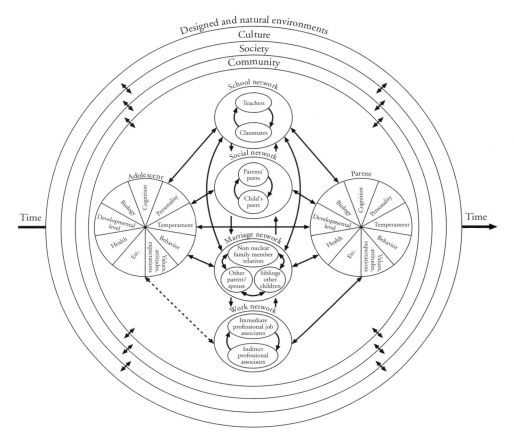

Figure 10.1   The developmental contextual view of human development: person–context relations (e.g., involving parents and children and interpersonal and institutional networks) are embedded in and influenced by specific community, societal, cultural, and designed and natural environments, all changing interdependently across time (with history).

The bioecological model

In his 1979 book *The Ecology of Human Development*, Bronfenbrenner explained the importance of the interrelated ecological levels, conceived as nested systems, for human ontogeny. Each of the ecological systems was explained to have an important impact on the child, the parent, the larger family, and, in fact, on the quality of life in society.

Bronfenbrenner (1977, 1979, 2001) described the microsystem as the setting within which the individual behaves at a given moment in his or her life (e.g., the home, school, club, or team) and the mesosystem as the set of microsystems constituting the individual's developmental niche within a given period of development (e.g., for a young adolescent, the mesosystem might be the home, school, peer group, after-school club, relatives' homes, religious institutions, the shopping mall, movie theaters and other entertainment centers, friends' homes, and family vacation spots). The exosystem is composed of contexts that, while not directly involving the developing person (e.g., the workplace of a child's parent), influence the person's behavior and development (e.g., as may occur when the parent has had a stressful day at work and, as a result, has a reduced capacity to provide quality caregiving to the child). The macrosystem is the superordinate level of the ecology of human development; it is the level involving culture, macro-institutions (such as the federal government), and public policy. The macrosystem influences the nature of interaction within all other levels of the ecology of human development.

Since the 1979 specification of these tiers within the developmental system, Bronfenbrenner (1994, p. 1645; see also Bronfenbrenner, 2001) has broadened his conception of the microsystem to include:

> a pattern of activities, social roles, and interpersonal relations experienced by the developing person in a given face-to-face setting with particular physical, social, and symbolic features that invite, permit, or inhibit, engagement in sustained, progressively more complex interaction with, and activity in, the immediate environment. (Bronfenbrenner, 1994, p. 1645)

Bronfenbrenner notes that an emphasis on a redefined and expanded concept of the microsystem leads to the last defining property of the current formulation of his theory of human development. As indicated by Bronfenbrenner and Morris (1998, p. 995), time is a critical dimension of the ecology of human development. As such, the dimension of time is included in his model:

> The 1979 volume scarcely mentions [time], whereas in the current formulation, it has a prominent place at three successive levels – micro-, meso-, and macro-. Microtime refers to continuity versus discontinuity within ongoing episodes of proximal process. Mesotime is the periodicity of these episodes across broader time intervals, such as days and weeks. Finally, macrotime focuses on the changing expectations and events in the larger society, both within and across generations, as they affect and are affected by, processes and outcomes of human development over the life course.

From concepts to methodological foci

Both the developmental contextual and the bioecological instances of developmental systems theory converge in specifying that several different levels of organization should be included in the appraisal of the context of human development. These levels range from social groups (e.g., dyads, triads) and the microsystems (families, school class-rooms, sports teams) within which the person may interact, to the macrosystem that affects (e.g., through public policies) the social relationships of other tiers (Lerner et al., 2003).

To understand these contextual levels, it is useful to differentiate among units of analysis suggested by the ideas derived from both developmental contextualism and bioecological theory. Units of contextual analysis may include groups, and these may involve dyads within the family or peer group, or involve student–teacher, child–coach, child–mentor, or youth–employer relationships. Triads or larger groups may be involved as well, as, for instance, may occur in the study of the family system or such peer structures as cliques, crowds, or liaisons. Any of these groups may be studied as parts of the person's micro-, meso-, or macrosystem.

To illustrate, whether one assesses a dyad, a triad, or a larger group depends on the conceptual and empirical issues being addressed. For instance, assessment of the mother–infant relationship in the context of questions about attachment theory (Ainsworth et al., 1978) would involve dyadic assessment, whereas questions about social relationships in adolescence might involve assessments of adolescent cliques or crowds, which by definition involve three or more individuals (Rubin, Bukowski, & Parker, 1998).

One might study attachment in the mother–infant relationship because of an interest in only this dyad, and thus one would in this case be concerned with one instance of the person's microsystem. However, one might also study the mother–infant dyad because of an interest in the relationship between the quality of the infant's attachment to his or her mother and functioning in a preschool or child care context. If so, this interest would reflect a concern for the mesosystem. Similarly, a study of the adolescent's behavior within a clique or crowd would involve an assessment of a microsystem. However, an appraisal of the implications of behavior in one group on behavior in the other would involve an interest in the mesosystem.

Numerous tools exist to measure such instances of the context. These include naturalistic observation, participant observation, ethnography, controlled observation, for example, involving contrived settings such as the "Strange Situation" (Ainsworth et al., 1978) or the use of the event sampling or "beeper technique" method (Csikszentmihalyi & Larson, 1987), and experimental observations. Questionnaires, interviews, or surveys may be appropriate to use when, for instance, attitudes about or perceptions of the context are the target of analysis.

Settings within which these assessments may be made include the home, schools, playgrounds, malls, campgrounds, places of employment, neighborhoods, and communities. When particular settings, such as neighborhoods, are measured at the exosystem level (e.g., as in Leventhal & Brooks-Gunn, 2004; Sampson, Morenoff, & Earls, 1999), then units of analysis that extend beyond the individual level of organization are appraised. For example, population density or maps of community liabilities (e.g., crime concentrations, inadequate housing) and community assets or strengths (e.g., civic organizations, affordable/high quality housing, faith institutions, schools) may be indexed (Leventhal & Brooks-Gunn, 2004).

Other units of contextual analysis include the natural and designed ecology, the ideational context of human development (involving, typically, the assessment of the meaning, or semiotic systems of the person; his or her values, attitudes, and beliefs or ideology; his or her appraisals of the physical world, including aesthetic sensitivity; and the person's understanding of the norms and mores of society and culture) (e.g., see Bornstein & Bradley, 2003). Public policy, part of the macrosystem of human development, can be assessed through various forms of macro-evaluation research (Jacobs & Kapuscik, 2000; Jacobs, Wertlieb, & Lerner, 2003), for instance, through the appraisal of cohort changes in behaviors (e.g., reported incidence of child abuse) thought to be the behavioral change sought by particular policies (e.g., home visiting programs for teenage mothers). In turn, policy (or program) evaluation can be used to assess individual level behavior changes occurring in the context of changes of social policy (Jacobs, 2003).

At this macro-level, the effects of historical changes in behavior – of individuals or cohorts – can be the appropriate target of contextual analysis. Various time-sensitive research designs may be used to assess the effects of historical change on individual or group development. Simple longitudinal or panel designs are the most well-known and frequently used of these methods. In addition, sequential designs (either longitud-inal or cross-sectional), time lag designs (see chapter 2), as well as various instances of demographic cohort analysis may be available for use. Analytic methods appropriate to exploit data derived from such designs include Structural Equation Methods (SEM; for example, LISREL or EQS; see chapter 17), Hierarchical Linear Modeling (HLM) procedures (see chapter 18), and several procedures discussed by von Eye and his colleagues (von Eye, 1990a, b; von Eye & Clogg, 1996; von Eye & Schuster, 2000) as useful for the analysis of quantitative longitudinal data, for example, event history analysis, cohort analysis, hazard analysis, time series analysis, and longitudinal Configural Frequency Analysis (CFA).

Conclusions about methods used to study the context of development

Depending on the context in question, an array of units of analysis may be indexed through a wide range of methods. While it is of course desirable to triangulate any assessment of the context that is used, even with such validation none of the methodo-logical foci we have noted is useful in understanding the relations within the devel-opmental system. As noted above, a measure of the context must be coupled with a measure of the individual – and, ideally, of the bidirectional, person–context relation (represented as the person↔context relation) – in order to begin to bring theoretically relevant data to bear on this system (e.g., Lerner et al., 2003; Magnusson & Stattin, 1998).

The Person↔Context Relation: Concepts and Methodological Options

Relations among levels of organization are the focus of inquiry in developmental systems theories. Changes in these relationships constitute the basic process of human develop-ment. Although changing relations among levels of organization ranging from biology through history would need to be indexed in order to assess the system fully, few studies have the resources and power to accomplish this task. At a minimum, changing relations between two levels have to be assessed (Lerner et al., 2003). The foci of such analysis can involve any two levels within the developmental system, e.g., the relation between the child and the parent, or teacher, the family and the community, or the community and the state/province or nation can be appraised (e.g., Eccles, 2004; Eccles, Wigfield, & Byrnes, 2003; Lerner et al., 2003). The goal of these analyses should be, ideally, to evaluate how individual and contextual variables coalesce to comprise the person↔context relation, and not primarily to study how variation across people explains relations among variables (e.g., Magnusson, 1999a, b).

Thus, when the study of human development is predicated on the relational ideas of developmental systems theory, the ideal target of analysis in research is the person↔context relation (Lerner, 2002; Overton, 1998). Context has been operationalized most often as small group (e.g., child–parent) exchanges and/or assessments of microsystem or mesosystem relations. The person characteristics related to the context have involved the study of an array of psychological (e.g., personality, cognitive, emotional) variables, behavioral attributes (e.g., temperament, aggression, dependence, assertiveness, sociability, etc.), and/or physical characteristics (e.g., puberty level, attractiveness, sex, physical ability status) (Damon, 1998). The array of methods used to index the individual level of organization has involved the range of tools that have been noted above to be involved in the appraisal of the context (see too Lerner et al., 2003).

However, just as the measurement of the context alone does not suffice to index the developmental system, so too the appraisal of the individual, even when accomplished in a study wherein the context is also measured, is not adequate to provide a view of this system. We have emphasized already that, unless the appraisals of the person and the context are integrated through a relational unit of analysis, the developmental system cannot be appraised.

Such person–context relational units are not easy to develop, especially when one recognizes that the metrics used must in some way be integrated (Lerner et al., 2003; Lerner, Skinner, & Sorell, 1980; Lewis & Lee-Painter, 1974). To illustrate, it may be appropriate to measure differences in infant language development in the second year of life by measuring weekly changes in active vocabulary. At the same time, to measure self-esteem in a parent who is raising a normatively developing infant will involve a measure other than words in one's active vocabulary and, probably, time divisions other than weeks. At this writing, it is not clear how to form a unit of analysis of the *relation* between vocabulary growth and self-esteem (as compared to a unit that is just composed of these two elements; see Lewis & Lee-Painter, 1974, for a foundational discussion of this issue). It is also uncertain how to form a relational unit when the time divisions associated with the elements in the relation are widely discrepant (Lerner, 2002; Lerner, Skinner, & Sorell, 1980). The incommensurate nature of the temporal parameters of measures is an instance of a more general problem of a lack of *measurement equivalence* between measures (Baltes, Reese, & Nesselroade, 1977).

In some instances, researchers have attempted to devise person↔context relational measures indices by computing discrepancy (or difference) scores between psychometrically equivalent measures of person and context (e.g., Windle & Lerner, 1986). For example, measures have been developed of the "goodness of fit" between attributes of behavioral individuality (e.g., regarding temperament or academic abilities; Chess & Thomas, 1999; Eccles, 2004; Eccles & Midgley, 1989; Eccles, Wigfield, & Byrnes, 2003; Eccles et al., 1993; Lerner & Lerner, 1983) and the demands for behavior present in the home or school. The size of the differences or discrepancies between scores has been used to index the degree of match or congruence that exists in the person–context relation.

However, the computational procedures involved in such relational scores have statistical problems. For instance, when the components involved in the computation of change scores are positively correlated, difference/change scores are less reliable than the components; this feature of measurement constrains the predictive validity of these indices.

In turn, several multivariate statistical innovations in relational and or systems analyses have been introduced, ranging from the categorical procedures involved in configural frequency analysis (von Eye, 1990a, b; von Eye & Schuster, 2000) to the procedures for assessing dynamic behaviors, cognitions, or skills (Fischer & Bidell, 1998; Molenaar, 1986; Thelen & Smith, 1998). To illustrate, in configural frequency analysis (von Eye, 1990b) one is able to identify patterns of multiple category membership that occur at frequencies greater than expected (these patterns are called "types") and less than expected ("antitypes"). Since either types or antitypes may include categories that include both individual-level behaviors (e.g., the presence or absence of delinquent or violent behaviors, passing grades in school, or safe sexual practices) as well as contextual variables (e.g., the presence or absence in a child's life of authoritative or authoritarian parents, a safe neighborhood, or a well-funded school), configural frequency analysis can be used to identify patterns of person–context covariation (e.g., Taylor et al., 2002a, b, 2003, 2004).

In addition, qualitative research (e.g., Burton, 1990; Jarrett, 1998; Taylor, 1990, 1993), including ethnographic and cultural anthropological methods (Mistry & Saraswathi, 2003; Rogoff, 1998), have been employed to assess the person–context system. For instance, structured, open-ended interviews with youth and older family members may be coded for the presence of themes that portray individuals' relations with features of their context (e.g., the role of neighborhood social support in facilitating healthy development among poor children and parents; Jarrett, 1998). Nevertheless, no measurement procedure or statistical analysis technique has elicited a consensus among scholars in regard to constituting the preferred means through which to assess the developmental system.

One reason for this lack of agreement about methods to be used is that there has been no specification of the design criteria for devising such methods and no comparison between extant measures and these criteria. At this writing, what may be most useful in helping to further the assessment of person–context relations within the developmental system is discussion of these design criteria. That is, what precisely are the issues that must be addressed for a method to be useful in generating knowledge of the dynamic system of human development? The ideas associated with bioecological theory and developmental contextualism are again useful in addressing this question.

Methodological Challenges for Studying the Developmental System

How should research be conducted in order to appraise appropriately the person–context developmental system? Bronfenbrenner (2001; Bronfenbrenner & Morris, 1998) and Lerner (1991, 1995, 1996, 1998b, 2002) suggest that the person↔context relational process must be studied as it is embedded across time in broader developmental systems (that is, in relation to the other levels of organization constituting the developmental system).

For instance, Bronfenbrenner and Morris (1998) propose a Process–Person–Context–Time (or PPCT) model for conceptualizing the integrated developmental system and for designing research to study the course of human development. Similarly, in Lerner's theory of developmental contextualism (1991, 1995, 1996, 1998b), there is a corresponding focus on the dynamic (reciprocal) person↔context relations as developed across time. From the perspective of both instances of developmental systems theory, three issues, or design criteria, suggest themselves as necessary in devising methods to adequately assess the developmental system. These issues are relationism, probabilism, and temporality.

Relationism

The issue of relationism pertains to the interdependency – and indeed the dynamic reciprocity – of all change processes in the developmental system. Processes from all levels of analysis – from the inner/biological to the sociocultural/historical – change in reciprocal relation to one another. Thus, changes in processes of a given target level affect changes in all other levels. This change then provides feedback to the target level. Because such interactions involve constant alterations through time, returning to an initial point is not possible. The dynamism of relationism underscores the rationale for a focus on reciprocal relations among dynamically interacting elements, and not on the elements themselves, which are the units of analysis used in developmental systems research.

Relationism has implications for generalizability. Results of empirical inquiries may not be casually shifted from one context to another as it is the context that provides the basis for the change. Change phenomena are, therefore, relational to the loci in time and place that they occur (cf. Elder, Modell, & Parke, 1993; Looft, 1973; Overton, 1998). Several methodological issues are associated with relationism.

External validity Because of the relational nature of change, the primary concern in developmental systems research must be one of external validity. From this perspective, even a completely internally valid (Campbell & Stanley, 1963) determination of the contribution of a given ("target") individual or contextual variable to the variation in a developmental outcome is not sufficient for understanding the role of that target variable in the full system of changes constituting human development (Hultsch & Hickey, 1978).

Analogous to conventions for interpreting main and interaction effects in an analysis of variance (wherein one does not interpret a significant main effect when it is embedded in a higher-order significant interaction), relationism requires that understanding of a "target" feature of individual behavior or development (e.g., a 5-year-old's temperament style, or a middle school student's motivation for mathematics achievement) or of the context (e.g., parents' demands for their children's behavior, or cultural expectations for mathematics achievement for children of a given gender, respectively) must be integrated with other individual and contextual variables fused together in the developmental system. Without reference to such integrated levels, valid understanding of the role of the individual or contextual target variable in the developmental process will remain incomplete, lack generalizability, and hence be externally invalid (Meacham, 1977).

For example, Chess and Thomas (1999; Thomas & Chess, 1977) present data suggesting that a child's temperamental processes have meaning for individual development only in the context of "goodness of fit" with parental processes. The same temperamental characteristics (e.g., those that make a child "difficult" for middle class, European American parents to rear) may, when expressed in contexts composed of people of different socioeconomic backgrounds, or racial or ethnic characteristics, or cultural values (e.g., regarding child rearing), or combinations of these attributes, present either no difficulty or be a boon to positive parent–child relations (Chess & Thomas, 1999).

Research design and data analysis While issues of internal validity cannot be ignored, developmental systems research should emphasize the use of methods enabling the observation and analysis of the contributions of contextual variables to a target change process. As noted above, data analytic methods such as configural frequency analysis, cohort analysis, event history analysis, and hazard analysis are useful in such research (e.g., see Elder, 1998, 1999; Featherman & Lerner, 1985; von Eye & Schuster, 2000). For example, Elder's (1999) classic work on children of the Great Depression illustrates how embeddedness in a birth cohort that experienced a nonnormative historical event (the devastating economic changes that occurred in the United States after the stock market crash of 1929) either during childhood or during adolescence differentially affected the immediate and later-life psychological and social behavior and development of youth.

Sequential designs (see chapter 2) may be useful for collecting data pertinent to such analyses. These designs enable descriptions of the age-, history-, and time-of-testing-related components of change functions. When used in conjunction with measures of the precise variables constituting historical (or cohort), time (or period), and age-related effects, these designs may provide data suggesting how the confluence of individual and contextual variables coalesces to produce a particular change. For example, relations may exist among molecular, inner/biological events (e.g., adrenocorticoid hormone release and neuronal transmissions; Suomi, 1999), between these changes and those at other, more molar levels (e.g., aversive interpersonal exchanges promoting a stress reaction; Suomi, 1999), and between molar levels themselves (e.g., war and battles existing between two countries; Garbarino, Kostelny, & Dubrow, 1998).

Measurement From the design and data analytic perspective noted above, description rests on indexing multiple variables from multiple levels within the developmental system. Given that dynamic, reciprocal interchanges can exist within and between levels of analysis, methods of observation capable of recording changes in both molecular and molar variables are needed. As discussed earlier, relational, person-centered or person↔context-centered measures need to be developed to link levels within the developmental system.

As such, given that relations are the focus of research within this perspective, appropriate developmental research must be multivariate in character (i.e., at the minimum, a measure of individual and contextual levels must exist) and thus as a consequence necessarily multilevel. In addition, multidisciplinary research may be needed to provide the expertise to construct an adequate relational unit of analysis linking the levels involved in change within the developmental system. For example, collaborations among biologists, psychologists, and sociologists may be involved in developing measures linking, say, the hormonal changes of puberty with changes in young adolescents' emotional exchanges in peer group and family settings (e.g., see Magnusson & Stattin, 1998).

Probabilism

The second issue to be considered in regard to design criteria is probabilism, derived from the probabilistic epigenetic character of change within the developmental system. Because of the evolving, reciprocal nature of systems change, relations among variables, either between or within persons, do not exist statically over time; as all processes change across time, an interrelation that once existed cannot be repeated. There are several methodological issues raised by probabilism.

Conceptualization of the research question The goal of research should not be to uncover static, universal laws, regularities that apply across time and context. Although it certainly may be possible to generalize across time and context, research should address whether such statements are empirically warranted. Research should not begin with the a priori assumption that generalizability is the case. Change trajectories associated with person, context, person↔context relations, and time should become the focus of research.

Since any one endeavor cannot assess all of the parameters of all of the variables coalescing to provide the basis of a target change, a single effort will not suffice to chart a change trajectory. Accordingly, programmatic research should seek to depict a sample of the parameters of the coalesced variables constituting the person–context–time change process.

In short, a research effort should not be conceived of as an attempt to discover a fixed and completely generalizable regularity associated with a process. Rather, it should be construed as an effort to provide a probabilistic statement about the boundaries, or confidence intervals, of a process imposed by the parameters of change of the other processes within which the target process (e.g., person↔context relations, family↔neighborhood relations, etc.) is embedded (Jaccard & Guilamo-Ramos, 2002).

External validity The focus on confidence limits derived from probabilism suggests that while exact replications cannot be achieved (because of constant change), predictions of changes-within-ranges may be made. Generalizations within ranges can also be made insofar as the research program has an estimate of the change parameters of the variables providing the context of a target change. Again, an alternative to the traditional view of external validity is raised. Valid inferences from a given data set can be made only when the change trajectory of a target process is understood as a probabilistic phenomenon limited by the parameters of the other changes within which it exists.

Such probabilistic limitations have implications for the goals of explanatory research. Causation is seen as bidirectional or configural within a developmental systems perspective (Ford & Lerner, 1992; Thelen & Smith, 1998). Causes are associated with the prevailing context of the developmental event. Thus, making causal statements involves specification only of the sufficient conditions for change. Because of the impossibility for precise replicability, the variables that are necessary to cause change at one time in history may not be necessary (or present) at others. Indeed, if we take an evolutionary perspective we must remain quite open-ended even about the inner/biological "determinants" of development.

Measurement In establishing confidence intervals for the person↔context relational process and its parameters, two measurement issues are raised: "What constitutes a significant change in the relational process?" and "What constitutes a significant change in the parameters (person and context)?" Simply, "How much time matters?" The empirical answers to these questions are dependent on the degree to which the index of a target relation is reliably sensitive to change in both the relation and its components. Yet, since all of these are assumed to constantly change, issues of measurement equivalence (cf. Baltes, Reese, & Nesselroade, 1977) – across time, settings, and organisms, as well as, of course, within an organism – are raised in the form of the above two questions.

Timing

The third prototypic issue, timing, may be understood by recognizing that the issue of probabilism implies that change processes occurring at one point in time will lead to a different outcome than they would have had they occurred at other points in time. Occurring at different points in time, changes are inherently different processes. The dynamically interactive (fused) milieu providing the basis of the change processes is different and, therefore, the processes cannot be parametrically the same.

For example, Gould (1977) has argued that changes in timing are major evolutionary determinants. He contends that the slower ontogeny among humans, relative to their ancestral species (i.e., human "neoteny"), occurring as a consequence of phylogenetic changes in the timing of growth, is in itself the core principle of human adaptation. The observable dissimilarities between humans and chimps, contradictory in the face of their almost identical genetic structures, may be attributable to such heterochronic change.

Conceptualization of the research question The issue of timing has methodological import for developmentalists. Change is alteration over time, and since time is constant, nothing exists in precisely the same manner across time. Changes represent the outcome of the confluence of all relations in the developmental system. However, since that which is produced and that which produces are continually altered, the timing of an interrelation becomes a superordinate parameter of all changes (Bronfenbrenner & Morris, 1998;

Elder, 1998; Lerner, 1978; Schneirla, 1957). A key question for developmentalists is how much the timing of variables being indexed in the system makes a difference in the outcome of a given person↔context relation. To address such a concern, we may usefully capitalize on Wohlwill's (1973) suggestion that time become the dependent variable in developmental research. For instance, given different points in a person↔context relational process, what ontogenetic points are likely to "result"?

Research design Although criteria for what constitutes a difference are inevitably value-laden, the issue of timing again indicates that the measurement of historical and period effects, as may be implemented through sequential methods or through other techniques (e.g., hazard analysis, event history analysis, time series analysis, or longitudinal CFA), is a core requirement of any complete developmental effort. Assessing variables from all levels of analysis that together may constitute such timing effects becomes not just a methodological nicety of elaborate research, but a theoretically necessary component of any empirical attempt to discern the nature of the sources of change in person↔context relations.

The nonequivalent temporal metric Measuring change simultaneously at multiple levels of analysis, with the hope of showing how the timing of these changes constitutes a source of development, poses methodological challenges. These challenges are subsumed under the issue of the nonequivalent temporal metric. Rates of process changes within and across levels of analysis are not necessarily the same. On the individual/psychological level, for instance, cognitive, personality, and emotional changes do not necessarily proceed at comparable rates, either intra- or interindividually (cf. Riegel, 1977). Despite such within-level differences, it may be the case that months or years represent a useful (i.e., sensitive) developmental division ("along the x-axis") to measure changes in individual/psychological processes. Decades, or, perhaps even centuries, might be the smallest sensible temporal division on the historical level. For example, Sarason (1973) raised this point in regard to why intellectual interventions aimed at the individual/psychological level of analysis can be evaluated for their effectiveness along temporal divisions of "months" or "years-to-change," while biocultural interventions (e.g., Project Head Start) may need to be evaluated with divisions of decades or even centuries.

Data analysis Whether time constitutes the x-axis in a given analysis (as is most often the case in extant developmental research), or if time is used as the y-axis, as Wohlwill (1973) suggested, it remains the case that the index of changes in the person↔context relations spanning the multiple levels of analysis included in a developmental system research effort necessarily involves different metrics. Within any given effort, the temporal divisions optimally sensitive to index change may differ substantially from level to level. If this is the case, reciprocities among, for example, molecular, inner/biological changes and molar, sociocultural/historical ones, represent a crucial issue (cf. Riegel, 1977). What may be the optimal time division on the former level (e.g., a week) may be irrelevant at the historical level. In turn, the optimal division on this level (e.g., a century) might be too broad to even have meaning at the inner/biological level. Accordingly, important changes at one level of organization may be invisible at another level.

Conclusions

In our view, developmental systems theories broaden the conceptual focus of developmental science, suggesting to scholars that they ask new questions about the human life cycle and that new ways be devised to answer these questions. However, just as new questions are certainly not answered as of yet, all revisions in the discovery component of the scientific method (as we have argued are suggested by the prototypic issues raised by developmental systems formulations) have not been devised.

Such theories do have import for: (1) emphases on external as opposed to internal validity; (2) conceptualization of research questions; (3) the validity of developmental measurement; (4) the validity of developmental research designs; (5) observing processes contributing to developmental change functions; and (6) the analysis of developmental data. In fact, currently the most heuristic methodological implication of developmental systems theories is that they sensitize developmentalists to the need for development-specific methodologies. By insisting that all behavior and contexts exist as interrelated change phenomena, only methods suitable to the appraisal of development can be seen as appropriate for research (cf. Baltes, Reese, & Nesselroade, 1977).

Developmental systems theory brings a new, multicomponent research question to the fore of developmental inquiry: what relational (person↔context) scores, from what measures of person and context, administered at what ontogenetic, situational, and historical times, may be used in what analyses, to address what substantive questions, among people of what characteristics? By addressing such a multicomponent question, developmental scientists may be able to meet the challenges of describing, explaining, and optimizing the lives of changing people in a changing world. Developmental systems theory may be the necessity constituting the mother of methodological invention appropriate to face this challenge.

Acknowledgments

The preparation of this chapter was supported in part by grants from the W. T. Grant Foundation and the National 4-H Council.

References

Ainsworth, M. D. S., Blehar, M. C., Water, E., & Wall, S. (1978). *Patterns of attachment.* Hillsdale, NJ: Lawrence Erlbaum Associates.

Baer, D. M. (1976). The organism as host. *Human Development, 19,* 87–9.

Baltes, P. B. (1979). Life-span developmental psychology: Some converging observations on history and theory. In P. B. Baltes & O. G. Brim, Jr. (eds.), *Life-span development and behavior* (vol. 2, pp. 255–79). New York: Academic Press.

Baltes, P. B. (1983). Life-span developmental psychology: Observations on history and theory revisited. In R. M. Lerner (ed.), *Developmental psychology: Historical and philosophical perspectives* (pp. 79–112). Hillsdale, NJ: Lawrence Erlbaum Associates.

Baltes, P. B. (1987). Theoretical propositions of life-span developmental psychology: On the dynamics between growth and decline. *Developmental Psychology, 23*, 611–26.

Baltes, P. B. (1997). On the incomplete architecture of human ontogeny: Selection, optimization, and compensation as foundations of developmental theory. *American Psychologist, 52*, 366–80.

Baltes, P. B., Lindenberger, U., & Staudinger, U. M. (1998). Life-span theory in developmental psychology. In W. Damon (series ed.) & R. M. Lerner (vol. ed.), *Handbook of child psychology*, vol. 1: *Theoretical models of human development* (5th edn., pp. 1029–1144). New York: John Wiley.

Baltes, P. B., Reese, H. W., & Nesselroade, J. R. (1977). *Life-span developmental psychology: Introduction to research methods*. Monterey, CA: Brooks/Cole.

Baltes, P. B., Staudinger, U. M., & Lindenberger, U. (1999). Life span psychology: Theory and application to intellectual functioning. In J. T. Spence, J. M. Darley, & D. J. Foss (eds.), *Annual Review of Psychology* (vol. 50, pp. 471–507). Palo Alto, CA: Annual Reviews.

Bijou, S. W. (1976). *Child development: The basic stage of early childhood*. Englewood Cliffs, NJ: Prentice-Hall.

Bijou, S. W. & Baer, D. M. (eds.) (1961). *Child development: A systematic and empirical theory*. New York: Appleton-Century-Crofts.

Bijou, S. W. & Baer, D. M. (eds.) (1965). *Child development: Universal stage of infancy* (vol. 2). Englewood Cliffs, NJ: Prentice-Hall.

Bloom, L. (1973). *One word at a time: The use of single word utterances before syntax*. The Hague: Mouton.

Bornstein, M. H. & Bradley, R. H. (eds.) (2003). *Socioeconomic status, parenting, and child development*. Mahwah, NJ: Lawrence Erlbaum Associates.

Bowers, K. S. (1973). Situationism in psychology. *Psychological Review, 80*, 307–36.

Brandtstädter, J. (1998). Action perspectives on human development. In W. Damon (series ed.) & R. M. Lerner (vol. ed.), *Handbook of child psychology*, vol. 1: *Theoretical models of human development* (5th edn., pp. 807–63). New York: John Wiley.

Brandtstädter, J. (1999). The self in action and development: Cultural, biosocial, and ontogenetic bases of intentional self-development. In J. Brandtstädter & R. M. Lerner (eds.), *Action and self-development: Theory and research through the life-span* (pp. 37–65). Thousand Oaks, CA: Sage.

Bronfenbrenner, U. (1974). Developmental research, public policy, and the ecology of childhood. *Child Development, 45*, 1–5.

Bronfenbrenner, U. (1977). Toward an experimental ecology of human development. *American Psychologist, 32*, 513–31.

Bronfenbrenner, U. (1979). *The ecology of human development*. Cambridge, MA: Harvard University Press.

Bronfenbrenner, U. (1994). Ecological models of human development. In T. Husen & T. N. Postlewaite (eds.), *International encyclopedia of education* (2nd edn., vol. 3, pp. 1643–47). Oxford: Pergamon Press/Elsevier Science.

Bronfenbrenner, U. (2001). The biological theory of human development. In N. J. Smelser & P. B. Baltes (eds.), *International encyclopedia of the social and behavioral sciences* (pp. 6963–70). Oxford: Elsevier.

Bronfenbrenner, U. & Morris, P. A. (1998). The ecology of developmental process. In W. Damon (series ed.) & R. M. Lerner (vol. ed.), *Handbook of child psychology*, vol. 1: *Theoretical models of human development* (5th edn., pp. 993–1028). New York: John Wiley.

Bubolz, M. M. & Sontag, M. S. (1993). Human ecology theory. In P. G. Boss, W. J. Doherty, R. LaRossa, W. R. Schumm, & S. K. Steinmetz (eds.), *Sourcebook of family theories and methods: A contextual approach* (pp. 419–48). New York: Plenum Press.

Burton, L. M. (1990). Teenage childbearing as an alternative life-course strategy in multigeneration black families. *Human Nature*, *l(2)*, 123–43.

Cairns, R. B. (1998). The making of developmental psychology. In W. Damon (series ed.) & R. M. Lerner (vol. ed.), *Handbook of child psychology*, vol. 1: *Theoretical models of human development* (5th edn., pp. 419–48). New York: John Wiley.

Campbell, D. T. & Stanley, J. C. (1963). *Experimental and quasi-experimental designs for research.* Chicago, IL: Rand McNally.

Chess, S. & Thomas, A. (1999). *Goodness of fit: Clinical applications from infancy through adult life.* New York: Brunner/Mazel.

Collins, W. A., Maccoby, E. E., Steinberg, L., Hetherington, E. M., Bornstein, M. H. (2000). Contemporary research on parenting: The case for nature and nurture. *American Psychologist*, 55, 218–32.

Csikszentmihalyi, M. & Larson, R. (1987). Validity and reliability of the experience-sampling method. *Journal of Nervous and Mental Disease, 175(9)*, 526–36.

Damon, W. (ed.) (1998). *Handbook of child psychology* (5th edn.). New York: John Wiley.

Dixon, R. A. & Lerner, R. M. (1999). History and systems in developmental psychology. In M. Bornstein & M. Lamb (eds.), *Developmental psychology: An advanced textbook* (4th edn., pp. 3–45). Mahwah, NJ: Lawrence Erlbaum Associates.

Eccles, J. S. (2004). Schools, academic motivation, and stage-environment fit. In R. M. Lerner & L. Steinberg (eds.), *Handbook of Adolescent Psychology* (2nd edn.) New York: John Wiley.

Eccles, J. S. & Midgley, C. (1989). Stage–environment fit: Developmentally appropriate classrooms for young adolescents. In C. Ames & R. Ames (eds.), *Research on motivation in education. Goals and cognitions* (vol. 3, pp. 139–86). New York: Academic Press.

Eccles, J. S., Wigfield, A., & Byrnes, J. (2003). Cognitive development in adolescence. In I. R. Weiner (editor-in-chief) & R. M. Lerner, M. A. Easterbrooks, & J. Mistry (vol. eds.), *Handbook of psychology*, vol. 6: *Developmental psychology* (pp. 325–50). New York: John Wiley.

Eccles, J. S., Wigfield, A., Harold, R., & Blumenfeld, P. B. (1993). Age and gender differences in children's self- and task perceptions during elementary school. *Child Development, 64*, 830–47.

Elder, G. H., Jr. (1974). *Children of the Great Depression: Social change in life experiences.* Chicago, IL: University of Chicago Press.

Elder, G. H., Jr. (1979). Historical change in life patterns and personality. In P. B. Baltes & O. G. Brim, Jr. (eds.), *Life-span development and behavior*, vol. 2. New York: Academic Press.

Elder, G. H., Jr. (1980). Adolescence in historical perspective. In J. Adelson (ed.), *Handbook of adolescent psychology* (pp. 3–46). New York: John Wiley.

Elder, G. H., Jr. (1998). The life course and human development. In W. Damon (series ed.) & R. M. Lerner (vol. ed.), *Handbook of child psychology*, vol. 1: *Theoretical models of human development* (5th edn., pp. 939–91). New York: John Wiley.

Elder, G. H., Jr. (1999). *Children of the Great Depression: Social change in life experiences* (2nd edn.). Boulder, CO: Westview Press.

Elder, G. H., Jr., Modell, J., & Parke, R. D. (eds.). (1993). *Children in time and place: Developmental and historical insights.* New York: Cambridge University Press.

Erikson, E. H. (1968). *Identity, youth and crisis.* New York: Norton.

Featherman, D. L. & Hauser, R. M. (1978). *Opportunity and change.* New York: Academic Press.

Featherman, D. L. & Lerner, R. M. (1985). Ontogenesis and sociogenesis: Problematics for theory about development across the lifespan. *American Sociological Review, 50*, 659–76.

Fischer, K. W. (1980). A theory of cognitive development: The control and construction of hierarchies of skills. *Psychological Review, 87*, 477–531.

Fischer, K. W. & Bidell, T. (1998). Dynamic development of psychological structures in action and thought. In W. Damon (series ed.) & R. M. Lerner (vol. ed.), *Handbook of child psychology*, vol. 1: *Theoretical models of human development* (5th edn., pp. 467–561). New York: John Wiley.

Fisher, C. B. & Lerner, R. M. (eds.). (1994). *Applied developmental psychology*. New York: McGraw-Hill.

Ford, D. L. & Lerner, R. M. (1992). *Developmental systems theory: An integrative approach*. Newbury Park, CA: Sage.

Garbarino, J., Kostelny, K., & Dubrow, N. (1998). *No place to be a child: Growing up in a war zone*. San Francisco, CA: Jossey-Bass.

Gesell, A. L. (1946). The ontogenesis of infant behavior. In L. Carmichael (ed.), *Manual of child psychology* (pp. 295–331). New York: John Wiley.

Gollin, E. S. (1981). Development and plasticity. In E. S. Gollin (ed.), *Developmental plasticity: Behavioral and biological aspects of variations in development* (pp. 231–51). New York: Academic Press.

Gottlieb, G. (1970). Conceptions of prenatal behavior. In R. Aronson, E. Tobach, D. S. Lehrman, & J. S. Rosenblatt (eds.), *Development and evolution of behavior: Essays in memory of T. C. Schneirla* (pp. 111–37). San Francisco, CA: Freeman.

Gottlieb, G. (1983). The psychobiological approach to developmental issues. In M. M. Haith & J. Campos (eds.), *Handbook of child psychology*, vol. 2: *Infancy and biological bases* (pp. 1–26). New York: John Wiley.

Gottlieb, G. (1991). The experiential canalization of behavioral development: Theory. *Developmental Psychology*, *27*, 4–13.

Gottlieb, G. (1992). *Individual development and evolution: The genesis of novel behavior*. New York: Oxford University Press.

Gottlieb, G. (1997). *Synthesizing nature–nurture: Prenatal roots of instinctive behavior*. Mahwah, NJ: Lawrence Erlbaum Associates.

Gottlieb, G., Wahlsten, D., & Lickliter, R. (1998). The significance of biology for human development: A developmental psychobiological systems view. In W. Damon (series ed.) & R. M. Lerner (vol. ed.), *Handbook of child psychology*, vol. 1: *Theoretical models of human development* (5th edn., pp. 233–73). New York: John Wiley.

Gould, S. J. (1977). *Ontogeny and phylogeny*. Cambridge, MA: Belknap Press of Harvard.

Haeckel, E. (1868). *Naturliche Schopfringsgeschichte*. Berlin: Reimer.

Haeckel, E. (1876). *The history of creation: or, the development of the earth and its inhabitants by the action of natural causes: a popular exposition of the doctrine of evolution in general, and of that of Darwin, Goethe and Lamarck in particular*. New York: D. Appleton.

Haeckel, E. (1905). *The wonders of life*. New York: Harper.

Hall, G. S. (1904). *Adolescence: Its psychology and its relations to physiology, anthropology, sociology, sex, crime, religion, and education*, vols. 1 and 2. New York: Appleton.

Hernandez, D. J. (1993). *America's children: Resources for family, government, and the economy*. New York: Russell Sage Foundation.

Hirsch, J. (1997). Some history of heredity-vs.-environment, genetic inferiority at Harvard (?), and *The* (incredible) *Bell Curve*. *Genetica*, *99*, 207–24.

Horowitz, D. F. (2000). Child development and the PITS: Simple questions, complex answers and developmental theory. *Child Development*, *71*, 1–10.

Hultsch, D. F. & Hickey, T. (1978). External validity in the study of human development: Theoretical and methodological issues. *Human Development*, *21*, 76–91.

Jaccard, J. & Guilamo-Ramos, V. (2002). Analysis of variance frameworks in clinical child and adolescent psychology: Advanced issues and recommendations. *Journal of Clinical Child Psychology*, *31*, 278–94.

Jacobs, F. H. (2003). Child and family program evaluation: Learning to enjoy complexity. *Applied Developmental Science*, 7, 62–75.

Jacobs, F. & Kapuscik, J. (2000). *Making it count: Evaluating family preservation services.* Medford, MA: Family Preservation Evaluation Project, Tufts University.

Jacobs, F., Wertlieb, D., & Lerner, R. M. (eds.) (2003). *Enhancing the life chances of youth and families: Public service systems and public policy perspectives.* Volume 2 of R. M. Lerner, F. Jacobs, & D. Wertlieb (eds.), *Handbook of applied developmental science: Promoting positive child, adolescent, and family development through research, policies, and programs.* Thousand Oaks, CA: Sage.

Jarrett, R. L. (1998). African American children, families, and neighborhoods: Qualitative contributions to understanding developmental pathways. *Applied Developmental Science*, 2, 2–16.

Kohlberg, L. (1978). Revisions in the theory and practice of moral development. *New Directions for Child Development*, 2, 83–8.

Kuo, Z.-Y. (1976). The dynamics of behavior development: An epigenetic view. New York: Plenum Press.

Lerner, J. V. & Lerner, R. M. (1983). Temperament and adaptation across life: Theoretical and empirical issues. In P. B. Baltes & O. G. Brim, Jr. (eds.), *Life-span development and behavior* (vol. 5, pp. 197–231). New York: Academic Press.

Lerner, R. M. (1978). Nature, nurture, and dynamic interactionism. *Human Development*, 21, 1–20.

Lerner, R. M. (1986). *Concepts and theories of human development* (2nd edn.). New York: Random House.

Lerner, R. M. (1991). Changing organism–context relations as the basic process of development: A developmental-contextual perspective. *Developmental Psychology*, 27, 27–32.

Lerner, R. M. (1995). *America's youth in crisis: Challenges and options for programs and policies.* Thousand Oaks, CA: Sage.

Lerner, R. M. (1996). Relative plasticity, integration, temporality, and diversity in human development: A developmental, contextual perspective about theory, process, and method. *Developmental Psychology*, 32, 781–6.

Lerner, R. M. (ed.) (1998a). *Theoretical models of human development.* Volume 1 of W. Damon (editor-in-chief) *Handbook of Child Psychology* (5th edn.). New York: John Wiley.

Lerner, R. M. (1998b). Theories of human development: Contemporary perspectives. In W. Damon (series ed.) & R. M. Lerner (vol. ed.), *Handbook of child psychology*, vol. 1: *Theoretical models of human development* (pp. 1–24). New York: John Wiley.

Lerner, R. M. (2002). *Concepts and theories of human development* (3rd edn.). Mahwah, NJ: Lawrence Erlbaum Associates.

Lerner, R. M. & Tubman, J. (1989). Conceptual issues in studying continuity and discontinuity in personality development across life. *Journal of Personality*, 57, 343–73.

Lerner, R. M., Fisher, C. B., & Weinberg, R. A. (1997). Editorial: Applied developmental science: Scholarship for our times. *Applied Developmental Science*, 1, 2–3.

Lerner, R. M., Fisher, C. B., & Weinberg, R. A. (2000a). Toward a science for and of the people: Promoting civil society through the application of developmental science. *Child Development*, 71, 11–20.

Lerner, R. M., Fisher, C. B., & Weinberg, R. A. (2000b). Applying developmental science in the twenty-first century: International scholarship for our times. *International Journal of Behavioral Development*, 24, 24–9.

Lerner, R. M., Jacobs, F., & Wertlieb, D. (eds.) (2003). *Applying developmental science for youth and families: Historical and theoretical foundations.* Volume 1 of R. M. Lerner, F. Jacobs, &

D. Wertlieb (eds.), *Handbook of applied developmental science: Promoting positive child, adolescent, and family development through research, policies, and programs*. Thousand Oaks, CA: Sage.

Lerner, R. M., Skinner, E. A., & Sorell, G. T. (1980). Methodological implications of contextual/dialectic theories of development. *Human Development, 23*, 225–35.

Lerner, R. M., Anderson, P. M., Balsano, A. B., Dowling, E., & Bobek, D. (2003). Applied developmental science of positive human development. In I. B. Weiner (editor-in-chief), R. M. Lerner, M. A. Easterbrooks, & J. Mistry (vol. eds.), *Handbook of psychology*, vol. 6: *Developmental psychology* (pp. 535–58). New York: John Wiley.

Leventhal, T. & Brooks-Gunn, J. (2004). Diversity in developmental trajectories across adolescence: Neighborhood influences. In R. M. Lerner & L. Steinberg (eds.), *Handbook of Adolescent Psychology*. New York: John Wiley.

Lewis, M. & Lee-Painter, S. (1974). An interactional approach to the mother–infant dyad. In M. Lewis & L. A. Rosenblum (eds.), *The effect of the infant on its caregivers* (pp. 21–48). New York: John Wiley.

Looft, W. R. (1973). Socialization and personality throughout the life-span: An examination of contemporary psychological approaches. In P. B. Baltes & K. W. Schaie (eds.), *Life-span developmental psychology: Personality and socialization* (pp. 25–52). New York: Academic Press.

Magnusson, D. (1995). Individual development: A holistic integrated model. In P. Moen, G. H. Elder, & K. Lusher (eds.), *Linking lives and contexts: Perspectives on the ecology of human development* (pp. 19–60). Washington, DC: APA.

Magnusson, D. (1996). Interactionism and the person approach in developmental psychology. *European Child and Adolescent Psychiatry, 5*, 18–22.

Magnusson, D. (1999a). On the individual: A person-oriented approach to developmental research. *European Psychologist, 4*, 205–18.

Magnusson, D. (1999b). Holistic interactionism: A perspective for research on personality development. In L. A. Pervin & O. P. John (eds.), *Handbook of personality: Theory and research* (2nd edn., pp. 219–47). New York: Guilford.

Magnusson, D. & Stattin, H. (1998). Person–context interaction theories. In W. Damon (series ed.) & R. M. Lerner (vol. ed.), *Handbook of child psychology*, vol. 1: *Theoretical models of human development* (5th edn., pp. 685–759). New York: John Wiley.

Mayer, K. U. & Huinink, J. (1990). Age, period, and cohort in the study of the life course: A comparison of classical A-P-C analysis with event history analysis or farewell to Lexis? In D. Magnusson & L. R. Bergman (eds.), *Data quality in longitudinal research* (pp. 211–32). Cambridge, MA: Cambridge University Press.

McCandless, B. R. (1967). *Children*. New York: Holt, Rinehart & Winston.

McCandless, B. R. (1970). *Adolescents*. Hinsdale, IL: Dryden Press.

Meacham, J. A. (1977). A transactional model of remembering. In N. Datan & H. W. Reese (eds.), *Life-span developmental psychology: Dialectical perspectives on experimental research* (pp. 261–83). New York: Academic Press.

Mistry, J. & Saraswathi, T. S. (2003). Cultural context of child development. In R. M. Lerner, M. A. Easterbrooks, & J. Mistry (eds.) *Comprehensive Handbook of Psychology*, vol. 6: *Developmental Psychology*. New York: John Wiley.

Molenaar, P. C. M. (1986). On the impossibility of acquiring more powerful structures: A neglected alternative. *Human Development, 29*, 245–51.

Novikoff, A. B. (1945a). The concept of integrative levels of biology. *Science, 62*, 209–15.

Novikoff, A. B. (1945b). Continuity and discontinuity in evolution. *Science, 101*, 405–6.

Overton, W. (1998). Developmental psychology: Philosophy, concepts, and methodology. In W. Damon (series ed.) & R. M. Lerner (vol. ed.), *Handbook of child psychology*, vol. 1: *Theoretical models of human development* (5th edn., pp. 107–87). New York: John Wiley.

Overton, W. F. & Reese, H. W. (1973). Models of development: Methodological implications. In J. R. Nesselroade & H. W. Reese (eds.), *Life-span developmental psychology: Methodological issues.* New York: Academic Press.

Plomin, R. (2000). Behavioural genetics in the 21st century. *International Journal of Behavioral Development, 24,* 30–4.

Reese, H. W. & Overton, W. F. (1970). Models of development and theories of development. In L. R. Goulet & P. B. Baltes (eds.), *Life-span developmental psychology: Research and theory.* New York: Academic Press.

Riegel, K. F. (1977). The dialectics of time. In N. Datan & H. W. Reese (eds.), *Life-span developmental psychology: Dialectical perspectives on experimental research.* New York: Academic Press.

Rogoff, B. (1998). Cognition as a collaborative process. In W. Damon (series ed.) & D. Kuhn & R. S. Siegler (vol. eds.), *Handbook of Child Psychology,* vol. 2: *Theoretical models of human development* (5th edn., pp. 679–744). New York: John Wiley.

Rowe, D. C. (1994). *The limits of family influence: Genes, experience, and behavior.* New York: Guilford.

Rubin, K. H., Bukowski, W., & Parker, J. G. (1998). Peer interactions, relationships, and groups. In W. Damon & N. Eisenberg (eds.), *Handbook of Child Psychology,* vol. 3: *Social, emotional, and personality development* (pp. 619–700). New York: John Wiley.

Rushton, J. P. (1999). *Race, evolution, and behavior* (special abridged edition). New Brunswick, NJ: Transaction.

Sameroff, A. J. (1983). Developmental systems: Contexts and evolution. In W. Kessen (ed.), *Handbook of child psychology,* vol. 1: *History, theory, and methods* (pp. 237–94). New York: John Wiley.

Sampson, R. J., Morenoff, J. D., Earls, F. (1999). Beyond social capital: Spatial dynamics of collective efficacy for children. *American Sociological Review, 64,* 633–60.

Sarason, S. B. (1973). Jewishness, Blackish-ness and the nature–nurture controversy. *American Psychologist, 28,* 962–71.

Schaie, K. W. (1965). A general model for the study of developmental problems. *Psychosocial Bulletin, 64,* 92–107.

Schaie, K. W. & Strother, C. R. (1968). A cross-sequential study of age changes in cognitive behavior. *Psychological Bulletin, 70,* 671–80.

Schneirla, T. C. (1956). Interrelationships of the innate and the acquired in instinctive behavior. In P. P. Grasse (ed.), *L'instinct dans le comportement des animaux et de l'homme* (pp. 387–452). Paris: Masson et Cie.

Schneirla, T. C. (1957). The concept of development in comparative psychology. In D. B. Harris (ed.), *The concept of development* (pp. 78–108). Minneapolis, MN: University of Minnesota.

Shweder, R., Goodnow, J., Hatano, G., Le Vine, R. A., Markus, H., & Miller, P. (1998). The cultural psychology of development. One mind, many mentalities. In W. Damon (series ed.) & R. M. Lerner (vol. ed.), *Handbook of child psychology,* vol. 1: *Theoretical models of human development* (5th edn., pp. 865–933). New York: John Wiley.

Skinner, B. F. (1938). *The behavior of organisms.* New York: Appleton.

Skinner, B. F. (1964). Behaviorism at fifty. In T. W. Wann (ed.), *Behaviorism and phenomenology: Contrasting bases for modern psychology* (pp. 79–108). Chicago, IL: University of Chicago Press.

Sørensen, B., Weinert, E., & Sherrod, L. R. (eds.) (1986). *Human development and the life course: Multidisciplinary perspectives.* Hillsdale, NJ: Lawrence Erlbaum Associates.

Spanier, G. B. (1976a). Measuring dyadic adjustment: New scales for assessing the quality of marriage and similar dyads. *Journal of Marriage and the Family, 38,* 15–28.

Spanier, G. B. (1976b). Use of recall data in survey research on human sexual behavior. *Social Biology*, 23, 244–53.

Spanier, G. B. & Glick, P. C. (1980). The life cycle of American families: An expanded analysis. *Journal of Family History*, 5, 97–111.

Suomi, S. J. (1999). Developmental trajectories, early experiences, and community consequences: Lessons from studies with Rhesus monkeys. In D. P. Keating & C. Hertzman (eds.), *Developmental health and the wealth of nations* (pp. 185–200). New York: Guilford.

Taylor, C. S. (1990). *Dangerous society*. East Lansing, MI: Michigan State University Press.

Taylor, C. S. (1993). *Girls, gangs, women, and drugs*. East Lansing, MI: Michigan State University Press.

Taylor, C. S., Lerner, R. M., von Eye, A., Balsano, A. B., Dowling, E. M., Anderson, P. M., Bobek, D. L., & Bjelobrk, D. (2002a). Stability of attributes of positive functioning and of developmental assets among African American adolescent male gang and community-based organization members. In R. M. Lerner, C. S. Taylor, & A. von Eye (eds.), *Pathways to positive development among diverse youth* (*New directions for youth development: Theory, practice and research*, no. 95, pp. 35–56). San Francisco, CA: Jossey-Bass.

Taylor, C. S., Lerner, R. M., von Eye, A., Balsano, A. B., Dowling, E. M., Anderson, P. M., Bobek, D. L., & Bjelobrk, D. (2002b). Individual and ecological assets and positive developmental trajectories among gang and community-based organization youth. In R. M. Lerner, C. S. Taylor, & A. von Eye (eds.), *Pathways to positive development among diverse youth* (*New directions for youth development: Theory, practice and research*, no. 95, pp. 57–72). San Francisco, CA: Jossey-Bass.

Taylor, C. S., Lerner, R. M., von Eye, A., Bobek, D. L., Balsano, A. B., Dowling, E., & Anderson, P. M. (2003). Positive individual and social behavior among gang and nongang African American male adolescents. *Journal of Adolescent Research*, 16, 547–74.

Taylor, C. S., Lerner, R. M., von Eye, A., Bobek, D. L., Balsano, A. B., Dowling, E., & Anderson, P. M. (2004). Internal and external developmental assets among African American male gang members. *Journal of Adolescent Research*, 19, 303–22.

Terman, L. M. (1916). *The measurement of intelligence*. Boston, MA: Houghton.

Terman, L. M. (1925). *Genetic studies of genius: Mental and physical traits of a thousand gifted children*. Stanford, CA: Stanford University Press.

Thelen, E. & Smith, L. B. (1994). *A dynamic systems approach to the development of cognition and action*. Cambridge, MA: MIT Press.

Thelen, E. & Smith, L. B. (1998). Dynamic systems theories. In W. Damon (series ed.) & R. M. Lerner (vol. ed.), *Handbook of child psychology*, vol. 1: *Theoretical models of human development* (5th edn., pp. 563–633). New York: John Wiley.

Thomas, A. & Chess, S. (1977). *Temperament and development*. New York: Brunner/Mazel.

Thorndike, E. L. (1904). The newest psychology. *Educational Review*, 28, 217–27.

Tobach, E. & Greenberg, G. (1984). The significance of T. C. Schneirla's contribution to the concept of levels of integration. In G. Greenberg & E. Tobach (eds.), *Behavioral evolution and integrative levels* (pp. 1–7). Hillsdale, NJ: Lawrence Erlbaum Associates.

von Bertalanffy, L. (1933). *Modern theories of development*. London: Oxford University Press.

von Bertalanffy, L. (1968). *General systems theory: Foundations, development, applications*. New York: G. Braziller.

von Eye, A. (1990a). *Statistical methods in longitudinal research: Principles and structuring change*. New York: Academic Press.

von Eye, A. (1990b). *Introduction to Configural Frequency Analysis: The search for types and antitypes in cross-classifications*. Cambridge: Cambridge University Press.

von Eye, A. & Clogg, C. C. (eds.). (1996). *Categorical variables in developmental research: Methods of analysis*. San Diego. CA: Academic Press.

von Eye, A. & Schuster, C. (2000). The road to freedom: Quantitative developmental methodology in the third millennium. *International Journal of Behavioral Development*, *24*, 35–43.

Vygotsky, L. S. (1978). *Mind in society: The development of higher psychological processes*. Cambridge, MA: Harvard University Press.

Wapner, S. & Demick, J. (1998). Developmental analysis: A holistic, developmental, systems-oriented perspective. In W. Damon (series ed.) & R. M. Lerner (vol. ed.), *Handbook of child psychology*, vol. 1: *Theoretical models of human development* (5th edn., pp. 761–805). New York: John Wiley.

Watson, J. B. (1914). *Behavior: An introduction to comparative psychology*. New York: Holt.

Watson, J. B. (1928). *Psychological care of infant and child*. New York: Norton.

Werner, H. (1957). The concept of development from a comparative and organismic point of view. In D. B. Harris (ed.), *The concept of development* (pp. 125–48). Minneapolis, MN: University of Minnesota Press.

White, S. H. (1968). The learning–maturation controversy: Hall to Hull. *Merrill-Palmer Quarterly*, *14*, 187–96.

Windle, M. & Lerner, R. M. (1986). The goodness of fit model of temperament–context relations: Interaction or correlation? In J. V. Lerner & R. M. Lerner (eds.), Temperament and social interaction during infancy and childhood. *New Directions for Child Development* (vol. 31, pp. 109–20). San Francisco, CA: Jossey-Bass.

Wohlwill, J. F. (1973). *The study of behavioral development*. New York: Academic Press.

Zigler, E. (1999). A place of value for applied and policy studies. *Child Development*, *69*, 532–42.

Zigler, E. (2003). Foreword. In R. M. Lerner, F. Jacobs, & D. Wertlieb (eds.), *Handbook of applied developmental science: Promoting positive child, adolescent, and family development through research, policies, and programs*, vol. 1: *Applying developmental science for youth and families: Historical and theoretical foundations*. (pp. xvii–xx). Thousand Oaks, CA: Sage.

PART III

Developmental Intervention: Traditional and Emergent Approaches in Enhancing Development

CHAPTER ELEVEN

Enhancing Children's Socioemotional Development: A Review of Intervention Studies

Femmie Juffer, Marian J. Bakermans-Kranenburg, and Marinus H. van IJzendoorn

Introduction

In the past few decades many early intervention programs have been launched with the objective to support parents in their child-rearing task, and with the more or less explicit claim that their children's development should benefit from these intervention efforts. In this chapter we will review studies that aimed at optimizing those parental behaviors that are assumed to enhance children's social and emotional development. The narrative review will be presented after discussing some methodological considerations. Furthermore, we will discuss our own experimental intervention study as an illustration of an intervention involving mothers with an insecure mental representation of attachment.

From a scientific perspective, intervention programs are highly interesting since the results may shed light on both theoretical and clinical issues. The *theoretical relevance* of the study of intervention programs becomes evident in its contribution to the development and refinement of prevalent theories. Through the experimental manipulation of a well-defined variable deemed causally related to an outcome behavior, theories and hypotheses can be tested in a robust way. For example, through manipulating parental sensitivity with interventions aimed at enhancing sensitivity, it can be tested whether the predicted outcome, a higher percentage of securely attached children, is actually found. The association between parental sensitivity and infant–parent attachment assumed in attachment theory (Bowlby, 1982), and empirically established in meta-analyses of correlational studies (Atkinson et al., 2000; de Wolff & van IJzendoorn, 1997; Goldsmith & Alansky, 1987), can thus be tested with respect to its causal nature. In this way, intervention studies can contribute substantially to our knowledge of factors that are causally related to aspects of children's development. Therefore, questions about the internal validity of the intervention experiments are crucial.

The *clinical relevance* of the study of interventions is most apparent when practical consequences and effects of a program are discussed. The needs of at-risk children or parents with problems may be immense and challenging (Bronfenbrenner, 1974), thus urging researchers and clinicians to design intervention programs that meet these needs (e.g., Marvin et al., 2002; Moran et al., 2000). For example, interventions have been conducted with families of children referred for sleeping or feeding disorders, with the objectives to help parents cope with these disrupting behaviors, and to facilitate a more optimal adjustment in the child (e.g., Robert-Tissot et al., 1996). It is crucial to know whether the intervention turns out to be successful in reducing the targeted behavioral symptoms. It is, however, also important to determine whether an effective intervention can be generalized outside the experimental setting, serving the needs of a larger group with similar problems. Consequently, questions concerning the external validity of the intervention studies come to the fore.

Since the publication of one of the first comprehensive reviews on the effectiveness of early childhood interventions on cognitive development (Bronfenbrenner, 1974), several reviews and meta-analyses on early interventions have documented their effectiveness in enhancing parental child-rearing attitudes and practices, and children's socioemotional development (Beckwith, 2000; Benasich, Brooks-Gunn, & Clewell, 1992; Bradley, 1993; Egeland et al., 2000; Heinicke, Beckwith, & Thompson, 1988; Lagerberg, 2000; Lojkasek, Cohen, & Muir, 1994; MacLeod & Nelson, 2000; van IJzendoorn, Juffer, & Duyvesteyn, 1995). In this chapter we present our review of the extant literature on early childhood interventions with a special emphasis on parental sensitivity and/or children's attachment.

Review of Intervention Studies on Parent–Child Interaction

In this section we review intervention studies that aimed at promoting positive parent–child interactions in early childhood. Although the review is probably not exhaustive, we tried to collect as many relevant studies as possible. Pertinent studies were collected systematically, using at least three different search strategies (Mullen, 1989). First, PsycINFO, Dissertation Abstracts, and Medline were searched with keywords "attachment," "sensitivity" (or related terms such as "responsiveness"), and "intervention" (or related terms such as "preventive" or "therapeutic"). Second, the references of the collected papers, books, and book chapters were searched for relevant intervention studies. Third, experts in the field were asked to mention intervention studies related to sensitivity or attachment. Our selection criteria were rather broad, in order to include as many intervention studies as possible, regardless of research design qualities. Unpublished studies or interventions that were only reported at meetings or conferences were excluded. Brief, postnatal Brazelton interventions were excluded as well (see Das Eiden & Reifman, 1996, for a meta-analysis of this type of intervention). Not only intervention studies using the classical Ainsworth sensitivity rating scales (Ainsworth, Bell, & Stayton, 1974) were included, but also studies with post-tests based on the HOME (Caldwell & Bradley, 1984), the Nursing Child Assessment Teaching Scale (NCAST; Barnard et al., 1988), the Erickson rating scales for maternal sensitivity/supportiveness (Egeland et al., 1990; Erickson, Sroufe, & Egeland, 1985), or related measures. The intervention studies were not restricted to a specific population, e.g., middle-class families with healthy infants, and clinical populations were included as well.

We collected intervention studies that aimed at enhancing positive parental behaviors, such as responsiveness, sensitivity, or involvement, presuming that these behaviors are beneficial for the child's concurrent and later social and emotional development. For example, the relevance of sensitivity as a determinant for the developing child–parent attachment relationship is well documented (de Wolff & van IJzendoorn, 1997). As we were interested in actual changes in parenting behavior rather than parent-reported evaluations or attitudes, we restricted our review to studies that used observational measures.

Because the review is limited to the child's socioemotional development, we will not describe intervention studies that concentrated on the child's cognitive development only (for reviews of cognitively oriented programs, see Farran, 1990, 2000; Zigler & Hall, 2000; for an overview of educational interventions directed at children with disabilities, see Guralnick, 1997). Several of the intervention studies that we did include presented cognitive outcome data as well, such as the child's Bayley scores, but these data are not reviewed.

We examined 70 intervention studies that matched our criteria (see also Bakermans-Kranenburg, van IJzendoorn, & Juffer, 2003). We will compare and discuss these studies with the objective of highlighting some general trends or conclusions rather than reviewing each separate study thoroughly.

Sample: The recipients of the intervention

In only a small minority of the studies the intervention was targeted towards *middle-class, normal parents with healthy children* (e.g., Dickie & Gerber, 1980; Lambermon & van IJzendoorn, 1989; Leitch, 1999; Metzl, 1980; Scholz & Samuels, 1992). In these studies the effect of parent education through videotapes or brochures was tested. Given the fact that in the general population many well-baby clinics and parent education facilities provide parents with lots of written or videotaped information, it is noteworthy that the research on this particular topic is lagging behind.

As an example, an intervention program directed towards normal parents was conducted by Scholz and Samuels (1992), who visited 32 first-time Australian families in their home at 4 weeks postpartum. The fathers and the mothers together were given a demonstration of baby bathing and massage, and shown a videotape about this subject. At the post-test at 12 weeks postpartum, positive effects on parental warmth and infant responsiveness were reported.

In most studies the intervention was implemented in a special, clinical or multirisk group. Intervention programs were designed for groups of *infants* at risk for problematic socioemotional development, for *parents* in adverse circumstances, or for families with *both* problematic parents and at-risk children.

The studies involving special groups of *children* consisted of families with premature infants (Barrera, Rosenbaum, & Cunningham, 1986; Bustan & Sagi, 1984; Kang et al., 1995; Meyer et al., 1994; Spiker, Ferguson, & Brooks-Gunn, 1993; Wijnroks, 1994), clinically referred children (Cohen et al., 1999; Robert-Tissot et al., 1996), children with developmental disabilities (Mahoney & Powell, 1988; Seifer, Clark, & Sameroff, 1991), anxious-withdrawn preschoolers (Lafreniere & Capuano, 1997), or internationally adopted infants (Juffer et al., 1997; Rosenboom, 1994).

An illustration of a large, comprehensive intervention study directed towards parents of low-birth-weight, premature infants can be found in Spiker, Ferguson, and Brooks-Gunn (1993). In the Infant Health and Development Program (IHDP; see also: Bradley et al., 1994; Klebanov, Brooks-Gunn, & McCormick, 2001) involving 985 participants, intervention parents received three modalities of services, including home visits, a center-based curriculum, and parent support group meetings. The goals of the home visits were to provide emotional and social support to the parents, and to help them develop interactional skills and knowledge. Spiker, Ferguson, and Brooks-Gunn (1993) found small but significant effects of the IHDP intervention at 30 months ($n = 683$). The interaction of mother and child was rated as more synchronous compared to a control group.

An example of a study involving clinically referred children can be found in Robert-Tissot et al. (1996). The study examined a clinical group of 75 parents and their children under 30 months of age who were referred for sleeping, feeding, and behavioral disorders (e.g., aggression). The families were randomly assigned to two treatment groups, and assessed in pre- and post-tests. A control group was not included in the study. The first treatment consisted of psychodynamic mother–infant psychotherapy. During the sessions the therapist listened to the mother's complaints and anxieties while remaining attentive to the ongoing interactions, and actively searching for a focus of intervention, for example by discussing similarities between current problems and conflicts in the mother's past history. The second treatment consisted of interaction guidance through the use of video-assisted coaching (McDonough, 1993). In this approach, no explicit reference was made to the mother's past history. The therapist remained in the "here and now" frame and capitalized on the reinforcement of favorable interactions. According to mother-report a significant reduction of infant symptoms, e.g., sleeping difficulties, was established in both treatment groups. Observational ratings revealed that maternal sensitivity to the infant's signals had increased after treatment in both intervention groups, but interaction guidance brought about a greater improvement than psychodynamic mother–infant psychotherapy. Also, the infants in both treatment groups had become more cooperative, less compulsive-compliant, less difficult, and displayed more positive affect during dyadic interactions.

The studies with special groups of *parents* comprised samples with low socioeconomic status (SES) mothers (e.g., Palti et al., 1984), studies with multirisk mothers (e.g., Armstrong et al., 1999), studies with adolescent mothers (e.g., Osofsky, Culp, & Ware, 1988), studies with depressed mothers (e.g., Cicchetti, Toth, & Rogosch, 1999), and a study with highly anxious mothers (Barnett et al., 1987).

Black and Teti (1997) described a particular nonintensive intervention focusing on sensitive parenting, for adolescent mothers. In a randomized trial the intervention group consisting of 26 African American adolescent mothers viewed and received a copy of a videotape titled *Feeding Your Baby With Love*. At the post-test two weeks later, intervention mothers and 33 control mothers were videotaped feeding their baby. The intervention mothers were significantly more involved with their babies during feeding, compared to the control group.

An example of a more intensive intervention program directed towards low-SES mothers with the focus on sensitivity was described by Riksen-Walraven et al. (1996). In the Netherlands, 37 lower-class ethnic minority families with a 1-year-old child participated in '*Instapje*', a parent-focused intervention program. During 16 weekly home visits, a lay intervenor of the same ethnic Surinam-Dutch background showed the mother a program book and a set of play materials to be used in the interactions. The intervenor also acted as a role model, by playing with the child and explaining to the mother the way she reacted. The mother was then asked to play regularly with her child during the next week. At 18 months, at the post-test, the intervention mothers scored higher than a comparison group of 38 ethnic minority mothers on three out of four dimensions of parental support: supportive presence, respect for the child's autonomy, and structure and limit setting.

An illustration of an intervention program directed towards multirisk mothers that aimed at enhancing sensitivity, affecting parents' representations, and providing social support can be found in Heinicke et al. (1999). The mothers in this study were poor and lacked support, and other risk factors such as histories of abuse were frequently present. The primary goal of the intervention was to offer the mother the experience of a stable, trustworthy relationship, and to promote her sense of self-efficacy. At the post-test at 12 months, the infants of the intervention group ($n = 31$) were more often securely attached in the Strange Situation Procedure (Ainsworth et al., 1978), and their mothers were more responsive, compared to a control group ($n = 33$).

Some interventions were directed at *parents in difficult circumstances with at-risk infants*. Several combinations were found, such as samples of premature children with low-SES or adolescent mothers (Beckwith, 1988; Field et al., 1980; Kang et al., 1995; Ross, 1984) or low-SES mothers with insecurely attached or irritable infants (Lieberman, Weston, & Pawl, 1991; van den Boom, 1994).

In Field et al.'s (1980) study, black adolescent mothers of preterm infants were provided a home-based parent-training intervention. Weekly home visits were made over an 8-month period by a trained intervenor and a black adolescent student. The goal of the intervention was to educate the mothers on child-rearing issues, to teach them age-appropriate stimulation of their infants, and to facilitate harmonious mother–child interactions. At a first follow-up assessment at 4 months postpartum, the scores of the intervention mothers compared favorably to the scores of the control mothers with respect to their reciprocal face-to-face interaction. At the post-test at 8 months, the 27 intervention mothers received significantly higher ratings on the HOME than the 25 control mothers. The specific HOME ratings which contributed to these differences were emotional and verbal responsiveness and maternal involvement with the infant.

Intervention focus, method and intensity

Intervention programs should be designed to meet the unique needs of a particular sample. Moreover, they are frequently based on diverging theoretical assumptions and empirical evidence about the parameters that influence children's development. These theoretical perspectives are reflected in a different focus of intervention, and translated in diverging intervention methods and intensities. Following Egeland et al. (2000), we distinguish interventions directed at the parent's sensitive behavior, programs that focus on the parent's mental representation, and intervention efforts that attempt to stimulate or provide social support for parents.

Many interventions with the ultimate goal of promoting children's emotional and social development, especially their attachment security, attempt to do so by enhancing maternal *sensitivity* or *responsiveness*. These interventions are based on attachment theory (Bowlby, 1982; Ainsworth et al., 1978) and draw on an extensive body of relevant knowledge and research. In this type of intervention the parent's behavior towards the child is the focus of the intervention. Ainsworth et al. (1978) defined sensitivity as the ability to perceive the child's signals correctly, and to react to these signals promptly and adequately. Some interventions appear to start at the most basic level of sensitivity: in order to make the parents "better perceivers" they are taught observational skills. This goal can be reached in several ways, for example through stimulating parents to fill in a workbook about the behavior of their child (Riksen-Walraven, 1978), or by encouraging parents to engage in "speaking for the baby" (Carter, Osofsky, & Hann, 1991). Obviously, the latter method of providing "subtitles" or verbal comments on the child's signals and expressions may help parent to become better observers. The intervenor may also encourage the parent to perceive the child's behavior in a more correct, objective way, that is, without distortions, by explaining salient issues about the child's development. Many interventions that focus on parental sensitivity concentrate on the second part of Ainsworth's definition. In this case, the intervenor teaches or demonstrates prompt and adequate responding, for example through discussing parenting brochures or by modeling the desired behaviors (e.g., Mahoney & Powell, 1988). Another strategy to enhance sensitivity is by reinforcing sensitive and responsive behaviors that the parents already show to their child, for example with video feedback (e.g., Bakermans-Kranenburg, Juffer, & van IJzendoorn, 1998; Juffer et al., 1997; Seifer, Clark, & Sameroff, 1991; Ziegenhain et al., 1999).

Interventions that focus on the parent's sensitivity sometimes imply rather short-term programs. For example, only one session was implemented in a few studies (e.g., Black & Teti, 1997; Kang et al., 1995; Riksen-Walraven, 1978), three or four sessions in several studies (e.g., Bustan & Sagi, 1984; van den Boom, 1994), and six to eight sessions in some other studies (e.g., Krupka, 1995; Seifer, Clark, & Sameroff, 1991).

An illustration of sensitivity interventions was described by Juffer (1993; Juffer et al., 1997). The intervention, implemented by three intervenors, aimed at supporting parental sensitivity, with the ultimate goal of promoting secure attachment and infant competence. In a sample of 90 mothers with internationally adopted infants, 30 mothers received a personal book, 30 received the book and three sessions with video feedback, and 30 mothers were in the control group (receiving a brochure about adoption). The personal book program was based on Riksen-Walraven's (1978) "workbook for parents" intervention. In the personal book for adoptive families the role of sensitive responsiveness was explained, and suggestions were given for playful interaction, and for holding and comforting the baby. In order to promote the mother's observational skills, she was invited to fill in observations of her own baby. In the more intensive intervention mothers were provided the same book and three sessions of video feedback. The intervenor showed a videotape of the mother interacting with her child, and commented on selected fragments of the film. Sensitive responses of the mother were reinforced with positive comments, where the intervenor emphasized the beneficial effects of these responses on the child's behavior. The intervenor also commented on the infant's signals and responses by verbalizing the baby's reactions and expressions, with the objective of promoting the mother's observational abilities and empathy. At the post-test at 12 months, the mothers who received the book as well as video feedback were more sensitive, and their children were more often securely attached compared to the control group.

In the second type of intervention the efforts are directed towards the parent's *representation of attachment*, and the focus of change is the parent's representational model or working model of attachment (Bowlby, 1982). Many of these intervention programs base their approach on the work of Selma Fraiberg (Fraiberg, Adelson, & Shapiro, 1975). Fraiberg's famous metaphor of "ghosts in the nursery" has inspired developers of interventions to design interventions that are typically insight-oriented, therapeutic, and often lengthy. The idea that parents are apt to "re-enact" or repeat the parenting behavior of their own parents, even unconsciously and involuntarily, led to the hypothesis that maladaptive parenting behavior should be changed through changing parents' mental representations of attachment or inner working models. In this type of intervention parents are involved in discussions about their past and present attachment experiences and feelings (Bakermans-Kranenburg, Juffer, & van IJzendoorn, 1998), in child–parent psychotherapy (Cicchetti, Toth, & Rogosch, 1999; Cohen et al., 1999; Lieberman, Weston, & Pawl, 1991), or in psychodynamic therapy (Cooper & Murray, 1997; Robert-Tissot et al., 1996). These discussions or therapy sessions aim at re-structuring the parent's mental representation of attachment towards a more secure and balanced view on relationships. During the sessions the intervenor or therapist serves as a secure base for the parent from which he or she can explore attachment problems, and try out new ways of relating to others, including the child. Often these interventions take a long time, e.g., 50 sessions (Lieberman, Weston, & Pawl, 1991), although some interventions attempt to pursue their goal in a shorter period of time, e.g., four to ten sessions (Bakermans-Kranenburg, Juffer, & van IJzendoorn, 1998; Cooper & Murray, 1997; Robert-Tissot et al., 1996).

An example of an intervention that focused on the parent's representation was described by Cohen et al. (1999). One of the two treatments evaluated in this study was psychodynamic psychotherapy (PPT), a parent–infant therapy for clinically referred infants. During center-based sessions mother and infant were invited to play. The mother and therapist agreed to talk together, but they would also try to attend to the infant's activities. In this representational approach the therapist made use of psychodynamic transference, repetition of the past, re-experiencing of affect, and interpretation. In this approach it was assumed that therapy modifies the mother's mental model of her relationship with her infant by exploring the assumptions derived from her relationship with her own parents. The focus was on the mother gaining insight into herself and how she related to her child, for example by differentiating the needs of her infant from her own needs. In this treatment, the primary work was between the mother and the therapist.

The basic process was the same as in adult psychotherapy, except that the therapy focused on the difficulties the mother was experiencing with her child (Cohen et al., 1999). For example, while discussing the child's feeding problems, the therapist might ask how the mother herself was nurtured as a child, and subsequently explore her thoughts and feelings about this subject. Ultimately, the mother might understand that her current problems with respect to feeding her baby could be connected with the inadequate care she experienced from her own parents.

In the second treatment, Watch, Wait, and Wonder, (WWW; Cohen et al., 1999), a representational approach was combined with a behavioral approach. The authors described WWW as infant-led psychotherapy: mothers were given the opportunity to explore with the therapist intergenerational (representational) issues, although a specific and ultimate goal of WWW was to enable the mother to follow her infant's lead (behavioral approach). For half of each session the mother was instructed to get down on the floor, to observe her infant, and to interact only at her child's initiative. According to the authors, this method places the mother in the position of being (more) sensitive and responsive.

Cohen et al. (1999) reported that after about 15 sessions both PPT and WWW were successful in reducing infant-presenting problems, and in reducing maternal intrusiveness. The infants in the WWW group showed a greater shift towards a more organized and secure attachment, and their emotion regulation improved more than in the PPT group. The study did not include a control group. The changes that were reported were differences and gains between pre- and post-treatment assessments.

Stimulating or providing *social support* to parents is included in the third type of intervention. The importance of practical and emotional support from relatives or friends for the parent's functioning and subsequently the child's developmental outcome has been supported by ample empirical evidence (Crnic et al., 1983; Crockenberg, 1981). Less well examined is Crnic and Greenberg's (1987) hypothesis on the developmental nature of social support. The authors pose that social support may be most influential at particular times in the parent's development. They suggested that, for example, the transition to parenthood, as a period of considerable change in routines, expectations, and behaviors, requires numerous adjustments, both physically and emotionally. In such a transition period parents may be not only more needy of help, but also more receptive for support from others (see also Cowan & Cowan, 1987).

Several studies made use of social support primarily, sometimes by giving practical help and advice (Barnett et al., 1987), offering individualized services (Gowen & Nebrig, 1997), by providing information about community services (Luster et al., 1996), or by stimulating the parents to extend their social network. Other intervention studies combined the provision or enhancement of social support with another focus of intervention, for example by aiming to promote sensitive parenting as well as providing general support (Barnard et al., 1988; Beckwith, 1988; Gelfand et al., 1996; Lafreniere & Capuano, 1997; Letourneau, 2000). Still other intervention studies combined the provision of social support with both a behavioral focus of intervention and a representational approach. For example, in project STEEP (Steps Toward Effective and Enjoyable Parenting; Egeland & Erickson, 1993; Egeland et al., 2000), mothers not only received practical support and advice, but also video feedback in order to increase sensitive parenting, and help to examine and discuss their own childhood experiences. Compared to the control group, the STEEP program had a positive impact on a number of outcome measures, e.g., the mother's sensitivity and her understanding of infant development, although no positive effects were found on attachment security.

Some intervention programs providing or enhancing social support take substantial periods. For example, mothers participated in the intervention programs described by Barnard et al. (1988) and Barnett et al. (1987) for at least one year. The results of the studies using social support (whether or not combined with another focus of intervention) were mixed: in many studies positive effects on maternal sensitivity were found (e.g., Barnard et al., 1988; Beckwith, 1988; Luster et al., 1996), but in other cases the intervention was not successful (Barnett et al., 1987).

Design and methodological problems

A large part of the intervention studies we reviewed had robust designs, with random assignment to an experimental group and a control group. In some studies no control group was used, mostly in view of ethical reasons (Brinich, Drotar, & Brinich, 1989), that is, the problem of withholding from at-risk families a potential beneficial program. Although the rationale of this consideration is clearly understandable, these designs are seriously flawed because they lack a comparison group. The possibility of providing the control group with a dummy treatment that is largely similar to the intervention group's program and lacks only one or two ingredients should be seriously considered. For example, the control group could be provided a general brochure about children's development (the dummy intervention), while the experimental group receives (also) a more specific brochure about the relevance of sensitive parenting for children's attachment security. The effectiveness of the specific aspect(s) of the intervention can thus be tested without failing in one's duties towards the control group. This approach combines two advantages that characterize adequate designs: if the intervention is more successful than the dummy treatment, we know more specifically what ingredient did the work. Second, differential attrition can be prevented, and ethical problems with abstaining from support to families at-risk do not arise (see van IJzendoorn & Bakermans-Kranenburg, 2002).

When studies without a control group report pre- and post-test data, the gain between pre- and post-test can be utilized, as the pre-test scores provide a baseline with which to compare the post-test-scores (e.g., Cohen et al., 1999; Lambermon & van IJzendoorn, 1989; Mahoney & Powell, 1988; Robert-Tissot et al., 1996). As we discussed before, these designs are less robust compared to true experimental designs. Apart from randomization, methodological problems were discerned in several studies. Differential attrition, especially in the control group, was a problem in some studies (Barnard et al.,

1988; Beckwith, 1988; Brophy, 1997). Also, a ceiling effect, due to high percentages of secure infant–mother attachments in the control group, was suspected in a few studies (Juffer et al., 1997; Meij, 1992; Rosenboom, 1994). In one study it was reported explicitly that the coders of the outcome behaviors were not blind to the intervention or control condition of the subjects (Weiner, Kuppermintz, & Guttmann, 1994). Obviously, this raises questions about the reliability and the validity of the study's outcomes.

A Case Study: The Leiden Attachment Intervention Study

In this section, our own ongoing attachment-based intervention study will serve as a case of early intervention. Our preventive intervention attempts to break the intergenerational cycle of insecure attachment in a group of mothers who are at risk for developing an insecure attachment relationship with their child because of their own insecure mental representations of attachment (Bakermans-Kranenburg, Juffer, & van IJzendoorn, 1998). Since insecure infant–parent attachment is associated with less optimal sequelae for the child in the preschool years and middle childhood (Elicker, Englund, & Sroufe, 1992; Lewis et al., 1984; Stams, Juffer, & van IJzendoorn, 2002; Weinfield et al., 1999), it is important that parents be supported in order to develop a (more) secure attachment relationship with their child in infancy.

To reach this goal, we distinguished two types of interventions: interventions directed at the behavioral level and interventions directed at the representational level. First, many studies have shown that parental sensitivity is a key variable in the development of secure attachment (de Wolff & van IJzendoorn, 1997; Goldsmith & Alansky, 1987). Therefore, intervention efforts may be directed at enhancing parents' sensitive behavior. Second, insecure mental representations of attachment were found to be associated with parental insensitive responses to the infant's attachment signals and with insecure infant–parent attachment (Main, Kaplan, & Cassidy, 1985; van IJzendoorn, 1995). Therefore, intervention efforts may also focus on the representational level, that is, on parents' mental representations of attachment, in order to pave the way for subsequent behavioral changes.

In our study these two types of intervention were provided. The first program, Video Intervention to promote Positive Parenting (VIPP), aims at enhancing maternal sensitive behavior through providing personal video feedback, combined with brochures on sensitive responding in daily situations. The second intervention (VIPP-R, that is, VIPP combined with Representational efforts) includes additional discussions about past and present attachment, aiming at affecting the mother's mental representation of attachment. Moreover, building a supporting relationship between the intervenor and the mother is considered a crucial element of both types of intervention (Bowlby, 1988). The two programs are short term and home based: during four home visits the interventions are implemented by three female intervenors. In both types of intervention there are specific themes for each session, and guidelines for each session are described in a protocol (Bakermans-Kranenburg, Juffer, & van IJzendoorn, 1998; for a case study, see Juffer, van IJzendoorn, & Bakermans-Kranenburg, 1997).

Video feedback (VIPP)

The method of video feedback was developed in a previous study (Juffer, 1993), based on attachment theory (Ainsworth et al., 1978; Bowlby, 1982). The intervention appeared to be successful in promoting maternal sensitivity and infant–mother attachment in families with first adopted children (Juffer et al., 1997). For the Leiden attachment intervention study, this method was further developed into the current Video Intervention to promote Positive Parenting (VIPP).

In the VIPP program, mother and infant are videotaped during daily situations at their home, e.g., playing together or bathing the baby. On reviewing the tape at the institute, the intervenor prepares her future comments. During the next visit the videotape is shown to the mother, and the intervenor discusses some selected fragments with her. Video feedback provides the opportunity to focus on the baby's videotaped signals and expressions, thereby stimulating the mother's observational skills and empathy for her child. It also enables positive reinforcement of the mother's moments of sensitive behavior shown on the videotape. Before or after the video feedback the mother receives a brochure on sensitive responding, e.g., about crying and comforting, or about playing together.

VIPP consists of four themes that are elaborated successively during the four home visits: (1) the baby's contact-seeking and explorative behavior, (2) the accurate perception of the baby's (subtle) signals and expressions, (3) the relevance of prompt and adequate responding to the baby's signals, and (4) affective attunement and sharing of emotions. By explicitly acknowledging the mother as an expert on her own child, she is encouraged to participate in the discussion actively. For example, when the intervenor attempts to "speak for the baby" (Carter, Osofsky, & Hann, 1991), the mother is invited to take part, and provide "subtitles" for the baby's behavior.

Video feedback and representational discussions (VIPP-R)

In the second intervention modality, video feedback and brochures are accompanied by discussions about the mother's attachment experiences in her own childhood, and their possible influences on her present parenting behavior. Discussions about past and present attachments may enable parents to reconsider their childhood experiences and explore the link between those experiences and the developing relationship with the baby (Fraiberg, Adelson, & Shapiro, 1975). The mother is invited to reflect on her own childhood experiences by completing short questionnaires or projective material, followed by a discussion about a specific theme. For example, during one visit the mother is invited to read three fictional attachment biographies, and to elaborate on these stories and her own experiences with her parents. The material and discussion themes are based on attachment theory (Bowlby, 1982, 1988), and inspired by the biographies of "earned secure" persons (Pearson, Cohn, & Cowan, 1994). Persons with earned secure representations of attachment report to have had a hard or unloving childhood, but they nevertheless succeeded in restructuring their thoughts and feelings about these negative experiences. Ultimately, they appear to be able to reflect on their childhood experiences coherently, thus showing a secure representation of their attachment biography (Main & Goldwyn, in press).

The VIPP-R attachment discussions consist of four themes, which are elaborated during four home visits: (1) separations in the past, experienced as a child, and separations from the baby in the present, (2) parenting in the past, experienced as a child, and parenting in the present, experienced as a mother, (3) the process of breaking away during adolescence, and defining adult relationships with the parents, including the mother's own experiences with her parents, as well as her expectations of the future relationship with her child, and (4) the explicit link between "being the child of my parents" and "being the parent of my child," focusing on which childhood experiences the mother wants to pass or not to pass to her child.

Participants in our study were mothers with insecure mental representations of attachment, as measured with the Adult Attachment Interview (AAI) (George, Kaplan, & Main, 1985; Hesse, 1999). On the basis of the AAI, two types of insecure representations of attachment can be distinguished: insecure dismissing and insecure preoccupied attachment. In contrast to secure parents, who are able to reflect on positive or negative childhood experiences in a coherent way, insecure dismissing parents idealize their childhood experiences or devalue the importance of attachment relationships for their own lives. Insecure preoccupied parents, who are still angrily or passively involved with their past relationships, seem mentally entangled with their parents. Insecure dismissing mothers as well as insecure preoccupied mothers were randomly assigned to one of the two intervention groups or to the control group.

The intervention sessions were implemented between the baby's 7th and 10th months of age. As the intervenors did not know the mother's AAI, they were blind to the mother's type of insecurity (dismissing or preoccupied). At 6 months (pre-test) and at 11 months (post-test) video observations were made of the mother–infant dyads in the home to rate the mothers' sensitivity. At the post-test these observations were made by a co-worker unknown to the mother. At 12 months, a second AAI was administered to the mother by a different interviewer. At 13 months, mother and child were invited to the institute to assess the quality of the infant–mother attachment relationship in the Strange Situation procedure (Ainsworth et al., 1978), and to assess the mother's sensitive responsiveness during free play with Ainsworth, Bell, and Stayton's (1974) rating scale for sensitivity. All coders were blind to other data concerning the dyads.

Since our study is still in progress, the results are preliminary (see also Bakermans-Kranenburg, Juffer, & van IJzendoorn, 1998). In the small subsample for which data are available, the interventions did not yield a significant effect on infant–parent attachment. Both types of intervention, VIPP and VIPP-R, turned out to be effective in enhancing the mother's sensitive responsiveness at the post-test. Intervention mothers received significantly higher sensitivity scores than control mothers ($d = 0.87$, $p = 0.01$). No difference was found between the two intervention programs, nor between dismissing or preoccupied intervention mothers. Interestingly, insecure dismissing mothers tended to profit most from VIPP, the intervention program with video feedback only, whereas insecure preoccupied mothers tended to profit most from VIPP-R, the program with video feedback and attachment discussions (interaction effect: $d = 0.65$, $p = 0.19$). Maybe the different interventions meet the different needs of dismissing and preoccupied mothers (Bakermans-Kranenburg, Juffer, & van IJzendoorn, 1998). An insecure dismissing mother may profit most from an intervention with a clear focus on behavior that provides her with helpful tips to be used in the daily interaction with her child. An insecure preoccupied mother, who is still involved with her own attachment experiences, may profit most from an intervention with an additional representational approach that aims at (re-)structuring her thoughts and feelings with respect to attachment.

In sum, some interesting positive effects of VIPP and VIPP-R were found in a first study using these interventions. Of course, data from the larger group of mothers in our study are needed before strong conclusions can be drawn about, for example, the differential effects of the two intervention programs. Outcome data concerning the other measures, such as the AAI, are needed, too. Findings from the post-test AAI's can show whether changes in the mother's representation of attachment were achieved through the intervention, especially the VIPP-R intervention.

Conclusions

In this chapter we reviewed early intervention programs that aimed at supporting parents with the ultimate goal to enhance their children's social and emotional development. Our review shows that the study of early intervention in the service of children's socioemotional development involves thousands of families with multiple problems. Also, huge investments are made by intervenors using a wide array of intervention methods. Nevertheless, interventions appear to have a varying degree of success in reaching their intervention goals. From a population health perspective, society can profit from the results of successful early intervention programs, as childhood experiences appear to affect subsequent health status in profound and long-lasting ways (Hertzman & Wiens, 1996).

For the study of early intervention a few strands of research seem appealing for the future. More research is needed to study the long-term effects of early interventions, not only until the intervention children reach middle childhood (Stams et al., 2001), but also in adolescence (Riksen-Walraven & Van Aken, 1997) and in adulthood. It will be interesting to know, for example, how early intervention experiences may shape the parenting behavior of former intervention children. Also, it seems important that "booster" sessions should be conducted in successful intervention programs to keep the positive change intact, and to prevent the intervention groups from regressing into their old, maladadaptive, patterns of parenting. In fact, Bronfenbrenner's (1974) idea of a stepwise and long-range intervention program with several intervention stages throughout the first 12 years of life still seems to be most promising.

More research is also needed to examine the feasibility and effectiveness of interventions that intend to change parental representations, since the majority of intervention studies are directed at the behavioral level. For example, is it worthwhile to attempt to restructure parents' overall representation of attachment? Should intervention efforts (also) be directed at parents' more specific representations of their child and the parent–child relationship?

Furthermore, few studies have examined the benefits that intervention programs may produce for other family members. Theoretically, parental changes should benefit not only the target children involved in the intervention, but also their younger siblings. To date these "diffusion" effects (Seitz & Apfel, 1994) are largely unknown. Finally, new studies are emerging about the effects of early intervention on psychophysiological functioning of children, not only immediately after the intervention (Field et al., 1998; Fisher et al., 2000), but also six to eight years after treatment (Raine et al., 2001). These preliminary results about the influence of early enrichment on (later) psychophysiological functioning (see also Epstein, 2001) are promising for the field of early intervention and need to be replicated with different types of interventions in different groups of parents and their children.

Note

Address for correspondence: Leiden University, Center for Child & Family Studies, PO Box 9555, 2300 RB Leiden, The Netherlands. Email addresses: juffer@fsw.Leidenuniv.nl, bakermans@fsw.Leidenuniv.nl, and vanijzen@fsw.Leidenuniv.nl.

References

Ainsworth, M. D. S., Bell, S. M., & Stayton, D. J. (1974). Infant-mother attachment and social development. In M. P. Richards (ed.), *The introduction of the child into a social world* (pp. 99–135). London: Cambridge University Press.

Ainsworth, M. D. S., Blehar, M. C., Waters, E., & Wall, S. (1978). *Patterns of attachment. A psychological study of the Strange Situation.* Hillsdale, N. J.: Lawrence Erlbaum Associates.

Armstrong, K. L., Fraser, J. A., Dadds, M. R., & Morris, J. (1999). A randomized, controlled trial of nurse home visiting to vulnerable families with newborns. *Journal of Paediatric Child Health*, 35, 237–44.

Atkinson, L., Niccols, A., Paglia, A., Coolbear, J., Parker, K. C. H., Poulton, L., Guger, S., & Sitarenios, G. (2000). A meta-analysis of time between maternal sensitivity and attachment assessments: Implications for internal working models in infancy/toddlerhood. *Journal of Social and Personal Relationships*, 17, 791–810.

Bakermans-Kranenburg, M. J., Juffer, F., & van IJzendoorn, M. H. (1998). Interventions with video feedback and attachment discussions: Does type of maternal insecurity make a difference? *Infant Mental Health Journal*, 19, 202–19.

Bakermans-Kranenburg, M. J., van IJzendoorn, M. H., & Juffer, F. (2003). Less is more: Meta-analyses of sensitivity and attachment interventions in early childhood. *Psychological Bulletin*, 129, 195–215.

Barnard, K. E., Magyary, D., Summer, G., Booth, C. L., Mitchell, S. K., & Spieker, S. (1988). Prevention of parenting alterations for women with low social support. *Psychiatry*, 51, 248–53.

Barnett, B., Blignault, I., Holmes, S., Payne, A., & Parker, G. (1987). Quality of attachment in a sample of 1-year-old Australian children. *Journal of the American Academy of Child and Adolescent Psychiatry*, 26, 303–7.

Barrera, M. E., Rosenbaum, P. L., & Cunningham, C. E. (1986). Early home intervention with low-birth-weight infants and their parents. *Child Development*, 57, 20–33.

Beckwith, L. (1988). Intervention with disadvantaged parents of sick preterm infants. *Psychiatry*, *51*, 242–7.

Beckwith, L. (2000). Prevention science and prevention programs. In Ch. H. Zeanah (ed.), *Handbook of infant mental health* (2nd edn., pp. 439–56). New York: Guilford.

Benasich, A. A., Brooks-Gunn, J., & Clewell, B. C. (1992). How do mothers benefit from early intervention programs? *Journal of Applied Developmental Psychology*, *13*, 363–76.

Black, M. M. & Teti, L. O. (1997). Promoting mealtime communication between adolescent mothers and their infants through videotape. *Pediatrics*, *99*, 432–7.

Bowlby, J. (1982). *Attachment and loss*, vol. 1: *Attachment* (2nd edn.). New York: Basic Books.

Bowlby, J. (1988). *A secure base: Clinical applications of attachment theory*. London: Routledge.

Bradley, R. H. (1993). Children's home environments, health, behavior, and intervention efforts: A review using the HOME inventory as a marker measure. *Genetic, Social, and General Psychology Monographs*, *119*, 439–90.

Bradley, R. H., Whiteside, L., Mundfrom, D. J., Casey, P. H., Kelleher, K. J., & Pope, S. K. (1994). Contribution of early intervention and early caregiving experiences to resilience in low-birthweight, premature children living in poverty. *Journal of Clinical Child Psychology*, *23*, 425–34.

Brinich, E., Drotar, D., & Brinich, P. (1989). Security of attachment and outcome of preschoolers with histories of nonorganic failure to thrive. *Journal of Clinical Child Psychology*, *18*, 142–52.

Bronfenbrenner, U. (1974). Is early intervention effective? *Teachers College Record*, *76*, 279–303.

Brophy, H. E. (1997). Adolescent mothers and their infants: A home-based crisis prevention effort. *Dissertation Abstracts International*, *58*, 3309.

Bustan, D. & Sagi, A. (1984). Effects of early hospital-based intervention on mothers and their preterm infants. *Journal of Applied Developmental Psychology*, *5*, 305–17.

Caldwell, B. M., & Bradley, R. H. (1984). *Home observation for measurement of the environment*. Little Rock, AR: University of Arkansas at Little Rock.

Carter, S. L., Osofsky, J. D., & Hann, D. M. (1991). Speaking for the baby: A therapeutic intervention with adolescent mothers and their infants. *Infant Mental Health Journal*, *12*, 291–301.

Cicchetti, D., Toth, S. L., & Rogosch, F. A. (1999). The efficacy of toddler–parent psychotherapy to increase attachment security in offspring of depressed mothers. *Attachment and Human Development*, *1*, 34–66.

Cohen, N. J., Muir, E., Parker, C. J., Brown, M., Lojkasek, M., Muir, R., & Barwick, M. (1999). Watch, Wait, and Wonder: Testing the effectiveness of a new approach to mother–infant psychotherapy. *Infant Mental Health Journal*, *20*, 429–51.

Cooper, P. J. & Murray, L. (1997). The impact of psychological treatments of postpartum depression on maternal mood and infant development. In L. Murray & P. J. Cooper, *Postpartum depression and child development* (pp. 201–61). New York: Guilford.

Cowan, C. P. & Cowan, P. A. (1987). A preventive intervention for couples becoming parents. In C. F. Z. Boukydis (ed.), *Research on support for parents and infants in the postnatal period* (pp. 225–51). Norwood, NJ: Ablex.

Crnic, K. A. & Greenberg, M. T. (1987). Maternal stress, social support, and coping: Influences on the early mother–infant relationship. In C. F. Z. Boukydis (ed.), *Research on support for parents and infants in the postnatal period* (pp. 25–40). Norwood, NJ: Ablex.

Crnic, K. A., Greenberg, M. T., Ragozin, A. S., Robinson, N. M., & Basham, R. B. (1983). Effects of stress and social support on mothers and premature and full-term infants. *Child Development*, *54*, 209–17.

Crockenberg, S. B. (1981). Infant irritability, mother responsiveness, and social influences on the security of infant–mother attachment. *Child Development*, *52*, 857–65.

Das Eiden, R. & Reifman, A. (1996). Effects of Brazelton demonstrations on later parenting: A meta-analysis. *Journal of Pediatric Psychology, 21*, 857–68.

De Wolff, M. S. & van IJzendoorn, M. H. (1997). Sensitivity and attachment: A meta-analysis on parental antecedents of infant attachment. *Child Development, 68*, 571–91.

Dickie, J. R. & Gerber, S. C. (1980). Training in social competence: The effect on mothers, fathers, and infants. *Child Development, 51*, 1248–51.

Egeland, B. & Erickson, M. F. (1993). Attachment theory and findings: Implications for prevention and intervention. In S. Kramer & H. Parens (eds.), *Prevention in mental health: Now, tomorrow, ever?* (pp. 21–50). Northvale, NJ: Jason Aronson, Inc.

Egeland, B., Erickson, M. F., Clemenhagen-Moon, J., Hiester, M. K., & Korfmacher, J. (1990). *24 months tools coding manual: Project STEEP revised 1990 from mother–child project scales.* Minneapolis: University of Minnesota (manuscript).

Egeland, B., Weinfield, N. S., Bosquet, M., & Cheng, V. K. (2000). Remembering, repeating, and working through: Lessons from attachment-based interventions. In J. D. Osofsky & H. E. Fitzgerald (eds.), *Handbook of infant mental health*, vol. 4: *Infant mental health in groups at high risk* (pp. 35–89). World Association for Infant Mental Health. New York: John Wiley.

Elicker, J., Englund, M., & Sroufe, L. A. (1992). Predicting peer competence and peer relationships in childhood from early parent–child relationships. In R. Parke & G. Ladd (eds.), *Family–peer relationships: Modes of linkage* (pp. 77–106). Hillsdale, NJ: Lawrence Erlbaum Associates.

Epstein, H. T. (2001). An outline of the role of brain in human cognitive development. *Brain and cognition, 45*, 44–51.

Erickson, M. F., Sroufe, L. A., & Egeland, B. (1985). The relationship between quality of attachment and behavior problems in preschool in a high-risk sample. In I. Bretherton & E. Waters (eds.), *Growing points of attachment: Theory and research. Monographs of the Society for Research in Child Development, 50*, 147–66. Chicago, IL: University of Chicago Press.

Farran, D. C. (1990). Effects of intervention with disadvantaged and disabled children: A decade review. In J. P. Shonkoff & S. J. Meisels (eds.), *Handbook of early childhood intervention* (pp. 501–39). Cambridge: Cambridge University Press.

Farran, D. C. (2000). Another decade of intervention for children who are low income or disabled: What do we know now? In J. P. Shonkoff & S. J. Meisels (eds.), *Handbook of early childhood intervention* (2nd edn., pp. 510–48). Cambridge: Cambridge University Press.

Field, T. M., Widmayer, M., Stringer, S., & Ignatoff, E. (1980). Teenage, lower-class, black mothers and their preterm infants: An intervention and developmental follow-up. *Child Development, 51*, 426–36.

Field, T. M., Scafidi, F., Pickens, J., Prodromidis, M., Pelaez-Nogueras, M., Torquati, J., Wilcox, H., Malphurs, J., Schanberg, S., & Kuhn, C. (1998). Polydrug-using adolescent mothers and their infants receiving early intervention. *Adolescence, 33*, 117–43.

Fisher, P. A., Gunnar, M. R., Chamberlain, P., & Reid, J. B. (2000). Preventive intervention for maltreated preschool children: Impact on children's behavior, neuroendocrine activity, and foster parent functioning. *Journal of the American Academy of Child and Adolescent Psychiatry, 39*, 1356–64.

Fraiberg, S., Adelson, E., & Shapiro, V. (1975). Ghosts in the nursery: A psychoanalytic approach to the problems of impaired infant–mother relationships. *Journal of the American Academy of Child Psychiatry, 14*, 387–422.

Gelfand, D. M., Teti, D. M., Seiner, S. A., & Jameson, P. B. (1996). Helping mothers fight depression: Evaluation of a home-based intervention program for depressed mothers and their infants. *Journal of Clinical Child Psychology, 25*, 406–22.

George, C., Kaplan, N., & Main, M. (1985). *Adult attachment interview.* Berkeley, CA: University of California (unpublished manuscript).

Goldsmith, H. H. & Alansky, J. A. (1987). Maternal and infant predictors of attachment: A meta-analytic review. *Journal of Consulting and Clinical Psychology, 55*, 805–16.

Gowen, J. W. & Nebrig, J. B. (1997). Infant–mother attachment at risk: How early intervention can help. *Infants and Young Children, 9(4)*, 62–78.

Guralnick, M. (ed.) (1997). *The effectiveness of early intervention.* Baltimore, MD: Paul H. Brookes.

Heinicke, C. M., Beckwith, L., & Thompson, A. (1988). Early intervention in the family system: A framework and review. *Infant Mental Health Journal, 9*, 111–41.

Heinicke, C. M., Fineman, N. R., Ruth, G., Recchia, S. L., Guthrie, D., & Rodning, C. (1999). Relationship-based intervention with at-risk mothers: Outcome in the first year of life. *Infant Mental Health Journal, 20*, 349–74.

Hertzman, C. & Wiens, M. (1996). Child development and long-term outcomes: A population health perspective and summary of successful interventions. *Social Science and Medicine, 43*, 1083–95.

Hesse, E. (1999). The Adult Attachment Interview: Historical and current perspectives. In J. Cassidy & P. Shaver (eds.), *Handbook of attachment: Theory, research and clinical applications* (pp. 395–433). New York: Guilford.

Juffer, F. (1993). Verbonden door adoptie. Een experimenteel onderzoek naar hechting en competentie in gezinnen met een adoptiebaby [Attached through adoption: An experimental study on attachment and competence in families with an adopted baby]. Utrecht, The Netherlands: Utrecht University (dissertation).

Juffer, F., van IJzendoorn, M. H., & Bakermans-Kranenburg, M. J. (1997). Intervention in transmission of insecure attachment: A case study. *Psychological Reports, 80*, 531–43.

Juffer, F., Hoksbergen, R. A. C., Riksen-Walraven, J. M. A., & Kohnstamm, G. A. (1997). Early intervention in adoptive families: Supporting maternal sensitive responsiveness, infant–mother attachment, and infant competence. *Journal of Child Psychology and Psychiatry, 38*, 1039–50.

Kang, R., Barnard, K., Hammond, M., Oshio, S., Spencer, C., Thibodeaux, B., & Williams, J. (1995). Preterm infant follow-up project: A multi-site field experiment of hospital and home intervention programs for mothers and preterm infants. *Public Health Nursing, 12*, 171–80.

Klebanov, P. K., Brooks-Gunn, J., & McCormick, M. C. (2001). Maternal coping strategies and emotional distress: Results of an early intervention program for low birth weight young children. *Developmental Psychology, 37*, 654–67.

Krupka, A. (1995). The quality of mother–infant interactions in families at risk for maladaptive parenting. London, Ontario: University of Western Ontario (dissertation).

Lafreniere, P. J. & Capuano, F. (1997). Preventive intervention as means of clarifying direction of effects in socialization: Anxious-withdrawn preschoolers case. *Development and Psychopathology, 9*, 551–64.

Lagerberg, D. (2000). Secondary prevention in child health: Effects of psychological intervention, particularly home visitation, on children's development and other outcome variables. *Acta Paediatric Supplements, 434*, 43–52.

Lambermon, M. W. E. & van IJzendoorn, M. H. (1989). Influencing mother–infant interaction through videotaped or written instruction: Evaluation of a parent education program. *Early Childhood Research Quarterly, 4*, 449–58.

Leitch, D. B. (1999). Mother–infant interaction: Achieving synchrony. *Nursing Research, 48(1)*, 55–8.

Letourneau, N. (2000). Promoting optimal parent–infant interactions with keys to caregiving. *NCAST National News, 16(3)*, 1–6.

Lewis, M., Feiring, C., McGuffog, C., & Jaskir, J. (1984). Predicting psychopathology in six-year-olds from early social relations. *Child Development, 55,* 123–36.

Lieberman, A. F., Weston, D. R., & Pawl, J. H. (1991). Preventive intervention and outcome with anxiously attached dyads. *Child Development, 62,* 199–209.

Lojkasek, M., Cohen, N., & Muir, E. (1994). Where is the infant in infant intervention? A review of the literature on changing troubled mother–infant relationships. *Psychotherapy, 31,* 208–20.

Luster, T., Perlstadt, H., McKinney, M., Sims, K., & Juang, L. (1996). The effects of a family support program and other factors on the home environment provided by adolescent mothers. *Family Relations, 45,* 255–64.

MacLeod, J. & Nelson, G. (2000). Programs for the promotion of family wellness and the prevention of child maltreatment: A meta-analytic review. *Child Abuse and Neglect, 24,* 1127–49.

Mahoney, G. & Powell, A. (1988). Modifying parent–child interaction: Enhancing the development of handicapped children. *Journal of Special Education, 22,* 82–96.

Main, M. & Goldwyn, R. (in press). Adult attachment scoring and classification systems. In M. Main (ed.), *Assessing attachment through discourse, drawings, and reunion situations (working title).* New York: Cambridge University Press.

Main, M., Kaplan, S., & Cassidy, J. (1985). Security in infancy, childhood, and adulthood: A move to the level of representation. *Monographs of the Society for Research in Child Development, 50,* 66–104.

Marvin, R., Cooper, G., Hoffman, K., & Powell, B. (2002). The circle of security project: Attachment-based intervention with caregiver-preschool child dyads. *Attachment and Human Development, 4,* 107–24.

McDonough, S. (1993). Interaction guidance: Understanding and treating early infant–caregiver relationship disturbances. In C. H. Zeanah (ed.), *Handbook of infant mental health* (pp. 414–26). New York: Guilford.

Meij, J. Th. (1992). Sociale ondersteuning, gehechtheidskwaliteit en vroegkinderlijke competentie-ontwikkeling [Social support, attachment, and early competence]. Nijmegen, The Netherlands: Catholic University (dissertation).

Metzl, M. N. (1980). Teaching parents a strategy for enhancing infant development. *Child Development, 51,* 583–6.

Meyer, E. C., Coll, C. T. G., Lester, B. M., Boukydis, C. F. Z., McDonough, S. M., and Oh, W. (1994). Family-based intervention improves maternal psychological well-being and feeding interaction of preterm infants. *Pediatrics, 93,* 241–6.

Moran, G., Pederson, D. R., Krupka, A., & Avison, W. R. (2000, July). Promoting resilience through secure attachment: A brief intervention for adolescent mothers and their infants. Poster presented at the ICIS conference, Brighton, UK.

Mullen, B. (1989). *Advanced basic meta-analysis.* Hillsdale, NJ: Lawrence Erlbaum Associates.

Osofsky, J. D., Culp, A. M., & Ware, L. M. (1988). Intervention challenges with adolescent mothers and their infants. *Psychiatry, 51,* 236–41.

Palti, H., Otrakul, A., Belmaker, E., Tamir, D., & Tepper, D. (1984). Children's home environments: Comparison of a group exposed to a stimulation intervention program with controls. *Early Child Development and Care, 13,* 193–212.

Pearson, J. L., Cohn, D. A., & Cowan, P. A. (1994). Earned-security and continuous-security in adult attachment: Relation to depressive symptomatology and parenting style. *Developmental Psychopathology, 6,* 359–73.

Raine, A., Venables, P. H., Dalais, C., Mellingen, K., Reynolds, C., & Mednick, S. A. (2001). Early educational and health enrichment at age 3–5 years is associated with increased autonomic and central nervous system arousal and orienting at age 11 years: Evidence from the Mauritius Child Health Project. *Psychophysiology, 38,* 254–66.

Riksen-Walraven, J. M. A. (1978). Effects of caregiver behavior on habituation rate and self-efficacy in infants. *International Journal of Behavioral Development, 1,* 105–30.

Riksen-Walraven, J. M. A. & van Aken, M. A. G. (1997). Effects of two mother–infant intervention programs upon children's development at 7, 10, and 12 years. In W. Koops, J. B. Hoeksma, & D. C. van den Boom (eds.), *Development of interaction and attachment: Traditional and non-traditional approaches* (pp. 79–91). Amsterdam: North-Holland.

Riksen-Walraven, J. M. A., Meij, J. Th., Hubbard, F. O., & Zevalkink, J. (1996). Intervention in lower-class Surinam-Dutch families: Effects on mothers and infants. *International Journal of Behavioral Development, 19,* 739–56.

Robert-Tissot, C., Cramer, B., Stern, D. N., Serpa, S. R., Bachmann, J. P., Palacio-Espasa, F., Knauer, D., de Muralt, M., Berney, C., & Mendiguren, G. (1996). Outcome evaluation in brief mother–infant psychotherapies: Report on 75 cases. *Infant Mental Health Journal, 17,* 97–114.

Rosenboom, L. G. (1994). Gemengde gezinnen, gemengde gevoelens? Hechting en competentie van adoptiebaby's in gezinnen met biologisch eigen kinderen [Mixed families, mixed feelings? Attachment and competence of adopted infants in families with biological children]. Utrecht, The Netherlands: Utrecht University (dissertation).

Ross, G. S. (1984). Home intervention for premature infants of low-income families. *American Journal of Orthopsychiatry, 54,* 263–70.

Scholz, K. & Samuels, C. A. (1992). Neonatal bathing and massage intervention with fathers, behavioral effects 12 weeks after birth of the first baby: The Sunraysia Australia intervention project. *International Journal of Behavioral Development, 15,* 67–81.

Seifer, R., Clark, G. N., & Sameroff, A. J. (1991). Positive effects of interaction coaching on infants with developmental disabilities and their mothers. *American Journal on Mental Retardation, 96,* 1–11.

Seitz, V. & Apfel, N. H. (1994). Parent-focused intervention: Diffusion effects on siblings. *Child Development, 65,* 677–83.

Spiker, D., Ferguson, J., & Brooks-Gunn, J. (1993). Enhancing maternal interactive behavior and child social competence in low birth weight, premature children. *Child Development, 64,* 754–68.

Stams, G. J. J. M., Juffer, F., & van IJzendoorn, M. H. (2002). Maternal sensitivity, infant attachment, and temperament predict adjustment in middle childhood: The case of adopted children and their biologically unrelated parents. *Developmental Psychology, 38,* 806–21.

Stams, G. J. J. M., Juffer, F., van IJzendoorn, M. H., & Hoksbergen, R. A. C. (2001). Attachment-based intervention in adoptive families in infancy and children's development at age seven: Two follow-up studies. *British Journal of Developmental Psychology, 19,* 159–80.

van den Boom, D. C. (1994). The influence of temperament and mothering on attachment and exploration: An experimental manipulation of sensitive responsiveness among lower-class mothers with irritable infants. *Child Development, 65,* 1457–77.

van IJzendoorn, M. H. (1995). Adult attachment representations, parental responsiveness, and infant attachment: A meta-analysis on the predictive validity of the Adult Attachment Interview. *Psychological Bulletin, 117,* 387–403.

van IJzendoorn, M. H. & Bakermans-Kranenburg, M. J. (2002). Disorganized attachment and the dysregulation of negative emotions. In B. Zuckerman, A. Lieberman, & N. Fox (eds.), *Socioemotional regulation: Dimensions, developmental trends and influences* (pp. 159–81). New York: Johnson & Johnson Pediatric Institute.

van IJzendoorn, M. H., Juffer, F., & Duyvesteyn, M. G. C. (1995). Breaking the intergenerational cycle of insecure attachment: A review of the effects of attachment-based interventions on maternal sensitivity and infant security. *Journal of Child Psychology and Psychiatry, 36*, 225–48.

Weiner, A., Kuppermintz, H., & Guttmann, D. (1994). Video home training (the Orion project): A short-term preventive and treatment intervention for families with young children. *Family Process, 33*, 441–53.

Weinfield, N. S., Sroufe, L. A., Egeland, B., & Carlson, E. A. (1999). The nature of individual differences in infant–caregiver attachment. In J. Cassidy & P. R. Shaver (eds.), *Handbook of attachment: Theory, research, and clinical applications* (pp. 68–88). New York: Guilford.

Wijnroks, L. (1994). Dimensions of mother–infant interaction and the development of social and cognitive competence in preterm infants. Groningen, The Netherlands: University of Groningen (dissertation).

Ziegenhain, U., Wijnroks, L., Derksen, B., & Dreisörner, R. (1999). Entwicklungspsychologische Beratung bei jugendlichen Müttern und ihren Säuglingen: Chancen früher Förderung der Resilienz [Psychological counseling for adolescent mothers and their infants: chances for early promotion of resilience]. In G. Opp & A. Freytag (eds.), *Von den Stärken der Kinder: Erziehung zwischen Risiko und Resilienz* [*Competent children: Child-rearing between risk and resilience*]. Munich: Reinhardt.

Zigler, E. F. & Hall, N. W. (2000). *Child development and social policy: Theory and applications.* Boston, MA: McGraw-Hill.

CHAPTER TWELVE

Early Childhood Education: The Journey from Efficacy Research to Effective Practice

Craig T. Ramey and Sharon L. Ramey

During the past decade there has been a steady increase in scientific evidence that establishes the undeniable importance of the early years in human development (see Shonkoff, & Phillips, 2000). This evidence is particularly strong with respect to school readiness for children from families of limited education and low income (Ramey & Ramey, 1998). Language and literacy skills and their relation to other aspects of child development have been identified as key areas for further scientific concern and systematic policy formulation (Hart & Risley, 1995; Lyon, 2002).

A series of experimental trials using early childhood education, family support, and pediatric care has demonstrated that high-risk children can be prepared for initial success in school. When this increased school readiness is coupled with adequate school programs the initial positive effects persist into adolescence and adulthood. The magnitude of the effects produced by various preschool interventions is systematically related to characteristics of the preschool programs themselves (Ramey & Ramey, 1998a). Important program characteristics include (1) having a well-specified curriculum, (2) having programs of a half-day or longer, (3) beginning early in the child's life and developing a strong communication pattern between adults and children, and (4) focusing on cognitive development as well as linguistic and social competence.

The purpose of this chapter is to highlight specific findings from several of our preschool programs and to advocate a new type and level of inquiry to make successful programs available to all children who need them. What is needed from the research community is a shift in the central question being asked in contemporary early childhood education research. We need to realize that the old question of whether the development of high-risk children *can* be positively changed has been answered with a resounding "yes." We must now move on to more refined questions concerning the relative influence of different types of programs including practical questions concerning age of onset, intensity, and duration of treatment, as well as the effects of various specific educational curricula. During this transition we need to study and to improve, where needed, the existing early childhood programs.

We need to develop new partnerships of scientists and educators to improve the quality of existing preschool educational programs. If significant progress is made in the availability of high-quality preschool programs we believe that these improvements will affect not only children and parents who are disadvantaged, but the taxpayers who support their education. It is our belief that high quality early childhood education and rigorous science is a powerful combination that can provide benefits to our whole society.

Now for some specific results which have led us to this point of view.

Each year hundreds of thousands of children enter kindergarten unprepared to meet the intellectual demands of school (Carnegie Report, 1995). Lack of cognitive readiness bodes ill for future school performance. Poor school readiness predicts increased likelihood of low levels of academic achievement and high levels of retention in grade, special education placement, and ultimately school dropout. In turn, school dropouts are at much elevated risk for unemployment, teen pregnancy, juvenile delinquency, social dependency, and poor parenting practices. These patterns are repeated intergenerationally (Carnegie Report, 1995).

Poor school performance is foreshadowed by subaverage performance on cognitive, linguistic, and social functioning during the years prior to kindergarten.

Remedial special education to improve cognitive development and academic achievement that is begun in the elementary school years faces an enormous challenge. In essence, for special education to be effective, the base rate of cognitive development must be altered if the progressive gap between normal and subaverage cognitive development is to be arrested and intellectual development is to be established at normative trajectories. If genuine *catch-up* is to occur, the rate of development during treatment must actually exceed the normative rate. Thus, the shorter the period of remedial intervention, the more powerful it must be. This point is illustrated in Figure 12.1.

Unfortunately, little is known about how to accelerate cognitive development beyond normative or typical rates. Thus, the initial hopes and expectations for remedially oriented special education often go unmet.

A policy alternative to remedial or typical special education is primary prevention. Primary prevention entails the identification of high-risk individuals in the general population and the provision of the hypothesized missing essential experiences for normative development.

A large body of observational research suggests that children who evidence delayed cognitive development have insufficient frequency of exposure to particular adult–child transactional experiences (e.g., Bradley et al, 1989; Huttenlocher et al., 1991; Ramey & Ramey, 2000). These transactional experiences are particularly lacking in some low socioeconomic status families and are reliably missing beginning in the second year of life and sometimes earlier. (Yeates et al., 1983; Huttenlocher et al., 1991). These transactional experiences have been summarized by Ramey and Ramey (1992) and are presented

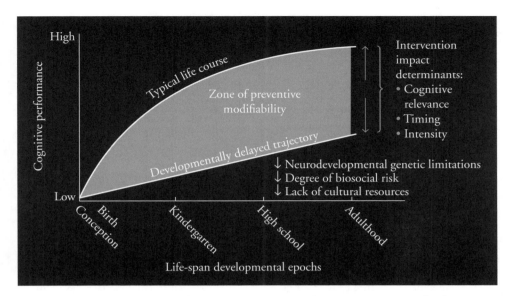

Figure 12.1 Hypothetical range of reaction for experience-driven cognitive neurodevelopment. (From Ramey & Ramey (1998). Copyright 1998 by the American Psychological Association. Adapted with permission.)

in Table 12.1. These *developmental priming mechanisms* are part of a theoretical framework derived from general systems theory and applied to two-generational early intervention programs by Ramey et al. (1995). Insufficient exposure to these developmental priming mechanisms is hypothesized to negatively affect developmentally appropriate cortical neuronal connections and synaptic efficiency associated with cognitive, linguistic, and social development. In turn these changes are hypothesized to be reflected in summative performance on norm-referenced measures of cognitive, linguistic, and social competence.

To test the hypothesis that provision of these theoretically critical experiences can potentially prevent progressive cognitive delay we have conducted two single-site randomized trials and one multisite randomized controlled trial with high-risk children and their families. These projects and their cognitive outcomes are the focus of the remainder of this chapter.

The Early Intervention Programs

Certain programmatic commonalities run throughout the Abecedarian Project (Ramey & Campbell, 1992), Project CARE (Ramey et al., 1985), and the Infant Health and Development Program (IHDP; Ramey et al., 1992). These early childhood education programs were multidisciplinary, intergenerational, individualized for children and their families, contextually embedded in local service delivery systems, research-oriented, and organized around key concepts underpinning randomized controlled trials.

Table 12.1   Developmental priming mechanisms

---

1. Encouragement of exploration
To be encouraged by adults to explore and to gather information about their environments
2. Mentoring in basic skills
To be mentored (especially by trusted adults) in basic cognitive skills, such as labeling, sorting, sequencing, comparing, and noting means–ends relationships
3. Celebration of developmental advances
To have their developmental accomplishments celebrated and reinforced by others, especially those with whom they spend a lot of time
4. Guided rehearsal and extension of new skills
To have responsible others help them in rehearsing and then elaborating upon (extending) their newly acquired skills
5. Protection from inappropriate disapproval, teasing, or punishment
To avoid negative experiences associated with adults' disapproval, teasing, or punishment for those behaviors that are normative and necessary in children's trial-and-error learning about their environments (e.g., mistakes in trying out a new skill, unintended consequences of curious exploration or information seeking). Note: this does not mean that constructive criticism and negative consequences cannot be used for other child behaviors which children have the ability to understand are socially unacceptable
6. A rich and responsive language environment
To have adults provide a predictable and comprehensible communication environment, in which language is used to convey information, provide social rewards, and encourage learning of new materials and skills. Note: although language to the child is the most important early influence, the language environment may be supplemented in valuable ways by the use of written materials
7. Guidance and limitation
To have adults keep children safe and to teach what is acceptable, and what is not – the rules of being a cooperative, responsive, and caring person.

The research design and associated key concepts that have guided our efforts have derived from the evolving literature on randomized controlled trials concerned with efficacy of treatments. That is, can a given program work under nearly idealized research conditions? Guiding concepts for our efficacy trials worthy of special mention include:

1   recruitment from prespecified populations to enhance generality of findings;
2   random assignment to treatment and control groups to establish initial group equivalence;
3   application and documentation of receipt of a replicable compound of services including specific educational curricula;
4   minimization of attrition to prevent biased estimates of treatment effects;
5   independent assessment of outcomes by observers masked to treatment conditions of participants;
6   preplanned statistical analyses of hypothesized outcomes with adequate sample sizes for appropriate statistical power to detect statistically and practically meaningful group differences;

7   replication of key findings in independent samples of children and families;
8   publication of findings in peer-reviewed journals;
9   dissemination of findings to key policy makers and the general public after publication in peer-reviewed journals.

Participants and Programs

The first two projects (The Abecedarian Project ($N = 111$ children) and Project CARE ($N = 63$ children) were single-site randomized controlled trials which enrolled children at birth who were biologically healthy but who came from very poor and undereducated families. For example, the mean maternal education in both projects was approximately 10 years of schooling. Approximately 75 percent of the mothers were unmarried. Control group families (sometimes referred to as follow-up families) were not a totally untreated group, however. Rather, those children received pediatric follow-up services on a schedule recommended by the American Academy of Pediatrics. In addition the children were provided unlimited iron fortified formula. Families of control group children also received social work services and home visits. These sources were provided due to ethical and research concerns. Their provision, we should note, makes the demonstration of group differences less likely due to their presumed positive influence on the control group children and families.

The early intervention groups received the same services just mentioned for the control groups plus they received an Early Childhood Education Program known as Partners for Learning (Sparling, Lewis, & Ramey, 1995) within the context of a specially developed Child Development Center. This Center admitted children after 6 weeks of age and maintained low child/teacher ratios (e.g., 3:1 for children <1 year; 4:1 for children between 1 and 3 years) and an ongoing inservice curriculum training and technical assistance program for teachers. Parent involvement was facilitated by home visits and parent groups. A fuller description of the preschool program can be found in articles by Ramey and Campbell (1992) and Ramey and Ramey (1998a). In general, program features in the Abecedarian and CARE projects foreshadowed those that are now recommended by the National Association for the Education of Young Children.

Partners for Learning can be described as an educational curriculum that is concerned with 31 child development areas and consistently oriented toward adult–child transactions involving well-formed and conversational language about topics of everyday interest to young children (McGinness & Ramey, 1981; Ramey et al., 1981). *Partners for Learning* acts both as a child program resource and as a staff development resource and provides a means to individualize the educational program for each child.

The IHDP ($N = 985$) was a slightly modified version of that program used in the Abecedarian and CARE projects. Modifications included establishing the program as an eight-site randomized controlled trial, and limiting enrollment to infants who were born at <2,500 grams and <37 weeks gestational age. Thus all child participants were to varying degrees of low birthweight and prematurity. Weekly home visits were the main early intervention component until children were 12 months of age (corrected for prematurity). At 12 months of age children began attending Child Development Centers that were replicas of the one used for the Abecedarian and CARE projects. Fuller descriptions of the IHDP can be found in Infant Health and Development Program (1990) and Ramey et al. (1992).

Cognitive Results from these Early Education Programs

Figure 12.2 shows Bayley Mental Development Index (MDIs) scores and Stanford-Binet (S-B) IQ scores by age and treatment conditions during the first 3 years of life for both the Abecedarian project (Figure 12.2a) and Project CARE (Figure 12.2b). The top of the gray area represents the mean performance on the control group's cognitive assessments at the ages identified on the horizontal axis while the top of the black area represents the mean performance of the early childhood education group. Thus, the amount of black represents the cognitive value added due to the influence of the early childhood education. In both of these graphs there is a divergence of the curves favoring the early intervention groups over the control groups during the first 18 months. Consistent with the random assignment of children to treatment and control conditions, a strong causal inference is justified concerning the preventive power of the early educational curriculum. By 36 months the mean IQ scores in the Abecedarian Project were 101 and 84 for the early education and control groups, respectively (Ramey & Campbell, 1984). In Project Care the comparable 36-month scores were 105 and 93 (Ramey et al., 1985).

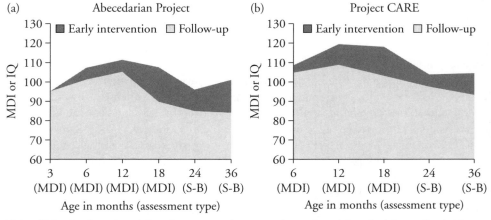

Figure 12.2   Bayley Mental Development Index scores (MDIs) and Stanford-Binet (S-B) IQ scores by age and treatment conditions during the first 3 years of life for (a) the Abecedarian project and (b) Project CARE.

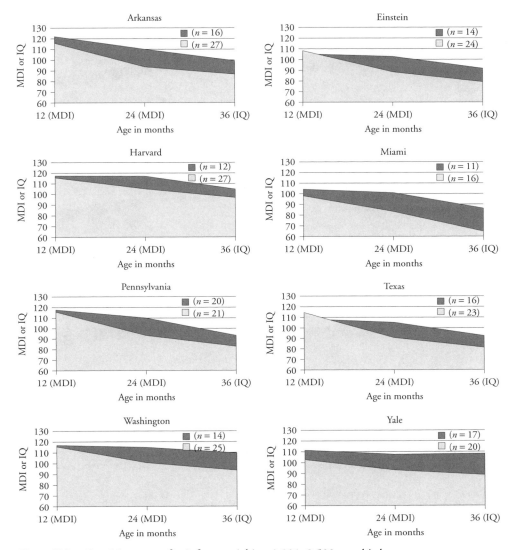

Figure 12.3 Cognitive scores for infants weighing 2,001–2,500 g at birth.

Figure 12.3 contains plots for the most comparable IHDP children to the Abecedarian and CARE children – those closest to full birthweight (2,001–2,500 grams) at each of the eight sites. These eight graphs all show similar divergence to 36 months with an overall mean difference of 13.2 IQ points favoring the early intervention groups at 36 months. Comparable plots (Figure 12.4) for the lighter low birthweight groups (<2,001 grams) reveal similar trends in seven of the eight comparisons (the Harvard site being the exception) but with a somewhat diminished magnitude of difference between the early intervention and control (follow-up) groups (overall mean difference = 6.6 IQ

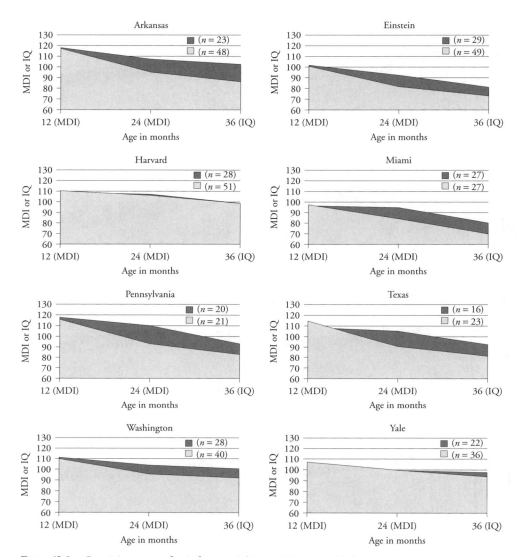

Figure 12.4 Cognitive scores for infants weighing <2,001 g at birth.

points at 36 months). Thus 17 of the 18 comparisons at 36 months across the Abecedarian, CARE, and IHDP projects support the hypothesis that intensive early intervention is associated with higher cognitive performance relative to randomized controls.

Figure 12.5 illustrates that children's cognitive performance at 36 months is positively related to mothers' education levels in the IHDP control group and that the positive effects of the early intervention are greater for the children of lesser educated mothers. That is, those children at greatest cognitive risk due to low family educational resources benefited the most. These were benefits in addition to the cognitive ones. These benefits are summarized in Table 12.2. The symbol "NS" means that the characteristic described

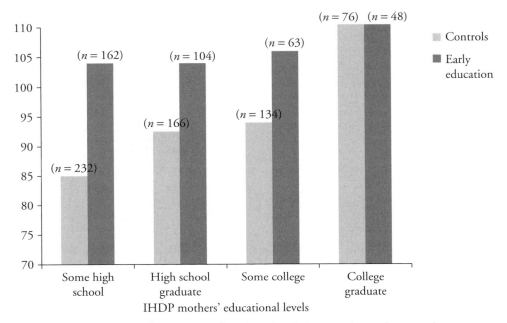

Figure 12.5 Cognitive performance as a function of early intervention and maternal educational level.

Table 12.2 Developmental outcomes affected positively by the Infant Health and Development Project

	Age in months		
	12	*24*	*36*
Cognitive development	NS	*	*
Adaptive and prosocial behavior	–	–	*
Behavior problems	–	*	*
Vocabulary	–	*	*
Receptive language	–	*	*
Reasoning	–	–	*
Home environment	NS	*	*
Maternal interactive behavior	–	–	*
Maternal problem solving	–	–	*

* = *p* < 0.01
– = Not measured
NS = Not significant
Source: Gross, Spiker, & Haynes (1997), *Helping Low Birth Weight, Premature Babies: The Infant Health and Development Program*. Stanford, CA: Stanford University Press

Table 12.3   Brief summary of Abecedarian results during preschool period

Positive effects on	*No effects on*
IQ performance	Maternal attachment
Learning and cognitive performance	Parental child rearing attitudes
Language development	Home environments
Resilience to non-optimal biological and behavioral conditions	
Social responsiveness	*Decreased effects*
Academic locus of control	Incidence of intellectual subnormality
Maternal education	
Maternal employment	

Source: Summarized from Ramey, MacPhee, & Yeates, 1982

was measured and the two groups were not significantly different by statistical test. The symbol "−" means that the characteristic was not measured at that age. The symbol "*" means that the characteristic was measured and in all instances, without exception, the differences favored the early childhood education group over the follow-up group. Thus, at 36 months of age the Early Childhood Education group had, on average, higher cognitive development across and showed more adaptive and prosocial behaviors. The educationally treated group also had fewer behavior problems, larger vocabularies, better receptive language, and better reasoning skills. Their home environments were rated as developmentally more supportive, their mothers interacted with them more in developmentally appropriate ways, and their mothers were better at solving everyday problems concerning childrearing. Thus, a comprehensive early childhood and family support program produced broad and positive developmental outcomes for both the child and family while it was in operation during the first three years of life, at which point it was terminated.

The Abecedarian and CARE Projects continued with the Early Childhood Educational Program until the children entered public kindergarten. The cognitive differences between the treated and control groups continued to persist at statistically significant levels (Burchinal et al., 1997). Table 12.3 presents a summary of results from the Abecedarian Project during the preschool period.

Similarly to the Infant Health and Development Program, the Abecedarian Program produced a broad array of positive effects both on participating children and their parents. It is noteworthy that in these programs and with other high-quality early education projects, so far, there have been no reports of negative side effects on the children, their families, or the attachment between children and families.

Follow-Up Results

The Infant Health and Development Program was terminated at age 3 and produced a somewhat disappointing pattern of cognitive results thereafter. Longitudinal analyses

Table 12.4   Summary of Abecedarian K-2 transition program

Individualized focus on academic and learning activities in school and at home
Emphasis on reading, mathematics, and writing
Master Home/School Resource Teachers (12 children and families per teacher)
Development of an individualized and documented supplemental curriculum for each child
Explicit attention and action relevant to family circumstances, as needed
Summer camps with academically relevant experiences

of these children's development showed that by 5 and 8 years of age, the overall IQ differences between the treatment and comparison groups decreased to such an extent that it was no longer educationally significant (Brooks-Gunn et al., 1994; McCarton et al., 1997). However, it is noteworthy that the *heavier* low birthweight children continued to have significantly higher IQ scores at age 5, and by age 8 the early intervention group scored 4.4 points higher than the comparison. The follow-up researchers involved in this study concluded that early cessation of services at age 3 was likely to have contributed to the loss of early benefits and that additional interventions are indicated for low birthweight infants to sustain earlier gains. In short, stopping intervention at age 3 for these highly vulnerable infants is not a good idea.

In the Abecedarian Project we decided to examine the effects of an additional educational treatment that we began at kindergarten entry and continued for the first 3 years of school. To address this issue we randomly divided each of the two preschool groups. One half of each group received an enriched educational program from kindergarten entry through second grade. This allowed a practical test of three major educational policy alternatives with respect to timing and duration of early intervention services. This allowed a practical test of three major educational policy alternatives with respect to timing and duration of early intervention services: early intervention only; early intervention followed by transition intervention; later intervention only.

Table 12.4 provides a brief summary of the services delivered during the school-age phase of the intervention. A fuller description of this aspect of the Abecedarian Project can be found in Ramey and Campbell (1992). In essence, the K-2 program was intensive, focused on home and school continuity, emphasized reading, math, and writing, and was conducted year around. Parents, teachers, and children participated enthusiastically.

The overall research design on the Abecedarian Project is presented in schematic form in Figure 12.6. At the end of the second grade a stair-step pattern of performance on reading and math was found that indicated a proportional response to the intensity of the treatment. This is illustrated for reading in Figure 12.7. The majority of the effect was captured, however, by whether the children had participated in the preschool program. The school-age program, by itself, was of marginal added value although it seems to have had a slight protective role for those children who had the preschool program.

Follow-up assessments of the Abecedarian children have now been completed at 8, 12, 15, and 21 years of age. With respect to standardized measures of intelligence, the differences between the treatment and comparison groups narrowed but continued to be statistically and educationally meaningful at approximately 5 IQ points. Perhaps more

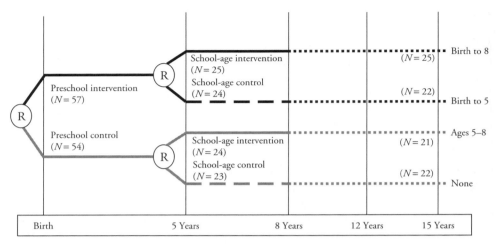

Figure 12.6   Two-phase design of Abecedarian Project.

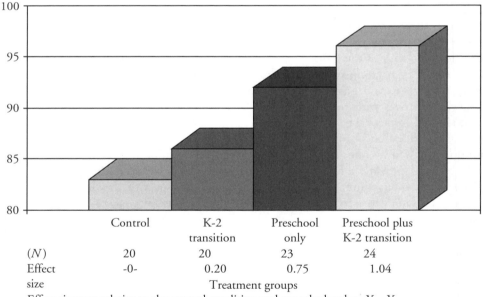

(N)   20   20   23   24
Effect   -0-   0.20   0.75   1.04
size   Treatment groups

Effect sizes are relative to the control condition and are calculated as $\bar{X} - \bar{X}$, where: $\bar{X}$ = mean, T = treatment condition, C = control condition, S.D. = standard deviation.

Figure 12.7   Abecedarian Project. Woodcock-Johnson age-referenced reading standard scores at age 8.

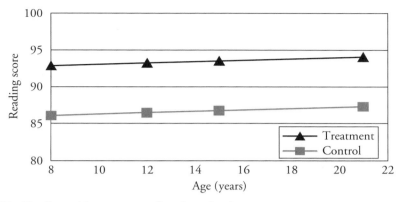

Figure 12.8 Reading achievement as a function of early treatment.

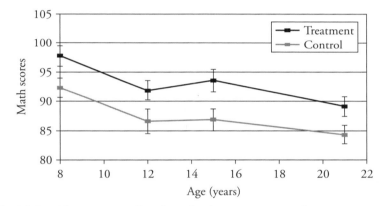

Figure 12.9 Math achievement as a function of early treatment over time.

germane to education, however, are the results from reading and math achievement assessments. At all ages from 8 to 21, the preschool treatment group had significantly higher academic achievement scores in both reading and mathematics. Figure 12.8 shows the results for reading performance for Abecedarian children and Figure 12.9 shows the math performance.

In the follow-up study at age 21 (Campbell et al., 2002) it was found that not only did the children in the preschool treatment group earn significantly higher scores on intellectual and academic measures as young adults but they were also more likely to have attained more years of total education, were three times more likely to attend a four-year college (12 percent versus 36 percent), and showed a reduction in teenaged births compared to preschool controls. An earlier follow-up at age 15 had demonstrated that they were 47 percent less likely to be retained in grade and 75 percent less likely to be placed in special education (Ramey et al., 2000). Thus, the cognitive benefits that began with a good preschool education better prepared these high-risk children to be ready to develop the reading and math skills that the schools were prepared to teach. In turn the children mastered these two gateway skills and, as a group, did better through-out school and into young adulthood. In short, risk for poor cognitive development was offset to a considerable degree by high-quality preschool education focused on cognitive development, conversational skills, and social competence.

Summary and Conclusions

These results, although somewhat larger in magnitude of positive effects, are consistent with earlier findings from the Consortium of Longitudinal Studies (Lazar & Darlington, 1982) and from other randomized trials of high-quality early childhood educational programs (see Ramey & Ramey, 1998b, for a detailed review). We think it plausible that the greater intensity and duration of our preschool component accounts for their larger effects when compared to less intensive preschool interventions. In summary, we believe that the efficacy question of whether early childhood education can have meaningful positive impact on at-risk children has been answered with a clear *yes*. The obvious question is, where do we go from here?

Based on the research evidence in hand we believe that four actions are timely and important.

First, our country should provide appropriate levels and types of early childhood programs to those children in greatest need of additional high-quality preschool education. To do this we need better population-based studies of risk and careful empirical research on the specific benefits of different educational practices and curricula.

Second, existing program standards need to be reviewed and upgraded where guide-lines are not consistent with scientific evidence for program effectiveness. We believe that this should be accompanied by high-quality teacher training and technical assistance to improve teacher knowledge and skills.

Third, we should create a nationwide network of model demonstration programs that have been certified as demonstrating exemplary high standards and practices.

Fourth, we should provide useful and appealing public information that is scientifically based on the importance of roles and activities of parents and teachers in the development of young children.

These four courses of action are ones that can begin immediately and that can reinforce one another in improving children's competence. The theoretical systems and technologies are available to facilitate high-quality and practical scientific inquiry. We can readily create the infrastructures to transfer the scientific knowledge to where it will be useful and to monitor its impact on children and families.

As our knowledge about the importance of early childhood cognitive development, literacy, and social competence increases so does our responsibility to act upon this knowledge to improve the conditions that can maximize positive child cognitive out-comes and social competence. We are confident that this can be done effectively and efficiently. If conducted well, we believe that our society, as a whole, will benefit by reducing the number of children who do not develop anywhere near their full potential.

References

Bradley, R. H., Caldwell, B. M., Rock, S. L., Ramey, C. T., Barnard, K. E., Gray, A., Hammond, M. A., Gottfried, A., Siegel, L. S., & Johnson, D. L. (1989). Home environment and cognitive development in the first 3 years of life: A collaborative study involving six sites and three ethnic groups in North America. *Developmental Psychology, 25*, 217–35.

Brooks-Gunn, J., McCarton, C. M., Casey, P. H., McCormick, M. C., Bauer, C. R., Bernbaum, J. C., Tyson, J., Swanson, M., Bennett, F. C., Scott, D. T., Tonascia, J., & Meinert, C. (1994). Early intervention in low-birth-weight premature infants: Results through age 5 years from the Infant Health and Development Program. *Journal of the American Medical Association, 272(16)*, 1257–62.

Burchinal, M. R., Campbell, F. A., Bryant, D. M., Wasik, B. H., & Ramey, C. T. (1997). Early intervention and mediating processes in cognitive performance of children of low-income African American families. *Child Development, 68*, 935–54.

Campbell, F. A., Ramey, C. T., Pungello, E., Sparling, J., & Miller-Johnson, S. (2002). Early childhood education: Outcomes as a function of different treatments. *Applied Developmental Science, 6*, 42–57.

Carnegie Report (1995). *Years of Promise: A Comprehensive Learning Strategy for America's Children.* New York: Carnegie Corporation.

Gross, R. T., Spiker, D., & Hayes, C. (eds.) (1997). *Helping Low Birth Weight, Premature Babies: The Infant Health and Development Program.* Stanford, CA: Stanford University Press.

Hart, B. & Risley, T. R. (1995). *Meaningful experiences in the everyday experiences of young American children.* Baltimore, MD: Paul H. Brookes.

Huttenlocher, J., Haight, W., Bryk, A., Seltzer, M., & Lyons, T. (1991). Early vocabulary growth: Relation to language input and gender. *Developmental Psychology, 27*, 236–48.

Infant Health and Development Program (1990). Enhancing the outcomes of low-birth-weight, premature infants. *Journal of the American Medical Association, 263*, 3035–42.

Lazar, I. & Darlington, R. (1982). Lasting effects of early education. *Monographs of the Society for Research in Child Development, 47* (serial no. 195) (2/3): 1–151.

Lyon, R. (2002). Cognition, reading and school readiness. Presentation at President's Summit on Cognitive Development, Georgetown University, Washington, DC.

McCarton, C. M., Brooks-Gunn, J., Wallace, I. F., Bauer, C. R., Bennett, F. C., Bernbaum, J. C., Broyles, R. S., Casey, P. H., McCormick, M. C., Scott, D. T., Tyson, J., Tonascia, J., & Meinert, C. L. (1997). Results at age 8 years of early intervention for low-birth-weight premature infants: The Infant Health and Development Program. *JAMA, 277*, 126–32.

McGinness, G. & Ramey, C. T. (1981). Developing sociolinguistic competence in children. *Canadian Journal of Early Childhood Education, 1*, 22–43.

Ramey, C. T. & Campbell, F. A. (1984). Preventive education for high-risk children: Cognitive consequences of the Carolina Abecedarian Project. *American Journal of Mental Deficiency, 88(5)*, 515–23.

Ramey, C. T. & Campbell, F. A. (1992). Poverty, early childhood education, and academic competence: The Abecedarian experiment. In A. Huston (ed.), *Children in poverty* (pp. 190–221). NY: Cambridge University Press.

Ramey, C. T. & Ramey, S. L. (1998a). Prevention of intellectual disabilities: Early interventions to improve cognitive development. *Preventive Medicine, 27*, 224–32.

Ramey, C. T. & Ramey, S. L. (1998b). Early intervention and early experience. *American Psychologist, 53*, 109–20.

Ramey, C. T., McGinness, G., Cross, L., Collier, A., & Barrie-Blackley, S. (1981). The Abecedarian approach to social competence: Cognitive and linguistic intervention for disadvantaged preschoolers. In K. Borman (ed.), *The social life of children in a changing society* (pp. 145–74). Hillsdale, NJ: Lawrence Erlbaum Associates.

Ramey, C. T., Bryant, D. M., Sparling, J. J., & Wasik, B. H. (1985). Project CARE: A comparison of two early intervention strategies to prevent retarded development. *Topics in Early Childhood Special Education, 5,* 12–25.

Ramey, C. T., Bryant, D. M., Wasik, B. H., Sparling, J. J., Fendt, K. H., & LaVange, L. M. (1992). Infant Health and Development Program for low birth weight, premature infants: Program elements, family participation, and child intelligence. *Pediatrics, 89,* 454–65.

Ramey, C. T., MacPhee, D., & Yeates, K. O. (1982). Preventing developmental retardation: A general systems model. In J. M. Joffee & L. A. Bond (eds.), *Facilitating infant and early childhood development* (pp. 343–401). Hanover, NH: University Press of New England.

Ramey, C. T., Ramey, S. L., Gaines, R., & Blair, C. (1995). Two-generation early interventions: A child development perspective. In I. Siegel (series ed.) & S. Smith (vol. ed.), *Two-generation programs: A new intervention strategy,* vol. 9: *Advances in applied developmental psychology* (pp. 199–228). Norwood, NJ: Ablex.

Ramey, C. T., Campbell, F. A., Burchinal, M., Skinner, M. L., Gardner, D. M., & Ramey, S. L. (2000). Persistent effects of early childhood education on high-risk children and their mothers. *Applied Developmental Science, 4,* 2–14.

Ramey, S. L. & Ramey, C. T. (1992). Early educational intervention with disadvantaged children – To what effect? *Applied and Preventive Psychology, 1,* 131–40.

Ramey, S. L. & Ramey, C. T. (2000). Early childhood experiences and developmental competence. In J. Waldfogel & S. Danziger (eds.), *Securing the future: Investing in children from birth to college* (pp.122–50). NY: Russell Sage Foundation.

Shonkoff, J. P. & Phillips, D. A. (2000). *From neurons to neighborhoods: The science of early childhood development.* Washington, DC: National Academy Press.

Sparling, J. J., Lewis, I., & Ramey, C. T. (1995). *Partners for learning: Birth to 36 months.* Lewisville, NC: Kaplan Press.

Yeates, K. O., MacPhee, D., Campbell, F. A., & Ramey, C. T. (1983). Maternal IQ and home environment as determinants of early childhood intellectual competence: Developmental analysis. *Developmental Psychology, 19,* 731–9.

CHAPTER THIRTEEN

Fostering Early Communication and Language Development

Steven F. Warren and Dale Walker

The central role of communication and language abilities to human social and cognitive functioning is abundantly clear when these abilities fail to develop as expected or are impaired due to accident, disease, heredity, teratogens, impoverished input or combinations of these or other risk factors. Communication and language problems originating during early childhood can have a ripple effect throughout development and have been frequently identified as contributing factors to later identified learning disabilities, behavior disorders, mental retardation, and school failure (Aram & Hall, 1989; Fey, Catts, & Larrivee, 1995; Kaiser & Hester, 1997; Walker et al., 1994). Delays and disorders of communication and language development account for over 70 percent of children aged 3–5 years identified with a disability (Wetherby & Prizant, 1992) and is the single most common reason for special education referral (Casby, 1989).

It is likely that as we move deeper into the "information age," the central role of communication and language abilities will further expand, at least in post-industrial societies. In societies that increasingly tie economic success with levels of literacy development, even relatively mild communication and language disorders may directly influence an individual's job prospects, social opportunities, and overall quality of life. Furthermore, children with severe communication disorders or mental retardation who fail to acquire effective communication skills may endure lives of undue dependency, and relative social isolation irrespective of whatever other abilities they possess.

In the face of these challenges, it is important to note the impressive achievements that have been steadily reported in our knowledge of both typical and atypical communication and language development, our ability to identify delays and disorders early in development, and our ability to foster and enhance optimal communication and language development. Within this context, the intent of this chapter is threefold. First, we describe the framework of a developmental model of communication and language intervention that is emerging in the research literature. Second, we discuss in more depth two promising areas of early intervention research: fostering prelinguistic communication development in very young children with developmental delays, and fostering language development in young children developmentally at risk due to impoverished environments. We conclude with a discussion of future research directions.

Research on methods to enhance the communication and language development of children has been ongoing since the early 1960s. Scores of studies have been conducted over this time period, the vast majority aimed at testing various procedures or intervention "packages" with relatively small numbers of children for very limited periods of time. This "technology building" period is receding and the framework of a developmental model for fostering early communication and language is emerging. This model supports the use of different approaches at different points in a child's development.

Premises of the Developmental Intervention Model

There are two basic premises of the developmental model of communication and language intervention. First, the rate and quality of language input that a child receives is viewed as crucially important to their optimal development. Second, the most effective intervention approach depends on the child's developmental level and the nature of the intervention goal. Each premise encapsulates much of what has been learned about early language development and intervention across three decades of research.

Rate and quality of language input matters

This premise is important because of the possibility that inadequate input might cause or contribute to language delay and, conversely, that enhanced input may foster development. Since the 1970s, proponents of the social interactionist perspective of language development (e.g., Bruner, 1975; Chapman, 2000; Gallaway & Richards, 1994; MacWhinney, 1999; Nelson, 1989; Snow, 1984; Tomasello, 1992) have been building the case that adults can play an important role in children's language acquisition. They have noted that from birth onward children are exposed to an ocean of language. Hour after waking hour, day after day, month after month, the child encounters the natural curriculum provided by exposure to his native language (Hart & Risley, 1999). Furthermore, the millions of words and sentences that children experience are not just undifferentiated noise. Much of this natural curriculum is specifically adjusted and fine tuned (Baumwell, Tamis-LeMonda, & Bornstein, 1997; Bruner, 1975; Sokolov, 1993) to the child's language comprehension level. A wide range of teaching devices have been detected in common use by adults, including expansions, models, contingent imitations, growth recasts, use of concrete, simplified vocabulary, slower rate of articulation, use of higher pitch and exaggerated intonation, a focus on objects and events to which the child is attending, etc. (Hart & Risley, 1999; Hoff-Ginsburg, 1986; Menyuk, 1988; Nelson, 1991; Snow, Perlmann, & Nathan, 1987; van Kleeck, 1994). Adjustments, termed "parentese" or "motherese" (i.e., simplified vocabulary, higher pitch), appear to aid the acquisition of linguistic and communicative competence. The rate at which adults talk to children (Huttenlocher et al., 1991; Hart & Risley, 1995; Wells, 1985), the rate at which children themselves talk (e.g., Hart & Risley, 1980, 1995; Nelson, 1973), and the responsiveness of parents to their child's communication attempts (Yoder & Warren, 1998, 1999a, 2001) have all been shown to correlate with faster acquisition of various components (e.g., vocabulary growth) of language acquisition.

Counter arguments have been put forth that language input is a relatively unimportant variable. These arguments have largely been based on the fact that most children ultimately acquire adult syntax irrespective of their circumstances or the nature of the input they received as children (Pinker, 1994). However, such arguments may miss the point, at least for children who are at risk for language delays, mental retardation, and developmental disabilities. There is evidence that input can affect the rate and quality of language development for both typically and atypically developing children. Moreover, development can be enhanced for at least some critical components of the language system (e.g., vocabulary) via modifications in input. Finally, optimal input may have a far greater effect on the ultimate language development of children at risk for developmental disabilities than on typically developing children (Landry et al., 1997; Snow, 1984). The issue from the perspective of language intervention researchers is not "does input matter?" but rather how can it be made to matter the most.

How input is provided matters too

The second premise is that the most effective form of intervention depends on the developmental level of the child as well as learning style and/or temperament issues in some cases (e.g., autism). Twenty-five years ago language intervention approaches were developed almost independent of any concern about how they might best match up to different phases in the child's development or different characteristics of the language skills to be mastered (e.g., pragmatics versus syntactic rules). However, as an increasing array of approaches and techniques have become available, families of techniques have emerged that vary along a small number of important dimensions. Some of the key variables include whether a procedure is based on "following the child's attentional lead," whether specific or general goals are targeted, whether elicited imitation prompts are used, whether growth recasts are used, etc. We will briefly review the support for three of the primary "families" of techniques that have emerged from the research. These are the responsive interaction approach, milieu teaching, and direct instruction. We have selected these intervention approaches because they differ from one another in theoretically important ways that exemplify how various approaches can have differential effectiveness at different points along the developmental continuum.

Responsive interaction Many terms are used to describe the responsive interaction approach in the literature, including the interactive model (Tannock, & Girolametto, 1992) and the conversational model (MacDonald, 1985). This approach is widely used in parent training throughout North America. Its major immediate goals are to increase the child's social communication skills and facilitate grammar by enhancing the quality of interaction between the adult and child. Interaction is usually initiated and controlled by the child. Adults follow the child's attentional lead and respond contingently to the child's behavior in a manner that is congruent with the child's immediate interest. Modeling, recasting, and expansions of the child's communication attempts are encouraged (Nelson, 1989), while the use of directives (e.g., elicited imitation, mands, testing questions) is discouraged because it is assumed that they will disrupt the flow of interaction and the child's attentional engagement (Harris et al., 1986). Thorough descriptions of the responsive interaction approach can be found in Nelson (1989) and Wilcox and Shannon (1998).

Responsive interaction approaches are particularly well suited for facilitating the acquisition of higher level morphological and syntactic skills that can be made salient through growth recasts (e.g. Baker & Nelson, 1984; Camarata, Nelson, & Camarata, 1994; Fey et al., 1993). A growth recast is a specific expansion or modification of a child's immediately preceding utterance in which new syntactic or semantic information is added. Theoretically, the temporal proximity and semantic overlap of the recast and the child's utterance aids the child in making comparisons between his own utterance and the recast. Such comparisons may make differences between the two utterances salient. If this comparison is made at a time when the child is "ready" to acquire the new semantic or grammatical structure (Nelson, 1989), or if the child notices this difference repeatedly in similar linguistic contexts (Camarata, 1995), the child should acquire the structure. Finally, responsive interaction approaches are relatively easy for parents and early childhood teachers to learn and can be used virtually anywhere and at any time.

Several recent studies have found that responsive interaction approaches are more effective than milieu teaching (discussed below) with children who have a mean length of utterance (MLU) above 2.5, but less effective than milieu teaching with children who have an MLU under 2.0 (the treatments are nonsignificantly different between MLU 2.0 and MLU 2.5) (Yoder et al., 1995). Children with MLUs above 2.5 likely have the attentional and memory resources necessary to efficiently learn from recasts that require them to compare their own utterance with the following adult utterance (Yoder et al., 1995).

The relative ineffectiveness of the responsive interaction approach below MLU 2.0 may be due to its prohibition on the use of elicited production prompts by adults (e.g., "say cup," "what's that?" etc.). These types of prompts may be a particularly powerful learning strategy at this point in development (Speidel & Nelson, 1989). Also, a growing body of literature demonstrates that the use of directives (as opposed to redirectives like "look here") in the context of joint-attention routines (interactions in which both the child and adult focus their attention on the same action or activity) aids learning and social engagement in both typically and atypically developing children (de Kruif et al., 2000; McCathren, Yoder, & Warren, 1995). Finally, test questions about the child's attentional focus (e.g., "what is that?" "what are you doing?") may aid children in verbally participating in activities while giving adults a window into the child's thoughts that allows them to construct teaching episodes about the child's focus of attention (Yoder et al., 1994).

Milieu teaching   Milieu approaches are characterized by the use of dispersed teaching episodes that are embedded in ongoing activities and interactions. The term "milieu" means environment and was first used to describe this approach in 1978 (Hart &

Rogers-Warren, 1978). This approach subsumes several specific techniques, including incidental teaching (e.g., Hart & Risley, 1980) and the mand-model procedure (e.g. Warren, McQuarter, & Rogers-Warren, 1984). These procedures share several common features, including (a) teaching follows the child's attentional lead; (b) prompting child production indirectly through environmental arrangement (e.g., placing a desired toy out of reach) or directly through explicit prompts as necessary (e.g., "what's that?"); (c) natural consequences are used (e.g. continued interaction, access to a desired toy, assistance); and (d) specific skills are targeted (e.g., vocabulary growth; two-term semantic relations such as agent–action, or action–object word combinations; prelinguistic communication functions such as requesting and commenting). The incidental teaching and mand-model procedures are complementary and follow the same basic steps in prompting and supporting newly emerging words and forms. The distinction between the two procedures centers on who (the adult or the child) initiates the instructional episode. In the mand-model procedure, the adult initiates the episode by manding (e.g., asking a question) about something the child presently has his attention focused on (e.g., "what's that?"). In the incidental teaching procedure, the child initiates the episode (e.g., by vocalizing about something, or perhaps pointing at something to recruit the adult's attention). The adult then evokes the target response (e.g., vocabulary) by prompting a more elaborate response (Warren, 1992).

The responsive interaction and milieu teaching approaches are similar in many ways, but vary substantially on one important dimension. Responsive interaction emphasizes the use of growth recasts to teach new responses, whereas milieu teaching uses elicited prompts for the initial productions of target forms and/or functions. In a typical interaction, the adult's decision to elicit a more complete response from the child (e.g., with a mand) is incompatible with expanding what the child said; you can do one or the other, but not both simultaneously. For example, the child might initiate the word "push," to which the adult might respond "push what?" in milieu teaching (an elaborative question), or "push car" (an expansion) in responsive interaction.

As noted above, milieu teaching interventions seem to be particularly effective in teaching prelinguistic communication functions, basic vocabulary, and initial two- and three-term semantic relationships (e.g., action–object combinations like "push car") to children with MLUs of 2.0 or lower (Kaiser, Yoder, & Keetz, 1992; Wilcox, Kouri, & Caswell, 1991). This is probably due to the constraints in children's attentional and memory resources at this point in development, which make elicited production techniques relatively more effective when combined with the conversational scaffolds that are part of milieu teaching (e.g., modeling, time delay). Like responsive interaction techniques, milieu teaching can be embedded into routines at home (e.g., Kaiser, 1993), activity-based preschool curriculum models (e.g., Bricker, Pretti-Frontczak, & McComas, 1998), and book-reading formats (e.g., Whitehurst et al., 1992), and can be intensively applied in contexts that support a high degree of social interaction (e.g., game playing routines) or spread episodically across the day (Hart, 1985).

Direct teaching Direct teaching, sometimes referred to as didactic or direct instruction, has a long history as a language intervention approach (e.g., see Schiefelbusch & Lloyd, 1974). It is typically characterized by the use of specific prompts and reinforcement, rapid massed trial instruction, the frequent direct assessment of learning, and the use of task analysis to break targeted skills down into small, easily learned parts (e.g., Guess, Sailor, & Baer, 1974). In contrast to responsive interaction and milieu teaching, direct teaching is adult directed and the specific content of teaching is usually prespecified. Child engagement is maintained by well-organized instructional materials, rapid pacing, and immediate, contingent feedback (Klinder & Carnine, 1991). Well-developed curricula, most notably the DISTAR Language Program (Englemann & Osborn, 1976), have been widely utilized in schools to teach higher level language skills at the early childhood and elementary school levels. Carefully prescribed programs have also been developed for children with moderate to severe levels of mental retardation (e.g., Guess, Sailor, & Baer, 1974).

Direct teaching has some clear strengths. With language instruction, it can be used to assure those specific skills and concepts that are difficult to teach conversationally are actually taught and learned (e.g., some very complex uses). Indeed, the more abstract and specific the skill, the more effective direct instruction may be (Connell, 1987; Cole, 1995). Research has indicated that direct instruction is relatively more effective than milieu teaching (Yoder, Kaiser, & Alpert, 1991) and more effective than mediated instruction (an approach that is very similar to responsive interaction) (Cole & Dale, 1986; Cole, Dale, & Mills, 1991), particularly with more developmentally advanced children. The results of these studies run counter to the conventional wisdom that children who are more severely disabled benefit more from greater amounts of structure and children who are high functioning are more equipped to learn from interactive, child-directed instruction (Snow, 1989). This may be because highly structured and scripted interventions are difficult for lower functioning children because they are less able to follow the adult's lead (Cole, 1995), while milieu teaching approaches are easier for them to learn from because they are based on following the child's lead (McCathren, Yoder, & Warren, 1995).

An impressive amount of research has supported the efficacy of direct teaching with children with developmental delays or mild levels of mental retardation and MLUs above 2.5 (Klinder & Carnine, 1991; White, 1988). On the other hand, direct teaching is not likely to be effective in most circumstances at the prelinguistic or early language levels because it requires attentional resources and other cognitive skills (e.g., ability to learn from a decontextualized format), which developmentally young children typically have not yet acquired. Indeed, Yoder, Kaiser, and Alpert (1991) found that milieu teaching was more effective than direct instruction for teaching early vocabulary. Furthermore, direct instruction is likely to be of little use for teaching pragmatic skills, and its inherent emphasis on structure and form may impede generalization of learning if it is not supplemented by activities designed to make newly taught skills meaningful for children (Spradlin & Siegel, 1982).

An optimal continuum of intervention approaches

Our intention in this brief review has been to trace the outlines of an emerging model of communication and language intervention that is based on what types of "input" are optimally effective at different points in development. This model posits that no single approach or family of techniques (e.g., milieu teaching) is appropriate for the wide range of skills that develop as the child progresses from initial prelinguistic communication to sophisticated linguistic development and reading. Instead, a continuum of specific approaches is likely to be optimal, particularly when applied against the backdrop of an environment populated with highly responsive adults who continually engage the child in positive, stimulating forms of social interaction. This continuum favors specific approaches during prelinguistic and early language development that utilize elicited production prompts, models, and contingent input techniques intended to foster initial receptive and productive vocabulary development and two- and three-term semantic relationships. As the child's MLU exceeds 2.0, emphasis should switch from elicited production techniques to techniques like growth recasts that require a child to compare their utterance and the adult's recast of it. Finally, as the child's syntactic skills advance and their language becomes increasingly decontextualized and abstract, direct teaching techniques may also be utilized to facilitate the acquisition of specific forms. Such direct teaching techniques might be used in combination with responsive interaction techniques.

Fostering Prelinguistic Communication Development

The onset of intentional communication late in the first year of life marks an infant's active entry into their culture and ignites important changes in how others regard and respond to them. A significant delay in the onset of intentional communication is a strong indicator that the onset of productive language also will be delayed (McCathren, Warren, & Yoder, 1996). Such a delay may hold the infant in a kind of developmental limbo because the onset of intentional communication triggers a series of transactional processes that support the emergence of productive language just a few months later. In this section, we discuss the research of Yoder and Warren on the effects of prelinguistic communication interventions aimed at teaching infants and toddlers to be clear, frequent prelinguistic communicators. Although a large amount of research has been conducted on the effects of early language intervention, very little has been done on the effects of prelinguistic communication intervention.

The transactional model of development and intervention

The premises and hypotheses of Yoder and Warren's prelinguistic intervention research are based on a transactional model of social communication development (McLean & Snyder-McLean, 1978; Sameroff & Chandler, 1975). The model presumes that early social and communication development is facilitated by bidirectional, reciprocal interactions between the child and their environment. For example, a change in the child such as the onset of intentional communication may trigger a change in the social environment, such as increased linguistic mapping by their caregivers. These changes then support further development in the child (e.g., increased vocabulary), and subsequently further changes by the caregivers (e.g., more complex language interaction with the child). In this way both the child and the environment change over time and affect each other in reciprocal fashion as early achievements pave the way for subsequent development.

A transactional model may be particularly well suited to understanding social communication development in young children because caregiver–child interaction can play such an important role in this process. The period of early development (age birth to 3 years) may represent a unique time during which transactional effects can have a substantial impact on development: the young child's relatively restricted repertoire during this early period can make changes in their behavior more salient and easily observable to caregivers. This in turn may allow adults to be more specifically contingent with their responses to developing skills of the child than is possible later in development when the child's behavioral repertoire is far more expansive and complex. During this natural window of opportunity the transactional model may be employed by an experienced practitioner to multiply the effects of relatively circumscribed interventions and perhaps alter the very course of the child's development in a significant way. But the actions of the practitioner may need to be swift and intense, or they may be muted by the child's steadily accumulating history.

To appreciate the true potential of transactional effects, it is necessary to consider the relentless manner by which cumulative advantages and deficits may develop during the first few years of life. For example, an input difference in positive affect expressed by a parent toward their child of 10 events per day (a difference of less than 1 event per waking hour on average) will result in a cumulative difference of 10,950 such events over a three-year period. If a child who experiences less positive affect, also experiences cumulatively more negative affect (e.g., "stop that," "get out of there," "shut your mouth up," "you're a bad baby"), it is easy to conceive of the combination of these qualitative and quantitative experiential differences contributing to deficits in attachment, exploratory behavior, self-concept, language development, later school achievement, etc.

What evidence do we have that such large cumulative deficits occur, and/or that they play havoc with social and communication development? While the evidence is virtually all correlational, it is nevertheless compelling. There is substantial evidence that typically developing young children experience large differences in terms of the quantity and quality of language input they receive, and these differences correlate with important indicators of development later in childhood (e.g., vocabulary size, IQ, reading ability, school achievement) (Feagans & Farran, 1982; Gottfried, 1984; Hart & Risley, 1992; Prizant & Wetherby, 1990; Walker et al., 1994). Because they often display low rates of initiation and responsiveness, (Rosenberg, 1982; Yoder, Davies, & Bishop, 1994), young children with developmental delays or sensory disorders also experience input that differs substantially in quantity and quality from the input that high-achieving, typically developing children receive despite the best intentions and efforts of their caregivers (Brooks-Gunn & Lewis, 1984; Crawley & Spiker, 1983). The challenges faced by young children who initiate relatively infrequently may be further multiplied if their caregiver(s) are relatively unresponsive (e.g., Hart & Risley, 1995).

Caregivers who are unresponsive to their young child's initiations and who often display depressed or negative affect toward the child may represent a risk factor in terms of their child's emotional, social, and communication development (Landry et al., 1997). Unresponsive caregivers often have children who are insecurely attached (Ainsworth et al., 1978), which is a risk factor for poor social–emotional development (Bornstein & Tamis-LeMonda, 1989). Furthermore, there is evidence that low responsive caregivers can negate or minimize the positive transactional effects of early intervention efforts because they fail to respond to changes in their child's repertoire being generated by the intervention (Mahoney et al., 1998; Yoder & Warren, 1998). In short, the generation of transactional effects likely depends on sensitive, responsive caregivers who notice and nurture the child's growth.

The generation of strong transactional effects in which the growth of emotional, social, and communication skills is scaffolded by caregivers can have a multiplier effect in which a relatively small dose of early intervention may lead to long-term effects. These effects are necessary when we consider that a relatively "intensive" early intervention by a skilled practitioner may represent only a few hours a week of a young child's potential learning time (e.g., 5 hours per week of intensive interaction would represent just 5 percent of the child's available social and communication skill learning time if we assume the child is awake and learning for 100 hours per week). Thus, unless direct intervention accounts for a large portion of a child's waking hours, transactional effects are mandatory for early intervention efforts to achieve their potential.

Effects of prelinguistic communication intervention

In their initial explorations of the effects of prelinguistic communication intervention, Yoder and Warren demonstrated that increases in the frequency and clarity of prelinguistic requesting by children with developmental delays as a result of the intervention, covaried with substantial increases in linguistic mapping by teachers and parents who were naïve as to the specific techniques and goals of the intervention (Warren et al., 1993; Yoder et al., 1994). These studies also demonstrated strong generalization effects in that the intentional requesting function they taught was shown to generalize across people, settings, communication styles, and time. Based on the promising results of these initial studies, Yoder and Warren (1998, 1999a, b, 2001) conducted a longitudinal experimental study of the effects of prelinguistic communication intervention on the communication and language development of children with general delays in development. This study represented an experimental analysis of the transactional model of social communication development.

Fifty-eight children between the ages of 17 and 32 months (mean = 23; SD = 4) with developmental delays and their primary parent participated in the study. The children were recruited from three early intervention centers. Fifty-two of the children had no productive words at the outset of the study; the remaining six children had between one and five productive words. All children scored below the 10th percentile on the expressive scale of the Communication Development Inventory (Fenson et al., 1994). All of the children fit the Tennessee definition of developmental delay (i.e. at least a 40 percent delay in at least one developmental domain, or at least a 25 percent delay in at least two developmental domains).

The children were randomly assigned to one of two treatment groups. Twenty-eight of the children received an intervention termed "prelingusitic milieu teaching" (PMT) for 20 minutes per day, three or four days per week, for 6 months. The other 30 children received an intervention termed "responsive small group" (RSG). PMT represented an adaptation of milieu language teaching. It was based on following the child's attentional lead, building social play routines (e.g., turn-taking interactions like rolling a ball back and forth), and using prompts such as time delays (e.g., interrupting a turn-taking routine such as rolling the ball back and forth by not taking your turn until the child initiates a request for you to continue), as well as models and natural consequences to teach the form and functions of requesting and commenting. RSG represented an adaptation of the responsive interaction approach. The adult played with the child in a highly responsive manner and commented on what the child was doing, but never attempted to directly elicit or prompt any communication function or form. These interventions are described in detail elsewhere (e.g., Warren & Yoder, 1998). Caretakers were kept naïve as to the specific methods, measures, records of child progress, and child goals throughout the study. This allowed Yoder and Warren to investigate how change in the children's behavior as a result of the interventions might affect the behavior of the primary caretaker, and how this in turn might affect the child's development later in time. Data were collected at five points in time for each dyad: at pre-treatment, at post-treatment, and 6, 12, and 18 months after the completion of the intervention.

Both interventions had generalized effects on intentional communication development. However, the treatment that was most effective depended on the pre-treatment maternal interaction style and the education level of the mother (Yoder & Warren, 1998, 2001). Specifically, Yoder and Warren (1998) found that for children of highly responsive, relatively well-educated mothers, PMT was effective in fostering generalized intentional communication development. However, for children with relatively unresponsive mothers, RSG was relatively more successful in fostering generalized intentional communication development.

The two interventions differ along a few important dimensions that provide a plausible explanation for these effects. PMT uses a child-centered play context in which communication prompts for more advanced forms of communication are employed as well as social consequences for target responses such as specific acknowledgement and compliance. The RSG emphasized following the child's attentional lead and being highly responsive to child initiation while avoiding the use of direct prompts for communication. Maternal interaction style may have influenced which intervention was most beneficial because children may develop expectations concerning interactions with adults (including teachers and interventionists) based on their history of interaction with their primary caretaker. Thus, children with responsive parents may learn to persist in the face of communication breakdowns, such as might be occasioned by a direct prompt or time delay, because their history leads them to believe that their communication attempts will usually be successful. On the other hand, children without this history may cease communicating when their initial attempt fails. Thus, children of responsive mothers in the PMT group persisted when prompted and thus learned effectively in this context while children with unresponsive parents did not. But when provided with a highly responsive adult, who virtually never prompted them over a 6-month period, children of unresponsive mothers showed greater gains than children of responsive parents receiving the same treatment.

The effects of maternal responsivity as a mediator and moderator of intervention effects rippled throughout the longitudinal follow-up period. Yoder and Warren demonstrated that children in the PMT group with relatively responsive mothers received increased amounts of responsive input from their mothers in direct response to the children's increased intentional communication (Yoder & Warren, 2001). Furthermore, the effects of the intervention were found on both requests and comments (Yoder & Warren, 1999a), became greater with time, and impacted expressive and receptive language development 6 and 12 months after intervention ceased (Yoder & Warren, 1999b, 2001). It is important to consider this finding in light of the substantial number of early intervention studies in which the effects were reported to wash out over time (Farran, 2000). Finally, the finding that the amount of responsive input by the primary caregiver was partly responsible for the association between intentional communication increases and later language development (Yoder & Warren, 1999a) coupled with the longitudinal relationship between maternal responsivity and expressive language development (Yoder & Warren, 2001) supports the prediction of the transactional model that a child's early intentional communication will elicit the mother's linguistic mapping, which in turn will facilitate the child's vocabulary development.

Implications

The research by Yoder and Warren represents a relatively rare experimental example of child influence on adults' use of behavior that in turn fosters the child's further development (Bell & Harper, 1977). It hints at the potential power of the transactional model, at least during the early period of development, when children's behavior repertoires are small and their developmental history relatively short. Unfortunately, except for Wilcox and her colleagues (Wilcox & Shannon, 1998), there has been very little additional research reported on prelinguistic communication interventions. Furthermore, given that the research of Yoder and Warren purposefully restrained the potential efficacy of prelingusitic intervention by only providing the intervention a few times a week in an isolated context without parent involvement, the potential efficacy of very early communication interventions must be viewed as highly promising.

Fostering Language Growth in At-Risk Children

There is ample evidence suggesting that infants and young children who experience environmental risk factors are more likely to have constraints on their later language performance. For example, infants from extreme poverty backgrounds have been found to produce fewer vocalizations (e.g., Oller et al., 1995), while young children exposed to violence have been reported to sometimes regress in their use of language (e.g., Osofsky, 1995), and to use language infrequently (e.g., Groves, 1997; Walker, 2000). Infants who are exposed to fewer language-learning opportunities in their homes are at risk for developing more limited vocabularies, using language less frequently (Hart & Risley, 1999), and, later, for low performance on receptive and expressive language and early literacy measures (Walker et al. 1994). Children who experience environmental risks appear to have more prohibitions and correspondingly fewer positive comments directed toward them, thus increasing the likelihood that they will produce fewer vocalizations and, later, fewer words compared to children who have more positive experiences (e.g., Hart & Risley, 1999; Walker & Hart, 1996; Warren & Rogers-Warren, 1982). Finally, infants who experience multiple environmental risks including prenatal exposure to substance abuse have lower developmental trajectories compared to infants who experience fewer or no risk factors (Carta et al., 2001).

Evidence of differential language learning opportunities

Research with at-risk children conducted through the Juniper Garden's Children's Project at the University of Kansas for the past 40 years (e.g., Greenwood et al., 1989, 1992; Greenwood, Delquadri, & Hall, 1984; Hart & Risley, 1968) has emphasized the role of interactions within the child's environment as having the potential to either accelerate or decelerate development. Work reported by Carta and colleagues (Carta, 1991; Atwater et al., 1994) examining risks in early intervention settings has emphasized the development of interventions to improve the overall classroom ecology and teacher behaviors to increase children's level of active engagement. Children experiencing these interventions have typically surpassed control peers on measures of developmental growth, vocabulary, and social competence, and were more likely to be placed in regular kindergarten classes.

Research on child-rearing practices related to language development has focused on the relation between practices that influence the language-learning environments of young children, and child outcomes in terms of language development and production (Hart & Risley, 1992; 1995; Huttenlocher et al., 1991). In a longitudinal study investigating how children learn to talk through interactions that parents have with their infants and toddlers between the ages of 7 and 36 months, Hart and Risley (1992, 1995) found large differences among typically developing children's early language learning experiences in their homes. In monthly naturalistic observations, verbal production was assessed for infants and their families for over 30 months. Among their key findings were that those children who heard more talk, heard richer and more varied vocabularies, heard more affirmatives (e.g., "good," "I like that"), more open-ended questions, and experienced more positive affect had substantially larger vocabularies at age 3 (Hart & Risley, 1995, 1999). Conversely, children who heard less talk, were exposed to limited vocabulary, heard more prohibitions (e.g., "no," "shut up"), heard fewer questions, and experienced more negative affect developed much smaller vocabularies.

Hart and Risley (1999) emphasized the extreme contrasts in the amount of interaction between parents and children from advantaged, working-class, and disadvantaged backgrounds. On average, they reported that in the most advantaged homes, parents addressed an average of 2,100 words per hour to their children compared to 1,200 words per hour in the working-class families and 600 per hour to children in the poorest families. Children from high-risk backgrounds were much more likely to have caregivers who interacted with them infrequently (Hart & Risley, 1995). When caregivers did interact, those interactions were more often characterized by the use of more prohibitions or negative comments compared to affirmative or positive comments (e.g., Hart & Risley, 1992, 1995).

In a subsequent longitudinal study of the children from the Hart and Risley sample, Walker et al. (1994) found that the early home measures of language-related experience predicted child performance in early elementary school. These results demonstrated that early language experiences in the home between the ages of 7 and 36 months were highly predictive of receptive and spoken language when children were between 5 and 10 years old. Those children who entered elementary school at a disadvantage in terms of the amount and quality of language-related interactions and outcomes continued to be at a disadvantage throughout early elementary school in areas specific to language (e.g., receptive vocabulary, reading) (Walker et al., 1994).

Following observations of the children from both of their longitudinal studies, Walker and Hart conducted an analysis of those children who had the lowest scores on a composite of risk factors (i.e., family income, parent education, parental age at birth of child, number of siblings, extended family or support network, job status, neighborhood, family stability in terms of moves, parent vocabulary, and general parenting quality) (Walker & Hart, 1996). They compared children who had the greatest number of risk factors present when they were between 7 and 36 months of age with those children who experienced few or no risk conditions. Children who were at highest risk based on their risk composite heard affirmative or neutral feedback (e.g., "wow," "look at you") in their homes on average for only 41 percent of all feedback addressed to them. Thus, when those children were spoken to in their homes, prohibitions (e.g., "no," "don't do that") comprised 59 percent of the feedback heard. For the children with few or no risk factors, affirmative statements comprised approximately 78 percent of all feedback compared to prohibitions, which comprised 22 percent of the feedback delivered.

Observations of teacher–child interactions conducted when the children from the original Hart and Risley sample reached kindergarten through 3rd grade yielded disturbing results. Children with the highest risk score heard approval statements from their teachers for only 2.27 percent of observations (approximately 5 minutes per day) and heard disapproval statements on average three times more often (5.74 percent or approximately 13 minutes per day). Children who received primarily negative feedback early in their lives continued to experience more negative feedback than positive in school. These findings suggested that general patterns of behavior first evident in the home continued through the context of schooling, resulting in some children hearing more negative than positive feedback throughout their early years of development. Walker and Hart (1996) concluded that although these children may have engaged in behavior that perhaps evoked some negative feedback from caregivers and teachers, there were surely many missed opportunities for receiving positive feedback early on at home and later in school.

Promising intervention approaches

Language intervention procedures considered to be successful with young children who are at risk for language delay have been developed not only to promote communication and language development of at risk children, but to do so while accounting for their individual differences and the unique environments in which they learn language. Incidental language teaching, shared book reading interventions, and the provision of high-quality infant and toddler care appear particularly promising for increasing the language skills of children from impoverished environments.

The early intervention research of Hart and Risley (1980) demonstrated that through the use of incidental teaching procedures, they were able to increase the amount of talking during the free play of preschool children from poverty backgrounds to a level that matched their more advantaged peers' rates. Incidental teaching procedures emphasize following the child's lead or interest during brief, naturalistic episodes to maximize the chances that the child will be interested in the topic. The environment is arranged to promote a child's interest, the adult waits for the child to initiate, and then a series of graduated prompting procedures (e.g., requests for elaboration, imitation) and natural consequences follow (e.g., identification of the item requested, or receiving the item). Incidental teaching has been used successfully to promote the use of nouns and adjectives during free play (Hart & Risley, 1974), compound sentence use during free play (Hart & Risley, 1975), and new vocabulary words (Hart & Risley, 1980) with disadvantaged preschoolers. Hart and Risley's incidental teaching approach was the basis for the development of the milieu language teaching approach discussed earlier in the chapter.

Shared book-reading interventions have been developed over the past decade with the intent of increasing children's opportunities to practice and develop oral language and literacy-related skills (e.g., Dale et al., 1996; Hockenberger, Goldstein, & Haas, 1999; Lonigan & Whitehurst, 1998; Snow, Burns, & Griffin, 1998). These interventions are characterized by the use of procedures similar to incidental language techniques, including the use of open-ended questions (e.g., who, what, when, where, and why), repeats and recasts of child verbalizations, following the child's interest or lead, provision of assistance when necessary, and delivery of praise along with other literacy-promoting activities. Lonigan and Whitehurst (1998) reported a shared book-reading intervention intended to increase expressive language and emergent literacy skills. This intervention was implemented in childcare centers and homes with 100 preschool-aged children from low-income backgrounds. They compared the effectiveness of center, home, and combined implementation formats of a dialogic reading intervention. While both child-care teachers and parents produced significant positive changes in the development of oral language of the low-income children participating in the study, stronger effects for vocabulary development were found for the centers with the highest rate of intervention implementation, and for children who were exposed to dialogic reading both at home and in centers. Children in the parent-only intervention group, however, made the largest gains in descriptive use of language. While many factors appeared to influence the ultimate results achieved, shared book-reading interventions appear to be a promising context for language learning.

Early intervention programs designed to improve the developmental outcomes of at-risk children have emphasized the importance of high-quality child care and preschool experiences to later language and cognitive outcomes (e.g., Abecedarian Project: Ramey & Campbell, 1992; CARE: Wasik et al., 1991; Consortium for Longitudinal Studies: Lazar et al., 1982). These programs provided intensive and generally comprehensive interventions to disadvantaged infants, young children, and their families with the purpose of improving later school performance. These model programs demonstrated that outcomes for disadvantaged children and their families could be markedly improved with social, economic, and educational support. The comprehensive components of these programs have since been incorporated into service models for young children (e.g., transportation, nutrition and health services, home visiting and parent education, and community-linked services). These programs were, however, typically well funded, requiring tremendous resources to implement and sustain – resources generally not available in community-based programs serving disadvantaged children.

Interventions emphasizing the role of the parent in promoting the communication and language development of their infants and young children have also been found to be successful. The Parents as Teachers program, for example, designed to support needy women and their young children (National Diffusion Network, 1996), provides information about child development, and infant and toddler care, and teaches parents how to respond to their infant's cues and to use commenting related to their child's interest. Findings suggest that by age 3, children involved in the Parents as Teachers program have marked improvement on measures of cognitive and language development. Further, in a study conducted to promote high-quality parent–child interactions with homeless families, parent advocates were successful in providing feedback to parents to increase the quality of their interactions (e.g., use of positive comments, following the child's lead, imitation) with their young children (Kelly, Buehlman, & Caldwell, 2000). Common across these studies was a comprehensive approach to intervention; one in which family needs were met within a supportive framework designed to decrease the strains of environmental deprivation while emphasizing the importance of responsive caregiver–child interactions.

Perhaps the most general form of intervention for children at risk due to poverty and related factors is to ensure that they receive high quality child care. Relatively strong associations have been reported between quality of care and child outcomes in terms of cognitive and language development (e.g., Howes, Phillips, & Whitebook, 1992; NICHD Early Child Care Research Network, 1996; Phillips et al., 1994). For example, the NICHD Child Care Research Network (1998) reported that the quality of interaction between child-care provider and child was related to better cognitive and language scores when toddlers were between 15 and 36 months. Investigating the structural quality aspects of child care, Burchinal and colleagues (Burchinal et al., 2000) reported that at-risk children who experience adult:child ratios within recommended guidelines tended to have higher receptive and overall language scores (with moderate effect scores) (see also NICHD Child Care Research Network, 1999, 2000). This association can be explained by the viewpoint that scaffolded conversations with adults that include individualized language models and responsive turn-taking are particularly important to early language development (e.g., Hoff-Ginsburg, 1990), and are very difficult for a caregiver to do with individual children if the number of children exceeds the recommended ratio (Burchinal et al. 2000). Likewise, the incidental teaching, shared book-reading or the parent-led interventions described above are unlikely to be feasible in settings with improperly trained or unsupported caregivers.

Conclusions

Enormous progress has been made in the science and practice of fostering early communication and language development. It is obvious, however, that further development of effective approaches for fostering early communication and language development will require the commitment of many more highly trained scientists and the provision of substantial resources over the long haul. Longitudinal intervention designs that utilize random assignment and maintain a high degree of treatment fidelity simply cannot be done (and should not be done) without these supports. The challenges ahead are clear and substantial, but can surely be met in time. We have touched on only a few of the areas of relevant research in this report, and cast these in a context of overall progress. Given the central roles that communication and language play in human development and behavior across the life span, the potential payoff of expanding the research agenda in this domain is unquestionably substantial.

Acknowledgments

Grants from the National Institute of Child Health and Human Development (HD02528-34) and the Office of Special Education Programs of the US Department of Education (D324C990040, H324D980066) provided support for the preparation of this manuscript. However, the opinions expressed are solely those of the authors.

References

Ainsworth, M. D., Blehan, M. C., Waters, E., & Wall, S. (1978). *Patterns of attachment: A psychological study of the strange situation.* Hillsdale, NJ: Lawrence Erlbaum Associates.

Aram, D. M. & Hall, N. E. (1989). Longitudinal follow-up of children with preschool communication disorders: Treatment implications. *School Psychology Review, 18,* 487–501.

Atwater, J. B., Orth-Lopes, L., Elliott, M., Carta, J. J., & Schwartz, I. S. (1994). Completing the circle: Planning and implementing transitions to other programs. In M. Wolery & J. Wilbers (eds.), *Including children with special needs in early childhood programs* (pp. 167–88). Washington, DC: National Association for the Education of Young Children.

Baker, N. & Nelson, K. (1984). Recasting and related conversational techniques for triggering syntactic advances by young children. *First Language, 5,* 3–22.

Baumwell, L., Tamis-LeMonda, C. S., & Bornstein, M. H. (1997). Maternal verbal sensitivity and child language comprehension. *Infant Behavior and Development, 20(2),* 247–58.

Bell, R. & Harper, L. (1977). *Child effects on adults.* Hillsdale, NJ: Lawrence Erlbaum Associates.

Bornstein, M. H. & Tamis-LeMonda, C. S. (1989). Maternal responsiveness and cognitive development in children. In M. H. Bornstein (ed.), *Maternal responsiveness: Characteristics and consequences* (pp. 803–9). San Francisco, CA: Jossey-Bass.

Bricker, D., Pretti-Frontczak, K., & McComas, N. (1998). *An activity-based approach to early intervention* (2nd edn.). Baltimore, MD: Brookes.

Brooks-Gunn, J. & Lewis, M. (1984). Maternal responsiveness in interactions with handicapped infants. *Child Development, 55,* 782–93.

Bruner, J. S. (1975). The ontogenesis of speech acts. *Journal of Child Language, 2,* 1–19.

Burchinal, M. R., Roberts, J. E., Riggins, R., Jr., Zeisel, S. A., Neebe, E., & Bryant, D. (2000). Relating quality of center-based child care to early cognitive and language development longitudinally. *Child Development, 71,* 339–57.

Camarata, S. C. (1995). A rationale for naturalistic speech intelligibility intervention. In M. Fey, J. Windsor, & S. Warren (eds.), *Language intervention: Preschool through the elementary years* (pp. 63–84). Baltimore, MD: Brookes.

Camarata, S. C., Nelson, K., & Camarata, M. (1994). Comparison of conversational-recasting and imitative procedures for training grammatical structures in children with specific language impairment. *Journal of Speech and Hearing Research, 37,* 1414–23.

Carta, J. J. (1991). Education for young children in inner-city classrooms. *American Behavioral Scientist, 34,* 440–53.

Carta, J. J., Atwater, J. B., Greenwood, C. R., McConnell, S. R., McEvoy, M. A., & Williams, R. (2001). Effects of cumulative prenatal substance exposure and multiple environmental risks on children's developmental trajectories. *Journal of Clinical and Consulting Psychology, 30,* 327–37.

Casby, M. W. (1989). National data concerning communication disorders and special education. *Language, Speech, and Hearing Services in the Schools, 20,* 22–30.

Chapman, R. (2000). Children's language learning: An interactionist perspective. *Journal of Child Psychology and Psychiatry, 41,* 33–54.

Cole, K. N. (1995). Curriculum models and language facilitation in the preschool years. In M. Fey, J. Windsor, & S. Warren (eds.), *Language intervention: Preschool through the elementary years.* (pp. 39–62). Baltimore, MD: Brookes.

Cole, K. N. & Dale, P. S. (1986). Direct language instruction and interactive language instruction with language delayed preschool children: A comparison study. *Journal of Speech and Hearing Research, 29,* 206–17.

Cole, K., Dale, P. S., & Mills, P. E. (1991). Individual differences in language delayed children's responses to direct and interaction preschool instruction. *Topics in Early Childhood Special Education, 11,* 99–124.

Connell, P. J. (1987). An effect of modeling and imitation teaching procedures on children with and without specific language impairment. *Journal of Speech and Hearing Research, 30,* 105–13.

Crawley, S. & Spiker, D. (1983). Mother–child interactions involving two-year-olds with Down' syndrome: A look at individual differences. *Child Development, 54,* 1312–23.

Dale, P. S., Crain-Thoreson, C., Notari-Syverson, A., & Cole, K. (1996). Parent–child book reading as an intervention technique for young children with language delays. *Topics in Early Childhood Special Education, 16,* 21–35.

de Kruif, R. E. L., McWilliam, R. A., Ridley, S. M., & Wakely, M. B. (2000). Classification of teachers' interaction behaviors in early childhood classrooms. *Early Childhood Research Quarterly, 15,* 247–68.

Englemann, S. & Osborn, J. (1976). *Distar Language.* Chicago, IL: Science Research Associates.

Farran, D. C. (2000). Another decade of intervention for children who are low income or disabled: What do we know now? In J. P. Shonkoff & S. J. Meisels (eds.) *Handbook of early children intervention* (2nd edn., pp. 510–48). New York: Cambridge University Press.

Feagans, L. & Farran, D. C. (1982). *The language of children reared in poverty: Implications for evaluation and intervention.* New York: Academic Press.

Fenson, L., Dale, P. S., Reznick, J. S., Bates, E., Thal, D. J., & Pethick, S. J. (1994). *Variability in early communicative development. Monographs of the Society for Research in Child Development,* *59,* (5, serial no. 242).

Fey, M. E., Catts, H., & Larrivee, L. S. (1995). Preparing preschoolers for the academic and social challenges of school. In M. E. Fey, J. Windsor, & S. Warren (eds.), *Language Intervention: Preschool through the elementary years* (pp. 225–90). Baltimore, MD: Brookes.

Fey, M. E., Cleave, P., Long, S., & Hughes, D. (1993). Two approaches to the facilitation of grammar in language-impaired children: An experimental evaluation. *Journal of Speech and Hearing Research, 36,* 141–57.

Gallaway, C. & Richards, B. J. (1994). *Input and interaction in language acquisition.* Cambridge: Cambridge University Press.

Gottfried, A. W. (1984). Home environment and early cognitive development: Integration, meta-analysis, and conclusions. In A. W. Gottfried (ed.), *Home environment and early cognitive development: Longitudinal research* (pp. 329–42). New York: Academic Press.

Greenwood, C. R., Delquadri, J., & Hall, R. V. (1984). Opportunity to respond and student academic performance. In W. Heward, T. Heron, D. Hill, & J. Trap-Porter (eds.), *Behavior analysis in education* (pp. 58–88). Columbus, OH: Charles E. Merrill.

Greenwood, C. R., Carta, J. J., Hart, B., Thurston, L., & Hall, R. V. (1989). A behavioral approach to research on psychosocial retardation. *Education and Treatment of Children, 12,* 330–46.

Greenwood, C. R., Carta, J. J., Hart, B., Kamps, D., Terry, B., Arreaga-Mayer, C., Atwater, J., Walker, D., Risley, T., & Delquadri, J. (1992). Out of the laboratory and into the community: 26 years of applied behavior analysis at the Juniper Gardens Children's Project. *American Psychologist, 47,* 1464–74.

Groves, B. M. (1997). Growing up in a violent world: The impact of family and community violence on young children and their families. *Topics in Early Childhood Special Education, 17,* 74–102.

Guess, D., Sailor, W., & Baer, D. M. (1974). To teach language to retarded children. In R. L. Schiefelbusch & L. L. Lloyd (eds.) *Language perspectives: Acquisition, retardation, intervention* (pp. 477–516). Baltimore, MD: University Park Press.

Harris, M., Jones, D., Brookes, S., & Grant, J. (1986). Relations between non-verbal context of maternal speech and rate of language development. *British Journal of Developmental Psychology, 4,* 261–8.

Hart, B. (1985). Naturalistic language training techniques. In S. F. Warren & A. K. Rogers-Warren (eds.), *Teaching functional language.* Baltimore, MD: University Park Press.

Hart, B. & Risley, T. R. (1968). Establishing the use of descriptive adjectives in the spontaneous speech of disadvantaged preschool children. *Journal of Applied Behavior Analysis, 1,* 109–20.

Hart, B. & Risley, T. R. (1974). The use of preschool materials for modifying the language of disadvantaged children. *Journal of Applied Behavior Analysis, 7,* 243–56.

Hart, B. & Risley, T. R. (1975). Incidental teaching of language in the preschool. *Journal of Applied Behavior Analysis, 8,* 411–20.

Hart, B. & Risley, T. R. (1980). *In vivo* language intervention: Unanticipated general effects. *Journal of Applied Behavioral Analysis, 13,* 407–32.

Hart, B. & Risley, T. R. (1992). American parenting of language learning children: Persisting differences in family child interaction observed in natural home environments. *Developmental Psychology, 28,* 1096–1105.

Hart, R. & Risley, T. R. (1995). *Meaningful differences in the everyday experiences of young American children.* Baltimore, MD: Brookes.

Hart, B. & Risley, T. R. (1999). *The social world of children learning to talk*. Baltimore, MD: Brookes.

Hart, B. & Rogers-Warren, A. (1978). Milieu language training. In R. L. Schiefelbusch (ed.), *Language intervention strategies* (pp. 193–235). Austin, TX: Pro-Ed.

Hockenberger, E. H., Goldstein, H., & Haas, S. L. (1999). Effects of commenting during joint book reading by mothers with low SES. *Topics in Early Childhood Special Education, 19*, 15–27.

Hoff-Ginsburg, E. (1986). Function and structure in maternal speech: Their relation to the child's development of syntax. *Developmental Psychology, 22(2)*, 155–63.

Hoff-Ginsburg, E. (1990). Maternal speech and the child's development of syntax: A further look. *Journal of Child Language, 17*, 85–90.

Howes, C., Phillips, D. A., & Whitebook, M. (1992). Thresholds of quality: Implications for the social development of children in center-based child care. *Child Development, 53*, 449–60.

Huttenlocher, J., Haight, W., Bryk, A., Seltzer, M., & Lyons, T. (1991). Early vocabulary growth: Relation to language input and gender. *Developmental Psychology, 27*, 236–48.

Kaiser, A. (1993). Parent-implemented language intervention: An environmental system perspective. In A. Kaiser & D. Gray (eds.), *Enhancing children's communication: Research foundations for intervention.* (pp. 6–84). Baltimore, MD: Brookes.

Kaiser A. P. & Hester, P. P. (1997). Prevention of conduct disorders through early intervention: A social-communicative perspective. *Behavioral Disorders, 22*, 117–30.

Kaiser, A. P., Yoder, P. J., & Keetz, A. (1992). Evaluating milieu teaching. In S. Warren & J. Reichle (eds.), *Causes and effects in communication and language intervention* (pp. 9–47). Baltimore, MD: Brookes.

Kelly, J. F., Buehlman, K., & Caldwell, K. (2000). Training personnel to promote quality parent–child interaction in families who are homeless. *Topics in Early Childhood Special Education, 20(3)*, 174–85.

Klinder, D. & Carnine, D. (1991). Direct instruction: What it is and what it is becoming. *Journal of Behavioral Education, 1*, 193–213.

Landry, S. H., Smith, K. E., Miller-Loncar, C. L., & Swank, P. R. (1997). The relation of change in maternal interaction styles to the developing social competence of full-term and preterm children. *Child Development, 69*, 105–23.

Lazar, I., Darlington, R., Murray, H., Royce, J., & Snipper, A. (1982). Lasting effects of early education: A report from the Consortium for Longitudinal Studies. *Monographs of the Society for Research in Child Development, 47* (2/3, serial no. 195).

Lonigan, C. J. & Whitehurst, G. J. (1998). Relative efficacy of parent and teacher involvement in a shared-reading intervention for preschool children from low-income backgrounds. *Early Childhood Research Quarterly, 13*, 263–90.

MacDonald, J. (1985). Language through conversation: A model for intervention with language delayed children. In S. Warren & A. Rogers-Warren (eds.), *Teaching functional language* (pp. 89–122). Austin, TX: Pro-Ed.

MacWhinney, B. (ed.) (1999). *The emergence of language*. Mahwah, NJ: Lawrence Erlbaum Associates.

Mahoney, G., Boyce, G., Fewell, R. R., Spiker, D., & Wheeden, C. A. (1998). The relationship of parent–child interaction to the effectiveness of early intervention services for at-risk children and children with disabilities. *Topics in Early Childhood Special Education, 18*, 5–17.

McCathren, R. B., Warren, S. F., & Yoder, P. J. (1996). Prelinguistic predictors of later language development. In K. Cole, D. Thal, & P. Dale (eds.), *Assessment of Communication and Language* (pp. 57–76). Baltimore, MD: Brookes.

McCathren, R. B., Yoder, P. J., & Warren, S. F. (1995). The role of directives in early language intervention. *Journal of Early Intervention, 19*, 91–101.

McLean, J. & Snyder-McLean, L. (1978). *A transactional approach to early language training.* Columbus, OH: Charles E. Merrill.

Menyuk, P. (1988). *Language development: Knowledge and use.* Glenview, IL: Scott, Foresman.

National Diffusion Network (1996). *Educational Programs that Work* (22nd edn.). Longmont, CO: Sopris West.

Nelson, K. (1973). *Structure and strategy in learning to talk. Monographs of the Society for Research in Child Development,* 38, (1–2, serial no. 149).

Nelson, K. E. (1989). Strategies for first language teaching. In M. Rice & R. L. Schiefelbusch (eds.), *The teachability of language* (pp. 263–310). Baltimore, MD: Brookes.

Nelson, K. E. (1991). On differentiated language-learning models and differentiated interventions. In N. Krasnegor, D. Rumbaugh, R. Schiefelbusch, & M. Studdert-Kennedy (eds.), *Biological and behavioral determinants of language development* (pp. 399–429). Hillsdale, NJ: Lawrence Erlbaum Associates.

NICHD Early Child Care Research Network (1996). Characteristics of infant child care: Factors contributing to positive caregiving. *Early Childhood Research Quarterly,* 11, 269–306.

NICHD Early Child Care Research Network (1998). Relations between family predictors and child outcomes: Are they weaker for children in child care? *Developmental Psychology,* 34, 1119–28.

NICHD Early Child Care Research Network (1999). Child outcomes when child care center classes meet recommended standards for quality. *American Journal of Public Health,* 89, 1072–7.

NICHD Early Child Care Research Network (2000). Characteristics and quality of child care for toddlers and preschoolers. *Applied Developmental Science,* 4, 116–35.

Oller, D. K., Eilers, R. E., Basinger, D., Steffens, M. L., & Urbano, R. (1995). Extreme poverty and the development of precursors to the speech capacity. *First Language,* 15, 167–87.

Osofsky, J. D. (1995). The effects of exposure to violence on young children. *American Psychologist,* 50, 782–8.

Phillips, D. A., Voran, M., Kisker, E., Howes, C., & Whitebook, M. (1994). Child care for children in poverty: Opportunity or inequity? *Child Development,* 65, 472–92.

Pinker, S. (1994). *The language instinct.* New York: Morrow.

Prizant, B. & Wetherby, A. (1990). Toward an integrated view of early language and communication development and socioemotional development. *Topics in Language Disorders,* 10, 1–16.

Ramey, C. T. & Campbell, F. A. (1992). Poverty, early childhood education, and academic competence: The Abecedarian experiment. In A. Huston (ed.), *Children in poverty.* New York: Cambridge University Press.

Rosenberg, S. (1982) The language of the mentally retarded: Development, progress, and intervention. In S. Rosenberg (ed.), *Handbook of applied psycholinguistics* (pp. 329–93). Hillsdale, NJ: Lawrence Erlbaum Associates.

Sameroff, A. J. & Chandler, M. J. (1975). Reproductive risk and the continuum of caretaking casualty. In F. D. Horowitz, M. Hetherington, S. Scarr-Salapatek, & G. Siegel (eds.). *Review of child development research* (vol. 4, pp. 187–244). Chicago, IL: University of Chicago Press.

Schiefelbusch, R. L. & Lloyd, L. L. (1974). *Language perspectives: Acquisition, retardation, and intervention.* Baltimore, MD: University Park Press.

Snow, C. (1984). Parent–child interaction and the development of communicative ability. In R. L. Schiefelbusch & J. Pickar (eds.), *The acquisition of communicative competence* (pp. 69–108). Baltimore, MD: University Park Press.

Snow, C. E. (1989). Imitativeness: A trait or a skill? In G. E. Speidel & K. E. Nelson (eds.), *The many faces of imitation in language learning* (pp. 73–90). New York: Springer-Verlag.

Snow, C. E., Burns, S., & Griffin, P. (eds.) (1998). *Preventing reading difficulties in young children.* Washington, DC: National Academy Press.

Snow, C. E., Perlmann, R., & Nathan, D. (1987). Why routines are different: Toward a multiple factors model of the relation between input and language acquisition. In K. E. Nelson & A. van Kleeck (eds.), *Child language* (vol. 6, pp. 65–97). Hillsdale, NJ: Lawrence Erlbaum Associates.

Sokolov, J. L. (1993). A local contingency analysis of the fine-tuning hypothesis. *Developmental Psychology, 29(6)*, 1008–23.

Speidel, G. E. & Nelson, K. E. (1989). A fresh look at imitation in language learning. In G. Speidel & K. E. Nelson (eds.) *The many faces of imitation in language learning* (pp. 1–21). New York: Springer-Verlag.

Spradlin, J. E. & Siegel, G. M. (1982). Language training in natural and clinical environments. *Journal of Speech and Hearing Disorders, 47*, 2–6.

Tannock, R. & Girolametto, L. (1992). Reassessing parent-focused language intervention programs. In S. F. Warren & J. Reichle (eds.), *Causes and effects in communication and language intervention* (pp. 49–79). Baltimore, MD: Paul H. Brookes.

Tomasello, M. (1992). *First verbs.* Cambridge: Cambridge University Press.

Van Kleeck, A. (1994). Potential cultural bias in training parents as conversational partners with their children who have delays in language development. *American Journal of Speech-Language Pathology, 31*, 67–78.

Walker, D. (2000). Resilience in families affected by substance abuse and domestic violence. In J. Atwater (chair), Identification of experiences that promote resilience for young children at risk. Symposium presented at the Conference on Research Innovations in Early Intervention, San Diego, CA, April.

Walker, D. & Hart, B. (1996). Does early experience impact a lifetime? A combined longitudinal analysis of children's early language-learning experiences and later schooling experiences. Paper presented in J. J. Carta (chair), Longitudinal studies exploring contextual influences on children's behavioral development in urban settings. Symposium conducted at the meeting of the Annual Convention of the Association for Behavior Analysis, San Francisco, CA, May.

Walker, D., Greenwood, C. R., Hart, B., & Carta, J. J. (1994). Improving the prediction of early school academic outcomes using socioeconomic status and early language production. *Child Development, 65*, 606–21.

Warren, S. (1992). Facilitating basic vocabulary acquisition with milieu teaching procedures. *Journal of Early Intervention, 16*, 235–51.

Warren, S. F. & Rogers-Warren, A. (1982). Language acquisition patterns in normal and handicapped children. *Topics in Early Childhood Special Education, 2*, 70–77.

Warren, S. F. & Yoder, P. J. (1998). Facilitating the transition from preintentional to intentional communication. In A. Wetherby, S. Warren, & J. Reichle (eds.), *Transitions in prelinguistic communication* (pp. 365–384). Baltimore, MD: Brookes.

Warren, S. F., McQuarter, R. A., & Rogers-Warren, A. (1984). The effects of mands and models on the speech of unresponsive language delayed preschool children. *Journal of Speech and Hearing Disorders, 49*, 42–52.

Warren, S. F., Yoder, P. J., Gazdag, G. E., Kim, K., & Jones, H. A. (1993). Facilitating prelinguistic communication skills in young children with developmental delay. *Journal of Speech and Hearing Research, 36*, 83–97.

Wasik, B. H., Ramey, C. T., Bryant, D. M., & Sparling, J. J. (1991). A longitudinal study of two early intervention strategies: Project CARE. *Child Development, 61*, 1682–96.

Wells, G. (1985). *Language development in the preschool years.* New York: Cambridge University Press.

Wetherby, A. M. & Prizant, B. M. (1992). Profiling young children's communicative competence. In S. F. Warren & J. Reichle (eds.), *Causes and effects in communication and language intervention* (pp. 217–53). Baltimore, MD: Paul H. Brookes.

White, W. A. T. (1988). A meta-analysis of effects of direct instruction in special education. *Education and Treatment of Children, 11*, 364–74.

Whitehurst, G. J., Fischel, J. E., Arnold, D. S., & Lonigan, C. J. (1992). Evaluating outcomes with children with expressive language delay. In S. F. Warren and J. Reichle (eds.) *Causes and effects in communication and language intervention* (pp. 277–313). Baltimore, MD: Paul H. Brookes.

Wilcox, M. J. & Shannon, M. S. (1998). Facilitating the transition from prelinguistic to linguistic communication. In A. Wetherby, S. F. Warren, & J. Reichle (eds.) *Transitions in prelinguistic communication* (pp. 385–416). Baltimore, MD: Brookes.

Wilcox, M. J., Kouri, T., & Caswell, S. (1991). Early language intervention: A comparison of classroom and individual treatment. *American Journal of Speech-Language Pathology, 1*, 49–62.

Yoder, P. J., Davies, B., & Bishop, K. (1994). Adult interaction style effects on the language sampling and transcription process with children who have developmental disabilities. *American Journal on Mental Retardation, 99*, 270–82.

Yoder, P. J. & Warren, S. F. (1998). Maternal responsivity predicts the extent to which prelinguistic intervention facilitates generalized intentional communication. *Journal of Speech, Language, and Hearing Research, 41*, 1207–19.

Yoder, P. J. & Warren, S. F. (1999a). Maternal responsivity mediates the relationship between prelinguistic intentional communication and later language. *Journal of Early Intervention, 22*, 126–36.

Yoder, P. J. & Warren, S. F. (1999b). Self-initiated proto-declaratives and proto-imperatives can be facilitated in prelinguistic children with developmental delays. *Journal of Early Intervention, 22*, 337–54.

Yoder P. J. & Warren, S. F. (2001). Relative treatment effects of two prelinguistic communication interventions on language development in toddlers with developmental delays vary by maternal characteristics. *Journal of Speech, Language, and Hearing Research, 44*, 224–37.

Yoder, P. J., Kaiser, A. P., & Alpert, C. (1991). An exploratory study of the interaction between language teaching methods and child characteristics. *Journal of Speech and Hearing Research, 34*, 155–67.

Yoder, P. J., Warren, S. F., Kim, K., & Gazdag, G. E. (1994). Facilitating prelinguistic communication skills in young children with developmental delay II: Systematic replication and extension. *Journal of Speech and Hearing Research, 37*, 841–51.

Yoder, P. J., Kaiser, A. P., Goldstein, H., Alpert, C., Mousetis, L., Kaczmarek, L., & Fisher, R. (1995). An exploratory comparison of milieu teaching and responsive interaction in the classroom. *Journal of Early Intervention, 19*, 218–42.

CHAPTER FOURTEEN

Enhancing Social Competence

Elizabeth A. Stormshak and Janet A. Welsh

Social Competence: A Developmental Framework

Defining social competence

Although there is no universally accepted definition of social competence, in general it can be defined as the capacity to elicit desirable social outcomes and avoid negative ones across a variety of social contexts (Dodge & Murphy, 1984). Socially competent children are those who possess both repertoires of socially appropriate behaviors and the social–cognitive capabilities that allow them to execute these behaviors in a manner that is sensitive and responsive to the demands of particular social situations. Generally, socially competent children are those who get along well with others and avoid negativity and conflict in relationships (Dodge & Murphy, 1984).

Although specific social behaviors, such as prosocial acts, positive orientation toward others, good play skills, good problem-solving, and the ability to regulate emotions, are often viewed as indices of social competence, the behaviors required for social competence vary somewhat with gender, development, and contextual factors. Being a good playmate, for example, may be indicative of social competence at one developmental stage but not at another, and more adaptive in some contexts than in others. Therefore, it is important when evaluating social competence to consider contextual and developmental factors, rather than viewing specific social skills in isolation.

Normative trends in social development

During the preschool period, most peer interactions involve shared play activities, particularly fantasy play. Socially competent preschoolers are those who can sustain their attention to the game and demonstrate positive affect and an agreeable disposition toward their playmates. The ability to regulate emotions despite high levels of arousal and to communicate clearly are critical ingredients to social success for preschool children (Hymel & Rubin, 1985). Because social behavior is not as well coordinated for preschoolers as it is at later ages, interactions are less sustained, and disputes and conflicts are fairly common. Similarly, although aggression is correlated with peer dislike during the preschool years, it is typically less strongly related than during middle childhood (Coie, Dodge, & Kupersmidt, 1990; Bierman, 1986).

As children enter middle childhood, fantasy play declines and rule-based games become more common contexts for peer interaction. Correspondingly, the ability to understand and follow rules as well as regulate emotions during competitive interactions become critical components of social competence (Hartup, 1983). Children who display friendly, positive behaviors and good sportsmanship are generally well liked, while those who continue to display aggression or immature behaviors such as whining, cheating, and tattling are increasingly subjected to peer rejection (Coie, Dodge, & Kupersmidt, 1990; Hymel & Rubin, 1985; Pope, Bierman, & Mumma, 1989). In addition, stable "best friendships" begin to emerge in middle childhood, almost exclusively with same-gender peers, and these friendships are more stable and less contextually bound than those of younger children. In these relationships, being a good play partner is no longer sufficient; grade school children also develop expectations that their friends be helpful, trustworthy, loyal, and dependable (Bukowski & Hoza, 1989; Furman & Bierman, 1984).

During the preadolescent and early adolescent years, play declines dramatically (with the exception of participation in organized sports), and young people spend much of their free time "hanging out" with friends. Communication via notes and talking on the phone becomes prominent, and intimate self-disclosure becomes a central component of friendship, especially for girls (Laursen, 1993). Adolescent peer conflicts typically involve relationship problems such as gossip, disclosure of secrets, or loyalty issues (Hartup & Laursen, 1989).

Adolescents become increasingly aware of peer group norms, and strive to "fit in" by using peer standards to evaluate their own and others' social behavior (O'Brien & Bierman, 1988). As young people move out of the self-contained classroom of the elementary school and into the much larger and more diffuse peer group of secondary school, they confront numerous possibilities regarding peer group affiliation. Although some groups value and reinforce prosocial norms and helpful, friendly, cooperative behaviors, others do not. Therefore, the types of behaviors and characteristics regarded as "socially competent" may vary considerably from one peer group to another. Youth exhibiting chronic problems with aggression, poor achievement, and antisocial behavior may be rejected from mainstream peer groups and affiliate with deviant groups, which may endorse antisocial and delinquent activities (Dishion et al., 1991).

In addition to developmental changes, normative patterns of social competence are influenced by gender differences, which emerge in early childhood and continue throughout life. Boys generally play in larger groups and prefer active, competitive games, while girls typically seek dyadic or triadic relationships and engage in more sedate activities (Eder & Hallinan, 1978; Hartup, 1983). Similarly, cultural and subcultural affiliation influences the behaviors and characteristics required for social success. Different cultural groups vary considerably in their acceptance of aggression, cooperation, competition, affection, reticence, and other social traits. For example, one study found that US children were more verbally and physically aggressive than Polish or Finnish children, and that inner city African American children (the lowest SES group in the sample) rated themselves and were nominated by peers as the most aggressive (Ostermann et al., 1994). Similarly, cultural differences may exist in withdrawal and internalizing behavior, which appear less related to social competence in Asian cultures than in the US (Chen, Rubin, & Li, 1995). Interestingly, these differences may be artifacts of measurement. That is, in each culture certain behaviors are valued and other behaviors are discouraged. Raters such as teachers and parents may under- or over-rate behaviors based on cultural norms. For example, Weisz et al. (1995) found that Thai children were rated by teachers as more aggressive than US children, but were observed to engage in lower levels of aggression than their US counterparts. Overall, individuals who display social behaviors considered normative to the peer group or culture tend to be accepted by the group, whereas those who violate group norms are likely to experience rejection or ostracism (Stormshak et al., 1999a; Wright, Giammarino, & Parad, 1986).

Finally, when considering social competence, it is important to keep in mind that there are multiple aspects of this construct. For example, social competence in school-aged children is often indexed by the degree to which they are accepted or rejected by their peer group (Parker & Asher, 1987). However, group acceptance is distinct from friendship, which makes its own, unique contributions to social competence. It is possible for children to be generally well-liked by peers but lacking in supportive friendships; conversely, it is possible for children to have one or two good-quality friendships but be ignored or rejected by the peer group as a whole (Coie & Dodge, 1988). In addition, as mentioned above, the norms and values of the larger cultural group and the peer social network may play a substantial role in defining and shaping social competence.

The importance of social competence for development

Several decades of clinical and developmental research have documented the significance of social competence in childhood for outcomes later in life. In particular, it has become clear that children who experience chronic, serious difficulties with social adjustment are at risk for a myriad of negative outcomes, including poor school achievement and dropout, mental health disorders, and delinquency (Parker & Asher, 1987; Parker et al., 1995). Impaired social relations constitute a core diagnostic criterion for several child and adolescent psychiatric disorders defined in the *Diagnostic and Statistical Manual of Mental Disorders*, fourth edition (DSM-IV), including Conduct Disorder, Oppositional-Defiant Disorder, Attention Deficit/Hyperactivity Disorder, and pervasive developmental disorders (American Psychiatric Association, 1994). Furthermore, retrospective studies of adults with significant emotional and behavioral problems often indicate early histories of poor social competence (see Parker et al., 1995).

Conversely, developmental research has also demonstrated the benefits of good social adjustment for other areas of development. Normatively, as children age, they spend more time interacting with peers. Peer activities such as shared fantasy and role play help to develop perspective-taking skills, the critical skills of negotiation and cooperation, and assist in the understanding of social norms and conventions (Parker et al., 1995). Children deprived of opportunities to develop good-quality relationships with others are thus also deprived of contexts in which to develop and refine communication skills, empathy, social-cognitive abilities, and self-regulatory capacities. In addition, children without supportive friends or those who experience hostility and victimization at the hands of peers are vulnerable to loneliness, social alienation, and depression (Boivin, Hymel, & Bukowski, 1995).

Factors contributing to social competence

Developmental research suggests that family interaction patterns and parental discipline strategies may play a key role in the development of social competence. A fair amount of evidence exists linking parenting style to children's competence with peers. Most specifically, parents who use consistent, authoritative discipline practices that emphasize self-control are more likely to have socially competent children (Maccoby, 1980; Hinde & Tamplin, 1983). Parents who engage in harsh, inconsistent, or retaliatory discipline practices seem to train their children in aggressive, power-oriented interpersonal strategies that create difficulties in peer settings (Stormshak et al., 2000a; Bierman & Smoot, 1991; Dishion, 1990; Dodge, Bates & Pettit, 1990).

Similarly, research has demonstrated that many skills critical to social competence, such as emotional self-regulation, impulse control, and social adaptability, are related to the quality of the early parent–child relationship, which serves as a prototype for later relationships (Greenberg, Kusche, & Speltz, 1991). Children who experience consistent, sensitive caregiving in the early years are less irritable, less anxious, and better emotionally regulated; these characteristics may contribute to greater social competence later in life (Berlin & Cassidy, 1999; Elicker, Englund, & Sroufe, 1992; Ainsworth et al., 1978). By contrast, children who form insecure attachments to caregivers because of inconsistent, inappropriate caregiver behavior are at risk for developing negative social characteristics such as anxiety, withdrawal, or hostile, intrusive behaviors that contribute to social difficulties outside the family (Jacobvitz & Sroufe, 1987).

In addition to discipline practices and the quality of the parent–child relationship, other parenting characteristics relevant to the development of social competence have been identified by developmental researchers. Specifically, some parents facilitate social competence by serving as "gatekeepers" for their children's social interactions, providing opportunities for peer contacts, monitoring, and assistance with negotiation and conflict resolution (Ladd & Hart, 1992). Children who enter school with a number of positive peer contacts in their classroom show improved academic as well as social adjustment (Ladd, 1990; Ladd & Price, 1987).

Social competence may also be influenced directly by child characteristics such as temperament, activity level, and communicative ability. Children who are positive, flexible, and capable of good self-regulation and clear communication are more likely to be socially successful than those who are temperamentally difficult, irritable, poorly regulated, or have impaired communication skills (Gottman, 1983; Wills, Windle, & Cleary, 1998).

The influence of social networks and community characteristics on social competence

Finally, research has shown that children's social competence is influenced by the characteristics of their communities and peer social networks. One of the most robust predictors of problem behavior and later delinquency is the association with peers engaged in similar forms of behavior (see Dishion, French, & Patterson, 1995). Consistent with the work of Elliott and Menard (1996), there seems to be a reciprocal causation between problem behavior and involvement in a deviant peer group. The general set of findings presents somewhat of a paradox in the literature. In early childhood, aggressive behavior and social competence deficits in children lead to peer rejection and isolation (Coie, Belding, & Underwood, 1988; Dishion, 1990; Dodge, 1983). However, involvement in a deviant peer network is one of the strongest correlates of antisocial behavior (Patterson & Bank, 1989), delinquent behavior (Elliot, Huizinga, & Ageton, 1985; Patterson & Dishion, 1985), and substance use (Dishion, Capaldi, & Yoerger, 1999; Dishion & Loeber, 1985).

Recent research attempts to clarify this paradox. Contrary to popular belief, antisocial boys do establish friendships characterized by positive interactions (Dishion, Andrews, & Crosby, 1995). In particular, children attending school in high-risk classrooms characterized by aggression tend to socialize each other to the positive aspects of aggressive behavior; that is, in these classrooms aggression and violence are associated with peer acceptance, not rejection (Stormshak et al., 1999a). It is within these positive exchanges that the socialization of deviance occurs. Dishion et al. (1995) coded the discussion topics of boys with their best friends. They found deviant dyads based their relationship on the discussion of substance use and problem behavior. Positive affect in those relationships was only in reaction to deviant talk, in contrast to the well-adjusted boys and their friends, who were not positive around the discussion of deviancy. This process of deviancy training in adolescence was associated with escalation in both subsequent delinquency and substance use from early to middle adolescence. Similarly, Stormshak and Webster-Stratton (1999) examined the quality of the peer relations of at-risk preschool children, and found that aggressive children escalated with their "best friends," socializing each other to aggression, and that escalation in this context was related to both home and school behavior problems. During the preadolescent and early adolescent years, youth rejected by mainstream peer groups may be particularly attracted to the norms and behaviors of deviant peers, which include substance use, delinquency, and school dropout (Dishion et al., 1991). Clearly, these youth tend to form affiliations with others like themselves, who often share and reinforce antisocial or aggressive orientations (Cairns, Neckerman, & Cairns, 1989).

Community characteristics may also support and reinforce different aspects of social behavior. While middle class communities may provide monitoring, positive recreational outlets, and strong social institutions (such as schools or youth clubs) that promote adaptive social behavior, impoverished communities are often physically unsafe and lacking in sources of positive social support for families and children. In these communities, the context of violence and stress may contribute significantly to lack of social competence with peers (Attar, Guerra, & Tolan, 1994). In these contexts, deviant groups such as youth gangs may also pose significant threats to the social adaptation of young people (Scheier, Botvin, & Miller, 1999) as well as provide some youth with organized social support (Vigil & Yun, 1996).

History of Interventions to Promote Social Competence

Following the increased awareness of the importance of social competence for healthy development were interventions designed to ameliorate the problems of children and youth experiencing social difficulties. Early prevention and intervention efforts tended to focus in one of three areas – training in social skills, training in social cognitive strategies, and parent training – and to be fairly limited in scope. For example, some programs, recognizing that children experiencing social difficulties seemed to be lacking in specific social skills, made social skills training the focus of the intervention. Most of these early studies included elementary-aged boys involved in short-term social skill training groups employing a "coaching" model, in which adult facilitators used didactic teaching, modeling, and reinforcement of targeted social skills (Bierman & Furman, 1984; Oden & Asher, 1977). While participants in these studies often showed improvements in the behaviors targeted, these rarely translated into overall improvements in their peer status (Putallaz & Wasserman, 1990).

Several other child-focused programs have emphasized the development of social-cognitive skills such as emotional understanding, self-control, and problem solving rather than instruction in particular social behaviors. These programs have been delivered as a school-based curriculum as well as in a group therapy format. Among these are the Interpersonal Cognitive Problem Solving (ICPS) program (Shure & Spivack, 1982, 1988), Lochman's social relations intervention program for rejected children (Lochman et al., 1993; Lochman, 1992), and a social problem solving program developed by Weissberg et al. (1981) and implemented in the schools. All of these programs have proved effective at improving social cognitive skills and reducing impulsivity and negative behaviors; however, none has yielded long-lasting results for children with severe deficits in social competence.

Based upon research demonstrating the relationship between parenting style and social competence in children, many programs have targeted parenting skills rather than child behavior. Over the past two decades, numerous projects have demonstrated the short-term effectiveness of parent education and parent training interventions emphasizing the use of nonpunitive, authoritative discipline approaches, knowledge of child development, parent anger management strategies, and parent–child communication (Forehand & McMahon, 1981; Patterson, 1982; Patterson, Chamberlain, & Reid, 1982; Webster-Stratton, Kolpacoff, & Hollinsworth, 1988). Although these programs have been found to improve parenting, there is little evidence that parent training alone has led to long-term improvements in children's social competence, particularly when children are past preschool age. In addition, parent education and training approaches are unlikely to be of much help when significant poverty, vocational instability, substance abuse, parent psychopathology, and domestic violence are present in the family (Patterson, 1983; Webster-Stratton & Hammond, 1990).

While many early programs yielded positive results, most were modest and failed to demonstrate long-term improvements in children's social competence. One limitation may have been the unidimensional nature of these programs, which sometimes failed to consider the child or family as part of a larger, dynamic social system, and potential obstacles to the generalization of newly acquired skills. For example, although social skill training programs often resulted in the acquisition of new, socially adaptive behaviors by children, they did not address the negative attitudes and expectations of the peer group or the poor quality of the parent–child relationship, both of which may have contributed significantly to the child's poor social competence.

Finally, a number of studies, primarily with adolescents, have revealed the potentially hazardous effects of well-intentioned programs which bring high-risk youth together for group activities designed to foster social competence. In several such programs, youth in the intervention groups showed significantly higher rates of problem behavior than those in the control groups, indicating that the powerful, negative effects of deviant peer group affiliation outweighed the benefits of any intervention approach (Dishion & Andrews, 1995; McCord, 1992).

Developmental-Ecological Models of Intervention for Social Competence

It is clear from the aforementioned research that social competence problems rarely develop in isolation but instead co-occur with a variety of other problems, including disrupted family relationships, problems with self-regulation, and general behavior problems across both the home and school environment. As a result, current intervention efforts have been designed to target social competence both directly and indirectly across different domains and contexts of development. Social competence interventions are embedded within a larger intervention package designed to promote change across a variety of different developmental domains. This ecological perspective on intervention has been primarily adapted from Bronfenbrenner's (1979) seminal theoretical work on the ecological model. Within this model, interventions target not only the individual child but the family, peer system, school context, and community. Indeed, some of the most effective intervention efforts change the context in which problems occur, which in turn alters the interactions among lower system levels. This focus leads to more comprehensive intervention packages that target multiple domains of development.

The school is clearly one of the most important contexts for the development of social competence. Although parenting and family management have significant effects on social competence, these effects play out in interactions among peers, which usually occur in the school environment. Additionally, school contexts may impact the acceptability of certain behaviors. For example, aggression in early childhood may be acceptable to peers in some contexts (e.g., highly aggressive classrooms; Stormshak et al., 1999a). This acceptability of certain behaviors in some contexts has implications for prevention and intervention. If interventions target only the individual child, then changes in the child create a "lack of fit" between the child and environment. For example, interventions in which children are removed from their environment and trained in social problem solving appear to have little or no impact on subsequent delinquency and social problems (Guerra & Slaby, 1990). Therefore, the most effective interventions aimed at enhancing social competence include both a school and a home component. The following summarizes some of the intervention research that has specifically targeted social competence as one outcome and includes interventions focused around multiple contexts of development.

Preschool and early childhood interventions

Interventions in early childhood typically emphasize a prevention model in which children are supported in the development of prosocial behaviors prior to establishing behaviors that are more embedded in the child and environment, and, hence, more difficult to change. In preschool, socially competent children should be able to engage in parallel play with other children, ask questions, support peers, and share. Although conflicts are frequent, children begin to develop skills in conflict negotiation and management of emotions within these interactions. At this age, complex problem solving and cognitive interventions are not appropriate; however, interventions targeting social skills directly have shown positive effects in improving the peer relations of children this age (Mize & Ladd, 1990; Stevahn et al., 2000).

Social competence interventions in early childhood that are driven by the ecological model have typically focused on at-risk groups, such as single, adolescent mothers, low-income children enrolled in Head Start programs, and families of children with early behavior problems. Early intervention efforts that target only parents or only children are less successful at enhancing social outcomes than those targeting both the child and the family (Yoshikawa, 1995). Thus, intervention efforts with the most success have primarily targeted both children and families, and have been embedded in preschools or early intervention programs. For example, the Nurse-Family Partnership Program (Olds, 1997) provides individualized, home-based interventions to young, pregnant women beginning during their second trimester of pregnancy and following up for two years after the child's birth. This intervention targets the social ecology of the child quite broadly, beginning with the prenatal environment. Subsequent focus includes infant health and safety, the child's emotional and cognitive development, positive parenting practices, and the personal development of the mother, which often resulted in fewer subsequent children and increased educational and socioeconomic status of the family. Longitudinal findings from the Nurse-Family Partnership Program showed significant improvements in the health, development, social competence, and behavioral and academic adjustment of the children whose mothers received regular visitations from nurses.

As young children move into the preschool setting, effective interventions target children in the preschool context and link changes at school with home behavior. In a classroom-based intervention for preschoolers developed by Webster-Stratton (1991), children received a social skills curriculum called "Dinosaur School" (Webster-Stratton, 1991). In this program, children watch videotapes of attractive characters modeling a variety of prosocial skills. Children also learn problem solving, emotions, and conflict negotiation. The videotape curriculum is led by co-leaders who use matching puppets to interact with children. Games and activities reinforce skills and promote generalization. The curriculum follows a developmental model, starting with social skills such as helping and sharing and then moving on to more complex models of problem solving. Parents received parent training using her widely recognized videotaped parenting program (Webster-Stratton, 1981, 1990). Children who received social skills training showed improvements in problem solving, conflict management skills, and peer interactions. Parents who received assistance with parenting and support showed improvements in parenting and reductions in child behavior problems at home. Combinations of child social skills training and parent training were more effective at reducing later problems and were related to greater improvements in behavior one year later then were social skills training or parent training alone (Webster-Stratton & Hammond, 1997).

There have been several preschool programs developed as early intervention models which have specifically targeted social competence and aggressive behavior in early childhood. Many of these programs have successfully reduced risk in short-term follow-up assessments of children conducted as children enter elementary school; however, very few programs have followed children into adolescence and adulthood to examine the potential impact of early intervention. Some examples of successful programs which followed children into adolescence include the Perry Preschool Project (Berruta-Clement et al., 1984) and the Syracuse Family Development Research Project (Lally, Mangione, & Honig, 1988). These programs were focused on reducing long-term risk among low-income, high-risk children and families. They were ecological in that interventions targeted multiple domains of development, including classroom behavior, home and family problems, and achievement. Longitudinal follow-up of children and families suggested reductions in delinquent behavior up to 27 years later. Short-term outcomes associated with these programs included enhanced social competence, cognitive skills, and parent–child relationships. These short-term outcomes served as mediators in a longitudinal model that reduced delinquent behavior and enhanced social competence (Yoshikawa, 1994).

Intervention programs implemented in community agencies and preschool programs, such as Head Start, have been particularly successful at enhancing social competence for at-risk children. Social competence is a primary focus of the Head Start mission, and thus an ideal target for interventions which support the existing Head Start curriculum (Raver & Zigler, 1997). Project STAR (Steps to Achieving Resilience: Kaminski et al., 2002; Stormshak et al., 1999b) was developed as a comprehensive intervention aimed at reducing the risk of later substance use. The intervention targeted risk factors during the preschool years linked to later substance use in adolescence and adulthood. These factors included social competence, school bonding (defined at this age as parent involvement), parenting skills, early literacy, and self-regulation of behavior (e.g., ability to sustain attention and regulate emotions). Head Start classrooms were randomly assigned to either the intervention or control group. Children and families were followed into the kindergarten year. A classroom-based curriculum was developed to enhance social competence and increase self-regulation and delivered by Head Start teachers, who received a number of training workshops and continued consultation. The curriculum included 20 sessions of skill-based instruction as well as Activity Based Intervention training for teachers, which encouraged embedding skill-based learning into everyday activities (Bricker & Woods-Cripe, 1992). Classroom lessons focused on sharing, problem solving, turn-taking, talking and playing with friends, and learning letters. Parent training and home visiting were also provided to intervention families. Parents received parenting classes and a curriculum developed by Webster-Stratton (1991), which included educational material on play, praise, limit setting, and handling misbehavior. Home visits assisted families at implementing the skills learned in the parenting groups at home and with siblings. Improvements in social competence, reported by teachers and parents, were maintained over two years. Parenting skills such as positive parenting as well as parent-school involvement also increased and effects were maintained into the kindergarten year (Kaminski et al., 2002).

These findings have implications for prevention and intervention with this age group. In preschool, social competence is integrally related to other domains of development, thus interventions which target parents, children, and schools are the most effective. Community interventions that enhance existing programming for at-risk children are particularly successful. Programs lasting at least two years and following children through adolescence provide needed information on both short-term effects and longer term outcomes.

School-age interventions

As children enter school, social competence becomes more complex and involves skills such as negotiating complex peer interactions and emotional conflicts. The competitive play which is characteristic of social games at this age contributes to the difficulty that some children have with peers. A review of the literature on intervention and social competence suggests that the majority of intervention packages have been developed at the elementary school age to target both individual child skills as well as the classroom environment. There are several reasons for the importance of targeting this age group. First, social competence problems at this age are predictive of later problems, which tend to be less responsive to intervention as children develop. Second, children are in the same classroom all day, which makes the implementation of a school-based curriculum straightforward in terms of assessment and consultation. Additionally, because children are contained in the same classroom, ratings of peer acceptance can be easily assessed as well as changes in the classroom environment.

Several examples of programs will be discussed and highlighted here, including both universal programs designed to benefit all students and targeted interventions focused on children at risk. A summary of some of the key ingredients across programs is provided in Table 14.1. The first is PATHS (Promoting Alternative Thinking Strategies: Greenberg

Table 14.1 Summary of key ingredients included in social skills programs in elementary school

Basic skills
  Making friends
  Sharing
  Helping
  Listening
  Cooperation
  Negotiating conflict
  Teamwork
  Talking with peers
Identification of feelings
  Labeling emotions
  Understanding emotions
  Empathy
  Managing anger
Problem-solving
  Understanding social problems
  Generating solutions
  Generating alternatives
  Role-plays: acting out problems
Self-regulation
  Stop and think models
  Evaluating consequences of solutions
  Evaluating emotions during problem solving
Links with classroom environment
  Problem solving in the classroom
  Talking to peers about problems
  Involving teachers
Maintaining friendships
  Supporting friends
  Keeping friends

& Kusche, 1993). PATHS is a universal, classroom-based intervention that was initially developed for use with deaf children in order to support the development of emotional understanding and problem solving. The curriculum is primarily focused around enhancing social competence, and includes training in problem solving, emotional understanding, and self-regulation. A strong emphasis on feeling identification and communication is embedded in the curriculum, which begins by having children learn all the feelings and place a "feeling face" on their desks that identifies how they are feeling that day. Emotional understanding, empathy, and discussion of feelings with peers are then emphasized throughout the lessons, which are taught by teachers with support from consultants. The curriculum is embedded in the school and lasts all year. PATHS has been effective at improving self-control, emotional understanding, and the use of more effective conflict resolution skills and increased social competence (Greenberg et al., 1995). When the effects of PATHS were assessed on a large school population of first graders, PATHS was found to decrease both observed aggression and peer ratings of aggression when compared to control classrooms (Conduct Problems Prevention Research Group, 1999b). Additionally, dosage analyses revealed an effect on classroom environment; that is, more lessons taught were related to a positive classroom environment. Although PATHS was administered at only the classroom level, the success of PATHS is significant because both individual and contextual changes in the environment were examined and impacted by this intervention. That is, individual children reduced their levels of aggression and these changes in behavior matched the positive classroom environment that was created by the intervention. PATHS is an example of a program which attempts to change individual behavior by targeting the context in which behavioral interactions occur (e.g., the first grade classroom).

The universal PATHS program was included as part of a larger intervention package for at-risk school-aged children called FAST Track (Families and Schools Together: Conduct Problems Prevention Research Group, 1992). Children in FAST Track were identified in kindergarten as "at-risk" using a multiple gating procedure based on a combination of both teacher and parent reports of behavior (Lochman & The Conduct Problems Prevention Research Group, 1995). FAST Track is an example of a multifocused intervention program designed to decrease later delinquency and antisocial behavior. FAST Track is based on a long-term intervention model with targeted intervention delivered through middle school. The success of this model is dependent on building competencies and protective factors in the child, family, school, and community. One strength of FAST Track was its comprehensive design. School-wide participation was achieved at each site and thus teachers and parents were recruited in part by schools to participate in the project. When families refused to attend the intervention, school-wide data was collected and analyzed as part of the ongoing relationship between FAST Track, schools, and communities. Thus, high-risk families who refused participation were still included in some of the school-wide assessment and outcomes of the project. Rather than focus results on only those who participated in the more intense intervention efforts (e.g., parent training, social skills training, home visiting), FAST Track took a public health perspective on the development of delinquency and conduct problems, focusing on the larger school population in many of the outcomes reported.

Designed around a developmental model of conduct problems, an important target of FAST Track in early childhood was social competence, in addition to behavior problems and family management. Social competence was specifically targeted through PATHS (discussed above) and a social skills coaching intervention administered during first through fourth grades ("Friendship group"). This intervention included training in positive social interactions, social problem solving, and emotional understanding. Children met in groups of 5–6 for 22 sessions over the course of the first grade year. The curriculum took a developmental approach to teaching social competence, starting with beginning skills such as building teamwork and group cohesion and then moving on to more difficult skills such as cooperation and competition. Therapists for the groups were trained in using "induction" techniques which promoted practicing skills during the sessions and listening to peer feedback instead of over-control and management of behavior. For example, children were encouraged to listen to their peers and practice the new skills learned during conflicts and episodes of behavioral dysregulation. Group support for achievement of skills such as emotional control and positive peer interaction was facilitated. Parents and children received a variety of additional services, including a 22-session parenting group, home visits, and tutoring. The parenting curriculum focused on home–school involvement, parental self-control, developmentally appropriate expectations for children, and parenting skills that promote parent–child interaction and decrease problem behavior. Home visits paralleled the parenting curriculum and provided individual support to families with additional needs. Children received individualized tutoring to promote early reading skills three times a week throughout the first grade year.

Overall, results of FAST Track after first grade suggest that the intervention was successful at enhancing social competence, with intervention children showing more positive interactions with playmates at school and increased social preference scores compared to a high-risk control group (Conduct Problems Prevention Research Group, 1999a). Results of the first three years indicate significant reductions in special education referrals and aggression both at home and at school for the targeted children (Conduct Problems Prevention Research Group, 1998, 1999a, b).

Another example of a successful, universal ecological intervention is the LIFT program, which included a school-based classroom curriculum, a playground component, and a parenting intervention (Linking the Interests of Families and Teachers: Reid et al., 1999). The LIFT program included a social competence, school-based curriculum that focused on training in problem solving, feeling identification, and self-control. The curriculum was administered by trained interventionists in 20 sessions over the school year to first and fifth graders. This curriculum specifically targeted playground behavior in a "playground component" with a modified version of the Good Behavior Game, in which children earned rewards as a group for positive behavior and negative behaviors were subtracted from their group scores. At the beginning of the program, children within each classroom were divided into teams. These groups earned positive rewards by engaging in prosocial behavior on the playground and collecting armbands (which children wore when they behaved in an overtly positive manner). These armbands were then collected and put in a jar. When the jar was full, a reward was earned. Each time a child was observed behaving negatively, the behavior was noted in a log book. Negative points were subtracted from a preset positive point score, and total points at the end of recess led to rewards such as stickers and prizes. Parents attended parenting groups that met for six weekly sessions. The curriculum targeted problem solving, parenting skills, and education in developmentally appropriate social behaviors. Parents were also encouraged to become active in the school. A phone line was installed in each classroom and teachers were encouraged to leave brief messages about activities and homework on the phone message machine. Parents were encouraged to call the message machine and leave messages for the teacher. Weekly contact with families by intervention staff promoted involvement in the school and integration of school and home activities.

The results of this intervention suggest immediate improvements in social competence and behavior during playground observations, particularly for the most aggressive children (Eddy, Reid, & Fetrow, 2000). Effects on negative parenting and teacher ratings of behavior were also found. Additionally, at three-year follow-up the effects of this intervention were maintained in less severity of behavior problems for the first graders and lower initiation of deviant peer associations for middle-schoolers when compared to a matched control group.

In summary, research on effective school-age interventions demonstrates the value of a simultaneous focus on the individual child, the family, and the classroom environment. While universal programs alone can enhance the classroom climate and improve the general social competence of most children, these are generally insufficient for children with significant social skill deficits and behavioral problems. Changes in the child and/or family without concurrent changes in the school may be effective at reducing short-term conduct problems but are not the most effective in changing the peer interactions of children, which occur primarily in the school setting. Interventions that provide opportunities for practicing skills, include interventions across several years of development, and assess children for years after the intervention are the most effective.

Adolescent interventions

In adolescence, social competence is defined more broadly than in early childhood. For some children, social competence may involve avoiding deviant peers and selecting friends based on socially appropriate behavior. At this age, some youth have solidified a pattern of socially incompetent behavior (e.g., "life-course persistent" adolescents; Moffitt, 1993) whereas others are simply experimenting with deviant behavior and may benefit from prevention efforts which broadly target peer difficulties characteristic of this age (e.g., drug and alcohol use, intimacy). Interventions must focus not only on social competence generally, but must pay special attention to the contexts in which adolescents interact and skills that may be used in these contexts to decrease social risk.

Interestingly, group therapy or "anger management" training is one of the most widely offered interventions for at-risk adolescents. However, research in this area tends to be scant, and findings that suggest a long-term positive impact for adolescents who receive this type of intervention have been limited. There have been several studies in which adolescents are taught problem solving and social cognitive skills in order to increase their ability to engage positively with peers. For example, Guerra and Slaby (1990) administered a 12-session program to adolescent offenders in a state correctional institution. The intervention focused on teaching a number of positive skills, such as attending to relevant information, generating responses to problems, seeking additional information in problem situations, and prioritizing responses to problems. The intervention also focused on the development of self-control techniques and modifying beliefs that supported the use of aggression. Although youth showed improvements in cognitive skills at follow-up, no long-term effects on aggression or recidivism were found. Similar to other research, short-term changes in cognitions or self-control skills were not related to long-term changes in behavior (Feindler, Marriott, & Iwata, 1984).

This research has resulted in questions around the efficacy of such approaches to interventions. For example, research by Dishion and colleagues suggests that offering social skills interventions in a group format may be problematic in that "iatrogenic" effects of placing at-risk youth in a group together and training them to engage positively with each other only creates a context for deviant peer associations. In fact, in their research using the Adolescent Transitions Program (ATP), Dishion and colleagues found that families who participated in parent training without child group therapy showed the greatest improvements. However, for youth who participated in the group training behavior actually worsened over time (Dishion et al., 1996; Dishion & Andrews, 1995). This research suggests that group formats for intervention at this age may not be the best way to train children with social skills deficits. Instead, interventions that target families and school are likely to be more effective and create less risk of promoting deviant behavior, particularly for children with long-term problems whose difficulties stem from family management and parenting deficits that began in early childhood (Moffitt, 1993).

One aspect of social competence in adolescence involves choosing appropriate peers and refusing to engage in risky and/or deviant behavior. Most successful adolescent intervention programs have targeted social competence as a mediator of risk behaviors such as substance use and school failure. These programs generally fall into one of two categories: school-based prevention curricula that target students directly and are implemented by classroom teachers or guidance counselors, and extracurricular programs that target parents and youth together.

Parent–youth programming in schools Programs targeted at parents are based on developmental models emphasizing the significant protective impact of close ties to family and school during the adolescent years, and the value of parent–child communication and parental monitoring at enhancing competence and reducing risk for adolescents. Examples of these include Preparing for the Drug Free Years (PDFY; Spoth, Redmond, & Shin, 1998), which is a universal family-focused preventive intervention designed to increase parenting skills related to the reduction of problem behavior in adolescence by enhancing family management skills. The intervention is delivered in five weekly parenting sessions, including a session in which youth participate with parents to learn skills at resisting antisocial peer influences. Results from a series of studies using PDFY suggest that the program enhances parent–child interaction and short-term parenting interactions, as well as reducing the growth of problem behavior over time (Kosterman et al., 1997; Spoth, Redmond, & Shin, 1998; Mason et al., 2003).

The Adolescent Transition Program (ATP) is a tiered, multilevel family intervention delivered within a middle school setting (Dishion & Kavanagh, 2003). The intervention is based on an ecological model of child development and incorporates assessments and interventions that link the multiple systems in which youth and families interact, including home, schools, and peers. The first level of the intervention involves creating a family resource center within the middle school environment. Staffed with a parent consultant, the family resource center serves as a point of contact and a universal intervention for parents and teachers concerned about youth behavior. The goals of the parent consultant in the family resource center are to: (a) provide an infrastructure for collaboration with school staff and parents, (b) deliver universal interventions, (c) support norms for protective parenting practices, and (d) disseminate information encouraging family management practices in adolescence. This approach to school-based intervention has been successful at reducing the risk of problem behavior, preventing the onset of substance use, and reducing risk behavior at school, including contacts with deviant peers (Dishion et al., 2002; Stormshak et al., in press).

A broad-scale field trial currently underway, the PROSPER Project (Promoting School–Community–University Partnerships to Enhance Resilience; Spoth, Greenberg, & Bierman, 2002) has attempted to increase the ecological validity of these adolescent interventions by combining classroom-based and family-focused programming in a coordinated, district-wide fashion. While these universal programs are not sufficient to meet the needs of youth with well-established behavioral and substance use problems, they can enhance social competence and reduce risk for many young people. For seriously troubled youth, intensive, family-focused, case-management-style interventions such as Mutisystemic Therapy (Henggeler et al., 1998) appear to be the most promising.

Programs targeting youth through school-based curricula   There is currently a bewildering abundance of published, school-based programs designed to enhance youth social competencies and reduce risk. However, relatively few have evidence of long-term effectiveness based on scientifically rigorous evaluations. Empirically validated programs generally incorporate several different types of skill development, including resistance training, decision making, and goal clarification, and normative education in their curricula. For example, the Life Skills Training Program (LST: Botvin, 1996) includes 18 lessons that focus on decision making, coping with negative emotions, communication and social skills, normative information regarding substance use, and assertiveness. Using a slightly different conceptual model, the All Stars Program (Giles, Harrington, & Fearnow-Kenney, 2001) involves 14 lessons emphasizing future plans and aspirations, commitment, bonding to prosocial groups, and clarification of social norms. Recognizing the risks of aggregating groups of at-risk youth, programs such as LST and All Stars are implemented in the socially relevant context of the school as universal prevention. These programs have been successful at reducing drug and alcohol use for adolescents, which involves mediators such as setting appropriate personal goals, choosing appropriate peers, and engaging in socially appropriate behavior (Botvin, 1996; Botvin et al., 1992; Harrington et al., 2001).

Social Competence Interventions in the Next Decade: Past Findings and Future Implications

The previous review of intervention research can be summarized into a few key findings and recommendations for future research. First, interventions which target children across home and school as well as include specific training for children in social skills are the most effective interventions for enhancing social competence. Second, the longer the intervention lasts, the earlier it begins, and the more follow-up assessments that are conducted, the more effective intervention appears to be at reducing risk and enhancing skills. One reason for this finding is that social competence changes across development and may be conceptualized as a risk factor early in childhood for a variety of different outcomes. Finally, future research into social competence interventions is likely to emphasize the importance of implementation quality and the challenges associated with implementing evidence-based programs in real-life settings such as schools and communities.

Several contexts of development have been largely ignored and will likely be part of the next generation of intervention research. The first is the neighborhood, which may be an important context for the development of social competence for many children. Researchers have begun to move beyond specific behaviors that predict risk to systematic investigations that examine the structure of neighborhoods and social networks as contexts of risk. For example, the perceived hassles around poverty in the context of neighborhoods impact the development of antisocial behavior in middle childhood, whereas detachment from high-risk neighborhoods may protect some children from the development of behavior problems (Seidman et al, 1998, 1999). Additionally, research on neighborhood peer networks suggests that they are complex, and often times the highest risk peers are central to these networks, creating a context for the development of antisocial behavior. Research in the area of peer relations has begun to examine not only peer acceptance and rejection as important constructs but the social networks of youth and the implications of placement within the network on adjustment. For example, mapping the social networks of youth can lead to understanding the important qualities of influential peers and the characteristics of the peer network that may lead to antisocial behavior. Xie, Cairns, and Cairns (1999) found that aggressive youth were central to the networks of inner city boys. Similarly, highly antisocial youth may be the most popular when one examines peer network "centrality" rather than simply looking at peer ratings. For example, when children are asked to place each other in groups as well as rank peers using peer nomination techniques, some aggressive youth emerge as central to their peer networks (Rodkin et al., 2000).

Additionally, recent research on sibling relationships as a potential influence on social competence is also emerging. Intervention research may target the family broadly, but few studies specifically focus on siblings within the family. It is clear that siblings may provide a context for both the development of risk as well as protection from deviancy (Stormshak et al., 1996, 2000b; Stormshak, Comeau, & Shepard, in press). For example, in elementary school many children with social skills deficits are rejected from peers. In turn, this leads children to spend additional time with siblings. These siblings may serve as role models and social support, or they may create a context for the promotion of deviant behavior and modeling of inappropriate social skills. Research exists to support both of these potential models (East & Rook, 1992; Lewin et al., 1993; Bank, Patterson, & Reid, 1996). Intervention research which focuses on siblings will be important in newly developed models of intervention.

Social competence in the next decade will likely be defined even more broadly, including early social skills and competencies with peers as well as behaviors deemed "competent" by adults, such as academic achievement and limited risk taking. Interventions will continue to focus on social competence as it is embedded in a complex developmental system. Interventions which target multiple indicators of adjustment will likely have the most impact on social competence across development.

References

Ainsworth, M. D. S., Blehar, M. C., Waters, E., & Wall, S. (1978). *Patterns of attachment.* Hillsdale, NJ: Lawrence Erlbaum Associates.

American Psychiatric Association (1994). *Diagnostic and statistical manual of mental disorders* (4th edn.). Washington, DC: American Psychiatric Association.

Attar, B. K., Guerra, N. G., & Tolan, P. H. (1994). Neighborhood disadvantage, stressful life events, and adjustment in urban elementary-school children. *Journal of Clinical Child Psychology, 23(4)*, 391–400.

Bank, L., Patterson, G. R., & Reid, J. B. (1996). Negative sibling interaction patterns as predictors of later adjustment problems in adolescent and young adult males. In G. Brody (ed.), *Sibling relationships: Their causes and consequences – Advances in applied developmental psychology* (pp. 197–22). Norwood, NJ: Ablex.

Berlin, L. J. & Cassidy, J. (1999). Relations among relationships: Contributions from attachment theory and research. In J. Cassidy & P. R. Shaver (eds.), *Handbook of attachment: Theory, research, and clinical applications.* (pp. 688–712). New York: Guilford.

Berruta-Clement, J. R., Schweinhart, L. J., Barnett, W. S., Epstein, A. S., & Weikart, D. P. (1984). *Changed lives: The effects of the Perry Preschool Program on youths through age 19.* Ypsilanti, MI: High Scope Press.

Bierman, K. L. (1986). The relationship between social aggression and peer rejection in middle childhood. In R. Printz (ed.), *Advances in behavioral assessment of children and families,* (vol. 2, pp. 151–78). Greenwich, CT: JAI Press.

Bierman, K. L. & Furman, W. (1984). The effects of social skills training and peer involvement on the social adjustment of preadolescents. *Child Development, 55*, 151–62.

Bierman, K. L. & Smoot, D. L. (1991). Linking family characteristics with poor peer relations: The mediating role of conduct problems. *Journal of Abnormal Child Psychology, 19*, 341–56.

Boivin, M., Hymel, S., & Bukowski, W. M. (1995). The roles of social withdrawal, peer rejection, and victimization by peers in predicting loneliness and depressed mood in childhood. *Development and Psychopathology, 7*, 765–85.

Botvin, G. J. (1996). Substance abuse prevention through life skills training. In R. D. Peters & R. J. McMahon (eds.), *Preventing childhood disorders, substance abuse, and delinquency* (pp. 215–40). Thousand Oaks, CA: Sage.

Botvin, G. J., Dusenbury, L., Baker, E., & James-Ortiz, S. (1992). Smoking prevention among urban minority youth: Assessing effects of outcome and mediating variables. *Health Psychology, 11*, 290–99.

Bricker, D. & Woods-Cripe, J. J. (1992). *An activity-based approach to early intervention.* Baltimore, MD: Paul H. Brookes.

Bronfenbrenner, U. (1979). *The ecology of human development: Experiments by nature and design.* Cambridge, MA: Harvard University Press.

Bukowski, W. & Hoza, B. (1989). Popularity and friendship: Issues in theory, measurement and outcome. In T. J. Berndt & G. W. Ladd (eds.), *Peer relationships in child development* (pp. 15–45). New York: John Wiley.

Cairns, R. B., Neckerman, H. J., & Cairns, B. D. (1989). Social networks and the shadows of synchrony. In G. R. Adams, T. P. Gulotta, & R. Montmayor (eds.), *Advances in adolescent development* (vol. 1, pp. 275–305). Newbury Park, CA: Sage

Chen, X., Rubin, K. H., & Li, Z. (1995). Social functioning and adjustment in Chinese children: A longitudinal study. *Developmental Psychology, 31*, 531–9.

Coie, J. D. & Dodge, K. A. (1988). Multiple sources of data on social behavior and social status in the school: A cross-age comparison. *Child Development, 59*, 815–29.

Coie, J. D., Belding, M., & Underwood, M. (1988). Aggression and rejection in childhood. In B. B. Lahey & A. E. Kazdin (eds.), *Advances in clinical child psychology*. New York: Plenum Press.

Coie, J. D., Dodge, K. A., & Kupersmidt, J. B. (1990). Peer group behavior and social status. In S. R. Asher & J. D. Coie (eds.), *Peer rejection in childhood* (pp. 17–59). Cambridge: Cambridge University Press.

Conduct Problems Prevention Research Group (1992). A developmental and clinical model for the prevention of conduct disorders: The FAST Track Program. *Development and Psychopathology, 4*, 509–27.

Conduct Problems Prevention Research Group (1998). Results of the Fast Track Prevention Project: Grade 3 Outcomes. Paper presented at the American Psychological Association, San Francisco, CA, August.

Conduct Problems Prevention Research Group (1999a). Initial impact of the Fast Track Prevention trial for conduct problems: I. The high-risk sample. *Journal of Consulting and Clinical Psychology, 67*, 631–47.

Conduct Problems Prevention Research Group (1999b). Initial impact of the Fast Track Prevention trail for conduct problems: II. Classroom effect. *Journal of Consulting and Clinical Psychology, 67*, 648–57.

Dishion, T. J. (1990). The family ecology of boys' peer relations in middle childhood. *Child Development, 61*, 874–92.

Dishion, T. J. & Andrews, D. W. (1995). Preventing escalation in problem behaviors with high-risk young adolescents: Immediate and 1-year outcomes. *Journal of Consulting and Clinical Psychology, 63*, 538–48.

Dishion, T. J. & Kavanagh, K. (2003). *Intervening in Adolescent Problem Behavior: A Family Centered Approach*. New York: Guilford.

Dishion, T. J. & Loeber, R. (1985). Male adolescent marijuana and alcohol use: The role of parents and peers revisited. *American Journal of Drug and Alcohol Abuse, 11*, 11–25.

Dishion, T. J., Andrews, D. W., & Crosby, L. (1995). Antisocial boys and their friends in early adolescence: Relationship characteristics, quality, and interactional process. *Child Development, 66*, 139–51.

Dishion, T. J., Capaldi, D. M., & Yoerger, K. (1999). Middle childhood antecedents to progression in male adolescent substance use: An ecological analysis of risk and protection. *Journal of Adolescent Research, 14*, 175–206.

Dishion, T. J., French, D. C., & Patterson, G. R. (1995). The development and ecology of antisocial behavior. In D. Cicchetti & D. Cohen (eds.), *Manual of developmental psychopathology* (pp. 421–71). New York: John Wiley.

Dishion, T. J., Patterson, G. R., Stoolmiller, M., & Skinner, M. (1991). Family, school, and behavioral antecedents to early adolescent involvement with antisocial peers. *Developmental Psychology, 27*, 172–80.

Dishion, T. J., Capaldi, D. M., Spracklen, K. M., & Li, F. (1995). Peer ecology of male adolescent drug use. *Development and Psychopathology, 7*, 803–24.

Dishion, T. J., Andrews, D. W., Kavanagh, K., & Soberman, L. H. (1996). Preventive interventions for high-risk youth. In R. D. Peters & R. J. McMahon (eds.), *Preventing childhood disorders, substance abuse, and delinquency* (pp. 184–214). Thousand Oaks, CA: Sage.

Dishion, T. J., Kavanagh, K., Schneiger, A., Nelson, S., & Kaufman, N. K. (2002). Preventing early adolescent substance use: A family-centered strategy for the public middle school. *Prevention Science, 3*, 191–201.

Dodge, K. A. (1983). Behavioral antecedents of peer status. *Child Development, 51,* 162–70.

Dodge, K. A. & Murphy, R. R. (1984). The assessment of social competence in adolescents. *Advances in Child Behavior Analysis and Therapy, 3,* 61–96.

Dodge, K. A., Bates, J. E., & Pettit, G. S. (1990). Mechanisms in the cycle of violence. *Science, 250,* 1678–83.

East, P. L. & Rook, K. S. (1992). Compensatory patterns of support among children's peer relationships: A test using school friends, non-school friends, and siblings. *Developmental Psychology, 28,* 163–72.

Eddy, J. M., Reid, J. B., & Fetrow, R. A. (2000). An elementary-school based prevention program targeting modifiable antecedents of youth delinquency and violence: Linking the Interests of Families and Teachers (LIFT). *Journal of Emotional and Behavioral Disorders, 8,* 165–76.

Eder, D. & Hallinan, M. T. (1978). Sex differences in children's friendships. *American Sociological Review, 43,* 237–50.

Elicker, J., Englund, M., & Sroufe, L. A. (1992). Predicting peer competence and peer relationships in childhood from early parent–child relationships. In R. D. Parke & G. W. Ladd (eds.), *Family–peer relationships: Modes of linkages* (pp. 77–106). Hillsdale, NJ: Lawrence Erlbaum Associates.

Elliott, D. S. & Menard, S. (1996). Delinquent friends and delinquent behavior: Temporal and developmental patterns. In J. D. Hawkins (ed.), *Delinquency and crime: Current theories. Cambridge Criminology Series* (pp. 28–67). New York: Cambridge University Press.

Elliott, D. S., Huizinga, D., & Ageton, S. S. (1985). *Explaining delinquency and drug use.* Beverly Hills, CA: Sage.

Feindler, E. L., Marriott, S. A., & Iwata, M. (1984). Group anger control training for junior high school delinquents. *Cognitive Therapy and Research, 8,* 299–311.

Forehand, R. & McMahon, R. J. (1981). *Helping the noncompliant child: A clinician's guide to effective parent training.* New York: Guilford.

Furman, W. & Bierman, K. L. (1984). Perceived determinants of friendship: A multidimensional study of developmental changes. *Developmental Psychology, 20,* 925–31.

Giles, S. M., Harrington, N. G., Fearnow-Kenney, M. (2001). Evaluation of the All Stars program: Student and teacher factors that influence mediators of substance use. *Journal of Drug Education, 31,* 385–97.

Gottman, J. M. (1983). How children become friends. *Monographs of the Society for Research in Child Development, 48,* (2, serial no. 201).

Greenberg, M. T. & Kusche, C. A. (1993). *Promoting social and emotional development in deaf children: The PATHS project.* Seattle, WA: University of Washington Press.

Greenberg, M. T., Kusche, C. A., & Speltz, M. (1991). Emotional regulation, self-control, and psychopathology: The role of relationships in early childhood. In D. Cicchette & S. L. Toth (eds.), *Rochester Symposium on Developmental Psychopathology,* vol. 2: *Internalizing and externalizing expressions of dysfunction* (pp. 21–55). Hillsdale, NJ: Lawrence Erlbaum Associates.

Greenberg, M. T., Kusche, C. A., Cook, E. T., & Quamma, J. P. (1995). Promoting emotional competence in school-aged children: The effects of the PATHS curriculum. *Development and Psychopathology, 7,* 117–36.

Guerra, N. G. & Slaby, R. G. (1990). Cognitive mediators of aggression in adolescent offenders: Intervention. *Developmental Psychology, 26,* 269–77.

Harrington, N. G., Giles, S. M., Hoyle, R. H., Feeney, G. J., & Yungbluth, S. C. (2001). Evaluation of the All Stars character education and problem behavior prevention program. Effects on mediator and outcome variables for middle school students. *Health Education & Behavior, 29,* 533–46.

Hartup, W. W. (1983). The peer system. In E. M. Hetherington (vol. ed.), *Handbook of child psychology* (4th edn.), vol. 4: *Socialization, personality and social development* (pp. 103–96). New York: John Wiley.

Hartup, W. W. & Laursen, B. (1989). Contextual constraints and children's friendship relations. Paper presented at the biennial meeting of the Society for Research in Child Development, Kansas City, MO, March.

Henggeler, S., Schoenwald, S. K., Borduin, C. M., Rowland, M. D., & Cunningham, P. B. (1998). *Multisystemic treatment of antisocial behavior in children and adolescents*. New York: Guilford.

Hinde, R. & Tamplin, A. (1983). Relations between mother–child interaction and behavior in preschool. *British Journal of Developmental Psychology*, *1*, 231–57.

Hymel, S. & Rubin, K. (1985). Children with peer relationship and social skills problems: Conceptual, methodological and developmental issues. In G. J. Whitehurst (ed.), *Annals of Child Development* (vol. 2, pp. 251–97). Greenwich, CT: JAI Press.

Jacobvitz, D. & Sroufe, L. A. (1987). The early caregiver–child relationship and attention deficit disorder with hyperactivity in kindergarten: A prospective study. *Child Development*, *58*, 1496–1504.

Kaminski, R., Stormshak, E. A., Good, R., & Goodman, M. (2002). Prevention of substance abuse with rural Head Start children and families: Results of project STAR. *Psychology of Addictive Behaviors*, *16*, S11–S26.

Kosterman, R., Hawkins, J. D., Spoth, R., Haggerty, K. P., & Zhu, K. (1997). Effects of a preventive parent-training intervention on observed family interactions: Proximal outcomes from preparing for the Drug Free Years. *Journal of Community Psychology*, *25*, 337–52.

Ladd, G. W. (1990). Having friends, keeping friends, making friends, and being liked by peers in the classroom: Predictors of children's early school adjustment? *Child Development*, *61*, 1081–1100.

Ladd, G. W. & Hart, C. H. (1992). Creating informal play opportunities: Are parents' and preschoolers' initiations related to children's competence with peers? *Developmental Psychology*, *28*, 1179–87.

Ladd, G. W. & Price, J. P. (1987). Predicting children's social and school adjustment following the transition from preschool to kindergarten. *Child Development*, *58*, 16–25.

Lally, J. R., Mangione, P. L., & Honig, A. S. (1988). The Syracuse University Family Development Research Project: Long-range impact of an early intervention with low-income children and their families. In D. R. Powell (ed.), *Annual advances in applied developmental psychology*, vol. 3: *Parent education as early childhood intervention: Emerging directions in theory, research, and practice* (pp. 79–104). Norwood, NJ: Ablex.

Laursen, B. (1993). Conflict management among close peers. In B. Laursen (ed.), *Close friendships in adolescence* (pp. 39–54). San Francisco, CA: Jossey Bass.

Lewin, M. L., Hops, H., Davis, B., & Dishion, T. J. (1993). Similarity in siblings' school social behavior: A comparison of teacher and peer ratings and direct observations. *Developmental Psychology*, *29*, 963–9.

Lochman, J. E. (1992). Cognitive-behavioral intervention with aggressive boys: Three-year follow-up and preventive effects. *Journal of Consulting and Clinical Psychology*, *60*, 426–32.

Lochman, J. E. & the Conduct Problems Prevention Research Group (1995). Screening of child behavior problems for prevention programs at school entry: Gender and race effects. *Journal of Consulting and Clinical Psychology*, *63*, 549–59.

Lochman, J. E., Coie, J. D., Underwood, M. K., & Terry, R. (1993). Effectiveness of a social relations intervention program for aggressive and nonaggressive, rejected children. *Journal of Consulting and Clinical Psychology*, *61*, 1053–8.

Maccoby, E. (1980). *Social development: Psychological growth and the parent–child relationship.* New York: Harcourt Brace Jovanovich.

Mason, A. W., Kosterman, R., Hawkins, J. D., Haggerty, K. P., & Spoth, R. L. (2003). Reducing adolescents' growth in substance use and delinquency: Randomized trial effects of a parent-training prevention intervention. *Prevention Science, 4,* 203–12.

McCord, J. (1992). The Cambridge-Sommerville Study: A pioneering longitudinal-experimental study of delinquency prevention. In J. McCord & R. Tremblay (eds.), *Preventing antisocial behavior: Interventions from birth to adolescence* (pp. 196–209). New York: Guilford.

Mize, J. & Ladd, G. W. (1990). A cognitive-social learning approach to social skill training with low status preschool children. *Developmental Psychology, 26,* 388–97.

Moffitt, T. E. (1993) Adolescence-limited and life-course-persistent antisocial behavior: A developmental taxonomy. *Psychological Review, 100(4),* 674–701.

O'Brien, S. F. & Bierman, K. L. (1988). Conceptions and perceived influence of peer groups: Interviews with preadolescents and adolescents. *Child Development, 59,* 1360–65.

Oden, S. & Asher, S. R. (1977). Coaching children in social skills. *Child Development, 48,* 495–506.

Olds, D. (1997). The Prenatal/Early Infancy Project: Fifteen years later. In G. W. Albee & T. P. Gullotta (eds.), *Primary prevention works. Issues in children's and families' lives* (vol. 6, pp. 41–67). Thousand Oaks, CA: Sage.

Ostermann, K., Bjorkvist, K., Lagerspetz, K. M., & Kaukianen, A. (1994). Peer and self estimated aggression and victimization from five ethnic groups. *Aggressive Behavior, 20,* 411–28.

Parker, J. G. & Asher, S. R. (1987). Peer acceptance and later personal adjustment: Are low-accepted children at risk? *Psychological Bulletin, 102,* 357–89.

Parker, J. G., Rubin, K. H., Price, J. M., & DeRosier, M. E. (1995). Peer relationships, child development, and adjustment: A developmental psychopathology perspective. In D. Cicchetti & D. Cohen (eds.) *Developmental Psychopathology,* vol. 2: *Risk, disorder and adaptation* (pp. 96–161). New York: Wiley.

Patterson, G. R. (1982). *Coercive family process.* Eugene, OR: Castalia.

Patterson, G. R. (1983). Stress: A change agent for family process. In N. Garmezy & M. Rutter (eds.), *Stress, coping and development in children* (pp. 235–64). New York: McGraw-Hill.

Patterson, G. R. & Bank, L. (1989). Some amplifying mechanisms for pathologic processes in families. In M. R. Gunnar & E. Thelen (eds.), *Systems and development: The Minnesota Symposia on Child Psychology* (vol. 22, pp. 167–209). Hillsdale, NJ: Lawrence Erlbaum Associates.

Patterson, G. R. & Dishion, T. J. (1985). Contributions of families and peers to delinquency. *Criminology, 23,* 63–79.

Patterson, G. R., Chamberlain, P., & Reid, J. B. (1982). A comparative evaluation of a parent-training program. *Behavior Therapy, 13,* 638–50.

Pope, A. W., Bierman, K. L., & Mumma, G. H. (1989). Relations between hyperactive and aggressive behavior and peer relations at three elementary grade levels. *Journal of Abnormal Child Psychology, 3,* 253–67.

Putallaz, M. & Wasserman, A. (1990). Children's entry behaviors. In S. R. Asher & J. D. Coie (eds.), *Peer rejection in childhood.* New York: Cambridge University Press.

Raver, C. & Zigler, E. F. (1997). Social competence: An untapped dimension in evaluating Head Start's success. *Early Childhood Research Quarterly, 12,* 363–85.

Reid, J. B., Eddy, J. M., Fetrow, R. A., & Stoolmiller, M. (1999). Description and immediate impacts of a preventive intervention for conduct problems. *American Journal of Community Psychology, 27,* 483–519.

Rodkin, P., Farmer, T., Pearl, R., Van Acker, R. (2000). Heterogeneity of popular boys: Antisocial and prosocial configurations. *Developmental Psychology, 36,* 14–24.

Scheier, L. M., Botvin, G. J., & Miller, N. L. (1999). Life events, neighborhood stress, psychosocial functioning, and alcohol use among urban minority youth. *Journal of Child and Adolescent Substance Abuse, 9*, 19–50

Seidman, E., Yoshikawa, H., Roberts, A., Chesir-Teran, D., Allen, L., Friedman, J., & Aber, L. (1998). Structural and experiential neighborhood contexts, developmental stage, and antisocial behavior among urban adolescents in poverty. *Development and Psychopathology, 10*, 259–81.

Seidman, E., Chesir-Teran, D., Friedman, J., Yoshikawa, H., Allen, L., & Roberts, A. (1999). The risk and protective functions of perceived family and peer microsystems among urban adolescents in poverty. *American Journal of Community Psychology, 27*, 211–37.

Shure, M. B. & Spivack, G. (1982). Interpersonal problem solving in young children: A cognitive approach to prevention. *American Journal of Community Psychology, 10*, 341–56.

Shure, M. B. & Spivack, G. (1988). Interpersonal cognitive problem solving. In R. H. Price, E. L. Cowen, R. P. Lorion, & J. Ramos-McKay (eds.), *14 Ounces of Prevention* (pp. 69–82). Hyattsville, MD: American Psychological Association.

Spoth, R., Greenberg, M. T., & Bierman, K. L. (2002). Project PROSPER: Promoting School–Community–University Partnerships to Enhance Resilience. Grant proposal funded by the National Institute of Drug Abuse.

Spoth, R., Redmond, C., & Shin, C. (1998). Direct and indirect latent-variable parenting outcomes of two universal family-focused preventive interventions: Extending a public health oriented research base. *Journal of Consulting and Clinical Psychology, 66*, 385–99.

Stevahn, L., Johnson, D. W., Johnson, R. T., Oberle, K., & Wahl, L. (2000). Effects of conflict resolution training integrated into a kindergarten curriculum. *Child Development, 71*, 772–84.

Stormshak, E. A. & Webster-Stratton, C. (1999). The peer relations of children with conduct problems: Differential correlates with self-report measures and behavioral problems. *Journal of Applied Developmental Psychology, 20*, 295–317.

Stormshak, E. A., Comeau, C. A., & Shepard, S. (in press). The relative contribution of sibling deviance and peer deviance in the prediction of substance use across middle childhood. *Journal of Abnormal Child Psychology*.

Stormshak, E. A., Bellanti, C. J., Bierman, K. L., & the Conduct Problems Prevention Research Group (1996). The quality of the sibling relationship and the development of social competence and behavioral control in aggressive children. *Developmental Psychology, 32*, 79–89.

Stormshak, E. A., Bierman, K. L., Bruschi, C. J., Dodge, K. A., Coie, J. D., & the Conduct Problems Prevention Research Group (1999a). The relation between behavior problems and peer preference in different classroom contexts. *Child Development, 70*, 169–82.

Stormshak, E. A., Kaminski, R., Good, R., & Goodman, M. R. (1999b). Substance abuse prevention in preschool: Support for at-risk children in Head Start centers across rural Oregon. Presented at the Society for Research in Child Development, Albuquerque, NM, April.

Stormshak, E. A., Bierman, K. L., McMahon, R. J., Lengua, L., & the Conduct Problems Prevention Research Group (2000a). Parenting practices and child disruptive behavior problems in early elementary school. *Journal of Clinical Child Psychology, 29*, 17–29.

Stormshak, E. A., Keck, L., Shepard, S., & Comeau, C. (2000b). High risk siblings as predictors of substance use. Presented at the Western Psychological Association, Portland, OR, April.

Stormshak, E. A., Dishion, T. J., Light, J., & Yasui, M. (in press). Implementing family-centered interventions within the public middle school: Linking service delivery to change in problem behavior. *Journal of Abnormal Child Psychology*.

Vigil, J. D. & Yun, S. C. (1996). Southern California gangs: Comparative ethnicity and social control. In C. R. Huff (ed.), *Gangs in America* (2nd edn., pp. 139–56). Thousand Oaks, CA: Sage.

Webster-Stratton, C. (1981). Video-tape modeling: A method of parent education. *Journal of Clinical Child Psychology, 10*, 93–8.

Webster-Stratton, C. (1990). Long-term follow-up of families with young conduct problem children: From preschool to grade school. *Journal of Clinical Child Psychology, 19*, 1344–9.

Webster-Stratton, C. (1991). Dinosaur social skills and problem solving training manual. Unpublished manuscript.

Webster-Stratton, C. & Hammond, M. (1990). Predictors of treatment outcome in parent training for families with conduct problem children. *Behavior Therapy, 21*, 319–37.

Webster-Stratton, C. & Hammond, M. (1997). Treating children with early-onset conduct problems: A comparison of child and parent training interventions. *Journal of Consulting and Clinical Psychology, 65*, 93–109.

Webster-Stratton, C., Kolpacoff, M., & Hollinsworth, T. (1988). Self-administered videotape therapy for families with conduct-problem children: Comparison with two cost-effective treatments and a control group. *Journal of Consulting and Clinical Psychology, 56*, 558–66.

Weissberg, R. P., Gersten, E. L., Carnike, C. L., Toro, P. A., Rapkin, B. D., Davidson, E., & Cowen, E. L. (1981). Social problem solving skills training: A competence building intervention with second to fourth grade children. *American Journal of Community Psychology, 9*, 411–23.

Weisz, J. R., Chaiyasit, W., Weiss, B., Eastman, K. L., & Jackson, E. W. (1995). A multimodal study of problem behavior among Thai and American children in school: Teacher reports versus direct observation. *Child Development, 66*, 402–15.

Wills, T. A., Windle, M., & Cleary, S. D. (1998). Temperament and novelty seeking in adolescent substance use: Convergence of dimensions of temperament with constructs from Cloninger's theory. *Journal of Personality and Social Psychology, 74*, 387–406.

Wright, J. C., Giammarino, M., & Parad, H. W. (1986). Social status in small groups: Individual-group similarity and the social "misfit". *Journal of Personality and Social Psychology, 50*, 523–36.

Xie, H., Cairns, R., & Cairns, B. (1999). Social networks and configurations in inner-city schools: Aggression, popularity, and implications for students with emotional and behavior disorders. *Journal of Emotional and Behavioral Disorders, 7*, 147–55.

Yoshikawa, H. (1994). Prevention as cumulative protection: Effects of early family support and education on chronic delinquency and its risks. *Psychological Bulletin, 115*, 28–54.

Yoshikawa, H. (1995). Long-term effects of early childhood programs on social outcomes and delinquency. *The Future of Children, 5(3)*, 51–75.

CHAPTER FIFTEEN

NICU-Based Interventions for High-Risk Infants

Christine Reiner Hess

Ongoing improvements in neonatal medical technology have led to increased survival rates for preterm, low-birth-weight, medically fragile infants (Hack & Fanaroff, 1999; O'Shea et al., 1997). These advancements have come at a price, however, in that there are greater numbers of preterm, low-birth-weight children at high risk for significant developmental delays and learning behavior problems than ever before (Hack et al., 2000; Hack, Klein, & Taylor, 1995). A recent prospective study of extremely preterm children (<26 weeks gestation) showed that 50 percent of this group manifested developmental delays as early as 3 years of age (Wood et al., 2000). Indeed, the need has never been greater for intervention programs designed to promote development in such children.

With the authorization of the Individuals with Disabilities Act (1986, reauthorized in 1997), the federal government extended early intervention and special education services to infants and toddlers (birth to 3 years) who have developmental delays and disabilities, and their families. With this legislation, states also have the option of providing services to at-risk children. This legislation reflects the widespread belief that intervention programs should begin as early in the child's life as possible, in order to have the best chance of preventing developmental delays. To this end, several intervention research programs have been conducted with high-risk infants beginning shortly after discharge from the neonatal intensive care unit (NICU) and have been associated with improved child development (e.g., Barrera et al., 1991; Field et al., 1980). Perhaps most notable was the Infant Health and Development Program, a randomized clinical trial of home- and center-based intervention including 985 children, which found cognitive gains favoring the intervention group (Infant Health and Development Program, 1990). For families who had high participation rates, cognitive gains for children who received the intervention were still apparent at age 8 (Hill, Brooks-Gunn, & Waldfogel, 2003).

Many high-risk infants begin their lives in the NICU, however, and can remain in there for several months prior to discharge, making it possible to begin working with parents and infants very shortly after birth. Further, when parents are included as participants in NICU-based programs, there is the added advantage of helping parents become more involved in their infants' care at a time when their infants' care is primarily in the hands of professionals. Traditional discharge planning begun only a few days prior to infant discharge from the NICU often falls short of meeting parents' information needs (Meck et al., 1995), emphasizing the need for parental participation to begin early. In addition, NICU-based intervention research programs should be ecologically valid. That is, demonstration projects designed to examine the efficacy of various types of interventions should contain program elements that can be easily incorporated into daily NICU routines in order to successfully translate research into practice.

This chapter examines NICU-based intervention programs targeted to preterm, low-birth-weight children, a population that is known to be at risk for developmental problems. The efficacy of these programs is evaluated, and examples of programs that have been successfully incorporated into standard NICU practices are described. Interventions are divided into four categories based on the primary goal of the programs: infant supplemental stimulation, infant developmentally supportive care, parent support/adjustment, and parent education programs. The present review focuses on intervention programs published since 1980 since several reviews of intervention programs, especially supplemental stimulation programs, conducted prior to this time are abundant in the literature (e.g., Cornell & Gottfried, 1976; Field, 1980; Ottenbacher et al., 1987). Only programs that included a control/comparison group were included in this review in order to be able to evaluate the efficacy of the intervention programs. Programs were identified using keyword searches in the PsycINFO, MEDLINE, PubMed, ERIC, Academic Search Premier, and Academic Search Elite databases.

Infant Supplemental Stimulation Programs

Supplemental stimulation interventions targeted to preterm, low-birth-weight infants are based on the premise that these infants are deprived of sensory stimulation in the NICU environment. Because of the medical fragility of these infants when hospitalized in the NICU, the belief is that they do not experience the same amount of tactile, auditory, and visual stimulation that full-term infants experience from interacting with their caregivers shortly after birth. Stimulation programs are therefore designed to compensate for the isolation that infants are assumed to experience in the NICU. Some stimulation programs focus primarily on one sensory modality, while others include multiple sensory modalities. A total of 25 programs were identified that evaluated the efficacy of supplemental stimulation: 12 tactile stimulation programs (tactile or tactile/kinesthetic), 3 auditory stimulation programs, and 10 multimodal stimulation programs.

Most programs found benefits of supplemental stimulation for preterm infants compared to controls, regardless of which sensory modality was targeted. For 12 programs, stimulation was delivered solely as massage (Rausch, 1981; Jay, 1982; Field et al., 1986;

Scafidi et al., 1990; Scafidi, Field, & Schanberg, 1993; Wheeden et al., 1993; Acolet et al., 1993; Harrison et al., 1996, 2000; Ferber et al., 2002; Dieter et al., 2003; Modrcin-Talbott et al., 2003). In 11 of these programs, massage was administered by professionals. In the remaining program, massage was administered either by professionals or by the mothers of the preterm infants, depending on experimental group assignment (Ferber et al., 2002). As an example of a stimulation program, Field and colleagues (e.g., Field et al., 1986) used a structured protocol of infant massage consisting of 5 minutes of tactile stimulation using a sequential head-to-toe progression, followed by 5 minutes of passive arm and leg movements, followed by 5 minutes of tactile stimulation. Their massage protocol was delivered by professionals three times per day over a 10-day period. Eleven of the infant massage programs examined infant growth as an outcome variable. Six of these eleven programs (all of which used the Field massage protocol) found increased weight gain as a result of infant massage (Field et al., 1986; Scafidi et al., 1990; Scafidi, Field, & Schanberg, 1993; Wheeden et al., 1993; Ferber et al., 2002; Dieter et al., 2003), and one program that used a massage protocol similar to that of Field and colleagues found a trend approaching significance for weight gain favoring the intervention group (Rausch, 1981). Based on work with animal models, Field (2001) has speculated that the underlying mechanism to explain growth may be increased vagal activity associated with massage that facilitates release of food-absorption hormones, thereby promoting weight gain. The four programs that used a "gentle human touch" protocol (originally introduced by Jay, 1982) consisting of massaging infant head and buttocks or head and arm/shoulder did not find an effect of massage on infant weight gain (Jay, 1982; Harrison et al., 1996, 2000; Modrcin-Talbott et al., 2003). Differential effects of weight gain may have been due to differences in the degree of pressure applied during massage (Field's protocol recommends firmer strokes) and the differences in number of infant body parts targeted for massage in the two protocols (a greater number of body parts were targeted in the Field protocol).

Four programs examined infant system regulation and maturity as outcomes as measured by the Brazelton Neurobehavioral Assessment Scale (NBAS: Brazelton, 1973). Three of these four programs found improved infant system maturity in areas of motor, attention, self-regulation, and/or habituation for massaged infants compared to non-massaged infants (Field et al., 1986; Scafidi et al., 1990; Wheeden et al., 1993). The one program that assessed length of NICU stay found that massaged infants were discharged an average of six days earlier than non-massaged infants with average cost savings of $3,000 per child (Field et al., 1986), which translates to approximately $10,000 in today's costs (Field, 2001).

Although massage programs by Field and colleagues (Field et al., 1986; Scafidi et al., 1990; Dieter et al., 2003) were associated with increased alertness and activity and decreased sleep for infants (which has the benefit of allowing infants to be more available for interactions with caregivers), others (Acolet et al., 1993; Harrison et al., 1996, 2000; Jay, 1982; Modrcin-Talbott et al., 2003) reported a calming effect of massage as evidenced by reduced active sleep and decreased motor activity. Differences in stimulation protocols (e.g., Field and colleagues had an additional kinesthetic stimulation component, massaged more infant body parts, and appeared to use firmer pressure), and in frequency and duration of stimulation, may account for this difference in infants' activity levels. The five programs examining physiological effects of massage found that massage was not aversive or harmful to the medically stable preterm, low-birth-weight infants since infants maintained physiological stability (e.g., no changes in oxygen saturation levels, oxygen requirements, heart rate, no increased bradycardia) during or after massage (Acolet et al., 1993; Harrison et al., 1996, 2000; Jay, 1982; Kuhn et al., 1991). One program found lower cortisol levels for infants following massage, suggesting a calming effect of massage (Acolet et al., 1993), while another program found increased epinephrine and norepinephrine levels following massage, suggesting greater sympathetic nervous system maturity (Kuhn et al., 1991, which presented additional results from the program of Scafidi et al., 1990).

For three programs, stimulation was delivered solely in the auditory modality (Caine, 1991; Cassidy & Standley, 1995; Coleman et al., 1997). These three programs used music or a combination of music and speaking as auditory stimulation. For example, one program exposed infants to three consecutive hours of auditory stimulation consisting of 30 minutes of vocal lullabies and children's music alternating with 30 minutes of NICU noise across a three-day period (Cassidy & Standley, 1995). Two programs examined infant weight gain, caloric intake, and length of hospital stay as outcome measures, and both found increased weight gain, increased caloric intake, and shorter hospital stays for infants given auditory stimulation compared to infants in the control group (Caine, 1991; Coleman et al., 1997). Auditory stimulation in the form of music had a calming effect on infants as evidenced by lower heart and respiratory rates and higher oxygen saturation levels in two programs (Cassidy & Standley, 1995; Coleman et al., 1997), and reduced stress behaviors and activity levels in two programs (Caine, 1991; Coleman et al., 1997). Thus, auditory stimulation in the form of singing and speaking does not appear to be harmful to medically stable preterm infants, although positive effects may only be very short term, as evidenced by acclimation to music by preterm infants after the first day of music therapy in the Cassidy and Standley (1995) program.

In 10 programs, stimulation was delivered through multiple modalities (Brown et al., 1980; Leib, Benfield, & Guidubaldi, 1980; Williams, Williams, & Dial, 1986; White-Traut & Goldman, 1988; White-Traut & Nelson, 1988; White-Traut et al., 1993, 1997, 1999; Standley, 1998; Whipple, 2000). For example, one program used a combination of structured infant massage (tactile), female humming (auditory), eye-to-eye contact (visual), and rocking (vestibular) for one 15–30 minute session administered 1–2 times weekly beginning at recruitment until the infant was discharged (minimum of three days) (Standley, 1998). Four programs examined infant alertness and activity as outcome measures. All four programs found that infants exposed to multimodal stimulation had increased alertness and activity compared to infants who were not exposed to the stimulation protocol (White-Traut & Nelson, 1988; White-Traut et al., 1993, 1997, 1999). Four programs examined infant development as an outcome variable, and two found improved development for infants exposed to multimodal stimulation compared to infants who did not receive multimodal stimulation (Leib, Benfield, & Guidubaldi, 1980; Williams, Williams, & Dial, 1986). In three programs, parents learned to administer the multimodal stimulation protocols with their infants. Benefits of parent participation included more frequent visitation to hospitalized infants (other than during intervention sessions) (Brown et al., 1980; Whipple, 2000) and better maternal–infant interactions (White-Traut & Nelson, 1988), suggesting positive consequences for parent–child relationships. Multimodal stimulation was not found to be aversive or harmful to the medically stable, preterm infants. The four programs that examined physiological measures found increased heart and respiratory rates and reduced oxygen saturation levels during massage, but these values remained within normal limits for preterm infants and returned to baseline levels upon termination of stimulation (White-Traut & Goldman, 1988; White-Traut et al., 1993, 1997, 1999). However, when comparing multimodal stimulation to tactile only or auditory only, White-Traut et al. (1997) found that tactile-only stimulation may be too arousing for some infants compared to other forms of stimulation since pulse rates greater than 180 were more likely with tactile-only stimulation. By contrast, auditory-only stimulation was soothing for infants as evidenced by increased quiet sleep following stimulation (White-Traut et al., 1997).

Strengths of these programs included use of structured stimulation protocols that were replicated across studies, increasing the reliability of findings using specific protocols (Field and colleagues; White-Traut and colleagues, Harrison and colleagues). The study by Ferber et al. (2002) was particularly interesting in that an independent research team used a modified version of the Field massage protocol and found similar results in terms of weight gain and alertness for preterm infants in Israel, while also demonstrating that mothers can be just as effective in delivering the structured massage protocol as professionals. Another strength of the infant stimulation studies was the generalizability of results to different preterm populations since programs were conducted using preterm infants with cocaine exposure (Wheeden et al., 1993), respiratory distress syndrome (Jay, 1982), and periventricular leukomalacia (White-Traut et al., 1999), and with medically fragile preterm infants (Modrcin-Talbott et al., 2003) in addition to medically stable, healthy preterm infants. Limitations included the use of only male preterm infants and very small sample size in the study by Acolet et al. (1993), use of weaker phase-lag designs in some studies rather than randomized controlled trials (Jay, 1982; Leib, Benfield, & Guidubaldi, 1980; Rausch, 1981; Williams, Williams, & Dial, 1986), and the fact that some mothers in the White-Traut and Nelson (1988) study who were assigned to the talking-only group also held and rocked infants so that these infants had multimodal stimulation rather than auditory stimulation only. Additionally, several studies had small sample sizes, and several used only short-term evaluations so it is unclear whether stimulation has longer term effects. It is unclear from multimodal stimulation programs whether the positive effects are associated with specific modes of stimulation or from the entire multimodal stimulation package.

The majority of programs included in this review conducted interventions with only medically stable infants and found that supplemental stimulation was not harmful to them. In fact, studies have indicated that although medically fragile preterm infants respond to handling during routine care procedures with distress such as accelerated heart and respiration rates, crying, gaze aversion, vomiting, and decreased oxygen saturation levels outside the normal range (Gorski et al., 1983; Long, Philip, & Lucey, 1980; Morrow et al., 1991; Norris, Campbell, & Brenkert, 1982), the infants respond much more favorably to massage (Morrow et al., 1991). Indeed, Modrcin-Talbott et al. (2003) found that their sample of more medically fragile preterm infants did not have an aversive reaction to massage and showed behavioral cues that massage had a calming effect. It is important to note that many of the supplemental stimulation programs reviewed here had protocols for carefully gauging infant distress to stimulation and terminated stimulation for infants showing distress symptoms above a certain level. Medically unstable preterm infants may not tolerate supplemental stimulation to the same degree as medically stable preterm infants and become overstimulated and distressed more easily (Dieter & Emory, 1997; Eckerman et al., 1994, 1995; Oehler, 1985; Oehler, Eckerman, & Wilson, 1988). Some researchers have found that exposing fragile preterm infants to only small amounts of stimulation in only the auditory modality (speaking, singing) results in favorable responses, but that multimodal stimulation leads to physiological and behavioral instability for these sicker infants (Oehler, 1985; Oehler, Eckerman, & Wilson, 1988). Thus, several researchers have suggested waiting until preterm infants are medically stable before exposing them to supplemental stimulation (e.g., Acolet et al., 1993; Dieter & Emory, 1997; Eckerman et al., 1994; Glass, 1999). When supplemental stimulation is warranted for medically stable infants, Harrison et al. (2001) have also suggested using individualized criteria for setting monitor alarm limits to detect infant physiological responses (e.g., heart rate, respiratory rate, oxygen saturation level) as opposed to standard criteria values in order to individualize developmental care to each unique infant.

Developmentally Supportive Care Interventions

In contrast to the view that preterm infants are isolated and deprived of appropriate sensory stimulation in the NICU, others have proposed that preterm infants are actually overstimulated in the NICU environment due to handling during routine care procedures and excessive noise and light levels. Zahr and Balian (1995) found that routine nursing procedures and NICU noise levels were associated with physiological and behavioral instability in the form of decreased oxygen saturation levels and frequent state changes for preterm infants. Glass (Glass, 1990; Glass et al., 1985) found that NICU light levels were associated with retinopathy of prematurity for preterm infants. Linn, Horowitz, and Fox (1985) have argued that NICU environments are not characterized by deprivation or overstimulation to the preterm infant; rather, there is an inappropriate pattern of stimulation that infants are exposed to in NICUs. Based on their review of studies of the ecology of NICU environments, as well as their own empirical research, Linn, Horowitz, & Fox (1985) describe the NICU environment "as providing little cross-modal stimulation, few temporally patterned stimuli, and little diurnal rhythmicity" and note that "the premature infant may have few opportunities to control the environment, contrary to the full-term infant's experiences" (p. 420). This emphasizes the need to first assess the level of stimulation in the NICU prior to designing intervention programs so that intervention programs can be best suited to addressing infants' developmental needs. Glass (1999) has emphasized that preterm infants are not a homogenous group, therefore determining what level of stimulation to provide should be based on the individual infant's medical and physiological stability, neurological maturation, and social and physical needs. Additionally, because some sensory systems mature earlier than others, Glass (1999) has suggested that interventions focus on providing protective care for the infant, then gradually introduce stimulation, beginning initially with the most mature sensory systems (i.e., hearing, touch) and using low-intensity stimulation.

Consistent with these recommendations, many have advocated the use of interventions that provide individualized developmentally supportive care to preterm infants in the NICU after first assessing infant responses to the NICU environment (e.g., Als et al., 1986, 1994). These researchers have tested the efficacy of the Neonatal Individualized Developmental Care Assessment Protocol (NIDCAP) developed by Als and Gibes (1986). This intervention strategy focuses on individualized nursing care to NICU infants by responding to infants' behavioral cues and altering care practices in response to infant cues and needs. Infants are formally observed for a minimum of 20 minutes prior to care procedures, all during care procedures, and for a minimum of 20 minutes after care procedures to assess their stress responses and self-regulatory behaviors. Based on these observations, care plans are written for intervention infants with the goal of synchronizing stimulation and routine care procedures with infant sleep/wake cycles, and to help promote infant self-regulatory behavior. Care plans address three major areas: distal and proximal physical environment of the infant, direct caregiving to the infant, and discharge planning. Examples of strategies employed to support preterm infants' development include decreasing light and noise in NICUs by covering isolettes and cribs; using positioning aids such as supports and nests to help with infant postures; promoting infant self-regulatory behaviors such as grasping, holding, and sucking; and involving parents in care and helping them to read and respond effectively to infant cues.

Developmentally supportive care interventions represent a more dynamic and family-centered approach to intervention than the supplemental stimulation programs described earlier. Families are encouraged and helped to participate in the infant's care, and the infant's responses are taken into account with adaptations made to accommodate the infant's individual needs and reactions. This type of intervention uses a model of relationship-based care, highlighting the mutuality of the infants, caregivers, and professionals, all of whom are involved in the child's care (Als, 1997).

Six programs were identified that examined developmentally supportive care interventions and all used the NIDCAP protocol (Als et al., 1986, 1994; Becker et al., 1991 with additional results reported in Becker et al., 1993; Fleisher et al., 1995; Westrup & Kleberg, 2000). Two of these programs used a phase-lag design in which the control group was recruited and completed the study, then after the control group was discharged from the NICU, the intervention group was recruited and completed the study (Als et al., 1986; Becker et al., 1991, 1993). Four programs utilized randomized controlled trials (Als et al., 1994; Fleisher et al., 1995; Buehler et al., 1995; Westrup & Kleberg, 2000).

The developmentally supportive care interventions, based on the NIDCAP protocol, were associated with improved system regulation and maturity in the five programs that investigated these outcomes (Als et al., 1986, 1994; Becker et al., 1991, 1993; Buehler et al., 1995; Fleisher et al., 1995). Five of the programs found that infants exposed to the NIDCAP protocol had shorter periods requiring ventilator assistance and/or oxygen therapy (only Buehler et al., 1995 did not find an effect). Four of the programs found that infants in the NIDCAP intervention had earlier graduation to bottle- or breast-feeding (Als et al., 1986, 1994; Becker et al., 1991, 1993; Fleisher et al., 1995). Additionally, both programs that examined brain activity found that NIDCAP interventions resulted in changes in brain activation and functioning favoring the intervention group (Als et al., 1994; Buehler et al., 1995). Findings suggested that individualized, developmentally supportive care, beginning shortly after birth, served to protect infants from inappropriate sensory stimulation of the NICU environment, and enhanced infant system maturity and brain development and functioning. Four programs examined the effect of NIDCAP interventions on length of hospital stay. Two of these programs found that NIDCAP interventions resulted in shorter hospital stays with significant cost savings (Als et al., 1994; Fleisher et al., 1995), while one found a trend for reduced hospital stays (Westrup & Kleberg, 2000). One program also found improvements in infant cognitive and motor development several months after intervention (Als et al., 1986), although another program found no such developmental improvements as a result of intervention (Als et al., 1994). The former program utilized a phase-lag design, however, so differences in developmental outcomes may have been a result of historical effects rather than the intervention. Alternately, longer follow-up periods may be necessary to see if developmental differences manifest over time.

Strengths of these interventions included replication of the NIDCAP protocol across several studies and in two different countries (USA and Sweden), increasing the reliability of findings. Additionally, positive benefits to infants were reported even when less-intensive interventions were used (Fleisher et al., 1995). The majority of studies targeted preterm infants at high risk for bronchopulmonary dysplasia due to extended mechanical ventilation and oxygen therapy. However, Buehler et al. (1995) examined the efficacy of this intervention with healthy, low-risk preterm infants and also found benefits, increasing the generalizability of the NIDCAP interventions for different populations of preterm infants. While the initial studies were conducted prior to the advent of surfactant drug therapy to improve lung maturity, two programs included infants who had been exposed to surfactant therapy (Fleisher et al., 1995; Westrup & Kleberg, 2000) and results were similar to those studies in which surfactant therapy was not used. Additionally, although the initial studies utilized phase-lag designs, later studies utilized more rigorous randomly controlled experimental designs and found similar results. Limitations of the NIDCAP studies included the fact that, due to the nature of developmentally supportive care, physicians and nurses who made decisions about infant care were often not blind to group assignment, which may have influenced their decisions regarding some of the dependent measures (e.g., terminating ventilation support, discharging infants). Additionally, although developmentally supportive care interventions are designed to be family-oriented, none of these studies evaluated parental outcomes such as adjustment or parent–infant interactions, so it is unclear how the interventions affected parents. Finally, the individualized approach to intervention makes it more difficult to evaluate the efficacy of the program from a research perspective, since specific protocols vary across infants, even though the same general intervention model is used for all infants. From a clinical perspective, however, the individualized approach to care is favorable to a regimented protocol since specific infant and family needs are addressed.

Parental Support/Adjustment Programs

Many parents are unprepared for the birth of a preterm, low-birth-weight child and experience an "acute emotional" reaction to this event (Kaplan & Mason, 1960). Parental responses to this event include anxiety, depressed affect, distress, and concern about the child's survival and future development (Bennett & Slade, 1991; McGettigan et al., 1994; Pederson et al., 1987; Teti, O'Connell, & Reiner, 1997). The goals of parent support/adjustment programs are to help parents deal with their emotional distress related to having a child hospitalized in the NICU and to identify and contact community resources who can help parents in the transition from hospital to home infant care. Some programs also focus on enhancing mother–child interactions. This approach to intervention is based on the premise that families' wellbeing must be adequate in order to promote positive parenting and to foster positive child outcomes. Seven programs were identified that used parent support/adjustment interventions (Minde et al., 1980, with follow-up results reported in Minde et al., 1983; Zeskind & Iacino, 1984; Beckwith, 1988; Cobiella, Mabe, & Forehand, 1990; Goetze et al., 1993; Roman et al., 1995; Preyde & Ardal, 2003).

Six of the seven programs provided mothers with formal support figures. The other program focused solely on maternal adjustment without formal support (Cobiella, Mabe, & Forehand, 1990). Programs differed in terms of who served as the formal support figure and in the duration and intensity of services. Three programs included veteran parents as support figures (Minde et al., 1980, 1983; Preyde & Ardal, 2003; Roman et al., 1995), while three programs included professionals such as nurses, early childhood educators, developmental specialists, or trained interventionists as support figures (Beckwith, 1988; Goetze et al., 1993; Zeskind & Iacino, 1984). Two programs were conducted solely in the NICU (Cobiella, Mabe, & Forehand, 1990; Minde et al., 1980, 1983), one program was conducted primarily in the NICU, and parents had the option of continuing contact with the veteran parent post-discharge (Preyde & Ardal, 2003), while the other four included home visits lasting from several weeks to a year. Despite these differences, six out of seven programs that examined the effect of formal support on maternal outcomes reported benefits to mothers receiving intervention. These benefits included improved attitudes and adjustment such as higher self-esteem, lower anxiety and depression, greater perceived social support, positive perceptions of the child's future prognosis, and more realistic appraisals of the child (Beckwith, 1988; Cobiella, Mabe, & Forehand, 1990; Minde et al., 1980, 1983; Preyde & Ardal, 2003; Roman et al., 1995; Zeskind & Iacino, 1984). Four programs examined some aspect of parenting behavior as an outcome variable. All four programs reported improved parenting behavior, including increased visitation, increased involvement, and/or better quality interactions (Beckwith, 1988; Minde et al., 1980, 1983; Roman et al., 1995; Zeskind & Iacino, 1984). One program also found that intervention families had more stimulating and enriching home environments (based on HOME by Caldwell & Bradley, 1979) than control families at program follow-up (Roman et al., 1995). Goetze et al. (1993) reported only minimal differences between high and low intensity groups and concluded that program costs greatly outweighed benefits. However, infants in their program were at higher medical risk than samples in the other parent-support interventions, and it is unclear whether mothers took advantage of other community resources as part of the intervention transition plan. More intense interventions may be necessary for groups at higher risk.

Strengths of these studies included follow-up periods that lasted beyond infant discharge from the hospital. In some cases, evaluations were conducted from several months to 2 years post-discharge. Because some programs had the goal of fostering better quality mother–child interactions, longer follow-up periods are especially important since interventions may set transactional processes between parent and child into motion that may take time to show effects (Sameroff & Chandler, 1975). Additionally, most of the programs were targeted specifically to parental needs, so parents determined what type of support they would receive from support figures (e.g., emotional, informational, educational), individualizing the intervention for families. Limitations were that Preyde and Ardal (2003) and Roman et al. (1995) used weaker designs (cohort design and phase-lag design, respectively) rather than a randomized controlled experimental design. Roman et al. (1995) had moderate attrition over time, Beckwith (1988) had differential attrition of the control group (but conducted attrition analyses), Cobiella, Mabe, & Forehand (1990) had attrition over time reducing their already small sample size, and Zeskind and Iacino (1984) had a small sample size in their study. Additionally, it is unclear if positive effects of intervention from Minde et al.'s (1980, 1983) program were due to support from group meetings, individual attention from the nurse, or both intervention components.

Parent Education Programs

Parent education programs focus on teaching parents about infant signals, abilities, and needs, as well as providing information that will help parents with the care and development of preterm infants. The goals of these programs typically include fostering better parent–infant relationships, as well as fostering infant development. Some of these programs focus primarily on the parent, while others use a more family-centered approach to care in which infant, parent, and family needs are addressed. Eight programs were identified that examined parent education interventions (Widmayer & Field, 1980, with follow-up results reported in Widmayer & Field, 1981; Nurcombe et al., 1984 with follow-up results reported in Rauh et al., 1988; Achenbach et al., 1990, 1993; Szajnberg et al., 1987; Resnick et al., 1987; Resnick, Armstrong, & Carter, 1988; Pfander & Bradley-Johnson, 1990; Parker et al., 1992, with additional results reported in Zahr, Parker, & Cole, 1992; Meyer et al., 1994).

The programs varied considerably in terms of program characteristics and goals. Some programs were conducted solely during the NICU period, while others began in the NICU but continued with home visits lasting from several weeks to 2 years. Some programs were solely parent-focused, with the goal of educating parents about infant signals and needs, and differences between preterm and full term infants. Other programs were more family-centered with a focus on fostering parental adjustment, enhancing parents' knowledge, behavior, and relationships with their children, as well as enhancing children's developmental outcomes (e.g., cognitive, motor, adaptive, interactive, and social abilities) through various activities, including supplemental stimulation and developmentally appropriate activities.

Various positive outcomes were reported for all eight intervention programs. Seven of the programs examined infant development as an outcome variable. Six of these seven programs found improved infant development (Widmayer & Field, 1980, 1981; Resnick et al., 1987; Resnick, Armstrong, & Carter, 1988; Rauh et al., 1988; Achenbach et al., 1990, 1993; Pfander & Bradley-Johnson, 1990; Parker et al., 1992 & Zahr, Parker, & Cole, 1992). Although Szajnberg et al. (1987) did not report developmental gains for intervention infants, this program only had parents watch one NBAS demonstration. Nurcombe et al. (1984) had a more intense program of longer duration, and found cognitive gains for intervention children that were not apparent until 3 years post-intervention (no differences from control at 6, 12, and 24 months). However, once apparent, these gains were consistent from 3 years through the 9-year follow-up (Rauh et al., 1988; Achenbach et al., 1990, 1993). This suggests the importance of using longer term follow-up when assessing effects of intervention programs. Five programs examined parenting behavior as an outcome variable, and all five reported improved parenting behavior for intervention parents, including increased maternal visiting frequency, more positive play and/or feeding interactions, and/or more enriching and stimulating home environments designed by parents (Meyer et al., 1994; Parker et al., 1992; Resnick, Armstrong, & Carter, 1988; Szajnberg et al., 1987; Widmayer & Field, 1980, 1981; Zahr, Parker, & Cole, 1992). Two programs examined parental wellbeing as an outcome variable, and both reported improved attitudes and/or adjustment for intervention parents compared to controls, including less depression, more positive attitudes about parenting and childrearing, higher parental confidence, and greater parenting satisfaction (Meyer et al., 1994; Nurcombe et al., 1984).

In general, programs that were more intense, of longer duration, and had multiple goals were associated with greater positive benefits for both parents and children. Strengths of these programs included longer term follow-up, often lasting for several months to several years post-intervention. Programs with longer term follow-up periods are desirable to help understand the effects of intervention on preterm infants, since interventions may set transactional processes between parent and child into motion that may take time to show effects (Sameroff & Chandler, 1975). Additionally, many of the programs were family-centered, rather than focusing solely on the parent or child, and included multiple goals, making the programs more comprehensive. Many programs were also tailored and individualized to best meet each family's needs while using the same general intervention model. Limitations were that Resnick, Armstrong, & Carter (1988) reported high attrition across the two-year follow-up period, randomization had to be abandoned for half of the participants in Parker et al.'s program (1992; Zahr, Parker, & Cole, 1992) due to changes in NICU discharge practices, and several studies had small sample sizes.

Recommendations for Intervention

The rapid growth and development during the first three years of life emphasizes the importance of beginning interventions as early as possible for preterm, low-birth-weight children. The NICU period presents an opportunity to begin interventions very shortly after birth while children are still hospitalized and can allow families to get involved early in the process. The issue then is how best to intervene to meet the needs of these at-risk children and their families.

Based on this review, it is recommended that programs be both parent-directed and infant-directed so that programs are more comprehensive and have a family-centered approach. The infant developmentally supportive care programs tended to be more family-centered than the infant stimulation programs, since they promoted family involvement. For example, families were strongly encouraged to participate in the child's care, were taught how to read and respond to infants' signals and needs, and were taught how to modify the child's environment to promote the child's self-regulation. For infant stimulation programs, parents can be taught how to provide infant stimulation and how to read and respond to infant signals, which has the benefit of making programs more family-centered. Additionally, five of the parent education programs were much more family-centered and included more dynamic, process-oriented approaches to intervention (Meyer et al., 1994; Parker et al., 1992; Nurcombe et al., 1984; Resnick et al., 1987; Resnick, Armstrong, & Carter, 1988). These five parent education programs included multiple goals targeted to the child and family in order to promote child development, parent–child relationships, and family adjustment and functioning, using components such as parent support, infant stimulation, developmentally appropriate activities, and parent education about infant signals, infant temperament, and infant needs. Including families in interventions, rather than focusing solely on the child or solely on the parent, helps set into motion transactional processes that may continue to benefit the family and child long after intervention ends.

Programs should also be individualized to the families and children receiving the intervention because programs that take into account family needs have the potential to be the most successful (Affleck et al., 1989). As seen in some of the reviewed studies, individualizing programs can be accomplished by using the same general program framework for all participants, but focusing on those issues or education modules of greatest concern to families. Examples of this individualized approach were used in the NIDCAP program by Als and colleagues, the parent support/adjustment program by Beckwith (1988), and the parent education programs by Meyer et al. (1994), Parker et al. (1992), Nurcombe et al. (1984), and Resnick and colleagues (1987, 1988).

In general, programs that were more intense, of longer duration, and extended services into the home after infant discharge were more beneficial to families than programs that were less intense and delivered solely in the NICU. Eight intervention programs reviewed here extended services into the home, varying in length of home services provided from six weeks to two years (Roman et al., 1995; Zeskind & Iacino, 1984; Beckwith, 1988; Goetze et al., 1993; Widmayer & Field, 1980; Nurcombe et al., 1984; Resnick et al., 1987; Resnick, Armstrong, & Carter, 1988). Home services had various goals, including addressing parental concerns once at home, helping parents contact and access community resources, improving parent–child relationships, teaching parents developmentally appropriate activities for children, giving parents anticipatory guidance, and providing parents with support. Providing home services at least for a few weeks helps parents' transition to becoming the child's primary caregivers, since the child's primary care in the NICU is provided by professionals. Traditional discharge planning often does not fulfill parents' informational needs, such that parents are making the transition to home care with many unanswered questions (Meck et al., 1995). Providing parents with services that bridge the transition from hospital to home can help facilitate family adjustment.

Lastly, intervention programs need to be ecologically valid. Programs that work in the demonstration phase, but contain program elements that cannot be sustained in regular NICU routines lack practical utility. Program components with the potential for ecological validity include NBAS demonstrations to help parents' understand infant abilities and needs. Serial NBAS demonstrations in which parents have hands-on practice tend to work better than single demonstrations (Widmayer & Field, 1980). Many NICUs already use NBAS examinations as clinical tools in regular NICU practice for clinicians to gain additional information about infants. Extending the clinical use of this tool as a demonstration intervention to parents would require minimal time, effort, and money. Additionally, infant tactile stimulation programs have been used extensively by Field and colleagues in hospitals in Miami, Florida for various populations of sick children, not just those born preterm (Field, 1995), and also have the potential to be ecologically valid. Based on the positive results of these studies, infant massage has been incorporated into regular practice in their hospitals (Field, 1995). Evidence that parents can be just as effective in delivering massage as professionals (Ferber et al., 2002) suggests that parents can be trained in infant massage as a cost effective means of delivering supplemental stimulation to a greater number of infants.

Parent-to-parent support programs are also widespread and incorporated into regular practice in many hospitals. Santelli et al. (1995) reported results of a national survey of 267 parent-to-parent support programs serving approximately 20,000 families in 47 of the 50 states. Lindsay et al. (1993) described a parent-to-parent support program that has been instituted in the Gerber Neonatal Intensive Care Unit at Butterworth Hospital in Michigan since 1976. In 1985, the NICU adopted the Perinatal Positive Parenting program as the model for their intervention. The study by Roman et al. (1995), reviewed in the section on parent support/adjustment programs, reported ongoing evaluation results of the program. To summarize, parent support was provided by veteran parents trained in a nurse-management model of care that focused on family coping, grief and loss, communication, developmental activities for preterm infants, parenting techniques, and support skills. Families were helped to access appropriate community resources. Volunteers contacted families, through phone calls and visits, a minimum of once weekly during the infant's NICU stay, then twice monthly after discharge. Additional contact was provided based on individual family needs. In 1993 when the article about the program was published, there were 110 volunteers who provided support. Funding was provided by Butterworth Hospital to cover coordinators' salaries and program costs. Costs for special projects and program expansion that exceeded the budget had been made up with funding sought through special grants. The program has benefited parents by improving adjustment and functioning (Lindsay et al., 1993; Roman et al., 1995). This shows that a parent-to-parent support program delivered by veteran parents of NICU infants can be an ecologically valid and successful intervention approach. Boukydis and Moses (1995) have provided information on how to establish and maintain parenting support programs for parents of NICU infants, with specific resource information to help institutions incorporate this type of intervention into regular clinical practice.

Although NBAS demonstration programs, infant stimulation programs, and parent support programs can be ecologically valid and successful intervention approaches, they tend to be limited in how family-centered they are. These are components that can be incorporated into more comprehensive intervention programs to better meet family needs. Two intervention programs that were successfully translated from research into practice that provided comprehensive, family-centered services with multiple goals are described next. These programs contain some of the ecologically valid program components described above. The first is a developmentally supportive care program that has been instituted as regular practice in Meriter Hospital in Madison, Wisconsin (Grunwald & Becker, 1991). The hospital has a level III NICU (NICU which has the ability to care for the sickest of infants) with 23 beds and is part of a university perinatal center. The program was adapted from the NIDCAP protocol developed by Als and colleagues described in the section on developmentally supportive care interventions. Initial training was provided by Brigham and Women's Hospital in Boston using the NIDCAP protocol. The NIDCAP protocol was modified so that training would be less intense and less expensive in order to train the entire NICU nursing staff and so that training could be done in-house. Formal evaluation of the training was conducted by comparing care procedures used by nurses after the training to care procedures used by nurses prior to program implementation. Results indicated that nurses used significantly more supportive measures specified in the program protocol after training than before training. Ongoing support is provided to staff, and a preceptor model is used to train and orient new staff to the program protocol. Grunwald and Becker (1991) reported that nurse response to the program was generally positive, although initial physician response was less enthusiastic. However, physicians became more comfortable with protocols when given time to adjust to the new procedures. In the initial program implementation phase, less emphasis was placed on parental involvement until nurses learned and became comfortable with the new care procedures. As nurses became more adept at using the developmentally supportive care procedures, greater emphasis was placed on family involvement. The initial evaluation phase of the program was conducted by Becker et al. (1991) and is described in the developmentally supportive care section. A summary of benefits for infants receiving the program indicated improvements in respiratory status, earlier normalized feeding behaviors, and better behavioral organization compared to infants who were assessed prior to program implementation. Thus, developmentally supportive care programs can be successfully incorporated into NICU care procedures to help improve developmental outcomes of preterm, low-birth-weight infants, using an individualized, family-centered approach to care.

The second program that has been translated from research into practice has been instituted by the Department of Pediatrics at Women's and Infant's Hospital in Providence, Rhode Island (Meyer et al., 1998). They developed the Infant Development Unit (IDU) as a clinical consultation service with the goal of providing comprehensive, family-centered, developmental services to high-risk infants. The clinical program was implemented based on results of a research study testing the efficacy of the program by Meyer et al. (1994) described in the parent education section. To summarize, the program addresses four areas: infant behavior and characteristics, family organization and functioning, caregiving environment, and home discharge and community resources. NBAS demonstrations for parents and the NICU Network Neurobehavioral Scale (Lester & Tronick, 1994), an exam used with high-risk infants to assess physiological stress and behavioral disorganization, are key intervention tools used by the IDU. Other common intervention strategies include "support and encouragement of a graduated parental caregiving role; supportive psychotherapy; access to a family resource library; mobilization of available social supports; short-term post-discharge follow-up; and coordination with community health care and early intervention providers" (p. 57). Services are individualized to families with a strong emphasis on issues of family-identified needs. They use an interdisciplinary team approach, and at the time of their publication, their staff included a developmental psychologist who served as director, a child and family psychiatrist, a clinical psychologist, a developmental pediatrician, a social worker, an occupational therapist, and a secretary. The IDU begins intervention services during the NICU and continues to provide services during the transition to home care. Thus, there is extensive collaboration between the NICU and IDU. Additionally, the IDU coordinates services with community resources to link parents with additional resources once they are at home.

Access to IDU services occurs through consultation requests that can be made by various nursing, physician, or social work personnel. Those children referred for services tend to be those at greatest risk due to multiple infant medical complications and families with high psychosocial needs. Funding for the program comes from various sources including third-party payers, Medicaid, and service contracts with the Rhode Island Department of Children, Youth, and Families. Billable services include evaluations for new patients, occupational therapy services, developmental testing, family psychotherapy, individual counseling, and case management. Additional funding is provided by the Department of Pediatrics. The evaluation phase found several benefits to families receiving the program, including positive maternal adjustment and functioning, and positive behaviors for both parents and infants in feeding interactions (Meyer et al., 1994). Thus, this comprehensive, individualized, family-centered program employed several components from intervention demonstration projects reviewed earlier and added some additional family-centered elements, resulting in improved outcomes for both high-risk children and their families.

It seems clear that NICU-based intervention programs that are family-centered, individualized to infant and family needs, and include multiple parent- and child-oriented goals have the greatest likelihood of improving child and family outcomes for preterm, low-birth-weight children. Intervention work should continue to move beyond research demonstration phases to translate successful research into successful clinical practice.

References

Achenbach, T. M., Phares, V., Howell, C. T., Rauh, V. A., & Nurcombe, B. (1990). Seven-year outcome of the Vermont intervention program for low-birthweight infants. *Child Development*, *61*, 1672–81.

Achenbach, T. M., Howell, C. T., Aoki, M. F., & Rauh, V. A. (1993). Nine-year outcome of the Vermont intervention program for low birth weight infants. *Pediatrics, 91(1),* 45–55.

Acolet, D., Modi, N., Giannakoulopoulos, X., Bond, C., Weg, W., Clow, A., & Glover, V. (1993). Changes in plasma cortisol and catecholamine concentrations in response to massage in preterm infants. *Archives of Disease in Childhood, 68,* 29–31.

Affleck, G., Tennen, H., Rowe, J., Roscher, B., & Walker, L. (1989). Effects of formal support on mothers' adaptation to the hospital-to-home transition of high-risk infants: The benefits and costs of helping. *Child Development, 60,* 488–501.

Als, H. (1997). Earliest intervention for preterm infants in the newborn intensive care unit. In M. J. Guralnick (ed.), *The effectiveness of early intervention* (pp. 47–75). Baltimore, MD: Paul H. Brookes.

Als, H. & Gibes, R. (1986). Neonatal individualized care and assessment program (NIDCAP). Unpublished manual. Boston Children's Hospital, Cambridge, MA.

Als, H., Lawhon, G., Brown, E., Gibes, R., Duffy, F. H., McAnulty, G., & Blickman, J. G. (1986). Individualized behavioral and environmental care for the very low birth weight preterm infant at high risk for bronchopulmonary dysplasia: Neonatal intensive care unit and developmental outcome. *Pediatrics, 78(6),* 1123–32.

Als, H., Lawhon, G., Duffy, F. H., McAnulty, G. B., Gibes-Grossman, R., & Blickman, J. G. (1994). Individualized developmental care for the very low-birth-weight preterm infant: Medical and neurofunctional effects. *Journal of the American Medical Association, 272(11),* 853–8.

Barrera, M. E., Kitching, K. J., Cunningham, C. C., Doucet, D., & Rosenbaum, P. (1991). A 3-year home intervention follow-up study with low birthweight infants and their parents. *Topics in Early Childhood Special Education, 10(4),* 14–28.

Becker, P. T., Grunwald, P. C., Moorman, J., & Stuhr, S. (1991). Outcomes of developmentally supportive nursing care for very low birth weight infants. *Nursing Research, 40(3),* 150–55.

Becker, P. T., Grunwald, P. C., Moorman, J., & Stuhr, S. (1993). Effects of developmental care on behavioral organization in very-low-birth-weight infants. *Nursing Research, 42(4),* 214–20.

Beckwith, L. (1988). Intervention with disadvantaged parents of sick preterm infants. *Psychiatry, 51,* 242–7.

Bennett, D. E. & Slade, P. (1991). Infants born at risk: Consequences for maternal post-partum adjustment. *British Journal of Medical Psychology, 64,* 159–72.

Boukydis, C. F. Z. & Moses, L. (1995). Establishing and maintaining a parenting network for parents of premature/high risk infants. *Infants and Young Children, 7,* 77–87.

Brazelton, T. B. (1973). *Neonatal Behavioral Assessment Scale.* London: Spastic International Medical Publications.

Brown, J. V., LaRossa, M. M., Aylward, G. P., Davis, D. J., Rutherford, P. K., & Bakeman, R. (1980). Nursery-based intervention with prematurely born babies and their mothers: Are there effects? *Pediatrics, 97(3),* 487–91.

Buehler, D. M., Als, H., Duffy, F. H., McAnulty, G. B., & Liederman, J. (1995). Effectiveness of individualized developmental care for low-risk preterm infants: Behavioral and electrophysiologic evidence. *Pediatrics, 96(5),* 923–32.

Caine, J. (1991). The effects of music on the selected stress behaviors, weight, caloric and formula intake, and length of hospital stay of premature and low birth weight neonates in a newborn intensive care unit. *Journal of Music Therapy, 28(4),* 180–92.

Caldwell, B. M. & Bradley, R. H. (1979). *HOME Observation for Measurement of the Environment.* Little Rock, AR: University of Arkansas at Little Rock.

Cassidy, J. W. & Standley, J. W. (1995). The effect of music listening on physiological responses of premature infants in the NICU. *Journal of Music Therapy, 32(4),* 208–27.

Cobiella, C. W., Mabe, P. A., & Forehand, R. L. (1990). A comparison of two stress-reduction treatments for mothers of neonates hospitalized in a neonatal intensive care unit. *Children's Health Care, 19(2)*, 93–100.

Coleman, J. M., Pratt, R. R., Stoddard, R. A., Gerstmann, D. R., & Abel, H. (1997). The effects of the male and female singing and speaking voices on selected physiological and behavioral measures of premature infants in the intensive care unit. *International Journal of Arts Medicine, 5(2)*, 4–11.

Cornell, E. H. & Gottfried, A. W. (1976). Intervention with premature human infants. *Child Development, 47*, 32–9.

Dieter, J. N. I. & Emory, E. K. (1997). Supplemental stimulation of premature infants: A treatment model. *Journal of Pediatric Psychology, 22(3)*, 281–95.

Dieter, J. N. I., Field, T., Hernandez-Reif, M., Emory, E. K., & Redzepi, M. (2003). Stable preterm infants gain more weight and sleep less after five days of massage therapy. *Journal of Pediatric Psychology, 28(6)*, 403–11.

Eckerman, C. O., Oehler, J. M., Medvin, M. B., & Hannan, T. E. (1994). Premature newborns as social partners before term age. *Infant Behavior and Development, 17*, 55–70.

Eckerman, C. O., Oehler, J. M., Hannan, T. E., & Molitor, A. (1995). The development prior to term age of very prematurely born newborns' responsiveness in en face exchanges. *Infant Behavior and Development, 18*, 283–97.

Ferber, S. G., Kuint, J., Weller, A., Feldman, R., Dollberg, S., Arbel, E., & Kohelet, D. (2002). Massage therapy by mothers and trained professionals enhances weight gain in preterm infants. *Early Human Development, 67*, 37–45.

Field, T. (1980). Supplemental stimulation of preterm neonates. *Early Human Development, 4(3)*, 301–14.

Field, T. (1995). Massage therapy for infants and children. *Developmental and Behavioral Pediatrics, 16(2)*, 105–11.

Field, T. (2001). Massage therapy facilitates weight gain in preterm infants. *Current Directions in Psychological Science, 10(2)*, 51–4.

Field, T. M., Widmayer, S. M., Stringer, S., & Ignatoff, E. (1980). Teenage, lower-class, black mothers and their preterm infants: An intervention and developmental follow-up. *Child Development, 51*, 426–36.

Field, T. M., Schanberg, S. M., Scafidi, F., Bauer, C. R., Vega-Lahr, N., Garcia, R., Nystrom, J., & Kuhn, C. M. (1986). Tactile-kinesthetic stimulation effects on preterm neonates. *Pediatrics, 77(5)*, 654–8.

Fleisher, B. E., VandenBerg, K., Constantinou, J., Heller, C., Benitz, W. E., Johnson, A., Rosenthal, A., & Stevenson, D. K. (1995). Individualized developmental care for very-low-birth-weight premature infants. *Clinical Pediatrics, 34(10)*, 523–29.

Glass, P. (1990). Light and the developing retina. *Documenta Ophthalmologica, 74*, 195–203.

Glass, P. (1999). The vulnerable neonate and the neonatal intensive care environment. In G. Avery, M. Fletcher, & M. MacDonald (eds.), *Neonatology: Pathophysiology and management of the newborn* (5th edn., pp. 91–108). Philadelphia, PA: Lippincott.

Glass, P., Avery, G. B., Subramanian, K. N., Keys, M. P., Sostek, A. M., & Friendly, D. S. (1985). Effect of bright light in the hospital nursery on the incidence of retinopathy of prematurity. *New England Journal of Medicine, 313*, 401–4.

Goetze, L. D., Immel, N., Escobar, C. M., Gillette, Y., Coury, D., & Hansen, N. (1993). Does more intensive neonatal intensive care unit follow-up service result in better outcomes? A cost-effect analysis. *Early Education and Development, 4(4)*, 275–89.

Gorski, P. A., Hole, W. T., Leonard, C. H., & Martin, J. A. (1983). Direct computer recording of premature infants and nursery care: Distress following two interventions. *Pediatrics, 72(2)*, 198–202.

Grunwald, P. C. & Becker, P. T. (1991). Developmental enhancement: Implementing a program for the NICU. *Neonatal Network, 9(6)*, 29–44.

Hack, M. & Fanaroff, A. A. (1999). Outcomes of children of extremely low birthweight and gestational age in the 1990s. *Early Human Development, 53(3)*, 193–218.

Hack, M., Klein, N. K., & Taylor, H. G. (1995). Long-term developmental outcomes of low birth weight infants. *The Future of Children, 5*, 176–96.

Hack, M., Wilson-Costello, D., Friedman, H., Taylor, G. H., Schluchter, M., & Fanaroff, A. A. (2000). Neurodevelopment and predictors of outcomes of children with birth weights less than 1000 g: 1992–1995. *Archives of Pediatrics and Adolescent Medicine, 154(7)*, 725–31.

Harrison, L., Olivet, L., Cunningham, K., Bodin, M. B., & Hicks, C. (1996). Effects of gentle human touch on preterm infants: Pilot study results. *Neonatal Network, 15(2)*, 35–42.

Harrison, L. L., Williams, A. K., Berbaum, M. L., Stem, J. T., & Leeper, J. (2000). Physiologic and behavioral effects of gentle human touch on preterm infants. *Research in Nursing and Health, 23*, 435–46.

Harrison, L., Berbaum, M. L., Stem, J. T., & Peters, K. (2001). Use of individualized versus standard criteria to identify abnormal levels of heart rate or oxygen saturation in preterm infants. *Journal of Nursing Measurement, 9(2)*, 181–200.

Hill, J. L., Brooks-Gunn, J., & Waldfogel, J. (2003). Sustained effects of high participation in an early intervention for low-birth-weight premature infants. *Developmental Psychology, 39(4)*, 730–744.

Infant Health and Development Program (1990). Enhancing the outcomes of low-birth-weight, premature infants. A multisite, randomized trial. The Infant Health and Development Program. *Journal of the American Medical Association, 263(22)*, 3035–42.

Jay, S. S. (1982). The effects of gentle human touch on mechanically ventilated very-short-term-gestation infants. *Maternal-Child Nursing Journal, 11(4)*, 195–256.

Kaplan, D. E. & Mason, E. A. (1960). Maternal reactions to premature birth viewed as an acute emotional disorder. *American Journal of Orthopsychiatry, 30*, 539–52.

Kuhn, C. M., Schanberg, S. M., Field, T., Symanski, R., Zimmerman, E., Scafidi, F., & Roberts, J. (1991). Tactile-kinesthetic stimulation effects on sympathetic and adrenocortical function in preterm infants. *Journal of Pediatrics, 119*, 434–40.

Leib, S. A., Benfield, G., & Guidubaldi, J. (1980). Effects of early intervention and stimulation on the preterm infant. *Pediatrics, 66(1)*, 83–90.

Lester, B. M. & Tronick, E. Z. (1994). NICU network neurobehavioral assessment scale. Unpublished manuscript. NICHD contract NO1-HD-2-3159.

Lindsay, J. K., Roman, L., Dewys, M., Eager, M., Levick, J., & Quinn, M. (1993). Creative caring in the NICU: Parent-to-parent support. *Neonatal Network, 12(4)*, 37–43.

Linn, P. L., Horowitz, F. D., & Fox, H. A. (1985). Stimulation in the NICU: Is more necessarily better? *Clinics in Perinatology, 12(2)*, 407–22.

Long, J. G., Philip, A. G. S., & Lucey, J. F. (1980). Excessive handling as a cause of hypoxemia. *Pediatrics, 65(2)*, 203–7.

McGettigan, M. C., Greenspan, J. S., Antunes, M. J., Greenspan, D. I., & Rubenstein, S. D. (1994). Psychological aspects of parenting critically ill neonates. *Clinical Pediatrics, 33(2)*, 77–82.

Meck, N. E., Fowler, S. A., Claflin, K., & Rasmussen, L. B. (1995). Mothers' perceptions of their NICU experience 1 and 7 months after discharge. *Journal of Early Education, 19*, 288–301.

Meyer, E. C., Coll, C. T. G., Lester, B. M., Boukydis, Z., McDonough, S. M., & Oh, W. (1994). Family-based intervention improves maternal psychological well-being and feeding interaction of preterm infants. *Pediatrics, 93(2)*, 241–6.

Meyer, E. C., Lester, B. M., Boukydis, C. F. Z., & Bigsby, R. (1998). Family-based intervention with high-risk infants and their families. *Journal of Clinical Psychology in Medical Settings, 5(1)*, 49–69.

Minde, K., Shosenberg, N., Marton, P., Thompson, J., Ripley, J., & Burns, S. (1980). Self-help groups in a premature nursery – a controlled evaluation. *Journal of Pediatrics, 96(5)*, 933–40.

Minde, K., Shosenberg, N., Thompson, J., & Marton, P. (1983). Self-help groups in a premature nursery – Follow-up at one year. In J. D. Call, E. Galenson, & R. L. Tyson (eds.), *Frontiers of infant psychiatry* (pp. 264–72). New York: Basic Books.

Modrcin-Talbott, M. A., Harrison, L. L., Groer, M. W., & Younger, M. S. (2003). The biobehavioral effects of gentle human touch on preterm infants. *Nursing Science Quarterly, 16(1)*, 60–67.

Morrow, C. J., Field, T. M., Scafidi, F. A., Roberts, J., Eisen, L., Larson, S. K., Hogan, A. E., & Bandstra, E. S. (1991). Differential effects of massage and heelstick procedures on transcutaneous oxygen tension in preterm neonates. *Infant Behavior and Development, 14*, 397–414.

Norris, S., Campbell, L. A., & Brenkert, S. (1982). Nursing procedures and alterations in transcutaneous oxygen tension in premature infants. *Nursing Research, 31(6)*, 330–36.

Nurcombe, B., Howell, D. C., Rauh, V. A., Teti, D. M., Ruoff, P., & Brennan, J. (1984). An intervention program for mothers of low-birthweight infants: Preliminary results. *Journal of the American Academy of Child Psychiatry, 23*, 319–25.

Oehler, J. M. (1985). Examining the issue of tactile stimulation for preterm infants. *Neonatal Network, 4*, 25–33.

Oehler, J. M., Eckerman, C. O., & Wilson, W. H. (1988). Social stimulation and the regulation of premature infants' state prior to term age. *Infant Behavior and Development, 11*, 333–51.

O'Shea, T. M., Klinepeter, K. L., Goldstein, D. J., Jackson, B. W., & Dillard, R. G. (1997). Survival and developmental disability in infants with birth weights of 501 to 800 grams, born between 1979 and 1994. *Pediatrics, 100(6)*, 982–6.

Ottenbacher, K. J., Muller, L., Brandt, D., Heintzelman, A., Hojem, P., & Sharpe, P. (1987). The effectiveness of tactile stimulation as a form of early intervention: A quantitative evaluation. *Journal of Developmental and Behavioral Pediatrics, 8(2)*, 68–76.

Parker, S. J., Zahr, L. K., Cole, J. G., & Brecht, M. (1992). Outcome after developmental intervention in the neonatal intensive care unit for mothers of preterm infants with low socioeconomic status. *Journal of Pediatrics, 120(5)*, 780–85.

Pederson, D. R., Bento, S., Chance, G. W., Evans, B., & Fox, M. (1987). Maternal emotional responses to preterm birth. *American Journal of Orthopsychiatry, 57(1)*, 15–21.

Pfander, S. & Bradley-Johnson, S. (1990). Effects of an intervention program and its components on NICU infants. *Children's Health Care, 19(3)*, 140–46.

Preyde, M. & Ardal, F. (2003). Effectiveness of a parent "buddy" program for mothers of very preterm infants in a neonatal intensive care unit. *Canadian Medical Association Journal, 168(8)*, 969–73.

Rauh, V. A., Achenbach, T. M., Nurcombe, B., Howell, C. T., & Teti, D. M. (1988). Minimizing adverse effects of low birthweight: Four-year results of an early intervention program. *Child Development, 59*, 544–53.

Rausch, P. B. (1981). Effects of tactile and kinesthetic stimulation on premature infants. *Journal of Obstetric and Gynecologic Nursing, XX*, 34–7.

Resnick, M. B., Armstrong, S., & Carter, R. L. (1988). Developmental intervention program for high-risk premature infants: Effects on development and parent–infant interactions. *Developmental and Behavioral Pediatrics, 9(2)*, 73–8.

Resnick, M. B., Eyler, F. D., Nelson, R. M., Eitzman, D. V., & Bucciarelli, R. L. (1987). Developmental intervention for low birth weight infants: Improved early developmental outcome. *Pediatrics, 80(1)*, 68–74.

Roman, L. A., Lindsay, J. K., Boger, R. P., DeWys, M., Beaumont, E. J., Jones, A. S., & Haas, B. (1995). Parent-to-parent support initiated in the neonatal intensive care unit. *Research in Nursing and Health, 18*, 385–94.

Sameroff, A. & Chandler, M. (1975). Reproductive risk and the continuum of caretaking casualty. In F. Horowitz (ed.), *Review of child development research*, vol. 4. Chicago, IL: University of Chicago Press.

Santelli, B., Turnbull, A. P., Marquis, J. G., & Lerner, E. P. (1995). Parent to parent programs: A unique form of mutual support. *Infants and Young Children, 8(2)*, 48–57.

Scafidi, F. A., Field, T. M., Schanberg, S. M., Baur, C. R., Tucci, K., Roberts, J., Morrow, C., & Kuhn, C. M. (1990). Massage stimulates growth in preterm infants: A replication. *Infant Behavior and Development, 13*, 167–88.

Scafidi, F. A., Field, T., & Schanberg, S. M. (1993). Factors that predict which preterm infants benefit most from massage therapy. *Developmental and Behavioral Pediatrics, 14(3)*, 176–80.

Standley, J. M. (1998). The effect of music and multimodal stimulation on responses of premature infants in neonatal intensive care. *Pediatric Nursing, 24(6)*, 532–8.

Szajnberg, N., Ward, M. J., Kraus, A., & Kessler, D. B. (1987). Low birth-weight prematures: Preventive intervention and maternal attitude. *Child Psychiatry and Human Development, 17(3)*, 152–65.

Teti, D. M., O'Connell, M. A., & Reiner, C. D. (1997). Parenting sensitivity, parental depression, and child health: The mediational role of parental self-efficacy. *Early Development and Parenting, 5(4)*, 237–50.

Westrup, B. & Kleberg, A. (2000). A randomized controlled trial to evaluate the effects of the Newborn Individualized Developmental Care and Assessment Program in a Swedish setting. *Pediatrics, 105(1)*, 66–72.

Wheeden, M. S., Scafidi, F. A., Field, T., Ironson, G., Valdeon, C., & Bandstra, E. (1993). Massage effects on cocaine-exposed preterm neonates. *Developmental and Behavioral Pediatrics, 14(5)*, 318–22.

Whipple, J. (2000). The effect of parent training in music and multimodal stimulation on parent–neonate interactions in the neonatal intensive care unit. *Journal of Music Therapy, 37(4)*, 250–68.

White-Traut, R. C. & Goldman, M. B. C. (1988). Premature infant massage: Is it safe? *Pediatric Nursing, 14(4)*, 285–9.

White-Traut, R. C. & Nelson, M. N. (1988). Maternally administered tactile, auditory, visual, and vestibular stimulation: Relationship to later interactions between mothers and premature infants. *Research in Nursing and Health, 11*, 31–9.

White-Traut, R. C., Silvestri, J. M., Nelson, M. N., Patel, M. K., & Kilgallon, D. (1993). Patterns of physiologic and behavioral response of intermediate care preterm infants to intervention. *Pediatric Nursing, 19(6)*, 625–9.

White-Traut, R. C., Cunningham, N., Nelson, M. N., Patel, M., & Silvestri, J. M. (1997). Responses of preterm infants to unimodal and multimodal sensory stimulation. *Pediatric Nursing, 23(2)*, 169–75.

White-Traut, R. C., Nelson, M. N., Silvestri, J. M., Patel, M., Vasan, U., Han, B. K., Cunningham, N., Burns, K., Kopischke, K., & Bradford, L. (1999). Developmental intervention for preterm infants diagnosed with periventricular leukomalacia. *Research in Nursing and Health, 22*, 131–43.

Widmayer, S. M. & Field, T. M. (1980). Effects of Brazelton demonstrations on early interactions of preterm infants and their teenage mothers. *Infant Behavior and Development, 3*, 79–89.

Widmayer, S. M. & Field, T. M. (1981). Effects of Brazelton demonstrations for mothers on the development of preterm infants. *Pediatrics, 67(5)*, 711–14.

Williams, P. D., Williams, A. R., & Dial, M. N. (1986). Children at risk: Perinatal events, developmental delays and the effects of a developmental stimulation program. *International Journal of Nursing Studies, 23(1)*, 21–38.

Wood, N. S., Marlow, N., Costeloe, K., Gibson, A. T., & Wilkinson, A. R. (2000). Neurological and developmental disability after extremely preterm birth. *New England Journal of Medicine, 343(6)*, 378–84.

Zahr, L. K. & Balian, S. (1995). Responses of premature infants to routine nursing interventions and noise in the NICU. *Nursing Research, 44(3)*, 179–85.

Zahr, L. K., Parker, S., & Cole, J. (1992). Comparing the effects of neonatal intensive care unit intervention on premature infants at different weights. *Developmental and Behavioral Pediatrics, 13(3)*, 165–72.

Zeskind, P. S. & Iacino, R. (1984). Effects of maternal visitation to preterm infants in the neonatal intensive care unit. *Child Development, 55*, 1887–93.

PART IV

Analytic Issues and Methods in Developmental Psychology

CHAPTER SIXTEEN

Assessing Growth in Longitudinal Investigations: Selected Measurement and Design Issues

Donald P. Hartmann

Introduction

This chapter is preliminary to those that consider analysis of the kinds of growth data produced by longitudinal investigations. In it I discuss some of the myriad issues that indeed are preparatory to the analysis of longitudinal data. Goldstein (1979), in his book on longitudinal studies, outlines many of these topics – and then addresses them in individual chapters of his book. These issues include sampling, measurement, time scales (defining temporal units), developmental standards or norms, data processing, planning and organization, tracing participants and gaining cooperation, piloting and quality control, checking, coding, and documentation, staffing, and ethical concerns such as confidentiality and informed consent. And this list is by no means exhaustive. To it could be added special data management problems as well as various design considerations.

Goldstein does not stand alone in devoting substantial portions of a book to these preliminary issues. Other recent monographs that address preparatory concerns include Baltes, Reese, and Nesselroade (1988), Cohen and Reese (1994), Collins and Horn (1991), Friedman and Haywood (1994), Gottman (1995), Magnusson and Casaer (1993), Menard (1991), Miller (1998), and Schaie et al. (1988).

While the development of our understanding of many of these issues would hardly be described as revolutionary, fairly dramatic changes have occurred in the conception of growth data and its analysis (e.g., Willett, 1988). Because these changes have implications for earlier components of longitudinal investigations, we briefly examine the nature of the changes that have occurred in our conception of growth data.

The older conception, sometimes referred to as the *incremental* view of change, emphasizes change as a series of starts and stops, rather than as a continuous process that takes place throughout the time span under investigation. This conceptualization is alleged to be responsible for creating many of the "problems in measuring change" (Harris, 1967). It has, according to Willett (1988, p. 347),

> Fostered an approach to change measurement that deals exclusively in "two-wave" designs, whose principal measures are the difference score and the residual-change score, whose predominant graphical displays are scatterplots of the posttest on the pretest, whose major group-level statistical summaries are correlations of the posttest and the pretest, whose overriding concerns are unreliability, invalidity, and regression to the mean. It is a conceptualization that, by virtue of its very existence, has retarded the *longitudinal* investigation of individual development. And it has prevented the generalization of traditional measures of change to *more* than two waves of data.

The incremental view of change has largely been superseded by the *process* view of change. The process approach views a person's scores as reflecting an ongoing underlying growth process, and scores are linked to the time they are obtained. The initial goal is to represent each individual's pattern of growth (the *intraindividual* portion of the model). According to Willett (1988) it is the use of mathematical growth modeling to represent individual growth that is at the heart of recent methodological advances. The second step is then to determine independent variables that are associated with the parameters that are used to describe the growth process – the *interindividual* part of the model (e.g., Francis, Schatschneider, & Carlson, 2000).

In this chapter on measurement and design issues, the section on measurement largely focuses on issues of reliability and measurement invariance. The design section is directed to sampling issues – a much-neglected topic in longitudinal or most any research. Before delving into the technical issues of measurement and design, a few words about the question or idea that prompted the study of growth.

Sources of research ideas

There are at least two, and perhaps three, bad sources of research ideas, largely related to methodology. The first might be called the measurement source of research ideas: "I have this incredible measurement device – test or apparatus. Which growth phenomena can I investigate in order to use my measurement device?" The second might be called the independent variable (IV) source of research ideas: "I have this compelling IV (e.g., gender or SES). Which growth phenomena can I investigate that might be related to this IV?" The third might be called the analysis source of research ideas: "I have this cutting-edge analytic tool, such as structural equation modeling or hierarchical linear modeling. Which growth phenomena can I investigate in order to use my statistical device?" These approaches to the generation of research ideas are not unlike the individual who receives a hammer, and searches for objects to pound. This tactic is perhaps acceptable for the acquisition of pounding skills, but not much else. The three approaches also illustrate a much-disdained investigative strategy: allowing the methodological tail to wag the substantive dog!

Most seasoned investigators choose their research ideas on the basis of theory – either illustrating the power of the theory or the utility of the theory in comparison to alternative conceptualizations of some phenomena. A second source of instigation is some practical issue that begs for an explanation, or at least explication.

Measurement

In this section we deal principally with three measurement-related issues: reliability, measurement equivalence, and the scheduling of assessment. Before doing so, however, we provide a brief overview of a wider array of measurement considerations and current controversies.

In general, measurement includes the operations that are used to obtain scores. In developmental research, the scores provided by measurements assess dependent variable performance, evaluate participant's independent variable statuses, and also determine their standing on other dimensions used to describe the research sample or to control for differences among individuals or groups. These research-related decision-making functions of measurement require that the resulting scores are both relevant and of high quality.

Measurement issues are particularly acute in developmental investigations, in part because of the vicissitudes of assessing participants occupying the ends of the developmental spectrum (Hartmann & George, 1999). Both youngsters and oldsters may pose challenges in establishing standard conditions of assessment, in capturing rapidly changing performance levels, and in ensuring invariance in the meaning of scores with changes in development. As a consequence, developmental investigators have singular responsibility to demonstrate that their measures meet these challenges.

The assessment of measurement worth or quality, not surprisingly, depends on the nature of the research and the specific questions put forward for investigation. Nevertheless, certain criteria are generally relevant to judgments of quality, including whether or not the measurement device is applied in a standard fashion, and whether or not the resulting scores are replicable (reliable) and measure what they are supposed to measure – the latter notion bears very close resemblance to the notion of construct validity.

Precisely how these criteria or standards are applied, and which are relevant, may also depend on various technical or theoretical considerations – sometimes referred to as measurement *facets* and *sources* (Messick, 1983; also see Baltes, Lindenberger, & Staudinger, 1998). The facets include the nature of the characteristics assessed – whether they are stable traits or changing states – structures or functions, and competence or typical performance. Other facets involve whether the scores are used for interindividual (normative) or intraindividual (ipsative) comparisons, and depend for their interpretation upon norms (norm-referenced) or upon objective performance standards (criterion-referenced). The sources of measurement include whether the assessment responses are based on self-reports, constitute test responses, or are reports of performance in naturalistic settings by participant or independent observers.

The quality of scores usually is judged by their conformity to standard psychometric criteria. These criteria include the standardization of administration and scoring procedures and the demonstration of acceptable levels of reliability and validity (American Psychological Association, 1985). Standardization is intended to insure that procedurally comparable scores are obtained for all participants assessed. Thus, standardization requires the use of equivalent administrative procedures, materials – such as items for tests or questionnaires and the timing and setting for observations – and methods of recording responses and of arriving at scores. Even slight variation from standardized procedures can introduce substantial noise into data and hence ambiguity into the interpretation of individual studies or even groups of studies, as has occurred, for example, in the literature on the assessment of children's fears using behavioral avoidance tests (Barrios & Hartmann, 1997).

Although all of the aforementioned psychometric criteria involve the interpretation or meaning of scores, validity is the psychometric criterion most directly relevant to their meaning. For a time, the litany of types of validity was expanding as rapidly as was the unvalidated uses of measuring instruments. The pendulum has swung back to a more unified conception of validity, subsumed by the concept of construct validity (e.g., Messick, 1994). Silva (1993, p. 69) has nicely summarized current notions of validity as well as highlighting the inadequacies of earlier formulations. Validity is associated with each inference made from assessment information. It is not the instrument that is validated but rather the interpretation of scores obtained from the instrument. Validity is an integrative judgment, reached after considering all of the information – both empirical evidence and theoretical rationales. It is not reducible to a coefficient or set of coefficients. Types and classes of validity are misnomers for types and classes of arguments – the concept of validity is essentially unitary. There is no limit to the range of data used to estimate validity. Any information may be relevant in the validation process – which is simply the process of hypothesis construction and testing. Also see Nunnally and Bernstein (1994), Pedhazur and Schmelkin (1991), Messick (1983), Wiggins (1973), and Miller (1998).

Before discussing the major topics of this section, a brief measurement caveat. Since the popularization of growth analysis, advocates of this position have been increasingly active in their criticisms – of our existing armamentarium of measures of important developmental phenomena, of traditional test construction techniques, as well as of some of our sacred psychometric principles (e.g., Collins & Sayer, 2000; Willett, 1988). Their dissatisfaction stems in large part from the individual difference approach that formed the basis for the development of most existent measures. A secondary basis of their disapproval stems from the continuing popularity of methods of expressing scores that remove variance and mean differences in their calculation (e.g., standard scores). These scores are far from optimum for assessing growth (e.g., Francis, Schatschneider, & Carlson, 2000).

While individual differences are of interest to growth-score analysts, their overarching interest is in describing intraindividual growth. Unfortunately, the dynamic nature of individual growth has not been adequately represented either in the instruments contained in our assessment inventory, or in the models of test construction that could be used to construct new assessment devices. Modest advances have been made in the development of new test construction models. These include the extension of Guttman scaling to the development of growth measures by Collins (e.g., 1996) as well as promising developments in item response theory (e.g., Embretson, 1991). Neither of these approaches has yet gained wide popularity. Thus, one cannot but agree with Collins and Sayer (2000) that "more measurement theories for dynamic variables, including guidelines for making up scales consisting of Likert items or other kinds of multicategory items, are needed" (p. 486).

Reliability

Aspects of reliability impact various parts of longitudinal research, including, for example, the selection of measures and their frequency of application. As is well known, reliability concerns the dependability, consistency, or generalizability of scores (e.g., Cronbach et al., 1972). Theoretical treatises on reliability decompose obtained scores (X) into at least two generic components: true or universe scores (X_t) and error scores (e_x).

$$X = X_t + e_x$$

The true score portion of one's obtained score is that part that remains constant across reliability assessments. This component is sometimes defined conceptually as the mean of an infinite number of measurements, or across all possible parallel forms of an instrument, or across all possible relevant measurement conditions (sometimes referred to as *facets*) such as occasions, scorers, and the like. The error component is the portion of one's score that changes across reliability assessments, and hence results in inconsistent performance. Inconsistent performance might be produced by any number of factors, including temporary states of the assessment setting, such as a clanging fire alarm, or of the participant (e.g., being ill), or idiosyncratic aspects of the measurement instrument such as inconsistent observer behavior or scorer error (Cronbach, 1984). Unfortunately, perhaps, the factors that produce consistent and inconsistent responding on measurement instruments vary depending on how reliability is assessed. For example, an illness might affect a child's playground aggression consistently across an observation session broken into temporal parts; aggression would thus be consistent or reliable across these parts. On the other hand, aggression would be inconsistent across observation sessions separated by longer intervals during which the child's health status changed.

As this discussion suggests, reliability may be assessed in a number of ways that differently divide obtained scores into true and error scores, including internal consistency reliability, interobserver reliability, parallel-form reliability, situational consistency, temporal reliability, and growth reliability.

Internal consistency reliability Internal consistency assesses the consistency of performance across a measure's internal or constituent parts. Internal consistency reliability is one of the few forms of reliability that does not require repeated administration or scoring of an instrument. A variety of internal consistency measures of reliability currently are available, the most common of which is coefficient alpha (e.g., Nunnally & Bernstein, 1994). The formula for coefficient alpha – $\alpha = [k/(k-1)][1 - (\Sigma\sigma_i^2/\sigma_x^2)]$, where k = number of components (e.g., items), $\Sigma\sigma_i^2$ = the sum of the component variances, and σ_x^2 = the variance of the composite scores – nicely illustrates the dependence of a composite score on the characteristics of its components. The reliability of a composite score can be estimated either by knowing the statistics for its component parts or directly via the "at least one more score" principle (see below). The reliability of the traditional difference scores is a case in point (see Willett, 1988).

Internal consistency is required for most applications of assessment instruments, including their use in longitudinal investigations. The scores obtained from an instrument composed of internally consistent parts assess a single characteristic or a set of highly interrelated characteristics. In contrast, assessment procedures containing internally inconsistent items, time periods, or analogous constituent parts measure a hodgepodge; as a result, scores obtained from them will not be comparable.

Interobserver reliability Interobserver (or interscorer) reliability assesses the extent to which observers or scorers obtain equivalent scores when assessing the same individual. Interobserver reliability is assessed or measured with agreement statistics (e.g., percent agreement or kappa) or with traditional reliability statistics (e.g., correlation coefficients). Hartmann and Wood (1990) and Suen (1988) discuss distinctions between these two classes of summary statistics.

Interobserver or scorer reliability likewise is requisite for the minimal interpretability of scores. Without adequate agreement between observers, the very nature of the phenomenon under study is unclear (Hartmann & Wood, 1990). Interobserver reliability is sometimes surprisingly low even when the phenomenon of interest is clearly defined and easily observed. When this occurs, it may be that differences between observers are confounded with setting differences. For example, parents and teachers may disagree about an easily observed behavior because the teacher observes the children in school and the parents observe their children at home (e.g., Achenbach, McConaughy, & Howell, 1987). In addition, if the same teacher rates all children, but a different parent rates each child, disagreements may occur because each parent may use the rating scale in an idiosyncratic manner (Hartmann & George, 1999).

Parallel-form reliability Parallel-form reliability assesses the degree to which alternate (parallel) forms of an instrument provide equivalent scores. Parallel-form reliability is to tests as interobserver reliability is to direct observations. Parallel-form reliability may play an important role for longitudinal investigators who intend to use parallel forms of assessment in the hopes of reducing the substantial testing effects that sometimes confound developmental changes in longitudinal investigations (e.g., Baltes, Reese, & Nesselroade, 1988).

Situational consistency Situational consistency or generalizability indexes the extent to which scores from an instrument are consistent across settings. For example, is the punctuality of children in the completion of their classroom assignments consistent with the punctuality with which they perform assigned chores at home? This form of reliability is analogous to the concept of the external validity of investigations. Situational consistency would be important to assess in a longitudinal investigation in which not all assessments were conducted in the same setting. Such would be the case if, for example, infants' attachment to their mothers were to be assessed in a typical university laboratory for some participants, but in a mobile research trailer for others.

Temporal reliability Temporal reliability measures the degree to which an instrument provides equivalent scores across time in the sense of "ordering" individuals consistently. Test–retest correlations frequently are used to assess the stability of a trait or behavior. Temporal stability consistently is found to be negatively correlated with the length of time between assessments. Indeed, the decreasing stability with increasing inter-assessment time (sometimes simplex in structure) has been observed so commonly in investigations of stability that it has assumed the character of a basic law of behavior.

Estimates of temporal stability can play an important role in determining the frequency with which a behavior must be sampled in a given time period in order to arrive at a stable estimate of its relevant characteristics. With even common behaviors of infants, the number of observation periods required to achieve stable estimates can be surprisingly large (e.g., De Weerth, van Geert, & Hoijtink, 1999). Test–retest statistics are sometimes used mistakenly. One frequent error is to describe stability without providing the interval over which it is assessed. A second common error occurs when developmental researchers interpret low test stability as evidence against measurement equivalence. The latter interpretation can be dangerous as test–retest correlations "confound issues of construct validity, instrument equatability over time, and interindividual differences in growth" (Willett, 1988, p. 362).

Growth reliability A final form of reliability is not part of the typical psychometric armamentarium: the reliability of growth. In the parlance of traditional reliability theory, this phrase is a bit of an oxymoron, as the notion of growth is incongruent with the notion of true score. When growth is described by some trend component, it may be unclear whether there are reliable interindividual differences in that trend component. Gathering an additional wave of data – one more than is required to estimate the value of the component – provides the information required in estimating the reliability of the component. I term this the principle of "at least one more score." Thus, for example, to assess the reliability of a slope requires three waves of data, and if one is interested in assessing the reliability of a quadratic trend, four measurement occasions are required. The additional score or measure provides the information necessary to assess the error variance associated with the component (e.g., Bryk & Raudenbush, 1992). Increasing the number of measurement waves still further has at least two additional advantages: It *increases* reliability as well as providing supplementary information about the nature of the growth process (Willett, 1988).

Despite the quite different types or forms of reliability, a single definition of reliability is common to most of them. Reliability is defined as one minus the ratio of error variance to obtained score variance ($r_{xx} = 1 - [\sigma_e^2/\sigma_x^2]$), where r_{xx} is the reliability coefficient, σ_e^2 is the variance of error scores, and σ_x^2 is the variance of obtained scores.

Examination of this expression clearly discloses that the conception of reliability confounds measurement imprecision (σ_e^2) with individual difference heterogeneity or σ_x^2 (Willett, 1988, p. 408). Thus, low reliability does not necessarily imply lack of precision (Rogosa, Brandt, & Zimowski, 1982).

Reliability gains general importance because it places a very specific limit on empirical validity in longitudinal as well as other forms of investigation. If validity is indexed by an instrument's correlation with a criterion (r_{xy}), and the instrument's reliability is expressed as r_{xx}, the upper limit of r_{xy} is $r_{xx}^{1/2}$. That is, $r_{xy} \leq r_{xx}^{1/2}$ – which is a form of the well-known correction for attenuation formula (Nunnally & Bernstein, 1994). Thus, a measuring instrument with $r_{xx} = 0.50$ could not expect to correlate greater than 0.707 with any criteria, even if the underlying constructs were perfectly correlated.

Measurement equivalence

Substantive interpretation of the scores in any developmental study – whether involving the comparison of different groups of participants or of the same individuals assessed on different occasions – requires that the scores for individuals in the groups or across the occasions assess the same construct. When the scores do not assess the same construct across groups or occasions, interpretation of score comparisons are at best muddied, and may result in inferences that are "potentially artifactual and . . . substantively misleading" (Widaman & Reise, 1997, p. 282).

Baltes, Reese, and Nesselroade (1988, chapter 17), in their classic monograph on developmental research methods, discuss a number of related forms of measurement nonequivalence that are of concern to longitudinal investigators. Two of these have been extensively discussed by Campbell and his associates under the general rubric of threats to internal validity (Campbell & Stanley, 1963; Cook & Campbell, 1979): threats due to *testing* and threats due to *instrumentation*. In the former case the measurement perturbation is due to changes that occur in the performance of the participant that result from repeated exposure to the assessment device. Baltes, Reese, and Nesselroade provide truly astonishing examples of the confounding of testing effects with developmental changes in the longitudinal assessment of cognitive performance in adolescents (p. 162). In the latter case the change in the meaning of scores is intrinsic to the instrument itself, and occurs, for example, when observers drift in their use of codes across an investigation (see, for example, Hartmann & Wood, 1990). Taplin and Reid (1973) provide a striking example of drift in longitudinal research conducted on family interactions at the Oregon Social Learning Center.

While these two causes of changes in the meaning of scores are of considerable concern to longitudinal investigators, a third type of measurement disturbance is often viewed as even more troublesome in its production of measurement nonequivalence. This third type is not due to reactive arrangement such as repeated assessments or to changes that are intrinsic to the measurement device, but rather to the interactions between development and the characteristics of the assessment device. This form of *developmental nonequivalence* is well known to investigators who study individuals during rapid transition periods, such as toddlerhood.

Consider, for example, a study intended to compare aggressiveness at ages 2, 4, and 6, using a cross-sectional, a longitudinal, or one of the sequential designs. Assume that the measure of aggression included only physical forms of aggression, such as hitting, pushing, and biting. If we observed a decrease in these aggression scores across age – as we likely would – it might be wrong to conclude that aggression decreased with development across this age span. The reason is clear: between ages 2 and 6 aggression changes its topography by becoming increasingly verbal. As a result, the numerical values obtained by the different-age children on the aggression measurement scale do not have equivalent or invariant meaning with regard to the latent construct of aggression. Other examples of this kind can be found in Hofstaetter (1954) and in Horn, McArdle, and Mason (1983).

Similarly, we may have difficulty arriving at substantive interpretations of differences in the correlations between the aggression scores and a variable such as "parental involvement" across these three ages. Differences in these correlations may merely reflect nonequivalence in the meaning of the aggression scores across time. Thus, we can see that the issue of developmental nonequivalence is of paramount importance in longitudinal studies, particularly those extending over a lengthy time period or over critical developmental transitions. In order to be interpreted substantively, scores obtained in these studies must assess the same construct. As Labouvie (1980, p. 493) notes,

> Studies of human development . . . need to consider the possibility that a given measure may apply to different concepts in different age/cohort populations and/ or that formally different measures may be required to tap the same concept across various groups. The question of . . . equivalence can be raised for both independent and dependent variables, antecedents, and consequents.

Because measurement equivalence falls under the general rubric of construct validation, its determination can involve a variety of theoretical and empirical arguments (e.g., Messick, 1994). Nevertheless, the primary approach to the assessment of measurement invariance has been "the study of similarities and differences in the covariation patterns of item–factor relations" (Windle, Iwawaki, & Lerner, 1988, p. 551). Furthermore, the preferred test of the hypothesis of measurement invariance appears to be by means of multiple-group confirmatory factor analysis (CFA), such as the estimation routines provided in LISREL (e.g., Reise, Widaman, & Pugh, 1993). Despite the growing popularity of using CFA for this purpose, Knight and Hill (1998) – in a very readable paper – suggest a number of informative strategies for assessing measurement equivalence (also see Eckensberger, 1973; Labouvie, 1980). To some degree, the specific strategies a researcher elects to utilize may depend on issues such as whether the researcher is attempting to develop equivalent measures or attempting to evaluate the equivalence of existing measures. The various strategies discussed by Knight and Hill (1998) might usefully be divided into those that involve the analysis of the internal structure of the measure versus those that involve cross-structure analysis. In the development that follows, we will assume that the developmental equivalence issue of concern involves within-participant comparison across occasions, though we could as well have chosen to examine between-participant comparisons as in a cross-sectional design.

Internal structure analysis Internal structure analysis can be construed as involving two very closely related forms of comparative analysis: the comparison of reliability coefficients and that of item–total-score correlations:

- *Comparison of reliability coefficients*: finding comparable internal consistency reliability coefficients across occasions provides strong presumptive evidence for measurement equivalence. The evidence may not be quite as compelling as that provided by the next form of internal structure analysis, however, as equivalent reliability can occur across waves of data collection by quite different combinations of interrelationships between the items that compose the assessment device. Conversely, substantially different values of internal consistency, say coefficient alphas, strongly suggest nonequivalence.
- *Comparison of item–total relations*: equivalent loadings of a measure's items on the latent construct across measurement occasions constitute, as previously indicated, sufficient evidence for developmental equivalence. Examination of the item–total-score correlations provides a crude approximation for the more sophisticated approaches involving Item Response Theory (IRT) or CFA. Similar item–total-score correlations across measurement occasions strengthen the measurement invariance interpretation, whereas dissimilar item–total-score correlations question the equivalence assumption.

Cross-structure analysis Cross-structure analyses operate on the relationships of the target measure with other measures external to it (e.g., convergent validity coefficients or empirical correlates). It is important to recognize that the results of cross-structure analyses may be ambiguous: discrepant results across repeated assessments may, for example, indicate the operation of different causal processes rather than measurement nonequivalence.

- *Evidence of convergent validity*: one method of cross-structure analysis involves operations identical to those used to demonstrate convergent validity (e.g., Campbell & Fiske, 1959). The target measure is correlated with one or more other measures that are presumed to assess the same construct. Consistent correlations with alternative measures of the same construct across repeated assessments of the target variable provide strong evidence of measurement invariance. Conversely, inconsistent convergent validity correlations across waves of data collection call into question the assumption of equivalence. The seriousness of the threat to equivalence produced by inconsistent values is a function of the available evidence for the continued construct validity of the alternative measures across measurement occasions.
- *Empirical correlates*: the final means of probing measurement invariance is conducted by comparing the correlations of the target measure with other external variables across waves of data collection. These other variables may be presumed determinants of the target variable or merely correlates. Knight and Hill (1998) describe three methods for conducting these cross-structure analyses of empirical correlates. The first, and simplest, method involves comparing parallel correlations from the multiple assessments with appropriate significant tests. The second method – of similar

complexity – involves examining measurement occasions as a moderator variable when regressing the target variable on the external variables using multiple regression analysis. Significant moderation poses a threat to the equivalence assumption. The final method employs structural equation modeling applied to the covariance matrix between the target and external measures. While SEM may be conceptually less available to many investigators, it has the advantage of considering an entire set of parallel coefficients rather than these coefficients taken two at a time across the two measurement occasions, as done by the preceding methods. Knight and Hill (1998) apply these procedures to data involving measurement equivalence *between* ethnic groups.

As Edelbrock (1994, p. 188) indicates, "Any doubts about measurement equivalence threaten the validity of inferences regarding developmental stability and change." It behooves investigators to demonstrate the equivalence of their measures across waves of data collection by the methods just described.

Sampling Issues in Longitudinal Research

This section focuses on a set of very important issues regarding sampling. Four sample issues loom large in any longitudinal investigation: (1) identifying the relevant population to which we hope to generalize, (2) selection of individuals who will represent that population, (3) recruitment and retention of the individuals we hope to select for that sample, and (4) accurate description of these procedures. These issues are critical for developmental investigators interested in examining longitudinal growth and change but are often overlooked.

Identifying the target population

An often overlooked, but foundational, issue in any investigation is that of defining the *target* population for the research. The target population should be the group of individuals to whom the investigator wishes to generalize the results of the study (Suen & Ary, 1989). The relevant population may be relatively limited and clearly defined, such as "graduate students who matriculated into our graduate program in developmental psychology between 1990 and 2000." Or it may be a much larger and perhaps amorphous population, such as all "normal" teenagers between the ages of 13 and 17 living in North America in the first decade of the 21st century. The nature of the target population requires careful reflection, because the decision as to what it constitutes serves two important functions: it defines the limits of the generality of the results of the study and it determines who we select to participate in our study to represent this population.

It sometimes seems that investigators assume that the results of their study apply to everyone, so that their target population is all living beings. And if that population definition is somewhat too broad, then certainly the target population includes everyone of the age that was included in their investigation. These population definitions seem to be based on very dangerous assumptions. Recall that this is the era in psychology where critical social theory and its allies are popular philosophies of science; contextualism is a major scientific approach; and interindividual and intraindividual differences as well as subject by treatment interactions are major topics of investigation (e.g., Lerner, 1998). None of these positions seems consistent with a universalist definition of the target population.

Selecting a group to represent the population

Formally, once the population is defined, *accessible* members of the population are identified and listed (the sampling frame), and a sample is drawn from this sampling frame using one of the standard method of drawing samples (e.g., random sampling, cluster sampling, or stratified sampling). These procedures seem rarely to be used in longitudinal research in developmental science. Instead, some method – infrequently described – is used to acquire a group of individuals who will represent some unspecified population. These sampling techniques are sometimes referred to as accidental sampling – though accidental perhaps suggests a greater degree of randomness than is implied in the actual procedure employed. Perhaps a more apt term is convenience or opportunistic sampling, as the sample drawn is often just that: a convenient or opportunistic aggregate of individuals that has some – often unclear – relationship to the substantive questions targeted in the research. Suen and Ary (1989, p. 44) indicate that samples such as these are:

> quite likely to be biased. However, the degree and nature of the biases are usually unknown and cannot be assessed. Inferential statistics will not be able to assess the representativeness of the sample with any degree of accuracy. At best, the data obtained . . . can only be tentative and should be used only as a guide for possible directions to be taken in a more rigorous study. At worst, data . . . may be misleading.

Indeed, the few studies that have compared the results of various sampling strategies suggest that convenience samples may provide more "advantaged" results (Hultsch et al., 2002). However, selection biases can not only misrepresent distributional characteristics such as means, variances, and covariance patterns; they can also misrepresent *relationships between variables*. Nesselroade (1988) points out "the ever-present threat of disparity between the sample that has been observed and the population or universe to which generalizations are attempted," and notes that "awareness of that threat . . . evidently continues to be in short supply in empirical research" (p. 14).

Our proclivity for generating "select-and-hope" samples is perhaps based on the erroneous notion that if enough investigators draw different convenience samples, the aggregate result will characterize the population of interest. This fatuous application of the central limit theorem will certainly lead to ambiguity and dissension – over whether a result is or is not consistent with prior research and how to intelligently interpret differences between studies.

If a random sampling method is not reasonable, as it certainly will not be for most studies, models other than accidental or convenience sampling models are described by Cook and Campbell (1979). These sensible approaches to sampling include the model of deliberate sampling for heterogeneity and the impressionistic modal instance model. In the model of deliberate sampling for heterogeneity, one identifies target classes of persons and insures that a wide range of instances from within each class is included in the study. In an investigation of the effects of pubertal status and popularity on dating, for example, one might choose a range of boys and girls from public and private schools located in rural, suburban, and city environments serving a diversity of SES and ethnic neighborhoods. The aim of this sampling method is to guarantee that the wide individual differences in children are included in the study. If the sample were sufficiently large, one would assess whether any of the participant dimensions were differentially related to outcome. This approach is entirely consistent with the sensible admonition of Abelson (1995, p. 12), who says that to generalize broadly within the confines of a single study requires broad sampling as well as the analysis of subject characteristics to determine whether they interact with outcome. If participant characteristics do correlate with outcome one can be pleased that they did not select a convenience sample with characteristics that differed from those of the target population on the dimensions correlated with outcome. For if they had done so, they would have misled.

The second sampling model described by Cook and Campbell (1979), the impressionistic modal instance model, requires investigators to explicate the kinds or classes of persons to which they *most* want to generalize and then to select instances of each class that are impressionistically similar to the class mode. Returning to the previous example, one might be particularly interested in children who attend "average" schools – average in size, SES and ethnic mix, expenditures, and the like. If schools can be assessed with respect to these dimensions, the schools that are most average would be selected for participation. This approach is perhaps most useful when the investigator can describe one or a few modal types that are of interest; it is not particularly suitable for the analysis of possible subtype differences. Whichever of these alternative models of sampling is selected, you as an investigator will be singular in that you will have *reflected* about population definitions, desired generalization, and sampling.

Recruiting and maintaining the intended participants

It is apparently well known that to maximize the validity and generalizability of findings, researchers conducting longitudinal studies must achieve high recruitment and retention rates for an appropriately selected target population (Capaldi et al., 1997). Despite the importance of these participant-related activities, Farrington et al. (1990, p. 145) noted with some irony that:

> more books and articles have been written about technical problems such as sampling, research design, and statistical analysis than about practical problems

that may be more difficult to solve and more important in their consequences for the validity of conclusions, such as tracing and securing cooperation.

The majority of work on recruiting and retaining samples traditionally has come from the literature on survey research (e.g., McAllister, Butler, & Goe, 1973). However, the recent upsurge in longitudinal research, particularly longitudinal studies with a prevention focus, has provided additional strategies for dealing with these crucial issues. Unfortunately, systematic empirical research on the effectiveness of these strategies for recruitment and retention is "generally not available" (Cauce, Ryan, & Grove, 1998, p. 157). Furthermore, few attempts appear to have been made to apply psychological theory to these issues (see Sproth & Redmond, 1995, for an exception). While recruitment and retention would seem to involve the development and maintenance of a special kind of relationship, the application of relationship theory to these sample issues appears to be generally overlooked. The book by Call, Otto, and Spenner (1982) and the recent and witty chapter by Cauce, Ryan, and Grove (1998) provide the most extensive treatments of sample recruitment and retention.

Recruitment A wide assortment of strategies has been suggested for increasing recruitment rates – though all strategies may not be equally effective in all studies, and it may be necessary to design the recruitment strategy specifically to suit the study population (e.g., Capaldi et al., 1997).

These strategies range from the commonplace to the exotic, and a number of them begin well before contact is established with potential participants. Kitson et al. (1982) recommend that publicity from newspaper articles providing favorable descriptions of the research and approval from influential individuals, such as a letter sent home from the school principal, can aid with recruitment. Capaldi et al. (1997) also emphasize the importance of building personal relationships with all community agencies involved in the studies. Still early in the recruitment process, Cauce, Ryan, and Grove (1998) suggest that even the name of the study may prove important for both recruitment and retention, especially if the study focuses on negative or risk activities. If introductory letters are sent to potential participants, project staff should be sensitive to their educational level, and these letters should be short, simple, and stress motivating factors (e.g., money), according to Capaldi and Patterson (1987).

These same investigators suggest that initial direct contact should be made with potential participants by visiting their homes. It is worth noting that these home visitors are provided with financial incentives for successful recruiting (Capaldi & Patterson, 1987). Cauce, Ryan, and Grove (1998) suggest that when home visits are not feasible, an alternative is to rent an interview site in the participants' community. If this strategy is followed, provide a map to this location, and make sure that parking is accessible and easy.

Numerous investigators emphasized that these initial contacts were critical in that they represented the beginning stage of the development of a personal relationship with the potential participant (e.g., see the review by Cauce, Ryan, & Grove, 1998). Survey researchers have directly compared response rates using varying approaches, and generally find the more personal the approach, the higher the response rate (e.g., Groves,

Miller, & Cannell, 1987). When Capaldi and Patterson (1987) used home visitors for these initial contacts, the home visitors were highly trained individuals who had substantial interpersonal communication skills (e.g., active listening) as well as the ability to set the potential participants at ease and establish good rapport. When recruiting families of high-risk children, this investigative team indicated that an added bonus occurred when the home visitors had children within the age range of those of the families recruited (and hence had ready-made shared topics of conversation).

It is universally believed that *the key* to successful recruitment is payment for participant's time (e.g., Cauce, Ryan, & Grove, 1998). The amount of the payment seems to be important as well. For example, Streissguth and Guinta (1992) found that increasing the payment rate per visit from $10 to $150 was credited for raising the recruitment rate from just under 60 percent to well over 80 percent!

The final strategy noted with some frequency is to persist. If even ordinary persistence fails, Cauce, Ryan, and Grove (1998, p. 160) wisely – and whimsically – suggest that:

> when all else seems to be failing, try running focus groups of potential participants to discuss recruitment issues. Focus groups may help to identify barriers to participation or potential incentives you would not have thought of on your own . . . If you are at your wits' end, talk to other researchers who have worked with similar population. Even when they cannot offer you wisdom, they may give you support.

Retention It is clear that the methods used to retain participants in longitudinal studies have not been entirely successful. According to Capaldi and Patterson (1987), approximately half (47 percent) of the initial participants in major American surveys with follow-up periods of 4–10 years were attriters. Attrition occurs for two reasons: because investigators lose contact with participants and because participants refuse to continue. Unfortunately, attriters from longitudinal investigations are usually not representative of all participants (see review by Farrington et al., 1990). A variety of strategies have been suggested in order to decrease both of these sources of participant loss – and based upon recent research, investigators appear to be increasingly sophisticated in the use of these methods as well as successful in retaining their samples.

The first key to successfully retaining participants is to monitor their whereabouts. Double-check the spelling of names, get a full birth date and place of birth, ask for phone numbers, place of employment, and driver's license number. Most investigators also report obtaining the addresses of relatives or friends who are likely to stay at their current address and with whom the participant or their family probably will stay in contact. Regular contact is also important, and this can be achieved by mailing participants a bimonthly newsletter with an address-correction stamp, and by sending holiday cards.

If these relatively simple methods of tracking participants fail, various investigators suggest most sophisticated tracking methods. Freedman, Thornton, and Camburn (1980) describe using business directories that contain detailed block maps with the addresses and telephone numbers of each dwelling unit (also see McAllister, Butler, & Goe, 1973). West, Hauser, and Scanlan (1998) emphasized the importance of keeping up with technological advances when tracking participants, such as Web- or CD-ROM-based address directories, as well as more familiar approaches, such as establishing toll-free phone numbers for respondents to contact researchers, offering monetary incentives, and developing special tracking networks.

The second key to participant retention is continued development of a personal relationship with the participant. Capaldi et al. (1997) encouraged recalcitrant participants by using personal visits that included friendly bantering and attention to how their lives are going; flowers and notes were given on occasions for which these would be appropriate. Individuals also were promised that they did not have to respond to questions that they did not care to answer, and child participants received their own newsletter, checks, and birthday cards. Perhaps an extreme of individualizing is the following, taken from a project run through the Oregon Social Learning Center (Capaldi et al., 1997, p. 485):

> Staff kept contact with a subject in jail on the East Coast who was due for release. He was not allowed back to his mother and stepfather's house due to a restraining order. Prior experience with this subject indicated that he would disappear into a dangerous part of town where we would be reluctant to send an interviewer and probably could not find him. Therefore, a motel room was reserved for him as soon as he was released, and an interviewer was immediately flown out to interview him.

One of the most critical retention strategies is providing the participants with financial incentives. As Cauce, Ryan, and Grove (1998) state it:

> Money, Money, Money: money grows in importance when the issue is retention; each participant is more precious than before because replacement is not possible. Reimbursement strategies that build in incentives for continued participation appear to be more effective.

Capaldi et al. (1997) provided families with up to $300 for each year of participation, and bonuses were given for keeping appointments and for completing the entire assessment.[1]

Other commonly mentioned characteristics of studies that are successful in retaining their sample are the enthusiasm, dedication, and persistence of the project staff. Freedman, Thornton, and Camburn (1980) attributed their successful 15-year survey of families to competence and dedication of the interviewing staff, active personal participation of the principal researchers in all phases of data collection, and the persistence of the staff in locating respondents and establishing rapport. Capaldi et al. (1997) also emphasize the value of a determined staff in keeping track of participants.

---

[1]   While some may take exception to this focus on money, Capaldi et al. (1997, p. 490) note that "it may be argued that it is unethical to ask subjects to give considerable time and effort to a research study *without* adequately compensating them for this effort."

The final technique for maintaining the sample was termed by Cauce, Ryan, and Grove (1998) "Keeping the Customer Satisfied." This strategy included making certain that the participant's tasks were not overly taxing, that interviews always ended on a positive note, and that participants were afforded flexibility in completing assessment. They also suggested the seemingly obvious strategy that if the study's refusal rate is higher than 10 percent, ask participants why they are refusing.

Describing sampling procedures

According to the American Psychological Association (1995, p. 13):

> The sample should be adequately described, and it should be representative (if it is not, give the underlying reasons) . . . When humans are the participants, report the procedures for selecting and assigning them and the agreements and payments made . . . If any [participants] did not complete the experiment, state how many and explain why they did not continue.

It is clear from even a cursory reading of the major psychological journals that many investigators are not following this prescription. Condon (1986) provides some evidence to substantiate this subjective impression: the "majority of research reports published in the major international psychiatric journals fail to state explicitly what proportion of subjects approached declined to participate. Instead, a variety of literary devices are used to convey an impression that the sample is representative of the group under study" (p. 87).

The spirit of the APA's prescription would seem to require that investigators report at least the following about their sampling:

- the definition of their target population;
- the method of selecting the pool of potential participants and the method of recruiting participants from this pool;
- the proportion of recruited individuals who agreed to participate, the reasons for refusing, and the proportion of refusers in each category of reasons;
- the proportion of individuals completing the study, the reasons for attrition, and the percentage of attriters within each category of reasons;
- the limitations on generalization of the results that are likely due to sample issues.

Compliance with these simple guidelines should produce congruence between the behaviors of investigators and the goals of the APA (1995, p. 13):

> Appropriate identification of research participants and clientele is critical to the science and practice of psychology particularly for assessing the results (making comparisons across groups), generalizing the findings, and making comparisons in replications, literature reviews, or secondary data analyses.

Summary

The tasks confronting longitudinal investigators who have important substantive questions to address – whether theoretically or practically motivated – are both irksome and challenging. In addition to a seemingly endless numbers of practical management concerns, they also must face a bewildering series of measurement, design, and analysis issues. This chapter has outlined many of the measurement and design issues – analysis issues are tackled in following chapters – and has discussed in some detail selected issues in these domains. These included measurement issues involving reliability and measurement equivalence. Both of these seem not to have occupied much of the attention of current developmental methodologists. The targeted design concern included a set of four sampling issues. It is perhaps the sampling issues that were addressed with the most concern, as sampling has long been the neglected child in most arenas of psychological research. I hope that the reminders provided on these topics might serve to improve the quality of our longitudinal research.

References

Abelson, R. P. (1995). *Statistics as principled argument*. Hillsdale, NJ: Lawrence Erlbaum Associates.

Achenbach, T. M., McConaughy, S., & Howell, C. (1987). Child/adolescent behavioral and emotional problems: Implication of cross-informant correlations for situation specificity. *Psychological Bulletin, 101*, 213–32.

American Psychological Association (1985). *Standards for educational and psychological tests*. Washington, DC: American Psychological Association.

American Psychological Association (1995). *Publication manual of the American Psychological Association* (4th edn.). Washington, DC: American Psychological Association.

Baltes, P. B., Lindenberger, U., & Staudinger, U. M. (1998). Life-span theory in developmental psychology. In W. Damon (series ed.) & R. M. Lerner (vol. ed.), *Handbook of child psychology*, vol. 1: *Theoretical models of human development* (5th edn., pp. 1029–143.). New York: John Wiley.

Baltes, P. B., Reese, H. W., & Nesselroade, J. R. (1988). *Life-span developmental psychology: Introduction to research methods*. Hillsdale, NJ: Lawrence Erlbaum Associates.

Barrios, B. & Hartmann, D. P. (1997). Fears and anxieties. In E. J. Mash & L. G. Terdal (eds.), *Behavioral assessment of childhood disorders* (2nd edn.). New York: Guilford.

Bryk, A. S. & Raudenbush, S. W. (1992). *Hierarchical linear models in social and behavioral research: Applications and data analysis methods*. Newbury Park, CA: Sage.

Call, V. R. A., Otto, L. B., & Spenner, K. I. (1982). *Tracking respondents: A multi-method approach*. Lexington, MA: Lexington.

Campbell, D. T. & Fiske, D. W. (1959). Convergent and discriminant validation by the multitrait-multimethod matrix. *Psychological Bulletin, 56*, 81–105.

Campbell, D. T. & Stanley, J. C. (1963). *Experimental and quasi-experimental designs for research*. Chicago, IL: Rand McNally.

Capaldi, D. M. & Patterson, G. R. (1987). An approach to the problem of recruitment and retention rates for longitudinal research. *Behavioral Assessment, 9*, 169–77.

Capaldi, D. M., Chamberlain, P., Fetrow, R. A., & Wilson, J. E. (1997). Conducting ecologically valid prevention research: Recruiting and retaining a "whole village" in multimethod, multiagent studies. *American Journal of Community Psychology, 25,* 471–92.

Cauce, A. M., Ryan, K. D., & Grove, K. (1998). Child and adolescents of color, where are you? Participation, selection, recruitment, and retention in developmental research. In V. C. McLoyd & L. Steinberg (eds.), *Studying minority adolescents: Conceptual, methodological, and theoretical issues* (pp. 147–66). Mahwah, MJ: Lawrence Erlbaum Associates.

Cohen, S. H. & Reese, H. W. (eds.) (1994). *Life-span developmental psychology: Methodological contributions.* Hillsdale, NJ: Lawrence Erlbaum Associates.

Collins, L. M. (1996). The analysis and quantification of change with age. In J. E. Birren & K. W. Schaie (eds.), *Handbook of the psychology of aging* (4th edn., pp. 38–56). San Diego, CA: Academic Press.

Collins, L. M. & Horn, J. L. (eds.) (1991). *Best methods for the analysis of change: Recent advances, unanswered questions, future directions.* Washington, DC: American Psychological Association.

Collins, L. M. & Sayer, A. G. (2000). Modeling growth and change processes: Design, measurement, and analysis for research in social psychology. In H. T. Reis & C. M. Judd (eds.), *Handbook of research methods in social and personality psychology* (pp. 478–95). New York: Cambridge University Press.

Condon, J. T. (1986). The "unresearched" – Those who decline to participate. *Australian and New Zealand Journal of Psychiatry, 20,* 87–9.

Cook, T. D. & Campbell, D. T. (1979). *Quasi-experimentation: Design and analysis issues for field settings.* Chicago, IL: Rand McNally.

Cronbach, L. J. (1984). *Essentials of psychological testing* (4th edn.). New York: Harper & Row.

Cronbach, L. J., Gleser, G. C., Nanda, H., & Rajaratnam, N. (1972). *The dependability of behavioral measurements.* New York: John Wiley.

De Weerth, C., van Geert, P., & Hoijtink, H. (1999). Intraindividual variability in infant behavior. *Developmental Psychology, 35,* 1102–12.

Eckensberger, L. H. (1973). Methodological issues of cross-cultural research in developmental psychology. In J. R. Nesselroade & H. W. Reese (eds.), *Life-span developmental psychology: Methodological issues.* New York: Academic Press.

Edelbrock, C. (1994). Assessing child psychopathology in developmental follow-up studies. In S. L. Friedman & H. C. Haywood (eds.), *Developmental follow-up: concepts, domains, and methods* (pp. 183–96). New York: Academic Press.

Embretson, S. E. (1991). Implications of a multidimensional latent trait model for measuring change. In L. M. Collins & J. L Horn (eds.), *Best methods for the analysis of change* (pp. 184–97). Washington, DC: American Psychological Association.

Farrington, D. P., Gallagher, B., Morley, L., St. Ledger, R. J., & West, D. J. (1990). Minimizing attrition in longitudinal research: method of tracing and securing cooperation in a 24-year follow-up study. In D. Magnusson & L. R. Bergman (eds.), *Data quality in longitudinal research* (pp. 122–47). Cambridge: Cambridge University Press.

Francis, D. J., Schatschneider, C., & Carlson, C. D. (2000). Introduction to individual growth curve analysis. In D. Drotar (ed.), *Handbook of research in pediatric and clinical child psychology: practical strategies and methods* (pp. 51–73). New York: Kluwer Academic/Plenum.

Freedman, D. S., Thornton, A., & Camburn, D. (1980). Maintaining response rates in longitudinal studies. *Sociological Methods and Research, 9,* 87–98.

Friedman, S. L. & Haywood, H. C. (eds.) (1994). *Developmental follow-up: Concepts, domains, and methods.* San Diego, CA: Academic Press.

Goldstein, H. (1979). *The design and analysis of longitudinal studies: Their role in the measurement of change.* London: Academic Press.

Gottman, J. M. (ed.) (1995). *The analysis of change*. Mahwah, NJ: Lawrence Erlbaum Associates.

Groves, R. M., Miller, P. V., & Cannell, C. F. (1987). Differences between the telephone and personal interview data. In O. Thornberry (ed.), *An experimental comparison of telephone and health interview survey*. Vital and health statistics, series 2, no. 106, DHHS pub. no. (PHS) 87–1380. Washington, DC: Public Health Survey.

Harris, C. W. (1967). *Problems in measuring change*. Madison, WI: University of Wisconsin Press.

Hartmann, D. P. & George, T. P. (1999). Design, measurement, and analysis in developmental research. In M. H. Bornstein & M. Lamb (eds.), *Developmental psychology: An advanced textbook* (4th edn., pp. 125–95). Mahwah, NJ: Lawrence Erlbaum Associates.

Hartmann, D. P. & Wood, D. D. (1990). Observational methods. In A. S. Bellack, M. Hersen, & A. E. Kazdin (eds.), *International handbook of behavior modification and therapy* (2nd edn., pp. 107–38). New York: Plenum Press.

Hofstaetter, P. R. (1954). The changing composition of intelligence: A study of the *t*-technique. *Journal of Genetic Psychology*, *85*, 159–64.

Horn, J. L., McArdle, J. J., & Mason, R. (1983). When is invariance not invariant: A practical scientist's view of the ethereal concept of factorial invariance. *The Southern Psychologist*, *1*, 179–88.

Hultsch, D. F., MacDonald, S. W. S., Hunter, M. A., Maitland, S. B., & Dixon, R. A. (2002). Sampling and generalisability in developmental research: Comparison of random and convenience samples of older adults. *International Journal of Behavioral Development*, *26*, 345–59.

Kitson, G. C., Sussman, M. B., Williams, G. K., Zeehandelaar, R. B., Shickmanter, B. K., & Steinberger, J. L. (1982). Sampling issues in family research. *Journal of Marriage and the Family*, *44(4)*, 965–81.

Knight, G. P. & Hill, N. E. (1998). Measurement equivalence in research involving minority adolescents. In V. C. McLoyd & L. Steinberg (eds.), *Studying minority adolescents: Conceptual, methodological, and theoretical issues* (pp. 183–210). Mahwah, NJ: Lawrence Erlbaum Associates.

Labouvie, E. W. (1980). Identity versus equivalence of psychological measures and constructs. In L. W. Poon (ed.), *Aging in the 1980s: Psychological issues* (pp. 493–502). Washington, DC: American Psychological Association.

Lerner, R. M. (ed.) (1998). *Handbook of child psychology*, vol. I: *Theoretical models of human development* (5th edn.). New York: Wiley.

Lykken, D. T. (1968). Statistical significance in psychological research. *Psychological Bulletin*, *70*, 151–9.

Magnusson, D. & Casaer, P. (eds.) (1993). *Longitudinal research on individual development: present status and future perspectives*. New York: Cambridge University Press.

McAllister, R. J., Butler, E. W., & Goe, S. J. (1973). Evolution of a strategy for the retrieval of cases in longitudinal survey research. *Sociology and Social Research*, *58*, 37–47.

Menard, S. (1991). *Longitudinal research*. Newbury Park, CA: Sage.

Messick, S. (1983). Assessment of children. In P. Mussen (ed.), *Handbook of child psychology*, vol. 1: *History, theory, and methods* (4th edn., pp. 477–526). New York: John Wiley.

Messick, S. (1994). Foundations of validity: Meaning and consequences in psychological assessment. *European Journal of Psychological Assessment*, *10*, 1–9.

Miller, S. A. (1998). *Developmental research methods* (2nd edn.). Upper Saddle River, NJ: Prentice-Hall.

Nesselroade, J. R. (1988). Sampling and generalizability: Adult development and aging research issues examined with the general methodological framework of selection. In K. W. Schaie, R. T. Campbell, W. Meredith, & S. C. Rawlings (eds.), *Methodological issues in aging research* (pp. 13–42). New York: Springer-Verlag.

Nunnally, J. C. & Bernstein, I. H. (1994). *Psychometric theory* (3rd edn.). New York: McGraw-Hill.

Pedhazur, E. J. & Schmelkin, L. P. (1991). *Measurement, design, and analysis: An integrated approach.* Hillsdale, NJ: Lawrence Erlbaum Associates.

Reise, S. P., Widaman, K. F., & Pugh, R. H. (1993). Confirmatory factor analysis and item response theory: Two approaches for exploring measurement invariance. *Psychological Bulletin, 114,* 552–66.

Rogosa, D. R., Brandt, D., & Zimowski, M. (1982). A growth curve approach to the measurement of change. *Psychological Bulletin, 90,* 726–48.

Schaie, K. W., Campbell, R. T., Meredith, W., & Rawlings, S. C. (eds.) (1988). *Methodological issues in aging research.* New York: Springer-Verlag.

Silva, F. (1993). *Psychometric foundations and behavioral assessment.* Newbury Park, CA: Sage.

Sproth, R. & Redmond, C. (1995). Parent motivation to enroll in parenting skills programs: A model of family context and health belief predictors. *Journal of Family Psychology, 9,* 294–310.

Streissguth, A. P. & Guinta, C. T. (1992). Subject recruitment and retention for longitudinal research: practical considerations for a nonintervention model. *NIDA Research Monographs, 177,* 137–54.

Suen, H. K. (1988). Agreement, reliability, accuracy, and validity: Toward a clarification. *Behavioral-Assessment, 10(4),* 343–66.

Suen, H. K. & Ary, D. (1989). *Analyzing quantitative behavioral observation data.* Hillsdale, NJ: Lawrence Erlbaum Associates.

Taplin, P. S. & Reid, J. B. (1973). Effects of instructional set and experimental influences on observer reliability. *Child Development, 44,* 547–54.

West, K. K., Hauser, R. M., & Scanlan, T. M. (eds.) (1998). *Surveys of children.* Washington, DC: National Academy Press.

Widaman, K. F. & Reise, S. P. (1997). Exploring the measurement invariance of psychological instruments: Applications in the substance use domain. In K. J. Bryant, M. Windle, & S. G. West (eds.), *The science of prevention: Methodological advances from alcohol and substance abuse research* (pp. 281–324). Washington, DC: American Psychological Association.

Wiggins, J. S. (1973). *Personality and prediction: Principles of personality assessment.* Reading, MA: Addison-Wesley.

Willett, J. B. (1988). Questions and answers in the measurement of change. In E. Z. Rothkopf (ed.), *Review of research in education 15: 1988–89* (pp. 345–422). Washington, DC: American Educational Research Association.

Windle, M., Iwawaki, S., & Lerner, R. M. (1988). Cross-cultural comparability of temperament among Japanese and American preschool children. *International Journal of Psychology, 23,* 547–67.

CHAPTER SEVENTEEN

Latent Growth Curve Analysis Using Structural Equation Modeling Techniques

John J. McArdle

The term "growth curve analysis" is a common research technique in developmental investigations. In a general sense, this term denotes the processes of describing, testing hypotheses, and making scientific inferences about the growth and change patterns in a wide range of time-related phenomena. Growth curve data have unique features: (a) the same entities are repeatedly observed, (b) the same procedures of measurement and scaling of observations are used, and (c) the timing of the observations is known. These features lead to unusual opportunities for developmental data analysis.

Formal models for the analysis of these kinds of growth curves have been developed in many different substantive domains. In this chapter we concentrate on the benefits of a *structural equation modeling* (SEM) approach. As an illustration, we present analyses of a longitudinal data collection on intellectual abilities over the life span – some of these data appear in the plot of Figure 17.1 (from McArdle & Hamagami, 1996; McArdle et al., 2000). The *y*-axis indexes the scores on "General Knowledge" and the *x*-axis is an index of the age-at-testing. The connected lines in this picture describes the pattern of General Knowledge scores for each of $N = 111$ individuals. From this collection of lines, often termed *growth curves*, we begin to see some overall trends of rapid rises in early childhood and adolescence to long periods of consistency at older ages. There are also different patterns of growth and change for some individuals. We illustrate some of the results using the data of Figure 17.1 and we highlight future issues of interest.

Researchers have found many creative ways to analyze average trends in growth data. When the observations are repeated entities on the same persons, research in the behavioral sciences has relied on advanced versions of the linear growth models formalized in terms of *analysis of variance* techniques (e.g., Pothoff & Roy, 1964; Bock, 1975). These classical methods provide powerful and accurate tests of "group trends." However, the introduction of individual differences in change analyses has led to a great deal of

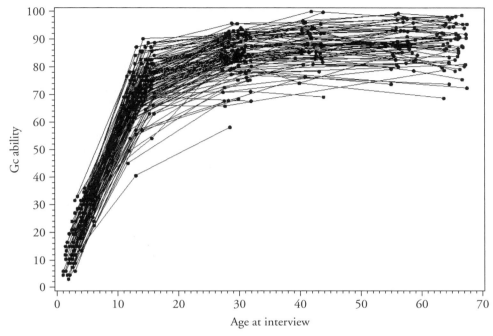

Figure 17.1 Plot of individual growth curves for the Bradway–McArdle longitudinal data
(*N* = 111).

statistical controversy in model fitting. For example, there are many published data analyses where the *observed difference scores* or *rates-of-change scores* ($\Delta Y_n/\Delta Age_n$) are used as outcomes in data analyses (e.g., McCrae, Arenberg, & Costa, 1987; Willett, 1990; Sullivan et al., 2000). Difference score calculations are relatively simple and theoretically meaningful. However, the potential confounds due to the accumulation of random errors has been a key concern in previous studies using observed change scores or rate of change scores (e.g., Bell, 1954; Bereiter, 1963; Cronbach & Furby, 1970; Burr & Nesselroade, 1990; Rogosa & Willett, 1985; Willett, 1990).

Early work on these problems led to the polynomial growth models by Wishart (1938) where an individual regression coefficient was used to describe a growth characteristic of the person (see Rogosa & Willett, 1985). However, other current techniques have roots in the important innovations by Meredith & Tisak (1990), who showed how the "Tuckerized curve" models (named in recognition of Tucker's contributions) could be represented and fitted using structural equation modeling based on restricted common factors. For these reasons, the term "latent growth models" seems appropriate for any technique that describes the underlying growth in terms of latent changes using the classical assumptions (e.g., independence of errors). These innovative techniques were important because this made it possible to represent a wide range of alternative growth and change models by adding the benefits of the structural equation modeling techniques (McArdle, 1986, 1997; McArdle & Epstein, 1987; McArdle & Anderson, 1990; McArdle & Hamagami, 1992).

During the past decade it has become possible to prove that all of these seemingly different models have identical properties. They are all based on fitting observed raw-score longitudinal growth data to the same theoretical model using the same likelihood-based techniques (as in Little & Rubin, 1987; McArdle, 1994; McArdle & Bell, 2000). These latent growth models have since been expanded upon and described by many others (McArdle & Woodcock, 1997; Willett & Sayer, 1994; Muthén & Curran, 1997; Metha & West, 2000). The contemporary basis of latent growth curve analyses can also be found in the recent developments of *multilevel models* (Goldstein, 1995; Bryk & Raudenbush, 1992) or *mixed-effects models* (Laird & Ware, 1982; Singer, 1998). In important work by Browne & du Toit (1991) classical nonlinear models were added as part of this same framework (see Cudeck & du Toit, 2001; McArdle & Hamagami, 1996, 2001; Pinherio & Bates, 2000). When these options are added to the latent variable path analysis models of SEM (e.g., McArdle & Prescott, 1992) many limitations apparent in previous growth research can be overcome.

The SEM techniques of this chapter are presented in three parts:

1   *Describing the Observed and Unobserved Longitudinal Data.* First we consider some useful ways to summarize the longitudinal data in Figure 17.1. These considerations lead us to consider how the SEM approach naturally permits us to consider the statistical information from both the complete and incomplete cases.

2   *Characterizing the Developmental Shapes of Both Individual and Groups.* In this part we try to adequately describe both the group and individual characteristics of the longitudinal data in Figure 17.1. We demonstrate how the SEM approach is generally easy and flexible. This flexibility is needed in this illustration because the data of Figure 17.1 do not easily fit a pattern described by linear or quadratic shapes.

3   *Examining the Predictors of Individual* and *Group Differences in Developmental Shapes.* Individual differences in growth may be the result of combinations of other measured variables. To study these possibilities we show how SEM can be used in a multilevel form, can be extended to include concepts from latent path analysis, and can provide empirical evidence for hypotheses about the precursors or correlates of individual longitudinal patterns.

In addition to these three issues, we discuss technical and substantive features of contemporary model fitting and the inferences that follow. The parameters in these kinds of models can be estimated using standard computer programs which allow appropriate constraints. Useful programs for these analyses include (1) the SAS and S-Plus packages (Littell et al., 1996; Singer, 1998; Verbeke & Molenberghs, 2000; Pinherio & Bates, 2000), (2) general SEM programs such as LISREL (McArdle & Epstein, 1987; Cudeck & du Toit, 2001), Mx (Neale et al., 1999), Mplus (Muthén & Muthén, 2002), and AMOS (Arbuckle & Wotke, 1999), and (3) specialized software such as MIXOR (Hedecker & Gibbons, 1996) and MLn (Goldstein, 1995), To simplify this presentation, we do not deal with these differences and simply state that the results for the classical SEM for latent growth curves will be the same no matter what program is used (for demonstration, see Ferrer, Hamagami, & McArdle, in press).

Describing the Observed and Unobserved Longitudinal Data

The Bradway–McArdle longitudinal data

In this research we describe a longitudinal analysis of intellectual abilities. The data we use come from the classic study of intellectual growth and change over 60 years. The persons in this study were first measured in 1931 when they were aged 2–7 as part of the larger standardization sample of the Stanford-Binet test ($N = 212$). They were measured again about ten years later by Katherine P. Bradway as part of her doctoral dissertation in 1944 ($N = 138$).

Many of these same persons were measured twice more by Bradway as adults at average ages of 30 and 42 using the Wechsler Adult Intelligence Scales ($N = 111$; for further details, see Bradway & Thompson, 1962; Kangas & Bradway, 1971). In 1984 and 1992, at average ages 57 and 65, the current author, working with Bradway, measured as many of these same subjects as we could locate (see McArdle & Hamagami, 1996; McArdle et al., 2000). About half ($N = 55$) of the adolescents tested in 1944 were measured again in 1984 at ages 55–57 and in 1993–97 at ages ranging from 64 to 72 (McArdle et al., 2000).

In prior research we have used comparable composite scores from the early Stanford-Binet tests (at ages of 4, 14, 30, and 42), as well as the WAIS tests (at average ages 30, 42, 56, and 64). In these analyses we only use a measure of General Knowledge or Crystallized Intelligence (g_c). These scores are in a comparable metric because they were based on an IRT Rasch-scaling of only selected items in each test (see Hamagami, 1998; McArdle & Nesselroade, 2003). Figure 17.1 is a display of individual growth curve data for this measure at each age-at-testing for $N = 111$ individuals.

Describing the observed data

The sample sizes, means, standard deviations, and correlations of these measures over six occasions are listed in Table 17.1. The overall subject participation shows a nearly continual loss of participants over the 60 years. The means and standard deviations show the simple pattern described earlier, with rapid rises in childhood and adolescence together with very little growth or decline in adulthood. The correlations over time, the unique statistical information of the longitudinal data, present a complex pattern of results, some correlations suggesting high stability of individual differences (e.g., $r > 0.9$) and others suggesting low long-term stability ($r < 0.1$). Figure 17.2 is a scatter plot matrix of the raw data at all occasions. In this figure the frequency histograms are placed on the main diagonal and the pairwise scatter plots are placed on the off-diagonals.

Results from dealing with incomplete information

The careful reader will note that the summary information presented in Table 17.1 and Figure 17.2 is not limited to only those participants with complete data at all six time

Table 17.1 Observed summary statistics based on the Bradway–McArdle longitudinal data at six time points ($N = 111$)

(a) Observed means, standard deviations, and ranges

Gc variable	N	Mean	Std dev.	Min.	Max.
Age 4	110	22.1	9.8	0.0	37.6
Age 14	111	72.2	9.3	40.6	90.2
Age 29	110	84.4	7.0	58.2	95.7
Age 42	49	87.9	6.7	69.2	100.0
Age 57	51	88.9	5.8	73.8	99.3
Age 65	51	88.1	7.1	68.7	98.6

(b) Observed correlations (each entry includes pairwise r and [pairwise n])

	Age 4	Age 14	Age 29	Age 42	Age 57	Age 65
Age 4	1.000 [111]					
Age 14	0.553 [110]	1.000 [111]				
Age 29	0.233 [109]	0.680 [110]	1.000 [110]			
Age 42	0.194 [48]	0.377 [48]	0.812 [48]	1.000 [48]		
Age 57	0.304 [51]	0.489 [51]	0.800 [50]	0.798 [37]	1.000 [51]	
Age 65	0.079 [51]	0.472 [51]	0.759 [50]	0.663 [33]	0.911 [36]	1.000 [51]

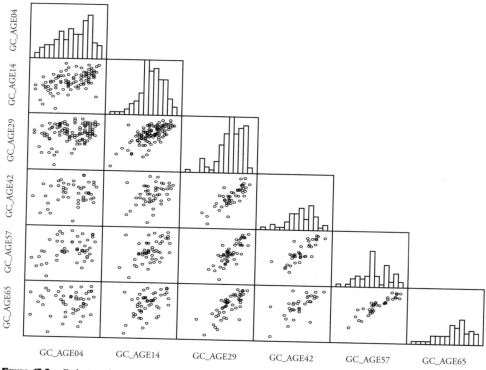

Figure 17.2 Relationships among the scores of the six "General Knowledge" (Gc) variables over time.

Table 17.2 Expected maximum likelihood estimated summary statistics from the Bradway–McArdle longitudinal data

(a) Patterns of complete (x) and incomplete (o) data

	1	2	3	4	5	6	7	8	9
Age 4	x	x	x	x	x	x	x	x	x
Age 14	x	x	x	x	x	x	x	x	x
Age 29	x	x	x	x	x	x	x	x	o
Age 42	o	x	o	x	o	x	o	x	x
Age 57	o	x	o	o	x	x	x	o	x
Age 65	o	x	x	o	o	o	x	x	x
Frequency	36	29	12	9	8	7	6	3	1

(b) Percentage of complete data (i.e., covariance coverage)

	Age 4	*Age 14*	*Age 29*	*Age 42*	*Age 57*	*Age 65*
Age 4	100.0					
Age 14	100.0	100.0				
Age 29	99.1	99.1	99.1			
Age 42	44.1	44.1	43.2	44.1		
Age 57	45.9	45.9	45.0	33.3	45.9	
Age 65	45.9	45.9	45.0	29.7	32.4	45.9

(c) Maximum likelihood estimates of expected means and SDs

	Age 4	*Age 14*	*Age 29*	*Age 42*	*Age 57*	*Age 65*
Mean	22.2	72.2	84.4	87.2	87.7	87.1
[SD]	[9.6]	[9.3]	[6.9]	[6.8]	[7.0]	[8.1]

(d) Maximum likelihood estimates of expected correlations

	Age 4	*Age 14*	*Age 29*	*Age 42*	*Age 57*	*Age 65*
Age 4	1.000					
Age 14	0.558	1.000				
Age 29	0.224	0.679	1.000			
Age 42	0.143	0.412	0.787	1.000		
Age 57	0.211	0.574	0.858	0.843	1.000	
Age 65	0.171	0.579	0.791	0.744	0.946	1.000

points of measurement. As is usual, we represent all available information about the observed means and variances and the "pairwise" correlations. To deal with this problem we present the additional information in Table 17.2. The first two sections describe the patterns of complete and incomplete data. Table 17.2a shows that there are only 9 different patterns of incomplete data (out of a possible set of 70 patterns), and most of the persons are either measured at all 6 times ($n = 29$) or only the first 3 times ($n = 36$). Table 17.2b shows the net effect of the incomplete data patterns on the "percentage of data" or "coverage" for each covariance of these scores – in some cases 100 percent of the participants are used but in others only 29.7 percent of the information is available (at ages 42 and 65).

In Table 17.2c and d we list some initial results from an "incomplete data" estimate of the sample means, standard deviations, and correlations based on an SEM-EM-type algorithm (Little & Rubin, 1987; McArdle, 1994; Cnaan, Laird & Slasor, 1997). This approach allows us to examine these summary statistics "as if all persons were measured at all occasions" (details are described later). By contrast to Table 17.1, these newly estimated statistics are fairly close to the pairwise estimates and this indicates that these data meet the minimal conditions of "missing at random" (MAR; Little & Rubin, 1987). Most importantly, these estimated statistics do not suffer from some common statistical problems (local linear dependency), and this also means that we can routinely use whatever information is available from every person (i.e., we do not select persons out of the $N = 111$ available).

Dealing with incomplete data as *unobserved but important scores* can alter inferences about growth and change. For example, from Table 17.1, the pairwise correlation of General Knowledge from age 4 to age 42 is only $r = 0.19$, and from age 4 to 65 only $r = 0.08$, and these are certainly not as high as comparable correlations recently reported elsewhere (e.g., Deary et al., 2000). It would be reasonable to critique our lower over-time correlations as being underestimated due to the loss of participants (i.e., selective attrition). This concern leads us to try to account for the patterns of incomplete data. It is interesting that when we do use contemporary technique to account for attrition we obtain similar results – the SEM-estimated correlation of General Knowledge from age 4 to age 42 is only $r = 0.14$, and from age 4 to 65 only $r = 0.17$ (from Table 17.2d). This new result implies that these *low correlations over time may be due to initial selection but are probably not attributable to subsequent attrition*. We view this analysis of incomplete data as an essential part of all models in this study.

Characterizing Developmental Shapes for Both Groups and Individuals

Linear growth models for repeated measures

Most growth curve analyses start by defining longitudinal data as having *repeated measurements* where we observe the Y variable at multiple occasions ($t = 1$ to T) on the same person ($n = 1$ to N) and we can symbolize the scores as $Y[t]_n$. In the most common approach we write a classical linear latent growth model as:

$$Y[t]_n = y_{0,n} + y_{s,n} \cdot Age[t]_n + e[t]_n \qquad (17.1)$$

In this *trajectory* equation the $Y[t]$ is formed for each group and individual and is composed of (a) the y_0, which are *unobserved or latent scores* representing the individual's initial level, (b) the y_s, termed the slopes, which are unobserved or latent scores representing the individual *linear change over time*, (c) the $Age[t]$, a set of group coefficients or *basis weights* which define the timing or *shape of the trajectory over time* (e.g., $Age[t] = t$, or as $A[t] = Age(t)$), and (d) the $e[t]$, which are unobserved but independent errors of measurements. The error terms are assumed to be normally distributed with mean zero and variance (σ_e^2) and are presumably uncorrelated with all other components.

One popular kind of *linear growth* model uses a fixed set of basis coefficients. In this example, we can make $A[t] = [Age[t]/10]$, yielding fixed values of $A[t] = [0.4, 1.4, 2.9, 4.2, 5.7, 6.5]$ so that it permits a practical interpretation of the slope parameters in terms of a *per-decade change*. In this longitudinal model the change score $(y_{s,n})$ is assumed to be constant *within* an individual but it is not assumed to be the same *between* individuals. The latent variables are written in lower case (y_0, y_s) because they are similar to the predicted scores in a standard regression equation – i.e., we do not use Greek notation because these scores will not be estimated. However, we usually do estimate several parameters to characterize these scores. It is typical to decompose latent scores into parameters representing a mean and a variance term:

$$y_{0n} = \mu_0 + d_{0n} \text{ and } y_{sn} = \mu_s + d_{sn} \tag{17.2}$$

where we have the fixed group means for intercept and slopes (μ_0, μ_s) but also implied random variance and covariance terms $(\sigma_0^2, \sigma_s^2, \sigma_{0s})$ describing the distribution of individual deviations (d_{0n}, d_{1n}) around those means. We also usually assume that there is only one random error variance (σ_e^2).

Growth models as SEM path diagrams

The path diagram of Figure 17.3 is an exact translation of the necessary matrix algebra of these models. These diagrams can be conceptually useful devices for understanding the basic modeling concepts. They are also practically useful because they can be used to represent the input and output of any of the SEM computer programs (see next section). These kinds of diagrams were originally used with regression models, but recent work has shown how they can be used in the context of growth and change (e.g., McArdle, 1986, McArdle & Epstein, 1987; McArdle & Anderson, 1990; McArdle & Woodcock, 1997). In this path diagram the observed variables are drawn as squares, the unobserved variables are drawn as circles, and the required constant (of equations (17.4) and (17.5)) is included as a triangle. Model parameters representing "fixed" or "group" coefficients are drawn as one-headed arrows while "random" or "individual" features are drawn as two-headed arrows. In this case the initial level and slopes are often assumed to be random variables with "fixed" means (μ_0, μ_s) but "random" variances (σ_0^2, σ_s^2) and correlations (ρ_{0s}). The standard deviations (σ_j) are drawn to permit the direct representation of the covariances as scaled correlations.

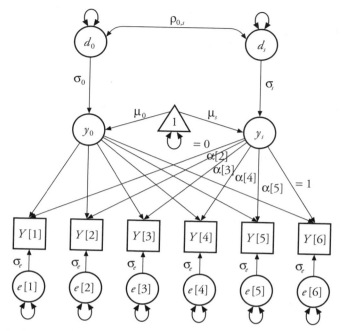

Figure 17.3   Path diagram of a latent "basis" growth model.

   This path diagram can also be interpreted as a two-common-factor model with means. The first latent factor score is an intercept or level score (labeled y_0), and the second latent factor score is a slope or change score (labeled y_s). The relationships between the latent levels y_0 and all observed scores $Y[t]$ are fixed at a value of 1. In contrast, the relationships between the latent slopes y_1 and all observed scores $Y[t]$ are assigned a value based on the time parameter $Age[t]$ which, depending on the application, may be fixed or estimated from the data. The random components $(e[t])$ have mean zero, constant deviation (σ_e), and are uncorrelated with all other components.

Growth models as expectations over time

In the models just presented the change within a person is initially represented by the latent means and variance terms in the growth models. In later interpretations, we can examine the relative size of these parameters and make substantive interpretations about the group and individual differences. These parameters also allow us to form the *expected growth curve charts* for both the observed and true scores. Detailed derivations are not presented here, but it is still useful to consider some key properties of the model (see McArdle, 1986, 1989; McArdle & Woodcock, 1997).
   To assist in interpretation of the model parameters we can use a Cartesian plot of the expected model trajectories – a few theoretical examples are given in the plots of Figure 17.4. Here $N = 3$ different individuals are presumed to have separate growth curves over the same units of age. In the first plot, Figure 17.4a, the three curves are

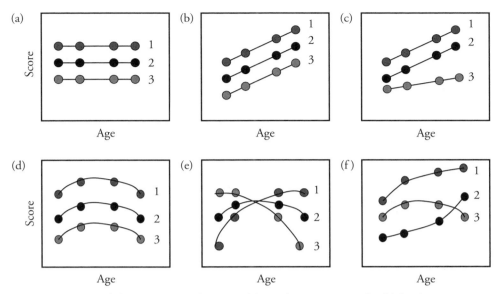

Figure 17.4 A set of alternative growth curves. (a) Level component only, (b) level component and slope mean, (c) level and slope components, (d) level component and shape mean, (e) shape component only, and (f) level and shape components.

parallel but displaced in height. The application of the growth model to these data yields only an initial level component with mean μ_0 and variance σ_0^2, but all other parameters would be zero. In the second plot, Figure 17.4b, the three curves are identically distributed but the curves are angled upward. This adds a slope mean $\mu_s > 0$ but still obtains slope variance $\sigma_s^2 = 0$ because all individuals have exactly the same shape. The third plot, Figure 17.4c, shows the "fan spread" apparent from a collection of growth curves with both shape and level components. In this model all parameters are required, including the correlation of levels and slopes ($\rho_{y[i],y[j]} > 0$ here).

In the first three plots of Figure 17.4 the curves are all linear (i.e., $A[t] = t$). However, the second set of plots in Figures 17.4d, e, and f are plots of collections of curves where the $A[t] = [1, 2, 2, 1]$ at the four occasions, and the group curve first increases then decreases. The three curves have differences in height, so $\sigma_0^2 > 0$, but all three people have the same slope, so $\sigma_s^2 = 0$. In the fifth plot, Figure 17.4e, the shapes for the individuals are different, so $\sigma_s^2 > 0$, but all three average out to the same score over these time points so $\sigma_0^2 = 0$. Conversely, these curves are all well above zero so the $\mu_0 > 0$ but the slopes average to zero so the $\mu_s = 0$. The sixth and final plot, Figure 17.4f, may be the more realistic scenario – all growth parameters are needed to capture the three change patterns.

Including nonlinearity in growth

The last three models of Figure 17.4 described above add complexity to the simple growth curve models (equation (17.1)) for the study of within-person changes. To deal with this complexity, Wishart (1938) introduced a useful way to examine a nonlinear shape – the use of power polynomials to better fit the curvature apparent in growth data. The individual growth curve (consisting of $t = 1, T$ occasions) is summarized into a small set of linear orthogonal polynomial coefficients based on a fixed power-series of time $(A[t], A[t]^2, A[t]^3, \ldots A[t]^p)$ describing the general nonlinear shape of the growth curve. A second-order (quadratic) polynomial growth model can be written as:

$$Y[t]_n = y_{0n} + y_{1n} \cdot Age[t] + \tfrac{1}{2}y_{2n} \cdot Age[t]^2 + e[t]_n \tag{17.3}$$

where a new set of component scores (e.g., y_p) are introduced to represent another level of change with a set of powered coefficients $(1/p \, A[t]^p)$. This leads to an implied change model where the change is linear with time (i.e., acceleration). Of course, a model of growth data might require this form of a second-order (quadratic), third-order (cubic), or even higher-order polynomial model fitted to the data. In all cases, additional variance and covariance terms are added to account for individual differences in latent scores. This polynomial growth curve approach remains popular (e.g., Bryk & Raudenbush, 1992).

We will deal with nonlinearity by introducing the concepts of *connected lines* or *splines* (Seber & Wild, 1989). As a simple example here, we could write a model for the same person at different occasions, where:

$$Y[t]_n = y_{0,n} + y_{1,n} \cdot A1[t]\{|age[t] < C\} + y_{2,n} \cdot A2[t]\{|age[t] > C\} + e[t]_n \tag{17.4}$$

where C is some critical age (i.e., C = 30 years), and there are two slope scores; y_1 before age C and y_2 after age C. This implies that the estimated parameters for the means and covariances of the intercept are now recentered to be at age C, and the slopes are before and after age C. These models can be combined with the polynomial models, and the critical cutoff ages (C_n) can be estimated as well. These concepts can create a potentially informative look at individual segments of growth (e.g., Cudeck & du Toit, 2001; Hamagami & McArdle, 2001).

An alternative form of the linear growth model was proposed by Rao (1958) and Tucker (1958, 1966) in the form of summations of "latent curves." The use of this latent growth curve offers a relatively simple way to investigate the shape of a growth curve. We allow the curve basis to take on a form based on the empirical data. For example, we could write a model for the same person at different occasions where:

$$\begin{aligned}
Y[1]_n &= y_{0,n} + y_{s,n} \cdot 0.4 + e[1]_n \\
Y[2]_n &= y_{0,n} + y_{s,n} \cdot \alpha[2] + e[2]_n \\
Y[3]_n &= y_{0,n} + y_{s,n} \cdot \alpha[3] + e[3]_n \\
Y[4]_n &= y_{0,n} + y_{s,n} \cdot \alpha[4] + e[4]_n \\
Y[5]_n &= y_{0,n} + y_{s,n} \cdot \alpha[5] + e[5]_n \\
Y[6]_n &= y_{0,n} + y_{s,n} \cdot 6.5 + e[6]_n
\end{aligned} \tag{17.5}$$

where the last four basis coefficients $\alpha[2]$, $\alpha[3]$, $\alpha[4]$, and $\alpha[5]$ are *free to be estimated*. The actual ages of the persons are known but the basis parameters are allowed to be freely estimated, and we end up with an optimal shape for the whole curve. In this model the $A[t]$ is estimated just like a common factor loading and thus has mathematical and statistical identification problems. In the typical case at least two entries of the $A[t]$ need to be fixed (e.g., $\alpha[1] = 0.4$ and $\alpha[2] = 6.5$) to provide a reference point for the changes in the other model parameters. There are many alternative ways to estimate these parameters (as demonstrated here) but, in general, the number of free parameters in the two-component growth model is $p = 6 + T - 1$. The use of an estimated basis has been termed a "meta-meter" or "latent time" scale, which can be plotted against the actual age curve for visual interpretation (Rao, 1958; McArdle & Epstein, 1987).

The choice between using a latent basis, or a polynomial, or a spline or other nonlinear model can be substantively important. The initial idea from Wishart (1938) was that the basic shape of each individual curve could be captured with a small number of fixed parameters and random variance components. In some cases a fixed-basis polynomial model is more parsimonious than a free-basis model. However, the polynomial model also (a) has a relatively fixed curvature and (b) requires an additional estimation of covariances among the new latent scores (y_p; this is true even if orthogonal polynomial coefficients are used). Thus, the polynomial model may add more complexity (via parameters to be estimated) than is actually needed, and the latent basis model may prove to be more efficient and interpretable. Although many recent textbooks overlook the latent basis model (e.g., Duncan et al., 1998; Singer & Willett, 2003), we always treat this as an empirical choice (McArdle & Bell, 2000; McArdle & Nesselroade, 2003).

Results from fitting standard latent growth models

We now describe the growth curve modeling results for the Bradway–McArdle data in Table 17.3. The first model of Table 17.3 is the *no-growth* model fitted (M_0) with only three parameters: an initial level mean ($\mu_0 = 68.6$), an initial standard deviation ($\sigma_0 < 0.1$), and an error variance ($\sigma_e^2 = 740$). The parameters also yield a model likelihood ($L^2 = -2276$). In this context, the MLE statistics of Table 17.2 represent an *unrestricted* or *fully-saturated* model with 27 statistics (6 means, 6 standard deviations, and 15 correlations), and these statistics collectively have a model likelihood ($L^2 = -1512$). The comparison of these two models shows the no-growth baseline is a poor fit compared to the totally unrestricted model ($\chi^2 = 1510$, df = 24).

The second *linear growth* model (M_1) has a fixed basis coefficient basis formed by taking $A[t] = [(Age[t]/10]$, or fixed values of $A[t] = [0.4, 1.4, 2.9, 4.2, 5.7, 6.5]$. This linear scaling is only one of many that could be used, but it was chosen to permit a practical interpretation of the slope parameters in terms of a *per-decade change*. This linear growth model also has three more free parameters: a slope mean (μ_s) and standard deviation (σ_s), and correlation (ρ_{0s}). This model fitted yields a new likelihood ($L^2 = -2092$) which is a large distance from the unrestricted model ($\chi^2 = 1142$ on df = 3) but is an improvement in fit over the previous baseline (M_1 versus M_0: $\Delta\chi^2 = 368$ on Δdf = 3). The resulting means describe a function that starts low at age 4 ($\mu_0 = 41.8$) but increases between ages 4 and 65 (by $\mu_s = 9.5$ per decade). The variance estimates of the

Table 17.3   Numerical results from latent growth models fitted to Bradway–McArdle longitudinal data at six time points ($N = 111$)

Parameters	M_0 Level	M_1 Linear	M_2 Quadratic	M_3 Latent
Fixed effects				
Basis $\alpha[04]$	1, 0	1, 0.4	1, 0.4, $\frac{1}{2}0.4^2$	1, 0.4
Basis $\alpha[14]$	1, 0	1, 1.4	1, 1.4, $\frac{1}{2}1.4^2$	1, 5.0 (0.6)
Basis $\alpha[29]$	1, 0	1, 2.9	1, 2.9, $\frac{1}{2}2.9^2$	1, 6.2 (0.07)
Basis $\alpha[42]$	1, 0	1, 4.2	1, 4.2, $\frac{1}{2}4.2^2$	1, 6.4 (0.08)
Basis $\alpha[57]$	1, 0	1, 5.7	1, 5.7, $\frac{1}{2}5.7^2$	1, 6.5 (0.08)
Basis $\alpha[65]$	1, 0	1, 6.5	1, 6.5, $\frac{1}{2}6.5^2$	1, 6.5
Level μ_0	68.6 (1.2)	41.8 (1.4)	47.8 (?)	17.9 (1.0)
Slope μ_s	–	9.5 (.40)	0.42 (?)	10.7 (0.19)
Accelerate μ_a	–	–	0.12 (?)	–
Random effects				
Error σ_e^2	740. (54)	345 (28)	41.3 (?)	17.4 (1.5)
Level σ_0	<0.01 (?)	<0.01 (?)	22.3 (?)	9.8 (0.79)
Slope σ_s	–	<0.01 (?)	29.3 (?)	1.5 (0.14)
Correl. ρ_{0s}	–	>0.99 (?)	−0.77 (?)	−0.77 (0.05)
Accelerate σ_a	–	–	15.9 (?)	–
Correl. ρ_{0a}, ρ_{sa}	–	–	0.33 (?), −0.84 (?)	–
Fit indices				
Num. para.	3	6	10	10
Deg. freedom	24	21	17	17
Log likelihood	−2276	−2092	−1830	−1583
Likelihood ratio ΔLL	1510	>1142	>617	122
RMSEA	0.75	0.69	0.56	0.23

intercept and slope parameters are too small to interpret ($\sigma_j < 0.02$), but the error variance has been reduced (from $\sigma_e^2\{M_0\} = 740$ to $\sigma_e^2\{M_1\} = 345$).

A quadratic polynomial model (M_2) was fitted next, including an additional slope variable (acceleration) defined by a fixed basis ($\frac{1}{2}A[t]^2$), one new mean, one new deviation, and two additional correlations. This 10-parameter model is still far worse than the unrestricted model ($\chi^2 > 617$ on df = 17) but is an improved fit compared to the linear model (M_2 versus M_1: $\Delta\chi^2 = 524$ on Δdf = 3). The error or unique variance has also been reduced substantially (from $\sigma_e^2\{M_2\} = 41.3$) but problems arose in the variance–covariance estimation ($\sigma_j < 0.02$), convergence was not achieved, and the model is likely to be less than adequate for these data.

Results from fitting a latent basis model

The fourth model fitted (M_3) was a latent basis growth model where some of the loadings, $A[t]$, are free to vary. For the purposes of estimation, we fixed $A[1] = 0.4$

(at Age = 4) and $A[65] = 6.5$ (at Age = 65), but the four other coefficients were estimated from the data. This results in a large improvement in the model likelihood ($L^2 = -1583$), which is much closer to the unrestricted model ($\chi^2 = 122$ on df $= 17$), and substantially better than the nested baseline model ($\Delta\chi^2 = 1386$ on Δdf $= 7$) and the nested linear model ($\Delta\chi^2 = 1018$ on Δdf $= 4$), and better than the non-nested quadratic model with the same numbers of parameters (-1830 versus 1583). The error variance has also been reduced ($\sigma_e^2\{M_3\} = 17.4$).

The interpretation of the model parameters is an important part of the latent growth analysis, and this is displayed in Figures 17.5 and 17.6. The estimated latent means are $\mu_0 = 17.9$ and $\mu_s = 10.7$, their deviations are $\sigma_0 = 9.8$ and $\sigma_s = 1.5$, and the two latent factors have correlation of $\rho_{0s} = -0.77$. These values are now written in on the new path diagram of Figure 17.5. The estimated basis coefficients were $A[t] = [0.4, 5.0, 6.2, 6.4, 6.5, 6.5]$, and these are repeated in Figure 17.5 also. These parameters can be combined to create expected means ($\mu_{y[t]} = \mu_0 + \mu_s A[t]$) here written as

$$\mu[04] = 17.9 + 10.7 \,\{0.4\} = 22.2 \tag{17.6}$$
$$\mu[14] = 17.9 + 10.7 \,\{5.0\} = 72.1$$
$$\mu[29] = 17.9 + 10.7 \,\{6.2\} = 84.4$$
$$\mu[42] = 17.9 + 10.7 \,\{6.4\} = 86.6$$
$$\mu[56] = 17.9 + 10.7 \,\{6.5\} = 87.6$$
$$\mu[65] = 17.9 + 10.7 \,\{6.5\} = 87.7$$

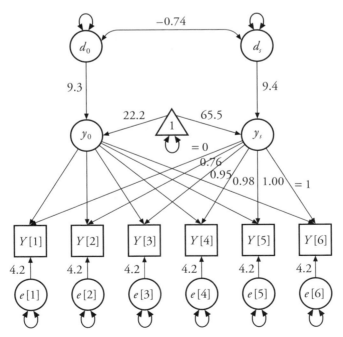

Figure 17.5 Path diagram of the numerical results of Model 4 from the Bradway–McArdle longitudinal data.

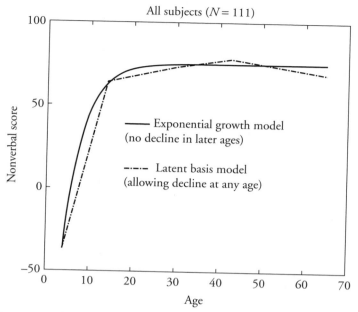

Figure 17.6 Latent growth score expectations for the General Knowledge scores in the Bradway–McArdle data.

which is a shape that rises quickly between ages 4 and 14, peaks at age 42, and exhibits no declines by age 65. All coefficients can be interpreted in terms of changes over decades, so the average 10-year change is 10.7 points, but a person who is 14 years old can be said to have the *latent age* of a 50-year-old (i.e., $A[14] = 5.0$). The individual differences in this model are seen in the variances for the level ($\sigma_0^2 = 9.5^2$) and the slope ($\sigma_s^2 = 1.5^2$) parameters. It is also important to note that the highest estimated coefficient never was higher than the fixed value at age 65 – this means that General Knowledge ability (Gc) does not decline within people repeatedly measured over this span of ages.

Additional results for models with further complexity

A study of model expectations shows that the previous model (M_3) fits fairly well, but it could fit better. It is now common practice to improve the model fit by freeing up one or more of the offending misfit covariances. This can easily be done here, and M_3 with a free "error variance" $\sigma(Gc\_14) > 30$ yields $\chi^2 = 66$ on df = 16. Similarly, M_3 with all free error variances yields $\chi^2 = 48$ on df = 12 with $\sigma(Gc\_04) < 0$. The problem with such model fitting is that fitting different sized error at different occasions does not seem to have any substantive or mathematical basis, and it has a potential to capitalize on chance in the data (i.e., as is often the case with models using the unfortunate term "correlated errors"; see Meredith & Horn, 2001). Also, while these post hoc results do

Table 17.4   Numerical results from alternative basis in latent growth models fitted to Bradway–McArdle longitudinal data

Parameters	M_3 *Latent*	M_4 *Unity*	M_5 *Ortho*	M_6 *Spline*
Fixed effects				
Basis α[04]	1, 0.4	1, 0	1, −2.8 (1.1)	1, 0, 0
Basis α[14]	1, 5.0 (0.6)	1, 0.76 (0.1)	1, 0.10 (0.26)	1, 1, 0
Basis α[29]	1, 6.2 (.07)	1, 0.95 (0.01)	1, 0.81 (0.04)	1, 1, 0.80 (0.03)
Basis α[42]	1, 6.4 (0.08)	1, 0.98 (0.01)	1, 0.93 (0.05)	1, 1, 0.98 (0.04)
Basis α[57]	1, 6.5 (0.08)	1, 1.00 0(0.01)	1, 1.00 (0.05)	1, 1, 1.01 (0.04)
Basis α[65]	1, 6.5	1, 1	1, 1	1, 1, 1
Level μ_0	17.9 (1.0)	22.2 (0.97)	70.3 (5.0)	22.2 (0.94)
Slope μ_s	10.7 (0.19)	65.5 (1.2)	17.4 (5.0)	50.0 (0.86)
Slope 2 μ_2	–	–	–	15.1 (0.86)
Random effects				
Error σ_e^2	17.4 (1.5)	17.4 (1.5)	17.4 (1.5)	8.3 (0.95)
Level σ_0	9.8 (0.79)	9.3 (0.75)	6.2 (0.47)	9.4 (0.69)
Slope σ_s	1.5 (0.14)	9.4 (0.84)	2.5 (0.76)	8.1 (0.69)
Correl. ρ_{0s}	−0.77 (0.05)	−0.74 (0.05)	0	−0.50 (0.08)
Slope 2 σ_2	–	–	–	7.1 (0.66)
Correl. ρ_{02}, ρ_{s2}	–	–	–	−0.60 (0.08), −0.04 (0.12)
Fit indices				
Num. para.	10	10	10	13
Deg. freedom	17	17	17	14
Likelihood ratio	122	122	122	46
RMSEA	0.23	0.23	0.23	0.14

Model 4b with free unique variance σ(Gc_14) > 30 yields χ^2 = 66 on df = 16;
Model 4c with all free unique variances yields χ^2 = 48 on df = 12 with σ(Gc_04) < 0.

improve the fit of the model, they do not substantially alter the previous parameters and afford us few useful insights.

We examine goodness-of-fit issues using a different approach. Table 17.4 is a list of results for a few alternative latent growth models. The first model (M_3) is simply the latent basis model carried over from Table 17.3. The second model (M_4) uses a slightly different set of basis coefficients, where a[04] = 0 and a[65] = 1, and this reflects a reinterpretation of the basis function in a different metric: $A[t]$ = [0.00, 0.76, 0.95, 0.98, 1.00, 1.00], with a new set of means (22.2 and 65.5) and variances (9.3 and 9.4). These new model parameters usefully re-express the model parameters by treating the age range between 4 and 65 as a full unit. If we consider this unit to be 100 percent of the changes between ages 4 and 65 (the observed period), it is now easy to say that 76 percent of all cognitive growth in knowledge occurred by age 14, 95 percent by age 42, and so on. This latent basis model (M_4) is no different than the first (M_3) because it creates exactly the same expectations as those in Table 17.3 and it fits exactly the same way (χ^2 = 122 on df = 17).

The next model (M_5) of Table 17.4 is also similar, except here we force the correlation among the latent scores to be fixed at zero and estimate five of the basis parameters (with $a[65] = 1$ still fixed for identification). This model yields the same expectations and the same fit ($\chi^2 = 122$ on df $= 17$) but we can see that the parameter for the basis at age 14 looks like a reasonable zero point for the intercept ($\alpha[14] = 0.1$), with parameters negative before ($\alpha[04] = -2.8$) and positive afterwards ($\alpha[29] = 0.81$). This leads us naturally to the idea for the next model (M_6), which is a spline model (equation (17.4)) composed of two latent slopes: one for changes up to age 14 and another for changes after age 14. The exact parameterization as listed shows a starting level of 22.2 at age 4 with a big average gain jump of 50 points (± 9.4) up to age 14, followed by a small steady gain of 15.1 points (± 8.1) from 14 to 65. However, this two-latent-slope spline should not be ignored because it shows much better fit overall ($\chi^2 = 46$ on df $= 14$) and when compared to the nested one-slope model (M_6 versus M_4: $\Delta\chi^2 = 76$ on Δdf $= 3$) is notable.

We do not need to make any specific decision about these model differences at this point. It is enough to say that the two-part linear slope model fits best, it is far better than the others considered, and it is far more interesting than simply adding unique variances or covariances to improve fit. However, the interpretation of the two-slope model is very similar to what we have already described in the one-slope model which changes direction. The one-latent-slope model (M_3, M_4 or M_5) may need to be reconsidered, and the complexity of individual differences should not be overlooked.

Studying Predictors of Individual Differences in Developmental Scores

The group mean parameters estimated in the previous analyses allow us to plot the group trajectory over time. Similarly, the estimated variance parameters allow us to consider the size of the between-group differences at each age. However, no prior information tells us about the *sources of this variance*. To further explore the differences between persons we need to expand the basic latent growth model. Let us assume a variable termed X indicates some measurable difference between persons (e.g., sex, educational level, etc.). If we measure this variable at one occasion we might like to examine its influence in the context of a growth model for $Y[t]$. One popular model is based on the use of "adjusted" growth parameters as popularly represented in the techniques of the *analysis of covariance*. In growth curve terms this model is written as:

$$Y[t]_n = y_{0:x,n} + y_{s::x,n} \cdot A[t] + \gamma[t]X_n + e[t]_n \tag{17.7}$$

where the γ are fixed (group) coefficients with some effect on the measured $Y[t]$ scores at each occasions, and the X is an independent observed (or assigned) predictor variable. In this case the growth parameters ($\mu_{0:x}$, $\mu_{s:x}$, $\sigma_{0:x}$, $\sigma_{s:x}$, $\sigma_{0,s:x}$) are conditional on the expected values of the measured X variable. The parameters of the changes may be defined by the resulting difference or differential equation, but the reduction of error variance (σ_{ex}) is often considered as a way to understand the overall impacts.

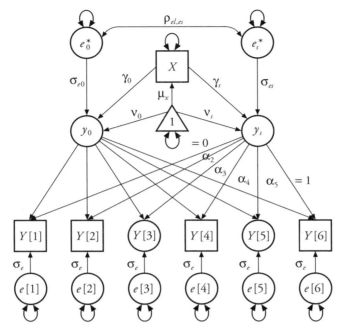

Figure 17.7 Latent growth as a path diagram with mixed-effect or multilevel predictors.

The apparent complexity of the covariance model leads to a simpler and increasingly popular way to add an external variable. We can write a *mixed* or *multilevel* model where the X variable has a direct effect on the parameters of the growth curve as:

$$Y[t]_n = y_{0n} + y_{sn} \cdot A[t] + e[t]_n \text{ with} \tag{17.8}$$
$$y_{0n} = v_0 + \gamma_0 X_n + e_{0n} \text{ and}$$
$$y_{sn} = v_s + \gamma_s X_n + e_{sn}$$

where the v are intercepts and the γ are regression slopes for the effect of X on the two latent components of $Y[t]$. This model is drawn as a path diagram in Figure 17.7. This diagram is the same as Figure 17.5 except here we have included the X as a predictor of the levels and slope components. It may be useful to write this as a reduced-form SEM so it is now clear that the three unobserved residual terms are not simply separable by standard linear regression or covariance equation (see McArdle & Hamagami, 1996).

This path diagram gives the basic idea of external variable models; several other more complex alternatives will be considered in later sections. In this simple linear model, as in more complex models to follow, we can always add predictors X for the intercepts and the slopes. In some areas of research these models have been termed *mixed-effects* models (Laird & Ware, 1982; Littell et al., 1996; Singer, 1998). In other areas of research these same models have been termed *random-coefficients* or *multilevel models*, or *slopes as outcomes* or *hierarchical linear models* (e.g., Bryk & Raudenbush, 1992). In other SEM research these models were considered using factor analysis terminology as *latent growth models with incomplete data and extension variables* (e.g., McArdle & Epstein, 1987; McArdle & Hamagami, 1992). Using any terminology, these models can be generically represented by the parameters in the path diagram of Figure 17.7, and this is a common way to understand the between-group differences in within-group changes. Once considered in this way, no new model fitting procedure is required.

Results for educational influences on latent scores

A variety of additional variables have been measured in the Bradway–McArdle collections, including demographic (e.g., gender, educational attainment by age 30 and 56, etc.), self reported health behaviors (e.g., smoking, drinking, physical exercise, etc.) and other problems (e.g., general health, illness, medical procedures, etc.), and personality measures (e.g., 16 PF factors). The SEM presented here include these variables into the latent growth curve analysis.

In the next set of analyses (Table 17.5) we consider four variables: (1) gender (effect coded as −0.5 for males and +0.5 for females), (2) the person's own educational level (at age 30 in years), (3) father's educational level (in years), and (4) mother's educational level (in years). Table 17.5 includes a list of summary statistics for these four variables, including information about the means and standard deviations (Table 17.5a), correlations within these variables (Table 17.5b), and the correlations between these variables and the six intellectual ability measures (Table 17.5c). Both the observed statistics and the expected statistics corrected for incomplete data (MLE) are presented.

We have studied a variety of group differences in the growth parameters, and the mixed-effect or multilevel models are easy to apply to these data. To be flexible here, we only fit the latent basis curve model with a 0–1 basis (M_4; as described above). We started with a baseline latent growth model with no predictors of the levels and slopes, but then added additional variables as predictors of these levels and slopes (see Figure 17.7). In these mixed models we added Gender as an effect-coded variable (i.e., $M = -0.5$ and $F = +0.5$), and the three indices of educational attainment centered at 12 years (see Table 17.5). In these mixed models we examined the raw coefficients, standard errors, and standardized estimates. A coefficient was considered accurate (significant) if the ratio of the parameter to its standard error was greater than 1.96 (at the 0.05 test level). We also compared the overall goodness-of-fit indices of multiparameter models, and we examined the change in the variance explained at the second level (see Snijders & Bosker, 1994). Two selected modeling results are listed in Table 17.6.

The first model (M_7) uses all four variables and has a misfit ($\chi^2 = 153$ on df = 33), which is a reasonable fit when compared to the free latent curve model (M_7 versus M_4: $\Delta\chi^2 = 32$ on Δdf = 16). This implies that the patterning of the correlations of predictors and outcomes (Table 17.2b) can be estimated using two latent variables (see McArdle & Prescott, 1992). The MLE parameters suggest the following interpretations: (0) the latent basis coefficients ($A[t]$) were unaffected by the inclusion of the predictors, (1) there are no accurate (significant) differences between males and females on either levels or slopes, (2) the persons' educational level (at age 30) was not predictive of the initial

Table 17.5 Additional summary statistics from the Bradway–McArdle longitudinal data at six time points ($N = 111$)

(a) Observed [and expected] means, SDs and ranges

Variable	N	Mean [MLE]	Std dev [MLE]	Min	Max
Gender	111	0.52 [0.52]	0.5 [0.5]	0.0	1.0
Educ_Per	110	13.7 [13.6]	2.3 [2.3]	7.0	22.0
Educ_Dad	76	10.3 [10.0]	3.1 [3.2]	6.0	17.0
Educ_Mom	75	11.1 [10.9]	2.8 [2.8]	6.0	17.0

(b) Observed [and expected] correlations of demographics (each entry includes pairwise *r* and pairwise *n*)

	Gender	Educ_Per	Educ_Dad	Educ_Mom
Gender	111 1.000			
Educ_Per	110 0.000 [0.001]	110 1.000		
Educ_Dad	76 0.182 [0.207]	76 0.244 [0.337]	76 1.000	
Educ_Mom	75 0.129 [0.123]	75 0.317 [0.395]	75 0.619 [0.644]	75 1.000

(c) Observed [and expected] correlations with cognitive abilities (each entry includes pairwise *r* and pairwise *n*)

	Gender	Educ_Per	Educ_Dad	Educ_Mom
Age 4	110 0.062 [0.074]	109 0.062 [0.056]	75 0.167 [0.204]	74 −0.024 [0.020]
Age 14	111 0.188 [0.193]	110 0.330 [0.330]	76 0.112 [0.204]	75 0.069 [0.156]
Age 29	110 0.187 [0.185]	110 0.491 [0.488]	76 0.267 [0.363]	75 0.221 [0.315]
Age 42	49 0.048 [−0.003]	48 0.522 [0.554]	38 0.298 [0.278]	38 0.154 [0.187]
Age 57	51 0.101 [0.132]	50 0.537 [0.551]	37 0.366 [0.308]	37 0.144 [0.203]
Age 65	51 0.058 [0.088]	50 0.322 [0.409]	37 0.222 [0.138]	37 0.153 [0.125]

Table 17.6 Numerical results from latent growth models with four extension variables fitted to Bradway–McArdle longitudinal data

Parameters	M$_7$ {Latent} Level	M$_7$ {Latent} Slope	M$_8$ {Latent} Level	M$_8$ {Latent} Slope
Fixed effects				
Basis A[t]	[= 0, 0.76, 0.95, 0.98, 1.00, = 1]		[= 0, 0.76, 0.95, 0.98, 1.00, = 1]	
Intercept γ_0	22.8 (1.5)[0]	62.6 (1.7)[0]	23.3 (1.5)[0]	62.6 (1.6)[0]
Regression from Gender γ_g	0.73 (2.0)[0.04]	1.63 (2.0)[0.09]	0	0
Regression Educ_Pers γ_p	0.20 (0.04)[0.048]	1.32 (0.47)*[0.32]	−0.13 (0.44)[−0.00]	1.44 (0.45)*[0.35]
Regression Educ_Dad γ_d	0.95 (0.47)*[0.32]	−0.68 (0.48)[−0.23]	58 (38) [0.19]	−0.24 (0.39)[−0.08]
Regression Educ_Mom γ_m	−0.78 (0.54)[−0.23]	0.65 (0.55)[0.19]	0	0
Random effects				
Residual σ_d	9.0 (0.75)	8.7 (0.82)	9.1 (0.75)	8.8 (0.82)
Error σ_e^2	17.4 (1.5)		17.5 (1.5)	
Correl. $\rho_{d0,ds}$	−0.81 (0.04)		−0.81 (0.04)	
Fit indices				
Num. para.	32		28	
Deg. freedom	33		37	
Likelihood ratio	153		159	
RMSEA	0.18		0.17	

Latent growth with all four predictors set to zero yields $L^2 = 195$ on df = 41.

cognitive level (at age 4) but was a positive indicator of overall changes in adulthood ($\gamma = 1.32$ [0.32]), (3) the educational level of the father (at age 14) was a positive contributor to the initial cognitive level ($\gamma = 0.95$ [0.47]) but not to the adult slope, and (4) the educational level of the mother (at age 14) was not related to the initial level or slope.

The second set of results (M_8) were based on a model where all coefficients for gender and mother's education were fixed at zero. This model fits the data just about as well as before (M_8 versus M_7: $\Delta\chi^2 = 6$ on $\Delta df = 4$), but the results obtained now differ in one respect – the coefficient for the father's education on initial level is no longer accurate. This is probably due to (a) the fact that the mother's education no longer has a direct effect, (b) it is positively correlated ($r = 0.62$) with father's education, and (c) the previous "suppression" effect has been eliminated and the coefficient is not as strong. In essence, the previous interpretation (M_7) needed to consider the negative coefficient of mother's education, and reinterpret the overall impact or do so in terms of the difference between parental educational levels.

At this point it seems the only direct educational influence found here is that of the person's educational level on their own slope. However, the model can be expanded to include more complex path representations, and this leads to a comprehensive series of mixed-model path equations. Assuming the three education variables are centered at grade 12, and we view the person's educational attainment as an outcome of the parent's educational attainment, we can estimate a simultaneous latent path model (M_9) where:

$$Y[t]_n = y_{0,n} + y_{s,n} \cdot A[t] + e[t]_n \qquad (17.9)$$
$$y_{0,n} = 21.9 + 0.2 \; EducPers_n + 9.3 \; d_{0,n}$$
$$y_{s,n} = 63.2 + 1.34 \; EducPers_n + 8.9 \; d_{s,n}$$
$$EducPers_n = 2.1 + 0.08 \; EducDad_n + 0.25 \; EducMom_n + 8.8 \; d_{0n}$$

with good overall fit of ($\chi^2 = 162$ on df = 39, so $\Delta\chi^2 = 3$ on $\Delta df = 2$). This result is substantively different than either previous model (M_7 or M_8) because it now emphasizes the positive but indirect effects of the mother (0.025×1.34) on the adult slopes of the children. This model is drawn as a SEM path diagram in Figure 17.8 to illustrate how the basic principles of multiple regression and path analysis follow directly from the latent variables of a growth model (see McArdle, 2001; McArdle & Hamagami, 2003).

Final Comments

This chapter was written to serve as an introduction to a general class of procedures that can be classified under the rubric of "latent growth curve modeling techniques." The brevity of this chapter cannot do justice to the broad applicability of these techniques. Hopefully, the analyses presented here have stimulated interest in this topic. Interested researchers can now proceed to consider natural additions, such as using SEM to examine measured group differences (e.g., femalesversus males) in growth (McArdle & Epstein, 1987; McArdle & Anderson, 1990; McArdle & Bell, 2000), or models dealing with

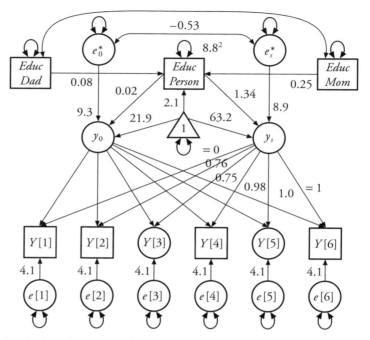

Figure 17.8   Results from latent growth with latent path predictors.

groups of families and twins (e.g., McArdle, 1986; McArdle et al., 1998; McArdle & Hamagami, 2003). It is also possible to examine group differences when the group membership is unknown or latent using latent growth "mixture" models (see Nagin, 1999; Muthén & Muthén, 2002; McArdle & Nesselroade, 2003). At the same time, we need to recognize that these SEM developments represent a limited class of longitudinal data analyses (e.g., Nesselroade & Baltes, 1979; Collins & Sayer, 2001). Indeed, some of the most difficult problems for future work on growth curves will not involve SEM statistical analysis or computer programming, but will be focused on the rather elusive meaning of the growth model parameters themselves (Zeger & Harlow, 1987; McArdle & Nesselroade, 2003). These substantive problems are among the most difficult dynamic challenges for future work.

Acknowledgments

The work described here has been supported since 1980 by the National Institute on Aging (grant no. AG-07137). I am especially grateful to the work of my close friend and colleague, Fumiaki Hamagami, and to my close collaboration with Kay Bradway. This research was also helped by the support of my many friends and colleagues, including Steven Aggen, Steven Boker, Emilio Ferrer-Caja, John Horn, Patty Hulick, Bill Meredith, John Nesselroade, Carol Prescott, and Dick Woodcock. Reprints can be obtained from the author at the Jefferson Psychometric Laboratory, PO Box 400400, Department of Psychology, University of Virginia, Charlottesville, VA 22904,

USA. Computer program input scripts used here can be found on our website at http://kiptron.psyc.virginia.edu.

References

Arbuckle, J. L. & Wotke, W. (1999). *AMOS 4.0 User's Guide*. Chicago, IL: Smallwaters.

Bell, R. Q. (1954). An experimental test of the accelerated longitudinal approach. *Child Development*, *25*, 281–6.

Bereiter, C. (1963). Some persisting dilemmas in the measurement of change. In C. W. Harris (ed.), *Problems in measuring change* (pp. 3–20). Madison, WI: University of Wisconsin Press.

Bock, R. D. (1975). *Multivariate statistical methods in behavioral research*. New York: McGraw-Hill.

Bradway, K. P. & Thompson, C. W. (1962). Intelligence at adulthood: A 25 year follow-up. *Journal of Educational Psychology*, *53(1)*, 1–14.

Browne, M. & du Toit, S. H. C. (1991). Models for learning data. In L. Collins & J. L. Horn, (eds.), *Best Methods for the Analysis of Change* (pp. 47–68). Washington, DC: APA Press.

Bryk, A. S. & Raudenbush, S. W. (1992). *Hierarchical linear models: Applications and data analysis methods*. Newbury Park, CA: Sage.

Burr, J. A. & Nesselroade, J. R. (1990). Change measurement. In A. von Eye (ed.), *Statistical Methods in Longitudinal Research* (pp. 3–34). Boston, MA: Academic Press.

Cnaan, A., Laird, N. M., & Slasor, P. (1997). Using the general linear mixed model to analyse unbalanced repeated measures and longitudinal data. *Statistics in Medicine*, *16*, 2349–80.

Collins, L. & Sayer, A. (eds.) (2001). *New methods for the analysis of change* (pp. 137–76). Washington, DC: APA Press.

Cronbach, L. J. & Furby, L. (1970). How we should measure change – or should we? *Psychological Bulletin*, *74*, 68–80.

Cudeck, R. & du Toit, S. H. C. (2001). Mixed-effects models in the study of individual differences with repeated measures data. *Multivariate Behavioral Research*, *31*, 371–403.

Deary, I. J., Whalley, L. J., Lemmon, H., Crawford, J. R., & Starr, J. M. (2000). The stability of individual differences in mental ability from childhood to old age: Follow-up of the 1932 Scottish Mental Survey. *Intelligence*, *28(1)*, 49–56.

Duncan, T. E., Duncan, S. C., Strycker, L. A., Li, F., & Alpert, A. (1998). *An introduction to latent variable growth curve modeling: Concepts, issues, and applications*. Mahwah, NJ: Lawrence Erlbaum Associates.

Ferrer, E., Hamagami, F., & McArdle, J. J. (in press). Modeling latent growth curves with incomplete data using different types of structural equation modeling and multilevel software. *Structural Equation Modeling*.

Goldstein, H. (1995). *Multilevel statistical models* (2nd edn.). New York: Oxford University Press.

Hamagami, F. (1998). A developmental-based item factor analysis. In J. J. McArdle & R. W. Woodcock (eds.), *Human abilities in theory and practice* (pp. 231–46). Mahwah, NJ: Lawrence Erlbaum Associates.

Hamagami, F. & McArdle, J. J. (2001). Advanced studies of individual differences linear dynamic models for longitudinal data analysis. In G. Marcoulides & R. Schumacker (eds.), *New developments and techniques in structural equation modeling* (pp. 203–46). Mahwah, NJ: Lawrence Erlbaum Associates.

Hedecker, D. & Gibbons, R. (1996). MIXOR: a computer program for mixed-effects ordinal regression analysis. *Computer Methods and Programs in Biomedicine*, *49*, 157–76.

Kangas, J. & Bradway, K. P. (1971). Intelligence at middle age: A thirty-eight year follow-up. *Developmental Psychology, 5(2)*, 333–7.

Laird, N. M. & Ware, J. H. (1982). Random effects models for longitudinal data. *Biometrics, 38*, 963–74.

Littell, R. C., Miliken, G. A., Stoup, W. W., & Wolfinger, R. D. (1996). *SAS system for mixed models*. Cary, NC: SAS Institute.

Little, R. J. A. & Rubin, D. B. (1987). *Statistical analysis with missing data*. New York: John Wiley.

McArdle, J. J. (1986). Latent variable growth within behavior genetic models. *Behavior Genetics, 16(1)*, 163–200.

McArdle, J. J. (1989). Structural modeling experiments using multiple growth functions. In P. Ackerman, R. Kanfer, & R. Cudeck (eds.), *Learning and individual differences: Abilities, motivation, and methodology* (pp. 71–117). Hillsdale, NJ: Lawrence Erlbaum Associates.

McArdle, J. J. (1994). Structural factor analysis experiments with incomplete data. *Multivariate Behavioral Research, 29(4)*, 409–454.

McArdle, J. J. (1997). Recent trends in modelling longitudinal business date by latent growth curve methods. In G. Marcoulides (ed.), *New statistical models with business and economic applications* (pp. 359–406). Mahwah, NJ: Lawrence Erlbaum Associates.

McArdle, J. J. (2001). A latent difference score approach to longitudinal dynamic structural analyses. In R. Cudeck, S. du Toit, & D. Sorbom (eds.), *Structural equation modeling: Present and future* (pp. 342–80). Lincolnwood, IL: Scientific Software International.

McArdle, J. J. & Anderson, E. (1990). Latent variable growth models for research on aging. In J. E. Birren & K. W. Schaie (eds.), *The handbook of the psychology of aging* (pp. 21–43). New York: Plenum Press.

McArdle, J. J. & Bell, R. Q. (2000). Recent trends in modeling longitudinal data by latent growth curve methods. In T. D. Little, K. U. Schnabel, & J. Baumert (eds.), *Modeling longitudinal and multiple-group data: practical issues, applied approaches, and scientific examples* (pp. 69–107). Mahwah, NJ: Lawrence Erlbaum Associates.

McArdle, J. J. & Epstein, D. B. (1987). Latent growth curves within developmental structural equation models. *Child Development, 58(1)*, 110–33.

McArdle, J. J. & Hamagami, E. (1992). Modeling incomplete longitudinal and cross-sectional data using latent growth structural models. *Experimental Aging Research, 18(3)*, 145–66.

McArdle, J. J. & Hamagami, F. (1996). Multilevel models from a multiple group structural equation perspective. In G. Marcoulides & R. Schumacker (eds.), *Advanced structural equation modeling techniques* (pp. 89–124). Hillsdale, NJ: Lawrence Erlbaum Associates.

McArdle, J. J. & Hamagami, F. (2001). Linear dynamic analyses of incomplete longitudinal data. In L. Collins & A. Sayer (eds.), *New methods for the analysis of change* (pp. 137–76). Washington, DC: APA Press.

McArdle, J. J. & Hamagami, F. (2003). Structural equation models for evaluating dynamic concepts within longitudinal twin analyses. *Behavior Genetics, 33(3)*, 137–59.

McArdle, J. J. & Nesselroade, J. R. (2003). Growth curve analyses in contemporary psychological research. In J. Schinka & W. Velicer (eds.), *Comprehensive handbook of psychology*, vol. 2: *Research methods in psychology* (pp. 447–80). New York: Pergamon Press.

McArdle, J. J. & Prescott, C. A. (1992). Age-based construct validation using structural equation models. *Experimental Aging Research, 18(3)*, 87–115.

McArdle, J. J. & Woodcock, J. R. (1997). Expanding test–rest designs to include developmental time-lag components. *Psychological Methods, 2(4)*, 403–35.

McArdle, J. J., Prescott, C. A., Hamagami, F., & Horn, J. L. (1998). A contemporary method for developmental-genetic analyses of age changes in intellectual abilities. *Developmental Neuropsychology, 14(1)*, 69–114.

McArdle, J. J., Hamagami, F., Meredith, W., & Bradway, K. P. (2000). Modeling the dynamic hypotheses of Gf-Gc theory using longitudinal life-span data. *Learning and Individual Differences, 12*, 53–79.

McCrae, R. R., Arenberg, D., & Costa, P. T. (1987). Declines in divergent thinking with age: Cross-sectional, longitudinal, and cross sequential analyses. *Psychology and Aging, 2(2)*, 130–37.

Meredith, W. & Horn, J. L. (2001). The role of factorial invariance in measuring growth and change In L. Collins & A. Sayer (eds.), *New methods for the analysis of change* (pp. 201–40). Washington, DC: APA Press.

Meredith, W. & Tisak, J. (1990). Latent curve analysis. *Psychometrika, 55*, 107–22.

Metha, P. D. & West, S. G. (2000). Putting the individual back into individual growth curves. *Psychological Methods, 5(1)*, 23–43.

Muthén, B. O. & Curran, P. (1997). General longitudinal modeling of individual differences in experimental designs: A latent variable framework for analysis and power estimation. *Psychological Methods, 2*, 371–402.

Muthén, L. K. & Muthén, B. O. (2002). *Mplus, the comprehensive modeling program for applied researchers: user's guide.* Los Angeles, CA: Muthen & Muthen.

Nagin, D. (1999). Analyzing developmental trajectories: Semi-parametric. Group-based approach. *Psychological Methods, 4*, 139–77.

Neale, M. C., Boker, S. M., Xie, G., & Maes, H. H. (1999). Mx statistical modeling (5th edn.). Unpublished program manual, Virginia Institute of Psychiatric and Behavioral Genetics, Medical College of Virginia, Virginia Commonwealth University, Richmond, VA.

Nesselroade, J. R. & Baltes, P. B. (eds.) (1979). *Longitudinal research in the study of behavior and development.* New York: Academic Press.

Pinherio, J. C. & Bates, D. M. (2000). *Mixed-effects models in S and S-PLUS.* New York: Springer-Verlag.

Pothoff, R. F. & Roy, S. N. (1964). A generalized multivariate analysis model useful especially for growth curve problems. *Biometrics, 51*, 313–26.

Rao, C. R. (1958). Some statistical methods for the comparison of growth curves. *Biometrics, 14*, 1–17.

Rogosa, D. & Willett, J. B. (1985). Understanding correlates of change by modeling individual differences in growth. *Psychometrika, 50*, 203–28.

Seber, G. A. F. & Wild, C. J. (1989). *Nonlinear models.* New York: John Wiley.

Singer, J. D. (1998). Using SAS PROC MIXED to fit multilevel models, hierarchical models, and individual growth models. *Journal of Educational and Behavioral Statistics, 23(4)*, 323–55.

Singer, J. D. & Willett, J. (2003). *Applied longitudinal data analysis.* New York: Oxford University Press.

Snijders, T. A. B. & Bosker, R. (1994). Modeled variance in two-level models. *Sociological Methods and Research, 22*, 342–63.

Sullivan, E. V., Rosenbloom, M. J., Lim, K. O., & Pfefferman, A. (2000). Longitudinal changes in cognition, gait, balance in abstinent and relapsed alcoholic men: Relationships to changes in brain structure. *Neuropsychology, 14(2)*, 178–88.

Tucker, L. R. (1958). Determination of parameters of a functional relation by factor analysis. *Psychometrika, 23*, 19–23.

Tucker, L. R. (1966). Learning theory and multivariate experiment: Illustration by determination of generalized learning curves. In R. B. Cattell (ed.), *Handbook of multivariate experimental psychology.* Chicago, IL: Rand McNally.

Verbeke, G. & Molenberghs, G. (2000). *Linear mixed models for longitudinal data.* New York: Springer-Verlag.

Willett, J. B. (1990). Measuring change: The difference score and beyond. In H. J. Walberg & G. D. Haertel (eds.), *The international encyclopedia of education evaluation* (pp. 632–7). Oxford: Pergamon Press.

Willett, J. B. & Sayer, A. G. (1994). Using covariance structure analysis to detect correlates and predictors of individual change over time. *Psychological Bulletin, 116*, 363–81.

Wishart, J. (1938). Growth rate determinations in nutrition studies with the bacon pig, and their analyses. *Biometrika, 30*, 16–28.

Zeger, S. L. & Harlow, S. D. (1987). Mathematical models from laws of growth to tools for biologic analysis: Fifty years of growth. *Growth, 51*, 1–21.

CHAPTER EIGHTEEN

Modeling Developmental Change Over Time: Latent Growth Analysis

Philip W. Wirtz

One of the more intriguing methodological advances in developmental research lies with the availability of valid techniques for research on differences in growth patterns among individuals. This advancement is relatively recent: in a 1994 review of five major software programs, Kreft, de Leeuw, and van der Leeden (1994) found that only the BMDP package had an integrated growth-modeling procedure. With the comparatively recent introduction of SAS Proc Mixed and SPSS Version 11.0, valid techniques which focus on individual – or "latent" – growth analysis (where the growth trajectory of an organism is explicitly modeled as a function of organism-specific characteristics) have now been integrated into widely used statistical packages.

There are several reasons why a researcher dealing with longitudinal data might wish to employ latent growth analysis rather than more traditional forms of analysis such as repeated measures ANOVA or repeated measures MANOVA. First among these is that proper application of repeated measures ANOVA to longitudinal data requires adherence to compound symmetry (or, more narrowly, sphericity) conditions. The compound symmetry conditions require (among other things) that the correlation of the dependent variable across any pair of time points be the same as the correlation across any *other* pair of time points. In many developmental models, it is much more common to expect a higher correlation between proximal time points than between distal time points; the compound symmetry assumption is often untenable in practice (see also, for example, Mendoza, Toothaker, & Crain, 1976; Rouanet & Lépine, 1970). Although several adjustments have been proposed and widely used (Greenhouse & Geisser, 1959; Huynh & Feldt, 1976), there is a considerable body of research demonstrating the weaknesses of these adjustments (e.g., Collier et al., 1967; Maxwell & Delaney, 2000; Stevens, 1992; Girden, 1992).

A second reason why a researcher dealing with longitudinal data might wish to employ latent growth analysis rather than more traditional forms of analysis such as repeated measures ANOVA or repeated measures MANOVA lies with the ANOVA/MANOVA-based requirement of no missing data; latent growth analysis imposes no such constraint. Third, unlike latent growth analysis, application of repeated measures MANOVA to longitudinal scenarios does not permit individual variation in the intervals between assessments. Fourth, neither form of classical repeated measures analysis provides a mechanism for the unbiased estimate of variability in growth trajectories across individuals. Ware (1985) provides a systematic comparison of latent growth analysis with classical repeated measures approaches.

The logic of latent growth analysis is best conveyed by example. Suppose an investigator wishes to investigate how firstborn children adjust to first-time siblinghood. Suppose further that, for each of a random sample of firstborn children who subsequently became siblings, the investigator has measures of attachment security to the mother (assessed by the Attachment Q-Set; Waters, 1995) taken at up to four points in time: just before the sibling's birth, approximately one month postpartum, approximately one year postpartum, and approximately two years postpartum. The "growth trajectory" for each child can be viewed graphically by plotting that child's attachment security to the mother (along the side) against time (along the bottom). Different children reflect different trajectories, as indicated by differences in the intercept and/or the slope of their growth curves (see Figure 18.1): some children reflect comparatively low (i.e., insecure) initial attachment which increases steeply with the passage of time; other children reflect comparatively high (i.e., secure) initial attachment which declines steeply with the passage of time; still

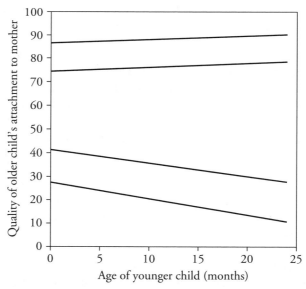

Figure 18.1 Linear growth trajectories of four children. Note: Quality of attachment was assessed with the Attachment Q-Set (Waters, 1995) and rescaled from 0 (extremely poor quality) to 100 (extremely good quality).

other children reflect maternal attachment security levels which remain relatively stable across time.

Three primary types of question form the basis for latent growth analyses of data such as these. First, how much variation in trajectory paths is there among the population of firstborn children adjusting to first-time siblinghood? Second, can some of that variation be attributed to characteristics of the child (such as the child's sex), or characteristics of the child's environment (such as the adequacy of attachment figures)? Third, how much residual variation remains even after accounting for the effects of such characteristics and of time?

In order to address these questions using latent growth analysis, it is necessary to assume a common relational form between time and attachment security to the mother. As a simple example, the investigator might be willing to assume that, for any given child, the relationship between time and attachment security to the mother is linear – that is, the change in attachment level between birth of the sibling and one year postpartum is the same as the change in attachment level between one year postpartum and two years postpartum. Under this assumption, any two children might vary in either the intercept or the slope (or both) of the straight line that describes the relationship. A more complex model might specify a nonlinear polynomial relationship: under a quadratic model, for example, children might vary in the intercept, linear, and/or quadratic terms.

Once the investigator has specified the relational form for the model, the equation describing each child is simple to present. In the case of a linear relational form, the relationship between Attachment Security to the mother (Y) and Age of the sibling for child *j* is described by

$$Y_{ij} = \pi_{0j} + \pi_{1j} Age_{ij} + e_{ij} \tag{18.1}$$

where π_{0j} represents the predicted value of Attachment Security two months prior to the birth of the sibling and π_{1j} represents the slope of the best-fitting regression line between Attachment Security of firstborn child *j* and Age of his/her first sibling.

A defining characteristic of latent growth analysis is the separation of (at least) two "levels" of effect: those effects which characterize each individual point in time at which an assessment was made (e.g., the age of the sibling at that time), and those effects which characterize the organism (e.g., sex). Equation (18.1) represents the former (known as "level 1"): note that the unit of analysis here is the individual assessment rather than the individual child. Thus, latent growth analysis is a form of the more general class of "hierarchical linear modeling" (HLM) procedures, because interest lies at two levels: the lower (individual assessment) level and the higher (individual child) level. We will return to this point subsequently, when we wish to model the effects of child-level attributes (such as gender) on assessment-level outcomes.

A second defining characteristic of this type of modeling procedure is that π_0 (the intercept) and π_1 (the slope) are permitted to be different for each child, as reflected by the *j* in the subscripts of the regression parameters (i.e., π_{0j} and π_{1j}). Thus, each child can reflect a unique "growth trajectory" (i.e., a unique intercept–slope pair); a primary objective of latent growth analysis is to test hypotheses about child-specific or environment-specific factors which influence these parameters.

In order to further explicate the model, it is often useful to expand Equation (18.1):

$$Y_{ij} = \pi_{0j} + \pi_{1j}Age_{ij} + e_{ij} \tag{18.1}$$

$$\pi_{0j} = \beta_{00} + r_{0j} \tag{18.2}$$

$$\pi_{1j} = \beta_{10} + r_{1j} \tag{18.3}$$

Under this explicated model, a given child's intercept is presumed to be composed of two sources: a fixed source, β_{00} (the intercept of the average child in the population) and a random source, r_{0j} (the difference between this child's intercept and the average child's intercept, due to unknown factors). Similarly, a given child's slope is presumed to be composed of two sources: β_{10} (the slope of the average child in the population) and r_{1j} (the difference between this child's slope and the average child's slope, due to unknown factors). We will shortly introduce additional variables into equations (18.2) and (18.3) in order to test hypotheses about factors which influence children's' intercepts and slopes.

In terms of equations (18.1)–(18.3), three primary questions of latent growth analysis emerge: (1) what is the variance of π_0 (intercepts) and of π_1 (slopes) across the members of the population? (2) Are π_0 and π_1 influenced by characteristics of the child (e.g., the child's sex) or of the child's environment (e.g., the adequacy of attachment figures in the child's environment)? (3) What is the variation of e_{ij} in the population? Latent growth analysis addresses each of these questions.

The vernacular of developmental science draws a sharper distinction between the concepts of "age" and "time" than is found in other social science substantive areas; as a result, it is important to clearly define what constitutes a "time point" in latent growth analysis. Under latent growth models, each person is assumed to be measured on more than one occasion. There is no requirement that these occasions be fixed in time: for example, it is not required that each child be first measured exactly two months prior to the birth of the sibling. Rather, the age of the sibling (e.g., −2 if the first assessment occurred exactly two months prior to the sibling's birth) is recorded as one of the measures taken on each occasion; this information is contained in the variable named "Age" in the present discussion. "Occasions" are frequently referred to as "time points" or "assessment points".

Similarly, this form of specification does not require that the time interval between assessments be fixed across children: conceivably, each child could be assessed at a unique set of occasions. The set of occasions at which a given child is assessed are assumed to be a random sample of all possible occasions at which the child could have been assessed; as a consequence, the set of sibling ages at which a given child is assessed are also assumed to be a random sample of all possible sibling ages at which the child could have been assessed. Under this specification, Age_{ij} contains the actual age of child j's sibling at assessment point i. This is a key distinction between a latent growth approach and the more traditional repeated measures ANOVA/MANOVA approaches, where assessments must be assumed (not necessarily correctly) to have been taken at fixed points in time relative to the birth of the sibling.

Note also that this form of specification also does not require each child to be assessed on the same *number* of occasions. Some children might be assessed on a number of occasions, while others might be assessed at only one. This is a second differentiating factor between a latent growth approach and a repeated measures MANOVA approach, where all subjects must be assessed on the same *number* of occasions.

In the formal jargon of statistics, Age is considered to be a "random effect" under a latent growth model, because the slope of the relationship between age and the outcome variable (attachment security to the mother) is assumed to vary from child to child – i.e., it is "random" rather than "fixed" across all children. It is also customary under a latent growth model to assume that the *intercepts* are random – that is, that children vary in their attachment security to the mother two months prior to the birth of the sibling. The explicit recognition under a latent growth model of both the Intercept and Age as *random* effects provides an additional basis for differentiating this approach from a repeated measures ANOVA/MANOVA model: the ability to estimate the variance of the intercept (π_0) and the slope (π_1) across the members of the population. In addition to being a distinguishing characteristic, this is a particularly salient feature of latent growth analysis, in that it provides a quantification of the effect of introducing other terms (such as sex of the individual or adequacy of the attachment figures) on variance reduction of the intercept or slope.

The conceptualization of the Intercept and of Age as random effects also provides the basis for specifying the null and alternative hypotheses. The null hypothesis associated with the Intercept specifies that if we had the *population* of all possible occasions on which we would measure each person in the *population* of people under study, and produced the best-fitting regression line for each person, each person would have the same Intercept. Based on equation (18.2) above, this becomes:

$$H_0 : \sigma_{r_0}^2 = 0$$

Similarly, the null hypothesis associated with Age specifies that if we had the population of time points for the population of people under study, and produced the best-fitting regression line for each person, the slope of that regression line would be identical for each person. Formally, this becomes:

$$H_0 : \sigma_{r_1}^2 = 0$$

The process of testing these two hypotheses is (in most circumstances) analytically more challenging than might immediately seem apparent, particularly when not all subjects are assessed on exactly the same number of occasions. This challenge delayed the introduction of generalized mixed-model analysis programs into major statistical computing packages such as SAS and SPSS. The "EM Algorithm" (Dempster, Laird, & Rubin, 1977), which forms the analytical core of most contemporary mixed-model implementations, leads to the generation of maximum likelihood estimates of π_0 and π_1 (and their respective variances and standard errors) for each child.

Regardless of whether or not the null hypotheses above are rejected, two additional parameter estimates (in addition to $\hat{\sigma}_{r_0}^2$ and $\hat{\sigma}_{r_1}^2$) are of interest: an estimate of the average intercept (β_{00}) and an estimate of the average slope (β_{10}) in the population. These two estimates define the "average" child in the population: β_{00} estimates the

Attachment Security level of the average child when Age = 0 (i.e., two months prior to the birth of the sibling), and β_{10} estimates the growth rate of the average child, where "growth rate" is operationalized as the slope of the relationship between Attachment Security (the dependent variable) and Age (the independent variable).

These four estimates form the starting point for latent growth analysis. β_{00} and β_{10} define the intercept and slope (respectively) of the "average" child, while $\hat{\sigma}_{r_0}^2$ and $\hat{\sigma}_{r_1}^2$ define how much variation there is in the intercept and slope (respectively) among the children in the population.

With these four estimates in hand, the next step in a latent growth analysis is to identify factors which might "explain" the variation in π_0 and π_1 among individuals. Suppose, for example, it is hypothesized that the growth rate of the average male differs from the growth rate of the average female. In order to test this hypothesis, it is useful to expand out the original equation (18.1):

$$Y_{ij} = \pi_{0j} + \pi_{1j} Age_{ij} + e_{ij} \tag{18.1}$$

$$\pi_{0j} = \beta_{00} + \beta_{01} Gender_j + r_{0j} \tag{18.4}$$

$$\pi_{1j} = \beta_{10} + \beta_{11} Gender_j + r_{1j} \tag{18.5}$$

Note that under this revised model, an individual child's intercept (π_{0j}) is a function of three elements: the average child's intercept (β_{00}), an effect of gender (β_{01}) on the child's intercept, and an error term (r_{0j}) which captures all the unmeasured effects on an individual child's intercept. Similarly, an individual child's linear growth (π_{1j}) is a function of three elements: the average child's linear growth (β_{10}), an effect of gender (β_{11}) on the child's linear growth, and an error term (r_{1j}) which captures all the unmeasured effects on an individual child's linear growth.

Now that Gender has been explicitly introduced into the model, r_{0j} and r_{1j} take on somewhat different interpretations: r_{0j} represents the effects of unmeasured variables on the intercept of child j, while r_{1j} represents the effects of unmeasured variables on the slope of child j. We continue to be interested in the variance of r_{0j} and of r_{1j}: with the introduction of additional variables (such as Gender) into the model, we would like to see a reduction in the variance of these two error terms. Under a latent growth model, these variances are often symbolized as τ_{00} and τ_{11}, respectively.

We are also typically interested in the values of β_{01} and β_{11}. These represent the (fixed) effects of Gender on the intercept and the growth (respectively).

Finally, depending on the context, we may or may not be interested in the values of β_{00} and β_{10}, which represent the intercept and growth (respectively) of the average member of the population whose Gender is coded as zero. The usefulness of β_{00} and β_{10} depends on whether or not there is interest in the intercept and the slope of the "average" person in the population defined by Gender = 0.

Returning to the central question of whether the growth rate of the average male differs from the growth rate of the average female, the corresponding null hypothesis is:

$$H_0: \beta_{11} = 0$$

Because latent growth analysis provides an estimate ($\hat{\tau}_{11}$) of the variance of r_{1j}, the standard error of β_{11} is estimable, and this hypothesis is testable. If the results of this hypothesis test reveal reasonable confidence that the null hypothesis is false, then an unbiased estimate ($\hat{\beta}_{11}$) of the difference in growth rates between the "average male" and the "average female" in the population can be calculated.

It may also be of interest to determine whether differences exist between males and females in the attachment level two months prior to the birth of the sibling. The corresponding null hypothesis is:

$$H_0 : \beta_{01} = 0$$

Here again, latent growth analysis provides an estimate ($\hat{\tau}_{00}$) of the variance of r_{0j}; the standard error of β_{01} is estimable, and this hypothesis is testable. If the results of this hypothesis test reveal reasonable confidence that the null hypothesis is false, then $\hat{\beta}_{01}$ provides an unbiased estimate of the difference in attachment levels between the "average male" and the "average female" in the population just prior to the sibling's birth.

Example[1]

For each of a random sample of 194 firstborn children who subsequently became siblings, attachment to the mother was measured at four points in time: just before the sibling's birth, approximately one month postpartum, approximately one year postpartum, and approximately two years postpartum. For presentational simplicity, attachment was rescaled such that the lowest quality attachment level was 0 and the highest quality attachment level was 100. Assuming a linear growth model, the estimated slope and intercept were calculated for each of the children in the sample using SAS Proc Mixed.

The average child in the population was estimated to have an initial attachment level of 59.3 and a slope of −0.24 ($t = -5.28$, df = 522, $p < 0.0001$); thus, on average, the attachment level of the average child in the population was estimated to decline by 0.24 units each month across the period of the study. As reflected in Figure 18.2, the slopes in this sample ranged from −0.71 to 0.21, were distributed approximately normally (Shapiro-Wilk $W = 0.99$, ns), and the estimated population standard deviation in slopes was found to be 0.09. Figure 18.3 presents the linear growth curves of the five children in the sample who reflected the most positive growth curves and the five children in the sample who reflected the most negative growth curves. The heavy line in the middle represents the estimated growth curve of the average child in the population. These results suggest that while attachment to the mother declines across time for the average child with the introduction of a sibling, children vary considerably in their response to this event.

One possible source of this variation may lie in the sex of the older child. In order to pursue this hypothesis, sex of the older child was introduced into the model. Based on

---

[1] The data for this example were graciously provided by Professor Douglas Teti of the University of Maryland at Baltimore County.

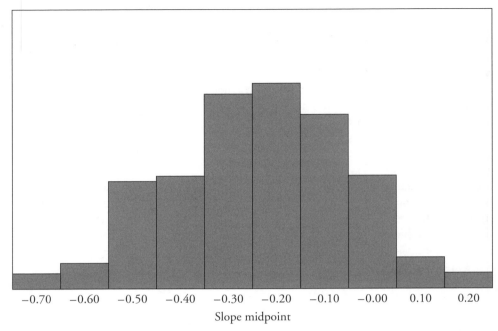

Figure 18.2   Distribution of slopes in the sample.

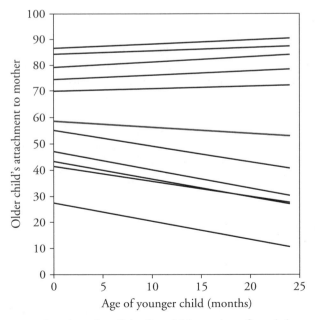

Figure 18.3   Linear growth trajectories of the five children who reflected the most extreme positive slopes and the five children who reflected the most extreme negative slopes. Note: The heavy line represents the average slope.

this analysis, the average slope of the male population was estimated to be −0.11 and the average slope of the female population was estimated to be −0.19. This difference was not found to be statistically significant ($t = -0.96$, df $= 521$, $p > 0.05$), providing no empirical support for the hypothesis that, on average, attachment to the mother declines at different rates for males and females.

Firstborn children's change in attachment to the mother in response to the birth of a sibling might also be related to mothers' perceptions of how adequate their intimate support network is, which was assessed just prior to birth of the sibling. It would be expected that firstborns' attachment to the mother would decline at a steeper rate among mothers with weaker intimate supports than among mothers with stronger supports, as suggested by relations empirically established between security of infant–mother attachment and quality of maternal supports (Belsky, 1999; Jacobson & Frye, 1991). In order to pursue this hypothesis, adequacy of the attachment figures was introduced into the model. Perceived adequacy of maternal attachment figures ranged between 0 (very poor: $n = 2$) and 12 (excellent: $n = 14$), with a mean of 8.2, a median of 9.0, and a standard deviation of 2.8. Based on this analysis, the average slope in child–mother attachment of the population with an adequacy of 0 was estimated to be −0.50; the average slope in child–mother attachment of the population with an adequacy of 12 was estimated to be −0.11. More specifically, a one-unit increase in mothers' perceptions of adequacy of intimate support was associated with a 0.03 increase in the slope; this effect was found to be statistically significant ($t = 2.07$, df $= 510$, $p < 0.05$). Thus, there is convincing evidence that the rate at which firstborns' quality of attachment to the mother declines with the advent of the first sibling may be slower for children of mothers with more adequate intimate supports (see Figure 18.4).

The requisite assumptions underlying the statistical tests employed in a latent growth analysis are similar to those associated with the t- and F-test in a general linear model framework. Specifically, the error terms (e_{ij}) are assumed to be independent, identically distributed (iid) normal random variables with a mean of 0 and a variance of σ^2. Additionally, the error terms associated with the intercept (r_{0j}) and the slope (r_{1j}) are assumed to be multivariate normal with zero means and variances/covariances of:

$$\begin{pmatrix} \tau_{00} & \tau_{01} \\ \tau_{10} & \tau_{11} \end{pmatrix}$$

In practice, these are usually reasonable assumptions. In the current example, it is reasonable to assume that fewer and fewer children will reflect a slope that is farther and farther away from the average slope (after controlling for adequacy of maternal attachment figures). Similarly, it is reasonable to assume that increasingly fewer children will reflect an intercept that is increasingly farther away from the average intercept (again, after controlling for adequacy of mothers' attachment figures). With respect to any particular child, his or her observed attachment at any given time point is likely to be relatively close to his or her growth trajectory line, with only occasional large departures.

Although the existence of this effect is of potential research importance in its own right, of additional interest is the question of magnitude: how *large* is the effect of

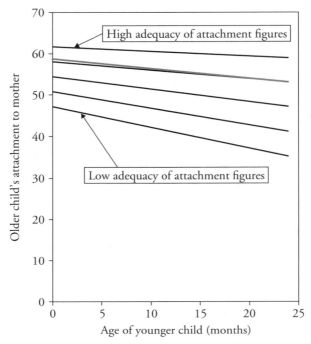

Figure 18.4   Linear growth trajectories in firstborn–mother attachment as a function of mothers' perceptions of the adequacy of their attachment figures.

adequacy of maternal attachment figures? One method for addressing this question is to compare the estimated variance in slopes before and after controlling for perceived adequacy of attachment. The estimated variance in slopes before controlling for adequacy of attachment was found to be 0.08876; the estimated variance in slopes after controlling for adequacy of attachment was found to be 0.07939. Thus, the introduction of adequacy of maternal attachment figures resulted in an 11 percent decrease in the variation in slopes.

Note that this is *not* the equivalent of the traditional R^2. This percentage only addresses the fraction of *explainable* variation that is explained. If the amount of original variation in slopes is small, then we are explaining 11 percent of very little. The unavailability of an R^2 equivalent is an unavoidable limitation of mixed-effect models in general, and of latent growth models in particular; see Snijders and Bosker (1994) for a fuller discussion on this issue.

Generalizations and Elaborations

Latent growth analysis provides for a number of important elaborations on the initial level presented here. For example, the investigator might have reason to suspect a nonlinear trajectory pattern; in the present context, perhaps most of the decline in attachment occurs shortly after the birth of the sibling, with attachment "leveling off" after a few months. Perhaps the investigator wishes to extend the hierarchical structure beyond the simple two-level model presented here; for example, suppose the effect on attachment of mothers' perceptions of how adequate their intimate support network is varies as a function of age of the mother. These represent straightforward generalizations of the basic model which can be easily accommodated by a latent growth analysis model.

When should the investigator consider employing a latent growth approach to the analysis of longitudinal data? An obvious advantage to this approach accrues to situations in which subjects vary either in terms of the number of observations or of the intervals between observations (or both). Under these circumstances, the requisite assumptions of the classical repeated measures ANOVA or MANOVA would be at least somewhat untenable.

However, it should be emphasized that the latent growth approach also requires adherence to a set of assumptions. For example, a common mathematical form that characterizes all subjects must be assumed: linear and quadratic polynomial forms are most frequently employed. Furthermore, the error terms are assumed to be normally distributed – and the r error terms must be uncorrelated with e.

These assumptions notwithstanding, it is clear that, with the introduction of latent growth analysis procedures into major statistical computing packages, the door has been opened for testing models which were, until very recently, methodologically intractable. Because of the centrality of longitudinal analyses in developmental science, this approach would appear to add another important methodological tool to the developmental scientist's arsenal.

Note

Correspondence concerning this report should be addressed to Philip W. Wirtz, Department of Management Science, George Washington University, 2115 G Street, NW, #403, Washington, DC 20015, USA. Electronic mail may be sent to pww@gwu.edu.

References

Belsky, J. (1999). Infant–parent attachment. In L. Balter & C. S. Tamis-LeMonda (eds.), *Child psychology: A handbook of contemporary issues* (pp. 45–63). Philadelphia, PA: Psychology Press/ Taylor & Francis.

Collier, R. O., Baker, F. B., Mandeville, G. K., & Hayes, T. F. (1967). Estimates of test size for several test procedures based on conventional variance ratios in the repeated measures design. *Psychometrika, 32*, 339–53.

Dempster, A. P., Laird, N. M., & Rubin, D. B. (1977). Maximum likelihood from incomplete data via the EM algorithm (with discussion). *Journal of the Royal Statistical Society, B39*, 1–38.

Girden, E. R. (1992). *ANOVA: Repeated measures* (Sage university paper series on quantitative applications in the social sciences, 84). Newbury Park, CA: Sage.

Greenhouse, S. W. & Geisser, S. (1959). On methods in the analysis of profile data. *Psychometrika*, *24*, 95–112.

Huynh, H. & Feldt, L. S. (1976). Estimation of the Box correction for degrees of freedom from sample data in randomised block and split-plot designs. *Journal of Educational Statistics, 1(1)*, 69–82.

Jacobson, S. W. & Frye, K. F. (1991). Effect of maternal social support on attachment: Experimental evidence. *Child Development, 62(3)*, 572–82.

Kreft, I. G., de Leeuw, J., & van der Leeden, R. (1994). Review of five multilevel analysis programs: BMDP-5V, GENMOD, HLM, ML3, VARCL. *The American Statistician, 48*, 324–35.

Maxwell, S. E. & Delaney, H. D. (2000). *Designing experiments and analyzing data*. Belmont, CA: Wadsworth.

Mendoza, J. L., Toothaker, L. E., & Crain, B. R. (1976). Necessary and sufficient conditions for F ratios in L × J × K factorial design with two repeated factors. *Journal of the American Statistical Association, 71*, 992–3.

Rouanet, H. & Lépine, D. (1970). Comparison between treatments in a repeated-measurements design: Anova and multivariate methods. *British Journal of Mathematical and Statistical Psychology, 23*, 147–63.

Snijders, T. A. B. & Bosker, R. J. (1994). Modeled variance in two-level models. *Sociological Methods and Research, 22(3)*, 342–63.

Stevens, J. (1992). *Applied multivariate statistics for the social sciences* (2nd edn.). Hillsdale, NJ: Lawrence Erlbaum Associates.

Ware, J. H. (1985). Linear models for the analysis of longitudinal studies. *American Statistician, 39(2)*, 95–101.

Waters, E. (1995). Appendix A: The Attachment Qset (Version 3.0). In E. Waters, B. E. Vaughn, G. Posada, & K. Kondo-Ikemura (eds.), *Caregiving, cultural, and cognitive perspectives on secure-base behavior and working models: New growing points of attachment theory and research. Monographs of the Society for Research in Child Development, 60* (nos. 2–3, serial no. 244), 234–46.

CHAPTER NINETEEN

Interdependence in Development: Data Analytic Strategies for Dyadic Designs

Deborah A. Kashy and Jennifer G. Boldry

One-on-one relationships with other people are integral to individual development. Such relationships typically begin with parents and progress to include other family members, peers, teachers, and eventually intimate partners. Indeed, perspectives on social and emotional development are rife with examples of the importance of interdependence in the developmental process. Consider the transactional model of development (Sameroff & Chandler, 1975), which argues that development is a complex function of the mutual, ongoing contributions of caregiver and child. In addition, although they suggest different processes, social learning theory (Bandura, 1977), psychoanalytic theories (Blos, 1967; Freud, 1949), and interdependence theory (Kelley, 1979; Kelley & Thibaut, 1978) all recognize the fundamental influence that ongoing reciprocal interactions with significant others have on an individual's development.

Developmental researchers often collect complex data sets. For example, Furman and Buhrmester (1992) investigated children's perceptions of their support networks. In this study, 4th grade students, 7th grade students, 10th grade students, and college-age students rated several components of their relationships with their mothers, fathers, oldest brothers, youngest brothers, oldest sisters, youngest sisters, grandparents, closest same-sex friends, and romantic partners. The authors were able to answer several interesting questions about age differences in children's perceptions of their relationships. However, because data were only collected from the children, questions about the interdependence of perceptions between parents and children were left unanswered. For example, how do mothers' perceptions of their relationships with their children impact children's perceptions of their relationships with their mothers? These data and others like them present numerous opportunities to further our understanding of how individuals influence one another throughout the developmental process. However, in order for the data to be used to their full potential, we must develop and apply data analytic tools explicitly designed to model the complex web of interdependence inherent in such data. In this chapter we describe several models especially designed to explore reciprocal dyadic processes. Data analytic techniques for dyadic research vary substantially depending on the nature of the observations. A critical question is whether each dyad generates one or two scores for each variable. For example, in Haviland and Lelwica's (1987) investigation of infants' reactions to their mothers, the central outcome variables (e.g., mouthing behavior, joy, interest) were measured only for the infants, and the predictor variables (affective states) were observed only for the mothers. Thus, every dyad generated only one score for each variable. Single scores for each dyad can also occur when the observation of interest is an emergent property of the dyad. For example, Strough and Berg (2000) observed interactions among pre-adolescents and recorded the proportion of high affiliation conversational exchanges in each dyad as a whole.

In cases for which only a single outcome score is observed for each dyad or each group (e.g., family or peer group), the data analytic strategy is straightforward, and traditional data analytic techniques, such as regression or ANOVA, can be applied. The dyad or group is treated as the unit of analysis, so the effective sample size is the number of dyads (or groups), not the number of individuals. For example, Strough and Berg (2000) used ANOVA to test whether the gender composition of the dyad (boys, girls, mixed) affected dyadic affiliation behavior. Indeed, traditional analytic techniques are appropriate for any analysis that focuses on only one member of a dyad or group (e.g., an ANOVA using an index of family functioning to predict adolescent social behavior in families with only one adolescent).

Cases for which each dyad member generates an observation on each variable present greater data analytic challenges. Such a situation might have occurred in Strough and Berg (2000) if they had measured the number of affiliative statements made by each child in a dyad rather than the number of affiliative exchanges made in a dyadic interaction. For an additional example, consider a sibling study in which both children report on the quality of their relationship with one another.

A further complication occurs in dyadic research when each individual participates as a member of multiple dyads, as is often the case in family and peer group contexts. For example, in a study of 32 four-person families, researchers videotaped every dyadic combination within the family (e.g., mother–infant, mother–preschooler, father–infant, and so on, with the exception of mother–father) and coded each person's play behavior (Stevenson et al., 1988). Similarly, in a study of 208 four-person families, each family member reported on his or her attachment style with every other family member (Cook, 2000). Examples of individuals participating in multiple dyads with peer research abound. For example, in Asher and Dodge (1986) as well as Parker and Asher (1993), every child in a class rated how much he or she liked to play with every other member of the class.

Another important issue in dyadic data analysis is whether there is a natural distinction between the two dyad members. If dyad members can be distinguished by a nonarbitrary variable such as gender (i.e., each dyad is comprised of one boy and one girl) then dyad members are said to be *distinguishable*. In the case of gender, boys' scores can be treated as observations on variable "X" and girls' scores can be treated as observations on variable "Y." Family relationships, in which each individual is identifiable by his or her family role (mother, father, oldest child, and so on), represent additional examples of distinguishable dyads. In this instance, the data generated by the mother in mother–oldest child dyads can be treated as "X" scores and the data generated by the oldest child can be treated as "Y" scores. However, there are many cases for which dyad members are not distinguishable. In developmental contexts, these cases arise most often in peer and friendship research. In the case of nondistinguishable dyads, assignment of individuals' scores as "X" or "Y" is arbitrary. Distinguishability of dyad members plays an important role in determining the appropriate data analytic approach.

In this chapter we explore the data analytic challenges involved in developmental research with dyads when both dyad members contribute outcome scores. In the first section of the chapter we discuss analytic strategies for data generated when both members of a dyad provide separate outcome scores, but each individual participates in only one dyad. In this section we touch on power and Type I error concerns that follow from the nonindependence typically inherent in this type of data. We then describe traditional techniques that are applicable to dyadic data analysis for some types of independent variables. Finally, we briefly introduce two new approaches for dyadic data analysis. The actor–partner interdependence model (Kashy & Kenny, 2000) illustrates how dyad members can influence both their own, and their partner's behavior. The second approach separates dyadic relationships into individual-level processes and dyad-level processes (Griffen & Gonzalez, 1995; Gonzalez & Griffin, 1999).

In the second part of the chapter, we turn our attention to instances in which each individual is a member of multiple dyads. We first introduce the social relations model (SRM; Kenny, 1994) when individuals in the group are not distinguishable, as is the case with peer groups. We then turn to the case when individuals within the group have distinct roles, as is the case in families. Because the data analytic methods that we describe are often computationally complex, we generally refrain from providing exact formulas and instead limit ourselves to providing sources when appropriate.

When Individuals Participate in Only One Dyad

In this section we discuss methods for analyzing dyadic data when each individual is a member of only one dyad, but both dyad members provide scores on the variables of interest. Consider a fictitious study of 100 non-twin sibling dyads. In the study, researchers collect a measure of attachment security from each child as well as a measure of how much each child enjoys spending time with his or her sibling. Some of the sibling dyads are same-sex and some are opposite-sex. In addition, imagine that half of the dyads come from dysfunctional families and the other half come from families that are not dysfunctional.

There are three types of variables represented in this example. Whether or not the siblings come from dysfunctional families is a *between-dyads* variable because both members of a dyad have the same score and so it varies only from dyad to dyad. Birth order (older or younger sibling) is a *within-dyads* variable because every dyad has one older sibling and one younger sibling. Within-dyad variables vary only within the dyad so that the dyad average is constant across dyads. Attachment security is a *mixed variable* because it varies both within dyads and between dyads, such that one child may be more secure than the other in some dyads, and some sibling pairs may have higher security on average than other sibling pairs. Gender is also a mixed variable because some dyads are same sex (boy–boy, girl–girl) and others are opposite sex (boy–girl). Note that the outcome measure (enjoyment) is also mixed, as is almost always the case.

Assessing nonindependence

Assessing the degree to which data from the two dyad members are related is one of the first steps in analyzing dyadic data. If dyad members are distinguishable, then the Pearson correlation between the two dyad members' outcomes scores provides a measure of nonindependence. In our example, the older sibling's enjoyment score might be assigned to be X and the younger sibling's enjoyment score would be Y. A significant correlation between X and Y, using a liberal alpha level for the statistical test of the correlation (an alpha of 0.20 is often recommended; e.g., Myers, 1979), indicates nonindependence.

If dyad members are indistinguishable, as is often the case with friendship dyads or twins, a Pearson correlation is not an appropriate measure of nonindependence because assignment of the dyad members to X and Y is arbitrary. Researchers sometimes use random assignment to categorize individuals as X or Y; however, any other random assignment would result in a different value for the Pearson correlation. In this case, the best measure of nonindependence is an intraclass correlation. This type of correlation provides a unique indicator of the strength of the relationship between scores for individuals who are indistinguishable. The intraclass correlation can be computed using an ANOVA-based technique (e.g., Kashy & Kenny, 2000) or a correlational technique (Griffin & Gonzalez, 1995).

Some common errors in dyadic data analysis

One common approach to analyzing data when individuals participate in only one dyad is to ignore the dyads altogether and treat the data as if it came from $2N$ individuals where N is the number of dyads in the study. For our example, a person's security, gender, birth order, and family status would predict his or her enjoyment (a sophisticated data analyst might even use the person's sibling's security as a predictor). Such an analysis treats the data as if there were 200 observations in the data set. This approach violates the independence assumption upon which most regression techniques, as well as other inferential tests such as ANOVA, are based because ratings of enjoyment are likely to be related within sibling pairs (i.e., if one child enjoys spending time with his or her sibling, it is more likely that the sibling also enjoys spending time with the child). Kenny and his colleagues (1995; Kenny, Kashy, & Bolger, 1998) have demonstrated that if the relationship between dyad members' outcome scores is positive, then significance tests tend to be overly liberal when the individual is erroneously treated as the unit of analysis. On the other hand, if the relationship between the dyad members' outcome scores is negative, then significance tests tend to be conservative and a loss of power occurs.

Another common approach is to average the dyad members' scores on each variable, and compute the analysis based on the dyad means. Thus, mean security, mean gender, and family status would predict mean enjoyment. Although this approach is not problematic in terms of the assumptions and is appropriate if all of the independent variables are between dyads, it is wasteful in terms of the effects of mixed independent variables because individual variation is lost. In addition, the correlations between averaged variables may be quite different from those obtained using each individual's scores (Gonzalez & Griffin, 1997).

Analysis of between-dyad independent variables

If all of the independent (or predictor) variables in a study vary only between dyads, appropriate data analytic techniques are straightforward. In this case, an average of the outcome variable is computed for each dyad by averaging over the two dyad members' scores, and that average score serves as the dependent (or outcome) variable in all analyses. Thus, if the independent variable is categorical or qualitative, independent groups *t*-tests or ANOVAs can test for the effects of the independent variables.[1] If the only independent variable of interest in our example were family dysfunction status, we would compute the average enjoyment score for each dyad, and then treat those averages as outcome scores in an independent groups *t*-test. If the independent variable is quantitative, a regression approach is appropriate. That is, the dyad average on the outcome serves as the criterion and the between-dyads independent variable serves as the predictor.

Analysis of within-dyad independent variables

If the independent variable of interest varies only within dyads, the approach is slightly different. If the variable is categorical, as is the case for the within-dyads variable in our example (birth order), we could simply use a correlated groups *t*-test, treating dyad as the unit of analysis.

If the within-dyads variable is continuous, a regression approach is appropriate. For example, if we measured the proportion of time spent talking by each child in a videotaped conversation between the two siblings, we would have a quantitative within-dyads variable (i.e., the sibling's proportions vary within a dyad, but for each dyad, the total is 1.0). Two difference scores are computed from these data: the difference between the dyad members' scores on the predictor variable (proportion of time spent talking) and the difference between the dyad members' scores on the outcome (enjoyment). The difference score on the predictor is then used in a regression predicting the difference

---

[1]   Note that using the dyad mean as the outcome is equivalent to treating dyad as a nested variable in an ANOVA. In this model there are three sources of variation: A (the independent variable), D/A (dyads nested within levels of the independent variable), and S/D/A (subjects within dyads). The test of the independent variable is conducted using the $MS_{D/A}$ as the error term. Note that the test of D/A, using the $MS_{S/D/A}$ as the error term, is actually the test of whether there is statistically significant nonindependence.

score on the outcome. Note that it is very important to be consistent in the direction of differencing across the two variables (i.e., if the predictor is differenced A − B then the outcome should also be computed as A − B). If the dyads are distinguishable, as in our example, and the differencing of both variables is done as older sibling minus younger sibling, then the intercept estimates the mean difference between the two dyad members' scores. In our example, the intercept reflects the mean difference in enjoyment for older versus younger siblings. If the dyads are not distinguishable, then the regression should be computed suppressing the intercept because the order of the differencing is arbitrary (see Kashy & Kenny, 2000).

Analysis of mixed independent variables

In this section, we describe two data analytic techniques appropriate for the study of dyadic data when individuals participate in only one dyad and the independent variable is mixed. Not only do these methods adjust for the statistical assumption of independence, they both explicitly model the interdependence between dyad members. The first approach is the actor–partner interdependence model (Kashy & Kenny, 2000; Kenny & Cook, 1999), and the second is a levels-of-analysis approach (Griffin & Gonzalez, 1995; Gonzalez & Griffin, 1999).

The actor–partner interdependence model   The actor-partner interdependence model (APIM; Kashy & Kenny, 2000; Kenny & Cook, 1999) is a generalization of a technique first proposed by Kraemer and Jacklin (1979) to study the effects of gender on play behavior. Kraemer and Jacklin observed play behavior in pairs of same- and opposite-sex children. These authors were interested in determining if a child's gender affected whether that child offered a toy to another child, and whether a toy was offered to him or her. They described the *actor effect* as reflecting how an individual's independent variable affects that individual's outcome variable, and the *partner effect* as reflecting how an individual's independent variable affects his or her partner's outcome variable. Specifically, the actor effect measures whether girls or boys were more likely to offer toys to others and the partner effect measures whether girls or boys were more likely to be offered toys.

Although Kraemer and Jacklin's (1979) approach was intuitively appealing, it was not widely applied. The model was restricted in potential applicability in part because it was initially limited to univariate analyses, and in part because it required that the independent variable be dichotomous. Building on Kraemer and Jacklin's model, the APIM is a multivariate solution that allows for both categorical and continuous predictor variables.

The APIM partitions the effects of any mixed predictor variable into actor and partner effects. In our sibling example, we can address whether a child's own level of attachment security predicts how much he or she enjoys spending time with his or her sibling (the actor effect). We can also determine whether a child's own level of attachment security predicts how much the sibling enjoys spending time with that child (the partner effect). Because gender is a mixed predictor variable in this example, we can also determine whether a person's gender affects his or her enjoyment as well as his or her sibling's enjoyment. In this analysis, we can further test whether family dysfunction or birth order interacts with either the actor or partner effect.

There are several approaches to estimating the APIM. The most versatile analysis technique uses multilevel modeling and is described in detail by Campbell and Kashy (2002). These authors provide a thorough description of how to estimate the APIM parameters using the statistical programs PROC MIXED (in SAS) and HLM5 (Raudenbush et al., 2001).

There are two alternatives to the multilevel modeling approach. The first alternative is a pooled regression technique that involves computing two regressions and then combining the results to estimate and test the actor and partner effects. Kashy and Kenny (2000) provide the details of this approach, including the calculation of actor and partner effects, pooled standard error, degrees of freedom, and statistical significance tests. This approach can be used with any statistical software package, and it can also be used for dyads that are not distinguishable as well as for those that are distinguishable. The pooled regression approach has the disadvantage of requiring hand computations to arrive at the final estimates and test statistics.

The final alternative is a structural equation modeling approach that can be applied only when dyad members are distinguishable, and is discussed by Kenny (1996). This method allows for direct tests of equality between the actor and partner effects, and does not require hand calculations.

Separating individual and dyadic effects An alternative approach to the analysis of mixed variables is presented by Griffin and Gonzalez (1995; Gonzalez & Griffin, 1999). These authors propose that the overall relationship between two mixed variables (variables that vary both between and within dyads) can be broken into two components: an individual-level correlation and a dyad-level correlation. The individual-level correlation measures the extent to which one dyad member's unique tendency on one variable relates to that individual's unique tendency on a second variable. So in the attachment security/enjoyment example, the individual-level correlation measures the extent to which one sibling's unique level of security relates to that same sibling's unique level of enjoyment. The dyad-level correlation measures the degree to which the two individuals' shared tendency or similarity on one variable relates to their shared tendency or similarity on a second variable. For the example, the dyad-level correlation would measure the degree to which the two individuals' similarity on attachment security relates to their similarity on enjoyment. This method is appropriate for both nondistinguishable dyads (Griffin & Gonzalez, 1995) and distinguishable dyads (Gonzalez & Griffin, 1999).

Research in which individuals are members of a single dyad holds a great deal of promise for the study of developmental issues. However, much of development occurs in relationships that exist within the context of a larger group – most notably family and peer groups. We now turn to data analytic strategies applicable to contexts in which individuals belong to multiple dyads within a group.

When Individuals Participate in Multiple Dyads

Multiple dyad designs occur in many forms (see Kenny, 1990 for a thorough discussion). One of the most common is a round-robin pattern in which every member of a group is paired with every other group member. Consider an example of a round-robin design in which researchers videotape each child in a playgroup interacting with every other child in the playgroup. In this example, researchers might observe the number of times each child exhibits verbal or physical aggression toward another child. Imagine that there are four children in a playgroup: **Anne**, **Bobby**, **Cindy**, and **David**. Researchers could videotape Anne's interactions with B, C, and D, and record the number of times each child exhibits aggression. Similarly, researchers could videotape Bobby's interactions with A, C, and D, and so on. Thus, there would be 6 separate dyadic combinations, each generating two data points (e.g., A's aggression toward B and B's aggression toward A) to result in a total of 12 aggressiveness scores (AB, AC, AD, BA, BC, BD, CA, CB, CD, DA, DB, and DC). To round out this hypothetical study, imagine that after the videotaped interactions, each child rates the degree to which he or she likes every other child in the group.

The social relations model for nondistinguishable dyads

The social relations model (SRM) is a general model of dyadic behavior, applicable to a number of multiple-dyad data structures, including the round-robin design. This model suggests that dyadic behavior is a function of the general tendencies that each individual brings to the dyad as well as the unique interaction that occurs between the two individuals. At heart, the SRM is a variance decomposition model that partitions the variation in dyadic scores into individual-level and dyad-level effects. Correlations among these effects can address important questions in development or other fields. Note that in this discussion of the SRM we use an example in which individuals within the group are not distinguishable.

The SRM proposes that any dyadic score (e.g., the number of times Anne aggresses against Bobby), can be broken into four components: the group mean, the actor effect, the partner effect, and the relationship effect. The *group mean* reflects the average level of a variable in a particular playgroup. For example, some groups may exhibit higher levels of aggressiveness than others. The *actor effect* assesses the degree to which a person's behavior is consistent across all of his or her partners. For example, does Anne act aggressively toward every other child in the group? The *partner effect* measures the degree to which a person elicits similar behavior from all others. For example, does everyone in the playgroup tend to aggress against Bobby?[2] Both actor and partner effects are individual-level effects. The *relationship effect* is inherently dyadic in that it refers to both Anne and Bobby, and measures the degree to which aggressiveness is a function of the unique relationship between two people. Anne's relationship effect with Bobby reflects the degree to which she aggresses against Bobby uniquely, more than she typically aggresses against others and more than Bobby is typically aggressed against by others.

As a second example, consider the meaning of the SRM components when children in our hypothetical study rate how much they like one another. For instance, in Anne's

---

[2]   Note that in the SRM the definitions of actor and partner effects differ from those introduced earlier in the description of the APIM.

rating of how much she likes Bobby, the group mean effect reflects the average rating of liking in the group (members of some groups may like one another more than members of other groups). The actor effect measures Anne's tendency to like everyone, the partner effect measures Bobby's tendency to be liked by everyone, and the relationship effect measures the degree to which Anne uniquely likes Bobby – more than she likes others and more than others like him. Note that for rating data, the actor effect is sometimes referred to as a rater effect and the partner effect is referred to as a target effect.

When only one set of ratings or observations per dyad is collected, relationship effects are confounded with error. It is possible to separate the true relationship effect from error if there are replications for each variable. For observational data, observing each dyad on more than one occasion provides multiple replications. For rating data, ratings on multiple indicators of each dimension provide multiple replications. When there are replications, estimates of the relationship effect are more precise because consistencies across observations or ratings are attributed to the relationship component and the inconsistencies are attributed to error.

Applications of the SRM

The SRM provides a novel method of addressing several important questions about dyadic behavior that are relevant to social development. Partitioning behavior into individual-level and dyad-level components allows us to determine the locus of the behavior. For example, we could determine the degree to which aggressive behavior is an individual difference variable. That is, it may be that some individuals are more aggressive than others (i.e., there are some bullies in the group). Large amounts of actor variance in aggression would indicate such behavioral consistencies. It may also be that some individuals are "victims" such that they consistently elicit aggression from everyone. Large amounts of partner variance would support such a hypothesis. Finally, aggressiveness may be an emergent property of the dyad so that interactions between two children may be aggressive regardless of the children's individual aggressive tendencies. Large amounts of relationship variance would suggest that aggressiveness is attributable to the dyad rather than the individuals who comprise the dyad.

When a behavior has a large individual component (i.e., there is a large degree of actor and/or partner variance) it may be theoretically meaningful to investigate dispositional correlates. In particular, we can correlate actor and partner effects with any individual-level variable. For instance, it may be that children who are more aggressive have lower self-esteem. A negative correlation between self-esteem and the actor effect for aggression would indicate such an effect. Similarly, a negative correlation between self-esteem and the partner effect for aggression would reflect that children who are consistently the targets of aggression have relatively low self-esteem.

The SRM also allows us to explore two types of reciprocity: generalized and dyadic reciprocity. At the individual level, *generalized reciprocity* measures whether aggressive children are more likely to be aggressed against by others. The correlation between an individual's actor effect on aggression and his or her partner effect on aggression provides an index of generalized reciprocity. *Dyadic reciprocity* measures whether when one child is especially aggressive against a second child, that second child is especially aggressive in return. The correlation between the relationship effects for the two dyad members (i.e., AB with BA) provides an index of dyadic reciprocity.

The SRM provides methods for assessing a number of other effects (see Kenny, 1994 for a thorough discussion). When analyzing ratings rather than observed behaviors, the variance in the actor effects provides an estimate of *assimilation* (i.e., the degree to which perceivers tend to see all targets as alike; perceiver A sees B, C, and D as highly likeable, but perceiver B sees A, C, and D as rather unlikable). The partner variance measures *consensus* (i.e., the degree to which perceivers agree in their perceptions of targets; perceivers A, B, and C agree that D is likeable, and perceivers A, C, and D agree that B is not likeable). Self-ratings can be correlated with actor and partner effects to measure *assumed similarity* (i.e., do I see others as I see myself?) and *self–other agreement* (i.e., do others see me as I see myself?), respectively.

We can address several additional questions when multiple variables are included in the same SRM study. For example, we can explore whether there is a relationship between partner effects in liking and partner effects in aggression. A negative correlation between these two partner effects in our hypothetical study would indicate that a person who is generally disliked by all group members is frequently aggressed upon by the other group members. Similarly, we could correlate relationship effects across variables to examine whether, if one child especially dislikes another, he or she exhibits especially high levels of aggression toward that child.

A particularly interesting multiple variable example arises if metaperception data are collected. Imagine that in addition to asking the children how much they like each other child in their playgroup, we also ask them how much they think each child in the group likes them. This metaperception data can also be broken into actor, partner, and relationship effects. The actor effect measures the degree to which a child thinks everyone likes him or her. The partner effect indicates the degree to which everyone thinks that a particular child likes them. The relationship effect measures the degree to which a child thinks that a particular child likes him or her, over and above the actor and partner effects. In addition to examining the variance partitioning for metaperception data, we can also address questions of meta-accuracy with such data. *Generalized meta-accuracy* measures whether a child who thinks everyone likes him or her is in fact liked by everyone. *Dyadic meta-accuracy* measures whether children know who in particular likes them and who does not.

The SRM has been used in a number of studies exploring developmental phenomena. For example, Malloy et al. (1996) explored agreement between self, peers, and teachers in perceptions of attractiveness, ability, and popularity in a three-year longitudinal study. Scarpati, Malloy, and Fleming (1996) studied attributions of skill efficacy and self-control among adolescents with learning disabilities. Ross and Lollis (1989) investigated conflict in toddler peer interactions, and Whitley, Schofield, and Snyder (1984) examined peer preferences across black and white children in a desegregated school.

The SOREMO statistical program (Kenny, 1999) analyzes round-robin data structures with group members who are not distinguishable. Although a detailed discussion of how to estimate the SRM components is beyond the scope of this chapter, the reader can consult Kashy and Kenny (2000) for a detailed example or Kenny and La Voie (1984) for details on the estimation of SRM parameters.

Although the SRM is designed for interval or ratio data, it can be used for other types of data. In the case of ranking data (e.g., if children ranked their peers in terms of popularity), the actor variance will be 0 because each individual by necessity provides the exact same range of responses. For example, when children in a 30-person class rank their peers, the values range from 1 to 29 for every "rater." There is little research examining the stability of SRM estimates with dichotomous data (e.g. if children nominate who in their class is popular); consequently, we suggest using an interval or ratio level of measurement whenever possible.

The SRM with families

One of the areas for which the SRM holds the greatest promise for developmental science is in research with families. Family relationships naturally fall into a round-robin form such that a person may have separate, but related relationships with his or her mother, father, and sibling(s). The SRM provides a method for modeling a number of patterns of interdependence within families. For example, there may be intragenerational similarities (Kashy & Kenny, 1990) such that parents are especially similar to one another (e.g., they perceive others in the same way or they are perceived by others in the same way) and siblings are likewise similar. It may also be the case that interdependence occurs as a function of the person's gender (e.g., mothers and daughters may be especially similar).

Typically, the SRM derives parameter estimates by pooling across nondistinguishable individuals (e.g., peers), first within groups and then across groups to estimate general levels of actor, partner, and relationship variance. If group members are distinguishable from one another on a nonarbitrary basis, as is the case with family members, pooling within the group (family) is not appropriate. Instead, the SRM for families estimates the variance components separately for each family role (e.g., mother, father, son, daughter), allowing us to glean important information about the interrelationships between family members.

As an example, consider a study of perceived social support within families in which there is an adolescent (A), a pre-adolescent (P), a mother (M), and a father (F). In this study, each family member reports on the degree to which they perceive every other family member as supportive. Thus, the adolescent provides three data points: how supportive the adolescent perceives the pre-adolescent to be (AP), how supportive the adolescent perceives the mother to be (AM), and how supportive the adolescent perceives the father to be (AF). Likewise, the pre-adolescent provides PA, PM, and PF. The mother and father provide similar data, resulting in a total of 12 data points.

For families (or any group in which the individuals fall into distinguishable roles) the SRM partitions the dyadic data into a family mean, separate actor and partner effects for each role, and relationship effects for each combination of roles. In our example, there will be an actor effect for the adolescent, estimating the degree to which the adolescent tends to see all family members as supportive. The adolescent will also have a partner effect that estimates the degree to which the adolescent is seen as supportive (or unsupportive) by all family members. In addition, there will be three relationship effects for the adolescent, one with each family member (AP, AM, AF). The adolescent–pre-adolescent relationship effect (AP), for example, measures the degree to which the adolescent sees his or her younger sibling as especially supportive (more supportive than he or she sees other family members, and more supportive than other family members see the pre-adolescent). Likewise, there will be actor and partner effects for the mother, father, and pre-adolescent, as well as relationship effects for each combination. The family mean is simply the average supportiveness score for the entire family.

The SRM for families pools data across families to estimate the actor, partner, and relationship variances for each role or combination of roles. Thus, a great deal of actor variance for the adolescent role would indicate that in some families the adolescent sees all family members as highly supportive, whereas in other families the adolescent sees all family members as unsupportive. High levels of partner variance for the adolescent would indicate that in some families, the adolescent is generally seen as supportive but in others he or she is seen as unsupportive. High levels of relationship variance would suggest that supportiveness is a dyadic construct and depends on who is involved in the relationship.

Applications of the SRM to families

The SRM variance partitioning can provide a great deal of information about family patterns and interrelationships. Simply examining the degree to which the variance in the data lies at the family mean level, the individual (actor and partner) level, and the dyad level can be theoretically important. It may be that social support in families is really a dyadic phenomenon. It may also be that some roles show greater individual-level variance than others. For example, all mothers may be seen as supportive (so there is little partner variance for mothers) whereas some fathers are seen as very supportive but others are seen as very unsupportive.

Correlations among the actor and partner effects can also be informative. For example, a significant correlation between the partner effects for mothers and fathers would indicate that parents are seen as having similar supportive styles. Similarly, a significant correlation between the actor effects for adolescents and pre-adolescents would suggest that children view their family members in a similar way. Generalized reciprocity can also be estimated separately for each role. The correlation between the adolescent's actor effect and his or her partner effect might indicate that adolescents who see family members as more unsupportive tend to be seen as unsupportive themselves. It is also possible to estimate dyadic reciprocity for each combination of roles (e.g., if an adolescent sees his or her mother as especially unsupportive, does the mother reciprocate that view?).

The SRM for families also allows us to examine relationships between the various effects and general measures of family functioning (e.g., the McMaster Family Assessment Device: Epstein, Baldwin, & Bishop, 1983; or the Family Adaptability and Cohesion Evaluation Scales: Olson, 1986). If such data were collected in our hypothetical social support example, we could determine whether families that are more supportive are better functioning (the correlation between the family mean on supportiveness and the measure of family functioning). We could also explore whether the partner effects for the various roles show differential correlations with measures of functioning. For example, a strong correlation between the mother's partner effect on supportiveness and functioning, in conjunction with relatively weak correlations between the other partner effects and family functioning would indicate that the supportiveness of the mother is the most critical factor in determining functioning, and that how supportive or unsupportive the other family members are is less important. In addition to family-level variables, we can also correlate individual difference variables with the various effects.

The SRM with families' has been used to study play behavior in families with infants and toddlers (Stevenson et al., 1988), affective style (Cook, Kenny, & Goldstein, 1991), and interpersonal control (Cook, 1993). Additionally, Manke and Plomin (1997) used the SRM to examine the relative contributions of genetic heritage versus environmental factors in the development of personal style.

A latent variable approach typically accomplishes the actual estimation of the SRM components for families (see Kashy, Jellison, & Kenny, 2004; Kashy & Kenny, 1990; Cook, 1994 for greater detail; see also chapter 17 in this volume). In this confirmatory factor analysis method, each dyadic score is treated as an indicator of two latent factors – an actor factor and a partner factor. For example, the AM rating of supportiveness is treated as an indicator of the adolescent actor factor and the mother partner factor. Similarly, the AF rating is an indicator of the adolescent actor factor and the father partner factor. The relationship variance is the variation in dyadic scores not explained by the latent factors. Like the general SRM, the relationship effects are confounded with error unless multiple measures are obtained for each dyad.

Conclusion

This chapter introduces several new methodological approaches to developmental researchers. The social relations model offers both a conceptual framework as well as a sophisticated data analytic model for the study of complex dyadic and group relationships. The actor–partner model and levels of analysis approach make a similar contribution. We realize that we have only briefly introduced these models, and hope that readers of this chapter will follow up our discussion by turning to the sources we have cited.

In the 1998 *Handbook of child psychology*, vol. 3, Parke and Buriel argued that researchers must make greater efforts to investigate interdependence in family relationships. They suggest that "Considerable progress has been made in describing the behavior of individual interactants within dyadic and to a lesser extent triadic settings, but less progress has been achieved in developing a language for describing interaction in dyadic or triadic terms" (p. 529). The data analytic approaches described in this chapter offer methods by which researchers can explore the interdependence described by Parke and Buriel. These methodological advancements allow for the investigation of the relationships among family members, friendship dyads and groups, teacher–child relations, and relations with significant others with an emphasis on the interdependence among people.

References

Asher, S. R. & Dodge, K. A. (1986). Identifying children who are rejected by their peers. *Developmental Psychology, 22*, 444–9.

Bandura, A. (1977). Self-efficacy: Toward a unifying theory of behavior change. *Psychological Review, 84*, 191–215.

Blos, P. (1967). *The second individuation process of adolescence: Psychoanalytic study of the child* (vol. 22). New York: International Universities Press.

Campbell, L. J. & Kashy, D. A. (2002). Estimating actor, partner, and interaction effects for dyadic data using PROC MIXED and HLM5: A user-friendly guide. *Personal Relationships, 9*, 327–42.

Cook, W. L. (1993). Interdependence and the interpersonal sense of control: An analysis of family relationships. *Journal of Personality and Social Psychology, 64*, 587–601.

Cook, W. L. (1994). A structural equation model of dyadic relationships within the family system. *Journal of Consulting and Clinical Psychology, 62*, 500–9.

Cook, W. L. (2000). Understanding attachment security in family context. *Journal of Personality and Social Psychology, 78*, 285–94.

Cook, W., Kenny, D. A., & Goldstein, M. J. (1991). Parental affective style risk and the family system: A social relations model analysis. *Journal of Abnormal Psychology, 100*, 492–501.

Epstein, N. B., Baldwin, L. M., & Bishop, D. S. (1983). The McMaster Family Assessment Device. *Journal of Marital and Family Therapy, 9*, 171–80.

Freud, A. (1949). *Psychoanalytic study of the child* (vol. 4). New York: International Universities Press.

Furman, W. & Buhrmester, D. (1992). Age and sex differences in perceptions of networks of personal relationships. *Child Development, 63*, 103–15.

Gonzalez, R. & Griffin, D. (1997). On the statistics of interdependence: Treating dyadic data with respect. In S. Duck (ed.), *Handbook of personal relationships: Theory, research, and interventions* (2nd edn., pp. 271–302). Chichester: John Wiley.

Gonzalez, R. & Griffin, D. (1999). The correlational analysis of dyad-level data in the distinguishable case. *Personal Relationships, 6*, 449–69.

Griffin, D. & Gonzalez R. (1995). Correlational analysis of dyad-level data in the exchangeable case. *Psychological Bulletin, 118*, 430–39.

Haviland, J. M. & Lelwica, M. (1987). The induced affect response: 10-week-old infants' responses to three emotional expressions. *Developmental Psychology, 23*, 97–104.

Kashy, D. A. & Kenny, D. A. (1990). Analysis of family research designs: A model of interdependence. *Communication Research, 17*, 462–82.

Kashy, D. A. & Kenny, D. A. (2000). The analysis of data from dyads and groups. In H. T. Reis & C. M. Judd (eds.), *Handbook of research methods in social psychology* (pp. 451–77). Cambridge: Cambridge University Press.

Kashy, D. A., Jellison, W. A., & Kenny, D. A. (2004). Modeling the interdependence among family members. *Journal of Family Communication, 4*(4).

Kelley, H. H. (1979). *Personal relationships*. Hillsdale, NJ: Lawrence Erlbaum Associates.

Kelley, H. H. & Thibaut, J. W. (1978). *Interpersonal relations: A theory of interdependence.* New York: John Wiley.

Kenny, D. A. (1990). Design issues in dyadic research. In C. Hendrick & M. S. Clark (eds.), *Review of personality and social psychology*, vol. 11: *Research methods in personality and social psychology* (pp. 164–84). Thousand Oaks, CA: Sage.

Kenny, D. A. (1994). *Interpersonal perception: A social relations analysis.* New York: Guilford.

Kenny, D. A. (1995). The effect of nonindependence on significance testing in dyadic research. *Personal Relationships, 2*, 67–75.

Kenny, D. A. (1996). Models of nonindependence in dyadic research. *Journal of Social and Personal Relationships, 13*, 279–94.

Kenny, D. A. (1999). SOREMO [computer program]. http://nw3.nai.net/~dakenny/kenny.htm.

Kenny, D. A. & Cook, W. (1999). Partner effects in relationship research: Conceptual issues, analytic difficulties, and illustrations. *Personal Relationships, 6*, 433–48.

Kenny, D. A. & La Voie, L. (1984). Separating individual and group effects. *Journal of Personality and Social Psychology, 48*, 339–48.

Kraemer , H. C. & Jacklin, C. N. (1979). Statistical analysis of dyadic social behavior. *Psychological Bulletin, 86*, 217–24.

Malloy, T. E., Yarlas, A., Montvilo, R. K., & Sugarman, D. B. (1996). Agreement and accuracy in children's interpersonal perceptions: A social relations analysis. *Journal of Personality and Social Psychology, 71*, 692–702.

Manke, B. & Plomin, R. (1997). Adolescent familial interactions: A genetic extension of the social relations model. *Journal of Social and Personal Relationships, 14*, 505–22.

Myers, J. L. (1979). *Fundamentals of experimental design* (3rd edn.). Boston, MA: Allen & Bacon.

Olson, D. H. (1986). Circumplex Model VII: Validation studies and FACES III. *Family Process, 25*, 337–51.

Parke, R. D. & Buriel, R. (1998). Socialization in the family: Ethnic and ecological perspectives. In W. Damon & E. Eisenberg (eds.), *Handbook of child psychology* (vol. 3, pp. 463–552). New York: John Wiley.

Parker, J. G. & Asher, S. R. (1993). Friendship and friendship quality in middle childhood: Links with peer group acceptance and feelings of loneliness and social dissatisfaction. *Developmental Psychology, 29*, 611–21.

Raudenbush, S. W., Bryk, A. S., Cheong, Y. F., & Congdon, R. (2001). *HLM 5: Hierarchical linear and nonlinear modeling* (2nd edn.). Lincolnwood, IL: Scientific Software International.

Ross, H. S. & Lollis, S. P. (1989). A social relations analysis of toddler peer relationships. *Child Development, 60*, 1082–91.

Sameroff, A. & Chandler, M. (1975). Reproductive risk and the continuum of caretaking casualty. In F. Horowitz (ed.), *Review of Child Development Research, vol. 4:* Chicago, IL: University of Chicago Press.

Scarpati, S., Malloy, T. E., & Fleming, R. (1996). Interpersonal perception of skill efficacy and behavioral control of adolescents with learning disabilities: A social relations approach. *Learning Disability Quarterly, 19*, 15–22.

Stevenson, M. B., Leavitt, L. A., Thompson, R. H., & Roach, M. A. (1988). A social relations model analysis of parent and child play. *Developmental Psychology, 24*, 101–8.

Strough, J. & Berg, C. A. (2000). Goals as a mediator of gender differences in high-affiliation dyadic conversations. *Developmental Psychology, 36*, 117–25.

Whitley, B. E., Schofield, J. W., & Snyder, H. N. (1984). Peer preferences in a desegregated school: A round robin analysis. *Journal of Personality and Social Psychology, 46*, 799–810.

CHAPTER TWENTY

Analysis of Behavioral Streams

Roger Bakeman, Deborah F. Deckner, and Vicenç Quera

In this chapter, we consider, step by step, how a research project concerned with observing and analyzing streams of behaviors itself unfolds. To keep matters concrete and relatively simple, our examples are drawn primarily from two sources, a recently published article (Lavelli & Poli, 1998) and the research in which we are currently involved with Lauren Adamson. In so doing, we take a narrative approach to explicate in some detail many of the tools and techniques required for such an endeavor (e.g., the GSEQ computer program; Bakeman & Quera, 1995a). Not all of our examples may apply directly to your work, but our intent in providing specific details is to help you visualize better how work of this sort proceeds. (For further discussion of observational studies, see Bakeman & Gottman, 1997; Bakeman, 2000a.)

The overall, brief summary of this chapter might be stated as follows. The systematic observation of behavior and its subsequent analysis is useful when investigators wish to capture aspects of relatively naturally occurring behavior as it unfolds in time. It is especially useful when process or dynamic aspects of that behavior are under study. It is often used for, but is not limited to, nonverbal behavior or beings that are nonverbal (i.e., human infants and non-humans). This chapter is not an alternative to other chapters in Part IV of this book that focus on analytic techniques, but could serve as a precursor to them. Similarly, the chapters on developmental designs in Part I of this volume might be considered as precursors to this chapter. In sum, in this chapter we focus primarily on concepts and tools that aid in extracting scores from observed streams of behavior; such scores then serve subsequent analyses.

Defining Basic Questions and Concepts

As with any worthy research study, the desire to analyze behavioral streams should be justified by a good question, which includes clear understanding and definitions of the concepts that the question references. As a first example, Lavelli and Poli (1998), who emphasized the importance of newborn feeding as the first instance of social interaction, asked whether patterns of mother–infant interaction during and after breastfeeding differed from those during and after bottle-feeding, and whether any such differences changed as infants aged from 3 days to 3 months. These investigators conceptualized early mother–infant interaction as representing the first occurrence of mother–infant dialog, emphasized its synchrony, and focused on such behaviors, among others, as mutual touches, gazes, smiles, and vocalizations.

As a second example, in earlier work with Adamson (e.g., Adamson & Bakeman, 1984, 1991; Bakeman & Adamson, 1984), joint attention was a central concept, usually defined as a state of attention shared between a mother (or any caregiver; we often use the word mother in its generic sense) and her infant, during which both shared their attention to a common object or event. Our concern with joint attention, and the way we conceptualized it, led us to develop our first joint attention coding scheme, which we describe shortly. In our current work (e.g., Adamson et al., 2000), we are focusing on the way language begins to infuse and transform joint attention just after infancy. By the end of infancy, a typically developing child usually has mastered the rudiments of conversation. We view this as an astonishing feat that entails, among other skills, the ability to engage with a social partner about a topic of mutual interest using a wealth of communicative acts, including language. We term this feat *symbol-infused joint engagement*, and our concern with its development has led us to observe slightly older children (in the second and third years of life as opposed to the first and second years) and to modify our first coding scheme, again in ways we describe shortly.

Developing Coding Schemes Tied to Questions and Concepts

We view coding schemes as the thermometers or rulers (i.e., the measuring instruments) of systematic observation, albeit ones that include a human component. Coding schemes are guided by the concepts that undergird the research and define the behaviors of interest in sufficient detail that observers could say with some assuredness, yes, they just saw an instance of a particular behavior defined by the scheme. Codes are often grouped into sets that, within the set, are mutually exclusive and exhaustive; that is to say, only one code applies to any thing coded (mutually exclusive) and some code applies to every thing coded (exhaustive). For example, we might code mothers as looking at their infant or not looking at their infant. Recording and analyzing codes defined and grouped into mutually exclusive and exhaustive sets often turns out to be quite useful, which is why such sets are frequently encountered. The term *coding scheme* can refer to a single set of mutually exclusive and exhaustive codes, or collectively to several sets of such codes, or to a group of codes, whether or not mutually exclusive and exhaustive, that are applied during one pass through a videotape (e.g., one pass might code a mother's behavior and another might code her infant's behavior).

Measurement occurs when a particular code is assigned to a particular entity in a systematic way. Usually that entity is an event of some sort (e.g., mother gazing at infant), although certainly codes can be assigned to objects as well (is it a red ball or a blue one?). For now, let us use the term *event* generically for the thing coded, although later we mention that time units could be coded as well. A useful distinction that we and others make (e.g., Altmann, 1974; Sackett, 1978) is between *momentary* and *duration events*. A momentary event may or may not last just a moment, but, by definition, its duration is not of interest to us and so we record only its occurrence, and perhaps its time of onset. By contrast, the amount of time devoted to duration events is of interest, and so we note how long they last, typically recording times of offset as well as times of onset.

One way of thinking about duration events is in terms of *behavioral states*. The usual assumption is that states reflect some underlying organization, so that an organism at any given time necessarily must be in one of a set of mutually exclusive and exhaustive states. One example would be the infant states of quiet alert, fussy, crying, rapid-eye movement sleep, and deep sleep (Wolff, 1966). Another would be the play states of unoccupied, onlooker, and solitary, parallel, associative, and cooperative play applied to preschoolers by Parten (1932).

The coding schemes used by Lavelli and Poli (1998) illustrate these notions nicely. Their coding schemes were motivated by a desire to explore differences in mother–infant interaction during breast- as compared to bottle-feeding. They coded four kinds of behavior: infant state, infant's feeding behavior, maternal behavior, and mother–infant interaction, which we present here in slightly simplified form. Following Wolff (1966) and Brazelton (1973), they defined five mutually exclusive and exhaustive states for the infant: sleeping, drowsy, alert, fussing, and crying. Another set of codes defined feeding behavior: coders noted whether or not a feeding episode was ongoing and if so whether the infant was sucking or not. Five additional codes were used to describe behavior when the infant was not actively sucking, including a cannot-observe code. Such a cannot-see or off-task code is often used to make a set exhaustive. Two sets of codes were used for maternal behavior. The first coded whether or not the mother was gazing at her infant. The second coded whether the mother was using tactile, auditory, or both tactile and auditory stimulation. Defining such combination codes (both tactile and auditory stimulation) is a common way to make codes mutually exclusive and, in this case, adding a fourth code (none of the above) would make the set exhaustive as well. Finally, Lavelli and Poli coded four dyadic, interactive behaviors – mutual touch, mutual gaze, mutual smile, and mutual vocalization – whose occurrence or frequency, but not duration, was of interest to them; thus we would regard them as momentary behaviors and not states.

In our own case, when we first began thinking about joint attention, the notion of state seemed to fit. The ages of the infants we observed (6–18 months) fell between those of Wolff and Parten. Moreover, some of Parten's codes seemed to apply. True, we were observing infants with their mothers whereas Parten observed preschoolers aged not quite 2 to almost 5 with each other but, like Parten, we wanted to characterize the child's engagement. After a bit of pilot work, we defined six codes. The first three came from Parten: *unengaged*, *onlooking*, and *objects* (solitary play with toys). The fourth, engagement with a *person*, usually the mother (no objects involved), was simply something afforded by the situation. The last two codes followed directly from the way we thought about joint attention. During infancy, the emergence of joint engagement appears not as a singular achievement but as a series of accomplishments. Broadly, the typical developmental progression begins with the two- to three-month-old establishing ways to interact with a social partner and then rapidly transforms as the four- to five-month-old becomes fascinated with handling objects. At this point, mothers may join the infant in exploring objects and in that sense the objects become shared. But this *supported joint engagement* does not require active joint attention to both object and mother from the infant. It is not until later in the first year and the beginning of the second that infants begin to coordinate attention to their mother and to an object close at hand, an accomplishment which we term *coordinated joint engagement*.

The coding scheme that is featured prominently in our current research represents a straightforward evolution of the one just described. It reflects our concern with how symbols, especially linguistic ones, begin to infuse the joint engagement of older infants and young children. After a bit of pilot work, we became convinced that adding five codes to our existing scheme would capture the phenomenon of symbol-infused joint engagement that we wished to study. In addition to the simple codes of object and person engagement, we added a code for symbol engagement, and in parallel with object and person engagement, we added two new codes for symbol-infused object-engagement and symbol-infused person engagement. These three codes seemed necessary to complete the logical possibilities, but we expected that they would occur fairly infrequently. Of considerably more theoretical interest to us were the two new codes for symbol-infused supported joint engagement and symbol-infused coordinated joint engagement.

Recording and Coding Behavioral Streams

Once design decisions are made (see Part I of this volume), and once a particular coding scheme has been developed, a series of practical and technical questions arise related to how coders will be trained and how they will record their decisions. If your aim is to observe behavior live, in real time, your choices for recording behavior include, in order of increasing technical complexity, simple pencil and paper; an audio recorder in which you speak codes for later transcription; some sort of hand-held electronic device into which you key codes (several are commercially available, e.g., the Psion); or a hand-held or laptop computer that you have had programmed for your particular purpose (Emerson, Reeves, & Felce, 2000).

However, it is more likely that you will record segments of the behavior of interest for later coding. Video (i.e., a visual and sound recording) has the merit of being subject to multiple viewings, in both real time and slow motion. Recordings can be stockpiled for later training of coders; they can be viewed by different observers on different occasions, each time coding different aspects of the behavior; and they can even be viewed by the same observer on different occasions to assess observer reliability over time. They permit reflection (and, literally, re-view) in a way live observation does not. Moreover, recording devices are relatively inexpensive, easy to use, and generally reliable.

Likely whatever recording apparatus you use, time will be recorded as a matter of course. It has not always been so. If you read older literature you will encounter *interval recording*, which is often called zero-one or partial-interval or simply time sampling (e.g.,

Altmann, 1974). Typically, rows on a paper recording form represented successive intervals (e.g., each could represent 15-second intervals; see Konner, 1976), columns represented particular behaviors, and observers noted with a tick mark the behaviors that occurred within each interval. The intent of the method was to provide approximate estimates of both frequency (how often specific behaviors occurred) and duration (what percentage or proportion of time behaviors occurred) in an era before readily available recording devices automatically preserved time. Thus the method was a compromise with desire, reflecting the technology of the time, and even then its shortcomings were clearly understood (e.g. Sackett, 1978).

With most recording devices in use today you will be able to record the onsets (i.e., the time of onset) of momentary behaviors and the onsets and offsets of duration behaviors economically. Organizing duration behaviors into sets of mutually exclusive and exhaustive code permits further efficiency; because the onset of one behavior in the set necessarily implies the offset of the previous behavior, only onsets of behaviors in a set need be recorded. For this reason we recommend that, when feasible, codes be organized into sets of mutually exclusive and exhaustive codes, as the examples from our work and from Lavelli and Poli (1998) illustrate.

Still, how exactly should time be recorded? When coding live using pencil and paper, time displayed on a stop watch could be written down, although, especially when the behavior of interest is fast moving and requires attention, this can unduly burden observers and distract from observation, thereby compromising data quality. However, almost any hand-held electronic device, including laptop computers, will record time automatically when a key is pressed. Thus the record preserved in the device represents a series of events and the times they occurred., When behavior is recorded with the devices available today (e.g., camcorders), a time code can almost always be incorporated in the video signal. This could be a visual time code, which is displayed on the screen when the tape is played back, or it could be an electronic code, which has an important advantage: on play back the time code can be read and stored in a data file automatically, freeing the observer of the need to key it in. This code is often called a VITC time code because it is stored in the vertical interval of the video signal, or a SMPTE code because it follows conventions defined by the Society of Motion Picture and Television Engineers.

Representing the Initial Data

If a no-tech approach to coding relies only on pencil and paper and the naked eye, and if a high-tech approach connects computers and video recordings, then a relatively low-tech approach to coding video material might assume video recording but rely on a visual time code and would require observers to record not just codes but also the time they occurred. Ultimately, we assume, data will be processed by computer so observers viewing video could use pencil and paper for their initial records and then enter the data in computer files later or key their observations directly into a computer as they work, whichever they find easier. Such a system retains all the advantages that accrue to coding previously recorded material and is attractive when budgets are constrained.

When feasible, a more high-tech approach has advantages, and a number of systems are available. Such systems combine video recordings, either analogue or digital, and computers in ways that serve to automate coding. Four examples are the systems developed by the James Long Company (Long, 1996), the PROCODER system (Tapp & Walden, 1993), the Observer (Noldus et al., 2000; for current information see http://www.noldus.com), and the ObsWin program (Martin, Oliver, & Hall, 1999; for current information see http://psgsuni.bham.ac.uk/obswin/obswin2.htm). Each of these four offers a range of different capabilities. Moreover, as with technical matters generally, their products change, and so any statements in a chapter such as this run the risk of becoming dated. Further, the Observer in particular offers a number of real-time capabilities, and all four offer data analytic possibilities, but here our comments are confined primarily to the capabilities these programs/systems have for coding previously recorded material. For a review of computer systems for recording observational data see Kahng & Iwata (2000).

Speaking somewhat generically, computer-based coding systems permit researchers to define the codes they use and their attributes. Then coders can view previously recorded information, in real time or slow motion, as they decide how the material should be coded. When they decide a code should be assigned (e.g., the baby just began crying), coders can either press a key or keys or else use the computer mouse to click that code on screen. The computer program then organizes the codes and their associated times into computer files. Coders can edit those files if, on reflection and reviewing, they think their initial coding should be changed. With appropriate equipment and software, the playback of a video recording can be controlled with mouse clicks on the screen. Researchers can even create a list of specific episodes to be played back, either for demonstration purposes or to permit other coders to recode them. In sum, such systems tend to the clerical tasks, freeing coders to focus on their primary task, which is making decisions as to how behavior should be coded. Their disadvantage is the amount of money the required equipment and software can cost, and the amount of time it can take to learn to use that equipment and software effectively.

No matter how you record and format your data initially, at some point those data need to be arranged into files suitable for preliminary computer processing. Probably you will also need to reduce those initial data before you conduct subsequent analyses with statistical packages such as SPSS or SAS. We have defined standard conventions for representing or formatting sequential data, which we call Sequential Data Interchange Standard (SDIS; Bakeman & Quera, 1995a; Quera & Bakeman, 2000). Files containing data that follow SDIS conventions are designed to be relatively intuitive, clear to read, and easy to use. Representing your data with these standard formats has an additional advantage: you can then use a program we have written to analyze SDIS formatted data that has considerable capability and flexibility. We call this program the Generalized Sequential Querier (GSEQ; Bakeman & Quera, 1995a; for current information see http://www.gsu.edu/~psyrab/sg.htm or http://www.ub.es/comporta/sg.htm).

Possible scenarios for representing your data include: you record data using pencil and paper and then enter it into computer files as SDIS data, or you collect data using an electronic device, which produces lists of codes and their time of occurrence, and then reformat this initial data according to SDIS conventions. Programs that reformat such data are relatively easy to write; for example, we have written programs that produce

SDIS data files from data files produced by the James Long Company system and by the Observer (Bakeman, 2000b; Bakeman & Quera, 2000). Or, you collect data with ObsWin (Martin, Oliver, & Hall, 1999), which has the capability to output data already in SDIS format. There is another possibility. Most data collection programs also have data analytic capabilities; this is true to varying extents for all three systems we have mentioned. If you find these capabilities sufficient for your purposes, there is no need to represent your data in SDIS format. We are somewhat biased, of course, but if you intend to pursue a variety of analytic options, we think it is worth your while to learn more about the capabilities and flexibility of GSEQ. Certainly one strength of GSEQ is the ease with which a variety of sequential indices can be defined and computed and then output for subsequent processing by packages such as SPSS or SAS, as we demonstrate later in this chapter.

First, we would like to provide some sense of what SDIS data files look like. Five data types are defined. The first and simplest we call *Event Sequential Data* (ESD), which consist of a single stream of codes recorded without time information. Here is what the first few lines of an ESD file might look like:

Event sleep drowsy alert fuss cry * sex (female male);
<infant #1> drowsy sleep drowsy fuss cry fuss alert . . . (female)/

The first line declares the data type and, optionally, lists permissible codes; the next line here lists the sequence of codes for a participant labeled "infant #1," who is female. A second type we term *Multi-Event Sequential Data* (MSD). It is used when an event is categorized by more than one dimension, but again without time information. For example, bids for a mother's attention might be categorized by antecedent (coded as Sol, Tog, or Oth), form (coded as Verb, Gest, or Both), and result (coded as Resp or None). Here is an example:

Multievent (Sol, Tog, Oth) (Verb, Gest, Both) (Resp, None);
<child #1> Sol Gest Resp . Sol Gest Rest . Oth Both None . . . /

Sets of mutually exclusive and exhaustive codes are declared by enclosing them in parentheses and episodes are separated with periods. A third type is *Interval Sequential Data* (ISD). It looks like MSD, except that commas are used to separate intervals. It is designed to accommodate investigators working with interval data (e.g., Bakeman et al., 1990), although earlier we characterized this method of data recording as seldom recommended today.

The final two types include time information and, as you might guess from our earlier comments, are the two we find most useful. The first is *State Sequential Data* (SSD), which assumes that your codes are organized into one or more sets of mutually exclusive and exhaustive codes. Here is an example (the codes represent unoccupied, onlooking, object, person, supported joint, and coordinated joint engagement):

State (un lo ob pe sj cj) * Visit (V1 V2 V3 V4 V5) Scene (turns music help);
<S125> ,0:41:29 un,0:41:29 sj,0:41:30 ob,0:42:02 un,0:43:26 sj,0:43:31 cj,0:43:46
ob,0:45:18 un,0:46:35 ,0:46:46 (V1,help)/

Time was represented as hh:mm:ss. In addition two conditions were defined, Visit and Scene; visits were labeled V1 to V5 and represented visits at different ages, and scenes (from a structured protocol) were labeled turns, music, and help. Following SDIS conventions, times are preceded by commas, and codes are followed by the times they began. Because these are state codes, the onset of a new state signals the offset of the preceding state.

The last data type, *Timed-Event Sequential Data* (TSD), is the most general, and can be viewed as an elaboration of SSD; any data expressed as SSD could be expressed as TSD, although a few more keystrokes would be required. For example, imagine that we defined *ix* as a momentary code for infant affective expression and that two occurred during the first episode of supported joint and one during the second episode of supported joint engagement. Then the TSD representation for the data just presented would be:

Timed (un lo ob pe sj cj) ix * Visit (V1 V2 V3 V4 V5) Scene (turns music help);
<S125> ,0:41:29 un,0:41:29- sj,0:41:30- ob,0:42:02- un,0:43:26- sj,0:43:31-
cj,0:43:46- ob,0:45:18- sj,0:45:30- ob,0:45:53- sj,0:46:30- un,0:46:35- & ix,0:41:37
ix,0:41:45 ix,0:43:36 ,0:46:46 (V1,help)/

In TSD, times for duration codes are indicated as *code, ontime-offtime*, but if no time occurs after the hyphen, it defaults to the next time encountered in the file.

One final example: Lavelli and Poli (1998) used Noldus' the Observer (Noldus et al., 2000). Imagine that their infant state codes were *sleep*, *drowsy*, *alert*, *fuss*, and *cry*; that their mother looking at infant codes were *look* and *nolook*; and that they recorded times to the nearest second. Then the start of the SDIS data file could look like this:

Timed (sleep drowsy alert fuss cry) (look nolook)
<subject id> 0, 0,sleep- 7,fuss- 12,cry- . . .
& 0,nolook- 4,look- 10,nolook-, 14,look- . . . ,29/

These examples do not exhaust all of the possibilities SDIS provides, but they should suffice to give you a reasonable sense of how your own data might be represented. This is an important step. Once the data you collect initially have been organized into computer files, then your first descriptive analyses can commence using all the power and accuracy that computers provide. However, first another important matter requires your attention: you need to convince yourself and others that those data were coded reliably.

Establishing Observer Reliability

When observers are asked to make categorical distinctions, the most common statistic used to establish interobserver reliability is Cohen's kappa (1960), a coefficient of agreement for categorical (i.e., nominal) scales. If a standard exists, which is assumed true, then observers can be compared with it. Otherwise, the usual assumption is, if two observers agree when independently coding the same material, then their data should accurately reflect the observed behavior, and hence be reliable. Either way, Cohen's kappa is useful both when training observers and later, when reporting their reliability in published reports. Moreover, it corrects for chance agreement and thus is much preferred to the percentage agreement statistics sometimes seen, especially in older literature.

Kappa

Kappa is an index that characterizes agreement in applying a set of mutually exclusive and exhaustive codes. A value of 1 indicates perfect agreement. Fleiss (1981) character-ized values over 0.75 as excellent, between 0.60 and 0.75 as good, and between 0.40 and 0.60 as fair. Values less than 0.60 are thus problematic; negative values are possible and would indicate systematic disagreement (or perhaps data entry errors). Kappa does not yield values for individual codes although useful information concerning sources of disagreement can be gleaned from the agreement matrix on which kappa is based. As an example, imagine that observers were asked to code infant states using Lavelli and Poli's (1998) codes. Imagine further that boundaries between states had already been identified so that coders approached their task with no ambiguity as to the thing (or unit) that they were coding. Speaking generally, let k represent the number of codes in the scheme, in this case five. Then agreement can be tallied in a $k \times k$ matrix, which is often called an agreement matrix or, simply, a kappa table. Rows represent the first coder, columns the second, and both are labeled identically with the k codes. When observers primarily agree, most tallies fall on the upper-left to lower-right diagonal. Off-diagonal cells indic-ate disagreements (e.g., what the first observer coded *sleep* the second observer coded *drowsy*), and noting off-diagonal cells with many tallies provides useful feedback when training observers.

For the infant state example, the agreement matrix might look like this:

Coder A	Coder B					
	Sleep	Drowsy	Alert	Fuss	Cry	Total
Sleep	12	2	0	0	0	14
Drowsy	2	7	1	1	0	11
Alert	0	0	15	0	0	15
Fuss	0	0	2	8	0	10
Cry	0	0	0	4	5	9
Total	14	9	18	13	5	59

In this example, 59 infant states were coded by two observers with what appears to be reasonably good agreement. For example, cry was never confused with sleep or drowsy or alert, and sleep was never confused with alert or fuss. The coders agreed 47 times (80 percent) and disagreed 12 times. Symmetric disagreements indicate that coders are equally confused whereas asymmetric disagreements indicate that coders may have different thresholds; thus, usually asymmetric disagreements are of greater concern. In this case, the coders disagreed about sleep versus drowsy four times, but twice Coder B coded a state sleep when Coder A coded it drowsy, and twice Coder A coded a state sleep when Coder B coded it drowsy, which is perfectly symmetric. In contrast, four times Coder B coded a state fuss when coder A coded it cry, but Coder A never coded a state cry that Coder B coded fuss. This suggests that Coder B has a higher threshold for what constitutes a cry and that the two coders need to become better calibrated through additional training.

The computation of kappa is fairly straightforward (for formulas see Bakeman & Gottman, 1997), although computer programs are available (e.g., the ComKappa program, which can be downloaded from http://www.gsu.edu/psychology/bakeman; Robinson & Bakeman, 1998). When codes are roughly ordinal or for other reasons investigators may wish to regard some disagreements as more serious than others, Cohen (1968) has specified a way of weighting disagreements; again, see Bakeman and Gottman for details.

Picturing observer agreement

For simplicity, our example using infant state codes assumed that boundaries between states had been marked previously so that coders needed only categorize states as though they were so many billiard balls to sort by color. This is a reasonable way to introduce kappa because a particular thing or entity is assigned a code, and the number of such things is the total number of tallies entered in the table. Rarely, however, are coders presented with already segmented streams of behaviors. Instead theirs is a twofold task: they need to both find the boundaries between states and then code the states so demarcated. A strict interpretation might be that the reliability of both these tasks should be established, but in fact rarely do coders even think of performing two separate tasks; instead, as they note onset times, the coding task seems seamless to them. And indeed, if we compute kappa based on seconds as the thing coded, then we capture in one agreement matrix both aspects of the coding task (we say *second* somewhat generically, for ease of exposition, but it could be any time unit that makes sense when coding a particular set of behaviors).

Recall that in our current research, we define eleven engagement codes: un, lo, ob, pe, sj, cj, sy, os, ps, ss, and cs for unengaged and onlooking; object, person, supported joint, and coordinated joint engagement; symbol-infused engagement alone; and symbol-infused object, person, supported joint, and coordinated joint engagement, respectively. When first training observers, and later when checking their reliability, we prepare SDIS files based on their coding. For example, here is the way one observer coded one of our contexts (i.e., conditions, in this case turn-taking) for one infant:

State (un lo ob pe sj cj sy os ps ss cs);
<192 V1 turns> un,0:28:55 lo,0:28:59 sj,0:29:11 cs,0:29:36 os,0:29:49 lo,0:30:07
ob,0:30:12 sj,0:30:18 os,0:31:00 sj,0:31:22 un,0:31:25 ob,0:32:34 sj,0:33:01
lo,0:34:16 ,0:34:27 /

```
GSW Plot for A192T.mds, data type State, 08/18/00, 3:22:39 PM
<turns> Unit 1, Session 1, 0:28:55-0:34:26

     0:28:50  0:29:00  0:29:10  0:29:20  0:29:30  0:29:40  0:29:50  0:30:00  0:30:10  0:30:20  0:30:30  0:30:40
     |----+----|----+----|----+----|----+----|----+----|----+----|----+----|----+----|----+----|----+----|----+----|----+----
un ...:.uuuu
lo ...:.    11111111111
ob ...:.                                                                    11111
pe ...:.                                                                          ooooo
sj ...:.              sssssssssssssssssssssss
cj ...:.                                                                                sssssssssssssssssssssssssssss
sy ...:.
os ...:.                                                 oooooooooooooooooooo
ps ...:.
ss ...:.
cs ...:.                                  cccccccccccc
```

Figure 20.1 Example of a data segment using the engagement state codes described in the text. This and subsequent plots were produced with the GSEQ for Windows (GSW) plot routine (Explore | Plot).

and here is the way a second observer coded the same context for the same infant:

State (un lo ob pe sj cj sy os ps ss cs);
<192 V1 turns> un,0:28:57 lo,0:29:03 sj,0:29:09 ss,0:29:36 os,0:29:49 ob,0:29:57
lo,0:30:07 ob,0:30:12 lo,0:30:18 sj,0:30:26 ss,0:31:02 un,0:31:25 ob,0:32:34
sj,0:33:02 un,0:34:13 ,0:34:25 /

For brevity, these two example files contain coding for only one condition and one infant, but the files for the two observers could contain many conditions for many infants. If we had wanted to visualize the observers' coding, we could have asked the GSEQ program to plot these files. Figure 20.1 shows the plot that GSEQ produces, here for the first two minutes of the first observer's coding (Explore | Plot). From it we can easily see that the session began with a few seconds of unoccupied, moved into a few more seconds of onlooking, and thence into a period of supported joint engagement, at least as coded by the first observer.

Given two files that represent coding for the same stream of behavior as performed independently by two different observers, the question now arises, how well do they agree? Figure 20.2 shows the output GSEQ produces (Tools | Compute Kappa), which consists, first, of a time-line plot showing where disagreements occurred and, second, of an agreement matrix along with the value of kappa computed. (The ampersand used to label the last row and column of the agreement matrix is used if there are any seconds for which no code was defined; in this case, there were none.) The GSEQ for Windows (GSW) kappa program permits users to define slippage, that is, an amount of time by which coders can disagree but still have their coding count as agreement. For this example, we defined slippage as plus or minus two seconds, which, in effect, counts a second as an agreement if the second coder agreed with the first within a five-second time window (the current second plus or minus two).

The time-line plot indicates each code with symbols the user chooses. Here we used the symbols u, l, o, p, s, c, Y, O, P, S, and C for un, lo, ob, pe, sj, cj, sy, os, ps, ss, and cs, respectively. The hh:mm:ss above the time line represent hours, minutes, and seconds, respectively. A hyphen underlies seconds that count as disagreements, and a period underlines seconds that would have counted as disagreements if we had not defined slippage; the hash sign simply underlies seconds that are not tallied in the agreement table because only one observer coded them. In this case, from the agreement matrix we see that three disagreements occurred for more than 10 seconds: between symbol-infused object and symbol-infused supported joint engagement (20 seconds), between symbol-infused supported joint and symbol-infused coordinated joint engagement (13 seconds), and between unengaged and onlooking (11 seconds). Further, from the time-line plot, we see exactly where these disagreements occurred, which is very helpful when we and the observers review tapes in an effort to figure out why disagreements occurred, what they might mean, and whether further training is needed.

By way of conclusion, we would like to reiterate a point made earlier: Observer reliability serves several functions. When training observers, not only does kappa provide a clear criterion towards which novice observers can strive, the agreement matrix, along with the time-line plots GSEQ produces, provides very useful feedback as to what kinds

```
GSW Agreement/Kappa, 08/18/00, 3:29:21 PM
Agreement plot:  line 1 is A192T, line 2 is B192T

0:28:50   0:29:00   0:29:10   0:29:20   0:29:30   0:29:40   0:29:50   0:30:00   0:30:10   0:30:20   0:30:30   0:30:40
|----+----|----+----|----+----|----+----|----+----|----+----|----+----|----+----|----+----|----+----|----+----|----+----
     uuulllllllllllllsssssssssssssssssssssssssCCCCCCCCCCCCCOOOOOOOOOOOOOOOOOOllllloooooossssssssssssssssssssssssssssssss
       uuuuuullllllsssssssssssssssssssssssssssSSSSSSSSSSSSSOOOOOOOOoooooooooollllloooooollllllllssssssssssssssssssssssss
     ##  --..      ..                         -------------        ..--------           ------..

0:30:50   0:31:00   0:31:10   0:31:20   0:31:30   0:31:40   0:31:50   0:32:00   0:32:10   0:32:20   0:32:30   0:32:40
|----+----|----+----|----+----|----+----|----+----|----+----|----+----|----+----|----+----|----+----|----+----|----+----
ssssssssssOOOOOOOOOOOOOOOOOOOOOOssuuuuuuuuuuuuuuuuuuuuuuuuuuuuuuuuuuuuuuuuuuuuuuuuuuuuuuuuuuuuuuuuuuuuuuoooooooooooooooo
ssssssssssssSSSSSSSSSSSSSSSSSSSSSSSSuuuuuuuuuuuuuuuuuuuuuuuuuuuuuuuuuuuuuuuuuuuuuuuuuuuuuuuuuuuuuuuuuuuuuuoooooooooooooooo
          ------------------------

0:32:50   0:33:00   0:33:10   0:33:20   0:33:30   0:33:40   0:33:50   0:34:00   0:34:10   0:34:20
|----+----|----+----|----+----|----+----|----+----|----+----|----+----|----+----|----+----|----+----
ooooooooooosssssssssssssssssssssssssssssssssssssssssssssssssssssssssssssssssssssssssssslllllllllll
oooooooooooosssssssssssssssssssssssssssssssssssssssssssssssssssssssssssssssssssssssuuuuuuuuuuuu
           .                                                                       ..----------##


Cohen's kappa =  0.7360, agreement =  80.49%, window = +|-  2
Rows: A192T, columns: B192T

              un       lo       ob       pe       sj       cj       sy       os       ps       ss       cs        &   Totals
------------------------------------------------------------------------------------------------------------------------------
     un       71        0        0        0        0        0        0        0        0        0        0        0       71
     lo       11       15        0        0        0        0        0        0        0        0        0        0       26
     ob        0        0       33        0        0        0        0        0        0        0        0        0       33
     pe        0        0        0        0        0        0        0        0        0        0        0        0        0
     sj        1        6        0        0      135        0        0        0        0        3        0        0      145
     cj        0        0        0        0        0        0        0        0        0        0        0        0        0
     sy        0        0        0        0        0        0        0        0        0        0        0        0        0
     os        0        0        8        0        2        0        0       10        0       20        0        0       40
     ps        0        0        0        0        0        0        0        0        0        0        0        0        0
     ss        0        0        0        0        0        0        0        0        0        0        0        0        0
     cs        0        0        0        0        0        0        0        0        0       13        0        0       13
      &        0        0        0        0        0        0        0        0        0        0        0        0        0
------------------------------------------------------------------------------------------------------------------------------
 Totals       83       21       41        0      137        0        0       10        0       36        0        0      328
               u        l        o        p        s        c        Y        O        P        S        C
```

Figure 20.2 Example of an agreement plot and kappa calculation; conventions for the plot are described in the text. This output was produced with the GSEQ for Windows (GSW) kappa routine (Tools | compute Kappa).

of disagreements might cause kappas to be low. Then, during data collection, reasonable values for kappa assure you that observers are continuing to code reliably, or lowering values may signal the need for additional training (typically, about 15–20 percent of a corpus is coded by more than one observer and observers should not know which of their work will be used to check reliability). Finally, when writing reports, once data are collected and analyzed, reporting values of kappa gives assurance to reviewers, editors, and eventually other readers that the data on which your analyses are based are sound.

Describing and Reducing Initial Data

In a previous section we talked about how the data-as-collected might be represented initially. We meant re-present literally – that is, the data are presented again, to the computer, for the first round of descriptive analyses. In saying this we make two assumptions: first, that often data are collected with somewhat more detail than is ultimately useful for even preliminary analyses and so some reduction is necessary at the outset (e.g., in the process of coding we find out that some codes occur very rarely or that some distinctions are difficult to make reliably); and second, that the very first analyses we do are primarily descriptive in nature, designed to give ourselves and readers a sense of our data, whereas subsequent analyses probe our data more deeply as, for example, we address specific hypotheses. In this section we focus on those initial, descriptive analyses and emphasize the advantages of and techniques for deriving new variables from the data-as-collected. These new, derived variables may both simplify our data and better reflect our conceptual concerns. Then, in the next section, we focus more on analyses that probe for patterns in the behavioral streams and emphasize ways in which variables can be combined into indices that both exploit sequential information in the data and permit answers to the research questions that motivated our investigations in the first place.

Basic descriptive statistics

Once data are collected the first step is to examine basic descriptive statistics for all our codes. For momentary codes, these include *frequencies* (how often did the observers use this code, i.e., to how many events was this code assigned?), *relative frequencies* (what proportion of the events were assigned this code?), and *rates* (how many times per hour, or other unit of time, did this event occur?). For duration codes, these include *frequencies*, *rates*, *probabilities* (for what proportion of total time did this event occur?), and *average durations* (how long, on average, did instances of this event last?). Relative frequencies can be computed for duration codes but usually the proportion of time is regarded as more informative (i.e., when behavior is timed usually it is more interesting to know that code A occurred 22 percent of the time than to know that 18 percent of all events were coded A). Note, however, that frequencies, probabilities, and average durations are redundant; if frequency is low and probability is high, the average duration necessarily must be long. Other statistics that can be computed for duration codes include minimum and maximum lengths (what was the shortest and longest length recorded for this event?). GSEQ computes other statistics as well (e.g., the average length of time between events; Version 3.7 and later), which some investigators might find useful.

Pooling

When first examining our data, it makes sense to pool over all cases because initially, as we make decisions about how best to reduce our data, we are concerned with how often codes were used and not yet with how individuals varied – that is, we want to view our data whole and not yet derive scores for individuals. GSEQ allows you to pool over cases (i.e., units, which may be infants, dyads, etc.), over conditions if any were given, or both. Assume, for example, that several mother–infant dyads were observed, that the observations of each dyad constitute a separate case in the SDIS data file, that one variable indicating the infant's sex was defined, that M and P were codes for momentary behaviors, and that A, B, and C were codes for a set of mutually exclusive and exhaustive duration behaviors. Then the declaration line for the SDIS file would look like this:

Timed (A B C) M P * sex (male female);

and the GSEQ commands:

Pool * sex;
Simple freq relf rate (M P);
Simple freq rate prob avgd (A B C);

would produce basic descriptive statistics for these data, pooled over all cases (the asterisk by itself on the Pool command would mean pool over all cases, separately for males and females; the word *sex* on the Pool command means pool over male and female cases as well). The benefit of proceeding this way – that is, producing basic descriptive statistics for your codes pooled over all cases (separately for each combination of levels for any variables, or pooled over levels of any variables if you so specify) – is that you gain a good overview of how often the behaviors of interest to you actually occurred in your coded corpus. With this knowledge, you can now proceed with data reduction.

Basic data reduction

There are at least three good reasons to reduce your data before proceeding with further analyses. First, you may have discovered during coding that observers could not reliably distinguish between two codes, yet when you combined those two codes into one superordinate code, the superordinate code was reliable, thus it makes sense to combine those two codes into one new one. Second, you may have discovered that some, relatively similar, codes occurred fairly infrequently. If treated as separate codes, scores would be zero for some cases and quite low numbers for others, but if combined into one code, that single code would be simpler and less problematic to analyze. Third, you may have solid, theoretical reasons for combining some codes into more encompassing variables.

Such reduction is easily accomplished with GSEQ. The Recode or Lump commands could be used, but for State and Timed-Event Sequential data, the Or command may be better. When new codes are introduced in the data with the Recode and Lump commands, the old codes are removed, whereas the Or command leaves the old codes intact, where they can be referenced later if the need arises. The Or command assigns the new code to a time unit if any one or more of the old codes was already assigned to that time unit. For example, recall that the eleven codes we use to code engagement state are un, lo, ob, pe, sj, cj, sy, os, ps, ss, and cs. First we examined simple, basic statistics for these codes, pooled over all cases. As we expected, in our corpus engagement with symbols alone (sy) occurred very rarely, as did symbol-infused object and person engagement (os, ps; these and subsequent statements are based on preliminary analyses of the first 24 mothers and infants in our study whose videotapes we had coded for engagement state). Thus we decided to create a single, symbol-infusement outside of joint engagement code that combined sy, os, and ps. For simplicity, we also decided to combine unengaged and onlooking (un, lo) because onlooking was not especially common and because the distinction between the two did not seem especially interesting.

Additionally, for theoretical reasons, we created one code that combined all joint engagement codes, whether supported or coordinated and whether or not symbol-infused (sj, cj, ss, cs); one code that represented that part of total joint engagement that was supported joint engagement (sj, ss), whether or not symbol-infused; and that part of total joint engagement that was symbol-infused (ss, cs), whether supported or coordinated. The GSEQ commands that created these new codes were:

```
File "C:\GSEQ\examples\ES24.mds";
OR syo = sy os ps;
OR unl = un lo;
OR jnt = sj cj ss cs;
OR sup = sj ss;
OR sij = ss cs;
Save "C:\GSEQ\examples\ES24mod.mds";
```

Earlier we had compiled the SDIS data file that contained data from these 24 mother–infant dyads (File | Open | Compile); this created an MDS or modified SDIS file (the SDIS data file is an ASCII file, easy to read and edit; the MDS file is a binary file, easier for GSEQ to process). This set of commands instructs GSEQ to open the file called ES24.mds, create five new codes, and save the results in a file called ES24mod.mds. Subsequently, we can refer to file ES24mod.mds and have available to us all of the codes in ES24.mds initially plus the five new ones created by these commands.

At this point, we would no longer want to pool over cases. Now that we have created new codes, reducing our data a bit, we want to derive and describe basic statistics for these new codes, and probably some old ones too, but consistent with usual practice, we would want to report means and variability for our sample (e.g., standard deviations and ranges) based on scores for individual cases. Later we will want to run other, more sophisticated analyses as well, and so it makes sense to learn now how to export data from GSEQ in a form that can be processed by standard statistical packages such as SPSS or SAS. For the present example, the GSEQ statements:

    File "C:\GSEQ\examples\ES24mod.mds";
    Simple freq prob avgd (unl ob pe syo jnt sje sij);
    Send "C:\GSEQ\examples\ES24fpa.dat" freq prob avgd tabs label overwrite;

would do two things. First, frequencies, probabilities, and average durations for the key behaviors of total unengaged (including onlooking), object and person engagement, symbol-infused outside of joint engagement, total joint engagement, total supported joint engagement, and total symbol-infused joint engagement would be computed for each case. Second, those simple statistics would be sent to a file (named here ES24fpa.dat) formatted so that they can be easily read by programs such as SPSS (in this case, each item in the file is separated with tabs, cases are identified with the label from the SDIS file, and any other data file of the same name is overwritten).

Here is an example, derived from one 5-minute observation in our corpus. The output created by the Simple command is:

```
Variable sex, condition male
Unit #7 label 'S107V1'.
Pooling over 1 session (maximum 1 session per unit).

SIMPLE statistics

Codes     FREQ      PROB        AVGD
        ---------------------------------------
ob   |    4       0.1688      13.25  |
pe   |    0       0.0000       0.00  |
syo  |    2       0.0350       5.50  |
unl  |    2       0.0637      10.00  |
jnt  |    7       0.7293      32.71  |
sup  |    9       0.4331      15.11  |
sij  |    2       0.1497      23.50  |
        ---------------------------------------
Totals:  26       1.5796

Total number of time units:     314
```

Note that although GSEQ computes simple statistics for each case in the SDIS data file, it does not also compute group summary statistics such as means, standard deviations, etc. We did not think it made sense to add abilities to GSEQ that already exist elsewhere. Instead we view GSEQ as a program that permits users to manipulate and reduce sequential data in quite flexible ways, often with an eye to computing scores and indices for individual cases. The various scores and indices are then delivered to general purpose statistical programs for subsequent, more sophisticated analyses. In the next section we elaborate on this theme further; first, however, we end this section with other, more sophisticated examples of data reduction.

Advanced data reduction

All examples of data reduction presented so far have used the Or command. This makes sense because the most common form of data reduction combines several codes into one, superordinate code, but GSEQ offers other possibilities as well, including the full complement of logical operations (i.e., And, Or, Not, Nor, and Xor). After the Or command, the And command is probably the most useful because, with it, you can identify those seconds (i.e., time units) that contain two or more named codes (the And command assigns the new code to a time unit if all of the old codes were already assigned to that time unit). For example, you might want to identify times when the mother is gazing at her infant and the infant is crying, which could be done with:

And GazeCry = GazeAt Cry;

In the next section we describe how co-occurrences can be tallied in two-dimensional tables, and how co-occurrence statistics (i.e., statistics derived from two-dimensional tables) can be computed, but sometimes it is advantageous to also form a specific co-occurrence code, as in this example, because then you can request simple statistics (with the Simple command) such as the average duration of episodes when mothers were gazing at an infant who was crying.

Some of the more interesting ways of effecting data reduction with GSEQ involve the Window command. With it, you can assign new codes to time units that are keyed to the onset and offset times of existing codes. For example, you could define a new code that included the second (or whatever time unit you use) when crying began and the following nine seconds, or a new code that included the five seconds before the onset of the infant entering the alert state, or a new code that included only the first (i.e. onset) second when that mother soothed her infant, and so forth. With such new codes, you can address questions such as, whether mothers begin to sooth their infants within five seconds of the infant beginning to cry, more so than at other times, and whether infants become alert within ten seconds of mothers' stimulating their infants, more so than at other times, and so forth.

Often investigators come to sequential analysis having read about lag-sequential analysis (Sackett, 1979) and, since their data include onset and offsets time for the behaviors of interest (i.e., they have state or timed-event sequential data), they attempt to apply the timed version of lag-sequential analysis using one-second lags. Almost always, in our experience, the questions such investigators have are better answered by forming new codes of the sort such described (using the Window command), and then computing indices as described in the next section. We say this because typically it is not so critical whether a mother responded to her infant's cry at a lag of two versus three versus five

```
GSW Plot for WinEx1.mds, data type Timed, 09/03/00, 11:57:29 AM
<Example 1> Unit 1, Session 1, 0:01-0:50

            0:00      0:10      0:20      0:30      0:40      0:50
            |----+----|----+----|----+----|----+----|----+----|----+----
      Cry . 		    ccccccc		               .........
    Sooth . 				 ssssss		       .........
 OnSooth . 				   o		               .........
   TenCry . 		    TTTTTTTTTT		               .........
   5B4Cry . 	   55555		                       .........
 p5aftCry . 		      pppppppppppp	               .........
 2nearEnd . 		        22222		               .........
```

Figure 20.3   Examples of new codes produced from original codes of Cry and Sooth using the data modification commands given in the text.

seconds, and so forth; what matters is whether she responded within a specified window of time. For many questions, treating each second as a separate lag applies too fine-grained a scale to the phenomenon of interest.

For example, imagine that Cry and Sooth were the codes used for infant crying and soothing, respectively. Then the following commands:

> Window OnSooth = (Sooth;
> Window TenCry = (Cry+9;
> Window 5B4Cry = (Cry-5,(Cry-1;
> Window p5aftCry = Cry+5;
> Window 2nearEnd = Cry)-2,Cry)+2;

would produce the new codes as shown in Figure 20.3. In this case, the onset of mother soothing occurred within five seconds after the offset of the one infant cry shown but not within ten seconds of the onset of infant crying. For the Window command, a left parentheses before a code indicates the onset second and a right parenthesis after a code indicates the offset second for that code, inclusive. Thus, here, the first Window command indicates the onset second for Sooth. The second Window command indicates the onset second for Cry and the following 9 seconds. The third Window command indicates the fifth second before the onset of Cry up to and including the first second before the onset of Cry. The fourth Window command indicates all seconds of Cry and the following five seconds. Finally, the fifth Window command indicates the 2 seconds before the offset of Cry up through and including the 2 seconds after the offset of cry. (For other examples using the Window command, see Bakeman and Quera, 1995a.)

The Window command, coupled with other GSEQ data modification commands, can be used in even more complex and useful ways, almost as a simple programming language. Examples are available on request from the authors. In general, we think that a thoughtful and sophisticated approach to data reduction and modification permits you to craft variables that are faithful to your research ideas. Such variables can themselves be combined into precisely targeted indices, which is the topic of the next section.

Describing and Analyzing Patterns in Behavioral Streams

In the previous section we suggested that, at least for the time-based data we have been discussing, thinking in terms of lag-sequential analysis where lags are associated with time units such as seconds applies too fine-grained a scale to be very useful (cf. Bakeman & Quera, 1995b). A more productive approach, we believe, involves developing targeted time-based indices in ways we demonstrate shortly. Such indices can be computed for individual participants (dyads, couples, etc.) and so can serve as scores in subsequent analyses that rely on any of the conventional techniques available in the standard statistical packages (e.g., analyses of variance, including repeated measured; multiple regression; structural equation modeling, etc.). Moreover, sequentially based indices can be combined in a data set with other sorts of scores (e.g., age, sex, and other background information; scores on various self-report scales; etc.). From this point of view, sequential analysis and the analysis of behavioral streams generally is not a separate statistical domain. Instead, as we noted earlier, it is a measurement approach, one of many that may contribute to a research endeavor.

For an example, let us return to the Lavelli and Poli (1998) study we mentioned earlier. Recall that they coded infant state (sleeping, drowsy, alert, fussing, and crying). These codes were regarded as mutually exclusive and exhaustive, so that one (and only one) was coded for every second of the observation. For this example, assume that they also coded when mothers were stimulating their infants with touch (tactile) or with any sort of vocalization or verbalization (auditory). Many research questions can assume the form: did Behavior B begin within a specified time window relative to Behavior A? For example, we might ask, did Behavior B begin within 10 seconds after Behavior A began, or within 15 seconds after Behavior A ended, or during a period of time that included when Behavior A was occurring and also 5 seconds after it ended? For the present example, assume that we want to know whether maternal stimulation appeared to result in infants becoming alert. More specifically, we want to know whether infants shifted to an alert state either during maternal auditory stimulation or within 5 seconds of its offset; likewise for tactile stimulation.

We would begin by creating two new codes. One would note whether or not an alert state began in each second, and the other would note whether or not each second was already coded for maternal stimulation or was within 5 seconds of the offset of such stimulation. After creating these new codes, we would ask GSEQ to tally them in appropriate 2 × 2 tables and compute appropriate statistics. The following GSEQ commands would create these codes, produce the required tables, and also produce an export file that could be imported into a statistical package such as SPSS:

```
File "C:\GSEQ\examples\LPex.mds";
Window OnAlert = (Alert;
Window MTS5 = Tactile+5;
Window MAS5 = Auditory+5;
Stats jntf odds lnor;
Target OnAlert &;
```

Given MAS5 &;
Target OnAlert &;
Given MTS5 &;
Export "C:\GSEQ\LPex.dat" jntf odds lnor tabs label append;

The new codes are OnAlert, which identifies onset seconds for the alert state, MTS5, which identifies seconds coded for maternal tactile stimulation and 5 seconds thereafter, and MAS5, which identifies seconds coded for maternal auditory stimulation and 5 seconds thereafter (Tactile+5 means all seconds coded for Tactile and the 5 following seconds; likewise Auditory+5). The Stats command requests that various statistics be computed for the tables that follow. In this case they are joint frequencies, the odds ratio, and the log odds, which are defined shortly (other statistics are also available; see Bakeman & Quera, 1995a). The Target and Given commands request that two 2 × 2 tables be produced. The columns for both tables are labeled the same: in the first column, seconds coded for the onset of alert (OnAlert) are tallied, whereas all other seconds (&, which here means, and everything else) are tallied in the second column. Similarly, in the first row for the first table, seconds coded for auditory stimulation or 5 seconds thereafter are tallied (MAS5), whereas all other seconds (&) are tallied in the second row. The second table is the same but for seconds coded for tactile stimulation or 5 seconds thereafter (MTS5). Finally, the Export command asks GSEQ to write a file that contains these statistics, separating items with tabs, using subject labels from the SDS file, and appending to any existing file with the name LPex.dat.

Imagine that the tables produced by GSEQ for a single 1-month old breastfed infant and her mother had the following tallies, first for auditory stimulation:

Mother	Infant		
	OnAlert	&	Total
MAS5	20	460	480
&	20	1300	1320
Total	40	1760	1800

and, second for tactile stimulation:

Mother	Infant		
	OnAlert	&	Total
MTS5	10	530	540
&	30	1230	1260
Total	40	1760	1800

These manufactured data assume that mothers spent approximately 27 percent and 30 percent of the time engaging in auditory and tactile stimulation, respectively, and that there were 40 episodes (hence 40 onsets) of an infant alert state during a 30-minute feeding observation for this particular mother and infant. As a descriptive matter we note that the probability of an infant becoming alert in any one second overall is 0.0222 (40/1,800), but that the conditional probability of any infant becoming alert during seconds coded for maternal auditory stimulation (or 5 seconds thereafter) is somewhat greater, 0.0417 (20/480); the comparable number for tactile stimulation is less, 0.0185 (10/540). Thus the probability of OnAlert is greater than its baseline for auditory stimulation, but less than baseline for tactile stimulation. Apparently, for this infant at least, auditory stimulation more effectively promoted an alert state than tactile stimulation.

Such 2 × 2 tables are broadly useful. We think that most of the time most investigators who have time-based sequential data will be able to define 2 × 2 tables like the ones exemplified here, one for each of several constructs of interest. Once such constructs are defined, once the appropriate new codes have been added to the sequential data file (usually using GSEQ's Window command), and once tallies have been entered into appropriate tables, indices can be computed that summarize the information in each table, separately for each participant. Values of these indices would then be entered into a data file, along with other information about each participant, and the data file would be analyzed using whatever statistical techniques (e.g., multiple regression, structural equation modeling, etc.) is appropriate.

Odds ratio

One of the best indices for descriptive purposes is the odds ratio. Imagine that we label the cells of a 2 × 2 table as follows:

a	b
c	d

Then, to use our example data, the odds of an alert state beginning during a second coded for auditory stimulation are 20:460 or 1 to 0.043 or 23 to 1, whereas the odds of an alert state beginning in seconds not coded for auditory stimulation are 20:1300 or 1 to 0.015 or 65 to 1. That is, the odds of an alert state beginning are about 2.83 times greater with auditory stimulation than without it, which is the ratio of the two odds (i.e., the odds ratio). Formally, the odds ratio is defined as:

$$\text{odds ratio} = \frac{a/b}{c/d} \tag{20.1}$$

(where a, b, c, and d refer to observed frequencies for the cells of a 2 × 2 table as noted earlier). To continue with our example, the odds ratio for maternal tactile stimulation is

0.774, which means that the odds of an alert state beginning during tactile stimulation is actually less than at other times.

The odds ratio can assume values from 0 (the odds for the first row are vanishingly small compared to the second row), to 1 (the odds for the two rows are the same), to infinity (the odds for the second row are vanishingly small compared to the first row). Especially when the odds ratio is greater than 1 (and it can always be made ≥1 by swapping rows), it has the merit, lacking in many indices, of a simple and concrete interpretation. Here, for example, because human minds seem to grasp numbers that are 1 or greater better than fractions less than 1, we might better say that the odds of an alert state beginning are 1.29 times greater without tactile stimulation than with it (i.e., 1/0.774 = 1.29), as say that the odds of an alert state are 0.774 times greater with than without tactile stimulation. However, we would reverse rows in this way only if we wanted to highlight one particular table; if our purpose were to compare several tables, all with similar row and column headings but from different participants, we would of course want them all organized the same.

Log odds

As useful as the odds ratio is descriptively, due to its odd distribution (from 0 to 1 to infinity), it is not the best choice as a score for subsequent analyses. A better choice is the natural logarithm (ln) of the odds ratio, which is estimated as:

$$\text{log odds ratio} = \ln\left(\frac{ad}{bc}\right) \tag{20.2}$$

and which extends from minus to plus infinity and equals 0 when there is no effect (i.e., when the odds in the two rows are the same). However, equation (20.2) estimates are biased. An estimate with less bias, which is also well defined when one of the cells is zero (recall that the log of zero is undefined), is obtained by adding $1/2$ to each cell:

$$\text{log odds ratio} = \ln\frac{(a + 1/2)(d + 1/2)}{(c + 1/2)(b + 1/2)} \tag{20.3}$$

(Wickens, 1989). Thus, when describing the pattern captured by a 2 × 2 table, we think the odds ratio has much to recommend it. However, when subjecting a 2 × 2 table summary score to subsequent parametric analyses, such as *t* tests, analyses of variance, multiple regression, and the like, we recommend the estimate of the log odds ratio, computed per equation (20.3).

For the present example, the log odds for auditory stimulation is 1.04 and for tactile simulation is −0.23. Although these numbers are logarithms (in this case exponents for *e*), for which most of us have little intuitive feel, these numbers do give the sense that the facilitating effect of auditory stimulation is greater than the inhibiting effect of tactile stimulation, although their purpose here is to serve as scores in subsequent parametric analyses (for a recent example of this approach see Deckner, Adamson, & Bakeman, 2003). Other statistics might also be used, for example, Yule's Q and the phi coefficient; for details, see Bakeman and Gottman (1997). In any case, attention should be paid to zero or low frequency cells in the 2×2 tables. Zero cells often result in computational problems. For example, if either b or c or both are zero, an odds ratio cannot be computed (divide by zero). Likewise, none of these statistics (except the log odds per equation (20.3)) can be computed if any of the marginals are zero. A zero in a single cell can be informative but a zero or even a very low marginal suggests that insufficient information is available to estimate a value for any of these statistics. Our own rule of thumb is this: if any marginal is less than 5, we do not compute statistics for that 2×2 table but instead regard their values as missing.

In sum, in order to describe patterns in behavioral streams, we recommend first defining a series of 2×2 tables that reflect the constructs and questions of your research. These 2×2 tables can be described with various statistics, although here we have emphasized the odd ratio. However, for parametric analysis, we recommend that scores be log odds ratios, for reasons given earlier. All of these statistics can be computed with GSEQ; we assume such scores will be integrated with other data sets containing scores from other sources, and that such merged data sets will ultimately be analyzed with standard statistical programs such as SPSS, SAS, LISREL, and the like.

Summary

Throughout this chapter we have discussed methods and means of analyzing information that may lie within behavioral streams, which we have presented as a series of seven steps. We began by discussing the need to begin with clear concepts and a clear sense of the research questions that motivate our work. We noted that coding schemes, which we view as the primary measuring instruments of observational research, are informed by those concepts and then honed in practice. We also provided several examples of coding schemes that we and others have found useful, and discussed how coding schemes are used to capture data from behavioral streams. Sometimes behavior is observed live, but more often it is first recorded, which permits reviewing. We emphasized that information concerning the timing and duration of behavior is highly desirable and, given current technology, easy enough to preserve. Even so, there are a variety of ways information about the timing and occurrence of behavior could be represented for subsequent analysis. We described a standard notation that we have developed (SDIS or the Sequential Data Interchange Standard; Bakeman & Quera, 1995a) and gave several examples of how sequential data would be expressed using SDIS conventions. We also noted the importance of demonstrating, to ourselves and others, that the observers on whom we rely code behavior reliably. We emphasized Cohen's kappa, in particular, and discussed the usefulness of visualizing observer agreement using time plots. Next we discussed ways to first describe and then reduce the data as collected initially. We provided several examples of how data description and reduction can be effected with a computer program we have developed (GSEQ or the Generalized Sequential Querier; Bakeman & Quera, 1995a). Some of these examples were quite basic but others were more complex. They demonstrated, first, the fairly unusual flexibility of GSEQ's data modification capabilities, but, more importantly, they suggested the importance of thoughtfully deriving scores from our data that truly reflect the concepts and questions that motivated our research in the first place. Once that is done, it is a relatively straightforward matter to describe and analyze whatever patterns exist in our sequential data. The approach we emphasized requires that 2 × 2 tables be defined for sequences of interest, that time units (seconds, usually) be tallied into these tables, and that various indices be derived from these tables (e.g., an odds ratio to describe the data, a log odds ratio to analyze it). Finally, such indices would be merged with other data sets and this ultimate data set would then contain scores derived from both behavioral streams and other sources. It would then serve as the basis for the usual sorts of analyses, such as multiple and logistic regression, analyses of variance and covariance, and structural equation modeling, as well for other more innovative analytic techniques such as those described in other chapters in Part IV.

Note

Correspondence concerning this article should be addressed to Roger Bakeman, Department of Psychology, Georgia State University, Atlanta, GA 30303, USA. Electronic mail may be sent to bakeman@gsu.edu.

References

Adamson, L. B. & Bakeman, R. (1984). Mothers' communicative actions: Changes during infancy. *Infant Behavior and Development, 7*, 467–78.

Adamson, L. B. & Bakeman, R. (1991). The development of shared attention in infancy. In R. Vasta (ed.), *Annals of Child Development* (vol. 8, pp. 1–41). London: Kingsley.

Adamson, L. B., Bakeman, R., Deckner, D. F., & Dunbar, B. (2000). A developmental perspective on the joint attention deficit in autism. In M. Harris (chair), *Typical and atypical pathways to symbolic communication*. Symposium presented at the biennial meeting of the International Conference on Infant Studies, Brighton, July.

Altmann, J. (1974). Observational study of behaviour: Sampling methods. *Behaviour, 49*, 227–67.

Bakeman, R. (2000a). Behavioral observations and coding. In H. T. Reis & C. K. Judd (eds.), *Handbook of research methods in social psychology* (pp. 138–59). New York: Cambridge University Press.

Bakeman, R. (2000b). VitcVert: A program for converting James Long Company data files to SDIS files (tech. rep. no. 16). Atlanta, GA: Georgia State University, Developmental Psychology Laboratory.

Bakeman, R. & Adamson, L. B. (1984). Coordinating attention to people and objects in mother–infant interaction. *Child Development, 55*, 1278–89.

Bakeman, R. & Gottman, J. M. (1997). *Observing interaction: An introduction to sequential analysis* (2nd edn.). New York: Cambridge University Press.

Bakeman, R. & Quera, V. (1995a). *Analyzing interaction: Sequential analysis with SDIS and GSEQ.* New York: Cambridge University Press.

Bakeman, R. & Quera, V. (1995b). Log-linear approaches to lag-sequential analysis when consecutive codes may and cannot repeat. *Psychological Bulletin, 118*, 272–84.

Bakeman, R. & Quera, V. (2000). OTS: A program for converting Noldus observer data files to SDIS files. *Behavior Research Methods, Instruments, and Computers, 32*, 207–12.

Bakeman, R., Adamson, L. B., Konner, M., & Barr, R. (1990). !Kung infancy: The social context of object exploration. *Child Development, 61*, 794–809.

Brazelton, T. B. (1973). *Neonatal behavior assessment scale.* Philadelphia, PA: Lippincott.

Cohen, J. A. (1960). A coefficient of agreement for nominal scales. *Educational and Psychological Measurement, 20*, 37–46.

Cohen, J. (1968). Weighted kappa: Nominal scale agreement with provision for scaled disagreement or partial credit. *Psychological Bulletin, 70*, 213–20.

Deckner, D. F., Adamson, L. B., & Bakeman, R. (2003). Rhythm in mother–infant interactions. *Infancy, 4*, 201–17.

Emerson, E., Reeves, D. J., & Felce, D. (2000). Palmtop computers for behavioral observation research. In T. Thompson, D. Felce, & F. J. Symons (eds.), *Behavioral observation: Technology and applications in developmental disabilities* (pp. 47–59). Baltimore, MD: Paul H. Brookes.

Fleiss, J. L. (1981). *Statistical methods for rates and proportions.* New York: John Wiley.

Kahng, S. W. & Iwata, B. A. (2000). Computer systems for collecting real-time observation data. In T. Thompson, D. Felce, & F. J. Symons (eds.), *Behavioral observation: Technology and applications in developmental disabilities* (pp. 35–45). Baltimore, MD: Paul H. Brookes.

Konner, M. J. (1976). Maternal care, infant behavior, and development among the !Kung. In R. B. DeVore (eds.), *Kalahari hunter-gathers* (pp. 218–45). Cambridge, MA: Harvard University Press.

Lavelli, M. & Poli, M. (1998). Early mother–infant interaction during breast- and bottle-feeding. *Infant Behavior and Development, 21*, 667–84.

Long, J. (1996). *Video coding system reference guide.* Caroga Lake, NY: James Long Company.

Martin, N., Oliver, C., & Hall, S. (1999). ObsWin: Observational data collection and analysis for Windows. *CTI Psychology Software News, 9*, 14–16.

Noldus, L. P. J. J., Trienes, R. J. H., Henriksen, A. H. M., Jansen, H., & Jansen, R. G. (2000). The Observer Video-Pro: New software for the collection, management, and presentation of time-structured data from videotapes and digital media files. *Behavior Research Methods, Instruments, and Computers, 32*, 197–206.

Parten, M. B. (1932). Social participation among preschool children. *Journal of Abnormal and Social Psychology, 27*, 243–69.

Quera, V. & Bakeman R. (2000). Quantification strategies in behavioral observation research. In Thompson, T., Felce, D., & Symons, F. J. (eds.), *Behavioral observation: Technology and applications in developmental disabilities.* (pp. 297–315). Baltimore, MD: Paul H. Brookes.

Robinson, B. F. & Bakeman, R. (1998). ComKappa: A Windows 95 program for calculating kappa and related statistics. *Behavior Research Methods, Instruments, and Computers, 30*, 731–2.

Sackett, G. P. (1978). Measurement in observational research. In G. P. Sackett (ed.), *Observing behavior*, vol. 2: *Data collection and analysis methods* (pp. 25–43). Baltimore, MD: University Park Press.

Sackett, G. P. (1979). The lag sequential analysis of contingency and cyclicity in behavioral interaction research. In J. D. Osofsky (ed.), *Handbook of infant development* (pp. 623–49). New York: John Wiley.

Tapp, J. & Walden, T. (1993). PROCODER: A professional tape control coding and analysis system for behavioral research using videotape. *Behavior Research Methods, Instruments, and Computers, 25*, 53–6.

Wickens, T. D. (1989). Multiway contingency tables analysis for the social sciences. Hillsdale, NJ: Lawrence Erlbaum Associates.

Wolff, P. (1966). The causes, controls, and organization of the neonate. *Psychological Issues, 5(17)*, special issue.

PART V

New Directions in Developmental Research

CHAPTER TWENTY-ONE

Emotion-Related Regulation:
The Construct and its Measurement

Nancy Eisenberg, Amanda Sheffield Morris, and Tracy L. Spinrad

Research on the topic of emotion regulation has increased dramatically in quantity and salience in the psychological literature in the past 10 to 20 years. Moreover, it is only in the past decade that there has been much concern with definitions of the construct (e.g., Cole, Martin, & Dennis, 2004; Cole, Michel, & Teti, 1994; Eisenberg et al., 1995; Thompson, 1994). Thus, measures of emotion-related regulation have varied considerably due to differences in the definitions used by investigators, as well as in variables such as the age of the child.

In this chapter, we discuss various aspects of emotion-related regulation (and related aspects of control) that researchers may want to assess, and then organize our review of methods around these definitional distinctions. In addition, types of methods are discussed (e.g., observational, child-report, adult-report, physiological) and illustrative examples of the various types of measures are provided.

Definitions and Differentiations

Most researchers who study emotion and behavioral regulation share an implicit understanding that emotion processes generally are adaptive and functional in nature (Campos et al., 1994). However, the outcome of an emotion can be very different from its intended adaptive function, and emotion-related regulation allows for control over emotional experience and the outcomes of emotions (Campos et al., 1994).

In thinking about emotion-related regulation at a conceptual level, it is useful to make at least three types of distinctions. The first distinction is between what we have labeled emotion regulation and emotion-related behavioral regulation. The second concerns the distinction between more effortful types of regulation and more passive, less voluntary types of control. The third and final distinction is between proactive regulation or coping and regulation/coping that occurs in response to an evocative situation.

Emotion regulation versus emotion-related behavioral regulation

Although definitions of emotion regulation clearly differ among researchers, most investigators believe it involves the regulation of both the internal experience of emotion and its outward expression. Eisenberg and colleagues (e.g., Eisenberg et al., 2000a) have defined emotion-related regulation as including both elements but also have differentiated the two for heuristic purposes. Thus, *emotion regulation* is defined as the process of initiating, avoiding, inhibiting, maintaining, or modulating the occurrence, form, intensity, or duration of internal feeling states, emotion-related physiological states, attentional processes, and motivational states of emotion in the service of accomplishing affect-related biological or social adaptation or achieving individual goals (Eisenberg & Morris, 2002). In brief, emotion regulation involves the management of internal emotional experience and related physiological and motivational processes. Mechanisms involved in emotion regulation include attentional processes (e.g., attention shifting and focusing; Rothbart, Ahadi, & Hershey, 1994), cognitive constructions (e.g., Mischel & Baker, 1972; Mischel, 2000), and sometimes even overt behaviors such as inhibiting movement toward an evocative object (Rothbart & Derryberry, 1981). Other people can also help to regulate a child's internal emotional states (e.g., through distraction); such attempts might be considered part of emotion regulation, albeit not emotion *self*-regulation.

In contrast, *emotion-related behavioral regulation* is defined as "the process of initiating, maintaining, inhibiting, modulating, or changing the occurrence, form, and duration of behavioral concomitants of emotion, including observable facial and gestural responses and other behaviors that stem from, or are associated with, internal emotion-related psychological, physiological states, and motivational states" (Eisenberg & Morris, 2002). This type of regulation (henceforth labeled behavioral regulation for brevity) generally involves the voluntary, effortful inhibition or activation of behavior linked to emotion and the overt expression of emotion. It also can involve active attempts to change the emotion-inducing context. Thus, instrumental or active coping – including attempts to actively change and manage a stress-inducing context – can be considered one aspect of emotion-related behavioral regulation, although it sometimes may be useful to distinguish between the regulation of the expression of emotion and attempts to alter an emotion-eliciting context. An additional complication is that active coping sometimes may be an attempt to manage internal emotions, so it may reflect emotion regulation as well as behavioral regulation. (Socializers may also provide external control of emotion-related behavior, but we feel that such controls should be separated conceptually from self-regulation of behavior.)

Clearly, emotional and behavioral regulation are intricately related. For example, attentional processes play some role in how behavior is managed and expressed. Nonetheless, the heuristic distinction helps to better pinpoint what aspect of control is of interest or being assessed.

Measures of emotion regulation and behavioral regulation often differ considerably. For example, typical measures of emotion regulation are tasks involving control of attention (e.g., computer games involving attention shifting or focusing; see Nigg, 2000) or adults' reports (or self-reports) of children's ability to shift and focus attention or cope by using cognitive distraction (e.g., thinking about something that is not distressing; Eisenberg et al., 2001; Rothbart, Ahadi, & Hershey, 1994; Sandler, Tein, & West, 1994). In contrast, measures of behavioral regulation typically include tasks that assess the child's ability to start and stop movements on command (e.g., Oosterlaan & Sergeant, 1998), children's ability to control their expression of emotion (e.g., Saarni, 1984), and adults' reports (or self-reports) of the ability to inhibit behavior when it is appropriate to do so. These types of measures are discussed further shortly.

Effortful versus less voluntary modes of control

Like a number of other investigators, we believe that well-regulated individuals are not overly controlled or undercontrolled (i.e., inhibited, not regulated). Rather, well-regulated people have the ability to respond to the ongoing demands of experience with a range of responses that are socially acceptable and sufficiently flexible to allow for spontaneity as well as the ability to delay spontaneous reactions as needed (Cole, Michel, & Teti, 1994). Accordingly, the second distinction that we believe to be important when thinking about conceptualizing and measuring emotion-related control is between voluntary, effortful regulation and less voluntary types of control. It is useful to think of *control* as a superordinate category that includes both voluntary or effortful and reactive (or less voluntary) control. Regulation is one type of control – the effortful, voluntary type. Therefore, regulation generally is viewed as adaptive (although it may not be in all situations) and can be differentiated from the level of a child's *control* of behavior, which may be adaptive or maladaptive, depending on its flexibility and whether it can be voluntarily managed. In contrast, involuntary, reactive control is viewed as less optimal (considered emotion dysregulation by some researchers; see Cole, Michel, & Teti, 1994; Cicchetti, Ackerman, & Izard, 1995).

Voluntary control or regulation overlaps substantially at a conceptual level with what Rothbart has labeled effortful control: "the ability to inhibit a dominant response to perform a subdominant response" (Rothbart & Bates, 1998, p. 137). Although occasionally Rothbart has defined effortful control so that it sometimes appears to pertain only to attentional regulation (she and Posner often talk about "executive attention"; Posner & Rothbart, 1998), measures of effortful control (including Rothbart's) typically involve attentional regulation (e.g., the ability to voluntarily focus attention as needed) and/or behavioral regulation, the ability to effortfully inhibit behavior as appropriate (called inhibitory control). Although not usually mentioned in discussions of effortful control, the ability to activate behavior when one does not desire to do so (e.g., get moving on a task in the morning when it would be nicer to stay in bed; Derryberry &

Rothbart, 1988) also would seem to be an aspect of the construct of effortful control if defined more broadly (i.e., not just in regard to the ability to "inhibit").

Effortful control is believed to involve executive functioning in the anterior cingulate gyrus and the prefrontal cortex (Mirsky, 1996; Posner & DiGirolamo, 2000). This part of the brain appears to be involved in subjective feelings of voluntary control of thoughts and feelings, and comes into play when resolving conflict, correcting errors, and planning new actions (Posner & Rothbart, 1998).

Executive attention (effortful attentional processes), which is a large part of effortful control, shows initial gains in development in the early months of life and at approximately 18 months of age (Diamond, 1991; Posner & Rothbart, 1998). Although effortful control is still quite immature at 24 months of age, marked improvements are seen in the third year of life, from about 24 to 33 or 36 months of age (Gerardi-Caulton, 2000; Kochanska, Murray, & Harlan, 2000; Posner & Rothbart, 1998). The ability to effortfully inhibit behavior on tasks such as "Simon Says" is fairly good by 4 years of age (Reed, Pien, & Rothbart, 1984). Although effortful control seems to be fairly well developed by 4 or 5 years of age, researchers have found that regulation continues to improve across childhood and into adulthood (Murphy et al., 1999; Williams et al., 1999).

In contrast to effortful types of regulation are aspects of control (or the lack thereof) that are less voluntary or so automatic that they are not usually under voluntary control. As mentioned previously, we consider these types of control to be less optimal than effortful control because of their involuntary, reactive nature. Because the individual has less control over such processes, he or she is less flexible and lack of control often may result in inhibition or approach behaviors that are not appropriate in a given context.

Derryberry and Rothbart (1997) have discussed this difference between active (effortful) and more passive or reactive types of responding; they suggested that behavioral inhibition (including constrained behavior and fearful reactions to novel or challenging situations) involves reactive anxiety or fear and reflects passive rather than effortfully controlled behavior. Thus, involuntary or passive types of control likely include behavioral inhibition (which is not the same as inhibitory control) as seen in overcontrolled children, who are timid, constrained, and lack flexibility in novel or stressful situations. At the other extreme of passive control is impulsive behavior that is not voluntarily controlled and is reactive in that it reflects approach tendencies and reward dominance (i.e., the tendency to move toward rewards). Mezzacappa et al. (1998) and Nigg (2000) also have noted distinctions between effortful executive control and what they have labeled motivational control, which includes behavioral inhibition. These forms of involuntary control, specifically overcontrol (behavioral inhibition) and undercontrol (impulsivity), have been linked to a variety of behavioral and emotional problems in children, highlighting the premise that these regulatory processes are less optimal than effortful processes and may place children at risk for the development of problem behavior (e.g., Biederman et al., 1990; Eisenberg et al., 2001; Kagan et al., 1999).

A number of theorists have discussed the neurological bases of inhibited and impulsive types of responses. Gray (1975, 1987) has argued that there is a behavioral inhibition system (BIS) that is activated in situations involving novelty and stimuli signaling punishment or frustrative nonreward, and the behavioral activation system (BAS), which involves sensitivity to cues of reward and cessation of punishment. Fowles (1987), Patterson and Newman (1993), DePue and Collins (1999), and others have proposed variations on Gray's BAS/BIS systems, but numerous investigators believe there are separate (albeit related) social withdrawal and social facilitation or approach systems. According to Gray (Pickering & Gray, 1999), impulsive behavior is associated with high BAS and relatively low BIS functioning, whereas the BIS system inhibits behavior (e.g., due to fear of punishment). Such reactive systems appear to be seated primarily in subcortical systems (e.g., the amygdala for inhibition and mesolimbic dopamine pathways for approach; Cacioppo, Gardner, & Berntson, 1999; Pickering & Gray, 1999). Research of this kind suggests that the neurological bases of effortful control (regulation) and more reactive types of control/undercontrol are different. It also suggests that measures that utilize reward and punishment may tap both BIS and/or BAS functioning.

Proactive versus reactive regulation/coping

A third distinction among various aspects of emotion-related regulation/control concerns when the control occurs – prior to the elicitation of emotion and emotion-related physiological responding or in response to an event likely to elicit emotion. Most research on emotion-related regulation/control in children concerns how children deal with emotion in the evocative situation as it is being elicited (or perhaps stopped from being elicited). This type of regulation/coping is reactive and happens after the emotion starts to occur. Yet emotion can be regulated long before it occurs. Processes and behaviors that serve to manage and modulate emotional reactions and emotion-related behaviors prior to an evocative situation have been labeled as antecedent emotion regulation (Gross, 1999) or proactive coping (Aspinwall & Taylor, 1997). Proactive coping is defined as "efforts undertaken in advance of a potentially stressful event to prevent it or to modify its form before it occurs" (Aspinwall & Taylor, 1997, p. 417). It is defined as nearly always active and as not involving positive reappraisals (thinking about something in a more positive light) or other methods of internal emotion soothing. Examples include selecting situations so as to avoid negative emotion or stress, or to maximize positive experiences (e.g., a shy person declining an invitation to a large party) or seeking information prior to an event so as to influence its outcome. In contrast, antecedent emotion regulation is defined as involving both proactive coping (e.g., the selection or modification of situations) and emotion regulation processes such as attention deployment or cognitive change (e.g., managing emotional reactions before they occur by using attention and cognitive processes to choose the situations that are focused upon and how they are interpreted; Gross, 1999).

Unfortunately, as yet there are few measures of antecedent emotion regulation or proactive coping in childhood, probably partly because it is difficult for observers to know which overt behaviors are chosen by a child to modify evocative situations before they occur. Moreover, children may have difficulty accurately reporting their use of attention in selecting situations to think about. Thus, the measures we discuss generally do not tap antecedent emotion regulation/proactive coping (although some measures of coping might).

Measurement

Many measures of emotion regulation tap a combination of emotionality and regulation, effortful control, or some combination of effortful control and reactive control processes. In this section, we focus primarily on effortful, voluntary measures of regulation, although we also discuss briefly some measures of involuntary regulation and measures that likely tap both voluntary and involuntary regulation. Because many indices of coping also may tap effortful control, we also briefly discuss measures of coping.

Emotion regulation

Emotion regulation can involve cognitive constructions, behavioral or cognitive avoidance, self-soothing, and related physiological processes. However, the most commonly assessed component of emotion regulation is attentional processes such as shifting and sustaining attention. Researchers typically assess infants' and toddlers' attentional regulation using parental report measures. Two widely known measures are the Infant Behavior Questionnaire (IBQ; Rothbart, 1981) and the Toddler Behavior Assessment Questionnaire (TBAQ; Goldsmith, 1996). These measures have dimensions labeled attention span/persistence (IBQ) or interest/persistence (TBAQ). Example items are, "How often in the last week did your infant play with one toy or object for 5–10 minutes?" for the IBQ and "How often did your child play alone with his or her favorite toy for 30 minutes or longer?" for the TBAQ. It is important to note that in early infancy, orienting toward people and objects may be involuntary; however, it is likely that with age, these constructs reflect more effortful attentional control. Thus, the meaning of these scales may change with development.

   In childhood and adolescence, researchers sometimes obtain both parents' and teachers' reports of attentional control. These measures, especially those developed by Rothbart and colleagues, likely tap a preponderance of effortful control. The Children's Behavior Questionnaire (CBQ; ages 3–7; Goldsmith & Rothbart, 1991; Rothbart, Ahadi, & Hershey, 1994; Rothbart et al., 2001) and the Early Adolescent Temperament Questionnaire (EATQ; ages 9–15; Capaldi & Rothbart, 1992) are the most widely used measures assessing attentional control. The CBQ has specific scales designed to tap attentional focusing and shifting; the EATQ has one scale for attentional control. (Additional subscales on the CBQ and EATQ tap other components of temperament, such as predispositions toward experiencing fear and frustration.) Examples of attention items include, "when drawing or coloring in a book, shows strong concentration," for the CBQ and "pays close attention when someone tells him or her how to do something," for the EATQ. The CBQ and EATQ are currently available in parent-report formats; others have adapted the CBQ for teachers (e.g., Eisenberg et al., 1997; Murphy et al., 1999). The EATQ was originally created as a self-report measure for early adolescents and has been recently revised (EATQ-R) to include two behavioral scales assessing depressed mood and aggression. The DOTs (or Revised Dimensions of Temperament Survey; DOTs-R; Windle & Lerner, 1986) is another parent-report measure that has an attention-related scale (task orientation); it also has an adolescent self-report version that contains distractibility and persistence subscales.

Numerous researchers have examined attentional regulation in infants, toddlers, and children using observational methods (there is little observational research on adolescents). In much of this work, investigators have observed infants and young children's persistence and their ability to resolve conflicts of attention between simultaneous stimulus events. For example, procedures from the Laboratory Temperament Assessment Battery (Lab-TAB; Goldsmith & Rothbart, 1999) have been used to measure attentional regulation in infants, toddlers, and children. In one task, infants and toddlers are given an opportunity to manipulate objects (blocks) for a period of time that is thought to become boring, and their task orientation and persistence (i.e., duration of looking, latency to look away, manipulation of objects) are coded. Although it is unclear whether this measure fully reflects effortful control in infancy, we would expect that these types of measures partly tap effortful control. In addition, Posner and Rothbart (1998) reported using a Stroop-like task designed for toddlers at age 2–3. In this task, objects were presented on one side of a screen and the child was required to respond by patting a button that matched the stimulus shown. The appropriate button could be on either side of the stimulant, such that toddlers were required to act on the identity of the stimulus rather than to press the button that was on the same side as the stimulus, irrespective of its identity. Children aged 36–38 months performed with high accuracy on this task. Moreover, Stroop-type tasks and other measures requiring inhibition and/ or switching of attention have been used to measure sustained attention and emotion regulation in school-aged children and young adolescents; these measures have been linked to low levels of externalizing problems such as aggression or delinquency and prosocial behavior (e.g., Lin, Hsiao, & Chen, 1999; Mezzacappa, Kindlon, & Earls, 1999; White et al., 1994; Wilson, 2003). Moreover, in a study of elementary school children, the tendency to quickly avert and then redirect one's gaze to a distressing film, which would be expected to reduce arousal, was related to lower levels of externalizing problems (Eisenberg et al., 1996).

Although attentional processes are important components of emotion regulation, additional emotion regulation strategies also have been measured (some of which likely involve attentional control). Kopp (1989) and Grolnick, Bridges, and Connell (1996), working with toddlers and young children, have identified emotion regulation strategies such as self-soothing (e.g., thumb or finger sucking, hand clasping, hair twirling) and comfort-seeking. In addition, some attentional strategies such as gaze aversion, orienting toward objects or people, and self-distraction have been examined in infants and toddlers. Stifter and Braungart (1995) found that, in response to frustrating tasks, self-comforting and orienting behaviors were exhibited during periods of decreased negative arousal, suggesting that these strategies may have been successful in regulating distress. Similarly, Grolnick, Bridges, and Connell (1996) observed 2-year-olds' strategies in response to a delay task and found that children who used active engagement with substitute objects (i.e., self-distraction) were the least distressed, whereas children who focused on the delay object tended to be highly distressed (also see Calkins & Dedmon, 2000; Gilliom et al., 2002). These studies support the notion that there are important individual differences in the strategies that infants, toddlers, and children use to regulate distress, and that some strategies seem to be more effective than others. It should be noted that some display of distress is appropriate in certain situations and researchers should consider contextual factors when examining effective regulation. Other important issues for future work include the degree to which the various control processes reflect voluntary control, involuntary control, or a combination of the two, and how this changes with age.

One task that on the surface appears to reflect inhibitory control may actually tap effortful attentional regulation as much as inhibitory control. Mischel (1974) examined children's ability to delay gratification when they would receive a more desirable reward for waiting a longer period of time (e.g., they are told they will receive one pretzel immediately versus two if they wait until the experimenter returns). Mischel and colleagues found that providing children with strategies to divert their attention or modify the consumatory qualities of the reward (e.g., think about a marshmallow as a cloud rather than as food) helped children to delay (Mischel & Baker, 1972; Mischel & Ebbesen, 1970; also see Krueger et al., 1996). The ability to delay gratification on this task, especially when children were not provided with a strategy for doing so, has been linked to social and cognitive competence in adolescence and early adulthood (Mischel, 2000; Mischel, Shoda, & Peake, 1988; Shoda, Mischel, & Peake, 1990). It is likely that children who shifted their attention or used other cognitive strategies to divert themselves lessened their emotional reactions to the desired commodities – what Metcalfe and Mischel (1999) have labeled the "hot, emotional 'go' system." Therefore, performance on this task may tap not only the ability to inhibit the desire to touch a desirable commodity and possibly toss it into one's mouth (inhibitory behavioral control), but also the ability to effortfully control attention. Moreover, because this task involves waiting for a reward, failure to do so may be partly due to reactive impulsivity based on approach to rewards (BAS responding). Thus, this measure may tap a combination of effortful and high involuntary approach (i.e., impulsivity).

It is likely that some other measures of control (or the lack thereof) involve involuntary aspects of attention. For example, focusing on recurring thoughts (rumination) could be viewed as an involuntary attentional focusing that cannot be easily modified by effortful attentional control (see Derryberry & Reed, 2002; MacLeod et al., 2002). Unfortunately, the processes involved in this type of involuntary regulation have not been explored in children.

Behavioral control

As with emotion regulation, behavioral regulation is believed to emerge in late infancy to the early toddler years (Kopp, 1982). Early obvious manifestations of voluntary behavioral control include compliance to commands and self-initiated inhibition. These abilities increase over the first three years of life (Kopp, 1982; Kuczynski & Kochanska, 1990; Vaughn, Kopp, & Krakow, 1984) and continue to develop throughout early childhood. Individual differences in effortful behavioral regulation relate to compliance, adjustment, and social competence (e.g., Eisenberg et al., 2001; Eisenberg et al., 2000b; Kochanska, Murray & Coy, 1997; Kochanska, Coy, & Murray, 2001; Rothbart, Ahadi, & Hershey, 1994; see Eisenberg et al., 2000a).

Kochanska and colleagues (1997; Kochanska, Murray, & Harlan, 2000) have devised batteries of observational tasks to measure inhibitory control in toddlers, preschoolers, and 5- to 6-year olds. Moreover, other researchers have used similar tasks to assess effortful inhibitory control in older children (Eisenberg et al., 2001; Olsen, Schilling, & Bates, 1999; White et al., 1994). Observational measures tend to assess toddlers' and children's ability to (a) comply with demands (e.g., to clean up), (b) delay gratification, (c) inhibit motor behavior, and (d) suppress or initiate activities. During these interactions, adult experimenters ask children to perform specific tasks, and compliance in these situations is contextually appropriate. Individual differences in performance on these types of tasks appear to predict later conscience development (Kochanska, 1991; Lytton, 1977) and degree of behavior problems in children (Shaw, Keenan, & Vondra, 1994).

Diverse methodologies have been used to measure children's ability to inhibit their motor behaviors in the preschool years and beyond. For example, researchers often have examined children's ability to inhibit fine and gross motor movements (Kochanksa, Murray, & Harlan, 2000; Maccoby et al., 1965; Olsen, Schilling, & Bates, 1999). Typically, the child is asked to walk a line (marked with tape on the floor) or to draw a line as slowly as possible. Or they might be asked to have a turtle and rabbit negotiate a path slowly and fast, respectively (and then look at the difference in timing from a baseline; Kochanska, Murray, & Harlan, 2000). Tasks designed to measure the ability to suppress and initiate activity to a signal also have been used. For example, Reed, Pien, & Rothbart (1984) had 40–49-month-old children play a simplified version of "Simon Says" to measure the child's ability to follow instructions given by one stuffed animal (initiate activity) and to ignore instructions given by a different stuffed animal (suppress activity). Tasks involving the ability to inhibit and activate motor behavior in school-aged children generally relate in predictable ways to outcomes (e.g., Mezzacappa, Kindlon, & Earls, 1999; Nigg, 1999; Oosterlaan & Sergeant, 1996, 1998). However, in certain observational tasks, children may appear regulated because they are overly inhibited in the experimental context.

Tasks designed to measure children's control of facial disappointment when it is socially inappropriate probably also tap effortful inhibitory control (although emotion regulation also may be involved). In these tasks, children's reactions (i.e., positive and negative emotions) to an unattractive prize are coded (Cole, Zahn-Waxler, & Smith, 1994; Eisenberg et al., 2001; Saarni, 1984). Children who are at risk for behavior problems have been found to express high levels of negative emotions in response to these types of disappointment tasks (Cole, Zahn-Waxler, & Smith, 1994; Eisenberg et al., 2001).

The aforementioned delay of gratification tasks in which a child is asked to wait to touch or play with an attractive toy or snack also have been used to measure behavioral regulation in toddlers and children (Grolnick, Bridges, & Connell, 1996; Kochanska, Murray, & Coy, 1997; Kochanska, Murray, & Harlan, 2000; Kochanska, Tjebkes, & Forman, 1998; Morales & Bridges, 1996; Silverman & Ragusa, 1992). In one task used with children, the child and experimenter place an M&M on their tongues and have a contest to see who can keep the candy there the longest – a task that certainly tests the limits of children's inhibitory control (Kochanska et al., 1996). These tasks involve inhibiting behavior upon command, rather than voluntarily making a choice to delay a reward and inhibiting behavior accordingly as in Mischel's paradigm. As for Mischel's measures of delay of gratification (see above), performance on tasks in which children are told to delay touching an attractive object likely reflect attentional as well as behavioral control, and reward dominance/impulsivity (BAS responding) as well as effortful control. It may be that failure to delay reflects primarily reward-related impulsivity, whereas the ability to delay reflects effortful behavioral or attentional control.

Other measures also are likely to measure a mix of attentional and behavioral control, as well as either effortful or low reactive control. For example, Eisenberg and colleagues (Eisenberg et al., 2001; Spinrad et al., 1999) had children attempt to assemble a jigsaw puzzle by putting their arms through sleeves that go into a box containing the puzzle; thus, they cannot see the puzzle. Children were instructed to try to complete the puzzle without looking at it and were told that if they finished the puzzle within the allowed time, they would receive a prize. Children's cheating (i.e., looking at the puzzle by lifting the sleeves) can be viewed as measuring low involuntary control (or high impulsivity due to BAS reward-dominance responding), whereas children's persistence on the puzzle task may measure effortful behavioral control (and attentional control).

Another type of measure of behavioral control that likely assesses involuntary control involves reward dominance games (Newman, Patterson, & Kosson, 1987; see also White et al., 1994). For example, using a computer, researchers have had children play a card game that involves rewards (adding "nickels") and punishments (losing "nickels"), and children can choose to discontinue the game at any time. Shortly into the game, there is a steadily increasing ratio of punishments to rewards. The number of trials that children play before discontinuing the game is coded. This assessment has been viewed as a marker of impulsivity or reward dominance and has been related to children's delinquent behavior (White et al., 1994) and externalizing problems (for children without comorbid anxiety problems; e.g., O'Brien & Frick, 1996).

In addition to observational measures of behavioral control, parents and teachers can rate behavioral control with the inhibitory control (voluntary control) and impulsivity (low reactive BIS control and/or high BAS responding) subscales of the CBQ. Inhibitory control measures the capacity for an individual to suppress inappropriate responses (e.g., "can wait before entering into activities if he or she is asked to"). Impulsivity measures the child's tendency to act without thinking (e.g., "sometimes interrupts others when they are speaking"). Parental reports of behavioral control have been positively related to children's effortful control using observational methods (Kochanksa, Murray, & Coy, 1997), and have been positively related to children's social competence and negatively related to children's problem behavior (Eisenberg et al., 2000a, 2001). Moreover, the combination of adult-reported effortful inhibitory control and attentional control (sometimes combined with behavioral measures of persistence) predict social competence and adjustment in school-aged children (e.g., Eisenberg et al., 2003; Valiente et al., 2003). It is likely that some parents cannot differentiate between inhibition due to effortful control and that due to temperamental behavioral inhibition (or high versus low inhibition); thus, adults' reports of inhibitory control sometimes may reflect a mix of effortful and passive control.

The revised version of the EATQ (Capaldi & Rothbart, 1992) also has a scale that taps inhibitory control in adolescence. As mentioned previously, the EATQ has self- and parent-report formats. Items on the inhibitory control scale tap adolescents' capacity to plan and to suppress socially inappropriate responses. Sample items include, "the more I try to stop myself from doing something I shouldn't, the more likely I am to do it" (reversed scored), and "I can stick with my plans and goals." Questions on this measure are designed to tap experiences common to adolescents.

Coping

Measures of coping with stress often involve the regulation of ongoing emotion (and less frequently assess proactive coping). In research on older children and adolescents, theorists have identified a long list of strategies for coping with stress, including problem-solving, information-seeking, cognitive restructuring, seeking understanding, catastrophizing, emotional release or ventilation, physical activities, acceptance, distraction, avoidance, self-criticism, blaming others, wishful thinking, humor, suppression, social withdrawal, resigned acceptance, denial, alcohol or drug use, seeking social support, and utilizing religious or spiritual support (Compas et al., 1999, 2001). Some of these strategies (e.g., cognitive distraction, cognitive restructuring) obviously involve attentional regulation; other strategies appear to involve activational control (getting a plan accomplished). Still others seem to reflect the lack of effortful attentional (catastrophizing) or behavioral regulation (emotional release or venting, if not done for instrumental purposes).

Researchers studying older children's and adolescents' coping often use self-report measures, typically assessing regulation in terms of children's coping responses to hypothetical vignettes involving emotion and emotion management strategies (e.g., Band & Weisz, 1988; Saarni, 1997). In addition, children's dispositional coping strategies have been measured by self-report using the Children's Coping Strategies Checklist (CCSC; Ayers et al., 1996; see Sandler, Tein, & West, 1994). With this measure, children rate how often they used particular coping behaviors when they had a problem in the last month. This measure has produced four factors:

1 Active strategies, including dimensions of cognitive decision making (e.g., "thought about what you could do before you did something"), direct problem solving (e.g., "you did something to make things better"), positive cognitive restructuring (e.g., "you reminded yourself that you are better off than a lot of other kids"), and seeking understanding (e.g., "you thought about why it happened").
2 Avoidant strategies, including items reflecting cognitive avoidance (e.g., "you tried to put it out of your mind") and avoidant actions (e.g., "you avoided the people who made you feel bad").
3 Distraction strategies, including distracting actions (e.g., "you listened to music") and physical release of emotions (e.g., "you played sports").
4 Support seeking strategies, including problem-focused support (e.g., "you asked your mother/father for help in figuring out what to do") and emotion-focused support (e.g., "you told your mother/father how you felt about the problem").

Moreover, a parent-report version of this questionnaire has been devised.

As already noted, although coping clearly can involve the regulation of internal emotion-related states and behaviors associated with emotion, it often is unclear if coping reactions reflect effortful regulation in these domains or reactive control (e.g., avoiding a situation because it is aversive or stressful). Further, it is not clear if all coping strategies are equally effective (see Compas et al., 2001). The effectiveness of coping depends somewhat on the situation and the individual. For example, research indicates that avoidant coping is viewed as a more adaptive strategy for younger than older children (Eisenberg et al., 1993, 1999; Kliewer, 1991). In addition, active coping is less likely to be a successful strategy when an individual has little or no control over a situation than in controllable contexts (Miller & Green, 1985). The relations of various modes of coping to other measures of regulation/control and the adaptive value of specific coping behaviors are issues for future theoretical and empirical inquiry.

Physiological Measures of Regulation

The experience of emotion and its regulation are controlled by the autonomic nervous system (Porges, Doussard-Roosevelt, & Maiti, 1994). Research on autonomic correlates of emotion has focused primarily on two branches of the nervous system: the sympathetic branch, which mobilizes the body to react in an emergency, and the parasympathetic branch, which conserves and maintains bodily resources. The parasympathetic branch works to regulate and decrease emotional arousal, and usually counteracts the activation of the sympathetic branch, which is responsible for arousal.

Researchers using physiological measures of regulation have relied primarily on indices of cardiac activity. Typically, heart rate variability that occurs at the frequency of breathing (respiratory sinus arrhythmia; RSA) is thought to be an estimate of parasympathetic influence (although some measures, often labeled vagal tone, have not actually measured respiration). Baseline cardiac vagal tone or RSA has been related to differences in infants' appropriate emotional reactivity (Porter, Porges, & Marshall, 1988; Stifter & Fox, 1990; Stifter, Fox, & Porges, 1989). In addition, high RSA has been associated with infants' attentional abilities (Porges, 1991; Richards, 1987; Stifter, Fox, & Porges, 1989) and with externalizing problems in 2-year-old boys (but not girls; Calkins & Dedmon, 2000).

In young school-aged children, vagal tone was positively related to measures of social competence, constructive coping, and low emotionality for boys, whereas the reverse was true for girls (Eisenberg et al., 1995). This pattern was somewhat weaker two years later (Eisenberg, et al., 1997). High RSA also has been linked to low antisocial behavior in adolescent boys (Mezzacappa et al., 1997; also see Pine et al., 1998).

Moreover, *changes* in cardiac activity or vagal tone appear to be related to regulation in infancy and childhood. In situations where regulation is required, one would expect a decrease in vagal tone (vagal suppression). Recent evidence supports the notion that vagal suppression is related to higher attentional and state regulation in infancy and childhood (Calkins & Dedmon, 2000; DeGangi et al., 1991; Gottman, Katz, & Hooven, 1996, 1997; Huffman et al., 1998; see Beauchaine, 2001). For example, Huffman et al.

(1998) found that 3-month-old infants who showed decreases in vagal tone (from baseline to social/attention challenges) were rated higher on maternal reports of orienting and soothability than were infants who showed increases in cardiac vagal tone. Moreover, in a sample of 2-year-olds, Calkins and Dedmon (2000) found that children classified by parents as displaying symptoms of aggressive/destructive behavior problems exhibited significantly lower RSA suppression during challenging situations than did children with few symptoms. Vagal suppression also has been associated with low levels of aggressive behavior with peers in school-aged children (Gottman, Katz, & Hooven, 1997).

It is likely that vagal (RSA) suppression partly taps effortful control. In fact, vagal modulation of respiratory drive, high frequency heart-rate variability, has been associated with executive control (i.e., effortful control) on behavioral tasks. In contrast, motivational control (e.g., passive avoidance, avoidance of punishment and low reward dominance) has been associated with sympathetic modulation of low-frequency heart-rate variability (Mezzacappa et al., 1998). Furthermore, low heart-rate variability, which is substantially negatively related to RSA/vagal tone, appears to be associated with involuntary behavioral inhibition (e.g., restrained behavior when dealing with novel or stressful situations; Kagan, 1998), which supports the notion that baseline heart rate measures of variability that are not examined in relation to respiration reflect high reactive control. It is possible that both resting RSA and heart rate variability do not tap effortful regulatory processes to the same degree as does vagal suppression or certain aspects of vagal tone (i.e., the part linked most closely to parasympathetic functioning; Mezzacappa et al., 1998).

Conclusion and Future Directions

In summary, there are numerous measures of emotion-related regulation that are being used in current research. However, in many cases it is unclear what aspects of emotion-related regulation/control are being assessed (behavioral or emotional) and if the control is voluntary or reactive. Thus, children may appear to be regulated when they simply are inhibited in stressful or novel situations. If children cannot effortfully control their attention, cognition, or actions, they cannot adapt to changing circumstances in flexible and appropriate ways. In addition, regulation that is effortful likely is more easily taught than is the control of reward-related approach tendencies or the relaxing of involuntary inhibition.

Investigators have begun examining the interrelations of various measures of regulation/control. Although findings are not highly consistent, there is some evidence that measures of reactive (less voluntary, motivational) control (or the lack thereof) group statistically whereas measures of effortful control also group together (Kindlon, Mezzacappa, & Earls, 1995; Olsen, Schilling, & Bates, 1999). However, the two types of measures also correlate; for example, adults' reports of children's impulsivity tend to be negatively related to their reports of inhibitory control (e.g., Eisenberg et al., 1995) and effortful inhibitory control is linked to low impulsivity in adulthood (Logan, Schachar,

& Tannock, 1997). Because effortful regulation likely can be used, at least to some degree, to inhibit reactive impulsivity, this relation should be expected. Nonetheless, it will be important to identify groups of measures that reflect similar aspects of control and map onto differences in neurological and autonomic functioning believed to underlie effortful control and reactive types of control.

As noted previously, there currently are few measures of proactive emotion regulation or proactive coping. However, some coping measures tap how children manage their cognitions when dealing with stress (e.g., positive cognitive restructuring or thinking about something in a more positive light; Sandler, Tein, & West, 1994); analogous measures might be constructed to assess conscious efforts to choose a priori the situations (or aspects of situations) that children focus upon. Moreover, measures of how children construct their worlds to minimize negative affectivity and enhance positive emotion could be devised. The development of measures of proactive regulation will provide a new window into how children manage their emotions and emotion-related behavior.

Acknowledgments

This research was supported by a grant (1 R01 MH60838) and a Research Scientist Award from the National Institutes of Mental Health (KO5 M801321) to Nancy Eisenberg.

References

Aspinwall, L. G. & Taylor, S. E. (1997). A stitch in time: Self-regulation and proactive coping. *Psychological Bulletin, 121*, 417–36.

Ayers, T. S., Sandler, I. N., West, S. G., & Roosa, M. W. (1996). A dispositional and situational assessment of children's coping: Testing alternative models of coping. *Journal of Personality, 64*, 923–58.

Band, E. B. & Weisz, J. R. (1988). How to feel better when it feels bad: Children's perspectives on coping with everyday stress. *Developmental Psychology, 24*, 247–53.

Beauchaine, T. (2001). Vagal tone, development, and Gray's motivational theory: Toward an integrated model of autonomic nervous system functioning in psychopathology. *Development and Psychopathology, 13*, 183–214.

Biederman, J., Rosenbaum, J. F., Hirshfeld, D. R., Faraone, S. V., Bolduc, E. A., Gersten, M., Meminger, S. R., Kagan, J., Snidman, N., & Reznick J. S. (1990). Psychiatric correlates of behavioral inhibition in young children of parents with and without psychiatric disorders. *Archives of General Psychiatry, 47*, 21–6.

Cacioppo, J. T., Gardner, W. L., & Berntson, G. G. (1999). The affect system has parallel and integrative processing components: Form follows function. *Journal of Personality and Social Psychology, 76*, 839–55.

Calkins, S. D. & Dedmon, S. E. (2000). Physiological and behavioral regulation in two-year-old children with aggressive/destructive behavior problems. *Journal of Abnormal Child Psychology, 28*, 103–18.

Campos, J. J., Mumme, D. L., Kermoian, R., & Campos, R. G. (1994). A functionalist perspective on the nature of emotion. In N. A. Fox (ed.), The development of emotion regulation:

Biological and behavioral considerations. *Monographs of the Society for Research in Child Development*, *59*, 284–303.

Capaldi, D. M. & Rothbart, M. K. (1992). Development and validation of an early adolescent temperament measure. *Journal of Early Adolescence*, *12*, 153–73.

Cicchetti, D., Ackerman, B. P., & Izard, C. E. (1995). Emotions and emotion regulation in developmental psychopathology. *Development and Psychopathology*, *7*, 1–10.

Cole, P. M., Martin, S. E., & Dennis, T. A. (2004). Emotion regulation as a scientific construct: Methodological challenges and directions for child development research. *Child Development*, *75(1)*, 313–14.

Cole, P. M., Michel, M. K., & Teti, L. O. (1994). The development of emotion regulation and dysregulation: A clinical perspective. *Monographs of the Society for Research in Child Development*, *59* (serial no. 240), 73–100.

Cole, P. M., Zahn-Waxler, C., & Smith, K. D. (1994). Expressive control during a disappointment task: Variations related to preschoolers' behavior problems. *Developmental Psychology*, *30*, 835–46.

Compas, B. E., Connor, J. K., Saltzman, H., Thomsen, A. H., & Wadsworth, M. G. (1999). Getting specific about coping: Effortful and involuntary responses to stress in development. In M. Lewis, and D. Ramsay (eds.), *Soothing and stress* (pp. 229–56). Mahwah, NJ: Lawrence Erlbaum Associates.

Compas, B. E., Connor, J. K., Saltzman, H., Thomsen, A. H., & Wadsworth, M. E. (2001). Coping with stress during childhood and adolescence: Problems, progress, and potential in theory and research. *Psychological Bulletin*, *127*, 87–127.

DeGangi, G., DiPietro, J., Porges, S. W., & Greenspan, S. (1991). Psychophysiological characteristics of the regulatory disordered infant. *Infant Behavior and Development*, *14*, 37–50.

DePue, R. A. & Collins, P. F. (1999). Neurobiology of the structure of personality: Dopamine, facilitation of incentive motivation, and extraversion. *Behavioral and Brain Sciences*, *22*, 491–599.

Derryberry, D. & Reed, M. A. (2002). Anxiety-related attentional biases and their regulation by attentional control. *Journal of Abnormal Psychology*, *111*, 225–36.

Derryberry, D. & Rothbart, M. K. (1988). Arousal, affect, and attention as components of temperament. *Journal of Personality and Social Psychology*, *55*, 958–66.

Derryberry, D. & Rothbart, M. K. (1997). Reactive and effortful processes in the organization of temperament. *Development and Psychopathology*, *9*, 633–52.

Diamond, A. (1991). Neuropsychological insights into the meaning of object concept development. In S. Carey & R. Gelman (eds.), *The epigenesis of mind: Essays on biology and cognition*. Hillsdale, NJ: Lawrence Erlbaum Associates.

Eisenberg, N. & Morris, A. S. (2002). Children's emotion-related regulation. In R. Kail (ed.), *Advances in child development and behavior* (vol. 30, pp. 190–229). Amsterdam: Academic Press.

Eisenberg, N., Fabes, R. A., Bernzweig, J., Karbon, M., Poulin, R., & Hanish, L. (1993). The relations of emotionality and regulation to preschoolers' social skills and sociometric status. *Child Development*, *64*, 1418–38.

Eisenberg, N., Fabes, R. A., Murphy, M., Maszk, P., Smith, M., & Karbon, M. (1995). The role of emotionality and regulation in children's social functioning: A longitudinal study. *Child Development*, *66*, 1239–61.

Eisenberg, N., Fabes, R. A., Guthrie, I. K., Murphy, B. C., Maszk, P., Holmgren, R., & Suh, K. (1996). The relations of regulation and emotionality to problem behavior in elementary school children. *Development and Psychopathology*, *8*, 141–62.

Eisenberg, N., Fabes, R. A., Shepard, S. A., Murphy, B. C., Guthrie, I. K., Jones, S., Friedman, J., Poulin, R., & Maszk, P. (1997). Contemporaneous and longitudinal prediction of children's social functioning from regulation and emotionality. *Child Development*, 68, 642–64.

Eisenberg, N., Fabes, R. A., Murphy, B. C., Shepard, S., Guthrie, I. K., Mazsk, P., Poulin, R., & Jones, S. (1999). Prediction of elementary school children's socially appropriate and problem behavior from anger reactions at age 4 to 6. *Journal of Applied Developmental Psychology*, 20, 119–42.

Eisenberg, N., Fabes, R. A., Guthrie, I. K., & Reiser, M. (2000a). Dispositional emotionality and regulation: Their role in predicting quality of social functioning. *Journal of Personality and Social Psychology*, 78, 136–57.

Eisenberg, N., Guthrie, I. K., Fabes, R. A., Shepard, S., Losoya, S., Murphy, B., Jones, S., Poulin, R., & Reiser, M. (2000b). Prediction of elementary school children's externalizing problem behaviors from attentional and behavioral regulation and negative emotionality. *Child Development*, 71, 1367–82.

Eisenberg, N., Cumberland, A., Spinrad, T. L., Fabes, R. A., Shepard, S. A., Reiser, M., Murphy, B. C., Losoya, S. H., & Guthrie, I. K. (2001). The relations of regulation and emotionality to children's externalizing and internalizing problem behavior. *Child Development*, 72, 1112–34.

Eisenberg, N., Valiente, C., Fabes, R. A., Smith, C. L., Reiser, M., Shepard, S. A., Losoya, S. H., Guthrie, I. K., Murphy, B. C., & Cumberland, A. (2003). The relations of effortful control and ego control to children's resiliency and social functioning. *Developmental Psychology*, 39, 761–76.

Fowles, D. C. (1987). Application of a behavioral theory of motivation to the concepts of anxiety and impulsivity. *Journal of Research in Personality*, 21, 417–35.

Gerardi-Caulton, G. (2000). Sensitivity to spatial conflict and the development of self-regulation in children 24–36 months of age. *Developmental Science*, 3, 397–404.

Gilliom, M., Shaw, D. S., Beck, J. E., Schonberg, M. A., & Lukon, J. L. (2002). Anger regulation in disadvantaged preschool boys: Strategies, antecedents, and the development of self-control. *Developmental Psychology*, 38, 222–35.

Goldsmith, H. H. (1996). Studying temperament via construction of the Toddler Behavior Assessment Questionnaire. *Child Development*, 67, 218–35.

Goldsmith, H. H. & Rothbart, M. K. (1991). Contemporary instruments for assessing early temperament by questionnaire and in the laboratory. In A. Angleitner & J. Strelau (eds.), *Explorations in temperament* (pp. 249–72). New York: Plenum Press.

Goldsmith, H. H. & Rothbart, M. K. (1999). *The Laboratory Temperament Assessment Battery* (locomotor version, edition 3.1). Madison, WI: University of Wisconsin-Madison.

Gottman, J. M., Katz, L. F., & Hooven, C. (1996). Parental meta-emotion philosophy and the emotional life of families: theoretical models and preliminary data. *Journal of Family Psychology*, 10, 243–68.

Gottman, J. M., Katz, L. F., & Hooven, C. (1997). *Meta-emotion: How families communicate emotionally*. Mahwah, NJ: Lawrence Erlbaum Associates.

Gray, J. A. (1975). *Elements of a two-process theory of learning*. New York: Academic Press.

Gray, J. A. (1987). Perspectives and anxiety and impulsivity: A commentary. *Journal of Research in Personality*, 21, 493–509.

Grolnick, W. S., Bridges, L. J., & Connell, J. P. (1996). Emotion regulation in two-year-olds: Strategies and emotional expression in four contexts. *Child Development*, 67, 928–41.

Gross, J. J. (1999). Emotion and emotion regulation. In L. A. Pervin & O. P. John (eds.), *Handbook of personality: Theory and research* (2nd edn., pp. 525–52). New York: Guilford.

Huffman, L. C., Bryan, Y., del Carmen, R., Pedersen, F., Dussard-Roosevelt, J., & Porges, S. W. (1998). Infant temperament and cardiac vagal tone: Assessments at twelve weeks of age. *Child Development*, 69, 624–35.

Kagan, J. (1998). Biology and the child. In W. Damon (series ed.) and N. Eisenberg (vol. ed.), *Handbook of child psychology*, vol. 3: *Social, emotional, and personality development* (pp. 177–235). New York: John Wiley.

Kagan, J., Snidman, N., Zentner, M., & Person, E. (1999). Infant temperament and anxious symptoms in school age children. *Development and Psychopathology*, 11, 209–24.

Kindlon, D., Mezzacappa, E., & Earls, F. (1995). Psychometric properties of impulsivity measures: Temporal stability, validity, and factor structure. *Journal of Child Psychology and Psychiatry and Allied Disciplines*, 36, 645–61.

Kliewer, W. (1991). Coping in middle childhood: Relations to competence, type A behavior, monitoring, blunting, and locus of control. *Developmental Psychology*, 27, 689–97.

Kochanska, G. (1991). Socialization and temperament in the development of guilt and conscience. *Child Development*, 62, 1379–92.

Kochanska, G., Coy, K. C., & Murray, K. T. (2001). The development of self-regulation in the first four years of life. *Child Development*, 72, 1092–111.

Kochanska, G., Murray, K., & Coy, K. (1997). Inhibitory control as a contributor to conscience in childhood: From toddler to early school age. *Child Development*, 68, 263–77.

Kochanska, G., Murray, K., & Harlan, E. T. (2000). Effortful control in early childhood: Continuity and change, antecedents, and implications for social development. *Developmental Psychology*, 36, 220–32.

Kochanska, G., Murray, K., Jacques, T. Y., Koenig, A. L., & Vandegeest, K. A. (1996). Inhibitory control in young children and its role in emerging internalization. *Child Development*, 67, 490–507.

Kochanska, G., Tjebkes, T. L., & Forman, D. R. (1998). Children's emerging regulation of conduct: Restraint, compliance, and internalization from infancy to the second year. *Child Development*, 69, 1378–89.

Kopp, C. B. (1982). Antecedents of self-regulation: A developmental perspective. *Development Psychology*, 18, 199–214.

Kopp, C. B. (1989). Regulation of distress and negative emotions: A developmental view. *Developmental Psychology*, 25, 343–54.

Krueger, R. F., Caspi, A., Moffitt, T. E., White, J., & Stouthamer-Loeber, M. (1996). Delay of gratification, psychopathology, and personality: Is low self-control specific to externalizing problems? *Journal of Personality*, 64, 107–29.

Kuczynski, L. & Kochanska, G. (1990). Development of children's noncompliance strategies from toddlerhood to age 5. *Developmental Psychology*, 26, 398–408.

Lin, C. C. H., Hsiao, C. K., & Chen, W. J. (1999). Development of sustained attention assessed using the continuous performance test among children 6–15 years of age. *Journal of Abnormal Child Psychology*, 27, 403–12.

Logan, G. D., Schachar, R. J., & Tannock, R. (1997). Impulsivity and inhibitory control. *Psychological Science*, 8, 60–64.

Lytton, H. (1977). Correlates of compliance and the rudiments of conscience in two-year-old boys. *Canadian Journal of Behavioral Science*, 9, 242–51.

Maccoby, E. E., Dowley, E., Hagen, J., & Dergerman, R. (1965). Activity level and intellectual functioning in normal preschool children. *Child Development*, 36, 761–70.

MacLeod, C., Rutherford, E., Campbell, L., Ebsworthy, G., & Holker, L. (2002). Selective attention and emotional vulnerability: Assessing the causal basis of their association through the experimental manipulation of attentional bias. *Journal of Abnormal Psychology*, 111, 107–23.

Metcalfe, J. & Mischel, W. (1999). A hot/cool-system analysis of delay of gratification: Dynamics of willpower. *Psychological Review, 106,* 3–19.

Mezzacappa, E., Kindlon, D., & Earls, F. (1999). Relations of age to cognitive and motivational elements of impulse control in boys with and without externalizing behavior problems. *Journal of Abnormal Child Psychology, 27,* 473–83.

Mezzacappa, E., Kindlon, D., Saul, J. P., & Earls, F. (1998). Executive and motivational control of performance task behavior, and autonomic heart-rate regulation in children: Physiologic validation of two-factor solution inhibitory control. *Journal of Child Psychology and Psychiatry, 39,* 525–31.

Mezzacappa, E., Tremblay, R., Kindlon, D., Saul, J., Arseneault, L., Seguin, J., Pihl, R., & Earls, F. (1997). Anxiety, antisocial behavior, and heart rate regulation in adolescent males. *Journal of Child Psychiatry and Psychology, 38,* 457–69.

Miller, S. M. & Green, M. L. (1985). Coping with stress and frustration: Origins, nature and development. In M. Lewis & C. Saarni (eds.), *The socialization of emotions* (pp. 263–314). New York: Plenum Press.

Mirsky, A. F. (1996). Disorders of attention: A neuropsychological perspective. In G. R. Lyon & N. A. Krasnegor (eds.), *Attention, memory, and executive function* (pp. 71–93). Baltimore, MD: Paul H. Brookes.

Mischel, W. (1974). Processes in delay of gratification. In L. Berkowitz (ed.), *Progress in experimental personality research* (vol. 3, pp. 249–92). New York: Academic Press.

Mischel, W. (2000). Attention control in the service of the self: Harnessing willpower in goal pursuit. Paper presented at the National Institute of Mental Health Self-Workshop, Bethesda, MD, June.

Mischel, W. & Baker, N. (1972). Cognitive appraisals and transformations in delay behavior. *Journal of Personality and Social Psychology, 31,* 254–61.

Mischel, W. & Ebbesen, E. B. (1970). Attention in delay of gratification. *Journal of Personality and Social Psychology, 16,* 329–37.

Mischel, W., Shoda, Y., & Peake, P. K. (1988). The nature of adolescent competencies predicted by preschool delay of gratification. *Journal of Personality and Social Psychology, 54,* 687–96.

Morales, M. & Bridges, L. J. (1996). Associations between nonparental care experience and preschooler's emotion regulation in the presence of the mother. *Journal of Applied Developmental Psychology, 17,* 577–96.

Murphy, B. C., Eisenberg, N., Fabes, R. A., Shepard, S., & Guthrie, I. K. (1999). Consistency and change in children's emotionality and regulation: A longitudinal study. *Merrill-Palmer Quarterly, 46,* 413–44.

Newman, J. P., Patterson, C. M., & Kosson, D. (1987). Response perseveration in psychopaths. *Journal of Abnormal Psychology, 96,* 145–8.

Nigg, J. T. (1999). The ADHD response-inhibition deficit as measured by the Stop Task: Replication with *DSM-IV* combined type, extension, and qualification. *Journal of Abnormal Child Psychology, 27,* 393–402.

Nigg, J. T. (2000). On inhibition/disinhibition in developmental psychopathology: Views from cognitive and personality psychology and a working inhibition taxonomy. *Psychological Bulletin, 26,* 220–46.

O'Brien, B. S. & Frick, P. J. (1996). Reward dominance: Associations with anxiety, conduct problems, and psychopathy in children. *Journal of Abnormal Child Psychology, 24,* 223–39.

Olsen, S. L., Schilling, E. M., & Bates, J. E. (1999). Measurement of impulsivity: Construct coherence, longitudinal stability, and relationship with externalizing problems in middle childhood and adolescence. *Journal of Abnormal Child Psychology, 27,* 151–65.

Oosterlaan, J. & Sergeant, J. A. (1996). Inhibition in ADHD, aggressive, and anxious children: A biologically based model of child psychopathology. *Journal of Abnormal Child Psychology, 24,* 19–36.

Oosterlaan, J. & Sergeant, J. A. (1998). Effects of reward and response cost on response inhibition in ADHD, disruptive, anxious, and normal children. *Journal of Abnormal Child Psychology, 26,* 161–74.

Patterson, C. M. & Newman, J. P. (1993). Reflectivity and learning from aversive events: Toward a psychological mechanism for the syndromes of disinhibition. *Psychological Review, 100,* 716–36.

Pickering, A. D. & Gray, J. A. (1999). The neuroscience of personality. In L. Pervin & O. John (eds.), *Handbook of personality* (pp. 277–99). San Francisco, CA: Guilford.

Pine, D., Wasserman, G., Miller, L., Coplan, J., Bagiella, E., Kovlenku, P., Myers, M., & Sloan, R. (1998). Heart period variability and psychopathology in urban boys at risk for delinquency. *Psychophysiology, 35,* 521–9.

Porges, S. W. (1991). Vagal tone: An autonomic mediator of affect. In J. Garber & K. A. Dodge (eds.), *The development of emotional regulation and dysregulation* (pp. 111–28). Cambridge: Cambridge University Press.

Porges, S. W., Doussard-Roosevelt, J. A., & Maiti, A. K. (1994). Vagal tone and the physiological regulation of emotion. In N. A. Fox (ed.), *Emotion regulation: Behavioral and biological considerations, Monographs of the Society for Research in Child Development, 59* (2–3, serial no. 240), 167–86.

Porter, F. L., Porges, S. W., & Marshall, R. E. (1988). Newborn pain cries and vagal tone: Parallel changes in response to circumcision. *Child Development, 59,* 495–505.

Posner, M. I. & DiGirolamo, G. J. (2000). Cognitive neuroscience: Origins and promise. *Psychological Bulletin, 126,* 873–89.

Posner, M. I. & Rothbart, M. K. (1998). Attention, self-regulation, and consciousness. *Philosophical Transactions of the Royal Society of London B, 353,* 1915–27.

Reed, M. A., Pien, D. L., & Rothbart, M. K. (1984). Inhibitory self-control in preschool children. *Merrill-Palmer Quarterly, 30,* 131–47.

Richards, J. E. (1987). Infant visual sustained attention and respiratory sinus arrhythmia. *Child Development, 58,* 488–96.

Rothbart, M. K. (1981). Measurement of temperament in infancy. *Child Development, 52,* 569–78.

Rothbart, M. K., Ahadi, S. A., & Hershey, K. L. (1994). Temperament and social behavior in childhood. *Merrill-Palmer Quarterly, 40,* 21–39.

Rothbart, M. K., Ahadi, S. A., Hershey, K. L., & Fisher, P. (2001). Investigations of temperament at three to seven years: The Children's Behavior Questionnaire. *Child Development, 72,* 1394–1408.

Rothbart, M. K. & Bates, J. E. (1998). Temperament. In W. Damon (series ed.) and N. Eisenberg (vol. ed.), *Handbook of child psychology*, vol. 3: *Social, emotional, and personality development* (pp. 105–76). New York: John Wiley.

Rothbart, M. K. & Derryberry, D. (1981). Development of individual differences in temperament. In M. E. Lamb & A. L. Brown (eds.), *Advances in developmental psychology* (vol. 1, pp. 37–86). Hillsdale, NJ: Lawrence Erlbaum Associates.

Saarni, C. (1984). An observational study of children's attempts to monitor their expressive behavior. *Child Development, 55,* 1504–13.

Saarni, C. (1997). Coping with aversive feelings. *Motivation and Emotion, 21,* 45–63.

Sandler, I. N., Tein, J., & West, S. G. (1994). Coping, stress and the psychological symptoms of children of divorce: A cross-sectional and longitudinal study. *Child Development, 65,* 1744–63.

Shaw, D. S., Keenan, K., & Vondra, J. I. (1994). Developmental precursors of externalizing behavior: Ages 1 to 3. *Developmental Psychology, 30*, 355–64.

Shoda, Y., Mischel, W., & Peake, P. K. (1990). Predicting adolescent cognitive and self-regulatory competencies from preschool delay of gratification: Identifying diagnostic conditions. *Developmental Psychology, 26*, 978–86.

Silverman, I. W. & Ragusa, D. M. (1992). A short-term longitudinal study of the early development of self-regulation. *Journal of Abnormal Child Psychology, 20*, 415–35.

Spinrad, T. L., Losoya, S. H., Eisenberg, N., Fabes, R. A., Shepard, S. A., Cumberland, A., Guthrie, I. K., & Murphy, B. C. (1999). The relation of parental affect and encouragement to children's moral behavior. *Journal of Moral Education, 28*, 323–37.

Stifter, C. A. & Braungart, J. M. (1995). The regulation of negative reactivity in infancy: Function and development. *Developmental Psychology, 31*, 448–55.

Stifter, C. A. & Fox, N. A. (1990). Infant reactivity: Physiological correlates of newborn and 5-month temperament. *Developmental Psychology, 26*, 582–8.

Stifter, C. A., Fox, N. A., & Porges, S. W. (1989). Facial expressivity and vagal tone in 5- and 10-month old infants. *Infant Behavior and Development, 12*, 127–37.

Thompson, R. A. (1994). Emotional regulation: A theme in search of definition. *Monographs of the Society for Research in Child Development, 59* (2–3, serial no. 240), 25–52.

Valiente, C., Eisenberg, N., Smith, C. L., Reiser, M., Fabes, R. A., Losoya, S., Guthrie, I. K., & Murphy, B. C. (2003). The relations of effortful control and reactive control to children's externalizing problems: A longitudinal assessment. *Journal of Personality, 71*, 1179–1205.

Vaughn, B. E., Kopp, C. B., & Krakow, J. B. (1984). The emergence and consolidation of self-control from eighteen to thirty months of age: Normative trends and individual differences. *Child Development, 55*, 990–1004.

White, J. L., Moffitt, T. E., Caspi, A., Bartusch, D. J., Needles, D. J., Stouthamer-Loeber, M. (1994). Measuring impulsivity and examining its relationship to delinquency. *Journal of Abnormal Psychology, 103*, 192–205.

Williams, B. R., Ponesse, J. S., Schachar, R. J., Logan, G. D., & Tannock, R. (1999). Development of inhibitory control across the life span. *Developmental Psychology, 35*, 205–13.

Wilson, B. (2003). The role of attentional processes in children's prosocial behavior with peers: Attention shifting and emotion. *Development and Psychopathology, 15*, 313–29.

Windle, M. & Lerner, R. M. (1986). Reassessing the dimensions of temperamental individuality across the life span: The Revised Dimensions of Temperament Survey (DOTS-R). *Journal of Adolescent Research, 1*, 213–30.

CHAPTER TWENTY-TWO

Person–Environment "Fit" and Individual Development

Theodore D. Wachs

The focus of this chapter is on the concept of person–environment fit, as it applies to various domains of children's development. The term "person–environment fit" refers to the concept that individual differences in adaptation are a joint function of the degree of fit (match) between the nature of the individual's characteristics and the nature of the individual's context. The concept of fit is inherent in the assumption promulgated by many of the early developmental researchers such as Baldwin, Gesell, Lewin, and Stern, that one cannot understand the process of development without understanding the joint contribution of both person and environment (Cairns, 1998). The concept of fit can also be seen in Piagetian theory, with regard to the hypothesis that outside stimulation will be assimilated into existing schemata only when there is an optimal level of fit between the informational complexity of outside stimulation and the developmental level of an individual's schemata (Hunt, 1961). Similarly, the concept of person–environment fit appears in the theoretical writings of Vygotsky, with specific reference to the need to facilitate development through providing stimuli to the child that are within the child's "zone of proximal development" (Kindermann, 2003). Outside of the social sciences the concept of organism–environment fit is also inherent in the evolutionary framework developed by Darwin, wherein reproductive success depends on how well individual organismic variation fits the demands of existing physical conditions (Lerner, Lerner, & Zabski, 1985).

In the area of child development the concept of person–environment fit has been most closely linked with the writings of Chess and Thomas (1991), who have focused on the developmental implications of individual differences in goodness of fit between an individual's temperament and their context. According to Chess and Thomas, successful adaptation and positive developmental outcomes occur when a child's temperament characteristics are well matched to contextual demands, values, and goals. Unsuccessful adaptation and negative developmental outcomes occur when a child's temperament characteristics are poorly matched to contextual demands, values, and goals.

Going beyond contemporary developmental research and theory, the implications of person–environment fit have been extensively studied in the area of industrial organizational psychology (Caplan & Van Harrison, 1993; Dawis & Lofquist, 1984; Kristof, 1996; Swanson & Fouad, 1999; Tinsley, 2000). Use of the construct of person–environment fit is also seen in the study of *gerontology* (Kahn, 1994; Rosowsky et al., 1997; Wallace and Bergeman, 1997), the study of quality of *marital relationships* (Steinglass, Tislenko, & Reiss, 1985; Wallerstein, 1996), *adjustment* of the severely handicapped (Schalock & Jensen, 1986), adult *reactivity* to life stress events (Suls, Martin, & David, 1998; Vachon & Stylianos, 1988), and is even seen in research on factors influencing *admission to graduate school* (Keith-Spiegel, Tabachnick, & Spiegel, 1994).

Nondevelopmental research and theory on person–environment fit not only illustrates the pervasiveness of this construct, but also provides alternative approaches to important methodological issues that must be considered when person–environment fit assessments are applied to the domain of child development. For example, nondevelopmental researchers have documented that relations between level of fit and outcome may be domain specific rather than general, that it is important to consider both level of person and contextual characteristics as well as level of fit, the need to use both objective and subjective measurements when assessing fit and the possibility that different outcomes may be sensitive to objective and subjective measures of fit (Caplan & Van Harrison, 1993; Edwards & Rothbard, 1999; Kristof, 1996; Tinsley, 2000; Vachon & Stylianos, 1988; Vitaliano et al., 1990). These issues will be considered at later points in this chapter.

Assessment of Person–Environment Fit

Whether conceptualized within the goodness of fit framework of Chess and Thomas (1989), or within alternative fit frameworks such as aptitude by treatment interaction (Cronbach & Snow, 1977), person–environment fit (Swartz-Kulstad & Martin, 2000; Tinsley, 2000) or stage–environment fit (Eccles, Lord, & Roeser, 1996), there appears to be general agreement that adequate assessment of fit requires detailed measurement of *both* individual as well as contextual characteristics. Without adequate measures of both context and individual, it becomes difficult to establish whether observed results reflect the operation of fit processes or some other underlying process. Thus, characterizing a child as having a very problematic or a very desirable temperament will tell us very little about the degree of person–environment fit for this child, until we also have information about the nature of the child's context (Paterson & Sanson, 1999). For example, while neonatal nurses' ratings of how much difficulty a given mother will have in dealing with their infant may accurately predict later child development (Riese & Matheny, 1990), such a measure tells us more about the validity of nurses' ratings than it does about the goodness of mother–environment fit. Similarly, stress in parent–child relations may reflect poor parent–child fit (Bogenschneider, Small, & Tsay, 1997), but it may also reflect a main effect due to less competent parenting. Unfortunately, all too often the requirement of measuring both individual and contextual characteristics has not been adequately met.

If it is essential to integrate measures of individual and contextual characteristics in the study of fit, a critical series of questions for developmental researchers are: *what* individual and contextual characteristics should be measured, *how* to best measure such characteristics, and *how* should we integrate our measures to most adequately define fit? These questions are dealt with in the following sections.

Assessment of individual characteristics

In regard to individual characteristics the "what" and "how" questions referred to above appear not to be a major issue. Characteristics that could be used to reflect the individual's contribution to fit usually involve standard measures of well-known individual difference variables such as temperament, stimulus preference styles, needs, values, level of cognitive capacity, specific cognitive strengths and weaknesses, and biological risk history such as preterm birth (Wachs, 1999). Individual differences in age-related physical characteristics such as level of pubertal maturation (Brooks-Gunn, Petersen, & Ichorn, 1985), or age-related differences in children's functional competencies (Kindermann, 1993) have also been used to define person contributions to fit. In addition, potentially relevant individual characteristics may also include deviations from normal developmental patterns, as seen in classroom fit studies involving children with attention deficit hyperactive disorder (Greene, 1995).

Assessment of contextual characteristics

In contrast to the identification and assessment of specific person characteristics, there is far more ambiguity and disagreement when it comes to assessing specific contextual characteristics that contribute to the level of person–environment fit.

Social address assessments One potential problem involves the use of what Bronfenbrenner & Crouter (1983) have characterized as social addresses. Social addresses such as socioeconomic status, rural versus urban rearing, or institutional versus non-institutional rearing, while describing where the child was reared, do not provide us with sufficient detail about the specific nature of the environmental demands, supports or stresses that a given child encounters at a given social address (Wachs, 1992). For example, while the general contextual characteristics of large versus small public schools have been identified (Schoggen & Schoggen, 1988), knowing the size of the school a child is attending rarely tells us much about what specific teacher practices or teacher demands a specific child encounters in classrooms within their school (Talbert & McLaughlin, 1999). Social address measures of context may be useful in addressing questions of fit in certain restricted situations, as in the case when children from minority groups encounter institutions from the larger culture such as schools, where the predominant values are distinctly different from those held by the child's family (Boyce & Boyce, 1988; Pachter & Harwood, 1996). However, for the most part, purely social address measures of context are not sufficiently detailed to tell us what specific contextual aspects the individual must fit into.

The objective context Contextual characteristics are traditionally defined in developmental research studies on the basis of specific *objective* social or stimulation aspects of the child's microsystem, such as level or type of parental control strategies, family routines or degree of caregiver positive or negative affect towards the child. In addition, physical characteristics of the child's microsystem can also be used in the assessment of person–environment fit. For example, the physical characteristics of objects that are available to the child may provide a greater or lesser degree of fit with the child's motor capacities (Smitsman, 1997). While the primary focus in developmental research has been on person–environment fit at the microsystem level, it is important to remember not only that the child's context involves multiple levels beyond the microsystem where fit processes may be operating (e.g., Kerr, 2001), but also the need to specify what contextual level the individual does or does not fit into (Kristof, 1996).

Although there is a certain level of categorical ambiguity, I also would include adult or peer beliefs about what specific characteristics make a child more or less desirable or valued as another example of an objective environmental measure. Unlike subjective perceptions of the environment, which reside in the mind of the individual child, these beliefs reside in the minds of other individuals besides the child. More critically, given available evidence it is not unreasonable to assume that adult or peer beliefs about the appropriateness or desirability of specific behaviors or characteristics will ultimately translate into how a given child with or without these characteristics is treated (Keogh, 1994).

The subjective context In defining contextual conditions that fit or do not fit individual characteristics, a number of researchers have argued that it is important to go beyond just objective environmental features and also consider the individual's "subjective" environment as well (Edwards & Rothbard, 1999; Lawton, 1999). The nature of the subjective environment is defined on the basis of an individual's perceptions, appraisals, and feelings about the characteristics of their objective physical environment (Wachs, 1999). For example, the level of sound in an individual's environment would be a measure of their objective environment, whereas the individual's perception of the sound as noisy or unpleasant would be a measure of the individual's subjective perception of their environmental context (Evans, 1999). While different methodologies are used to assess objective and subjective contexts, this does not imply that these dimensions of the environment are orthogonal. Rather, as suggested by Reeve (personal communication, December, 2001), these two dimensions are better conceived of as related constructs that require different assessment strategies.

In using subjective perceptions as an alternative way to measure the nature of the individual's environmental context, it is important to avoid what might be regarded as the subjective equivalent of social address measures. I refer here to the use of summed group perceptions rather than individual group members' perceptions of a given context, as in the case when an average pupil score is used to characterize the nature of a given classroom (Fraser & Fisher, 1983). The problem of course is that the average group perception of a given context such as a classroom may or may not be congruent with the perceptions of an individual student in this classroom (Fraser, 1991). Further, there is still considerable ambiguity in regard to the level of agreement between individuals that is needed to justify creating an aggregate perception of the environment (Kristof, 1996). Going beyond subjective social address measures, a variety of approaches have been proposed to allow accurate assessment of the individual's subjective perceptions of their objective environmental context, such as teacher report measures of the level of "collegiality" in their school (Talbert & McLaughlin, 1999) or children's perceptions of the "emotional climate" in different types of after-school care programs (Vandell & Posner, 1999).

Integrating individual and contextual characteristics to define level of fit

Assuming that we have valid measures of specific person and contextual characteristics, a critical question is how we integrate these two measures to come up with the degree of goodness or poorness of person–environment fit for a given individual.

Discrepancy scores Within the developmental literature perhaps the most popular approach has been the use of discrepancy or difference scores. Discrepancy scores are often based on other persons rating specific aspects of a child's behavior on a desirability scale (e.g., a 4-point scale ranging from highly undesirable to highly desirable for a given behavior). Then, using the same scale metric, the desirability score is subtracted from ratings of the degree to which the child actually displays these specific behavior patterns. The greater the discrepancy between the desirability score and the child's behavioral score, the poorer the fit between the child and his or her context. For example, in a series of studies young adolescents were administered a 54-item temperament questionnaire (DOTS-R) constructed so the child used a 4-point scale to rate the degree to which different behaviors are characteristic of them. Concurrently, the adolescent's parents or classmates were administered a parallel 4-point scale containing the same items (DOTS-R Ethnotheory), where they were to rate the desirability of each behavior or the degree to which they would have difficulty dealing with an individual with this behavior. Parent or peer DOTS-R Ethnotheory ratings were subtracted from the adolescent's DOTS-R temperament scores, with higher discrepancies between adolescent temperament and parent or peer preferences for specific temperaments being interpreted as poorer fit. Comparisons were then made to determine if there was greater prediction of child problem behaviors or child academic and social competence from the adolescent's temperament scores per se, versus the level of fit between temperament and parent and peer temperament preferences (Nitz et al., 1988; Talwar, Nitz, & Lerner, 1990).

An alternative approach that also involves using discrepancy scores occurs when adults are given a list of various types of child behaviors and asked to rank which five behaviors are the most or least desirable. Caregivers or other adults then rate the degree to which the child displays the most desired and undesired behaviors. If the majority of behaviors displayed by the child are rated as highly undesirable, the child would be considered as having a poor fit; if the majority of behaviors displayed by the child are rated as highly desirable the child would be considered as having a good fit (Feagans & Manlove, 1994). Discrepancy scores have also been used in skill analysis procedures, where observers rate what specific competencies are needed to succeed in a given context and then rate the percentage of these behavioral competencies possessed by the individual (Schalock & Jensen, 1986). When multiple measures of individual and context have been obtained, the use of measures of profile similarity as an index of fit has also been suggested (Kristof, 1996).

A few studies have also reported deriving discrepancy scores from subjective perception measures. One such approach is based on the child assessing the discrepancy between their own preferred needs on dimensions such as autonomy and their perceptions about the degree to which autonomy or other need-related behaviors are valued or not valued by teachers or parents (Juang et al., 1999). Alternatively, discrepancy type scores have also been derived from raters' perceptions about the degree to which physical characteristics of classrooms, along dimensions like crowding and openness, fit the behavioral patterns of children with specific types of behavioral problems such as attention deficit hyperactive disorder (Atkinson, Robinson, & Shute, 1997).

Non-discrepancy approaches to the assessment of fit Although not always presented in a person–environment fit framework, deriving person × environment interaction terms in hierarchical multiple regression analysis has been suggested as one approach to understanding how development is influenced by the interplay between person and contextual characteristics (Plomin and Daniels, 1984). Within this framework significant person × environment statistical interaction terms can be viewed as the equivalent of either poor or good fit, depending upon the directionality of the interaction. For example, Bates (2001) has reported that resistant children are more likely to show long-term externalizing behavior problems if their caregivers are low rather than high in limit-setting behaviors. These results could be used to suggest that the combination of resistant children and high parental limit setting represent a good person–environment fit, whereas the combination of resistant children and low parental control represents a case of poor fit.

A few studies have defined fit based on how the context adjusts to fit developmental changes in children's characteristics. Kindermann (1993) has used observation of mother–child transactions to assess the degree to which mothers adjust their behavior patterns to fit their child's developing competencies in areas like locomotion and self-care skills. A good fit is defined by mothers shifting their behavior patterns from dependence fostering to independence fostering as their child began to acquire a specific skill. A similar approach has been used by Midgley & Feldlaufer (1987), analyzing the degree to which developmental changes in adolescents' autonomy and social needs fit changes in the level of support offered by schools and parents for these needs.

Based on the concept of active organism–environment covariance (niche seeking; Plomin, DeFries, & Loehlin, 1977), it also has been suggested that level of person–environment fit could be defined as a function of the degree to which the individual is able to find an environment that is congruent with their primary needs and abilities (Swanson & Fouad, 1999; Wilk, Desmarais, & Sackett, 1995). Working within a subjective perception framework, the level of person–environment fit has also been defined on the basis of whether the coping strategies chosen by the individual actually fit the changeability of the perceived stressor (Rudolph, Dennig, & Weisz, 1995).

How well do current approaches allow an accurate assessment of fit?

Discrepancy scores While a variety of approaches to quantifying fit have been utilized, there is, at present, no generally accepted "gold standard" approach (Tinsley, 2000). To varying degrees, all of the available approaches used by developmental researchers to quantify fit can be seen as having methodological problems. Unfortunately a number of these problems are associated with the most popular approach used in developmental research to quantify fit, namely the use of discrepancy scores. Certain problems associated with the use of discrepancy scores, such as the problem of same-source measurement bias that is inherent when the same individuals rate the child's characteristics, environmental preferences, and outcomes, or the need to have equivalent content for person and environmental characteristic preference measures, can be overcome with relatively little difficulty. However, other problems inherent in the use of discrepancy scores are less amenable to quick fixes (Bates, 1989). Specifically, while discrepancy scores are relatively easy to calculate, our ability to actively interpret degree of fit from these scores is based upon a number of assumptions. These assumptions include: (1) equivalent influence of fit will occur for all levels of person and environment characteristics, and (2) equivalent influence of fit will occur regardless of directionality of fit, so that there will be no outcome differences when person characteristics are greater than environmental demands or preferences versus when environmental demands and preferences exceed person characteristics (Caplan & Van Harrison, 1993). Although the importance of these assumptions have generally not been considered by developmental researchers, they have received serious study by researchers in other areas such as industrial-organizational psychology. Reviews of the industrial-organizational literature indicate that the impact upon individual functioning of level of fit between what a person values or needs and the environmental resources available to meet the individual's values or needs need not be either linear or directionally equivalent (Edwards & Rothbard, 1999; Kristof, 1996). For example, when resources are below needs (poor fit), wellbeing generally increases as resources increase (better fit). However, when resources exceed needs (also poor fit) there are a variety of potential outcome patterns observed, depending upon the outcome area studied and the individual's level of resources and needs.

Such findings may be particularly troublesome for developmental researchers, given that all too often fit is based only on the absolute level of discrepancy and not the pattern of discrepancy (e.g., a discrepancy score of +3 is assumed to be equivalent to a discrepancy score of −3). Potential problems associated with looking just at absolute level of discrepancy are illustrated in a study by Erwin et al. (1993) relating children's adjustment to degree of fit between parent and daycare provider rearing strategies. Typically, in absolute discrepancy studies greater discrepancy is associated with more problematical outcomes. However, Erwin et al. (1993) report that *fewer* childhood adjustment problems were associated with greater discrepancies between parents and daycare providers' use of control through guilt and anxiety or loss of temper when children misbehave. While problematical from an absolute discrepancy viewpoint, these findings are quite meaningful when we go beyond absolute discrepancy and look at what these scores mean. Not surprisingly, in the case where there is congruence (fit) between multiple negative influences we would expect a poorer outcome, whereas discrepancy between home and daycare would mean that at least in one setting the child was experiencing some degree of developmentally facilitating experiences.

Interactions Different but nonetheless equally troubling methodological problems also appear when fit is defined on the basis of significant person × context interaction terms in a regression analysis. First, many person × context interaction studies are atheoretical, which all too often means that any significant interaction term can be interpreted as reflecting the operation of fit, regardless of the nature of the interaction. Further, there is ample discussion on how reduced person or context variability (range restriction) can sharply reduce our ability to detect existing person × environment interactions (Cronbach, 1991; McClelland & Judd, 1993). Thus, finding a nonsignificant person × context interaction does not necessarily mean that person–environment fit processes are not operating. Finally, based on the analytic strategy utilized, we may also wrongly conclude that fit processes are operating when in fact they are not. As discussed by Bates (1989, 2001), when fit is analyzed using regression approaches researchers may fail to make the distinction between whether a combined person–environment effect is additive (linear) or truly interactive (nonlinear), or whether person × environment interaction terms contribute unique variance after removing main effect variance associated with person and environment effects per se. For example, while Simeonsson et al. (1986) interpret their finding that better prediction of mother–infant interactions occurs when using multiple rather than single child and parent characteristic predictors as an example of goodness of fit, there was no test done for interaction among predictors. What their findings appear to reflect are an additive influence, rather than the influence of goodness of fit processes. While there are standard statistical procedures that can be used to differentiate between effects that are due to linear versus nonlinear combinations, all too often this differentiation is not made.

Niche seeking If we choose to focus on niche-seeking behavior as an index of fit, failure to find an appropriate niche does not necessarily reflect the operation of a poor fit between the person's individual characteristics and the characteristics of available contextual niches. In additional to individual characteristics, a variety of contextual factors such as parental divorce or reduced family income may also act to restrict the types of contextual niches that the individual encounters and can enter (Wachs, 2000).

The problem of conceptual ambiguity

For all of the above approaches used to define level of fit in developmental research there is also a common problem of conceptual ambiguity, in regard to the question of exactly what combinations of person and contextual characteristics should be most critical in defining good or poor fit. The fact that this problem occurs in regression approaches is not necessarily surprising, given that these approaches are often atheoretical in nature. We would expect such ambiguity to be far less of a problem in discrepancy approaches, given that these types of studies are often framed using the Chess and Thomas goodness of fit theory. However, what is not often recognized is that much of the evidence used by Chess and Thomas to define goodness or poorness of person–environment fit was based on clinical case studies (Chess & Thomas, 1991), wherein fit was defined by goodness of outcome and not on prior theoretically driven distinctions. That is, person–environment combinations that led to subsequent positive outcomes were viewed as reflecting good fit, whereas person–environment combinations that led to subsequent negative outcomes were viewed as reflecting poor fit. This approach allows for a highly flexible theory that can encompass potentially important factors, such as different cultural criteria for what types of behaviors are appropriate or not appropriate. This approach also has led to many useful clinical insights, as seen in the conclusion that highly inhibited children are more likely to have problems dealing with transitions to new school environments (Carey, 1998). However, by not including as an integral part of theory, decision rule criteria that would allow a priori specification of what specific person–environment combinations are likely to result in good or poor person–environment fit, there is an increased likelihood that any significant person–environment discrepancy effect can be interpreted as an example of the operation of goodness or poorness of fit processes (Wachs & Kohnstamm, 2001).

It is important to recognize that this problem is not inherent in all person–environment fit theories. Working within a Pavlovian framework, Strelau (2001; Strelau & Eliasz, 1994) has developed an arousal-based theory of fit which explicitly hypothesizes that highly stimulating environments will provide a poor fit for individuals with temperament characteristics defined by high stimulus sensitivity and low endurance, while low stimulation environments will provide a poor fit for individuals with temperaments characterized by low stimulus sensitivity and high endurance. Strelau's theory also leads to specific predictions about the types of environmental niches that will be sought out by individuals with these differing types of temperament characteristics. Within the field of industrial-organizational psychology the "gravitational" hypothesis leads to specific and validated predictions about the nature of occupational change that would occur as a function of different degrees of fit between individual abilities and job complexity (Wilk, Desmarais, & Sackett, 1995; Wilk & Sackett, 1996).

Empirical Evidence on the Developmental Consequences of Good and Poor Fit

Keeping in mind the above conceptual and methodological constraints, I now review evidence on the contributions of person–environment fit to child behavior and development. Following the previous discussion on assessing fit, this review will focus on both the findings and the methodological problems associated with discrepancy, interaction, and other types of fit-related studies. While much of the available research defines fit on the basis of individual differences in child temperament and the nature of the child's context, there also are a number of studies investigating the implications of the degree of fit between individual physical and psychological maturational changes or non-temperament individual characteristics and specific aspects of the individual's context. Finally, while all too little data is available on the issue of individual niche selection (active covariance) as a measure of fit, given its theoretical importance the few studies in this area will also be discussed.

Studies on temperament by context fit

Discrepancy studies Studies on the consequences of temperament–context fit indicate that, regardless of the age of child studied, the overall pattern of results tends to be disappointingly inconsistent. While some studies show that temperament–context fit provides a better prediction of outcomes than do main effects of temperament or context per se (Dollinger & Johnson, 1990; Nitz et al., 1988; Talwar, Nitz, & Lerner, 1990.), other studies show the reverse pattern (Bates & Labouvie, 1994; Keogh, 1994; Lernerz et al., 1987; Sprunger, Boyce, & Gaines, 1985; Windle et al., 1986.). Further, when significant temperament–context fit predictions occur, in all too many cases the influence of fit is moderated by a variety of theoretically unpredicted variables, including what temperament dimension is being considered, age or grade level of the child, and who is assessing the degree of fit. For example, results from a number of studies indicate that prediction of outcomes from temperament–context discrepancies will vary depending on the nature of the outcome measures assessed (Feagans, Merriwether, & Haldane, 1991; Lerner, Lerner, & Zabski, 1985; Paterson & Sanson, 1999). Some of the inconsistent results may reflect a restricted range, given that observed discrepancies were not seen as particularly undesirable in some studies (e.g., Nitz et al., 1988). However, other design and conceptual problems identified earlier must also be considered when interpreting this pattern of results. These other problems would include imprecise specification of what combinations of temperament and context best reflect poor fit, overreliance on one person being the sole source of all measures, not considering directionality when computing fit scores, and basing fit on overall group ratings and not on the ratings of the individual's specific peer group.

Temperament–context fit in cross-cultural perspective A few studies are available that analyze fit based on the degree of discrepancy between an individual's temperament characteristics and the demands and values of the culture within which the individual lives. While all too many of the studies in this area rely on post-hoc interpretations, the evidence does appear to suggest that children whose temperament characteristics are radically different from what their culture values have a reduced chance of survival under scarcity conditions (DeVries, 1994; Scheper-Hughes, 1987) as well as more problematical developmental outcomes (Kerr, 2001; Korn & Gannon, 1983; Super & Harkness, 1994).

Studies of temperament × context interactions Because of the relatively large number of temperament × context interaction studies that are potentially applicable to the question of fit, only a representative sample of these studies are discussed here. More detailed reviews of this literature can be found in a number of sources (e.g., Rothbart & Bates, 1998; Wachs, 2000). There are a number of studies reporting either theoretically predicted or replicated temperament × context interactions (Arcus, 2001; Bates, 2001; Gandour, 1989; Kochanska, 1997; Mangelsdorf et al., 1991; Strelau, 1989; Wachs, 1987). However, again we also find other studies indicating either little evidence for temperament × context interactions (Kawaguchi et al., 1998; Plomin & Daniels, 1984; Wallander, Hubert, & Varni, 1988), or highly complex findings that are not easily interpretable (Galambos & Turner, 1998; Grossman & Shigaki, 1994; Lumley et al., 1990), or nonpredicted temperament × context interactions (Hagekull & Bohlin, 1990; Miceli et al., 1998), or findings that vary based on the outcome measure assessed (Gordon, 1981; Park et al., 1997).

Given the numerous methodological problems that act to limit our ability to detect organism × context interactions in human research (Cronbach, 1991; McClelland & Judd, 1993; Rutter & Pickles, 1991; Wahlsten, 1990), it is not surprising to find inconsistency in interaction approaches to detecting fit. Indeed, what is surprising is the number of theoretically driven or replicated interactions that do appear. A critical question is what distinguishes those studies that are successful in finding temperament × context interactions from those that are not. Clearly, comparison across studies is difficult, given different methodologies and different age samples. However, what does seem to differentiate studies that were successful in detecting temperament × context interactions from studies that were unsuccessful is that successful studies were more likely to either have larger sample sizes, or to use direct (e.g., observational) rather than indirect (e.g., parental report) assessments of context. Further, among those studies that used direct contextual assessments, more interpretable results emerged either when assessments were based on repeated aggregated observations (Arcus, 2001; Bates, 2001; Gandour, 1989; Park et al., 1997; Wachs, 1987), or when controlled laboratory conditions were used (Gordon, 1981; Kochanska, 1997), or when contextual demand characteristics were high (e.g., Lumley et al., 1990; Strelau, 2001).

Why are interpretable interactions more likely to appear in studies fitting the conditions just described? An important reason involves the need for increased statistical power in order to detect existing interactions (Cronbach, 1991; McClelland & Judd, 1993). There are two well-known ways to increase statistical power. The first is to increase sample size, while the second is to increase the preciseness of one's measures (Wachs, 1991). Use of aggregated repeated measures, testing in controlled settings or testing under situations that stress the organism's coping capacities are precisely the conditions that are likely to increase the preciseness of our contextual or individual difference measurements.

One implication of the known link between statistical power and our ability to detect existing interactions is the all too often ignored conclusion that failure to find a significant temperament × context interaction term in no way means that such interactions are not actually operating. To deal with this issue the use of *confidence intervals* has been recommended when testing for interactions, as a means of estimating the likelihood of whether interaction processes are still possible but have not been detected in a given study (Cronbach, 1991; Rutter & Pickles, 1991).

Studies on fit between context and non-temperament characteristics

Fit between physical maturation and context A few studies have looked at the implications of concordance or discordance between physical changes occurring in adolescence and environmental demands upon the adolescent. For the most part this question has been studied using females in specialized contexts, such as highly competitive dance training or athletics. While physical maturational changes have been found to relate in the predicted direction to indices of body image (e.g., late physically maturing dancers have a better body image than early maturing dancers), few consistent behavioral or adjustment consequences have been found as a function of interactions between physical maturational characteristics and contextual expectations (Brooks-Gunn et al., 1989; Garguilo et al., 1987). In part this lack of consistent findings may reflect the use of "social address" measures of context (ballet training, type of sport) rather than direct measures of the specific demands encountered by individual adolescents.

Fit between psychological maturation and context Other studies have defined fit on the basis of discrepancies between what the developing adolescent wants from their context and what the context actually provides. For example, Eccles, Lord, and Roeser (1996) have hypothesized that adolescents who are making the transition to junior high school have increasing needs for social support and autonomy, as well as a greater sensitivity to the importance of self-worth, but that the junior high school context more often provides decreased social support, reduced opportunities for autonomous functioning, and more exposure to situations that could act to reduce feelings of self-worth. Eccles, Lord, and Roeser (1996) also have hypothesized that there would be a greater chance of mismatch between adolescent needs and the family decision structure in the case of early as opposed to later maturing females. In general, evidence has been supportive of the hypothesis that an increased level of developmental problems or a reduced level of school involvement will be associated with greater levels of discrepancy between changing adolescent needs and how well the school or family context responds to these needs (Eccles, Lord, & Roeser, 1996; Juang et al., 1999).

While the overall pattern of evidence is consistent, there remains some ambiguity as to how this pattern of findings should be interpreted. In part this reflects the fact that a lack of fit is sometimes inferred from main effects rather than direct assessments of fit (e.g., a reduced belief in one's ability to do well in math for adolescents who went from high- to low-efficacy teachers is interpreted in fit terms). In addition, while the observed pattern of results could be interpreted to mean that greater levels of mismatch lead to greater adjustment problems, given the heavy use of self-report measures this pattern of results also could be interpreted to mean that young adolescents with higher levels of behavior problems may be more likely to perceive greater mismatch between themselves and their family or school context. Similarly, it may be that the families of early maturing females may be more overprotective than are the families of later maturing females. Thus, whether this pattern of results reflects the operation of goodness of fit mechanisms or the operation of child effect processes (defined as either reactive covariance or differential perceptions) remains an open question.

School context studies The majority of studies using school as a context have focused on the question of whether fit interactions between student ability patterns and classroom instructional characteristics act to influence student school achievement. While some ability × instructional interactions have been reported (e.g., below-average students show higher achievement when working in heterogeneous groups containing above-average students, whereas above-average students show higher achievement when working in homogeneous groups with higher ability levels: Webb et al., 1998), reviews of this literature generally indicate either inconsistent findings or significant but highly complex interactions that are difficult to interpret (Cronbach & Snow, 1977; Snow, 1992).

Other person × school context fit studies have focused on the implications of student preferences for particular types of classroom environments versus the actual or perceived nature of the classroom environment. Results from this line of research generally indicate that the degree of fit between individual contextual preferences and classroom characteristics does add unique predictive variance to measures of school performance, learning style, and classroom behavior. However, the amount of unique variance associated with preference–context fit tends to be relatively modest, and it is still not clear whether achievement or attitudinal outcomes are more sensitive to this type of fit (Fraser & Fisher, 1983; Hattie & Watkins, 1988; Wong & Watkins, 1996, 1998).

Given the inconsistent, highly complex, and/or modest findings in the area of person × school context fit, there has been a good deal of discussion on methodological issues. One such issue is the use of relatively insensitive measures of context such as overall class ratings, rather than using individuals' perceptions of the nature of their classroom environment (Fraser, 1991). Cronbach has emphasized the need for large sample sizes if existing interactions are to be detected (Cronbach & Snow, 1977), as well as the possibility that specific person × classroom interactions may be moderated by higher-order interactions involving other person or classroom characteristics (Cronbach, 1991). While higher-order interactions have been found in some studies, the results are not always consistent with what was initially predicted, leading to a reliance on post-hoc explanations (Wong & Watkins, 1996). Further, detecting higher-order interactions requires higher levels of statistical power than is normally found in most studies.

Other individual–context fit studies There also are a scattered number of studies that do not fit into the above categories. Again, for these studies the mixed nature of findings tends to reflect what we have seen earlier. Thus, while Grotevant, McRoy, and Jenkins (1988) interpret their finding of better child adjustment and more positive perceptions of family relations in non-adoptive as opposed to adoptive families as due to better child–parent fit in non-adoptive families, the design used in this study does not allow us to distinguish between fit versus main effect contextual processes. Boivin, Dodge, and Coie (1995) hypothesized that the relation of children's interpersonal characteristics to peer social acceptance would vary depending on the interpersonal characteristics of the peer group, such that children whose characteristics are discordant from group characteristics should be less accepted. Of the three critical comparisons testing this hypothesis, one was supported (reactive aggression), one was in the correct direction but was not significant (prosocial behavior), and the third was significant but contrary to what was predicted (proactive goal-directed aggression). Using a controlled test procedure, Fanurik et al. (1993) provided training in either sensory focusing or distracting coping strategies to children who differed in their preference for focusing on or away from painful stimulation. It was hypothesized that training that matched the child's preferences would lead to better pain tolerance. While better pain tolerance was shown for fit conditions involving sensory focusing, the results were more inconsistent in regard to distraction coping strategies. Finally, Markstrom, Berman, and Brusch (1998) hypothesized that adolescents who lived in neighborhoods where the majority of residents had religious beliefs that matched those of the adolescents should show a stronger sense of personal, social, and religious identity than adolescents who lived in neighborhoods where the majority of residents had a different faith. Few predicted relations were found and of those that were found the relations were primarily for males.

The methodological concerns discussed earlier apply to the studies cited here as well. Again, we find either relatively weak measures of context (e.g., only 5 minutes of training in the Fanurik et al. study; heterogeneous levels and types of Jewish beliefs even in the primarily Jewish neighborhoods studied by Markstrom, Berman, & Brusch), as well as problematical measurement of individual characteristics (e.g., differences in the strength of different children's preferred coping styles were not considered by Fanurik et al.).

Niche selection/active covariance as an index of fit

Theoretically, the ability of individuals to find and enter contexts with characteristics that match their individual characteristics (niche seeking, active covariance) has been viewed as one index of organism–environment fit that should lead to better outcomes for such individuals (Strelau & Eliasz, 1994; Swartz-Kulstad & Martin, 2000). Empirically, there has been remarkably little evidence illustrating the operation of niche-seeking behavior as an index of fit. Much of the evidence that is cited as illustrating the operation of active covariance as fit is based on studies relating individual personality characteristics such as *sensation seeking* (Zuckerman, 1994), *inhibition* (Caspi, Elder, & Bem, 1988), *ego control* (Block, Block, & Keyes, 1988), *personal goals* (Nurmi, 1993), and *social conservatism and self-efficacy* (Schulenberg et al., 1996) to a variety of normal (e.g., age of career entry) and abnormal (e.g., drug use) outcomes. Other studies have utilized peer popularity ratings as evidence for the operation of person–peer group fit processes (East et al., 1992). The difficulty with utilizing these types of research studies as evidence for the operation of goodness of fit is that a variety of factors besides active covariance fit can influence links between personality and later outcomes. Further, best fit niches may not be freely available to an individual, regardless of individual preferences or characteristics. For example, the niches in which an individual is found may reflect a closing down of available niches by societal or interpersonal forces as a result of the individual's behavioral patterns (e.g., impulsivity, antisocial behavior) or individual characteristics (e.g., race or gender) rather than reflecting an active choice selection of best-fit niches (Strelau & Eliasz, 1994; Wachs, 2000). Rather than looking for main effect links between individual difference characteristics and either outcomes or niches, what is essential are process studies, looking at how individual characteristics translate into niche selection. An example of the type of study that is needed is seen in the work of Gunnar (1994), illustrating how inhibited and uninhibited preschool children act to structure their entry behavior into a novel preschool environment. Unfortunately, such studies require extensive observation of individual behavioral patterns at niche selection choice points and are all too rare at present.

Future Directions in Research on Organism–Environment Fit

As documented in the introductory section of this chapter, the concept of person–environment fit appears both in a number of major theories of human development as well as in theories from a variety of nondevelopmental disciplines. I would argue that the concept of person–environment fit is attractive to developmental theorists not only because it seems "intuitively" right, but also because, while parsimonious, it forces us to avoid oversimplistic single-cause explanations of human development. In addition, from an applied standpoint, increasing the level of person–environment fit has been viewed as a means of optimizing individual competence (Albin et al., 1996; Bates, Wachs, & Emde, 1994).

While the concept of person–environment fit is highly attractive, both from a theoretical and an applied perspective, as has also been documented in this chapter its empirical manifestations have something of a "will of the wisp" flavor. While there are a number of replicated examples of person–environment fit processes acting to influence various aspects of children's development, there are at least an equal number of examples when expected fit processes could not be found. When examples of fit processes are documented, all too often the effect sizes are weak or there is the possibility of alternative, non-fit, interpretations of observed findings. To improve the fit between theory and research evidence we need changes not only in how we investigate and conceptualize person–environment fit, but also in terms of the questions we are asking about the role played by fit processes in child development.

Methodological issues

A number of methodological concerns about how we are currently assessing fit have been presented in this paper. A summary of the main points raised earlier is presented in Table 22.1. Underlying much of what is in Table 22.1 is the fundamental rule that detection of existing fit processes requires precise measurement of both individual and contextual characteristics. While this requirement would seem to be so obvious as to not require continued restatement, all too often this requirement has not been met. The need for more precise measurement also relates to the importance of adequate statistical power, particularly when significance of person $\times$ context statistical interaction is used as the criterion for inferring the operation of fit processes. However, in addition to having adequate statistical power, it may be equally important to recognize the need to avoid type II errors in studies of person–environment fit, given the relatively brief history of

Table 22.1   Methodological issues in the assessment of the person–environment fit

1   A fundamental requirement is for precise measures of both individual and contextual characteristics.

2   Utilize direct repeated measurement of the individual's objective proximal physical and social environments. Use social address measurements only in conjunction with more detailed proximal measurements.

3   Go beyond the objective proximal environment to also assess the values and goals of the individual's larger cultural context and how these culturally driven values and goals act to moderate the impact of the individual's proximal environment.

4   Particularly for older children and adolescents integrate in the individual's subjective perceptions of their objective proximal environment as an additional assessment of context.

5   When assessing the subjective environment, avoid the use of average group perceptions since these may only weakly reflect individual perceptions.

6   In assessing individual characteristics, utilize multiple converging assessments rather than relying on single-source measurements.

7   Discrepancy scores that yield only an absolute level of discrepancy may be far less useful than valence-weighted scores or scores that also take into account the absolute level of person and contextual characteristics.

8   If assessment of fit is based on significance of statistical interaction terms it is essential to remember that greater levels of power are needed to detect interactions, particularly when non-extreme populations or contexts are being used. In this case confidence intervals may be an appropriate statistic in preliminary theory testing on person–context fit.

9   If assessment of fit is based on significance of statistical interaction terms it is essential to distinguish between additive versus interactive effects; the latter suggests the operation of fit, the former does not.

10   Power can be increased either by increasing sample size or by using more precise measures of person and contextual characteristics.

11   Regardless of the statistics used, truncated ranges of person or context variables will reduce our ability to detect the operation of person–context fit.

empirical research on this question. The statistical "ontological" conclusion of Rosnow and Rosenthal (1989) that "surely, God loves the .06 nearly as much as the .05" is clearly germane to the question of how best to analyze the current generation of research studies on person–environment fit.

Conceptual issues and critical questions

Even with state-of-the-art methodology and analytic techniques we may still be unable to identify existing person × context fit processes, or describe how good or poor fit translates into developmental variability, without prior consideration of some critical conceptual issues and questions. First and foremost there is the need for specification of what combinations of person and contextual characteristics are most likely to lead to good or poor fit. This means a greater emphasis on theory-driven research, with the theories of choice being those that have specific person–context characteristics as an integral part of the theory. As noted earlier, one such theory is that of Strelau (Strelau & Eliasz, 1994). Another would be that of Kochanska (1993), linking specific combinations of parent control strategies with specific dimensions of child temperament and attachment in the prediction of child compliance and socialization behaviors.

A related issue is the question of whether fit is best viewed as a linear or a threshold phenomenon, in terms of the relation of fit to development. Put another way, how much discrepancy between person and context leads to poor fit? Viewed in a linear framework, as discrepancy increases adequacy of fit should decrease. Viewed in a threshold framework, up to a certain point discrepancies between person and context characteristics would not lead to poorer fit; only after the discrepancy threshold was exceeded would poor fit become an influence on development. While virtually no developmental evidence is available on this question, research from the domain of organizational psychology suggests that neither a linear nor a threshold model will be sufficient. Rather, which model is more appropriate may depend on a variety of other factors, including what person and contextual characteristics are being measured and the level of these characteristics (Edwards & Rothbard, 1999).

A third critical conceptual issue is the need to consider fit within a temporal framework (Eccles, Lord, & Roeser, 1996; Horton & Bucy, 2000; Tinsley, 2000). Both children and their contexts change over time, which means that individual characteristics that fit the child's context at a given point in time may not provide a good fit at an earlier or later time. For example, in high-stress environments having a difficult temperament may be an advantage in infancy, but may be a major disadvantage when the infant becomes an adolescent (Gerhard, McDermott, & Andrade, 1994). Further, within a transactional perspective, changes in individual child characteristics may influence the child's context in ways that contribute to either a good or a poor fit, while changes in the child's specific context may act in the same manner with regard to child characteristics (Halverson & Deal, 2001). There also is the possibility that prior experiences may act to influence how the individual perceives themselves as fitting within their current context (Swartz-Kulstad & Martin, 2000). For example, prior stress can result in an individual's being either "sensitized" (vulnerable) or "steeled" (resistant) to later stress (Wachs, 2000). Understanding how previously sensitized or steeled individuals perceive themselves in relation to their current environment will require more than just defining current individual and contextual characteristics.

It also is important to conceptualize person–environment fit across a broader series of domains. One such domain is the fit of the individual to their culture (Super & Harkness, 1994). The literature in this area is small, but what there is clearly illustrates how cultural pressures can act to change an individual's characteristics in ways that provide a better fit to deeply rooted cultural values. Of particular interest here would be studies that looked at families who migrated to different cultures (Feldman & Rosenthal, 1990) or cultures undergoing acculturation pressure (Kagitcibasi, 1990), where traditionally valued individual characteristics were no longer viewed in the same way outside the family or by cultural change agents. Identification of the strategies that individuals and families use to adapt in ways that provide a better fit to a new or changing cultural context would provide a rich source of data that has both theoretical and practical implications in a rapidly changing world.

A final area of importance is that of niche selection (active covariance). As noted earlier, niche selection has the potential to provide a unique way of conceptualizing and assessing fit. However, few studies have given us sufficient detail on how individuals detect appropriate niches, how they select into such niches, the degree to which potential fit niches are closed off to individuals, and the developmental consequences of an individual's being in niches that provide varying degrees of fit with the individual's characteristics (Wachs, 2000). While some initial answers may come from perceptual studies addressing fundamental questions, such as how infants are able to detect the degree of fit between surface properties and their sensory-motor capabilities (Adolph, Eppler, & Gibson, 1993), far more research is needed in the area of niche identification and selection processes. Answers to such questions are essential if we are to truly understand the nature and impact of person–environment fit processes upon individual developmental variability.

Acknowledgment

Thanks are due to Professor Charlie Reeve for his most helpful comments on approaches to person–environment fit in the area of industrial-organizational psychology.

References

Adolph, K. E., Eppler, M. A., & Gibson, E. J. (1993). Development of perception of affordances. *Advances in Infancy Research, 8*, 51–98.

Albin, R. W., Lucyshyn, J. M., Horner, R. H., & Flannery, K. (1996). Contextual fit for behavioral support plan: A model for "goodness of fit." In L. K. Koegel & R. L. Koegel (eds.), *Positive behavioral support: Including people with difficult behavior in the community* (pp. 81–98). Baltimore, MD: Paul H. Brookes.

Arcus, D. (2001). Inhibited and uninhibited children: Biology in the social context. In: T. D. Wachs & G. Kohnstamm (eds.), *Temperament in context* (pp. 43–60). Mahwah, NJ: Lawrence Erlbaum Associates.

Atkinson, I. M., Robinson, J. A., & Shute, R. H. (1997). Between a rock and a hard place: An Australian perspective on education of children with ADHD. *Educational and Child Psychology, 14*, 21–30.

Bates, J. E. (1989). Applications of temperament concepts. In G. A. Kohnstamm, J. E. Bates, & M. K. Rothbart (eds.), *Temperament in childhood* (pp. 321–55). Chichester: John Wiley.

Bates, J. E. (2001). Adjustment style in childhood as a produce of parenting and temperament. In T. D. Wachs & G. Kohnstamm (eds.), *Temperament in context* (pp. 173–200). Mahwah, NJ: Lawrence Erlbaum Associates.

Bates, J. E., Wachs, T. D., & Emde, R. N. (1994). Toward practical uses for biological concepts of temperament. In J. E. Bates & T. D. Wachs (eds.), *Temperament: Individual differences at the interface of biology and behavior* (pp. 275–306). Washington, DC: American Psychological Association.

Bates, M. E. & Labouvie, E. W. (1994). Familial alcoholism and personality–environment fit: A developmental study of risk in adolescents. *Annals of the New York Academy of Sciences, 708,* 202–13.

Block, J., Block, J., & Keyes, S. (1988). Longitudinally foretelling drug use in adolescence. *Child Development, 59,* 336–55.

Bogenschneider, K., Small, S. A., & Tsay, J. C. (1997). Child, parent, and contextual influences on perceived parenting competence among parents of adolescents. *Journal of Marriage and the Family, 59,* 345–62.

Boivin, M., Dodge, K., & Coie, J. (1995). Individual-group behavioral similarity and peer status in experimental play groups of boys. *Journal of Personality and Social Psychology, 69,* 269–79.

Boyce, W. & Boyce, J. (1988). Acculturation and changes in health among Naajo boarding school students. *Social Science and Medicine, 17,* 219–26.

Bronfenbrenner, U. & Crouter, A. (1983). The evolution of environmental models in developmental research. In P. H. Mussen (series ed.) & W. Kessen (vol. ed.), *Handbook of child psychology,* vol. 1: *History, theory and methods* (pp. 357–414). New York: John Wiley.

Brooks-Gunn, J., Petersen, A. C., & Ichorn, D. (1985). The study of maturational timing effects in adolescence. *Journal of Youth and Adolescence, 14,* 149–61.

Brooks-Gunn, J., Attie, I., Burrow, C., & Rosso, J. T. (1989). The impact of puberty on body and eating concerns in athletic and nonathletic contexts. *Journal of Early Adolescence, 9,* 269–90.

Cairns, R. B. (1998). The making of developmental psychology. In W. Damon (editor-in-chief) & R. Lerner (vol. ed.), *Handbook of child psychology,* vol. 1: *Theoretical models of human development* (5th edn., pp. 25–105). New York: John Wiley.

Caplan, R. D. & Van Harrison, R. (1993). Person–environment fit theory: Some history, recent developments, and future directions. *Journal of Social Issues, 49,* 253–75.

Carey, W. B. (1998). Temperament and behavior problems in the classroom. *School Psychology Review, 27,* 522–33.

Caspi, A., Elder, G., & Bem, D. (1988). Moving away from the world: Life course patterns of shy children. *Developmental Psychology, 24,* 824–31.

Chess, S. & Thomas, A. (1989). Issues in the clinical application of temperament. In G. Kohnstamm, J. Bates, & M. Rothbart (eds.), *Temperament in childhood* (pp. 377–87). New York: John Wiley.

Chess, S. & Thomas, A. (1991). Temperament and the concept of goodness of fit. In J. Strelau & A. Angleitner (eds.), *Explorations in temperament* (pp. 15–28). New York: Plenum Press.

Cronbach, L. (1991). Emerging views on methodology. In T. D. Wachs & R. Plomin (eds.), *Conceptualization and measurement of organism–environment interaction* (pp. 87–104). Washington, DC: American Psychological Association.

Cronbach, L. & Snow, R. (1977). *Aptitudes and instructional methods.* New York: John Wiley.

Dawis, R. & Lofquist, L. (1984). *A psychological theory of work adjustment.* Minneapolis, MN: University of Minnesota Press.

DeVries, M. (1994). Kids in context: Temperament in cross-cultural perspective. In W. Carey & S. McDevitt (eds.), *Prevention and early intervention* (pp. 126–39). New York: Brunner/Mazel.

Dollinger, J. L. & Johnson, J. H. (1990). Predicting success in foster placement: The contribution of parent–child temperament characteristics. *American Journal of Orthopsychiatry, 60,* 585–93.

East, P. L., Lerner, R. M., Lerner, J. V., Soni, R., Ohannessian, C., & Jacobson, L. (1992). Early adolescent–peer group fit, peer relations, and psychosocial competence: A short-term longitudinal study. *Journal of Early Adolescence, 12,* 132–52.

Eccles, J. S., Lord, S. E., & Roeser, R. W. (1996). Round holes, square pegs, rocky roads, and sore feet: The impact of stage–environment fit on young adolescents' experiences in schools and families. In D. Cicchetti & S. L. Toth (eds.), *Adolescence: Opportunities and challenges. Rochester symposium on developmental psychopathology*, vol. 7 (pp. 47–92). Rochester, NY: University of Rochester Press.

Edwards, J. R. & Rothbard, N. P. (1999). Work and family stress and well-being: An examination of person–environment fit in the work and family domains. *Organizational Behavior and Human Decision Processes, 77*, 85–129.

Erwin, P. J., Sanson, A., Amos, D., & Bradley, B. S. (1993). Family day care and day care centres: Carer, family and child differences and their implications. *Early Child Development and Care, 86*, 89–103.

Evans, G. (1999). Measurement of the physical environment as stressor. In S. Friedman & T. D. Wachs (eds.), *Measuring environment across the life span* (pp. 249–78). Washington DC: American Psychological Association.

Fanurik, D., Zeltzer, L., Roberts, M., & Blount, R. (1993). The relationship between children's coping styles and psychological interventions for cold pressor pain. *Pain, 53*, 213–22.

Feagans, L. V. & Manlove, E. R. (1994). Parents, infants, and day-care teachers: Interrelations and implications for better child care. *Journal of Applied Developmental Psychology, 15*, 585–602.

Feagans, L. V., Merriwether, A. M., & Haldane, D. (1991). Goodness of fit in the home: Its relationship to school behavior and achievement in children with learning disabilities. *Journal of Learning Disabilities, 24*, 413–20.

Feldman, S. & Rosenthal, D. (1990). The acculturation of autonomy expectations in Chinese high schoolers residing in two western nations. *International Journal of Psychology, 25*, 259–81.

Fraser, B. J. (1991). Two decades of classroom environment research. In B. J. Fraser & H. J. Walberg (eds.), *Educational environments: Evaluation, antecedents and consequences* (pp. 3–27). Oxford: Pergamon Press.

Fraser, B. & Fisher, D. (1983). Student achievement as a function of person–environment fit. *British Journal of Educational Psychology, 53*, 89–99.

Galambos, N. L. & Turner, P. K. (1998). Parent and adolescent temperaments and the quality of parent–adolescent relations. *Merrill-Palmer Quarterly, 45*, 493–511.

Gandour, M. (1989). Activity level as a dimension of temperament in toddlers. *Child Development, 60*, 1092–8.

Garguilo, J., Attie, I., Brooks-Gunn, J., & Warren, M. P. (1987). Girls' dating behavior as a function of social context and maturation. *Developmental Psychology, 23*, 730–37.

Gerhard, A. L., McDermott, J. F., & Andrade, N. N. (1994). Variations in cultural influences in Hawaii. In W. B. Carey & S. C. McDevitt (eds.), *Prevention and early intervention: Individual differences as risk factors for the mental health of children: A festschrift for Stella Chess and Alexander Thomas* (pp. 149–57). New York: Brunner/Mazel.

Gordon, B. (1981). Child temperament and adult behavior: an exploration of "goodness of fit." *Child Psychiatry and Human Development, 11*, 167–78.

Greene, R. W. (1995). Students with ADHD in school classrooms: Teacher factors related to compatibility, assessment, and intervention. *School Psychology Review, 24*, 81–93.

Grossman, J. & Shigaki, I. S. (1994). Investigation of familial and school-based risk factors for Hispanic Head Start children. *American Journal of Orthopsychiatry, 64*, 456–67.

Grotevant, H., McRoy, R., & Jenkins, V. (1988). Emotionally disturbed adopted adolescents: early patterns of family adaptation. *Family Process, 27*, 439–57.

Gunnar, M. (1994). Psychoendocrine studies of temperament and stress in early childhood. In J. Bates & T. D. Wachs (eds.), *Temperament: Individual difference at the interface of biology and behavior* (pp. 175–98). Washington, DC: American Psychological Association.

Hagekull, B. & Bohlin, G. (1990). Early infant temperament and maternal expectations related to maternal adaptation. *International Journal of Behavioral Development, 13*, 199–214.

Halverson, C. & Deal, J. (2001). Temperamental change, parenting and the family context. In T. D. Wachs & G. Kohnstamm (eds.), *Temperament in context* (pp. 61–80). Mahwah, NJ: Lawrence Erlbaum Associates.

Hattie, J. & Watkins, D. (1988). Preferred classroom environment and approach to learning. *British Journal of Educational Psychology*, 58, 345–9.

Horton, C. B. & Bucy, J. E. (2000). Assessing adolescents: Ecological and person–environment fit perspectives. In W. E. Martin & J. L. Swartz-Kulstad (eds.), *Person–environment psychology and mental health: Assessment and intervention* (pp. 39–57). Mahwah, NJ: Lawrence Erlbaum Associates.

Hunt, J. McV. (1961). *Intelligence and experience.* New York: Ronald.

Juang, L. P., Lerner, J. V., McKinney, J. P., & von Eye, A. (1999). The goodness of fit of autonomy timetable expectations between Asian-Americans late adolescents and their parents. *International Journal of Behavioral Development*, 23, 1023–48.

Kagitcibasi, C. (1990). Family and home based intervention. In R. Brislin (ed.), *Family and home based intervention* (pp. 121–41). Newbury Park, CA: Sage.

Kahn, R. L. (1994). Opportunities, aspirations, and goodness of fit. In M. W. Riley & R. L. Kahn (eds.), *Age and structural lag: Society's failure to provide meaningful opportunities in work, family, and leisure* (pp. 37–53). New York: John Wiley.

Kawaguchi, M., Welsh, D., Powers, S., & Rostosky, S. (1998). Mothers, fathers, sons and daughters: Temperament, gender, and adolescent parent relationships. *Merrill-Palmer Quarterly*, 44, 77–96.

Keith-Spiegel, P., Tabachnick, B. G., & Spiegel, G. B. (1994). When demand exceeds supply: Second-order criteria used by graduate school selection committees. *Teaching of Psychology*, 21, 79–81.

Keogh, B. K. (1994). Temperament and teachers' views of teachability. In W. B. Carey & S. C. McDevitt (eds.), *Prevention and early intervention: Individual differences as risk factors for the mental health of children: A festschrift for Stella Chess and Alexander Thomas* (pp. 246–54). New York: Brunner/Mazel.

Kerr, M. (2001). Culture as a context for temperament. In T. D. Wachs & G. Kohnstamm (eds.), *Temperament in context* (pp. 139–52). Hillsdale, NJ: Lawrence Erlbaum Associates.

Kindermann, T. (1993). Fostering independence in mother–child interactions. *International Journal of Behavioral Development*, 16, 513–35.

Kindermann, T. (2003). Children's relationships and development of person–context relations. In J. Valsiner & K. J. Connolly (eds.), *Handbook of Developmental Psychology*. London: Sage.

Kochanska, G. (1993). Toward a synthesis of parental socialization and child temperament in early development of conscience. *Child Development*, 64, 325–47.

Kochanska, G. (1997). Multiple pathways to conscience for children with different temperaments. *Developmental Psychology*, 33, 228–40.

Korn, S. & Gannon, S. (1983). Temperament, cultural variation and behavior disorders in preschool children. *Child Psychiatry and Human Behavior*, 13, 203–12.

Kristof, A. (1996). Person–organization fit: An integrative review of its conceptualizations, measurement, and implications. *Personnel Psychology*, 49, 1–49.

Lawton, P. (1999). Environmental taxonomy. In S. Friedman & T. D. Wachs (eds.), *Measuring the environment across the life span* (pp. 91–126). Washington, DC: American Psychological Association.

Lerner, J. V., Lerner, R. M., & Zabski, S. (1985). Temperament and elementary school children's actual and rated academic performance: A test of a "goodness-of-fit". *Journal of Child Psychology and Psychiatry and Allied Disciplines*, 26, 125–36.

Lernerz, K., Kucher, J., Lerner, J., & Lerner, R. (1987). Contextual demands for early adolescent behavioral style. *Journal of Early Adolescence, 6,* 279–91.

Lumley, N., Ables, L., Melamed, B., Pistone, L., & Johnson, J. (1990). Coping outcome in children under going stressful medical procedures. *Behavioral Assessment, 12,* 223–38.

Mangelsdorf, S. C., Gunnar, M., Kestenbaum, R., Lang, S., & Andreas, D. (1991). Infant proneness-to-distress temperament, maternal personality, and mother–infant attachment: Associations and goodness of fit. *Annual Progress in Child Psychiatry and Child Development,* 312–29.

Markstrom, C. A., Berman, R. C., & Brusch, G. (1998). An exploratory examination of identity formation among Jewish adolescents according to context. *Journal of Adolescent Research, 13,* 202–22.

McClelland, G. & Judd, C. (1993). Statistical difficulties of detecting interactions and moderator effects. *Psychological Bulletin, 114,* 376–90.

Miceli, P., Whitman, T., Borkowski, J., Braungart-Rieker, J., & Mitchell, D. (1998). Individual differences in infant information processing: the role of temperamental and maternal factors. *Infant Behavior and Development, 21,* 119–36.

Midgley, C. & Feldlaufer, H. (1987). Students' and teachers' decision-making fit before and after the transition to junior high school. *Journal of Early Adolescence, 7,* 225–41.

Nitz, K., Lerner, R. M., Lerner, J. V., & Talwar, R. (1988). Parental and peer ethnotheory demands, temperament, and early adolescent adjustment. *Journal of Early Adolescence, 8,* 243–63.

Nurmi, J. (1993). Adolescent development in an age graded context. *International Journal of Behavioral Development, 16,* 169–89.

Pachter, L. M. & Harwood, R. L. (1996). Culture and child behavior and psychosocial development. *Journal of Developmental and Behavioral Pediatrics, 17,* 191–8.

Park, S., Belsky, J., Putnam, S., & Crnic, K. (1997). Infant emotionality, parenting and 3-year inhibition. *Developmental Psychology, 33,* 218–27.

Paterson, G. & Sanson, A. (1999). The association of behavioural adjustment to temperament, parenting and family characteristics among 5-year-old children. *Social Development, 8,* 293–309.

Plomin, R. & Daniels, D. (1984). The interaction between temperament and environment: Methodological considerations. *Merrill-Palmer Quarterly, 30,* 149–62.

Plomin, R., DeFries, J., & Loehlin, J. (1977). Genotype environment interaction and correlation in the analysis of human development. *Psychological Bulletin, 84,* 309–22.

Riese, M. & Matheny, A. (1990). Nurses' ratings of mother–infant dyads. Paper presented to the 7th International Conference on Infant Studies, Montreal, Quebec, April.

Rosnow, R. & Rosenthal, R. (1989). Statistical procedures and the justification of knowledge in psychological science. *American Psychologist, 44,* 1276–84.

Rosowsky, E., Dougherty, L. M., Johnson, C. J., & Gurian, B. (1997). Personality as an indicator of "goodness of fit" between the elderly individual and the health service system. *Clinical Gerontologist, 17,* 41–53.

Rothbart, M. & Bates, J. (1998). Temperament. In W. Damon (series ed.) & N. Eisenberg (vol. ed.), *Handbook of child psychology,* vol. 3: *Social, emotional, and personality development* (5th edn., pp. 105–76). New York: John Wiley.

Rudolph, K., Dennig, M., & Weisz, J. (1995). Determinants and consequences of children's coping in the medical setting. *Psychological Bulletin, 118,* 328–57.

Rutter, M. & Pickles, A. (1991). Person–environment interactions: Concepts, mechanisms and implications for data analysis. In T. D. Wachs & R. Plomin (eds.), *Conceptualization and measurement of organism–environment interaction* (pp. 105–41). Washington, DC: American Psychological Association.

Schalock, R. L. & Jensen, C. (1986). Assessing the goodness-of-fit between persons and their environment. *Journal of the Association for Persons with Severe Handicaps, 11,* 103–9.

Scheper-Hughes, N. (1987). A basic strangeness: Maternal estrangement and infant death. In C. Super (ed.), *The role of culture in developmental disorder* (pp. 131–53). San Diego, CA: Academic Press.

Schoggen, P. & Schoggen, M. (1988). Student voluntary participation and school size. *Journal of Educational Research, 81*, 288–93.

Schulenberg, J., Wadsworth, K., O'Malley, P., Bachman, J., & Johnston, L. (1996). Adolescent risk factors for binge drinking during the transition to young adulthood. *Developmental Psychology, 32*, 659–74.

Simeonsson, R. J., Bailey, D. B., Huntington, G. S., & Comfort, M. (1986). Testing the concept of goodness of fit in early intervention. *Infant Mental Health Journal, 7*, 81–94.

Smitsman, A. W. (1997). The development of tool use: Changing boundaries between organism and environment. In C. Dent-Read & P. Zukow-Goldring (eds.), *Evolving explanations of development: Ecological approaches to organism–environment systems* (pp. 301–29). Washington, DC: American Psychological Association.

Snow, R. E. (1992). Aptitude theory: Yesterday, today, and tomorrow. *Educational Psychologist, 27*, 5–32.

Sprunger, L. W., Boyce, W. T., & Gaines, J. A. (1985). Family–infant congruence: routines and rhythmicity in family adaptations to a young infant. *Child Development, 56*, 564–72.

Steinglass, P., Tislenko, L., & Reiss, D. (1985). Stability/instability in the alcoholic marriage: The interrelationships between course of alcoholism, family process, and marital outcome. *Family Process, 24*, 365–76.

Strelau, J. (1989). The regulative theory of temperament as a result of east–west influences. In G. Kohnstamm, J. Bates, & M. Rothbart (eds.), *Temperament in childhood* (pp. 35–48). New York: John Wiley.

Strelau, J. (2001). The role of temperament as a moderator of stress. In T. D. Wachs & G. Kohnstamm (eds.), *Temperament in context* (pp. 153–72). Mahwah, NJ: Lawrence Erlbaum Associates.

Strelau, J. & Eliasz, A. (1994). Temperament risk factors for type A behavior patterns of adolescents. In W. Carey & S. McDevitt (eds.), *Prevention and early intervention* (pp. 42–9). New York: Brunner/Mazel.

Suls, J., Martin, R., & David, J. (1998). Person–environment fit and its limits. *Personality and Social Psychology Bulletin, 24*, 88–98.

Super, C. M. & Harkness, S. (1994). Temperament and the developmental niche. In W. B. Carey & S. C. McDevitt (eds.), *Prevention and early intervention: Individual differences as risk factors for the mental health of children: A festschrift for Stella Chess and Alexander Thomas* (pp. 115–25). New York, NY: Brunner/Mazel.

Swanson, J. L. & Fouad, N. A. (1999). Applying theories of person–environment fit to the transition from school to work. *Career Development Quarterly, 47*, 337–47.

Swartz-Kulstad, J. L. & Martin, W. E. (2000). Culture as an essential aspect of person–environment fit. In W. E. Martin & J. L. Swartz-Kulstad (eds.), *Person–environment psychology and mental health: Assessment and intervention* (pp. 169–95). Mahwah, NJ: Lawrence Erlbaum Associates.

Talbert, J. & McLaughlin, M. (1999). Assessing the school environment. In S. Friedman & T. D. Wachs (eds.), *Measuring environment across the life-span* (pp. 197–228). Washington, DC: American Psychological Association.

Talwar, R., Nitz, K., & Lerner, R. M. (1990). Relations among early adolescent temperament, parent and peer demands, and adjustment: A test of the goodness of fit. *Journal of Adolescence, 13*, 279–98.

Tinsley, H. E. A. (2000). The congruence myth: An analysis of the efficacy of the person–environment fit model. *Journal of Vocational Behavior, 56*, 147–79.

Vachon, M. L. & Stylianos, S. K. (1988). The role of social support in bereavement. *Journal of Social Issues, 44,* 175–90.

Vandell, D. & Posner, J. (1999). Conceptualization and measurement of children's after school environment. In S. Friedman & T. D. Wachs (eds.), *Measuring the environment across the life span* (pp. 167–96). Washington, DC: American Psychological Association.

Vitaliano, P. P., DeWolfe, D. J., Maiuro, R. D., Russo, J., & Katon, W. (1990). Appraised changeability of a stressor as a modifier of the relationship between coping and depression: A test of the hypothesis of fit. *Journal of Personality and Social Psychology, 59,* 582–92.

Wachs, T. D. (1987). Specificity of environmental action as manifest in environmental correlates of infant's mastery motivation. *Developmental Psychology, 23,* 782–90.

Wachs, T. D. (1991). Synthesis: Promising research designs, measures and strategies. In T. D. Wachs & R. Plomin (eds.), *Conceptualization and measurement of organism–environment interaction* (pp. 162–82). Washington, DC: American Psychological Association.

Wachs, T. D. (1992). *The nature of nurture.* Newbury Park, CA: Sage.

Wachs, T. D. (1999). Celebrating complexity: Conceptualization and assessment of the environment. In S. Friedman & T. D. Wachs (eds.), *Measuring the environment across the life span* (pp. 357–92). Washington, DC: American Psychological Association.

Wachs, T. D. (2000). *Necessary but not sufficient: The respective roles of single and multiple influences on human development.* Washington, DC: American Psychological Association.

Wachs, T. D. & Kohnstamm, D. (2001). The bi-directional nature of temperament–context links. In T. D. Wachs & G. Kohnstamm (eds.), *Temperament in context* (pp. 201–22). Mahwah, NJ: Lawrence Erlbaum Associates.

Wahlsten, D. (1990). Insensitivity of the analysis of variance to heredity–environment interaction. *Behavior and Brain Sciences, 13,* 109–61.

Wallace, K. A. & Bergeman, C. S. (1997). Control and the elderly: "Goodness-of-fit." *International Journal of Aging and Human Development, 45,* 323–39.

Wallander, J. L., Hubert, N. C., & Varni, J. W. (1988). Child and maternal temperament characteristics, goodness of fit, and adjustment in physically handicapped children. *Journal of Clinical Child Psychology, 17,* 336–44.

Wallerstein, J. S. (1996). The psychological tasks of marriage: II. *American Journal of Orthopsychiatry, 66,* 217–27.

Webb, N. M., Nemer, K. M., Chizhik, A. W., & Sugrue, G. (1998). Equity issues in collaborative group assessment: Group composition and performance. *American Educational Research Journal, 35,* 607–51.

Wilk, S. & Sackett, P. (1996). Longitudinal analysis of ability–job complexity fit and job change. *Personnel Psychology, 49,* 937–67.

Wilk, S., Desmarais, L., & Sackett, P. (1995). Gravitation to jobs commensurate with ability: Longitudinal and cross-sectional tests. *Journal of Applied Psychology, 80,* 79–85.

Windle, M., Hooker, K., Lenerz, K., East, P., Lerner, J., & Lerner, R. (1986). Temperament, perceived competence, and depression in early and late adolescents. *Developmental Psychology, 22,* 384–92.

Wong, N. & Watkins, D. (1996). Self-monitoring as a mediator of person–environment fit. *British Journal of Educational Psychology, 66,* 223–9.

Wong, N. & Watkins, D. (1998). A longitudinal study of the psychosocial environmental and learning approaches in the Hong Kong classroom. *Journal of Educational Research, 91,* 247–54.

Zuckerman, M. (1994). Impulsive unsocialized sensation seeking. In J. Bates & T. D. Wachs (eds.), *Temperament: Individual differences at the interface of biology and behavior* (pp. 218–255). Washington, DC: American Psychological Association.

CHAPTER TWENTY-THREE

New Developments in the Study of Infant Memory

Patricia J. Bauer

Until not so very long ago, it was widely believed that the period of infancy was one during which the human organism was unable to engage in a type of mental act that most adults take for granted. That is, it was thought that infants were unable to encode, store, and subsequently retrieve memories of specific past events. If this were true, it would represent a striking deficit resulting in a profound discontinuity in development. Assumptions of just such a discontinuity nevertheless prevailed; they originated from no fewer than three sources: cognitive neuroscience, cognitive developmental theory such as that associated with Piaget, and ironically, research on adults' memories of early childhood. Moreover, the assumptions were hard to examine because of methodological issues.

Since Sigmund Freud first labeled it, the phenomenon of *infantile amnesia* has been one of the great curiosities in the field of memory. Infantile or childhood amnesia refers to the relative paucity among adults of verbally accessible memories from the first years of life. In his interviews with his adult patients, Freud noticed that few had memories from their early years. The memories that they did have were sketchy and incomplete. Freud termed this phenomenon "infantile amnesia" – "the amnesia that veils our earliest youth from us and makes us strangers to it" (1966, p. 326). Over the course of his career, Freud developed two hypotheses regarding the source of infantile amnesia. The more widely known is his hypothesis that early memories exist but are repressed due to their undesirable content. The other suggestion that he advanced was that early memories are mere fragments of experiences that are not organized in any coherent fashion. In the years since Freud identified infantile amnesia there have been numerous studies of adults' memories of their childhoods. They have yielded one of the most robust findings in the memory literature, namely that in Western culture, among adults, the average age of earliest verbalizable memory is 3 to $3^1/_2$ (see Weigle & Bauer, 2000, for a review; see Mullen, 1994, for evidence of later average earliest memories among Asian-American and Korean adults).

The suggestion that memories from early in life were repressed has not received empirical support (e.g., West & Bauer, 1999). However, the idea that adults have few memories from early in life because early experiences are not encoded in a coherent, adult-like manner is alive and well in the field of cognitive science; only recently has it begun to be challenged. The idea that infants and young children are not able to remember the events of their lives was consistent with the highly influential theory of Jean Piaget. Piaget (1952, 1962) developed the argument that for the first $1^{1}/_{2}$ to 2 years of life, infants live in a "here and now" world that includes objects and events available to the senses but which has no past and no future. Lacking the symbolic means to represent information not currently perceptually available (i.e., to *re-present* it), infants were thought unable to remember the past.

Although they may have been blissfully unaware of it, researchers in the field of cognitive neuroscience added fuel to the fire with their suggestions that the neural substrate supporting memory for specific past events was functionally late to develop. Initially, this conclusion was based on research with rats, in which one of the major neural structures implicated in memory for specific events, namely the hippocampus, is late to mature (see Nelson, 1995, for discussion). Application of the findings to humans led to the suggestion that the capacity for recall of specific past events would emerge late. This perspective held sway until the early 1980s, when it began to be challenged with research on human infants and non-human primates (see Schacter & Moscovitch, 1984, for discussion).

Finally, even as tenets attributed to Piagetian theory were being challenged on multiple fronts (e.g., Gelman & Baillargeon, 1983), and even as data suggesting earlier functional maturity of the neural circuitry supporting long-term memory were beginning to accrue, the suggestion that human infants were unable to remember specific events of their lives went unexamined for want of suitable methodology. In older children and adults, memory for specific past events is examined primarily through verbal report. For infants and young children, this is not a viable alternative. It is not until the fourth year of life that children become reliable partners in conversations about the past. That the average age of earliest reportable memory among adults is $3^{1}/_{2}$, and that age $3-3^{1}/_{2}$ marks the beginning of children's abilities to share past experiences verbally, "conspired" to create the impression that age 3 marked the onset of the ability to recall past events.

Whereas research on early memory development is primarily the purview of cognitive developmentalists, the extent to which infants carry forward the experiences of their lives is of interest beyond this subfield. It also is of interest to researchers and theoreticians who think about the impact of early experience more broadly. If early experiences either are not retained in an accessible format, or they are lost to consciousness over the course of development, then early experience will not be seen as a major determinant of later behavior. If, however, early experiences are consciously accessible and remain so over time (at least under some circumstances) then there is a proportionally larger role for them to play in explanations of later development. Another alternative is, of course, that early experiences are not consciously accessible but that they nevertheless have an impact on subsequent behavior (i.e., as implicit memories). Data on early memory, its development, and on the long-term accessibility of early memories, thus are of broad interest and significance.

In this chapter I summarize some of the research that has contributed to revision of the perspective that infants are unable to remember the past. Because questions of whether infants and young children are able to create, retain, and later retrieve coherent, organized memories of specific past experiences over periods of delay (as opposed to over the short term) is of central importance, data on long-term memory for specific events or episodes is featured. After discussion of methodological challenges and the data resulting from successful address of them, I turn to discussion of some of the promises in research on early memory development that are on the immediate horizon. Finally, I return to discussion of the question of whether early experiences are carried forward into childhood and beyond.

Methodological Challenges in the Study of Infant Memory

What kind of memory is it?

Most of what we think of when we talk about "memory for" or "remembering" a past event falls under the heading of a particular type of memory, namely, *declarative* memory (Zola-Morgan & Squire, 1993). Declarative memory involves the capacity for explicit recognition or recall of names, places, dates, events, and so on. In contrast, the type of memory termed *non-declarative* represents a variety of non-conscious abilities, including the capacity for learning procedures and skills, some forms of classical conditioning, and priming (i.e., facilitated processing of a stimulus as a result of previous exposure to it; see Parkin, 1997, for a review). A defining feature of non-declarative memory is that the impact of experience is made evident through a change in behavior or performance, but that the experience leading to the change is not consciously accessible (Zola-Morgan & Squire, 1993). Declarative memory is characterized as fast (e.g., supporting one-trial learning), fallible (e.g., memory traces degrade, retrieval failures occur), and flexible (i.e., not tied to a specific modality or context). Non-declarative memory is characterized as slow (i.e., with the exception of priming, it results from gradual or incremental learning), reliable, and inflexible (Squire, Knowlton, & Musen, 1993).

The distinction between different types of memory originally was derived from the adult cognitive and neuroscience literatures. As such, much of the work supporting the view that there are multiple memory systems comes from adult humans suffering from amnesia and from non-human primates. Some have argued that because human infants are neither brain-damaged adults nor monkeys, the distinction between memory systems is not relevant to human developmental science (e.g., Rovee-Collier, 1997). However, a long tradition of comparative psychology suggests that "lessons" learned from one population can, with appropriate care, be applied to others. Another caution in application of the multiple memory systems view to human cognitive development stems from use of the construct of conscious awareness as one of the criteria to differentiate declarative and non-declarative forms of memory. As noted by Rovee-Collier (1997) and Nelson (1997), it is not clear how consciousness can be assessed in a preverbal infant or non-human animal. As will be seen later, researchers have addressed this concern by designing tasks that bear the remaining characteristic features of declarative memory tasks and which produce behaviors that look quite different from those exhibited in non-declarative memory paradigms.

In spite of the cautions to application of the construct of "consciousness" to preverbal infants or nonverbal organisms, distinguishing different types of memory is crucial for two reasons. First, there is reason to believe that different types of memory are subserved by different neural substrates that mature at different rates and times (see Bauer, 2002; Carver & Bauer, 2001; Nelson, 1995, 1997, for discussion). Second, if we are going to talk about early experience having an impact on later behavior, then we need to know whether that early experience is potentially accessible or not, because only accessible memories are going to be verbalizable and available for examination. As Mandler (1990) has argued, we may speculate about or develop theories about unconscious procedures, but the fact that they are not conscious means that we cannot examine them directly. So, it is critical to know whether early experiences are consciously accessible, or not.

One of the most common ways to assess whether infants have encoded and retained information about a stimulus is to examine their patterns of looking or listening to material encountered before versus to material not previously encountered. For example, in visual paired comparison, infants are exposed to pairs of pictures of a stimulus. After a period of familiarization, infants are presented with the "familiar" picture along with a different, novel picture. Measures of the amount of time spent looking at each picture are taken. Based on such techniques, it is clear that from birth, infants register the effects of experience. After relatively brief periods of familiarization, infants show reliable preferential looking to novel stimuli, thereby indicating memory for the one to which they have been familiarized. In fact, the results of DeCasper and Spence (1986) suggest that even prenatal experiences later may manifest themselves in changes in behavior toward stimuli. Mere hours after birth, infants can distinguish between a novel story passage and one that their mothers read aloud during the last weeks of pregnancy (in this case, recognition was inferred based on differential rates and intensities of sucking behavior in response to the familiar versus a novel passage).

Not only do infants rapidly form memories, but they retain their experiences with stimuli over surprisingly long periods of time. For example, 5-month-olds have been shown to recognize face stimuli over a delay of 2 weeks (Fagan, 1973). Over long retention intervals, recognition may be evidenced by reliable visual preference for a familiar stimulus, rather than a novel one. In Bahrick and Pickens (1995), for example, when they were tested virtually immediately after familiarization with a novel object making a novel motion, 3-month-old infants demonstrated visual preference for a new stimulus, thereby indicating recognition of the old stimulus. Over intermediate periods of 1 day to 2 weeks, no preference was detected (i.e., amount of looking to familiar and novel stimuli did not differ). After 1 and 3 months, however, reliable preferences were observed for old stimuli, thereby indicating long-term recognition. The same pattern has been observed for auditory recognition of familiar versus novel nursery rhymes (Spence, 1996). The shifting distribution of attention is taken as evidence of the differential status of mnemonic (i.e., memory) traces over time. The assumption is that on the basis of a "fresh" memory trace, infants need not spend time processing familiar stimuli and consequently spend more time attending to what is novel. As the memory trace begins to fade, infants distribute their attentional resources more evenly, encoding the novel stimulus and updating their memories for the familiar stimulus. With further degradation of the memory representation, infants devote the majority of attentional resources to reconstruction of a mnemonic trace for the once-familiar stimulus (see Bahrick, Hernandez-Reif, & Pickens, 1997; Courage & Howe, 1998; for discussion). In summary, attentional preference techniques can be used to test infants' retention of particular stimuli; retention is demonstrated over both the short and the long term, and depending upon the circumstances of testing, recognition may be evidenced through greater attention to novel stimuli or through greater attention to familiar stimuli.

Whereas attentional preference techniques measure changes in infants' responses to previously encountered stimuli, it is unclear whether they measure the same type of recognition as evidenced when, for example, adults affirm or deny that they have seen a particular stimulus before. Mandler (1998) has suggested that infant recognition memory experiments actually are more analogous to adult priming studies than they are to adult recognition studies. Consider that in recognition memory tasks, adults are asked to reflect on their previous experience and make an explicit judgment as to whether a particular stimulus is "old" or "new," as a function of whether the item had or had not appeared on a list of studied items. In contrast, in infant recognition memory paradigms, no explicit judgment of whether an item has been encountered before is required. Rather, what is measured is whether processing of a stimulus is "facilitated" as a function of whether it had been encountered previously (i.e., infants spend proportionally less time processing stimuli with which they have been familiarized). In this respect, Mandler argues, the task is analogous to priming paradigms in which adults are tested to see whether their response times to judge whether, for example, strings of letters constitute words, are facilitated by previous study of the words. That a sense of familiarity or awareness need not accompany primed responses is evidenced by the fact that adults suffering from amnesia show normal priming even as they evidence pronounced deficits in recognition memory (Warrington & Weiskrantz, 1974). In summary, whereas differential responses to old and new stimuli indicate that information about the old stimulus has been stored, missing from the response is the component of explicit judgment of whether an item has been seen before.

Nelson (1995, 1997) has sounded a different note of caution to interpretation of infant attentional responses. He suggested that early preference for novelty, which is the most typical index of recognition memory, may actually be an obligatory response that is not under the organism's control. The suggestion is derived in part from findings that until about 8 months of age, infants' responses to novel stimuli are driven more by the frequency with which the stimuli are presented than by their novelty, per se (see Nelson & Collins, 1991, 1992, for discussion). For both Mandler and Nelson, the question raised is whether infant attentional preference studies evidence adult-like recognition, or some more "primitive" recognitory response. To address this issue, researchers have developed a nonverbal task that requires recall, rather than recognition, memory. Because recall entails accessing a cognitive structure based in past experience in the absence of ongoing perceptual support for that experience (Mandler, 1984), it provides unequivocal evidence of declarative memory processes.

Measuring declarative memory nonverbally: deferred and elicited imitation

Imitation of a model after a delay originally was suggested by Piaget (1952, 1962) as one of the hallmarks of the development of symbolic thought. Beginning in the middle 1980s, imitation-based techniques were developed as a means of testing mnemonic ability in infants and young children throughout the first 3 years of life (e.g., Bauer & Shore, 1987; Meltzoff, 1985). *Deferred imitation* involves using props to produce a single action or a multi-step sequence of actions and then, after a delay of seconds to months, inviting the infant or young child to imitate. *Elicited imitation* is a more generic term describing techniques in which infants or children may be permitted to imitate actions or multi-step sequences prior to imposition of a delay. Across laboratories and studies, there are a number of procedural variations on the theme of the imitation-based task. For example, in some cases single object-specific actions are demonstrated as many as three times, in silence, followed by a time-limited response period signaled only by presentation of the object to the infant (e.g., Meltzoff, 1988a). In other cases, sequences varying in length from two to nine steps are demonstrated two times, with narration, followed by a child-controlled response period signaled by presentation of the objects to the infant along with a verbal "reminder" of the sequences to be performed (e.g., Bauer, Hertsgaard, & Wewerka, 1995). In spite of these methodological variations, as discussed in detail elsewhere (e.g., Bauer, 1995, 1996, 1997; Mandler, 1990; Meltzoff, 1990), the conditions of learning and later testing in elicited and deferred imitation are conducive to formation of declarative memories but not non-declarative memories.

First, as noted earlier, declarative memory is characterized as fast. Numerous studies have revealed one-trial learning of modeled actions and action sequences (e.g., Bauer, 1992; Bauer & Hertsgaard, 1993; Mandler & McDonough, 1995; Meltzoff, 1988a, 1995). Moreover, the behaviors that index memory (i.e., reproduction of observed actions) are neither in the behavioral repertoire prior to exposure to the model (i.e., infants are tested on novel and in some cases (Meltzoff, 1988a), unusual actions) nor practiced during acquisition (i.e., infants merely observe a model; they do not participate as the action is demonstrated). Indeed, production of events prior to imposition of a delay is not necessary or even reliably facilitative of later reproduction (e.g., Bauer, Hertsgaard, & Wewerka, 1995; Carver & Bauer, 1999; Mandler & McDonough, 1995; Meltzoff, 1988a, b, 1995). These conditions are not conducive to non-declarative acquisition (Bachevalier, 1992; Mandler, 1990; Meltzoff, 1990; Schacter & Moscovitch, 1984; Squire, Knowlton, & Musen, 1993).

Second, declarative memory is characterized as fallible. That is, storage and retrieval failures, and thus forgetting, occur. Although as reviewed later, memory as tested via elicited imitation can be long lasting, forgetting also is in evidence. Indeed, significant forgetting is apparent after as few as 48 hours (Bauer et al., 2002; Bauer, Van Abbema, & de Haan, 1999). Studies in which infants and very young children are tested over different delay intervals (e.g., Bauer, 2002; Klein & Meltzoff, 1999) reveal a forgetting function quite similar to that observed in older children and even adults, namely an initial steep decline in performance followed by a more shallow forgetting function (see Schneider & Pressley, 1997, for a review).

Third, declarative memory is characterized as flexible. That is, memory can be demonstrated in contexts and under conditions that differ from those in which the material originally was learned. Infants have been shown to generalize imitative responses across changes in (a) the materials used to produce the modeled actions and sequences (i.e., changes in the size, shape, color, and/or material composition of objects used in demonstration versus test: Bauer & Dow, 1994; Bauer & Fivush, 1992; Lechuga, Marcos-Ruiz, & Bauer, 2002), (b) the appearance of the room at the time of demonstration of modeled actions and at the time of memory test (e.g., demonstration in a room decorated with large pink polka-dots on the walls followed by test in a plainly decorated room: Barnat, Klein, & Meltzoff, 1996; Klein & Meltzoff, 1999), (c) the setting for demonstration of the modeled actions and the test of memory for them (e.g., demonstration in a daycare setting followed by test in an infant's home: Hanna & Meltzoff, 1993; Klein & Meltzoff, 1999), and (d) the individual who demonstrated the actions and the individual who tested for memory for the actions (e.g., demonstration by a confederate peer followed by test by an adult experimenter: Hanna & Meltzoff, 1993). Infants are even able to use three-dimensional objects to produce events that they have only seem modeled on a television screen (Meltzoff, 1988c). Although there are suggestions that infants' memories as tested in the deferred imitation paradigm become more generalizable with age (Hayne, MacDonald, & Barr, 1997), infants as young as 9–10 months (Baldwin, Markman, & Melartin, 1993) have been shown to flexibly extend their knowledge across changes in stimuli. What is more, even as they show flexibility in their mnemonic responses, infants and young children provide evidence of memory for the original stimulus materials and locations, suggesting that flexibility in memory is not born of forgetting (Barnat, Klein, & Meltzoff, 1996; Bauer & Dow, 1994; Lechuga, Marcos-Ruiz, & Bauer, 2002).

In addition to being decontextualized, the memories formed in elicited imitation share another characteristic of declarative memories, namely they are verbally accessible. By necessity, evidence of verbal accessibility comes from children old enough to speak. As described in the section entitled "Verbal measures of recall", Bauer et al. (1998) analyzed the spontaneous verbalizations of children who, at the ages of 22 and 32 months, returned to the laboratory to be tested for memory for events to which they had been exposed at the ages of 16 and 20 months. Both age groups provided verbal evidence of memory for events that they had imitated prior to imposition of the 6 or 12 month delay. The 20-month-olds also provided mnemonic verbalizations about events that they had only watched prior to the delays (see Bauer & Wewerka, 1995, 1997, for additional evidence of verbally expressed event memory). That children subsequently are able to talk about events experienced in the context of imitation-based paradigms is strong evidence that the memories formed are declarative in nature.

Ideally, the logical argument that elicited imitation is mediated by declarative memory processes would be complemented by direct evidence of the neural basis for performance on the task. McDonough et al. (1995) tested adults with amnesia (in whom declarative memory processes are impaired) and control participants in a deferred imitation task using multi-step sequences. Whereas normal adults performed as expected on the task, patients with amnesia did poorly. Indeed, they performed no better than control participants who had never seen the events demonstrated. This finding strongly suggests that deferred imitation taps declarative memory.

Finally, deferred imitation taps recall memory, rather than recognition memory. The available props do provide perceptual support for performance. However, even in the case of single actions or the individual actions of multi-step event sequences, numerous control conditions make clear that the actions are not "discovered" by the infants and children through trial and error or problem solving, and that the objects themselves do not suggest or "afford" the actions to be performed with them (e.g., Bauer, 1992; Meltzoff, 1988a). In the case of multi-step event sequences, additional evidence that recall processes support performance comes from temporally ordered reproduction of modeled sequences. Consider that once an event sequence is modeled, no perceptual support for the order in which the actions are to be performed remains. To reproduce an ordered sequence, temporal order information must be encoded during presentation of the event sequence and subsequently retrieved from a representation of the event, in the absence of ongoing perceptual support. Particularly since retrieving temporal order information is thought to depend upon the integrity of the frontal lobes as well as connections between the medial temporal and frontal lobes (e.g., Shimamura, Janowsky, & Squire, 1991; Yasuno et al., 1999), and thus is thought to involve the entire neural network that subserves declarative memory, temporally ordered reproduction of multi-step sequences provides especially compelling evidence of declarative memory. For this reason, I pay particular attention to developments in ordered recall.

Declarative Memory in Infancy and Very Early Childhood

Elicited and deferred imitation have been used to test infants as young as 6 months and children as old as 36 months. Because the same technique has been used across such a wide age span, we are afforded a picture of developments in recall memory from infancy throughout the period of transition to early childhood. The developmental picture that has emerged from this research is of relatively early competence in recall over the short term, developments in long-term ordered recall near the end of the first year of life, and consolidation of the ability over the course of the second year of life.

Recall in the first year of life

To date, the youngest infants tested with deferred imitation of actions or action sequences are 6-month-olds. In Barr, Dowden, and Hayne (1996) infants were tested for immediate and 24-hour delayed recall of the three-step action sequence of pulling a mitten off a puppet's hand, shaking the mitten (which, at demonstration, contained a bell), and replacing the mitten on the puppet's hand. Barr and her colleagues found that 75 percent of 6-month-olds imitated at least one action after the 24-hour delay (i.e., pulling off the mitten). These data thus provide evidence of recall over the short term as early as 6 months. Interestingly, what was not apparent in Barr, Dowden, and Hayne's data was compelling evidence of ordered recall over the delay. Specifically, whereas 75 percent of 6-month-olds produced one action after 24 hours, only 25 percent of them provided evidence of memory for more than one step of the sequence. This "dissociation" between recall of content and recall of temporal order information is consistent with suggestions that, at this young age, the neural network that supports ordered recall has not as yet coalesced. Specifically, as discussed in Carver and Bauer (2001), most of the medial temporal and diencephalic components of the network may be relatively well developed. In contrast, other of the medial temporal components (i.e., the dentate gyrus of the hippocampus, which is implicated in consolidation of memories for long-term storage) and the frontal components (which are implicated in both long-term retrieval and recall of temporal order information) of the neural network are relatively immature (see Bauer, 2002; Nelson, 1997, for discussions).

By 9 months of age developments in ordered recall ability are readily apparent. In Carver and Bauer (1999), deferred imitation was used to test 9-month-old infants' long-term recall of novel two-step event sequences such as described in Table 23.1a. In the sample as a whole, after a 5-week delay, the infants showed evidence of recall of

Table 23.1 Examples of multi-step event sequences used in referenced research

---

(a) *Two-step sequence*

Sequence: Make Big Bird turn on the light
Materials: Small plastic car containing "Big Bird" character; clear plastic L-shaped base; plastic plunger extended from one end of the horizontal section of the base; small light bulb on end of horizontal section opposite plunger.
Steps: (1) Putting the car in the base (i.e., inserting it down the vertical section of the base), and (2) pushing in the plunger, thereby causing the car to roll to the other end and illuminate the light bulb.

(b) *Three-step sequence*

Sequence: Paddle rattle
Materials: Rectangular paddle with a handle; wooden block; nesting cup.
Steps: (1) Putting the block in the center of the paddle, (2) covering the block with the nesting cup, and (3) shaking the paddle by the handle, thereby causing the combination to rattle.

(c) *Four-step sequence*

Sequence: Make a gong
Materials: Base resembling the support for a swing set, small cup attached to one post of the swing-set-shaped base, bar resting in the cup, metal plate with a lip, small plastic mallet.
Steps: (1) Lifting the bar from the cup, (2) putting the bar across the posts (to form a crosspiece), (3) hanging the plate from the bar, and (4) hitting the plate with the mallet, thereby causing it to ring.

---

the individual target actions of the event sequences (e.g., in the example sequence "Make Big Bird turn on the light," putting the car in the base or pushing in the plunger). Furthermore, 45 percent of the infants also showed evidence of temporally ordered recall memory after the 5-week delay (i.e., they produced both actions of the sequence, in the correct temporal order); the remaining 55 percent of the infants did not show evidence of temporally ordered recall. This distribution since has been replicated in two separate samples of 9-month-olds (Bauer et al., 2001, 2003). What is more, Carver, Bauer, and Nelson (2000) reported an association between infant brain activity as measured by event-related potentials (ERPs) and behavioral evidence of ordered recall.[1] Infants who subsequently evidenced ordered recall earlier had shown evidence of differential ERP responses to pictures of event sequences to which they previously had been exposed and event sequences new to them. Infants who after 5 weeks did not show evidence of ordered recall did not produce ERP responses indicative of recognition memory. In a subsequent study, individual differences in recognition and ordered recall were linked to differences in the process of consolidation of memory traces, such that infants who subsequently evidenced ordered recall showed evidence of more robust consolidation (Bauer et al., 2003). To our knowledge, these are the first reports in the literature of use of multiple, converging measures to assess mnemonic function in early infancy.

Although it is not yet entirely clear precisely what the individual differences in long-term ordered recall and ERP responses mean, the data are indicative of developmental differences in infants' ability to store and/or retrieve information over extended periods of time (Bauer et al., 2003; Carver & Bauer, 1999; Carver, Bauer, & Nelson, 2000). That the differences are observed at 9 months suggests that this is an especially important period in development of long-term recall ability. This conclusion fits well with the proposed time frame for the coalescence of the declarative memory network (e.g., Carver & Bauer, 2001; Nelson, 1995, 1997; Schacter & Moscovitch, 1984). Additional evidence of important developments at this time comes from a study in which different infants were enrolled at the ages of 9 and 10 months, and tested for memory after delays of both 1 and 3 months (see Table 23.1a for a sample sequence; different event sequences were tested at each delay). As a group, the 9-month-olds showed evidence of memory for the temporal order of the events after 1 month but not after 3 months. In contrast, as a group, the 10-month-olds showed evidence of memory for temporal order after both the 1- and the 3-month delay intervals (Carver & Bauer, 2001). Together with the results of Barr, Dowden, and Hayne (1996), the data from 9- and 10-month-olds (Bauer et al., 2001, 2003; Carver & Bauer, 2001) are consistent with the suggestion that relatively early in development, mnemonic behaviors that can be supported by medial temporal lobe structures themselves (e.g., recall over the short term) will be in evidence, whereas behaviors that likely require further maturation of the neural substrate (e.g., recall of temporal order information and recall after long delay intervals) show a more protracted course of development.

---

[1]   ERPs are scalp-recorded voltage oscillations in the brain. Because they are time-locked to a particular stimulus, they are thought to reflect the cognitive processing of the stimulus (see Nelson & Monk, 2001, for discussion of use of ERPs in developmental research).

If long-term ordered recall is newly emergent near the end of the first year of life, it likely undergoes significant development and consolidation over the course of the second year. The results of a large-scale study of remembering and forgetting during the transition from infancy to early childhood bear out this suggestion.

Recall by 1- to 3-year-olds

Nonverbal measures of recall To date, the most comprehensive study of long-term recall memory throughout the second and into the third year of life is Bauer et al. (2000). Children were enrolled at the age of 13, 16, or 20 months. A total of 360 children participated, 180 of whom were 16-month-olds. All of the 13-month-olds and half of the 16-month-olds were tested on event sequences three steps in length; all of the 20-month-olds and half of the 16-month-olds were tested on event sequences four steps in length. Examples of three-step and four-step event sequences are provided in Table 23.1b and c, respectively. Differences in sequence length accommodated age-related changes in the lengths of sequences that children can accurately imitate (see Bauer, 1995, 1996, 1997, for reviews). At each of three sessions, spaced one week apart, the children were exposed to the same six event sequences. Three of the sequences they never were permitted to imitate; three of the sequences they were permitted to imitate one time, at the end of the third exposure session. (There were virtually no substantive differences in performance as a function of whether or not the children were permitted to imitate prior to the delay.) The children returned for delayed recall testing after delay intervals of either 1, 3, 6, 9, or 12 months (delay condition was a between-subjects manipulation). At the delayed recall session, the children were tested for recall of the six event sequences to which they previously had been exposed, as well as on three new events, as a within-subjects control. For all nine of the event sequences, the children first experienced a delayed-recall period during which they were prompted by the event-related props alone, after which they were provided with verbal reminders of the event sequences (see Bauer et al., 2000, for details of the procedure).

In Table 23.2 are the percentages of children at each age at enrollment who, at delayed testing, evidenced temporally ordered recall (i.e., higher levels of performance on previously experienced than on new event sequences). An asterisk indicates that the number of children with this pattern is greater than the number that would be expected by chance. Across age groups, the forgetting function is very similar to that seen in older children and even adults (Schneider & Pressley, 1997). That is, there was an initial relatively steep decline in performance, followed by a smooth, shallow declining function (see Klein & Meltzoff, 1999, for a similar forgetting function in children in this age range).

Although declines in performance as a function of delay were in evidence, for infants who had been 20 months of age at the time of exposure to the to-be-remembered event sequences, in all of the delay conditions, the number of children evidencing ordered recall was reliably greater than chance. For the children who had been 16 months of age at the time of experience of the event sequences, the percentage of children evidencing the pattern indicative of long-term ordered recall was reliably greater than chance in the

Table 23.2   Percentages of children showing evidence of ordered recall over retention intervals of 1 to 12 months (Bauer et al., 2000)

Age at experience	Delay interval (months)				
	1	*3*	*6*	*9*	*12*
20 months	100*	100*	83*	78*	67*
16 months	94*	94*	72*	50	61
13 months	78*	67	39	44	39

* The number of children exhibiting the pattern of ordered recall (i.e., higher level of performance on previously experienced than on new event sequences) was reliably greater than chance. Because determination of chance levels is affected both by the number of observations and by the number of tied observations, identical values will not necessarily yield identical outcomes (e.g., 20-month-old 12-month delay and 13-month-old 3-month delay).

1-, 3-, and 6- month delay conditions, but not in the 9- and 12-month delay conditions (the specific values are for 16-month-olds tested on four-step event sequences; the pattern applies to both groups of 16-month-olds; see Bauer et al., 2000, for details). Among the 13-month-olds, there was an even more rapid decline in performance across the delay conditions. Indeed, beyond 1 month, the number of 13-month-olds who performed at higher levels on previously experienced than on new event sequences was not greater than chance.

The data from Bauer et al. (2000) are reflective of increasing reliability in long-term ordered recall across the second year of life. At the short delay interval of 1 month, across age groups, there were a roughly equivalent proportion of children who contributed to the "memory" effect: 100 percent of 20-month-olds, 94 percent of 16-month-olds, and 78 percent of 13-month-olds showed higher levels of performance on previously experienced than on new event sequences. As the delay interval increased, fewer and fewer children maintained the information that they had learned about the events. The children "dropped out" faster the younger they were at the time of experience of the event sequences. For 20-month-olds, even at the longest delay interval, a random selection would yield a roughly 70 percent chance that the child would show temporally ordered recall. In contrast, for 13-month-olds, at 6 months and beyond, a random selection would yield a roughly 40–45 percent chance that the child would show temporally ordered recall.

In addition to evidence of increasingly reliable recall, Bauer et al. (2000) also provide evidence of increasingly *robust* memory over the course of the second year. Simply put, older children remembered more than younger children. Moreover, age-related differences in the amount remembered were particularly apparent under conditions of greater cognitive demand. For example, when the children were prompted by the event-related props alone, age differences were observed in all delay conditions. When the children were prompted by the event-related props and by the verbal reminders of the event sequences, age differences obtained only at the longer delay intervals of 9 and 12 months.

Thus, age effects in how much information was retained over the long term were observed (a) when the children had less support for recall (i.e., when they were prompted by event-related props alone), and (b) at longer retention intervals. Together, the data indicate that over the course of the second year of life, there are increases in the reliability and the robustness of long-term recall. The changes are highly suggestive of consolidation of long-term mnemonic function over this space of time.

Verbal measures of recall   One of the major methodological issues with use of deferred imitation as a measure of recall memory is that with development, infants and young children become better able to deduce, infer, or otherwise "figure out" how to create the target sequences (e.g., Bauer et al., 1999). As a result, it becomes difficult to use an exclusively nonverbal means to assess memory: recall over the long term is indexed by a difference between performance on events previously experienced and events new to the infant; high levels of performance on new event sequences reduces and may even eliminate differences on the two event types, even in the face of high levels of performance on previously experienced events.

Fortunately, just as children's increased deductive and inferential abilities seem to present insurmountable challenges, another ability, namely, language, reaches a point at which it can be exploited to aid in determination of whether or not children remember past events. As discussed in Bauer and Wewerka (1995, 1997), at the time their delayed recall was tested, some of the children in Bauer et al. (2000) used their newly developing language skills to talk about the materials in front of them and the events that the materials could be used to produce. In a number of cases sufficient to compel formal examination, the children's comments were indicative of memory for the event sequences that they had experienced 1 to 12 months previously. For example, with regard to the four-step sequence "Make a gong" (see Table 23.1c), the children (a) named or described the event (e.g., "it makes a loud noise"), (b) asked questions about or made statements regarding target actions of the event (e.g., "put that [indicating the metal plate] on there [indicating the cross piece]"), or (c) requested or commented on an as yet unseen prop or event (e.g., "can I see the bell?"). That the children produced more of these types of utterances in response to events that they had seen before relative to events that were new to them (i.e., control events), is verbal evidence of memory for the previously experienced event sequences.

As children's participation in conversations becomes more reliable, we can combine elicited imitation and verbal recall paradigms to test recall over extended periods of time. We adopted this approach in Bauer et al. (1998) and in Bauer, Wenner, and Kroupina (2002). When they were 3 years of age, we invited a subset of the children from Bauer et al. (2000) to return to the laboratory once again. Rather than rely on spontaneous verbalizations, we elicited from the children verbal descriptions about the event sequences to which they had been exposed at the ages of 13, 16, and 20 months. To elicit the reports, we placed the event-related props on the table in front of the children but did not permit them to interact with the props. Instead, we prompted the children to provide verbal descriptions of the events: "What was this one called?", "What did we do with this one?" As in previous related research (Bauer & Wewerka, 1997), we accepted as verbal evidence of event memory names of the events, questions about or statements regarding the events, and requests or comments on as yet unseen props or events. We found that at 3 years of age, children who had been 20 months of age at their first experience of the events were able to verbally describe them. The children who had been only 13 and 16 months of age were not (see Bauer et al., 1998; Bauer, Wenner, & Kroupina, 2002, for details). The combination of verbal and nonverbal techniques for assessing memory represents not only a methodological advance, but also has provided unique data that bear on the question of the long-term verbal accessibility of early memories.

On the Horizon in the Study of Infant Memory

Thus far, I have described studies in which the task of deferred imitation has been applied to questions concerning the development of long-term memory in normally developing infants and very young children. Particularly in light of the historical assumption that infants and very young children simply could not remember the past, focus on developments in long-term recall ability was necessary and appropriate. Now that it is well established that children younger than 3 "have a past," it is important to begin to extend inquiry to other issues in the study of early memory. In this section I describe two such extensions: to the study of short-term and working memory, and to theoretically interesting special populations of infants.

Short-term and working memory

Before it is consolidated as a long-term memory trace, information temporarily resides in a short-term memory store or is maintained in a temporary pattern of activation. The amount of information and the length of time over which infants are able to retain information in short-term memory have obvious implications for what they can remember over the long term: only information that persists beyond the brief temporal limits of short-term memory is potentially available for recall over the long term. This fact makes it imperative that we understand developmental changes in short-term memory. Using deferred imitation, we have found that over the course of the second and into the third year of life, there are reliable age-related increases in the length of event sequences that infants and children are able to remember over the short term. Whereas at 16 months of age, infants comfortably remember two-step event sequences (Bauer & Hertsgaard, 1993), by 24 months they remember four-step event sequences (Bauer et al., 2000), and by 30 months they remember event sequences that are as many as eight steps in length (Bauer & Fivush, 1992). In addition, there is suggestive evidence of differential early "mortality" of memories as a function of age. Whereas 16-month-olds show evidence of significant loss of information over delays of 24 hours (Bauer et al., 2002), 20-month-olds do not exhibit significant declines in performance until 48 hours have passed (Bauer, Van Abbema, & de Haan, 1999). Researchers are only just beginning to recognize and explore the potential impact on long-term recall of age-related differences in forgetting over the short term (see Bauer, Van Abbema, & de Haan, 1999, for discussion).

Table 23.3 Illustration of standard imitation and working memory paradigms

(a) *Standard imitation paradigm presentation of three separate multi-step sequences*

	Sequence A: Rattle	*Sequence B: Gong*	*Sequence C: Tools*
Step 1	Put block onto paddle	Put bar across posts	Open base
Step 2	Cover block with cup	Hang plate from bar	Fit top to base
Step 3	Shake handle	"Ring" with mallet	Hit nail through top

(b) *Working memory paradigm presentation of three multi-step sequences interleaved*

Step 1	Put block onto paddle		
Step 2		Put bar across posts	
Step 3			Open base
Step 4	Cover block with cup		
Step 5		Hang plate from bar	
Step 6			Fit top to base
Step 7	Shake handle		
Step 8		"Ring" with mallet	
Step 9			Hit nail through top

In some cases, even before it is transferred from short-term to long-term memory (or from a less to a more stable state of encoding), information must be manipulated in so-called working memory.[2] In older children, the ability to maintain the temporary activation of information in memory and simultaneously mentally manipulate it has been measured using techniques that require a great deal of verbal skill (e.g., repeating a number of sentences and then producing a list comprised of the last word in each of the sentences, in the order in which they occurred: Daneman & Carpenter, 1980). For this reason, tests of working memory function in infants and young children are relatively rare (see Diamond et al., 1997, for adaptation of the A not B paradigm as a test of working memory in infants). We have adapted the standard imitation paradigm as a nonverbal test of working memory. In the standard imitation paradigm, the steps for a given event sequence are presented in immediate succession (see Table 23.3a, for illustration of three separate event sequences). In the adaptation of the paradigm as a test of working memory, rather than presenting the steps of event sequences in succession, the steps of several different event sequences are interleaved, as illustrated in Table 23.3b. After interleaved demonstration, the infants are given the props for each separate

---

[2]   Although there is not universal agreement as to the definition of working memory (see Cowan, 1997, for a review), the concept of working memory differs from that of short-term memory in its recognition of a processing, in addition to a storage, feature of temporary mnemonic representation (e.g., Baddeley, 1999). Accordingly, tests of working memory require that information both be held "online" and that it be manipulated in some manner.

event sequence in turn. The interleaved presentation requires that infants hold in mind the individual steps of the events even as they integrate the information over time. The task has proven sensitive to developmental differences in working memory function across the 17–20-month age range (Starr, de Haan, & Bauer, 2003). Because the complexity of the task can be increased and decreased (i.e., by increasing or reducing the number of steps in each event sequence and/or the number of events interleaved), it is particularly promising as a measure of working memory throughout the period of transition from infancy to early childhood.

Early memory function in infants from special populations

Not all children experience a normal course of gestation or the "expectant" (Greenough, Black, & Wallace, 1987) early environment. Unfortunately, some early experiences are associated with deficits in cognitive and social development. Traditionally, assessments of cognitive function in young children from special populations have been based on rather global measures such as the Denver Developmental Scales and the Bayley Scales of Infant Development. Lower than normal scores on such measures cannot help to establish the specific source or sources of cognitive deficit, due to their global nature. We have used the deferred-imitation paradigm to test infants drawn from a number of special populations, to determine whether deficits in mnemonic function are apparent.

In de Haan et al. (2000) we used immediate and 10-minute deferred imitation to examine mnemonic function in otherwise healthy infants who had been born prematurely. Performance after the 10 minute delay was correlated with gestational age at birth (i.e., infants born prematurely performed poorly on the task, relative to full-term infants), suggesting that deferred imitation may be especially sensitive to subtle differences in cognitive function associated with premature birth. Similarly, in Kroupina et al. (2000), we found that children who as infants had been adopted from international orphanages showed deficits on the 10-minute deferred imitation task, relative to matched home-reared infants. We also have used both the 10-minute deferred and working memory tasks with infants born to mothers with diabetes. One result of maternal diabetes is that infants may experience iron deficiency prenatally. Consistent with suggestions that prenatal iron deficiency may compromise hippocampal function, at 12 months of age, infants born to mothers with diabetes show deficits in memory after a 10-minute delay (DeBoer et al., 2003). Finally, we have tested both 10-minute delayed recall and working memory in infants who have been physically abused or neglected, sexually abused, or both. Consistent with suggestions that childhood maltreatment may compromise frontal function, at 20 months, infants who have been maltreated show compromised performance on the working memory task (Bauer, Toth, & Cicchetti, 2003). Examination of performance on specific cognitive tasks by both normally developing children and by children whose declarative memory development may have been compromised can be expected to inform our theories of early mnemonic function. We also hold out hope that such tasks eventually may be used as an early diagnostic tool.

Conclusions and Implications

As recently as the middle 1980s, a fundamental discontinuity in mnemonic function was assumed. That is, it was widely believed that whereas older children and adults could recall the past, infants and very young children could not. Due largely to methodological advances, this assumption has been called into serious question. Researchers using deferred imitation, a nonverbal analogue to verbal recall, have demonstrated the emergence of long-term declarative memory late in the second half of the first year of life, with consolidation of mnemonic function over the second year. Moreover, once the words are available to them, children are able to verbally describe memories that in all likelihood originally were encoded without the benefit of language. Recent adaptations of the deferred imitation paradigm for tests of short-term and working memory, and for assessments with theoretically interesting special populations of infants, promise to provide a richer and more complete picture of the assembly and early function of declarative memory in the human infant.

What are the implications of these new data for questions regarding the preservation and later accessibility of early life experiences? We can say that prior to approximately 9 months of age, it is extremely unlikely that infants are able to encode specific event memories in a manner that will permit later access to them. Even at 9 months, the ability to recall over the long term is relatively fragile: it is apparent in only approximately 50 percent of infants (e.g., Bauer et al., 2003; Carver & Bauer, 1999) and it may require more than one experience of an event (Bauer et al., 2001). In contrast, by 20 months of age, long-term recall ability is both reliable and robust (Bauer et al., 2000). Moreover, at least under the conditions in which we have tested, children who were 20 months of age at the time of experience of specific events are able to provide verbal descriptions of them months later (Bauer et al., 1998; Bauer, Wenner, & Kroupina, 2002). Whether the ability of such young children to use language to talk about events experienced preverbally is more general is an open question. In one of the few available studies, Peterson and Rideout (1998) found no evidence of later verbal accessibility of early experiences when children were interviewed outside the context of the original event. In contrast, in Bauer et al. (2004), we found that 3-year-olds interviewed in their homes with props were able to verbally describe events experienced in the laboratory at 20 months of age.

Whether or not very early memories later are consciously and verbally accessible, there is evidence that early experience can leave an indelible mark. For example, in Myers, Clifton, and Clarkson (1987), at roughly 30 months of age, children who as infants had participated in auditory localization experiments in the first year of life showed greater tolerance for a condition in which the lights were turned off and they were plunged into total darkness, relative to their peers who had not had the early experience. Similarly, in Myers, Perris, and Speaker (1994), fully 50 months after a unique laboratory playroom experience, relative to naïve children, experienced children evidenced greater interest in and attention to toys that they had encountered before. In neither of these cases does the behavior of the experienced children indicate a consciously accessible memory of the earlier event (although see Myers, Clifton, & Clarkson, 1987, for suggestive evidence that at least one infant did have a declarative memory of the prior experience). Nevertheless, there were clear differences in behavior that can most reasonably be interpreted to be a result of specific early experiences. We as yet have a long way to go to establish the range of conditions under which early memories are retained over extended periods of time, in any form, and the conditions under which they are retained in accessible format.

Acknowledgment

Preparation of this chapter was supported by a grant from the National Institutes of Health (HD-28425).

Note

Correspondence may be addressed to Patricia J. Bauer, Institute of Child Development, 51 East River Road, University of Minnesota, Minneapolis, Minnesota 55455-0345, USA; pbauer@tc.umn.edu.

References

Bachevalier, J. (1992). Cortical versus limbic immaturity: Relationship to infantile amnesia. In M. R. Gunnar & C. A. Nelson (eds.), *Developmental behavioral neuroscience: The Minnesota Symposia on Child Psychology* (vol. 24, pp. 129–53). Hillsdale, NJ: Lawrence Erlbaum Associates.

Baddeley, A. D. (1999). *Essentials of human memory.* Hove, East Sussex: Psychology Press.

Bahrick, L. E., & Pickens, J. N. (1995). Infant memory for object motion across a period of three months: Implications for a four-phase attention function. *Journal of Experimental Child Psychology, 59,* 343–71.

Bahrick, L. E., Hernandez-Reif, M., & Pickens, J. N. (1997). The effect of retrieval cues on visual preferences and memory in infancy: Evidence for a four-phase attention function. *Journal of Experimental Child Psychology, 67,* 1–20.

Baldwin, D. A., Markman, E. M., & Melartin, R. L. (1993). Infants' ability to draw inferences about nonobvious properties: Evidence from exploratory play. *Child Development, 64,* 711–28.

Barnat, S. B., Klein, P. J., & Meltzoff, A. N. (1996). Deferred imitation across changes in context and object: Memory and generalization in 14-month-old children. *Infant Behavior and Development, 19,* 241–51.

Barr, R., Dowden, A., & Hayne, H. (1996). Developmental changes in deferred imitation by 6- to 24-month-old infants. *Infant Behavior and Development, 19,* 159–70.

Bauer, P. J. (1992). Holding it all together: How enabling relations facilitate young children's event recall. *Cognitive Development, 7,* 1–28.

Bauer, P. J. (1995). Recalling past events: From infancy to early childhood. *Annals of Child Development, 11,* 25–71.

Bauer, P. J. (1996). What do infants recall of their lives? Memory for specific events by 1- to 2-year-olds. *American Psychologist, 51,* 29–41.

Bauer, P. J. (1997). Development of memory in early childhood. In N. Cowan (ed.), *The development of memory in childhood* (pp. 83–111). Hove, East Sussex: Psychology Press.

Bauer, P. J. (2002). Long-term recall memory: Behavioral and neuro-developmental changes in the first 2 years of life. *Current Directions in Psychological Science*, 11, 137–41.

Bauer, P. J. & Dow, G. A. A. (1994). Episodic memory in 16- and 20-month-old children: Specifics are generalized, but not forgotten. *Developmental Psychology*, 30, 403–17.

Bauer, P. J. & Fivush, R. (1992). Constructing event representations: Building on a foundation of variation and enabling relations. *Cognitive Development*, 7, 381–401.

Bauer, P. J. & Hertsgaard, L. A. (1993). Increasing steps in recall of events: Factors facilitating immediate and long-term memory in 13.5- and 16.5-month-old children. *Child Development*, 64, 1204–23.

Bauer, P. J. & Shore, C. M. (1987). Making a memorable event: Effects of familiarity and organization on young children's recall of action sequences. *Cognitive Development*, 2, 327–38.

Bauer, P. J. & Wewerka, S. S. (1995). One- to two-year-olds' recall of events: The more expressed, the more impressed. *Journal of Experimental Child Psychology*, 59, 475–96.

Bauer, P. J. & Wewerka, S. S. (1997). Saying is revealing: Verbal expression of event memory in the transition from infancy to early childhood. In P. van den Broek, P. J. Bauer, & T. Bourg (eds.), *Developmental spans in event comprehension and representation: Bridging fictional and actual events* (pp. 139–68). Mahwah, NJ: Lawrence Erlbaum Associates.

Bauer, P. J., Hertsgaard, L. A., & Wewerka, S. S. (1995). Effects of experience and reminding on long-term recall in infancy: Remembering not to forget. *Journal of Experimental Child Psychology*, 59, 260–98.

Bauer, P. J., Toth, S., & Cicchetti, D. (2003). Explicit memory in young maltreated children. Paper presented to the Society for Research in Child Development, Tampa, Florida, April.

Bauer, P. J., Van Abbema, D. L., & de Haan, M. (1999). In for the short haul: Immediate and short-term remembering and forgetting by 20-month-old children. *Infant Behavior and Development*, 22, 321–43.

Bauer, P. J., Wenner, J. A., & Kroupina, M. G. (2002). Making the past present: Later verbal accessibility of early memories. *Journal of Cognition and Development*, 3, 21–47.

Bauer, P. J., Kroupina, M. G., Schwade, J. A., Dropik, P., & Wewerka, S. S. (1998). If memory serves, will language? Later verbal accessibility of early memories. *Development and Psychopathology*, 10, 655–79.

Bauer, P. J., Schwade, J. A., Wewerka, S. S., & Delaney, K. (1999). Planning ahead: Goal-directed problem solving by 2-year-olds. *Developmental Psychology*, 35, 1321–37.

Bauer, P. J., Wenner, J. A., Dropik, P. L., & Wewerka, S. S. (2000). Parameters of remembering and forgetting in the transition from infancy to early childhood. *Monographs of the Society for Research in Child Development*, 65 (4, serial no. 263).

Bauer, P. J., Wiebe, S., Waters, J. M., & Bangston, S. K. (2001). Reexposure breeds recall: Effects of experience on 9-month-olds' ordered recall. *Journal of Experimental Child Psychology*, 80, 174–200.

Bauer, P. J., Cheatham, C. L., Cary, M. S., & Van Abbema, D. L. (2002). Short-term forgetting: Charting its course and its implications for long-term remembering. In S. P. Shohov (ed.), *Advances in psychology research*, vol. 9 (pp. 53–74). Huntington, NY: Nova Science Publishers.

Bauer, P. J., Wiebe, S. A., Carver, L. J., Waters, J. M., & Nelson, C. A. (2003). Developments in long-term explicit memory late in the first year of life: Behavioral and electrophysiological indices. *Psychological Science*, 14, 629–35.

Bauer, P. J., Van Abbema, D. L., Wiebe, S. A., Cary, M. S., Phill, C., & Burch, M. M. (2004). Props, not pictures, are worth a thousand words: Verbal accessibility of early memories under different conditions of contextual support. *Applied Cognitive Psychology*, 18, 373–92.

Carver, L. J. & Bauer, P. J. (1999). When the event is more than the sum of its parts: Nine-month-olds' long-term ordered recall. *Memory, 7,* 147–74.

Carver, L. J. & Bauer, P. J. (2001). The dawning of a past: The emergence of long-term explicit memory in infancy. *Journal of Experimental Psychology: General, 130,* 726–45.

Carver, L. J., Bauer, P. J., & Nelson, C. A. (2000). Associations between infant brain activity and recall memory. *Developmental Science, 3,* 234–46.

Courage, M. L. & Howe, M. L. (1998). The ebb and flow of infant attentional preferences: Evidence for long-term recognition memory in 3-month-olds. *Journal of Experimental Child Psychology, 70,* 26–53.

Cowan, N. (1997). The development of working memory. In N. Cowan (ed.), *The development of memory in childhood* (pp. 163–99). Hove, East Sussex: Psychology Press.

Daneman, M. & Carpenter, P. A. (1980). Individual differences in working memory and reading. *Journal of Verbal Learning and Verbal Behavior, 19,* 450–66.

DeCasper, A. J. & Spence, M. J. (1986). Prenatal maternal speech influences newborns' perceptions of speech sounds. *Infant Behavior and Development, 9,* 133–50.

DeBoer, T., Wewerka, S., Bauer, P. J., Georgieff, M. K., & Nelson, C. A. (2003). Neurobehavioral sequelae of infants of diabetic mothers: deficits in explicit memory at 1 year of age. Manuscript in review.

de Haan, M., Bauer, P. J., Georgieff, M. K., & Nelson, C. A. (2000). Explicit memory in low-risk toddlers born between 27–42 weeks of gestation. *Developmental Medicine and Child Neurology, 42,* 304–12.

Diamond, A., Prevor, M. B., Callender, G., & Druin, D. P. (1997). Prefrontal cortex cognitive deficits in children treated early and continuously for PKU. *Monographs of the Society for Research in Child Development, 62* (4, serial no. 252).

Fagan, J. F. (1973). Infants' delayed recognition memory and forgetting. *Journal of Experimental Child Psychology, 16,* 424–50.

Freud, S. (1966). *Introductory lectures on psychoanalysis.* Translated and edited by J. Strachey. New York: Norton (originally published 1916–1917).

Gelman, R. & Baillargeon, R. (1983). A review of some Piagetian concepts. In J. H. Flavell & E. M. Markman (eds.), *Handbook of child psychology,* vol. III: *Cognitive development* (pp. 167–230). New York: John Wiley.

Greenough, W. T., Black, J. E., & Wallace, C. S. (1987). Experience and brain development. *Child Development, 58,* 539–59.

Hanna, E. & Meltzoff, A. N. (1993). Peer imitation by toddlers in laboratory, home, and day-care contexts: Implications for social learning and memory. *Developmental Psychology, 29,* 702–10.

Hayne, H., MacDonald, S., & Barr, R. (1997). Developmental changes in the specificity of memory over the second year of life. *Infant Behavior and Development, 20,* 233–45.

Klein, P. J. & Meltzoff, A. N. (1999). Long-term memory, forgetting, and deferred imitation in 12-month-old infants. *Developmental Science, 2,* 102–13.

Kroupina, M. G., Parker, S. W., Bruce, J., Gunnar, M. R., & Bauer, P. J. (2000). Assessing the cognitive development of internationally adopted children. Poster presented at the International Conference on Infant Studies, Brighton, UK, July.

Lechuga, M. T., Marcos-Ruiz, R., & Bauer, P. J. (2002). Episodic recall of specifics and generalization coexist in 25-month-old children. *Memory, 9,* 117–32.

Mandler, J. M. (1984). Representation and recall in infancy. In M. Moscovitch (ed.), *Infant memory: Its relation to normal and pathological memory in humans and other animals* (pp. 75–101). New York: Plenum Press.

Mandler, J. M. (1990). Recall of events by preverbal children. In A. Diamond (ed.), *The development and neural bases of higher cognitive functions* (pp. 485–516). New York: New York Academy of Sciences.

Mandler, J. M. (1998). Representation. In W. Damon (editor-in-chief) & D. Kuhn & R. S. Siegler (vol. eds.), *Handbook of child psychology*, vol. 2: *Cognition, perception, and language* (5th edn., pp. 255–308). New York: John Wiley.

Mandler, J. M. & McDonough, L. (1995). Long-term recall of event sequences in infancy. *Journal of Experimental Child Psychology*, *59*, 457–74.

McDonough, L., Mandler, J. M., McKee, R. D., & Squire, L. R. (1995). The deferred imitation task as a nonverbal measure of declarative memory. *Proceedings of the National Academy of Sciences*, *92*, 7580–84.

Meltzoff, A. N. (1985). Immediate and deferred imitation in fourteen- and twenty-four-month-old infants. *Child Development*, *56*, 62–72.

Meltzoff, A. N. (1988a). Infant imitation after a 1-week delay: Long-term memory for novel acts and multiple stimuli. *Developmental Psychology*, *24*, 470–76.

Meltzoff, A. N. (1988b). Infant imitation and memory: Nine-month-olds in immediate and deferred tests. *Child Development*, *59*, 217–25.

Meltzoff, A. N. (1988c). Imitation of televised models by infants. *Child Development*, *59*, 1221–9.

Meltzoff, A. N. (1990). The implications of cross-modal matching and imitation for the development of representation and memory in infants. In A. Diamond (ed.), *The development and neural bases of higher cognitive functions* (pp. 1–37). New York: New York Academy of Sciences.

Meltzoff, A. N. (1995). What infant memory tells us about infantile amnesia: Long-term recall and deferred imitation. *Journal of Experimental Child Psychology*, *59*, 497–515.

Mullen, M. K. (1994). Earliest recollections of childhood: A demographic analysis. *Cognition*, *52*, 55–79.

Myers, N. A., Clifton, R. K., & Clarkson, M. G. (1987). When they were very young: Almost-threes remember two years ago. *Infant Behavior and Development*, *10*, 123–32.

Myers, N. A., Perris, E. E., & Speaker, C. J. (1994). Fifty months of memory: A longitudinal study in early childhood. *Memory*, *2*, 383–415.

Nelson, C. A. (1995). The ontogeny of human memory: A cognitive neuroscience perspective. *Developmental Psychology*, *31*, 723–38.

Nelson, C. A. (1997). The neurobiological basis of early memory development. In N. Cowan (ed.), *The development of memory in childhood* (pp. 41–82). Hove, East Sussex: Psychology Press.

Nelson, C. A. & Collins, P. F. (1991). Event-related potentials and looking time analysis of infants' responses to familiar and novel events: Implications for visual recognition memory. *Developmental Psychology*, *27*, 50–8.

Nelson, C. A. & Collins, P. F. (1992). Neural and behavioral correlates of recognition memory in 4- and 9-month-old infants. *Brain and Cognition*, *19*, 105–21.

Nelson, C. A. & Monk, C. S. (2001). The use of event-related potentials in the study of cognitive development. In C. A. Nelson & M. Luciana (eds.), *Handbook of developmental cognitive neuroscience* (pp. 125–36). Cambridge, MA: MIT Press.

Parkin, A. J. (1997). The development of procedural and declarative memory. In N. Cowan (ed.), *The development of memory in childhood* (pp. 113–37). Hove, East Sussex: Psychology Press.

Peterson, C. & Rideout, R. (1998). Memory for medical emergencies experienced by 1- and 2-year-olds. *Developmental Psychology*, *34*, 1059–72.

Piaget, J. (1952). *The origins of intelligence in children*. New York: International Universities Press.

Piaget, J. (1962). *Play, dreams and imitation in childhood.* New York: Norton.

Rovee-Collier, C. (1997). Dissociations in infant memory: Rethinking the development of implicit and explicit memory. *Psychological Review, 104,* 467–98.

Schacter, D. L. & Moscovitch, M. (1984). Infants, amnesics, and dissociable memory systems. In M. Moscovitch (ed.), *Infant memory: Its relation to normal and pathological memory in humans and other animals* (pp. 173–216). New York: Plenum Press.

Schneider, W. & Pressley, M. (1997). *Memory development between two and twenty* (2nd edn.). Mahwah, NJ: Lawrence Erlbaum Associates.

Shimamura, A. P., Janowsky, J. S., & Squire, L. R. (1991). What is the role of frontal lobe damage in memory disorders? In H. D. Levin, H. M. Eisenberg, & A. L. Benton (eds.), *Frontal lobe functioning and dysfunction* (pp. 173–95). New York: Oxford University Press.

Spence, M. J. (1996). Young infants' long-term auditory memory: Evidence for changes in preferences as a function of delay. *Developmental Psychobiology, 29,* 685–95.

Squire, L. R., Knowlton, B., & Musen, G. (1993). The structure and organization of memory. *Annual Review of Psychology, 44,* 453–95.

Starr, R. M., de Haan, M., & Bauer, P. J. (2003). All in good time: Temporal integration and working memory in 17- and 20-month-old children. Manuscript in review.

Warrington, E. K. & Weiskrantz, L. (1974). The effect of prior learning on subsequent retention in amnesic patients. *Neuropsychologia, 12,* 419–28.

Weigle, T. W. & Bauer, P. J. (2000). Deaf and hearing adults' recollections of childhood and beyond. *Memory, 8,* 293–309.

West, T. A. & Bauer, P. J. (1999). Assumptions of infantile amnesia: Are there differences between early and later memories? *Memory, 7,* 257–78.

Yasuno, F., Hirata, M., Takimoto, H., Taniguchi, M., Nakagawa, Y., Ikejiri, Y., Nishikawa, T., Shinozaki, K., Tanabe, H., Sugita, Y., & Takeda, M. (1999). Retrograde temporal order amnesia resulting from damage to the fornix. *Journal of Neurology, Neurosurgery, and Psychiatry, 67,* 102–5.

Zola-Morgan, S. & Squire, L. R. (1993). Neuroanatomy of memory. *Annual Review of Neuroscience, 16,* 547–63.

CHAPTER TWENTY-FOUR

Understanding Children's Testimony Regarding their Alleged Abuse: Contributions of Field and Laboratory Analog Research

Michael E. Lamb and Karen L. Thierry

In this chapter, we discuss the ways in which two research strategies – laboratory analog and field studies – have been used to explore children's memories, particularly their recollection of abusive experiences. On the one hand, many researchers have studied children's memories of carefully staged events in order to isolate, manipulate, and evaluate the impact of specific factors that may affect encoding and retrieval. These studies have been extraordinarily valuable, but interpretation of their results is often complicated by doubts about their ecological validity: although interviews about staged events are meant to mimic questioning about abusive incidents, the staged incidents and interviews inevitably differ from those in the real world in many ways. In field studies, by contrast, researchers study children's accounts of real-world abusive incidents in order to elucidate the impact of uncontrolled and interdependent variables on encoding and retrieval. Field studies are typically non-experimental in nature, and the absence of control over potentially important factors may affect their conclusiveness as well. Our goal in this chapter is to highlight the strengths, weaknesses, and value of both approaches, demonstrating in the process that their contributions are complementary. As a result, neither approach should be gainsaid in efforts to understand better the development of memory and communication about experienced events. Divergent findings in field and analog settings can help researchers identify factors that might otherwise be overlooked or misunderstood. In addition, just as careful analog research can be particularly useful in defining cognitive processes and areas of competence, careful field research can make unique contributions to our understanding of basic developmental processes. Conclusions about the ways in which children's memorial and communicative abilities affect their performance in forensic interview contexts ought to be based on both laboratory analog and field studies to ensure both ecological validity and a sound empirical base.

In the first section of this chapter, we describe the media frenzy that helped stimulate an analysis of children's memory and suggestibility in the past two decades. We then review some of the most important results to emerge from laboratory analog studies on this topic. In the second section, we discuss criticisms of laboratory studies and limitations associated with field research before turning in the third section to a discussion of areas where the two lines of research converge and diverge to reveal important information about children's memorial and communicative capacities. Implications for practitioners and basic researchers are discussed in the final section.

High Profile Cases and the Studies they Spawned

McMartin, Little Rascals, and Wee Care

The enormous publicity accorded to allegations of multi-victim sexual abuse in daycare centers in the 1980s (Ceci & Bruck, 1995; Kelley, 1996; Nathan & Snedeker, 1995, Reinhold, 1990) helped prompt many researchers to study the accuracy of children's recollections and the unreliability of their responses when questioned (see Kuehnle, 1996, 1998; Poole & Lamb, 1998, for reviews). Law enforcement officials in these high-profile, multi-victim cases often appeared to have questioned children about their allegations suggestively or coercively by introducing details that had not been volunteered by the children, implying expected responses, and posing the same questions repeatedly, thereby raising doubts about the reliability of the children's "allegations."

In one particularly notorious case, members of the McMartin family were accused of abusing hundreds of children over a 10-year period (Reinhold, 1990). Interviewers and therapists confirmed that the children were asked suggestive questions, such as "Can you remember the naked pictures?" when the child had not mentioned either photography or nakedness (Garven et al., 1998, p. 348). In addition, Garven et al. (1998) noted that many questions were repeated even when the children had previously given unambiguous answers. For example, after a child responded that he/she did not remember any pictures of naked bodies, the interviewer repeated the question saying, "Can't remember that part?" Even after the child again responded "no," the interviewer persisted saying "Why don't you think about that for a while . . . Your memory might come back to you" (Garven et al., 1998, p. 349). Such statements suggest that the event really happened and convey that the interviewer is dissatisfied with the child's response. Another questionable tactic involved inviting children to pretend or imagine that something had happened (e.g., "Let's pretend and see what might have happened"). Children asked to imagine that events occurred sometimes have difficulty when later asked to distinguish between events that "really happened" and events that were just imagined (Foley & Johnson, 1985). In addition, children may later think that the interviewers are interested in reports of both experienced and imagined events.

Repeated suggestive questioning has characterized the investigation of other cases involving multiple alleged victims at the same daycare centers (see Ceci & Bruck, 1995). For instance, Kelly Michaels was accused of sexually abusing children at the Wee Care daycare center in New Jersey where she was a teacher (Ceci & Bruck, 1995). Suspicions first arose when a child having his temperature checked rectally remarked to the pediatrician that his teacher "does that" to him. When later questioned by an investigator, the child inserted his finger into the rectum of an anatomically detailed doll and indicated that other boys had their temperature taken too. Other children were repeatedly questioned about the alleged abuse in a series of interviews by police investigators and therapists; most of these children eventually alleged that Michaels had abused them. Similar techniques were used in other such cases. For example, when children made allegations of abuse by owners and workers at the Little Rascals daycare in Edenton, North Carolina, therapists and police officers began to interrogate all of the children who attended the center. Some of the children disclosed abuse after 10 months of "therapy" (Ceci & Bruck, 1995). In this case, none of the interviews were electronically recorded, but some of the coercive techniques were described to journalists or at trial.

Investigative interviewers in Kelly Michaels' case also capitalized on children's sensitivity to the high status of the interviewer, as when they commented, "I'm a policeman; if you were a bad girl, I would punish you wouldn't I? Police can punish bad people" (Ceci & Bruck, 1995, p. 152). Interviewers also induced negative stereotypes about Kelly Michaels by telling the children that she was "bad" or "scary." Further, interviewers in both the McMartin and Wee Care cases, among others, used peer pressure in their attempts to elicit disclosures. For example, they would tell the children that their friends had already identified the child as a victim. In addition, interviewers promised the children rewards – such as snacks or the termination of the interview – if they would make allegations.

Analysis of these notorious cases helped draw attention to such potentially problematic investigative techniques as repeated questioning and suggestion, references to the interviewer's high status, peer pressure, promises of rewards and threats, requests that children pretend or imagine that something occurred, and the use of anatomical dolls as interview aids. Such practices alarmed developmentalists and helped stimulate a number of laboratory analog studies in the 1980s and 1990s that clarified our understanding of suggestibility, children's memory processes, and forensic interview practices (Kuehnle, 1996; Lamb et al., 1999; Poole & Lamb, 1998), while fueling an intense controversy about the value of laboratory analog studies (e.g., Bruck & Ceci, 1999; Ceci & Bruck, 1995; Ceci & Friedman, 2000; Lyon, 1999, 2002). A selection of these analog studies are discussed in the next section.

Laboratory analog research

Laboratory analog studies played an especially important role in showing that the suggestive interview practices described above were indeed problematic, because young children were especially susceptible to suggestion (see Ceci & Bruck, 1993, for a review). Researchers have shown, for example, that young children acquiesce to misinformation because they avoid disagreeing with the suggestions of adult interviewers (Ceci, Ross, & Toglia, 1987; Lampinen & Smith, 1995). Ceci, Ross, and Toglia (1987) found, for example, that preschoolers are less likely to accept false suggestions made by 7-year-old children rather than by adults. In addition, Leichtman and Ceci (1995) showed that preschoolers who were repeatedly led to believe that a person was very clumsy acquiesced more easily over a 10-week period to allegations about that person than children who were given neutral information about him.

Young children are also more likely than older children and adults to incorporate false information into their memory of an event (Brainerd & Poole, 1997; Johnson, Hashtroudi, & Lindsay, 1993), perhaps because they do not understand the seriousness and purpose of forensic investigations and have poorer information-processing abilities (Ceci & Bruck, 1993). Both social factors, such as the superior status of the interviewer (Ceci, Ross, & Toglia, 1987; Zaragoza, Dahlgren, & Muench, 1992), and cognitive factors, including those relating to pretense or imagination (Reyna & Brainerd, 1997; Roberts & Blades, 2000; Titcomb & Reyna, 1995), may influence children's susceptibility to misinformation. Ceci et al. (1994), for instance, asked 3- to 6-year-olds to repeatedly imagine experiencing a fictitious event (e.g., getting their fingers caught in a mousetrap and going to the hospital to have it removed). Many children later claimed to have experienced these events, and even after debriefing, some of the children refused to accept that the events were only imagined. Such findings suggest that young children may have difficulty distinguishing fantasy from reality, and are suggestible in part because they tend to confuse the sources or origins (fantasy versus reality) of their knowledge (Ackil & Zaragoza, 1995; Roberts & Blades, 2000; Thierry, Spence, & Memon, 2001). When subjected to such suggestive techniques as repeated suggestion, instructions to imagine/pretend, and selective reinforcement in a series of interviews, preschool children assented to 95 percent of the false events (e.g., claiming that they witnessed the theft of food in their daycare) by the third interview session (Bruck, Hembrooke, & Ceci, 1997).

The use of anatomically detailed dolls when interviewing young children is also problematic because young children have difficulty simultaneously understanding that the doll is both an object and a representation of themselves (DeLoache, 1990). DeLoache and Marzolf (1995) thus found that 2- to 4-year-old children's responses (about games that they had played with an experimenter) were more likely to be correct when they were elicited without rather than with the aid of the doll. In addition, Bruck et al. (1995b) showed that the use of anatomically detailed dolls as interview aids increased 3-year-olds' tendencies to falsely report having experienced genital touching during a pediatric examination.

The results of such studies show that preschoolaged children are particularly suggestible. This led researchers such as Ceci and Bruck to argue that jurists should view with skepticism the testimonies of children in the Wee Care, Little Rascals, and McMartin cases because interviewers had wittingly or unwittingly exploited children's vulnerabilities when eliciting accounts from them. Such conclusions implied, of course, that the results of laboratory analog studies could and should be generalized to the interpretation of information provided by alleged victims in the course of forensic interviews. This assumption was quickly and vigorously challenged.

Laboratory Studies: How Ecologically Valid Are They?

The analog studies discussed in the previous section involved children's reports of staged events so that researchers knew exactly what had happened to the children – something that is seldom possible in the field. For obvious ethical reasons, however, the events studied lacked many characteristics of abusive incidents, leading to questions about their ecological validity. For example, getting a finger caught in a mousetrap and being sexually abused are quite different experiences with respect to both their nature and complexity. Additionally, some early analog studies tested children's memory for events that the children merely watched on a video (Dale, Loftus, & Rathbun, 1978; Wells, Turtle, & Luus, 1989) or heard about in stories that were read to them (Ceci, Ross, & Toglia, 1987). Of course, children may not remember events depicted in videos they watched or stories they heard as well as they recall events in which they were active participants. In fact, Rudy and Goodman (1991) showed that 4- and 7-year-olds were more likely to accept suggestions when they were mere observers rather than participants in a real-life event. Similarly, Tobey and Goodman (1992) found that 4-year-olds who participated in a real-life event were more resistant to suggestion and provided more accurate free-recall reports than those who just watched the event on a video.

Recognizing that studies involving events in which children are direct participants are likely to be more informative, some researchers have studied children's recall of pediatric examinations (Baker-Ward et al., 1993; Ornstein, Gordon, & Larus, 1992; Saywitz et al., 1991). In a study conducted by Saywitz et al. (1991), 5- and 7-year-old girls received a routine medical examination in which some of them had their genital and anal areas examined. One week or one month after the examinations, children were questioned about them. After a delay of one month, the 5-year-olds were more likely than the 7-year-olds to acquiesce to erroneous suggestions that the doctor touched their genital areas, although the overall rate of false reports was relatively low: only 3 percent falsely reported vaginal touches and 6 percent falsely reported anal touches. Many of the children failed to mention the genital touches in response to a general open-ended prompt, however, leading Saywitz et al. (1991) to speculate that children might not volunteer potentially embarrassing information unless prompted directly.

Of course, medical exams and follow-up questions by research assistants are not the same as instances of sexual abuse investigated by forensic interviewers. Children's responses to open-ended questions also vary greatly depending on the extent to which children understand the purpose of the interview and the value of the information they can provide. Unfortunately, we do not know whether the children studied by Saywitz et al. (1991) were recalling the specific examination under investigation or simply what usually happens when they go to the doctor. Children of this age form generic scripts of events, such as "doctor's office" or "medical check-up" scripts (Fivush, 1997; Nelson, 1993, 1996), so it is possible that children rely on their scripts when questioned about such examinations.

Although false reports were relatively uncommon even after the one-month delay in Saywitz et al.'s study (1991), children do have difficulty remembering specific details about events when there is some delay (e.g., 6 weeks) between the to-be-remembered event and questioning about it (Baker-Ward et al., 1993; Lamb, Sternberg, & Esplin, 2000; Ornstein, Gordon, & Larus, 1992). After longer delays (e.g., 2 years), the accuracy of the information recalled is even lower (Poole & White, 1993). Delay may be especially problematic when children have developed generic scripts for events that are similar to the to-be-remembered event. After a 12-week delay, for example, 6-year-olds tended to let details that were typical of medical check-ups but had not actually been experienced during a specific pediatric examination intrude into their memory of that exam, whereas atypical and similarly nonexperienced components of examinations were not incorporated into memory (Ornstein et al., 2001).

Children can also be led to make false reports about a medical exam when they are interviewed suggestively. For example, when Bruck et al. (1995a) interviewed 5-year-old children 1 week and 1 year after they had been inoculated in a pediatrician's office, children given repeated misleading information about the doctor's or research assistant's actions produced more false allegations (e.g., indicating that the research assistant had given the inoculation when, in fact, the pediatrician gave the inoculation) one year later than did children who were not misled.

Lyon (1999) has questioned the value of these laboratory analog studies, arguing that the interview techniques they employed do not represent typical forensic practices. He further noted that most sexual abuse cases involve a single victim whose abuser is a family member or relative, as opposed to the multiple alleged victims of daycare providers. He also emphasized that leading questions might sometimes be necessary to obtain disclosures of abuse from young children who are reticent to disclose because of fear, embarrassment, or loyalty to the perpetrator. For example, many of the children (especially the 7-year-olds) who had experienced genital touching during the pediatric examination studied by Saywitz et al. (1991) failed to report the touching in response to general open-ended questions (e.g., "tell me what happened during the doctor's examination"), perhaps because they were embarrassed to talk about genital touching. Lyon (1999) contended that embarrassment might make children less likely to make false allegations of abuse, even when they were asked leading questions. Of course, the evidence cited in support of this claim was obtained in an analog study (Saywitz et al., 1991), not in an analysis of forensic interviews in which children understood the seriousness of the investigation and the importance of their informativeness.

Lyon (1999) also criticized laboratory analog research on the grounds that most real-world cases of sexual abuse do not involve the coercive and suggestive practices used in many of these studies. For instance, Ceci and Bruck's studies explored the highly suggestive techniques used in the controversial daycare cases, including stereotype induction, repeated questioning, suggestion, and peer pressure (Bruck, Hembrooke, & Ceci, 1997; Ceci et al., 1994; Leichtman & Ceci, 1995). Lyon argued that option-posing questions, which give children the option of denying potentially false information in response to Yes/No questions or to select the correct option in response to forced choice questions, are less risky than questions that presuppose information not mentioned by the children. Most of the laboratory analog studies revealing high levels of suggestibility involved "highly misleading" suppositional-type questions. For example, Leichtman and Ceci (1995) asked children such questions as, "When Sam Stone ripped the book, did he do it because he was angry, or by mistake?" which make it more difficult for children to deny the misinformation (e.g., that the book was ripped) than do questions like "Did Sam Stone rip the book?" In particular, the former question requires children to correct the interviewer in resisting the misinformation, a difficult task for young children.

Similarly, Bruck, Hembrooke, & Ceci (1997) misled children by telling them about the fictitious events in the context of reinforcement and pretend/imagine instructions. Lyon argued that the suggestibility effects found in this analog study were "likely the least generalizable to the real world" (p. 1038), because such techniques are seldom used by forensic investigators. By contrast, he argued that the types of option-posing questions that occur in the real world (e.g., "Did he touch you there?") are not associated with high levels of error in analog studies (Goodman, Aman, & Hirschman, 1987; Saywitz et al., 1991), and thus should not be as problematic as suppositional questions in forensic contexts.

Descriptive studies of real-world interview practices in diverse agencies show that forensic interviewers frequently introduce topics and ask suggestive questions while rarely using open-ended prompts (Cederborg et al., 2000; Lamb et al., 1996b; Sternberg et al., 1996, 2001; Warren et al., 1996), however. Warren's analyses of interviews conducted by social workers in Tennessee revealed many suppositional-type suggestive questions (Ceci & Friedman, 2000). In addition, the suggestive questioning techniques used in Ceci and Bruck's work, including references to negative consequences for not disclosing and repeated questioning, were evident in many of the interviews studied by Warren (Warren et al., 2000). Even when interviewers ask only one suggestive question, the content, riskiness (e.g., suppositional versus option posing), and timing of the suggestive or problematic question must be examined carefully. Field studies show that option-posing questions elicit contradictory or erroneous information quite frequently, furthermore, indicating that it would be inappropriate to underestimate the riskiness of these prompts (Lamb & Fauchier, 2001; Orbach & Lamb, 2001), even though they are less risky than suppositional-type questions.

Similarly, Garven et al. (1998) showed that the exact techniques used in the McMartin Preschool case quickly led children to respond inaccurately. These researchers first examined transcripts of interviews conducted with alleged victims in the McMartin case, identifying such techniques as offering positive (or negative) consequences for making (or not making) allegations of abuse, posing the same repeated questions, and suggesting that other children had already disclosed. They then interviewed 3- to 6-year-old children about a staged event in which a male stranger visited children at their daycare center, read them a story, and handed out stickers and cupcakes. The children who were interviewed about the man's actions using a combination of highly suggestive techniques (e.g., rewards for making allegations plus repeated and suggestive questions) produced significantly more false accusations than children who were interviewed using only one suggestive technique. In fact, after being interviewed with multiple suggestive questioning techniques for only 4.5 minutes, children acquiesced to the false accusations nearly 60 percent of the time, whereas those interviewed using only one suggestive technique acquiesced 17 percent of the time.

Garven, Wood, and Malpass (2000) further showed that children interviewed suggestively using reinforcement made false allegations about mundane events (e.g., that a man said a bad word) 35 percent of the time, whereas those interviewed without such reinforcement made false allegations 12 percent of the time. Children who were reinforced also alleged fantastic events (e.g., that a man took a child on a helicopter ride) more often than children in the control group. Taken together, the results of these studies show that real-world interview practices are quite likely to elicit erroneous reports from young children.

Field studies: Are they adequately controlled?

Whereas the ecological validity or generalizability of results obtained in laboratory or analog studies must be demonstrated, not assumed, field studies are limited in the areas where analog studies are strongest. In laboratory analog studies, for instance, all participants in a given study see or participate in the same event under the same conditions and are interviewed after the same delay whereas field studies often involve child witnesses who may have experienced the same type of event (e.g., sexual abuse), but rather different specific events (e.g., fondling, intercourse) in varying circumstances and are interviewed after uncertain delays ranging from hours to years. Researchers seldom know what actually happened to the children included in field studies, making it impossible to draw any conclusions about the accuracy of the children's reports.

Field researchers have been able to document the extent to which forensic interviewers actually follow recommended interview practice guidelines (Home Office, 1992; Poole & Lamb, 1998), however. For example, Lamb and his colleagues found that, when interviewing alleged child abuse victims, Swedish, Israeli, British, and American investigators used many option-posing and suggestive questions but relatively few nonsuggestive, open-ended questions (Cederborg et al., 2000; Lamb et al., 1996a, b; Sternberg et al., 1996, 2001). Specifically, Lamb et al. (1996b) found that about 25 percent of the interviewers' prompts were option-posing (e.g., "Did he touch you there?" when touching had been mentioned by the child) and 9 percent of the interviewers' utterances were suggestive (e.g., questions in which interviewers assume details not revealed by children, such as, *Child*: "We laid on the sofa." *Interviewer*: "He laid on you or you laid on him?"). Only 2 percent of the interviewers' utterances were of the open-ended question type called for by best practice guidelines, even though the individual open-ended question types elicited 2.5 to 8 times more information from children than did individual focused and suggestive questions (Lamb et al., 1996a, b; Sternberg et al., 1996; Warren et al., 1996). Furthermore, both Lamb and Fauchier (2001) and Orbach and Lamb (2001) showed that suggestive and leading prompts were much more likely to elicit inaccurate information in the field, just as in laboratory analog contexts (e.g., Bjorklund et al., 1998; Cassel, Roebers, & Bjorklund, 1996; Dale, Loftus, & Rathbun, 1978; Dent, 1982; Dent & Stephenson, 1979; Goodman & Aman, 1990; Goodman et al., 1991a). Even when forensic interviewers are trained to use open-ended questions preferentially, this training often changes their knowledge about appropriate questioning strategies but not their actual questioning strategies (Aldridge & Cameron, 1999; Stevenson, Leung, & Cheung, 1992; Warren et al., 1996).

Moving beyond an either–or concept of generalizability

The heated rhetoric notwithstanding, it is clear that information obtained in analog studies *can* be generalized to real-world abuse cases. For example, laboratory studies of reinforcement and stereotype induction are relevant to those real-world uses of these suggestive measures. If these techniques are used by forensic interviewers, however, other factors surrounding the case must also be taken into account when considering implications of the analog research. For instance, the age of the child must be considered since many analog studies using these suggestive techniques involved only preschool-aged children as participants (Bruck, Ceci, & Francoeur, 2000; Bruck et al., 1995a, b; Leichtman & Ceci, 1995). Generalizability should thus be construed not as an either–or concept but as a continuum, with the specific circumstances surrounding the case affecting the relevance of particular analog studies.

From this perspective, laboratory analog and field studies should be viewed as complementary research techniques. Field studies help to guide the interpretation and applicability of analog research by highlighting factors important in the real world that experimentalists might not be able to address, as we illustrate below when we discuss the ability of young children to recall abusive events or the effects of taking children to the scene of their alleged abuse. Similarly, the control associated with laboratory studies allows researchers to offer valuable insight into factors that affect the accuracy of children's testimony, including suggestive questioning, the delay between the to-be-remembered event and questioning, and prior knowledge about events.

Because both research strategies have strengths and weaknesses, judicious use of both analog and field research designs can help to clarify the strengths and weaknesses of child witnesses. Points of convergence between the results obtained in the two types of research are particularly helpful in highlighting factors that influence children's memories of abuse. Points of divergence can meanwhile stimulate studies that further refine our knowledge of children's memory.

Implications of Laboratory and Field Research for Interview Practices and Child Development

We now discuss some of the most important findings to emerge from laboratory and field research on the ability to recall events. After reviewing findings obtained using both research strategies, we summarize the implications for forensic interview practices and highlight intriguing but unexpected insights into memory development processes.

Effects of suggestive questioning

Although it is usually impossible to measure accuracy in the field, field studies in which accuracy can be estimated show that open-ended questions yield more accurate information than option-posing and suggestive questions (Lamb & Fauchier, 2001; Orbach & Lamb, 2001), just as they do in laboratory analog studies (Bjorklund et al., 1998; Cassel, Roebers, & Bjorklund, 1996; Dent, 1982; Dent & Stephenson, 1979; Goodman & Aman, 1990; Goodman et al., 1991a). Lamb and Fauchier (2001) and Orbach and Lamb (2001) showed that option-posing (i.e., questions that require a choice among a specified set of alternatives, as in "Did he touch you?") and suggestive questions that imply information that has not been disclosed (e.g., "When he touched you, where were you?" when the child had not mentioned any touching) were more likely to elicit contradictory information from young children than were nonsuggestive, open-ended questions.

When children were questioned suggestively in analog studies about experienced but non-abusive events, particularly over repeated interview sessions, furthermore, they provided more inaccurate responses to specific questions (Ornstein, Gordon, & Larus, 1992; Saywitz et al., 1991) and in some cases, the suggested information actually intruded into their free-recall reports (Leichtman & Ceci, 1995). Similarly, children frequently do not correct investigative interviewers who distort details they report (Hunt & Borgida, 2001; Roberts & Lamb, 1999).

Open-ended prompts are also superior to closed-ended prompts (e.g., option-posing questions) with respect to the amount of information they elicit from alleged victims (Lamb et al., 1996a, b; Sternberg et al., 1996), although these free-recall accounts are often incomplete. In order to prevent contamination of children's memories and to elicit the highest quality of information, therefore, open-ended questions should be given priority when child witnesses are being interviewed.

Effects of delay

Regardless of the research setting, delay between the occurrence of the to-be-remembered event and questioning has adverse effects on the strength of the memory trace. In laboratory analog settings, children are more likely to be misled about an event (Ceci et al., 1994; Leichtman & Ceci, 1995) and tend to report fewer event details (Baker-Ward et al., 1993; Ornstein, Gordon, & Larus, 1992) the longer the delay. Similarly, Lamb, Sternberg, and Esplin (2000) have shown that after delays of more than 1 month, children report fewer new details about alleged abuse than do children recalling abuse that allegedly happened more recently. It is thus preferable to question child witnesses as soon as possible after the alleged incident(s). Interviewers should recognize that children interviewed after a substantial delay might require more time to retrieve details from recall memory, and they should also be more cautious when questioning children after long delays because such children are more susceptible to suggestion.

Developmental differences in responses to open-ended prompts

Older victims provide more forensically relevant details than do younger victims (Orbach et al., 2000a), just as older children remember more information in laboratory studies than younger children (Ornstein, Gordon, & Larus, 1992; Poole & Lindsay, 1995; Thierry, Spence, & Memon, 2001). Not surprisingly, therefore, older children also provide more details in response to open-ended prompts than younger children do (Orbach et al., 2000a). Despite agreement between laboratory and field researchers with respect to developmental differences in the number of details elicited using free-recall prompts, young children are, nevertheless, able to provide a good deal of information in response to open-ended questions, at least in field settings. Indeed, the proportion of details elicited in response to open-ended prompts as opposed to directive, option-posing, and suggestive prompts do not vary by age, indicating that even 4- to 6-year-olds can respond informatively to open-ended prompts (Lamb et al., 2003; Orbach et al., 2000a; Sternberg et al., 2001).

Interestingly, however, children (4- to 13-year-olds) who practice freely recalling neutral events during a presubstantive phase of a forensic interview later provide more details about the alleged abuse in response to open-ended prompts than do children not so trained, regardless of age (Orbach et al., 2000a; Sternberg et al., 2001). When given practice in freely recalling episodic details about neutral events, even preschoolers (4- to 5-year-olds) provide many details in response to open-ended prompts when asked about the alleged abuse (Lamb et al., 2003; Sternberg et al., 2001). Similar findings are not obtained when interviewers fail to follow best practice guidelines, however, suggesting that special steps must be taken to maximize the informativeness of young children.

Researchers have also shown that very young children are capable of recalling a remarkable amount of information about specific events (Fivush & Hamond, 1989; Hamond & Fivush, 1991; Orbach et al., 2000a; Sternberg et al., 2001). For example, children who visited Disney World when they were 3 to 4 years of age were interviewed about the event either 6 or 18 months later (Hamond & Fivush, 1991). Even after 18 months, children recalled many details about their trip, although the older children recalled more details and needed fewer cues than the younger children did. Similarly, Peterson and Whalen (2001) found that children who were 2 years old when they experienced an injury requiring emergency room treatment recalled many details about the injury five years later (and three years after a previous interview). Bahrick et al.'s (1998) study of Hurricane Andrew also illustrated detailed recall 6 years after an event. Such studies thus complement our observation that young children recall abusive experiences exceptionally well (e.g., Orbach et al., 2000a; Lamb et al., 2003; Sternberg et al., 2001).

Preschoolers typically do not say very much when responding to the very general prompts that are often used in analog studies (e.g., "Tell me what happened") and may omit information that adults consider important (e.g., Saywitz et al., 1991). Because alleged victims often give equally brief responses to similar prompts in clinical settings, some professionals (e.g. Hewitt, 1999) believe that young children (especially preschoolers) are incapable of responding to open-ended prompts and this conclusion has been used to justify the use of option-posing and suggestive prompts by forensic interviewers. The divergence between the results obtained by Lamb and his colleagues in interviews conducted using a structured interview protocol and the results obtained in both analog studies and standard forensic interviews suggests that children must be adequately and appropriately informed about the importance of providing detailed narrative responses, and that the open-ended questions must be responsive to the information already provided (Hershkowitz, 2001), not simply repeated. It is also clear that laboratory analog studies have seriously underestimated the ability of young children to extract details from recall memory.

The results of both analog and field studies also highlight important basic processes underlying children's memory, including the tendency to form scripts which help children organize event details in logical temporal sequences (Fivush & Hamond, 1989; Hamond & Fivush, 1991). Such findings also elucidate processes involved in young children's memories of abusive experiences. As Ornstein et al. (2001) found when examining children's memories of pediatric examinations, children's recollections become less accurate after delays because knowledge of what "typically" occurs in such situations intrudes into the memory of a specific event. Over time, memories of individual episodes of abuse might also become confused, and distinctive characteristics of specific experiences might become indistinguishable from details that the different incidents have in common, or from general knowledge about abuse.

Field and laboratory studies show that, although children are capable of recalling salient events accurately, their memories are nevertheless vulnerable to both internally (e.g., script-related intrusions) and externally (e.g., suggestions from interviewers) driven distortions. Memory development involves gaining more conscious recognition of one's own memory processes, such as being able to identify what actually happened during a particular event or episode, and distinguishing memories of real experiences from memories based on prior knowledge, imagination, or others' reports (Johnson, Hashtroudi, & Lindsay, 1993).

Effects of stress

Some of the discrepancies between laboratory analog and field studies with respect to the amount of information recalled by young children might reflect the fact that the to-be-remembered events in many laboratory studies do not have the emotional characteristics (e.g., stressfulness) of sexual abuse, but research on the effects of stress on children's event reports has been inconclusive. Some researchers have reported that high levels of stress are associated with improved memory in the laboratory (Goodman et al., 1991b; Warren & Swartwood, 1992), some have reported that high levels of stress are associated with poorer memory (Bugental et al., 1992; Merritt, Ornstein, & Spicker, 1994; Peters, 1987, 1991), and others have reported no relationship at all between stress and recall (Baker-Ward et al. 1993; Howe, Courage, & Peterson, 1994). For example, Howe, Courage, & Peterson (1994) found no relationship between the amount of stress (reported by the parents) and the amount of information recalled by their children either 3–5 days or 6 months after an emergency room procedure. By contrast, Goodman et al. (1991b) found that children who showed higher levels of arousal during a medical procedure reported the incident more accurately than children who simply had a washable tattoo applied. When Bahrick et al. (1998) classified 3- and 4-year-old children into high-, medium-, and low-stress groups based on the extent of their exposure to Hurricane Andrew, however, they found that children in the high- and low-stress groups recalled the least information about the hurricane whereas children in the medium-stress group recalled the most information, suggesting that some stress improves recall while too much stress impedes it. Even when stress enhances recall, however, memories are still susceptible to the deleterious effects of suggestion and delay (Sales, Goldberg, & Parker, 2001).

Few researchers have studied the association between the severity of abuse (presumably a correlate of stressfulness) and children's recall, probably because there is no consensus regarding the ways in which the severity of abuse should be measured, and a variety of events (ranging from exposure to rape at gunpoint) are defined as sexual abuse. Of course, these differences affect the conclusiveness of field research: because child witnesses recall different personally experienced events, many factors can make some events more memorable than others. In addition, whether or not the abuse is even stressful to children may vary depending on such factors as the age of the child and the identity of the perpetrator. With better definitions of child abuse and access to accounts of a larger number of cases, researchers may be able in the future to determine whether different types of abuse are recalled differently as a function of the many interrelated factors that characterize real-world experiences of abuse.

Effects of supportive interview techniques

The effects of context reinstatement on children's event recall have been studied extensively in both laboratory and field settings but the findings have been inconsistent. The prediction that contextual cues should enhance memory performance is based on Tulving's encoding specificity principle, whereby retrieval cues that were present during memory encoding help to bring into consciousness details of an event that might not have been retrieved without such cues (Tulving, 1983). Many researchers have shown in the laboratory that children recall more information, without adverse effects on accuracy, if they are interviewed where an event occurred (Gee & Pipe, 1995; Pipe & Wilson, 1994; Price & Goodman, 1990). Orbach et al. (2000b) reported no difference between the numbers of details reported by victims who were interviewed in the investigators' offices and at the scene of the alleged abuse, although mental context reinstatement did appear to facilitate the children's recall. Children aged 4 to 13 years old who were required to mentally reinstate the context of an alleged sexual abuse incident (children were instructed to "close your eyes and think about that time . . . think about sounds or voices you could hear . . . smells you could smell") produced proportionally more substantive details in response to open-ended invitations than children who were not given mental context reinstatement instructions (Hershkowitz et al., 2001). Because these were field studies, however, the accuracy of the details could not be assessed.

The contrasting effects of context reinstatement in the field and in the experimental laboratory illustrate why it is important to conduct both laboratory and field studies. Orbach et al. (2000b) speculated that children did not report more information at the scene of the alleged abuse because the context at the time that the abuse occurred differed from the context at the time of questioning. If abuse occurred in a shopping mall, for instance, the people, sounds, and smells at the time of the abuse would likely differ from those present at the time of questioning. In the laboratory, exact matches between encoding and retrieval (or interviewing) contexts can be recreated so that children are able to gain maximal benefits from contextual cueing. Such matches may not be feasible (or ethical) in the field. Analog studies may thus be needed to isolate and examine the effects of specific conditions or variables on basic memory processes while "real-world" realities may preclude capitalization in forensic contexts on the beneficial effects of such techniques as context reinstatement. Nevertheless, the enhancement of children's recall using mental context reinstatement instructions (Hershkowitz et al., 2001) suggests a promising technique that could be employed in field settings.

Conclusions

Laboratory and field researchers inform each other not only when they agree but also when they disagree. Each type of research has its strengths and weaknesses, and an accurate understanding of the multiple factors that determine how children will perform in a given situation cannot be obtained unless both types of research are conducted. Laboratory and field studies inform each other and consumers of the research with respect to the ways in which children can best be interviewed so as to maximize information retrieval and minimize inaccuracy. The results of laboratory studies which employ highly suggestive techniques (Bruck et al., 1995a; Garven et al., 1998) to show deleterious effects on children's accuracy are, of course, generalizable only to those real-word cases that actually utilize such suggestive techniques, and this underscores the value of field studies designed to increase the use of those nonsuggestive, open-ended questions which are most likely to elicit accurate information (Orbach et al., 2000a; Sternberg et al., 2001).

Field and laboratory studies have also informed each other with respect to developmental differences in the ability to freely recall events. Sternberg and colleagues (2001) have shown that, when questioned nonsuggestively using open-ended prompts, young witnesses can provide a considerable amount of information about alleged abuse, a finding that seems in conflict with the results of many laboratory studies indicating that young children freely recall very little. The discrepant findings may reflect many differences between the incidents and the interviewing strategies in field and laboratory analog studies, but at minimum they demonstrate both that performance and capacity should not be confused and that capacity is not always best illustrated in laboratory analog contexts, where children are asked to recall events of little significance to them after little or no effort is made to explain the importance of full and accurate recall. By contrast, laboratory studies permit a clearer test of the effects of physical context reinstatement on the amount of information retrieved. In field studies, contextual cueing is constrained because researchers lack control over the precise context.

Just as the real world helps to spark laboratory analog studies, so do laboratory studies help to spark field research. The remarkable performance of young children when responding to open-ended questions in the field (Lamb et al., 2003; Sternberg et al., 2001) may perhaps entice laboratory researchers to further investigate the factors (e.g., the nature of the events, type of questioning, or pre-interview preparation) that lead children to provide more details in response to open-ended questions in forensic contexts. Likewise, the conflicting findings of laboratory studies regarding the effects of stress on children's memory might lead field researchers to adopt more precise definitions of sexual and physical abuse so that associations between presumed correlates of stress or severity can be studied more extensively in the field. The two research strategies are complementary, with both helping to refine our understanding of the factors affecting children's memories of abuse and of how best to interview children so that the most accurate reports are obtained. In the process, complementary information about factors underlying the development of memory can also be obtained using both research strategies, contributing to both the applied and basic research literatures.

Acknowledgments

The authors are grateful to Maggie Bruck, Yael Orbach, Debra Poole, Thomas Lyon, Mel Pipe, and Amye Warren for helpful comments on earlier drafts.

Note

Correspondence should be sent to Michael E. Lamb, Section on Social and Emotional Development, National Institute of Child Health and Human Development, Rockledge One Center–Suite 8048, 6705 Rockledge Drive, Bethesda, MD 20892, USA. Telephone: +1 (301) 496-0420, fax: +1 (301) 480-5775, email: Michael_Lamb@nih.gov.

References

Ackil, J. K. & Zaragoza, M. S. (1995). Developmental differences in eyewitness suggestibility and memory for source. *Journal of Experimental Child Psychology, 60*, 57–83.

Aldridge, J. & Cameron, S. (1999). Interviewing child witnesses: Questioning strategies and the effectiveness of training. *Applied Developmental Science, 3*, 136–47.

Bahrick, L. E., Parker, J. F., Fivush, R., & Levitt, M. (1998). The effects of stress on young children's memory for a natural disaster. *Journal of Experimental Psychology: Applied, 4*, 308–31.

Baker-Ward, L., Gordon, B. N., Ornstein, P. A., Larus, D. M., & Clubb, P. A. (1993). Young children's long-term retention of a pediatric examination. *Child Development, 64*, 1519–33.

Bjorklund, D. F., Bjorklund, B. R., Douglas, R. B., & Cassel, W. S. (1998). Children's susceptibility to repeated questions: How misinformation changes children's answers and their minds. *Applied Developmental Science, 2*, 101–13.

Brainerd, C. J. & Poole, D. A. (1997). Long-term survival of children's false memories: A review. *Learning and Individual Differences, 9*, 125–51.

Bruck, M. & Ceci, S. J. (1999). The suggestibility of children's memory. *Annual Reviews of Psychology, 50*, 419–39.

Bruck, M., Ceci, S. J., & Francoeur, E. (2000). Children's use of anatomically detailed dolls to report genital touching in a medical examination: Developmental and gender comparisons. *Journal of Experimental Psychology: Applied, 6*, 74–83.

Bruck, M., Hembrooke, H., & Ceci, S. J. (1997). Children's reports of pleasant and unpleasant events. In D. Read & S. Lindsay (eds.), *Recollections of trauma: Scientific research and clinical practice* (pp. 199–219). New York: Plenum Press.

Bruck, M., Ceci, S. J., Francoeur, E., & Barr, R. (1995a). "I hardly cried when I got my shot!" Influencing children's reports about a visit to their pediatrician. *Child Development, 66*, 193–208.

Bruck, M., Ceci, S. J., Francoeur, E., & Renick, A. (1995b). Anatomically detailed dolls do not facilitate preschoolers' reports of a pediatric examination involving genital touching. *Journal of Experimental Psychology: Applied, 1*, 95–109.

Bugental, D. B., Blue, J., Cortez, V., Fleck, K., & Rodriguez, A. (1992). Influences of witnessed affect on information processing in children. *Child Development, 63*, 774–86.

Cassel, W. S., Roebers, C. E. M., & Bjorklund, D. F. (1996). Developmental patterns of eyewitness responses to increasingly suggestive questions. *Journal of Experimental Child Psychology, 61*, 116–33.

Ceci, S. J. & Bruck, M. (1993). Suggestibility of the child witness: A historical review and synthesis. *Psychological Bulletin, 113*, 403–39.

Ceci, S. J. & Bruck, M. (1995). *Jeopardy in the courtroom: A scientific analysis of children's testimony*. Washington, DC: American Psychological Association.

Ceci, S. J. & Friedman, R. D. (2000). The suggestibility of children: Scientific research and legal implications. *Cornell Law Review, 86*, 33–108.

Ceci, S. J., Ross, D. F., & Toglia, M. P. (1987). Suggestibility of children's memory: Psycholegal implications. *Journal of Experimental Psychology: General, 116*, 38–49.

Ceci, S. J., Loftus, E. F., Leichtman, M. D., & Bruck, M. (1994). The possible role of source misattributions in the creation of false beliefs among preschoolers. *International Journal of Clinical and Experimental Hypnosis, 42*, 304–20.

Cederborg, A., Orbach, Y., Sternberg, K. J., & Lamb, M. E. (2000). Investigative interviews of child witnesses in Sweden. *Child Abuse and Neglect, 24*, 1355–61.

Dale, P. S., Loftus, E. F., & Rathbun, L. (1978). The influence of the form of the question on the eyewitness testimony of preschool children. *Journal of Psycholinguistic Research, 7*, 269–77.

DeLoache, J. S. (1990). Young children's understanding of scale models. In R. Fivush and J. Hudson (eds.), *Knowing and remembering in young children* (pp. 94–126). New York: Cambridge University Press.

DeLoache, J. S. & Marzolf, D. P. (1995). The use of dolls to interview young children: Issues of symbolic representation. *Journal of Experimental Child Psychology, 60*, 155–73.

Dent, H. R. (1982). The effects of interviewing strategies on the results of interviews with child witnesses. In A. Trankell (ed.), *Reconstructing the past: The role of psychologists in criminal trials* (pp. 279–97). Stockholm: Norstedt.

Dent, H. R. & Stephenson, G. M. (1979). An experimental study of the effectiveness of different techniques of questioning child witnesses. *British Journal of Social and Clinical Psychology, 18*, 41–51.

Fivush, R. (1997). Event memory in early childhood. In N. Cowan (ed.), *The development of memory in childhood*. Hove, East Sussex: Psychology Press.

Fivush, R. & Hamond, N. R. (1989). Time and again: Effects of repetition and retention interval on 2-year-olds' event recall. *Journal of Experimental Child Psychology, 47*, 259–73.

Foley, M. A. & Johnson, M. K. (1985). Confusion between memories for performed and imagined actions. *Child Development, 56*, 1145–55.

Garven, S., Wood, J. M., & Malpass, R. S. (2000). Allegations of wrongdoing: The effects of reinforcement on children's mundane and fantastic claims. *Journal of Applied Psychology, 85*, 38–49.

Garven, S., Wood, J. M., Malpass, R. S., & Shaw, J. S. (1998). More than suggestion: The effect of interviewing techniques from the McMartin Preschool case. *Journal of Applied Psychology, 83,* 347–59.

Gee, S. & Pipe, M.-E. (1995). Helping children to remember: The influence of object cues on children's accounts of a real event. *Developmental Psychology, 31,* 746–58.

Goodman, G. S. & Aman, C. (1990). Children's use of anatomically detailed dolls to recount an event. *Child Development, 61,* 1859–71.

Goodman, G. S., Aman, C., & Hirschman, J. (1987). Child sexual and physical abuse: Children's testimony. In S. J. Ceci, M. P. Toglia, & D. F. Ross (eds.), *Children's eyewitness memory* (pp. 1–23). New York: Springer-Verlag.

Goodman, G. S., Bottoms, B. L., Schwartz-Kenney, B. M., & Rudy, L. (1991a). Children's testimony about a stressful event: Improving children's reports. *Journal of Narrative and Life History, 1,* 69–99.

Goodman, G. S., Hirschman, J. E., Hepps, D., & Rudy, L. (1991b). Children's memory for stressful events. *Merrill Palmer Quarterly, 37,* 109–57.

Hamond, N. R. & Fivush, R. (1991). Memories of Mickey Mouse: Young children recount their trip to Disney World. *Cognitive Development, 6,* 433–48.

Hershkowitz, I. (2001). Children's responses to open-ended utterances in investigative interviews. *Legal and Criminological Psychology, 6,* 49–63.

Hershkowitz, I., Orbach, Y., Lamb, M. E., Sternberg, K. J., & Horowitz, D. (2001). The effects of mental context reinstatement on children's accounts of sexual abuse. *Applied Cognitive Psychology, 15,* 235–48.

Hewitt, S. K. (1999). *Assessing allegations of sexual abuse in preschool children: Understanding small voices.* Thousand Oaks, CA: Sage.

Home Office (1992). *Memorandum of good practice on video recorded interviews with child witnesses for criminal proceedings.* London: Her Majesty's Stationery Office.

Howe, M. L., Courage, M. L., & Peterson, C. (1994). How can I remember when "I" wasn't there: Long-term retention of traumatic experiences and emergence of the cognitive self. *Consciousness and Cognition, 3,* 327–55.

Hunt, J. S. & Borgida, E. (2001). Is that what I said?: Witnesses' responses to interviewer modifications. *Law and Human Behavior, 25,* 583–604.

Johnson, M. K., Hashtroudi, S., & Lindsay, D. S. (1993). Source monitoring. *Psychological Bulletin, 114,* 3–28.

Kelley, S. J. (1996). Ritualistic abuse of children. In J. Briere, L. Berliner, J. Bulkley, C. Jenny, & T. Reid (eds.), *The APSAC handbook on child maltreatment* (pp. 90–99). Thousand Oaks, CA: Sage.

Kuehnle, K. (1996). *Assessing allegations of child sexual abuse.* Sarasota, FL: Professional Resource Press/Professional Resource Exchange.

Kuehnle, K. (1998). Child sexual abuse evaluations: The scientist-practitioner model. *Behavioral Sciences and the Law, 16,* 5–20.

Lamb, M. E. & Fauchier, A. (2001). The effects of question type on self-contradictions by children in the course of forensic interviews. *Applied Cognitive Psychology, 15,* 1–9.

Lamb, M. E., Sternberg, K. J., & Esplin, P. W. (2000). Effects of age and delay on the amount of information provided by alleged sex abuse victims in investigative interviews. *Child Development, 71,* 1586–96.

Lamb, M. E., Hershkowitz, I., Sternberg, K. J., Boat, B., & Everson, M. D. (1996a). Investigative interviews of alleged sexual abuse victims with and without anatomical dolls. *Child Abuse and Neglect, 20,* 1251–9.

Lamb, M. E., Hershkowitz, I., Sternberg, K. J., Esplin, P. W., Hovav, M., Manor, T., & Yudilevitch, L. (1996b). Effects of investigative utterance types on Israeli children's responses. *International Journal of Behavioral Development, 19*, 627–37.

Lamb, M. E., Sternberg, K. J., Orbach, Y., Hershkowitz, I., & Esplin, P. W. (1999). Forensic interviews of children. In A. Memon & R. Bull (eds.), *Handbook of the psychology of interviewing* (pp. 253–77). New York: John Wiley.

Lamb, M. E., Sternberg, K. J., Orbach, Y., Esplin, P. W., Stewart, H., & Mitchell, S. (2003). Age differences in young children's responses to open-ended invitations in the course of forensic interviews. *Journal of Consulting and Clinical Psychology, 71*, 926–33.

Lampinen, J. M. & Smith, V. L. (1995). The incredible (and sometimes incredulous) child witness: Child eyewitnesses' sensitivity to source credibility cues. *Journal of Applied Psychology, 80*, 621–7.

Leichtman, M. D. & Ceci, S. J. (1995). The effects of stereotypes and suggestion on preschoolers' reports. *Developmental Psychology, 31*, 568–78.

Lyon, T. D. (1999). The new wave in children's suggestibility research: A critique. *Cornell Law Review, 84*, 1003–87.

Lyon, T. D. (2002). Expert testimony on the suggestibility of children: Does it fit? In B. L. Bottoms, M. B. Kouera, & B. D. McAuliff (eds.), *Children and the law: Social science and policy* (pp. 378–411). New York: Cambridge University Press.

Merritt, K., Ornstein, P. A., & Spicker, B. (1994). Children's memory for a salient medical procedure: Implications for testimony. *Pediatrics, 94*, 17–23.

Nathan, D. & Snedeker, M. (1995). *Satan's silence.* New York: Basic Books.

Nelson, K. (1993). The psychological and social origins of autobiographical memory. *Psychological Science, 4*, 7–14.

Nelson, K. (1996). *Language in cognitive development: The emergence of the mediated mind.* New York: Cambridge University Press.

Orbach, Y. & Lamb, M. E. (2001). The relationship between within-interview contradictions and eliciting interviewer utterances. *Child Abuse and Neglect, 25*, 323–33.

Orbach, Y., Hershkowitz, I., Lamb, M. E., Sternberg, K. J., Esplin, P. W., & Horowitz, D. (2000a). Assessing the value of structured protocols for forensic interviews of alleged child abuse victims. *Child Abuse and Neglect, 24*, 733–52.

Orbach, Y., Hershkowitz, I., Lamb, M. E., Sternberg, K. J., & Horowitz, D. (2000b). Interviewing at the scene of the crime: Effects on children's recall of alleged abuse. *Legal and Criminological Psychology, 5*, 135–47.

Ornstein, P. A., Gordon, B. N., & Larus, D. (1992). Children's memory for a personally experienced event: Implications for testimony. *Applied Cognitive Psychology, 6*, 49–60.

Ornstein, P. A., Staneck, C. H., Agosto, C. D., & Baker-Ward, L. (2001). Differentiating between what happened and what might have happened: The impact of knowledge and expectation on children's memory. Paper presented to the biennial meeting of the Society for Research in Child Development, Minneapolis, MN, April.

Peters, D. P. (1987). The impact of naturally occurring stress on children's memory. In S. J. Ceci, M. P. Toglia, & D. F. Ross (eds.), *Children's eyewitness memory* (pp. 122–41). New York: Springer-Verlag.

Peters, D. P. (1991). The influence of stress and arousal on the child witness. In J. L. Doris (ed.), *The suggestibility of children's recollections* (pp. 60–76). Washington, DC: American Psychological Association.

Peterson, C. & Whalen, N. (2001). Five years later: Children's memory for medical emergencies. *Applied Cognitive Psychology, 15*, S7–S24.

Pipe, M.-E. & Wilson, J. C. (1994). Cues and secrets: Influences on children's event reports. *Developmental Psychology, 30*, 515–25.

Poole, D. A. & Lamb, M. E. (1998). *Investigative interviews of children: A guide for helping professionals.* Washington, DC: American Psychological Association.

Poole, D. A. & Lindsay, D. S. (1995). Interviewing preschoolers: Effects of nonsuggestive techniques, parental coaching and leading questions on reports of nonexperienced events. *Journal of Experimental Child Psychology, 60*, 129–54.

Poole, D. A. & White, L. T. (1993). Two years later: Effects of question repetition and retention intervals on the eyewitness testimony of children and adults. *Developmental Psychology, 29*, 844–53.

Price, D. W. W. & Goodman, G. S. (1990). Visiting the wizard: Children's memory of a recurring event. *Child Development, 61*, 664–80.

Reinhold, R. (1990). How lawyers and media turned the McMartin case into a tragic media circus. *New York Times*, January 25, p. 1D.

Reyna, V. F. & Brainerd, C. J. (1997). Fuzzy-trace theory: An interim synthesis. *Learning and Individual Differences, 7*, 1–75.

Roberts, K. P. & Blades, M. (2000). *Children's source monitoring.* Mahwah, NJ: Lawrence Erlbaum Associates.

Roberts, K. P. & Lamb, M. E. (1999). Children's responses when interviewers distort details during investigative interviews. *Legal and Criminological Psychology, 4*, 23–31.

Rudy, L. & Goodman, G. S. (1991). Effects of participation on children's reports: Implications for children's testimony. *Developmental Psychology, 27*, 527–38.

Sales, J. M., Goldberg, A., & Parker, J. F. (2001). Children's recall of a stressful event after a six-year-delay. Poster presented at the biennial meeting of the Society for Research in Child Development, Minneapolis, Minnesota, April.

Saywitz, K. J., Goodman, G. S., Nicholas, E., & Moan, S. (1991). Children's memories of physical examinations involving genital touch: Implications for reports of child sexual abuse. *Journal of Consulting and Clinical Psychology, 59*, 682–91.

Sternberg, K. J., Lamb, M. E., Hershkowitz, I., Esplin, P. W., Redlich, A., & Sunshine, N. (1996). The relation between investigative utterance types and the informativeness of child witnesses. *Journal of Applied Developmental Psychology, 17*, 439–51.

Sternberg, K. J., Lamb, M. E., Orbach, Y., Esplin, P. W., & Mitchell, S. (2001). Use of a structured investigative protocol enhances young children's responses to free recall prompts in the course of forensic interviews. *Journal of Applied Psychology, 86*, 997–1005.

Stevenson, V. M., Leung, P., & Cheung, K. M. (1992). Competency-based evaluation of interviewing skills in child sexual abuse cases. *Social Work Research and Abstracts, 28*, 11–16.

Thierry, K. L., Spence, M. J., & Memon, A. (2001). Before misinformation is encountered: Source monitoring decreases child witness suggestibility. *Journal of Cognition and Development, 2*, 1–26.

Titcomb, A. L. & Reyna, V. F. (1995). Memory interference and misinformation effects. In F. Dempster & C. Brainerd (eds.), *Interference and inhibition in cognition* (pp. 263–94). San Diego, CA: Academic Press.

Tobey, A. E. & Goodman, G. S. (1992). Children's eyewitness memory: Effects of participation and forensic context. *Child Abuse and Neglect, 16*, 779–96.

Tulving, E. (1983). *Elements of episodic memory.* Oxford: Clarendon Press.

Warren, A. & Swartwood, J. (1992). Developmental issues in flashbulb memory research: Children recall the Challenger event. In E. Winograd & U. Neisser (eds.), *Affect and accuracy in recall* (pp. 95–120). New York: Cambridge University Press.

Warren, A. R., Woodall, C. E., Hunt, J. S., & Perry, N. W. (1996). "It sounds good in theory, but . . .": Do investigative interviewers follow guidelines based on memory research? *Child Maltreatment, 1*, 231–45.

Warren, A. R., Garven, S., Walker, N. E., & Woodall, C. E. (2000). Setting the record straight: How problematic are "typical" child sexual abuse interviews? Paper presented at the Biennial Meeting of the American Psychology-Law Society, New Orleans, LA, March.

Wells, G. L., Turtle, J. W., & Luus, C. A. E. (1989). The perceived credibility of child eyewitnesses: What happens when they use their own words? In S. J. Ceci, D. F. Ross, & M. P. Toglia (eds.), *Perspectives on children's testimony* (pp. 23–46). New York: Springer-Verlag.

Zaragoza, M. S., Dahlgren, D., & Muench, J. (1992). The role of memory impairment in children's suggestibility. In M. L. Howe, C. J. Brainerd, & V. F. Reyna (eds.), *Development of long-term retention* (pp. 184–216). New York: Springer-Verlag.

CHAPTER TWENTY-FIVE

New Research Methods in Developmental Science: Applications and Illustrations

Marc H. Bornstein, Chun-Shin Hahn, O. Maurice Haynes, Nanmathi Manian, and Catherine S. Tamis-LeMonda

Introduction

The topics of developmental research vary from laboratory to laboratory, but a small number of overarching concerns are common to developmental investigators. By and large developmental research is directed to describing and explaining behavior over time. Researchers *describe* the nature of development by specifying children's abilities, behaviors, and experiences within and across ages. Descriptions normally focus on individual variation and group norms, as well as continuity and change in individuals and in groups over time. Researchers *explain* development by focusing on transactions among individuals and their experiences in relation to developmental outcomes. Explanatory goals include attempts to model normative changes as well as individual variation. The research methods presented in this chapter address these two primary objectives in developmental science in a number of ways:

- *Growth curve modeling*, as implemented in multilevel modeling, can be used to describe individual growth functions and examines factors that contribute to variation in the start points of the function and to their rates of change. One prominent theme in developmental science is change over time. Developmentalists are interested in trajectories of change in specific abilities or behaviors over age, and developmental research seeks to chart the nature of change.
- *Event history analysis* can be used to describe the likelihood of certain developmental milestones occurring at certain ages and to test group differences in those probabilities. Developmental research is concerned with onset of behavior or achievement of

milestones. Are there periods in the life course when a particular developmental event is most likely to occur? What factors contribute to variance in the developmental timing of events?

- *Item response theory* can be used to describe what children can and cannot do at different ages by evaluating the usefulness of different assessment procedures or tasks (items) in estimating the abilities of children in particular domains and in discriminating between children of differing abilities. A major issue in assessment concerns the discriminative properties of the actual tasks or items that are the focus of investigation. Given an array of items, which are more difficult for children to master relative to others? Which items best discriminate among children, how does their discriminative power change with age, and which items precede which others in development? Understanding the nature of the task is crucial to developing age-appropriate assessments.

In this chapter, we illustrate how several methodological advances in developmental science are applied to diverse issues of interest to us. We address successively, the application of multilevel modeling to fetal development, event history analysis to language development, and item response theory to the development of play. In general, each section first introduces a particular methodology and then illustrates its application with data from our program of research.

Multilevel Modeling and Fetal Development

Much of the data found in developmental science carry a hierarchical structure. A hierarchical data set consists of units that are grouped at different levels. A familiar example of hierarchically structured data is repeated measures nested within individuals. The measurement occasions (e.g., time or age points) are the level 1 units in a 2-level structure where the individuals are the level 2 units. In other common examples of 2-level structures, siblings may be the level 1 units where the level 2 units are the families, or families may be the level 1 units where the level 2 units are neighborhoods. Historically, ordinary multiple regression, analysis of variance, or some other statistical methods are common procedures with multilevel problems for which data are first aggregated or disaggregated into one single level of interest (Hox, 1995; Snijders & Bosker, 1999).

Two key elements which differentiate the multilevel modeling techniques from the conventional statistical tests were detailed by Raudenbush (1988, p. 86):

> First, . . . Under appropriate assumptions, such multilevel modeling solves, in principle, the problem of aggregation bias. Such bias occurs in part because a variable typically takes on different meanings and has different effects at different levels of aggregation, and in part because estimation of such effects is prone to selection bias at each level. . . . Second, these methods enable specification of appropriate error structures, including random intercepts and random coefficients. . . . In most settings, appropriate specification of error components solves the problems of

misestimated precision which have plagued hypothesis testing in nested, unbalanced data sets.

Multilevel modeling (MLM) is known in the literature under several names: covariance components models (Dempster, Rubin, & Tsutakawa, 1981), multilevel linear models (Mason, Wong, & Entwisle, 1984), mixed linear models (Goldstein, 1986), random coefficient models (Rosenberg, 1973), and hierarchical linear models (Strenio, Weisberg, & Bryk, 1983). Several software packages are now available for the multilevel analysis, including HLM, Varcl, and MLwiN/MLN, and structural equation modeling programs, such as EQS, Lisrel and MPlus.

We illustrate potential uses of multilevel analysis in research on fetal growth as implemented by HLM 5 (Raudenbush et al., 2001; for a review of the underlying theory and computations, see Bryk & Raudenbush, 1987; Raudenbush, 1988; Raudenbush & Bryk, 2002; see also chapter 18, this volume). Following Bryk and Raudenbush (1987), we evaluated the structure of mean growth trajectory, the extent of individual variation around mean growth trajectory, the correlation between rate of change and initial status, the reliability of assessment, and how personal characteristics predict status and change in the fetus.

Methods and procedures

The sample, admittedly small for MLM analysis but typical size in this area of research, consisted of 35 low-risk pregnant women and their singleton fetuses. Details of the fetal data collection methods are presented in Bornstein et al. (2002). Fetuses were tested at 24, 30, and 36 weeks gestational age. The original data set contained three fetal heart measures. For the sake of simplicity, we discuss only two of the measures, namely heart rate and heart rate variability. In addition to the fetal data, we collected background information of each dyad, from which we use family SES (see also Bornstein et al., 2003; Hollingshead Four-Factor Index of Social Status, 1975) to illustrate how a between-subjects predictor might be incorporated in the model.

Two MLMs were constructed for each fetal measure by varying the level 2 model in each model set. In the first model set, an unconditional level 2 model represented the mean of the fetal measure at 24 weeks and the fetal growth trajectory not controlling for any sociodemographic measure; in the second model set, a conditional level 2 model represented the mean of the fetal measure at 24 weeks and the fetal growth trajectory controlling for family SES.

Using the notation of Raudenbush and Bryk (2002), we posed a linear function of age for each fetal variable in the level 1 analysis. Take heart rate, for example:

$$Y_{ti} = \pi_{0i} + \pi_{1i} \, (gestational \; age_{ti} - 24) + \varepsilon_{ti} \tag{25.1}$$

where Y_{ti} is the heart rate at time t for fetus i, $i = 1, \ldots, 35$ (35 fetuses in the sample), and $t = 1, 2,$ and 3 (24, 30, and 36 weeks GA). The term $(gestational \; age_{ti} - 24)$ is the age of fetus i at time t minus 24 so that $(gestational \; age_{ti} - 24)$ is 0, 6, and 12 at 24, 30, and 36 gestational ages. π_{0i} is the intercept for fetus i, given the coding of (*gestational age$_{ti}$* − 24) and represents the heart rate at 24 weeks for fetus i, or initial status for fetus i. π_{1i} is the trajectory or linear trend in heart rate for fetus i, or growth rate for fetus i, from 24 to 36 weeks gestation. ε_{ti} is the deviation of fetus i from her or his growth trajectory at time t. These within-subjects errors are assumed to be mutually independent and normally distributed with mean of zero (Bryk & Raudenbush, 1987).

The focus of the level 2 unconditional models is on the distribution of growth parameters across fetuses:

$$\pi_{0i} = \beta_{00} + \mu_{0i} \tag{25.2}$$

$$\pi_{1i} = \beta_{10} + \mu_{1i} \tag{25.3}$$

In these models, both level 1 coefficients, the intercept (π_{0i}) and the linear trend (or slope, π_{1i}) are unconditionally predicted by the mean heart rate across fetuses (β_{00}) and the mean linear trend across fetuses in heart rate slope (β_{10}), respectively. The regression coefficients β_{00} and β_{10} are termed fixed effects. μ_{0i} is the random effect in estimating mean heart rate at 24 weeks, or the unique increment in the intercept, for fetus i. μ_{1i} is the random effect in estimating linear trend in mean heart rate, or the unique increment in the slope, for fetus i. μ_{0i} and μ_{1i} are assumed bivariate normal with zero means, variances τ_{00}, τ_{11}, and covariance τ_{01} (Bryk & Raudenbush, 1987). t statistics (the ratio of each estimate to its standard error) are employed to determine whether the mean for a fetal measure at 24 weeks (β_{00}) is significantly different from zero and whether the mean trajectory (β_{10}) is flat, increasing, or decreasing. Whether there was significant variation of individual fetuses around the mean or the mean growth trajectory was provided by separate χ^2 test of the null hypothesis that the variance estimate (τ_{00} and τ_{11}, respectively) was zero.

The effect of family socioeconomic status (SES, an overarching family characteristic) on the growth parameters was explored by entering family SES as a predictor in the level-2 models. The level-1 model remains as in equation (25.1). The level-2 model is expanded by entering terms for the effect of SES on the intercept (π_{0i}) and slope (π_{1i}):

$$\pi_{0i} = \beta_{00} + \beta_{01} \, (\textit{family SES})_i + \mu_{0i} \tag{25.4}$$

and

$$\pi_{1i} = \beta_{10} + \beta_{11} \, (\textit{family SES})_i + \mu_{1i} \tag{25.5}$$

In these models, family SES is centered around the grand mean for the Hollingshead Index so that β_{00} represents mean heart rate averaged over fetuses at 24 weeks in fetuses whose family SES is the mean of the Hollingshead Index and β_{01} is the change in beats per minute (bpm) for a unit deviation from the mean Hollingshead Index. β_{10} represents the linear trend in heart rate averaged over fetuses whose family SES is at the mean of the Hollingshead Index, and β_{11} is the change in mean heart rate slope for a unit deviation from the mean Hollingshead Index.

For each unconditional and conditional model, we calculated the estimated residual sums of squares (deviance) as an index of the variance in that measure that is not explained by the model. Using a likelihood-ratio test (χ^2, df = 2) to compare the deviance statistics of the two models, we evaluated whether the inclusion of family SES as a predictor contributed significantly to the explanation of variation in the mean of the fetal measure at 24 weeks or the fetal growth trajectory. Following significant likelihood-ratio test, the effects of family SES on the mean intercept at 24 weeks (β_{01}), and on the mean slope (β_{11}), are addressed by the t statistics.

Results and discussion

Table 25.1 summarizes the parameter estimates, their robust standard errors, the variance components, the corresponding test and p value, and the reliability estimates from the HLM output. Table 25.2 presents the estimated fixed-effects results of the effects of family SES on the growth parameters.

Mean growth trajectory On the average, fetuses had a heart rate of 144.89 bpm at 24 weeks, which declined by 0.56 bpm each week from 24 to 36 weeks gestation. Both parameters differed significantly from zero, $t(34)$s = 150.17 and −6.16, respectively, ps < 0.001, and, thus, are required for describing the mean growth trajectories for fetal heart rate. The average heart rate variability at 24 weeks gestation was 3.95 bpm, which increased by 0.15 bpm each week from 24 to 36 weeks gestation. Both parameters differed significantly from zero, $t(34)$s = 29.60 and 5.58, respectively, both ps < 0.001, and, thus, are required for describing mean growth trajectories for fetal heart rate variability.

Individual variation around mean growth trajectory Fetuses varied significantly in their heart rate at 24 weeks. The variance of individual fetal heart rates around the mean heart rate at 24 weeks – the error variance in the prediction of mean heart rate from heart rates for individual fetuses – was 18.80, $\chi^2(N = 35, \text{df} = 34) = 82.76$, $p < 0.001$. Fetuses did not vary in their heart rate decline: the variance of individual fetal trend estimates around the estimate of a linear trend in baseline fetal heart rate – the error variance in the prediction of a linear trend across fetuses from linear trends for individual fetuses – was 0.06, $\chi^2(N = 35, \text{df} = 34) = 43.86$, ns.

To account for the correlation between rate of change and initial status for fetal heart rate (see "Correlation between rate of change and initial status," below), two likelihood-ratio tests were conducted which confirmed the univariate χ^2 tests, $\chi^2(\text{df} = 2, N = 35) = 26.09$, $p < 0.001$, for heart rate at 24 weeks and $\chi^2(\text{df} = 2, N = 35) = 4.72$, ns, for heart rate decline.

For heart rate variability, fetuses varied significantly not only in initial status at 24 weeks, $\chi^2(\text{df} = 34, N = 35) = 53.34$, $p < 0.05$, but also in rates of change from 24 to 36 week gestation, $\chi^2(\text{df} = 34, N = 35) = 136.00$, $p < 0.001$. The variance estimate for the linear trend in heart rate variability implies an estimated standard deviation

Table 25.1   Linear growth models for fetal heart measures

Random effect	Variance component	df	χ^2	p
Mean initial status β_{00} (24 weeks gestation)				
Heart rate	144.89	0.96	150.17	<0.001
Heart rate variability	3.95	0.13	29.60	<0.001
Mean growth rate β_{10} (24–36 weeks gestation)				
Heart rate	−0.56	0.09	−6.16	<0.001
Heart rate variability	0.15	0.03	5.58	<0.001

Random effect	Variance component	df	χ^2	p
Initial status μ_{0i} (24 weeks gestation)				
Heart rate	18.80	34	82.76	<0.001
Heart rate variability	0.21	34	53.34	<0.05
Growth rate μ_{1i} (24–36 weeks gestation)				
Heart rate	0.06	34	43.86	ns
Heart rate variability	0.02	34	136.00	<0.001

Reliability of OLS regression coefficient estimate

Initial status, $_{0i}$ (24 weeks gestation)	
Heart rate	0.58
Heart rate variability	0.34
Growth rate, $_{1i}$ (24–36 weeks gestation)	
Heart rate	0.20
Heart rate variability	0.74

NB: Unconditional model.
β_{00}: the mean intercept across fetuses at 24 weeks gestation, equation (25.2).
β_{10}: the mean linear trend across fetuses from 24 to 36 weeks gestation, equation (25.3).
μ_{0i}: the random effect in estimating mean intercept at 24 weeks, or the unique increment in the intercept, for fetus *i*, equation (25.2).
μ_{1i}: the random effect in estimating linear trend from 24 to 36 weeks gestation, or the unique increment in the slope, for fetus *i*, equation (25.3).

which is the square root of 0.02 = 0.14. Fetuses whose increase in heart rate variability was one standard deviation above the average were expected to increase in that variability at a rate of 0.29 (0.15 + 0.14) bpm each week from 24 to 36 weeks gestation, whereas fetuses whose increase was one standard deviation below the average were expected to increase in variability at a rate of only 0.01 (0.15 − 0.14) bpm each week.

Correlation between rate of change and initial status   Under a linear individual growth model, the relation of change to initial status is the correlation between π_{1i} (the linear trend for each fetus) and π_{0i} (the intercept for each fetus) (Bryk & Raudenbush, 1987).

Table 25.2 Effects of family SES on growth parameters for fetal heart measures

Fixed effect	Coefficient	Standard error	t(33)	p
Initial status, $_{0i}$ *(24 weeks gestation)*				
Base, β_{00}				
Heart rate	144.89	0.96	150.86	<0.001
Heart rate variability	3.95	0.13	30.70	<0.001
Family SES, β_{01}				
Heart rate	0.05	0.09	<1	ns
Heart rate variability	0.02	0.01	1.62	ns
Growth rate, $_{1i}$ *(24–36 weeks gestation)*				
Base, β_{10}				
Heart rate	−0.56	0.09	−6.20	<0.001
Heart rate variability	0.15	0.03	5.93	<0.001
Family SES, β_{11}				
Heart rate	0.006	0.009	<1	ns
Heart rate variability	0.005	0.002	2.51	<0.05

β_{00}: the intercept averaged over fetuses at 24 weeks in fetuses whose family SES is the mean of the Hollingshead Index, equation (25.4).
β_{01}: the change in the mean intercept for a unit deviation from the mean Hollingshead Index, equation (25.4).
β_{10}: the linear trend averaged over fetuses whose family SES is at the mean of the Hollingshead Index, equation (25.5).
β_{11}: the change in the mean linear trend for a unit deviation from the mean Hollingshead Index, Equation (25.5).

For fetal heart rate, the estimated correlation between change and initial status was 0.70. This means that fetuses with a higher heart rate at 24 weeks showed smaller declines in their heart rate over time. There was no relation between heart rate variability at 24 weeks and increase in growth trajectory over time, $r = -0.01$.

Reliability of assessment Bryk and Raudenbush (1987) defined reliability as the ratio of the true parameter variance to the total observed variance (true parameter variance plus sampling variance). The reliability estimates, which are available from the HLM output, depend on two factors: the degree of heterogeneity among fetuses in the growth parameters (i.e., τ_{00}, which is an estimate of the variance of the intercept, and τ_{11}, which is an estimate of the variance of the slope) and the number of measurement occasions per fetus (Raudenbush & Chan, 1993). The reliability estimate increases as inter-fetus variability and the number of measurement occasions per fetus increase (see Raudenbush & Bryk, 2002, chapter 3, for computation details). The results (see Table 25.1) indicated that the reliability estimate was best for estimating slope in heart rate variability (0.74) and worst for estimating slope in heart rate (0.20). One possible reason for the lack of reliability in estimating heart rate slope is that the fetuses are relatively homogeneous with respect to their linear trend in heart rate change. However, all four of the reliability estimates were above the 0.05 criterion for treating the parameter estimates as fixed or nonrandomly varying (Raudenbush & Bryk, 2002).

Prediction of personal characteristics on status and change   The following analyses illustrate how differences in background (family SES) may account for variation among fetuses in initial status and rate of change. The results of the likelihood-ratio tests indicated that the conditional model controlling for family SES did not contribute significantly to the explanation of variation in fetal heart rate, $\chi^2(N = 35,$ df $= 2) = 0.93$, ns, but contributed significantly to a reduction in error in the prediction of the coefficients for heart rate variability, $\chi^2(N = 35,$ df $= 2) = 11.18$, $p < 0.005$.

Table 25.2 presents the estimated fixed-effects results of the effects of family SES on the growth parameters. Family SES did not improve the prediction of heart rate variability at 24 weeks gestation: changes in mean heart rate variability at 24 weeks for a unit change in the mean Hollingshead Index did not differ significantly from zero, $t(33) = 1.62$, ns. Family SES contributed to the explanation of the growth trajectory of heart rate variability: fetal heart rate variability increased at the rate of 0.005 bpm per week for each unit increase in the mean Hollingshead Index, $t(33) = 2.15$, $p < 0.05$.

This analysis of developmental trends as well as individual variation in fetal heart function showed that fetal heart rate shows developmental trends over three ages: normatively, mean heart rate decreased over the 24 to 36 weeks gestational age, whereas heart rate variability increased. That fetuses show individual variability in heart rate, where the normative developmental function is to increase heart rate variability, suggests that fetuses that are advanced in their development in these realms of cardiac function within the normal range, or that are developing at more rapid rates, are fetuses whose autonomic functioning in general or cardiac functioning in particular is more advanced. These fetuses could just as well be "ahead of the curve" in general development. Further to this point, those fetuses could also show advanced postnatal function (Bornstein et al., 2003).

Event History Analysis and Children's Achievement of Language Milestones

Considerable progress has been made in statistics applied to the treatment of longitudinal data over the past decade, and event history analysis (also referred to as survival analysis[1]) exemplifies such an advance (Allison, 1982; Willett & Singer, 1991, 1993; Yamaguchi, 1991). Event history analysis provides an innovative and apt statistical approach to modeling the timing of developmental events, as well as relations between predictors and the onsets of events. Two fundamental objectives of developmental science

---

[1]   The term "survival analysis" derives from its origins in actuarial science. Given the current emphasis on normative developmental processes, we prefer the more conceptually appropriate use of the term "event history analysis."

have been to describe the timing of meaningful events and to explain individual variation around their onset. When do children take their first steps or attain gender constancy? To what extent do children vary in the timing of those achievements, and what factors contribute to those differences? The purposes of event history analysis are to identify when in development a particular event or milestone occurs, and what factors predict the timing of those events (see also Cox & Oakes, 1983; Parmar & Machin, 1995). Additionally, it is a particularly useful tool because it accommodates censored data; that is, it can estimate the effect of predictors on the timing of events even when not all children have experienced the event by the end of data collection. This permits data collection to occur over briefer periods than required by statistical approaches such as ordinary linear regression, in which all participants must experience a particular event before the end of the study period.

We first define event history analysis and fundamental concepts and terms associated with the technique. We then illustrate its application in children's language acquisition. Clearly, no absolute age exists for the onset of developmental events. Rather, researchers talk about normative tendencies, or average ages of emergence, and recognize the limited information that means provide in the absence of information about variability. So, for example, children speak their first words at around 1 year of age. Standard deviations around this approximate age provide an appraisal of the spread among children. Often, average ages mask substantive and fascinating differences among children in patterns and timing of achievements.

In event history analysis, time is considered along its continuum, and the probability of the onset of a developmental event occurring is modeled across this continuum. Using this approach it is possible to ask: "What is the probability that a child will speak her or his first words at 9 months, 10 months, 11 months, and so on if s/he has not already done so?" The *baseline hazard function* depicts the unconditional probability of the onset of the target developmental event occurring at discrete ages. The shape of the hazard function depends on the nature of the event in question. If the event is equally likely to occur at any given age, the hazard function will be flat. Alternatively, there may be developmental periods during which the probability of the event peaks, indicating that its likelihood rises during a particular window of time. To the extent that the baseline hazard function peaks at discrete ages, it suggests that children are more likely to experience the event at certain ages than they are at others. Figure 25.1 depicts two hypothetical hazard functions, one for an event with equal likelihood across developmental time (Figure 25.1a) and another for an event characterized by a marked peak in the likelihood of its occurrence at 23 months (Figure 25.1b).

From baseline hazard probabilities, a second function, the *cumulative hazard function*, can also be plotted. The cumulative hazard function depicts the cumulative probability of an event occurring across successive ages. As a hypothetical example, if an investigator assesses a group of children monthly from 6 through 18 months, the cumulative probability of those children beginning to talk might be 0.00 at 6 months (as no children have yet achieved the milestone), 0.10 at 9 months, 0.15 at 10 months, 0.50 at 12 months, and so forth, until all children have achieved the milestone, at which point the cumulative hazard function reaches 1.00. Figure 25.2 presents the cumulative hazard function derived from the hypothetical hazard function in Figure 25.1b.

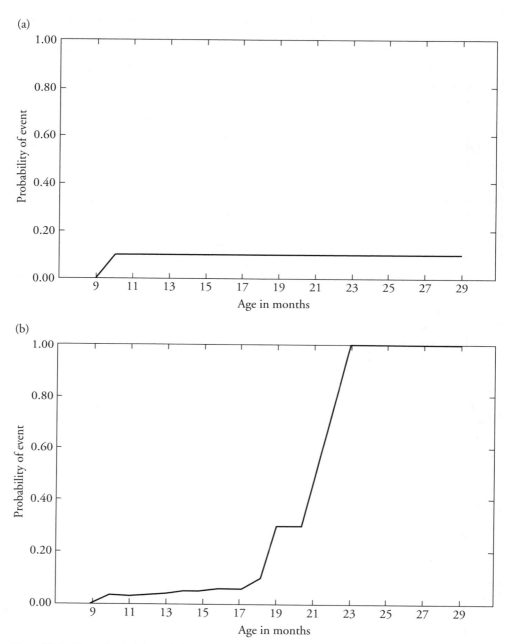

Figure 25.1   Hypothetical hazard functions (a) for event demonstrating equal likelihood of occurrence across discrete ages and (b) for event demonstrating a peak in its likelihood of occurrence around 23 months of age.

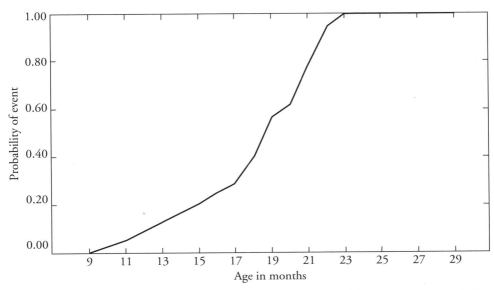

Figure 25.2 Hypothetical cumulative hazard function for the hazard function in Figure 25.1b.

The statistic *median lifetime* provides information as to when individuals achieve a given milestone on average. The median lifetime is defined as the point in the baseline survivor function at which the cumulative probability of the event reaches 0.50; that is, when half of the population experiences the target event. With respect to the hypothetical survivor function presented in Figure 25.2, the median lifetime can be seen as occurring at approximately 18 months.

Importantly, baseline hazard and survivor functions can be contrasted with *fitted hazard* and *survivor functions*, which provide estimates as to how much the timing of an event is displaced (i.e., moved forward or backward in time) given data on relevant predictors. Event history analysis can model the prediction of events from either discrete or continuous variables, and it provides parameter estimates that are conceptually and empirically useful in describing predictors of events (see Willett & Singer, 1991, 1993, for review).

Nested hierarchical χ^2 analyses are conducted in which the *baseline* hazard functions (i.e., hazard profiles in the absence of any predictors) are compared to *fitted* hazard functions, in which one or more predictors are included. A significant reduction in the χ^2 goodness-of-fit statistic indicates that model fit is improved when the predictor(s) is added to the baseline model. To examine the *unique* influences of two or more predictors over and above each other, fitted models that include two predictors (for example) are compared to models that include single predictors.

In standard regression applications, researchers ask about the amount of variance accounted for by a particular predictor or set of predictors. Using language as an example, researchers have asked how much children know at a fixed time in development and what predicts variability among children at that time. In event history analysis, the concept of variance becomes more pragmatic and tangible because fitted survivor functions model by precisely how much time a predictor displaces the median lifetime of an event. In addition, event history analysis may be used to model the timing of critical events for subgroups of individuals at extreme values of significant predictor variables (Willett & Singer, 1992), and the median lifetimes of the two subgroups can be contrasted. Parameter estimates of significant predictors at the 10th and 90th percentiles (a convention suggested for this statistical technique; Willett & Singer, 1993) are substituted in each of the hazard probability equations. The fitted survivor functions for these extreme values can be plotted, and differences in onset times of events can be compared.

Methods and procedures

The benefits of event history analysis are illustrated in our research on children's early language acquisition (Tamis-LeMonda & Bornstein, 2002; Tamis-LeMonda, Bornstein, & Baumwell, 2001; Tamis-LeMonda et al., 1998). Are differences among children in the timing of first imitations, first words, the vocabulary spurt, combinatorial speech, and language used in memory predicted by children's own earlier activities during interactions with their mothers and/or by dimensions of mothers' language responsiveness, and if so, by how much time do children at extremes of predictors differ in their onsets of these language milestones?

To address this question, maternal responsiveness and children's activities (e.g., vocalizations, play) were coded from videotaped interactions of mother–child free play at 9 and 13 months, and information about children's language acquisition was obtained through bi-weekly interviews with mothers from 9 through 21 months. The developmental onset of several language achievements in children were calculated based on the age in days at which children were reported to achieve these milestones.

Results and discussion

A series of nested hierarchical models, in which baseline hazard functions for children's language were compared to fitted hazard functions (containing various child and mother predictors), revealed that maternal responsiveness at 9 and 13 months predicted the timing of children's achieving language milestones over and above children's observed behaviors, but that responsiveness at 13 months was a stronger predictor of the timing of language milestones than was responsiveness at 9 months. Additionally, certain dimensions of responsiveness were more predictive of children's language onsets than were others.

After isolating significant predictors of children's language milestones, we modeled and plotted fitted hazard functions for values at the upper and lower 10th percentiles on key dimensions of maternal responsiveness at 13 months. Finally, in instances in which significant child and/or mother predictors of language milestones were identified, using these values and the parameter estimates for the significant predictors, we modeled two fitted hazard functions for each child language milestone – one for low levels of maternal

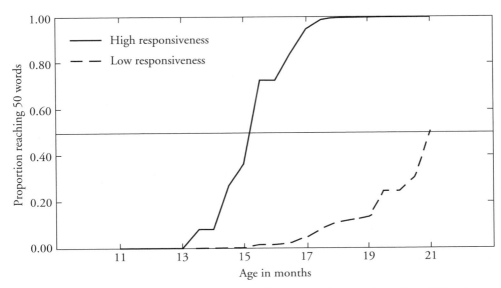

Figure 25.3 Modeling fitted hazard functions for the timing of 50 words: estimated function for high levels of maternal responsiveness to play and vocalizations at 13 months (upper 10th percentile) and estimated function for low levels of maternal responsiveness to play and vocalizations at 13 months (lowest 10th percentile).

responsiveness (i.e., the value at the 10th percentile of the relevant predictor(s)) and one for high levels of maternal responsiveness (i.e., the value at the 90th percentile of the predictor(s)).

As an example, for the milestone of achieving 50 words in expressive language, maternal responsiveness to children's vocalizations and play at 13 months were found to be significant predictors. We thus contrasted fitted hazard functions for high versus low responsiveness to vocalizations and play at 13 months. The estimates obtained from the fitted hazard functions for the two subgroups are presented in Figure 25.3. The point at which half the subgroup attains the milestone as well as in the percentages of children attaining each milestone by study end are evident. Specifically, half of the children with mothers high on responding to play and to vocalizations at 13 months are estimated to achieve 50 words in expressive language on average by 15.2 months, whereas half of the children whose mothers are low on responding to play and to vocalizations are estimated to achieve 50 words at 21 months, or nearly 6 months later.

This example from children's language development illustrates how event history analysis helps us to understand factors that contribute to normative developmental achievements. The data provided by this approach, such as median lifetimes on extreme values, are ecologically valid and meaningful. By modeling survivor functions for measures of maternal responsiveness, we showed that children are estimated to differ by as much as 6 months in the onset of achieving a critical language milestone when being reared in differentially responsive language environments.

Nonetheless, choosing event history analysis, as opposed to more traditional regression approaches, rests on the investigator's own perspective about the nature and meaning of the event that is being evaluated. Specific to language, if a particular milestone is viewed as an important and qualitatively distinct event in children's development, and if the nature of data collection permits evaluation of children's abilities at a number of discrete periods (e.g., monthly intervals), event history analysis can be particularly useful in evaluating factors that might displace the milestone forward or backward in time. If, however, the target event is considered an arbitrary point in a continuous process of growth, a regression approach might be more appropriate. We considered moments such as children's achieving their first 50 words in production to indicate important and transitional periods in language growth. Nonetheless, others might contend that such moments are not discrete events in the language-learning process, but are more continuous.

Item Response Theory and Children's Play Sophistication

Analytic tools to address questions of psychological interest are often developed well before they are implemented in mainstream developmental research. Item response theory (IRT), which has been in existence for more than half a century (Tucker, 1946), is one such example. IRT-based statistics identify items that provide maximum psychometric information and information pertaining to the difficulty of items relative to one another (Embretson & Reise, 2000; Hambleton & Swaminathan, 1991; Hambleton, Swaminathan, & Rogers, 1991; van der Linden & Hambleton, 1997). It is helpful to contrast IRT with classical measurement theory. In classical measurement theory, it is assumed that variation in observed scores is accounted for by an unobserved "true" score and by random error. The classical model assumes that all differences, other than random error, in the responses of individuals to items are attributable to the ability of the respondents. There is no role for differences in item difficulty so that items of average difficulty are typically searched for and employed. In contrast, IRT postulates that differences other than random error in the responses are separately attributable to individual differences in the respondents' ability and to differences in the difficulty and discriminability of items. The goal of IRT is to identify items that discriminate among individuals within each level of item difficulty.

IRT gained widespread popularity in educational testing, particularly in the realm of standardized aptitude and achievement testing, but has yet to achieve equal recognition in developmental science. Nonetheless, the potential relevance of IRT to developmental study is evident. Developmental researchers are interested in the extent to which certain tasks or abilities ("items") might serve as useful indicators of children's competence in a given area, and whether or not those items are ordered developmentally. As an example, a researcher might need to choose items that discriminate among children who differ on an underlying construct, such as cognitive development, and to create item sets that are increasingly difficult along this continuum. IRT addresses both goals by modeling the processes underlying an individual's responses to specific items (Thissen, 1991) both within and across age. In essence, IRT relates characteristics of items and characteristics of individuals to the probability of providing correct answers to specific items.

IRT models assume that an individual's performance is based on a latent trait of *ability*. IRT models also assume that the relationship between an individual's ability and her performance on an item can be characterized by a monotonically increasing function known as an item characteristic curve (ICC). The equation for the two-parameter logistic model of an ICC may be represented as:

$$P_i(\theta) = \frac{1}{1 + e^{-Da_i(\theta - b_i)}} \tag{25.6}$$

where θ is a latent trait of ability, $P_i(\theta)$ is the probability that an individual with ability θ answers item i correctly, e is the exponent of the natural logarithm, D is a scaling factor such that the logistic function approximates a normal function, a_i is the item discrimination parameter, and b_i is the item difficulty parameter. Performance of an individual of a given ability level, θ, on an item is some (logistic) function of a, the ability of the item to discriminate between individuals of equal ability, and b, the difficulty of the item. Equation (25.6) models a relation between performance and individual ability, item difficulty, and item discrimination.

We first discuss the psychometric parameters of IRT and the process of model testing using IRT methods. This discussion focuses on the commonly used two-parameter logistic model, which is applied when items are scored dichotomously (e.g., pass–fail). Next, we provide a developmental illustration of this statistical technique in the area of children's play competencies. This illustration focuses on identification of items that best discriminate among children who differ on the underlying construct of play ability, determination of the relative difficulty (i.e., ordering) of play items at a given age (here 9 months), and assessment of whether children's success with play items at earlier ages predicts underlying play ability later (at 21 months).

IRT models are used to assess the probability of an individual's response to a particular item (e.g., passing the item) given that individual's pattern of responses on an entire set of items from which the item is drawn. An individual's performance on the complete set of items is conceptualized as reflecting a continuous latent or unobserved construct of ability, θ (Hulin, Drasgow, & Parsons, 1983) which is assumed to be distributed as a standard normal variable (Harvey & Hammer, 1999). In essence, θ is analogous to an individual's "true score" on the dimension of interest. For example, in a two-parameter model of math achievement, the latent construct of mathematical ability (θ) is hypothesized to account for an individual's performance on each item of the test. The probability of an individual passing each successive math item is hypothesized to increase as θ increases. Items with high *discrimination* (parameter a) would be useful in differentiating among students with high versus low ability; in contrast, items with low discrimination would be equally likely to be passed by students varying in math competence, thus providing little useful information about math competency. If the math items vary in *difficulty* (parameter b), they would be ordered such that easy items would in probability be passed by everyone, hard items by students with high ability only.

The parameters of item discrimination and item difficulty are depicted by *item characteristic curves* (ICC), which show the expected probability of passing an item for different abilities. As such, ICCs depict relations between responses to each item and ability, with the assumption being that the latent construct of ability is the primary causal determinant of the observed responses to test items (Harvey & Hammer, 1999).

One limitation of the classical model of the true score is that it cannot be falsified and so it cannot be tested for how well it fits the data. In contrast, IRT models can be tested for their fit to the data using an iterative, maximum-likelihood procedure to estimate parameters of individuals' ability, item difficulty, and item discrimination. The discrimination and difficulty of items can be compared to one another formally by comparing the fits of nested models which differ in their assumptions about the equality of the difficulty and discrimination of items. One set of models is fit assuming that each item has *unique* difficulty and discrimination. Subsequent models are fit assuming that certain items have the *same* levels of difficulty and discrimination. The different models can then be compared by computing their likelihood ratio χ^2 fit statistics. To do so, parameter estimates are first obtained for an unconstrained model (i.e., in which all items are considered to be different from each other) and then for increasingly more constrained models in which the item discrimination parameters (parameter a_i for item i) and item difficulty parameters (parameter b_i) are set equal for selected items. After each successive model, the fit index of the less constrained model is subtracted from the fit index of the more constrained (nested) model. This difference score is distributed as χ^2 with degrees of freedom equal to the number of added constraints. Although unconstrained models will always provide the "best" fit, successive constraints that do not cause a significant reduction in fit are preferred, as they provide a more parsimonious explanation of the data and are more likely to be stable across samples. After obtaining the most parsimonious model of the item set, without sacrificing fit, the intercepts and slopes can be used to create ICCs for each of the items in the set. (See Hambleton, Swaminathan, & Rogers, 1991, and the website for Scientific Software, Inc.: http://www.ssicentral.com/. The general statistical package, SYSTAT 10, also has a module for binary test items which implements the one- and two-parameter logistic models.)

Methods and procedures

IRT is particularly useful in the domain of cognitive ability and testing. Given this history, we considered IRT methods appropriate to our investigations of children's play development, as children's play traverses a series of systematic changes over the course of the first 2 years which are thought to reflect advances in children's underlying cognitive competencies. Findings across a range of studies offer a detailed picture of young children's unfolding abilities in play: In early infancy, children mouth and manipulate; in the latter half of the first year, they engage in functional play and begin to combine objects in appropriate ways; near the start of the second year, symbolic play with objects emerges. Over the course of the second year, symbolic actions with objects become increasingly sophisticated (see Tamis-LeMonda & Bornstein, 1996, for review).

To systematically explore these and other progressions in children's play, we tested 114 children longitudinally on a set of 20 play items at 9, 13, 17, and 21 months of age. Play items were drawn from a list of object-actions thought to reflect emerging abilities

Table 25.3 Play items and examples

1 Mouthing	Mouth block
2 Manipulation	Look/touch block
3 Unitary functional play	Press buttons on phone
4 Inappropriate juxtapositions	Place dish on car
5 Perceptual juxtapositions	Stack toy plates
6 Functional juxtapositions	Put lid on teapot
7 Symbolic-self	Feed self with toy spoon
8 Symbolic-other	Rock doll
9 Sequence self	Pour in cup and drink
10 Substitute self	Wash self with block as a sponge
11 Vicarious	Make doll wave
12 Sequence other	Cover doll with blanket and pat to sleep
13 Substitute other	Feed doll with stick as spoon
14 Sequence substitute	Stir with stick and eat from stick
15 Sequence vicarious	Make bear walk to car and drive
16 Substitute vicarious	Make doll walk to cup and drive it as car
17 Sequence-other-substitute	Wash doll with sponge and dry
18 Sequence-vicarious substitute	Cloth on doll as a coat and make doll walk
19 Self-removed	Make doll kiss other doll
20 Emotive sequence	Make doll fall and cry

in children's object play as well as children's ability to combine separate units of action into integrated play episodes. Table 25.3 presents definitions and examples of the 20 items used in our assessment of children's object play. We began our investigation when children were 9 months of age, when emergent motor and cognitive competencies enable children to engage objects and most children evidence nonsymbolic play activities. Our assessments continued through 21 months when children exhibit relatively sophisticated forms of symbolic play and at least some exhibit all of the play items in the proposed scale.

During home visits, each child was observed in 10 minutes of solitary play and during play with an experimenter. Each child was credited with either passing or failing each of the 20 play items based on whether the child exhibited the play behavior in either play setting (i.e., alone or play with experimenter). During the solicited play session, the experimenter systematically probed for each play item by modeling the play action, handing toys to the child, and encouraging the child to engage in the action alone (i.e., "Can you do that?"). Each item was solicited twice.

From the pass–fail data across play items, a latent variable was calculated for each child at each age representing the child's underlying play competence at that point in time. Therefore, IRT enabled us to model the relative discrimination and difficulty of play items for each level of play competence. Specifically, three questions motivated the use of IRT methods in this investigation of children's developing object play: (1) Within each age, which play items best discriminate among children who are high versus low on the underlying construct of play competence? (2) What is the relative difficulty (i.e., ordering) of certain play items or groups of items with respect to one another at each age? (3) Across ages, which play items are most useful in distinguishing among children who are more or less advanced in play competence? These IRT analyses were guided by the assumptions that children would pass more items as they got older; more difficult items would be passed at later developmental stages or by fewer children; no item once achieved would be lost; and certain play items would be more revealing (i.e., discriminative) of children's play sophistication than others, both within and across age.

Results and discussion

We concentrate on findings obtained from the 9-month assessment and on the lagged relations between select play items and later play competencies. Unsurprisingly, and in line with the finding that virtually all 9-month-olds engage in play levels 1 and 2, and that virtually none exhibited play items 9 through 20, only play items 3 through 8 (in Table 25.3) were found to be useful indicators of children's play at 9 months. These six play items thus formed the basis for subsequent IRT analyses at this age.

We next proceeded to test the relative discrimination of play items 3 through 8 by comparing a model in which none of the slopes (parameter a) was constrained to a series of constrained models (i.e., a model in which slopes for items 1 and 2 were constrained to be equal; a model in which slopes for items 1 and 3 were constrained to be equal; a model in which slopes for items 1 and 4 were constrained to be equal; and so forth). In each pass, the χ^2 fit index of the less constrained model was subtracted from the fit index of the more constrained (nested) model, with degrees of freedom equal to differences in the number of constraints in the two models. The most parsimonious model was considered to be the one including maximum constraints without sacrificing fit.

In the current example, the best fitting model was one in which the six slopes for play items were constrained to be equal (i.e., were equally discriminating) at 9 months. Although these six items demonstrated equivalent "discrimination," they differed in their difficulty level, again revealed through the iterative process of contrasting the fit indices of nested models in which the intercepts (parameter b) were constrained to be equal. Based on the final model (in which difficulty of items 3 < 4 < 5, 6, and 7 < 8), the intercepts and slopes of each play item were used to create ICCs, visually depicting each item's relation to θ (see Figure 25.4). The intercepts and slopes for each item provide parameter estimates for difficulty and for discrimination. Specifically, the inflection point of the ICC for item 3 was to the left of those for items 4 through 8; the inflection point for item 4 was to the left of those for items 5 through 8; the inflection points for items 5, 6, and 7 were equivalent; and the inflection point for item 8 was to the right of the ICCs of the other play items. Conceptually, these trends could be interpreted as suggesting that unitary functional play is the easiest form of play; followed by inappropriate juxtapositions; followed by appropriate juxtapositions (both perceptual and functional) and self-directed symbolic play; followed by other-directed symbolic play. The equivalent difficulty of items 5 through 7 might suggest that they emerge in developmental tandem in children.

In summary, the most parsimonious model was one in which the six play items were constrained as equally discriminative, and items 5, 6, and 7 were constrained to be equal on the difficulty parameter.

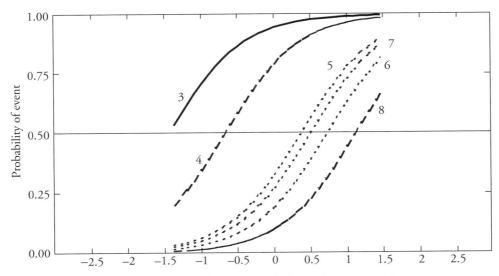

Figure 25.4   Item characteristic curves for six types of object play at 9 months.

Taking our example of children's play a step further, we then utilized IRT methods to assess whether children's overall play competence at 21 months could be determined from their earlier play abilities. To do so, a latent variable for play competence was calculated for each child at 21 months, and based on these values, children were classified into one of three competency groups: high play (upper quartile of children), medium play (middle 50 percent of children), and low play (lowest quartile of children). Figure 25.5a–f presents longitudinal data for children in each of these play groups in relation to the percentage of children who passed play items 3 through 8 at 9, 13, 17, and 21 months. None of the play items at 9 months discriminated among children with respect to their 21-month play. However, by 13 months, play items 5 (perceptual juxtapositions) and 8 (other-directed symbolic play) began to predict ultimate play competence: Specifically, a significantly greater percentage of children who ended up in the top quartile of play at 21 months had engaged in perceptual juxtapositions at 13 months when compared to children in the middle 50 percent and lowest quartile, $\chi^2(N = 114, df = 1) = 4.13, p < 0.05$. A significantly smaller percentage of children who ended up in the lowest quartile of play at 21 months had engaged in other-directed symbolic play when contrasted with children in the middle 50 percent or upper quartile, $\chi^2(N = 114, df = 1) = 8.63, p < 0.001$. These findings suggest that these two play items might be useful indicators of children's play competency over time, but that their developmental relevance does not emerge until 13 months and diminishes thereafter.

Several limitations of IRT have contributed to its relative obscurity in developmental science. These include limited accessibility, computational demands, expense, and sample-size requirements. However, computer improvements and refinements to software programs have led to growing availability and application of IRT. Another limitation is the relative lack of options for handling multidimensional data as well as for testing fits of

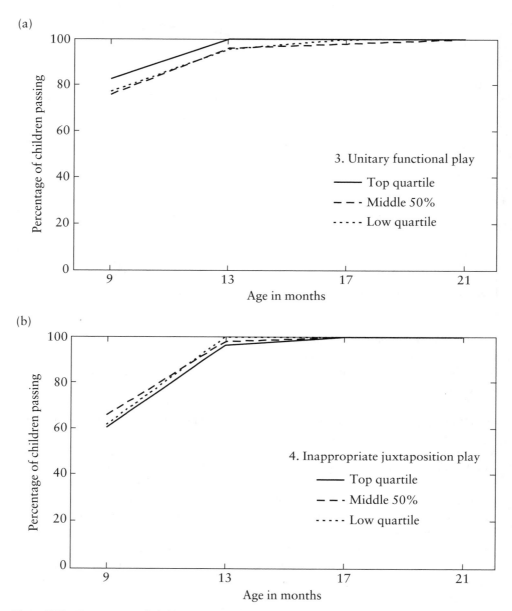

Figure 25.5   Percentages of children passing different play items at 9, 13, 17, and 21 months in relation to play sophistication at 21 months. Children at 21 months are grouped according to theta values at 21 months as high, medium or low in overall play. (a) Play item 3 (i.e., unitary functional play), (b) play item 4 (i.e., inappropriate juxtapositions).

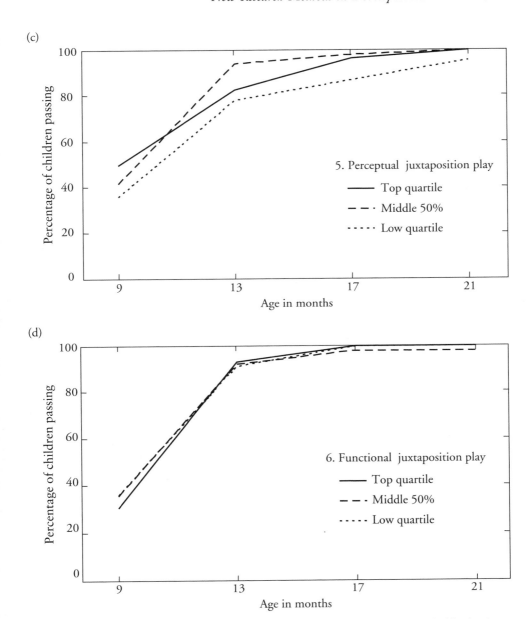

Figure 25.5 (*continued*) (c) play item 5 (i.e., juxtapositions based on perception), (d) play item 6 (i.e., juxtapositions based on function).

(e)

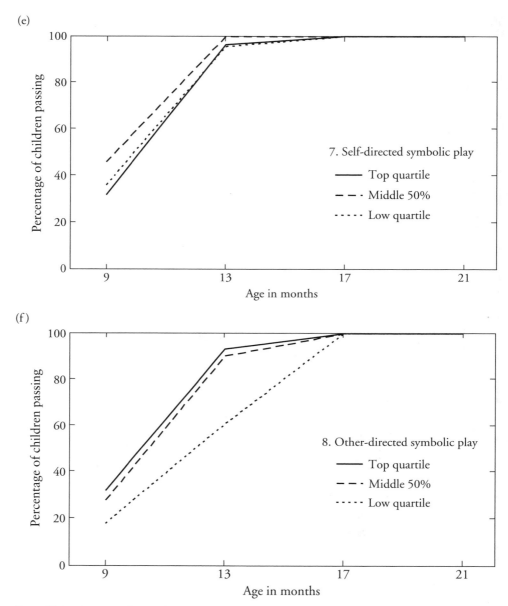

Figure 25.5   (*continued*) (e) play item 7 (i.e., self-directed symbolic play), and (f) play item 8 (i.e., other-directed symbolic play).

overall models. Unlike structural equation models, which avail various goodness-of-fit indices, fewer options for modeling the fit of IRT models exist (Harvey & Hammer, 1999). Nonetheless, there is a trend toward more sophisticated models (including those capable of modeling multidimensional data sets), greater flexibility and accessibility, and development of appropriate fit indices, all of which will no doubt lead to the enhanced use of IRT in the near future.

Finally, the use of IRT has been limited due to its large sample size requirements and the relatively large numbers of items within scales it requires to obtain accurate and stable estimates of unknown item parameters. Indeed, our sample of 114 children might be considered small by traditional IRT researchers. However, the requirement of large sample sizes has been reduced as a result of improved statistical algorithms. In fact, some have convincingly argued that sample size requirements for IRT are comparable to that of factor analysis and other such multivariate methods. Given the powerful potential of IRT for identifying items of meaningful relevance to developmentalists, benefits soon promise to outweigh its limitations.

Conclusions

The enterprise of developmental science in general, and the research program in child and family research in particular, addresses multiple substantive issues at multiple levels in multiple ways. This multivariate scientific domain has as its principal goals the description and explanation of constructs, structures, and functions through time. Because of its complex and sophisticated nature, the work begs equivalent complexity and sophistication in analytic response. In this chapter, we have reviewed a typical research program from developmental science and presented data sets on a variety of different topics. To address the research questions posed by these substantive areas, we have responded with a variety of modern analytic tools. More specifically, we showed how multilevel modeling can illuminate growth trajectories of fetal heart function, the unique role for event history analysis in children's achievement of language milestones, and item response theory's elucidation of play sophistication in childhood. We employ others as well, such as multimethod/multirespondent approaches and structural equation modeling. In general, we believe that these methodological and analytical advances testify to the increasing sophistication and future potential for developmental science.

Acknowledgments

This chapter summarizes selected aspects of ongoing research in child and family research in the National Institute of Child Health and Human Development, and portions of the text have appeared in previous scientific publications cited in the references. Order of authorship is alphabetical. We thank E. Beatty and C. Varron for assistance.

Note

Requests for reprints should be sent to Marc H. Bornstein, Child and Family Research, National Institute of Child Health and Human Development, National Institutes of Health, Suite 8030,

6705 Rockledge Drive, Bethesda MD 20892-7971, USA. Telephone: +1 (301) 496 6832; fax: +1 (301) 496 2766; email: Marc_H_Bornstein@nih.gov.

References

Allison, P. D. (1982). *Event history analysis.* Newbury Park, CA: Sage.

Bornstein, M. H., DiPietro, J. A., Hahn, C.-S., Painter, K. M., Haynes, O. M., & Costigan, K. A. (2002). Prenatal cardiac function and postnatal cognitive development: An exploratory study. *Infancy, 3,* 475–94.

Bornstein, M. H., Hahn, C.-S., Suwalsky, J. T. D., & Haynes, O. M. (2003). Socioeconomic status, parenting, and child development: The Hollingshead Four-Factor Index of Social Status and the Socioeconomic Index of Occupations. In M. H. Bornstein & R. H. Bradley (eds.), *Socioeconomic status, parenting, and child development* (pp. 29–82). Mahwah, NJ: Lawrence Erlbaum Associates.

Bryk, A. S. & Raudenbush, S. W. (1987). Application of hierarchical linear models to assessing change. *Psychological Bulletin, 101,* 147–58.

Cox, D. R. & Oakes, D. (1983). *The analysis of survival data.* New York: Chapman & Hall.

Dempster, A. P., Rubin, D. B., & Tsutakawa, R. K. (1981). Estimation in covariance components models. *Journal of the American Statistical Association, 76,* 341–53.

Embretson, S. E. & Reise, S. P. (2000). *Item response theory for psychologists.* Mahwah, NJ: Lawrence Erlbaum Associates.

Goldstein, H. (1986). Multilevel mixed linear model analysis using iterative generalized least squares. *Biometrika, 73,* 43–56.

Hambleton, R. K. & Swaminathan, H. (1991). *Item response theory: Principles and applications.* Boston, MA: Kluwer.

Hambleton, R. K., Swaminathan, H., & Rogers, H. J. (1991). *Fundamentals of item response theory.* Newbury Park, CA: Sage.

Harvey, R. J. & Hammer, A. L. (1999). Item response theory. *The Counseling Psychologist, 27,* 353–83.

Hollingshead, A. B. (1975). The four-factor index of social status. Unpublished manuscript, Yale University.

Hox, J. J. (1995). *Applied multilevel analysis.* Amsterdam: TT-Publikaties.

Hulin, C. L., Drasgow, F., & Parsons, C. K. (1983). *Item response theory: Application to psychological measurement.* Homewood, IL: Dow Jones-Irwin.

Mason, W. M., Wong, G. Y., & Entwisle, B. (1984). Contextual analysis through the multilevel linear model. In S. Leinhardt (ed.), *Sociological methodology 1983–1984* (pp. 72–103). San Francisco, CA: Jossey-Bass.

Parmar, M. K. B. & Machin, D. (1995). *Survival analysis: A practical approach.* New York: John Wiley.

Raudenbush, S. W. (1988). Educational applications of hierarchical linear models: A review. *Journal of Educational Statistics, 13,* 85–116.

Raudenbush, S. W. & Bryk, A. S. (2002). *Hierarchical linear models: Applications and data analysis methods.* Thousand Oaks, CA: Sage.

Raudenbush, S. W. & Chan, W.-S. (1993). Application of a hierarchical linear model to the study of adolescent deviance in an overlapping cohort design. *Journal of Consulting and Clinical Psychology, 61,* 941–51.

Raudenbush, S., Bryk, A., Cheong, Y. F., & Congdon, R. (2001). *HLM 5: Hierarchical linear and nonlinear modeling.* Lincolnwood, IL: Scientific Software International, Inc.

Rosenberg, B. (1973). Linear regression with randomly dispersed parameters. *Biometrika, 60,* 61–75.

Snijders, T. A. B. & Bosker, R. J. (1999). *Multilevel analysis: An introduction to basic and advanced multilevel modeling.* London: Sage.

Strenio, J. L. F., Weisberg, H. I., & Bryk, A. S. (1983). Empirical Bayes estimation of individual growth curve parameters and their relationship to covariates. *Biometrics, 39,* 71–86.

Tamis-LeMonda, C. S. & Bornstein, M. H. (1996). Variation in children's exploratory, nonsymbolic, and symbolic play: An explanatory multidimensional framework. In C. Rovee-Collier & L. P. Lipsitt (eds.), *Advances in infancy research* (pp. 37–78). Norwood, NJ: Ablex.

Tamis-LeMonda, C. S. & Bornstein, M. H. (2002). Maternal responsiveness and early language acquisition. In R. Kail (ed.), *Advances in child development and behavior* (vol. X, pp. 89–127). New York: Academic Press.

Tamis-LeMonda, C. S., Bornstein, M. H., & Baumwell, L. (2001). Maternal responsiveness and children's achievement of language milestones. *Child Development, 72,* 748–67.

Tamis-LeMonda, C. S., Bornstein, M. H., Kahana-Kalman, R., Baumwell, L., & Cyphers, L. (1998). Predicting variation in the timing of language milestones in the second year: An events history approach. *Journal of Child Language, 25,* 675–700.

Thissen, D. M. (1991). *MULTILOG user's guide. Multiple, categorical item analysis and test scoring using item response theory.* Lincolnwood, IL: Scientific Software International.

Tucker, L. R. (1946). Maximum validity of a test with equivalent items. *Pychometrika, 11,* 1–13.

van der Linden, W. J., & Hambleton, R. K. (eds.) (1997). *Handbook of modern item response theory.* New York: Springer-Verlag.

Willett, J. B. & Singer, J. D. (1991). From whether to when: New methods for studying student dropout and teacher attrition. *Review of Educational Research, 61,* 407–50.

Willett, J. B. & Singer, J. D. (1993). Investigating onset, cessation, relapse and recovery: Why you should, and how you can, use discrete-time survival analysis to examine event occurrence. *Journal of Consulting and Clinical Psychology, 61,* 952–65.

Yamaguchi, K. (1991). *Event history analysis.* Newbury Park, CA: Sage.

Name Index

Subject Index